A HISTORY OF
LATIN AMERICA

THE BLACKWELL HISTORY OF THE WORLD

General Editor: **R. I. Moore**

*Denotes title published

A HISTORY OF
LATIN AMERICA

c. 1450 to the Present

Second Edition

Peter Bakewell

350 Main Street, Malden, MA 02148-5020, USA
108 Cowley Road, Oxford OX4 1JF, UK
550 Swanston Street, Carlton, Victoria 3053, Australia

First edition published 1997
Second edition published 2004 by Blackwell Publishing Ltd
Reprinted 2004

Library of Congress Cataloging-in-Publication Data

Bakewell, P. J. (Peter John), 1943–
   A history of Latin America : c. 1450 to the present / Peter Bakewell.—2nd ed.
     p.   cm. — (The Blackwell history of the world)
   Includes bibliographical references and index.
   ISBN 0-631-23161-7 (alk. paper)—ISBN 0-631-23160-9 (alk. paper)
   1. Latin America—History.   I Title. II. Series.

   F1410 .B175   2004
   980—dc21   2002153415

A catalogue record for this title is available from the British Library.

Set in 10/12 pt Plantin
by Kolam Information Serrvices Pvt. Ltd, Pondicherry, India
Printed and bound in the United Kingdom
by T. J. International Ltd, Padstow, Cornwall

For further information on
Blackwell Publishing, visit our website:
http://www.blackwellpublishing.com

For Max and Nicholas
par nobile fratrum

CONTENTS

ILLUSTRATIONS

SERIES EDITOR'S PREFACE

There is nothing new about the attempt to understand history as a whole. To know how humanity began and how it has come to its present condition, to grasp its relation to nature and its place in the cosmos, is one of the oldest and most universal of human needs, expressed in the religious and philosophical systems of every civilization. Only in the last few decades, however, has it begun to appear both necessary and possible to meet that need by means of a rational and systematic appraisal of attainable knowledge. History claimed its independence as an autonomous field of scholarship, with its own subject matter and its own rules and methods, and not just a branch of literature, rhetoric, law, philosophy, or religion, in the second half of the nineteenth century. World History began to do so in only the closing decades of the twentieth. Its emergence was delayed on the one hand by simple ignorance – because the history of enormous stretches of space and time had been known not at all, or so patchily and superficially as not to be worth revisiting – and on the other by the lack of an acceptable basis upon which to organize and present what knowledge there was.

Both obstacles are now being rapidly overcome. There is almost no part of the world, or period of its history, that is not the subject of vigorous and sophisticated investigation by archaeologists and historians. It is truer than ever before that knowledge is growing and perspectives changing and multiplying more quickly than it is possible to assimilate and record them in synthetic form. Nevertheless, the attempt to grasp the human past as a whole can, and must, be made. A world which faces a common future of headlong and potentially catastrophic transformation needs its common history. At the same time, since we have ceased to believe, as the pioneers of "scientific" history did a century ago, that a complete or definitive account is ultimately attainable by the mere accumulation of information, we are free to offer the best we can manage at the moment. And since we no longer suppose that it is our business as historians to detect or proclaim "The End of History" in the fruition of any grand design, human or divine, there is no single path to trace, or golden key to turn. There is also a growing wealth of ways in which world history can be written. The oldest and simplest view, that world history is best understood as the history of contacts between peoples previously isolated from one another, from which (some think) all change arises, is now seen to be capable of application since the earliest times. An influential alternative focusses upon the tendency of economic exchanges to create self-sufficient but ever expanding "worlds" which sustain successive systems of power and culture. Another seeks to understand the differences between societies and cultures, and therefore the particular character of each, by comparing the ways in which they have developed their values, social relationships, and structures of power.

The Blackwell History of the World does not seek to embody any of these approaches, but to support them all, as it will use them all, by providing a modern, comprehensive, and accessible account of the entire human past. Its plan is that of a barrel, in which the indispensable narratives of very long term regional development are bound together by global surveys of the interaction between regions, and the great transformations which they have experienced in common, or visited upon one another. Each volume, of course, reflects the idiosyncrasies of its sources and its subjects, as well as the judgment and experience of its author. In combination some two dozen volumes will offer a framework in which the history of every part of the world can be viewed and most aspects of human activity can be compared, at different times and in different cultures. A frame imparts perspective; comparison implies respect for difference. That is the beginning of what the past has to offer to the future.

The history of Middle and South America is by no means easy to fit into a framework of world history. To an even greater extent than other histories it is dominated, at least in the imagination of outsiders, by a few spectacular images – the exotic splendor of the Aztec and Inca civilizations, and the fabulous wealth their destruction promised to the first European arrivals; the devastation of native populations by conquest and disease, and their replacement by African slaves; the miseries of plantation economies, the heady triumphs of early revolution and the failure of the nations born of them – especially by inevitable comparison with their North American counterparts – to establish stable and powerful political and economic structures in its wake. But if generalizations are easy the reality that lies behind them is bewilderingly complicated. A geography of extremes was uncongenial to communication, and its North/South axis made cultural transmission and adaptation much harder and slower than in Eurasia, where migrants from East to West had to cope with correspondingly more gradual changes in climate and conditions. An ecology in itself both various and fragile was devastated and remodeled by conquest and its consequences. Geography and ecology presented every imaginable combination of circumstance and environment to their human inhabitants, themselves infinitely variable in their cultural and ethnic inheritances. The dazzling civilizations encountered by the *conquistadores* had developed quite recently, for the Neolithic revolution had come late to the Americas, most of whose inhabitants retained much less developed lifestyles. The European colonists brought with them contrasting cultural and political inheritances, and constructed highly differentiated economies, which they supplied with labor on a vast scale from Africa, but also in the nineteenth century from India and China. Even without the conflicting pressures from the world beyond it is hardly remarkable that societies composed of such various ingredients have experienced such extremes of wealth and poverty, in their cultural and political as well as in their economic history. To the historian, whose most difficult task is always to strike the proper balance between the general and the particular, they pose a peculiarly unnerving challenge. Peter Bakewell has responded to it with an account of formidable composure and reassuring clarity.

R. I. Moore

SERIES EDITOR'S ACKNOWLEDGEMENTS

The Editor is grateful to all of the contributors to the *Blackwell History of the World* for advice and assistance on the design and contents of the series as a whole as well as on individual volumes. Both Editor and Contributors wish to place on record their immense debt, individually and collectively, to John Davey, formerly of Blackwell Publishing. The series would not have been initiated without his vision and enthusiasm, and could not have been realized without his energy, skill, and diplomacy.

PREFACE TO THE SECOND EDITION

The main change in this new edition is that, despite doubts expressed in the earlier preface, I have added a brief extra section outlining the history of Latin America between 1930 and the end of the twentieth century. To the text that appeared in the first edition hardly any change has been made, beyond the adjustments needed for the smooth insertion of the new chapter, correction of small factual errors and the addition of some new material to the bibliography. Although the original text could doubtless be improved, and new material usefully added to it, my feeling about it, to use that nicely terse Spanish phrase, is "He dicho." I have said what I wanted to say.

While writing the new section, I have continued to feel the nervousness about tackling recent history that led me to end the first edition around 1930. For that reason I have tried to do no more than show major economic and political trends, illustrating them with accounts of particular cases and participants. I hope that for the general reader these new pages will at least serve to open the landscape, and that teachers may find pegs in them on which to hang more detailed discussions. I am grateful to Alan Knight for his close reading of the new chapter.

PREFACE TO THE FIRST EDITION

Some readers of this book (including my professional colleagues – but it is not written for them) may find it odd that in a work proclaiming itself to be a general history of Latin America, the longest section is devoted to the sixteenth century. Most such histories have given greatest space to recent happenings, and progressively fewer pages to events and periods at increasing distance from the present.

My first explanation of the unusual balance of this book is that I have tried here to recount the history of Latin America (that is, Middle and South America since they began to be inhabited by speakers of Latin-based languages, principally the Spanish and the Portuguese) from the beginning forwards. A solid foundation therefore needed to be laid down. The second is my conviction that, in the history of Latin America, the sixteenth century is not only the most interesting but the most important period. That, indeed, seems to me a proposition that is very close to being axiomatic. The sixteenth century was the time when the Spaniards and Portuguese met with the people and the land of those parts of the "new" world that they were to colonize, and when interactions began that are still playing themselves out today. There are, to put it slightly differently, continuities between the sixteenth century and the present that give that century, the "founding" period, an enormous formative weight. Latin America is not, of course, solely the product of the unfolding of processes laid down four to five hundred years ago. There has been much innovation, from both within and without, as the book tries to show. Nonetheless, the long continuities are what impress me most.

I have brought the book to a close around 1930 because, accustomed as I have grown in my earlier work to dealing with longer and more distant sweeps of history, I am doubtful of my ability to make valid generalizations about the recent past. The study of Latin America over the past half century is, for me, the territory of political scientists, economists, sociologists, and other social scientists. They have written, and continue to do so, with enthusiastic energy; their works mount up mightily.

I am well aware of the limitations of this book, and acknowledge that in two senses it is a partial history. The first is that much that is important and interesting has been left out, or only briefly mentioned. Lack of space – or, more exactly, the demands imposed by readability and publishability – accounts to a degree for that. But the book is partial also because the omissions are in some measure the outcome of my own interests and biases. Some of those biases I recognize, and some are doubtless unconscious. I can say that the book follows no particular ideological scheme. It is simply a view of the workings of Latin American history that has developed in my mind over twenty years of teaching that history, and over thirty of doing research and writing on pieces of it.

For the existence and content of the book, I am indebted to far more people than I can mention, and probably more than I can remember, since it is in a broad sense the product of all my contact with Latin America, whether through living there or by consciously studying its past. My first thanks should go to the late Kenneth and Monica Wilden-Hart, who introduced me to Spanish, and fanned my early enthusiasm for the language. That interest eventually led me to Latin America. As an undergraduate I first learned about Latin American history from John Street, and about intellectual exhilaration from Theodore Boorman. John Elliott presided over my graduate work with a keen interest that was the best form of encouragement. Students in graduate seminars at the University of New Mexico and at Emory University have listened to my opinions and asked questions that often made me reconsider them. For help with specific points in the book I should like to thank Michael Conniff, Brooke Larson, David McCreery, Robert Pastor, Donna Pierce, Laurel Seth, Mary Elizabeth Smith, Susan Socolow, Karen Stolley, Sharon Strocchia, and William Taylor. All remaining errors are, of course, my own responsibility. I thank my editors, John Davey and R. I. Moore, for their toleration of my slow progress with the manuscript and for their encouragement.

To my wife, Susan, goes first my gratitude for her help with questions of art history; but a deeper appreciation of her forbearance and generosity in years when she had many demands on her own time and energy.

CONVENTIONS USED

References to the *Recopilación de Leyes de los Reinos de las Indias* are given in the order book, title, law. Thus *Recopilación* 1, 2, 3 means book 1, title 2, law 3.

"Peso" means the colonial Spanish *peso de a ocho*, or "piece of eight" (see glossary). Amounts given originally in some other denomination have been converted to pesos of this sort.

"Indian" is widely used to mean the people resident in the Americas before the arrival of Europeans, and the descendants of those same people. The term is of course inaccurate; Columbus was the perpetrator of the mis-identification. But other possibilities ("Amerinds," "Native Americans," "indigenes," and so on) are awkward or ugly.

Maps

BARBADOS
VENEZUELA
PANAMA
TRINIDAD
Caracas
Orinoco R.
GUYANA
COLOMBIA
SURINAME
LLANOS
Bogotá
Roraima
FRENCH
GUIANA
GUIANA HIGHLANDS
Pico da
Neblina
Quito
EQUATOR
Negro R.
Amazon R.
Chimborazo
Cuenca
Manaus
Belém
Iquitos
São
Luis
Marañón R.
Madeira R.
PERU
Lima
Cúzco
MATO GROSSO
PLATEAU
Recife
L. Titicaca
10° S
BOLIVIA
Salvador
Misti
La Paz
Brasilia
BRAZIL
Sajama
Cochabamba
ALTIPLANO
CHACO
Pico da
Bandeira
Pilcomayo R.
Paraguay R.
Paraná R.
São Francisco R.
BRAZILIAN HIGHLANDS
20° S
PACIFIC
OCEAN
Bermejo R.
GRAN
Paraíba R.
SERRA DO MAR
Rio de Janeiro
CHILE
PARAGUAY
Iguaçu R.
São Paulo
Asunción
Salado R.
TROPIC OF
CAPRICORN
Uruguay R.
ATLANTIC OCEAN
30° S
Aconcagua
PAMPAS
Santiago
URUGUAY
Buenos
Aires
Montevideo
Rio de
la Plata
ARGENTINA
Valdivia
40° S
PATAGONIA
FALKLAND ISLANDS
(ISLAS MALVINAS)
TIERRA DEL
FUEGO
50° S
kilometers
0   600
N
CAPE HORN
0   400
miles
Key
● Capitals
• Other towns
▲ Peaks
–·– Frontiers

MAP 1   South America – Mountains, Rivers, and Large Towns

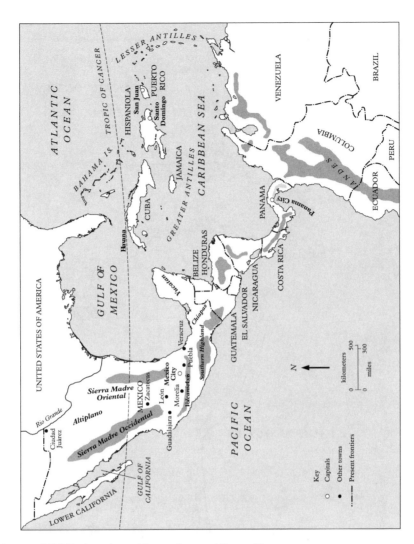

MAP 2   Middle America – Mountains, and Large Towns

Santa Fe

ATLANTIC OCEAN

(1550–1600)

1529–30

Zacatecas

1519

Tenochtitlan

1523

CUBA

HISPANIOLA

PUERTO RICO

1511

JAMAICA

1509

1508

1515–23

1509

Panama City

1536–7

1530–2

1536–8

Santa Fe de
Bogotá

Quito

1534

Cajamarca

1533

Cuzco

PACIFIC OCEAN

1540–1

Asunción

1537

1580

Santiago

Buenos
Aires

N

kilometers
0   500   1000

0   200 400 600
miles

MAP 3   Major Movements of Conquest and Settlement in Spanish America
(NB General directions, not precise routes, are shown)

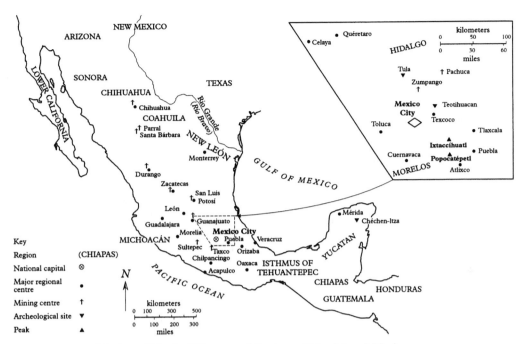

Key

Region	(CHIAPAS)
National capital	⊗
Major regional centre	•
Mining centre	↑
Archeological site	▼
Peak	▲

MAP 4 Mexico – Principal Towns and Regions, Colonial and Modern

CARIBBEAN SEA

TRINIDAD

PANAMA

PACIFIC OCEAN

Santa Marta

Cartagena

Coro

⊗ **Caracas**
✕ Carabobo

Portobelo

⊗ Panama City

Cúcuta

Orinoco R.

Angosturas
(Ciudad Bolívar)

Antioquia

VENEZUELA

• Socorro

• Quibdó

✕ Boyacá

**Santa Fe
de Bogotá** ⊗

Meta R.

Orinoco R.

Guaviare R.

COLOMBIA

• Popayán

• Pasto

Caquetá R.

Negro R.

Pichincha ✕ □ **Quito** ⊗

ECUADOR

Guayaquil •

• Cuenca

Iquitos •

Manaus •

Marañón R.

Tabatinga

Solimões R. (Amazon)

Cajamarca •

Juruá R.

Trujillo •

BRAZIL

Ucayali R.

Madeira R.

P E R U

✕ Junín

Urubamba R.

Lima □

↑

Ayacucho •

Huancavelica •

✕ Apurímac R.

Cuzco •

Beni R.

Guaporé R.

CHINCHA IS. ✕ †
• Pisco

L. Titicaca

BOLIVIA

• Arequipa

⊗ **La Paz**

• Cochabamba

• Santa Cruz

↑ Oruro

Arica

La Plata (Sucre)
□

↑ ↑
• † Potosí

CHILE

Porco •

PARAGUAY

• Tarija

Key

⊗ Modern capitals

● Major towns

□ Colonial *audiencia*

↑ Mining sites

✕ Battles in wars
of independence

N
↑

kilometers
0   100   300   500

0   100   200   300
miles

MAP 5   North-west South America

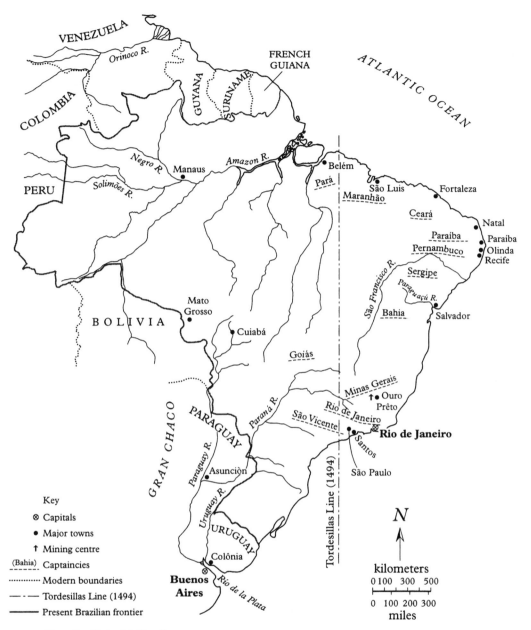

VENEZUELA

Orinoco R.

COLOMBIA

GUYANA

SURINAME

FRENCH
GUIANA

ATLANTIC OCEAN

Negro R.

Manaus

Amazon R.

• Belém

Pará

PERU

Solimões R.

São Luis
Maranhão

Fortaleza

Ceará

Natal

Paraíba
Olinda
Recife

Paraíba

Pernambuco

BOLIVIA

Mato
Grosso

Cuiabá

Sergipe

São Francisco R.

Paraguaçú R.

Bahia

Salvador

Goiás

GRAN CHACO

PARAGUAY

Paraná R.

Minas Gerais

† Ouro
Prêto

Rio de Janeiro

São Vicente

⊗ **Rio de Janeiro**

Santos

São Paulo

Paraguay R.

Asunción

Uruguay R.

URUGUAY

Colônia

Tordesillas Line (1494)

Key

⊗ Capitals

• Major towns

† Mining centre

(Bahia) Captaincies

·········· Modern boundaries

—·—· Tordesillas Line (1494)

▬▬ Present Brazilian frontier

⊗ **Buenos
Aires**

Rio de la Plata

N

kilometers

0 100 300   500

0   100 200 300
miles

MAP 6   Colonial Brazil

PART I

BASES

CHRONOLOGY OF PART I

AD 711   Moorish incursion into Spain begins

Ninth century *AD*   Decline of classic Maya culture

c. AD 1000   Norsemen reach North America

1200s   Moors expelled from Portugal. Moors in Spain restricted to the Emirate of Granada

Late 1200s   Catalan voyages to north-west Africa, and possibly a Genoese visit to the Canaries

1320–50   Tenochtitlan-Tlatelolco, the Aztec capital, begins to rise

1393   Castilian exploration of Canaries

Early 1400s   First caravels built in Iberian peninsula

1415   Portuguese capture of Ceuta in North Africa

1420s   Portuguese settle Madeira

Late 1420s   Formation of the Triple Alliance, the basis of Aztec expansion

1427   Definitive discovery of the Azores by the Portuguese

1440s   Start of Inca imperial expansion

1444   Portuguese reach Cape Verde, western-most point of Africa

1460s   Substantial settlement of Azores by Portugal

1469   Marriage of Isabella of Castile and Ferdinand of Aragon

1479   Treaty of Alcáçovas: Castile's rights to the Canaries, and Portugal's to the Azores, Cape Verdes, and Madeira, mutually accepted

1487   Dedication of the Great Temple in Tenochtitlan

1488   Bartolomeu Dias rounds southern Africa, for Portugal

1492   Spanish conquest of Granada; expulsion of Jews from Spain; Columbus's first voyage to America

1494   Treaty of Tordesillas: Castile and Portugal partition exploration and exploitation of the world (Portugal, east of *c.* 50 degrees west; Castile, west of that meridian)

1504   Death of Isabella

FURTHER READING FOR PART I

The basic work on Latin American geography is still Preston James, *Latin America.* (See the bibliography at the end of this book for full references.) Harold Blakemore and Clifford T. Smith (eds), *Latin America: Geographical Perspectives*, provides essays on regions by specialists.

The first volume of *The Cambridge History of Latin America* has chapters on native cultures before the arrival of Europeans. See also Alvin M. Josephy, Jr., *America in 1492*. Of the many works available on the Aztecs, the most engaging is Inga Clendinnen, *Aztecs. An Interpretation*. Less is available, at least in English, on the Incas; but María Rostworowski de Diez Canseco, *History of the Inca Realm*, is first-rate. The sixteenth-century view provided by Garcilaso de la Vega, *Royal Commentaries of the Incas*, remains fascinating. Aspects of Inca and Aztec culture are compared by Geoffrey W. Conrad and Arthur A. Demarest in *Religion and Empire*.

For Portuguese explorations, see Bailey W. Diffie and George D. Winius, *Foundations of the Portuguese Empire, 1415–1580*, and A. H. de Oliveira Marques, *History of*

Portugal. For Portugal and Spain, Charles Verlinden, *The Beginnings of Modern Colonization. Eleven Essays with an Introduction* (Cornell University Press, Ithaca, 1970). For Spain, Felipe Fernández-Armesto, *Ferdinand and Isabella*; Peggy K. Liss, *Isabel the Queen. Life and Times*, Oxford University Press, New York, 1992; J. H. Elliott, *Imperial Spain, 1469–1716*. And generally for exploration, John. H. Parry, *The Age of Reconnaissance* and *The Discovery of the Sea*.

[1] *LANDS AND CLIMATES*

"If you took the direct route, you would arrive in two days at Mazapil. But traveling by the water holes and along the carting road, the journey takes five or six days. Going as the crow flies, there is no road or water, which is the reason for following such a roundabout path as people use."[1] So wrote Domingo Lázaro de Arregui, a traveler in northern Mexico in the early 1620s, of the journey from the silver-mining city of Zacatecas to the outlying mining hamlet of Mazapil, 225 kilometers to the north-east. The territory to be crossed was high, though not particularly rugged; but it was dry, a typical section of the northern plateau, or *altiplano*, of Mexico. In moving about this semi-desert, especially with the animals essential for freighting trade goods, there was no choice but to go where the water was, even at the cost of doubling or tripling the time and length of the journey.

In different forms, it was a problem repeated time and time again in Middle and South America. The land was not, and still is not, helpful in most places to human habitation and activities. The struggle to live and thrive in it has produced over the past five thousand years or more some astonishingly ingenious human adaptations. But even today, with an unprecedented arsenal of technology at their disposal, people are far from taming it. Mountains still present a forbidding barrier to movement; the great rivers of South America are, with the exception of the Amazon, less easily navigated than the map might suggest, and still lead to places where rather few people want to go; deserts, both high and low, seriously reduce the area available to several countries for growing the food they need.

Enough variety can doubtless be found in most large regions of the world for the label "land of contrasts" to be aptly applied. But Latin America can surely lay a peculiarly strong claim to the title. In it, variations of terrain, climate, vegetation, and resources are tightly packed together in most of the nations occupying its territory. From the fully tropical, warm and wet city of Veracruz on the Gulf coast of Mexico it is only 120 kilometers to the permanent snows crowning the volcano that the Aztecs called Citlaltépetl, the Hill of the Star. This volcano, known now more commonly as the Pico de Orizaba, is, at 5,747 meters, the highest peak in Mexico. An even more striking transition is produced by the Sierra Nevada de Santa Marta, in north-eastern Colombia, which rises to snowy heights exceeding 5,500 meters within 50 kilometers of the luxuriantly vegetated Caribbean coast. Rapid changes also happen without any vertical movement. Particularly remarkable is the shift from humid tropical forest to sand desert, with a small intervening zone of savanna and scrub, that takes place over about 400 kilometers of the southern Ecuadorian and northern Peruvian coasts. Many other examples of swift change might be added. Among the obvious are the passage from high, cool semi-desert around the Bolivian capital of La Paz, over the snows of the eastern Cordillera Real of the Andes, and down into the humid, semi-tropical valleys called the *yungas* in the interior slopes of the mountains; or the rapid shift in Paraguay from the fertile, watered lands lying east of the River Paraguay, to the thorny scrub of the Gran Chaco west of it; or the move from the cool deciduous rainforests of southern Chile eastward over the Andes to the chill aridity of Patagonia, in the rain shadow of the mountains.

PHYSICAL GEOGRAPHY

As some of the examples just given suggest, the physical form of the land is a powerful influence on climate, land use, and living conditions in much of Middle and South America. The structure can be imagined simply as a mountainous spine (the western Sierra in Mexico, the Central American ranges, and the Andes in South America) running down the western side of the entire area; and east of this spine, a trunk consisting of lesser ranges and massifs, plains, and, in the Caribbean, large and small islands. But, for a sense of the influence of geography on Latin America's history, a closer study of the landforms repays the effort.

MIDDLE AMERICA AND THE CARIBBEAN

Broadly speaking, the geology and surface formations of North America continue down into northern and central Mexico.[2] The largest feature here is the plateau, or *altiplano*, which is some 1,200 meters high at the border with the United States at the Rio Grande. From there it rises gradually to reach about 2,400 meters at its southern end in central Mexico. The plateau is flanked on each side by mountains. The Sierra Madre Occidental, to the west, has peaks in excess of 3,000 meters.[3] The eastern range, the Sierra Madre Oriental, is generally a little lower. The Sierras do not reach the coasts. Low plains run from their feet to the sea.

The *altiplano* and its flanking ranges are abruptly cut off, at about 20 degrees north, by Mexico's most imposing physical feature. This is a line of volcanoes, termed the volcanic axis, running from the Pacific to the Gulf shore. Some of the volcanoes still bear their Nahuatl names. Particularly renowned are Popocatépetl (Smoking Mountain, 5,452 meters) and Ixtaccíhuatl (White Lady, 5,273 meters), which overlook from the south-east the broad valley in which Mexico City lies. It is alleged that on exceptionally smog-free days their snow-covered peaks, until recent decades one of the glories of the capital's site, can still be seen from the city. Some of the volcanoes along the axis are still active. And in 1943 their number grew when emerging lava split open the earth 300 kilometers west of Mexico City in the state of Michoacán, and a new cone, named Paricutín, began to rise.

South of the volcanic axis lies first a large area of old crystalline rock. Although the maximum heights here barely exceed 3,300 meters, long and heavy erosion has made these Southern Highlands one of the most rugged sections of Mexico's surface. A far larger separate structural region begins immediately south and east of the Highlands. This is "Old Antillia," so called because it is supposed to have been a single land mass that at one time linked the major Caribbean islands with Central America. It embraces not only the southern tip of Mexico, along with Guatemala and Honduras, but also, to the east, Jamaica, Cuba, Hispaniola (the island east of Cuba now occupied by Haiti and the Dominican Republic), Puerto Rico, and the Virgin Islands. Everywhere in this large zone are steep ranges and valleys, trending east and west, and formed by faulting and folding of the surface. Immediately north of Old Antillia is a different formation, an almost flat area of limestone known as the Antillean Foreland. Parts of this lie above sea level, forming the Yucatan peninsula of eastern Mexico, and the Bahama Islands to the north of Cuba. Because limestone is porous, Yucatan, especially in its northern half, has few surface streams. Water flows in underground channels, and can be reached only where the roofs of underground caverns have collapsed, leaving sink-holes, known locally as *cenotes*.[4] Yucatan provides the largest area of lowland plain in Mexico; but it is less useful than might be supposed because of the lack of accessible water and the poor quality of the soil that weathered limestone typically yields. More fertile is the Gulf coast lowland further north in eastern Mexico, which is a continuation of the coastal plain of the southern United States. Its greatest width, near the border in the north, is some 200 kilometers. By contrast, the coastal shelf in western Mexico is rarely more than 100 kilometers wide, and on the southern coast far less than that.

Joining Old Antillia to South America are two roughly parallel volcanic chains: to the east, the island-peaks of the Lesser Antilles, forming the outer limit of the Caribbean; and to the west, the ranges of the Pacific coast of Guatemala, El Salvador, Nicaragua, Costa Rica, and western Panama. Both these chains then connect to the Andes. The geology of eastern Panama has close similarities to that of a north-west projection of the Andes in Colombia; while the structure producing the Lesser Antilles meets the spur of the Andes that extends eastwards from Colombia to form the coastal ranges of Venezuela.[5]

SOUTH AMERICA

The Andes

The two rims of the Caribbean converge in the northern Andes. These great mountains then run southwards for almost 8,000 kilometers to Tierra del

Fuego at the tip of South America, forming the longest continuous series of ranges on the face of the earth. The Andes are not a single chain, but many, more or less closely connected. Added to this structural diversity is variety in formation. Over most of their length, the Andean ranges are the product of folding and faulting. But in three regions – southern Colombia and Ecuador, central and southern Peru together with the border zone of Bolivia and Chile, and south-central Chile (with nearby areas of western Argentina) – volcanic activity has added other peaks to the landscape. The highest mountain anywhere in the Andes (and in the Americas), Aconcagua (6,959 meters) in western Argentina, is volcanic. So are many other of the highest summits in Ecuador (Cotopaxi at 5,897 meters, and Chimborazo at 6,267); in southern Peru (Misti at 5,822 meters); and in north-western Bolivia (Sajama at 6,520 meters). Many volcanoes are still active, though eruptions may come only at long and unpredictable intervals. The effects of vulcanism generally extend considerably outwards from the peaks themselves, leaving lava-covered plateaux and thick layers of ash and tuff, often deeply incised by erosion.[6]

Though enormously long, the Andes are narrow, rarely exceeding 350 kilometers in width except in the center of their course, in Bolivia, where the distance across the ranges becomes almost 700 kilometers. Their narrowness is small consolation, however, to anyone trying to cross them: extreme ruggedness and steep slopes make for slow and difficult progress. Few are the east–west passes below 3,000 meters (in contrast with passes across the western ranges of North America, which are rarely higher than 2,000 meters). The deep valleys that separate parallel ranges often make east–west movement still more difficult. The problem is particularly severe in Colombia, where the Andes divide into three distinct cordilleras, with the valleys of the Cauca and Magdalena rivers between them. Less forbidding, but still challenging, is the physical structure of southern Peru and the entire highland zone of Bolivia. Here the traveler to the interior faces first a high coastal range, then a wide plateau (called *altiplano*, like the plateau of northern Mexico), and finally an inland *Cordillera Real* ("Royal Range") that is as high as the first range, and drops only gradually through broken terrain towards the central lowlands of South America. The ruggedness of the Andean heights, however, has its positive aspects as well. The valleys, troughs, and basins among the ranges, at altitudes generally between 2,500 and 4,000 meters, have often presented, and still present, living conditions favorable enough to attract and support surprisingly large populations.

Though rocks and faulting from many geological periods may be found in the Andes, the main uplifting and folding that produced the present mountains took place in very recent geological time, between four and fifteen million years ago.[7] Those same disturbances were accompanied by the volcanic activity that created, for example, the western range of southern Peru and Bolivia. One reason for the great height and brokenness of the Andes is precisely that, in geological terms, they are young; erosion has not yet greatly worn them down or softened their outlines. Volcanoes are still active in the Andes, as they are also in Central America and, to a lesser degree, in Mexico. The mountainous western spine of Middle and South America belongs, in fact, to the geologically unstable "ring of fire" around the Pacific. And the existence of that ring results from the fact that the Pacific shores generally mark the lines of meeting of great tectonic plates in the earth's crust. Where the edges of these plates come together, and move against each other, volcanoes and earthquakes are most likely to occur. The western Mexican and Central American coasts mark the boundary between the Cocos Plate, offshore, and the North American and Caribbean Plates. Almost the entire western coast of South America corresponds with the meeting of the Nazca Plate, underlying the Pacific, and the South American Plate – a large slab of the crust that forms not only the landmass of South America, but also the seabed eastwards to the mid Atlantic ridge in the South Atlantic.[8]

Lesser highlands of South America

By contrast with the Andes, the rest of South America is geologically ancient, and, thanks to its distance from jolting tectonic joints, stable. Most of South America east of the Andes can be described as highland, if a height of roughly 200 meters is taken as the boundary between plains and highlands; though the contrast with the Andes is clear if the maximum altitudes in the two major highland areas are considered: 3,014 meters at the Pico de Neblina at the extreme south of the Guiana Highlands, 1,000 kilometers south of Caracas on the Venezuelan–Brazilian border; and 2,890 meters at the Pico da Bandeira at the eastern edge of the Brazilian Highlands, 300 kilometers or so north-east of Rio de Janeiro.

The Highlands of Brazil occupy the entire east and south of the country. Most of the rest of Brazil falls in the Amazon basin, but the northern boundary takes in a part of the Guiana Highlands. These also form the inland sections of the three Guianas (from west to east, British, Dutch and French – of which only the French territory preserves that name, the other two having become Guyana and Surinam). But the country with the largest and highest area of the Guiana Highlands is Venezuela. There, they make up most of the eastern end of the national territory.

Both the Guiana and the Brazilian Highlands have a base of ancient crystalline rock, which the generally abundant rains falling on these regions have softened and decomposed. An undulating surface is the result, often covered with a deep layer of soil produced by the rain's dissolving action. Projecting above this rolling terrain here and there are the massive remains of old mountains, smoothly rounded by erosion. And in places, particularly in the interior, the crystalline base is covered by stratified formations, mostly of sandstone, that have resisted erosion and now appear as plateaux.[9] Not only in height, therefore, but also in the generally undramatic nature of their surfaces, are the interior highlands in contrast with the Andes. They have their spectacular moments, nonetheless. At the point where Brazil, Venezuela, and Guyana meet, for example, is Mt Roraima – not so much a mountain as a large, flat-topped plateau reaching 2,772 meters above sea level, and one of a number of such table-lands in the region that are supported by flat layers of sandstone. Small rivers rise on these plateaux, then plunge over their edges in enormous leaps. The highest of them, and in fact the highest waterfall in the world, is Angel Fall in Venezuela, with a drop of 980 meters.[10] Lesser in height, but vastly greater in volume, are the falls of southern Brazil, where rivers such as the Paraná and the Iguaçu drop over the sharp edges of a plateau formed in this case not of sandstone, but of diabase – a dark lava particularly resistant to erosion.[11] The diabase Paraná plateau and the several major rivers flowing over it provide a combination of gravity and water that can be transformed into vast quantities of hydroelectric power. Brazil and Paraguay have fully exploited this opportunity in recent decades.[12]

Plains of South America

Measured by the 200-meter upper limit suggested before, about a quarter of South America's surface is lowland plain. And half of this lies in the inland area drained by the Amazon and its tributaries. At the western boundary of Brazil with Bolivia, Peru, Ecuador, and Colombia, the plains of this basin extend some 1,400 kilometers north to south; but they narrow eastwards, so that, as the Amazon nears its multiple mouths, it flows through a gap barely 250 kilometers wide between the Guiana and Brazilian Highlands. The total area of the Amazon basin (including the Andean and other highland areas where the rivers originate, as well as the plains through which they flow) has been estimated as 6,133,000 square kilometers. It is remarkable how far west the Amazonian drainage area reaches: the headwaters of the Marañón, a major tributary, rise in the Peruvian Andes only 115 kilometers from the Pacific.

The Amazon basin abounds in water, both on the ground and falling from the sky. The average outflow at the river's entry into the Atlantic is calculated at 12,869,000,000 liters a minute, or a cubic kilometer of water about every 78 minutes. This amounts to roughly 11 percent of all the water draining from the world's continents into the oceans, and is the largest volume of water gathered by any river system.[13] The main stream of the river is navigable for ships of 6-meter draught up to Manaus, 1,450 kilometers from the coast, but only 30 meters above mean sea level; and for vessels drawing under 4.25 meters as far as Iquitos, in eastern Peru, which is 2,700 kilometers as the crow flies from the Amazon's mouths. Few of the tributaries, however, can be used by ships of any size far from the main stream, on account of falls and rapids where they cross formations of crystalline rock.[14]

North of Amazonia, beyond the Guiana Highlands, lies another lowland region, the plains, or *llanos*, of the Orinoco basin. The Orinoco River rises on the south-west slopes of the Highlands, and wraps around them northward before flowing east through Venezuela to enter the sea through a delta facing the island of Trinidad. The *llanos* are an enormous plain, almost 1,000 kilometers long by 325 kilometers from north to south, but of a lesser order of magnitude than the Amazon lowlands.

The third lowland area of the interior, however, is far more Amazonian in scale; and, considered as a scene of human and economic activity over the past several centuries, outranks Amazonia in importance. This is the basin drained by rivers – the Paraguay, Paraná, and Uruguay are the principal streams – that combine to form the Río de la Plata (a name that properly belongs only to the estuary through which the combined waters enter the South Atlantic). The basin includes the Chaco of western Paraguay and north-western Argentina, and also the fertile lowland plains, known as pampas, of southern Uruguay and central Argentina. Some 400 kilometers south of Buenos Aires the plains come to an end as the land rises into Patagonia.

In addition to its interior lowlands, South America has a perimeter of coastal plain, though this is remarkably narrow except in the few places where major rivers, such as the Orinoco, Amazon, and those of the Río de la Plata system, cut through ranges and massifs to reach the sea. There are regions in which the plain disappears altogether. This happens, for example, in the southern quarter of Chile, where mountains run down to, and indeed into, the sea, forming an archipelago of hundreds of islands.

On the east, the coastal plain of Brazil never exceeds 170 kilometers in width. It has an abrupt inland boundary where the Brazilian Highlands, broadly tilted as they are toward the interior, drop down from what are generally their maximum heights (excluding isolated peaks) in the 900 to 1,400 meter range, forming a steep escarpment. Seen from the coastward side, so much like a range of mountains does this scarp look, rather than the edge of the inland massif, that, at least in its southern part, it goes by the name of Serra do Mar, or Ocean Range.[15] Further south still, in Uruguay and central Argentina, the coastal lowland broadens greatly, as the pampas extend far inland back from the sea. But in southern Argentina, lowland along the shore all but disappears; here the Patagonian plateaux drop sharply into the ocean as cliffs.

Almost the entire coastal territory on the west, from half-way down the Pacific shore of Colombia to lower Chile, consists of a shelf between the Andes and the sea. Its maximum width at any point is some 180 kilometers, achieved in central Ecuador. It then narrows southward, so that at some points along the Peruvian coast, Andean foothills come down to within a kilometer or two of the water. The western coastal strip also varies considerably in height. In Ecuador it consists of low hills interspersed with swamps. In Peru, much of it is at sea level. But the northern and central coasts of Chile, extending over some 2,000 kilometers, consist of a marked plateau, between 300 and 2,000 meters high, which rises with extreme abruptness from the sea.

CLIMATE AND VEGETATION

MIDDLE AMERICA

Harsh weather conditions, and rapid variations of climate, mark many parts of Latin America. Northern Mexico is an example. Here, Lower California is a dry desert. This aridity carries across the Gulf of California to the mainland, until it is alleviated by the rising ground of the western Sierra Madre, which causes inflowing air to rise, cool, and drop its moisture. Inside the western ranges, though, on the Mexican *altiplano*, desert and semi-desert return, since the incoming air is now dry. The same happens with onshore winds from the Gulf of Mexico that meet the eastern Sierra Madre as they blow inland. The drying effect is greatest in northern Mexico, where the landmass is widest and the center of the *altiplano* farthest from the sea. There, for instance, a little south of the border towns of E1 Paso and Ciudad Juárez, lies a considerable area of sand desert. As the *altiplano* proceeds south-eastward, narrowing as Mexico as a whole narrows, rainfall increases, and the climate shifts from arid to semi-arid. Average temperatures on the *altiplano* tend to fall, also, to the south, because the land rises. So, even though the Tropic of Cancer crosses north-central Mexico 470 kilometers above Mexico City, summer temperatures in the capital are lower than in the inland towns of the far north of the country. An outcome of these changes is that vegetation gradually increases southward, passing from arid scrub and cactus in the far north, to thin grassland with stunted trees, and finally, south of the Tropic, to areas of denser woodland and of soil that, with some help from irrigation, can be profitably used for crop farming.

Conditions continue to improve southward. Central highland Mexico is, indeed, blessed with a strip of land, limited to the south by the volcanic axis, and extending into the *altiplano* perhaps 300 kilometers north of that line of peaks, that has long offered marvellously benign conditions for human living. In this zone many of the high cultures of pre-Spanish Mexico developed and thrived: Teotihuacán, the first of the mature, "classic," cultures of central Mexico, *c.*AD 0–750; after that, the Toltecs; the Tarascans, to the west in Michoacán; and the Aztecs, the last major culture before the Europeans came. And in this same favored zone, many of the major towns of modern Mexico lie: from east to west, Puebla, Mexico City, Toluca, Querétaro, Morelia, León, and Guadalajara, to name only the largest. The region is, judged by degrees of latitude, tropical. But it is neither hot nor humid. Its height, typically 2,100 to 2,400 meters, reduces temperatures to a level ideal for human comfort and the cultivation of temperate crops. And these moderate temperatures, thanks to the zone's location below the tropic, change little with the seasons. Mexico City's average temperature in January is, for instance, 12.2 °C; and in July, 16.1 °C. Isolation from the sea by coastal escarpments and ranges protects the region from excessive rain; but the barriers of distance and altitude are not so great as to keep out all moisture-bearing air, so that enough rain for agriculture usually falls in the summer months. Add to these benevolent climatic conditions a remarkable fertility of soil, owed first to long-weathered deposits of volcanic ash (contributing minerals), and second to the presence of large areas of dry lake-beds (contributing organic matter), and it is easy to see why this geographical center of Mexico has always been the demographic and cultural center also.

If the climate of central highland Mexico has the benefits of tropicality without the drawbacks, the same cannot be said of the coasts. The west coast, once the tropic is passed, becomes rapidly wetter southward. And the east coast is damp from the border with the USA down, and remarkably so south of the tropic, where warm and humid winds off the Gulf of Mexico run

FIGURE 1.1   The *altiplano* (*c.*2,400 meters) of northern Mexico, with the town of Río Grande (state of Zacatecas) in the middle distance.

FIGURE 1.2   The interior ranges of the Sierra Madre Occidental, Mexico: the valley of the Bolaños river (state of Jalisco).

FIGURE 1.3 The Bolivian *altiplano* (*c.* 4,000 meters) near La Paz, looking east to the peaks of the Cordillera Real of the Andes.

FIGURE 1.4 An Andean volcano: Misti (*c.* 5,800 meters) in southern Peru, with the town of Arequipa in the foreground.

FIGURE 1.5   The valley of the Urubamba river, in the Peruvian Andes a little north of Cuzco, seen from the Inca fortress of Ollantaytambo. This is one of many high valleys cultivated for thousands of years past in the central Andes.

FIGURE 1.6   The Cerro Rico (Rich Hill) of Potosí, Bolivia, seen from a square in an Indian quarter of the town.

FIGURE 1.7 Sucre, capital of Bolivia until the end of the nineteenth century, and before that, as La Plata, seat of the *Audiencia* of Charcas. The town retains much of its colonial air and form, not least in its straight streets and division into rectangular blocks.

FIGURE 1.8 An Andean *hacienda*: Cayara, in a high valley near Potosí, Bolivia. Note the terracing, now abandoned, on the surrounding slopes.

up against the slopes of the Southern Highlands and neighboring smaller ranges. The lower Gulf coast is Mexico's wettest area, with rainfall exceeding 3,000 millimeters a year on the sea-facing slopes of the Sierra Madre of Chiapas.[16] The natural vegetation on both coasts is what would be expected from the combination of heat, high humidity, and low latitude: tropical forest. On the Pacific side the forest is light; but the Gulf coast wears a full rainforest. This continues up into Yucatan, thinning only in the extreme north of the peninsula, where rainfall declines.

Broadly similar conditions to those of the Mexican coasts also apply in the large Caribbean islands and in Central America. Rainfall in Cuba, Jamaica, Hispaniola, and Puerto Rico lies generally in the 1,000–1,500 millimeter range. This, in combination with tropical heat, yields a vegetation of forest in the eastern ends of Cuba and Jamaica, and in most of Hispaniola and Puerto Rico. Central and western Cuba have a lighter vegetation of short-grass savanna and scattered woods of pine and palmetto.[17] Wooded savanna also covers western Jamaica.

The climatic unity of the Greater Antilles and Central America is suggested by the average July temperatures of Havana (Cuba), San Juan (Puerto Rico), and Panama City, which are identical at 27.8 °C. But most of Central America has far more rain than the Antilles. It is, indeed, the largest area of heavy rainfall anywhere in North and Middle America. The entire Caribbean coast of Central America (the eastern shores of Guatemala, Honduras, Nicaragua, Costa Rica, and Panama) receives over 2,000 millimeters of rain yearly. Colón, on the Caribbean coast of Panama, is doused with no less than 3,350 millimeters of rainwater annually.[18] Much of the Pacific coast is just as wet as the eastern side. The outcome in plant life is again forest, this time with a preponderance of full rainforest, but a lighter covering on the Pacific coast. Only in the lower temperatures of highland central Guatemala and southern Honduras does tropical woodland give way to mixed forest of conifers and broadleafed trees.

SOUTH AMERICA

Tropicality is again the dominant trait in South America, with a trifle under three-quarters of the subcontinent lying north of the Tropic of Capricorn. Small variations in temperature through the year are a result, just as in Middle America. But even more than in Middle America, conditions of climate and vegetation commonly thought of as tropical are modified by other environmental influences.

This is especially so on the west side of South America, where ocean winds and currents produce enormous variations in climate. At one extreme is northwestern Colombia. One site there, Quibdó, is reported to receive 10,500 millimeters of rain annually.[19] It is certainly the wettest place in Latin America. Heavy rain falls on the entire west coast of Colombia, though it decreases southward. The moisture is carried by winds blowing on to the coast after passing over the warm waters of the Equatorial Counter Current. Not only do these winds pick up great quantities of moisture as they move over the sea, but local conditions are such that they drop a double annual maximum of rainfall on the Colombian coast.

The north Ecuadorian coast also receives this double maximum (though with a smaller total volume of rain). But a short move southward in coastal Ecuador produces, within 4 degrees of latitude, an astonishing change in climate. At the tip of the Santa Elena Peninsula, 140 kilometers west of Guayaquil, rain is scarce. And at the Ecuadorian–Peruvian border, about the same distance south-west of Guayaquil, begins an arid zone that continues down the west coast for 3,200 kilometers, to a point a little north of Santiago, the capital of Chile.[20] This is the Peruvian coastal desert, where rain rarely falls; and its continuation in the Atacama desert of northern Chile, in parts of which rain never falls.

Other continental west coasts – southern and Lower California, south-west and north-west Africa, west Australia – have comparable desert zones; but the arid stretch in western South America is longer by far, starting much closer to the Equator (only 4 to 5 degrees of latitude below it) than the other cases. A combination of high atmospheric pressure offshore and ocean currents is responsible. From the south Pacific high-pressure cell, which is centered year-round some 1,600 kilometers off the coast of northern Chile, a little below the Tropic of Capricorn, cool and stable air moves toward the land. As it does so, it crosses two distinct cold currents. The first is the Peru Oceanic Current (until recently known as the Humboldt Current), flowing up from the south; and the second, shoreward from this, is the yet cooler Peruvian Coastal Current, also moving north, and the product of the upwelling of cold bottom-water to the surface. The already cool air from the high-pressure cell is further chilled as it flows over these two currents toward the coastline, and arrives there as a dense, dank, meteorologically inactive mass. An almost permanent temperature inversion exists, indeed, along the coast, preventing vertical development of rain-producing clouds. Cloud, though, is certainly abundant in the winter months (June to October) along the Peruvian shore, presenting a puzzling, almost contradictory, spectacle: lowering, heavy masses of water vapor sliding over a sand desert. A downpour seems imminent, but hardly ever comes. Frequently during the winter, though, a Scotch mist known as *garúa* covers parts of the coast; it is mainly this thick and dismal drizzle that produces Lima's average annual precipitation of 41 millimeters.

In summer the sun is strong enough to dissolve the cloud cover, and the weather turns warm and humid. But the temperature inversion generally stays in place, preventing warm air from rising and developing into convectional rainclouds. The only circumstance in which this atmospheric stability breaks down (and this demonstrates the immense influence on the coastal climate of the chilly waters offshore) arises when the cold upwelling weakens, and warmer water moves down from the north. Then instability in the air mass above the coast becomes possible, clouds form, and heavy, sometimes torrential, rains fall. The result is often disastrous, since the coastal land, being adapted to aridity, has no protection against the power of cloudbursts and heavy masses of surface water. Floods and erosion are the outcome. These changes in offshore flows and onshore precipitation are the phenomenon known in Peru as "El Niño" ("the Child"), since they often happen around Christmas, in midsummer. El Niño affects, however, only the northern half of the Peruvian coast. Further south the precipitating changes in currents do not occur.

The only part of the west coast that matches the common image of the tropics is the shore of Colombia and northern Ecuador, where exceptionally heavy rains stimulate the growth of rainforest. The Peruvian coast would be entirely bare of vegetation if its aridity were not slightly relieved by two other sources of moisture besides rain. One is the *garúa*, which in winter dampens the Pacific-facing slopes between 800 and 1,400 meters enough to support the growth of small plants and grasses over considerable areas (known as *lomas*).[21] Denser vegetation, however, appears where rivers dropping from the western heights of the Andes flow across the desert plain to the sea. About forty river-watered "oases" exist on the Peruvian coast. They are more extensive in the north, where the plain is at its widest. There also the rivers are larger than in the center and south. All these westward-flowing streams, however, are tiny in comparison with those that rise in the Andes and flow east to the interior. Many of the coastal rivers, indeed, flow only during the season of rains in the mountains, between December and March. The oases were originally wooded, but have for millennia past been intensively cultivated for food crops, the river waters being carefully diverted and distributed for irrigation.[22] In these coastal patches of greenery, indeed, arose some of Peru's, and America's, most accomplished native cultures; and today many of Peru's large towns occupy those same sites.

In the Atacama desert of northern Chile, even those coastal oases disappear, as the climate becomes more utterly arid. Indeed, only one river in northern Chile, the Loa, manages to reach the coast. Around 30 degrees south, however, where "Middle Chile" starts, the coast begins to receive some rainfall, as a climatic regime known as Mediterranean (for its resemblance to that pattern of mild, wet winters and dry, sunny summers) becomes dominant. (Analogous Mediterranean regimes, at distances between 30 and 40 degrees from the equator, occur on other continental west coasts.)[23] Here, over a distance north to south of some 700 kilometers, is the heart of Chile. In the Central Valley lying behind the coastal range is Santiago, the capital. Its removal from tropical South America is shown by the lowness, and wide variation, of its average seasonal temperatures: 7.6 °C in the coldest month, and 20 °C in the warmest.[24] Middle Chile offers highly favorable conditions for living and agriculture.

Typical continental west-coast conditions continue southward on the Chilean coast. Below 40 degrees south comes a zone of wet, stormy winters, and cool, unsettled summers. Valdivia, at almost 40 degrees south, receives 2,660 millimeters of rain annually. The division between Mediterranean Chile and the southern regime is abrupt, taking place roughly at the Bío Bío River, at some 37 degrees south. This was the frontier during colonial times between Spanish settlement in Middle Chile and the fiercely independent Araucanian people who lived among the dense broadleafed forests covering the humid south. Storms that result from the mixing of cold, antarctic air with more northerly, warmer air bring the heavy rains. Southern Chile is indeed among the most storm-lashed regions of the globe.[25] And its lower extremities also feel the effects of the Roaring Forties, the westward winds that encircle the globe at high southern latitudes. These were the winds that long made the passage from the Atlantic to the Pacific around Cape Horn at the tip of South America such a daunting nautical challenge. Not until the eighteenth century did ships become sufficiently weather resistant and maneuverable to tackle this transit with confidence.

Though the west coast presents great contrasts in climate and plant life along its length, these are found on the whole in large blocks. Just inland from the coast, on the other hand, in the Andes such changes can and do occur over very small distances. This is mainly because the mountains are steep, and temperatures change quickly with altitude; and also because orientation of small areas, such as slopes and valleys, to sun and prevailing winds can have dramatic effects on their immediate climate. "Microclimates" are indeed a common feature of the Andes – small regions where conditions may be quite different from what would be expected at a particular height and latitude.

Throughout the section of the Andes that falls within the tropics – some 4,300 kilometers following the curve of the ranges – height serves to reduce temperature, providing, in the mountain basins of medium altitude, conditions that have long encouraged human settlement and development. In the north, for example, are the high basins of the eastern range, or Cordillera Oriental, of Colombia. In one of these is the colonial and present capital of the country, Bogotá, at an altitude of 2,640 meters, and with an average year-round temperature of 14.5 °C (a figure that varies, owing to the city's tropical location, only 1 °C between the coldest and warmest month). Taking advantage of the farming potential of these basins, the Chibcha culture, the most advanced in the northern Andes, developed in them in pre-conquest times. The Spaniards brought in cattle, and added their own familiar wheat and barley to maize, the staple native grain.[26]

In Ecuador, the ten basins lying between the two parallel cordilleras that form the Andes were similarly the home of sedentary, agricultural peoples before the Europeans arrived. They continue to support much of the peasant population today. The basin partly occupied by Quito, the national capital, is the most heavily populated now. The city lies only 35 kilometers or so south of the equator. It perches on the basin's eastern rim at 2,850 meters. At that altitude wheat, barley, and potatoes grow well. Down below, on the valley floor at about 2,300 meters, maize and pasture-grasses for cattle flourish. The second most populous Andean basin in Ecuador is the southern valley of Cuenca, where, at some 2,500 meters, maize and dairy cattle again thrive.[27] In both cases altitude makes middle latitude farming possible almost on the equator.

It is above all in Peru that the Andes' provision of many varieties of climate and environment within a small space has been central to human development. The most obvious example of local modification of an environment is the land surrounding Lake Titicaca, part of which lies in Peru and part in Bolivia. The lake's surface is at slightly above 3,800 meters. Its maximum depth is 280 meters. It is 180 kilometers long and averages some 50 kilometers in width. It is by far the largest body of water at extreme altitude in the world. Its great volume has a moderating effect on the climate of the immediate surroundings, reducing the chill of great height and benefiting agriculture. This is one reason for the region's long having been a focus of dense and culturally advanced settlement in the central Andes.

Though on a much smaller scale, the valley of Cuzco, in the center-south of the Peruvian Andes, is another prime case of a benevolent combining of height, latitude, aspect, water, and soil. This narrow depression, barely more than 30 square kilometers in area, became the heart of the Inca empire, the largest and most finely organized of all American native states. The valley, some 3,400 meters above sea level, had been occupied for many centuries before the Incas entered it as a small, migrant tribe in the thirteenth century AD. They set their home community, Cuzco, at the head of the valley. From the 1430s the town grew rapidly in size and splendor, concurrently with an exterior expansion of Inca power up and down the Andes that by 1520 had carried the tribe's and the city's political authority as far afield as present northern Ecuador in one direction, and central Chile in the other.

As the Incas began to extend their hegemony, they took in other similar valleys close to Cuzco, such as those of Yucay and Ollantaytambo. The inhabitants of these valleys had long grown food on their alluvial floors and on irrigated terracing built into the adjacent mountainsides. But a particularly interesting part of the history of the southern sierra in Peru, the highest part of the central Andes, is the use made by the Incas and their predecessors of cultivable areas at a variety of other heights. The ranges of the southern sierra indeed offer the widest choice of local environments to be found in the Andes – the most extensive and complex "altitudinal zonation," as it has been called.[28] The highland communities took advantage of this to set up small "colonies" at different heights, using each small area so settled to grow particular foods. So, for example, at the height and latitude of the Cuzco valley, potatoes and other root crops could be grown. But maize, beans, and squash did better in lower, warmer places. And coca and fruits were best grown lower still. Conversely, above the level of Cuzco and other communities sited in high valleys, llamas and alpacas could be grazed on rough grasses.[29] *Puna* is the name given in Peru to the shallow slopes and occasional high plains between the mountains at altitudes running up from roughly 4,000 meters to the snowline at 5,000 meters.[30] This zone has been termed "high-altitude tundra."[31] It has a natural vegetation of *ichu*, a grass so coarse that only the native Andean camelids have the digestive apparatus necessary to benefit from it.

The Incas are the best-known practitioners of the technique of ecological colonization, and used it also for political purposes. So, for example, in the late fifteenth century they sent *mitimaes* (a Quechua term for colonists) from the imperial center to the valleys around Cochabamba in the eastern ranges of what are now the Bolivian Andes. There, at 2,500 meters, maize grew well; and the Cochabamba valleys became one the main granaries of the Inca state.[32] At the same time, however, the colonists served the political purposes of the empire: they contributed to the spread of the "state" language,

Quechua; they acted as models in behavior and farming practices for the conquered local people; and they were a constant reminder of Inca power.

The latitude of Cochabamba (the center of present-day Bolivia) is roughly the southern limit of vertical colonization by pre-Conquest communities. This is in large part because, with increasing latitude southwards, there is general cooling even at low altitude; and hence the range of useful microenvironments at different heights diminishes. An additional difficulty is that in southern Bolivia, northern Chile, and north-western Argentina, the extreme aridity of the coastal plateau reaches far up into the mountains. Almost the only moisture to be found is in the snowcaps of the highest volcanic peaks. In these conditions of high, cold desert, human habitation is hard pressed; although it has long been present to some small, if primitive, degree in the southern *altiplano* of Bolivia, for example. And a little further south, on the *puna* of the Argentine–Chilean border, under the volcanic summits, a pre-Inca Atacaman culture once existed.[33] In slightly less arid conditions a little to the east, where moisture from the Atlantic side of the subcontinent penetrates, the Humahuaca and Diaguita (or Calchaquí) farming cultures, again both pre-Inca, flourished in the high basins of north-western and north-central Argentina respectively.[34]

By the latitude of Santiago in central Chile, the snowline on the Andes has descended to between 4,000 and 4,500 meters.[35] On the slopes behind Valdivia, 700 kilometers further south, the snow is down to about 1,500 meters. And in the southernmost extremes of the country, in Tierra del Fuego, permanent snows start at 700 meters, and Andean glaciers drop icebergs directly into the sea.[36] Below the snows in these southern reaches of the Andes facing the Pacific, rain-drenched and gale-lashed forest is the natural cover of the slopes. Neither climate nor vegetation welcomes human settlement.

Nor do they in much of the interior of South America. Almost the whole of the immense Amazon drainage area has a natural flora of tropical rainforest. So, too, does most of the area of Guyana, Surinam, and French Guiana, together with parts of the interior of Venezuela and Colombia. In most of this forested area, rainfall is high (2,570 millimeters a year at Iquitos in Peruvian Amazonia, 2,030 millimeters at Manaus in north-central Brazil); so also are temperatures, though they are not as extreme as might be imagined. Manaus, for instance, slightly south of the equator, has an average January temperature of 26°C, while in Buenos Aires, 3,500 kilometers further south, the corresponding figure is only three degrees lower. It is at first view surprising that, being so largely tropical, South America has a far smaller area suffering many truly hot days (above 43 °C) than North America. But this is an expectable outcome of the greater continentality of the North American climates. Moreover, the part of South America most afflicted by sweltering heat (the Chaco region of northern Argentina and western Paraguay) is not equatorial, and in fact barely tropical.[37] Nevertheless, the combination in the tropical forests of high year-round heat and humidity does make them an uncomfortable environment for human dwelling. And to this disadvantage is added the general infertility of their soils. This, again, is connected with high and constant rainfall. The masses of descending water leach the soil of soluble minerals, so that when the trees are cleared, the ground will normally yield good crops only for a year or two.[38]

To the north and south of the Amazon basin, and on patches of higher terrain within it, lie areas of lighter tropical woodland, wooded savanna, and grass and shrub that in aggregate cover an area almost as large as the full rainforest itself. Some of these regions are decidedly unfriendly to settlement and prosperity. Such are the backlands of north-eastern Brazil, away from the humid coasts, where the dominant vegetation is *caatinga*, a scrub woodland. Broadly similar in flora and climate (with the exception of its extreme summer temperatures) is the Chaco of western Paraguay and northern Argentina, with an adjoining section of south-eastern Bolivia. This is not, to be sure, an economic wasteland. The hard *quebracho* ("break-ax") tree, the plant most commonly associated with the Chaco, has long been profitably exploited for its tannin, useful for processing hides provided by the cattle that find thin grazing in the Chaco. Limited crop farming is possible in the Argentine part of the region.[39]

Much more productive than the Chaco or the backlands is an ample band of savanna, with a natural covering of either grass or light woodland, that occupies the center-south of Brazil. It runs broadly north-east from the borders with Paraguay and Bolivia as far as the backlands of the Brazilian north-east itself. This, compared with the backlands or with the Chaco, is welcoming and fertile. On its interior, western, side, the savanna lies on the Mato Grosso plateau; further north and east it occupies the inner, westward-dipping, slopes of the Brazilian Highlands. In both cases altitude runs typically between 400 and 900 meters. Rainfall is moderate, in comparison with the Amazon basin to the north. And temperatures are agreeable. Brasilia, the new capital of the country, was built in the middle of this band from the late 1950s on; it has an average temperature in January of about 18°C, and in July of 14 °C. Partly under the stimulus of the new, interior focus of the country that Brasilia represents, the agricultural potential of the savanna is now beginning to be realized, with burgeoning farming, for instance, in the adjacent state of Goiás.

On the eastern side of Brazil, more typically tropical conditions again dominate, with proximity to the Atlantic making for greater rainfall and humidity. Light tropical forest is the natural vegetation of most of the inland-facing slopes of the Brazilian highlands to a distance varying between 200 and 400 kilometers from the coast. It was on these slopes, particularly in the hinterlands of Rio de Janeiro and São Paulo in the valley of the Paraíba River, that in the nineteenth century Brazil's immense coffee-growing industry developed.[40] For most of the colonial period, by contrast, it was the coastal plain itself, between the shore and the seaward-facing escarpment of the Highlands, that was both the economic and demographic focus of Brazil. Along most of this narrow strip the natural cover is dry tropical forest. In it, clearings were made, from almost the beginning of European settlement, for growing sugar cane. In the sixteenth and seventeenth centuries Brazil dominated world production of sugar, much as it came in the nineteenth to dominate coffee.

[2]   *AMERICAN PEOPLES*

AZTECS

When, three decades or so after Columbus's first voyage, the Spaniards began to penetrate the American mainlands, and to make contact with the great native cultures, they were impressed by what they found. These were a very different rank of people from the islanders of the Caribbean. Of the Aztec capital, Tenochtitlan, Hernán Cortés wrote to the Emperor Charles V in 1520, "I will say ... that these people live almost like those in Spain, and in as much harmony and order as there, and considering that they are barbarous and so far from the knowledge of God and cut off from all civilized nations, it is truly remarkable to see what they have achieved in all things."[1] Thirteen years later, the conquerors of Peru were equally struck by the Inca capital, Cuzco, telling the Emperor, "This city is the greatest and finest ever seen in this country or anywhere in the Indies. We can assure your Majesty that it is so beautiful and has such fine buildings that it would be remarkable even in Spain."[2]

By the time these reports were sent in, the conquering Spaniards already knew that these two cities were the hearts of great empires, though they still did not realize the full extent of the Aztecs' and Incas' reach. The Aztecs dominated most of Mexico south of Tenochtitlan, with an influence extending into what is now Guatemala, and a considerable area north-east of Tenochtitlan extending down to the Gulf coast. The total area was not far short of Spain's. Inca controls had a far lengthier span, running some 4,000 kilometers from present northern Ecuador to central Chile (a far greater distance than any dimension of Charles's Holy Roman Empire), though they were largely confined to the Andean highlands. Despite its narrowness, nonetheless, *Tahuantinsuyu* (Land of the Four Quarters), as the Incas called their domain, was the largest native American empire ever assembled, and has been reckoned the largest ever created in the world with Bronze Age technology.[3]

What was not immediately obvious to the Spaniards was that these two great states were quite new features on the American political and economic landscape. By remarkable coincidence, they both had essentially come into being – burst onto the scene, indeed – a century before the European invaders appeared. In both cases, their eruption brought to an end a long period, lasting

250–300 years, in which central Mexico and the central Andes were filled with small, jostling, polities. These, in turn, had been the residue of the collapse of earlier, centralizing states around 1200. In Mexico, Toltec rule and influence, centered on the city of Tula just beyond the northern end of the Valley of Mexico, subsided dramatically in the late twelfth century. And in the central Andes, the parallel power, Tiahuanacu, sited at the southern tip of Lake Titicaca, contracted quickly in the same years.

The reasons for the fall of Tula and Tiahuanacu are much disputed. Whatever the specific causes, in both cases the decline fits into a pattern of periodic concentration and dissolution of power and religious influence in central Mexico and the central Andes that extends back into the haze of time. Similarly disputed are the reasons for the refocusing of political, cultural, and religious authority that constitutes the emergence of the Aztec empire from the many city states of Mexico, and the rise of the Incas from among numerous more rural communities in what are now highland Peru and Bolivia.

There is broad agreement that the origin of the citizens of the Aztec imperial capital, Tenochtitlan, was a small tribe, calling itself the Mexica, that drifted into the Valley of Mexico late in the thirteenth century.[4] This was one minor group among many originating in the north and west who were drawn to the fertility and perhaps the sophistication of the Valley. Like many other of these migrants, the Mexica were crude in comparison with the peoples of the existing Valley towns, gatherers rather than growers, nomads rather than dwellers. The Valley was already full; no obvious niche awaited the Mexica. They survived for a while as mercenaries in the constant conflicts among the city states. Then they finally found refuge on what, according to their own history, were unoccupied swampy islands in the largest lake, Texcoco, on the Valley floor (though archaeologists have recently uncovered pre-Mexica remains on the island sites).[5] And there, somewhere between 1320 and 1350, they began to build what was for many years a twin town, Tenochtitlan-Tlatelolco.

Until well into the next century, the Mexica survived, indeed thrived, as fighting vassals, and then junior allies, of one of the leading forces in the Valley's power struggles: the Tepaneca, whose chief town was Azcapotzalco, on the shore of the lake, 8 kilometers or so north-west of Tenochtitlan. As the Mexica fought successfully for the Tepaneca, their society was gradually militarized. Warriors acquired an ever greater central power, tending to push aside the authority and practices of the *calpullin* (a Nahuatl term for traditional social groups, perhaps originally bound by ties of kin, whose members tended to live on and cultivate a common piece of land). The new, war-sanctioned supreme leaders, the *tlatoque* (singular, *tlatoani*: "he who speaks"), and an emergent nobility below them, the *pipiltin*, gained lands for themselves as reward for their efforts in the Tepaneca expansion.[6] This, by the early 1400s, had passed beyond the Valley's limits to the north and west, and had begun to take on an imperial tone.[7]

Finally the Mexica grew to possess such military strength, expertise, and confidence that they resolved to turn on their Tepaneca masters. A crisis of succession in Azcapotzalco in the late 1420s gave the opportunity. The Mexica joined forces with Texcoco, a leading city on the east side of the Valley that had long been in conflict with the Tepaneca; and to this basic union they added a smaller nearby town, Tlacopan, to form a famous "Triple Alliance." In 1428 this combination defeated the Tepaneca, and took over their lands. These, added to the territories of Texcoco, were the kernel from which sprang the rampant growth of the Aztec empire. "Aztec" denotes the common culture of the people of the Valley of Mexico. And the Valley was from this point onwards, until the Spaniards brought matters to a halt in 1519–21, ever more firmly in the grasp of the Triple Alliance.

Until its final decades, authority in the Alliance was shared between Texcoco and Tenochtitlan. Texcoco was the senior partner in age and sophistication.[8] But the fiery energy that drove the developing imperial machine was Tenochtitlan's. And this energy was not merely material and military, but, perhaps more tellingly, ideological.

For all the small polities of the Valley in the pre-imperial time, the model of cultured civilization remained the Toltecs; or, at least, the Toltecs as increasingly idealizing memory portrayed them. Ruling dynasties in the city states proudly proclaimed whatever genealogical links with the Toltecs they could muster.[9] Newcomers sought to create such connections. The Mexica, in the traditional account, did so in c.1372 by requesting from Culhuacan, a city state south of Tenochtitlan in the Valley whose rulers had strong Toltec links, a prince to lead them. The man in question, Acamapichtli, may have been the son of a Mexica father and a princess of Culhuacan.[10] In any case, he is seen as the first *tlatoani* of the Mexica. As such he was the initiator of a dynasty of supreme leaders whose Toltec ancestry gave them, and the Mexica under them, not only a sense of belonging in the Valley, but of holding a legitimate right to wield power to which the old *calpulli*-based government could not lay claim.

As Mexica power and self-esteem grew, so also did the status of their particular tribal god Huitzilopochtli ("Southern Hummingbird"). This figure, possibly the deification of some distant Mexica hero, was unique to them, and remained a minor god in the fourteenth century. The Mexica, indeed, as part of their assimilation of Valley culture, took up the cults of the great enduring divinities of central Mexico: Quetzalcoatl (Plumed Serpent), Tlaloc (the rain god), Tezcatlipoca (Smoking Mirror), and a multitude of only slightly lesser figures. But, as the Aztec empire gained in power after 1428, so too did Huitzilopochtli rapidly rise in public estimation to the level of the old great gods. It was in the reign of Moctezuma I (1440–68) that the first large temple of Huitzilopochtli was built. And the great pyramid that was dedicated, after several amplifications, in the center of Tenochtitlan in 1487 bore two shrines, one for the worship of Tlaloc, and the other for that of Huitzilopochtli.[11] As Aztec military and political successes multiplied, so did the Mexicas', and others', sense of the god's power. The exaltation of Huitzilopochtli that then seemed due led, it seemed, to still further imperial gains; and so on in a mutually reinforcing process. Further, Mexica history was quite consciously and purposely reinvented early on in the imperial expansion – during, in fact, the reign of Itzcoatl (1428–40), the *tlatoani* who had led the revolt against the Tepaneca – to promote Huitzilopochtli to the highest rank in the pantheon, as one of the four sons of the creator gods.[12] Another purpose of this rewriting or, more precisely, repainting of the Mexicas' past (the old picture histories were destroyed) was to establish as "fact" their Toltec heritage; and indeed generally to glorify their heritage in the eyes of their neighbors in the Valley.[13]

The propaganda may not have easily undone those neighbors' scorn of the Mexica as parvenus. But they all soon found themselves with the choice of bending either to that message or to the reality of Mexica force. For in Itzcoatl's years most of the Valley towns were overcome by the Triple Alliance, led by Mexica warriors, and more or less willingly incorporated into the expansive effort of the nascent empire. Moctezuma I, Itzcoatl's successor, then sent imperial forces outside the Valley, as did the four subsequent *tlatoque* – Axayacatl (1469–81), Tizoc (1481–6), Ahuitzotl (1486–1502), and Moctezuma II (1502–20) – down to the time of the Spanish conquest. Each new ruler, having been chosen by high councils for his promise as warrior and leader, was expected to prove his selection by making new conquests. These led to the broadening of the imperial bounds by 1519 on the scale already suggested. By the time the Spaniards came, only a few pockets of resistance held out against Aztec pressure in central and southern Mexico.

Exactly what it was that drove the Aztecs of the Valley of Mexico to expand so fast and so far is a matter of vigorous debate among archeologists and ethnohistorians. One persistent sort of explanation is demographic. It is possible that the growth of Mexica hegemony coincided with the rising phase of a slow population cycle that had characterized central Mexico for many centuries past.[14] By this argument, simple need for food in the Valley drove its inhabitants to conquer outside it, and to force their new subjects to provide tribute in kind and in labor. The phenomenal growth of the city of Tenochtitlan-Tlatelolco itself, which by the early sixteenth century held possibly 200,000 or even 300,000 people,[15] created perhaps a particularly urgent demand for tributes of food and other supplies. This would have been an especially strong stimulus for expansion, since Tenochtitlan was the city of the Mexica themselves, the warrior heart of the Aztec body.

The demographic explanation of expansion is vulnerable to arguments of imprecision and overgenerality. Who can say what the precise increase of demand for food was in the Valley between, say, 1350 and 1500; or if it was necessary for the Aztecs to overrun such a large area in order to meet it? To critics having such doubts, a stronger, but still materialist, line of explanation is that all levels of Aztec society clearly benefited from expansion. Supreme rulers – the *tlatoque* – were confirmed in power by conquests. The nobility – an almost wholly warrior class – gained wealth in land and tribute. Some of this wealth was passed on as patronage to subordinates, and so served to create political support. Influential middle groups in society, such as the priests and administrators whose ranks multiplied as the empire grew, were supported by booty taken in war and by the inflow of tribute that followed it. Social, as well as economic, gain went to the successful warrior. And in late Aztec times, in an ever more rigidly stratified society, martial prowess became the only practicable means of social ascent for the mass of people. Thus warfare and conquest, once embarked on, acquired a momentum of their own because many, or nearly all, saw chances for gain and glory in them.[16]

There is a danger, though, in advancing these pragmatic explanations for expansion. The risk is of making the Aztecs seem rational, twentieth-century people, responsive to calculations of profit and loss. In reality, their mental world was anything but rational (in the modern sense), and it may well be that a highly distinctive set of ideas about how the universe functioned, an ideology grounded in religion, was the deepest and truest source of their imperial drive. Huitzilopochtli, the minor tribal deity of the Mexica elevated in the fifteenth century to the highest heavenly circles, was central in this scheme of things. The Mexica, and the other members of their alliance, did not simply feel the nationalistic urge to spread his cult that might have been expected. Rather, conquest and empire became essential to the proper worship of Huitzilopochtli; and without that proper worship, belief was that the universe would cease to function.

One part of the exaltation of Huitzilopochtli was his close association with the warrior sun, Tonatiuh (as well as with the ancient, powerful, whimsical force of Tezcatlipoca, one of whose guises was as the young sun of spring and summer).[17] The passage of the sun across the sky was not seen as part of the perpetual natural order, but, in true Aztec fashion, as a constant battle. The battle, in this case, was against the stars' resistance. To keep up the fight, the sun (Huitzilopochtli-Tonatiuh) required to be fed with life itself, an essence to be found only in human blood. Hence, in practical terms, the working of the cosmos demanded continual offerings of blood, obtained by ritual killing.

The Aztecs, indeed, in acting out these beliefs, became perhaps the leading practitioners of human "sacrifice" of all time. And possibly the greatest of all Aztec ritual slaughters took place at the dedication of the great pyramid of Huitzilopochtli and Tlaloc, in the center of Tenochtitlan, in 1487. On that occasion as many as twenty thousand victims may have rendered up their life spirit to the gods.[18] Most of these, and most victims at any time, were captives taken in war. Only war could yield the needed supply of sacrificial blood. Thus conquest became part and parcel of the working of the Aztec universe. It is true that ritual battles, the famous "flowery wars" of Aztec Mexico, were staged among the three components of the Alliance, and between the Alliance and a few nearby polities, with the aim of yielding particularly valuable captives for subsequent offerings to the deities.[19] But in general, areas already overwhelmed could not be expected to continue supplying victims, except in the common enough case of rebellion, when military punishment would yield its crop. Territorial extension of combat, therefore, was inevitable.

It was convenient, of course, that expansion also produced tribute needed to sustain the Valley's dense population: foodstuffs, cotton cloth in immense amounts, cacao beans, gold dust, and not least feathers – feathers of tropical birds, especially those of the quetzal from the south. Pursuit of these, according to Mexica merchants, seems almost to be have been in itself a reason for conquest, so highly were they valued for picture making, their shimmering colors seeming to be "Shadows of the Sacred Ones" themselves.[20] Then again, the violence accompanying conquest, and the marching of armies across the land en route to the expanding frontier, had a usefully intimidating effect on previously subjugated polities. So did the constant cutting and plucking of captives' hearts and the cascading of their blood down the temple stairways in Tenochtitlan. Provincial leaders were often brought in to witness these sights. War, religion, politics, and economics thus intertwined to reinforce one another, and also what became, after 1428, Aztec triumphal expansionism. Some students suspect an element of design in this combination, seeing in it particularly the hand of Tlacaelel, a nephew of Itzcoatl, and a Machiavellian ideologue and kingmaker active almost to the end of the fifteenth century.[21] But it is hard to judge the role of design against that of circumstance in the creation of the Aztec "system."

Rational design seems in a sense, too, at odds with the Aztec mentality. These were an intensely religious people, or, better, a people who were intensely aware of inhabiting a world crowded with bustling, fickle, often malevolent spirits. The great god Tezcatlipoca was archetypical: "Smoking Mirror" was his name, and the fleetingness of vapors and of reflections in polished obsidian his protean nature. He was the creative force that gave children; but also a power that rejoiced to bring random, senseless destruction among humans.[22] In general, the sacred forces, large and small, that crowded in on everyday life were threatening; only constant appeasement through many minor rituals would keep them at bay. The guard must never be let down. The fierce Aztec prohibition of drunkenness, except on proper celebratory occasions, was aimed not so much at maintaining decorous public order as at denying hazardous spiritual forces an open doorway into human affairs.[23]

INCAS

The Inca world, too, was one of encircling spirituality, but the hallucinatory quality that tinctures our image of the Aztecs was absent from it. Certainly the Andean mountain world was full of holy places and holy objects, as it still is: the Quechua word _huaca_, denoting sacredness of site or thing, is still often heard today; and the little roadside shrine, or _apachita_, consisting of nothing more than a pile of stones, is a constant feature of highland journeys. But in religion, as in much else, the Incas seem sober, measured, subdued when placed beside the Aztecs, almost as if the greater physical height of their lands had cooled their psyches as much as it had the air that they breathed and in which their crops grew.

There was nothing subdued, of course, about the rate with which the Inca state expanded in the century before the European invasion. Its growth began suddenly in _c_.1440, two centuries or more after the Incas' arrival in the Cuzco valley of the southern Peruvian Andes, an event generally placed in _c_.AD 1200.[24] They were one among many small ethnic groups taking advantage of the favorable microclimates provided by the high valleys. Where they had come from is an open question. One of their own creation myths linked them to Lake Titicaca (some 300 kilometers south-east of Cuzco). But that is perhaps more indicative of a desire to connect themselves with the greatest of earlier polities in the southern sierra, Tiahuanacu, than it is of their real origin.

The early Incas and their neighbors shared a social organization whose features still persist strongly in the central Andes. Communities were small, no more than villages close to farming and grazing land. The basic unit of society, apart from the family, was the *ayllu*, which seems fundamentally to have been a clan, a group of people descended from some common ancestor. An *ayllu* might extend to more than one village, though its members were required to marry within the group. *Ayllus* in the later, imperial period were governed by hereditary *curacas*; though it is not clear when such positions became hereditary. *Ayllus* held land around their communities, which members could use as they needed it, to grow food and to pasture llamas and alpacas.[25]

Deeply ingrained into the communal life of these clans was the notion of mutual aid and responsibility, of a reciprocity that was an economic obligation, but even more a moral one.[26] People were expected to lend their labor to cultivate neighbors' land, and expected that neighbors would help them in due course. All capable people collaborated to support the incapable – orphans, widows, the sick – with food and housing. They also collaborated to produce food offerings to local deities. Early leaders could perhaps call on the labor of *ayllu* members for their own, and communal, purposes. *Curacas* of imperial times and later certainly did so, and they in turn had a responsibility to reward their subjects in various ways. But what services the early leaders could legitimately expect is unclear, as is much else in the pre-expansionary history of the Incas.

One thing is obvious enough, though: that these many small highland polities were in competition for land and water, and beyond this engaged in constant raiding and looting of each other, becoming increasingly militaristic as they did so. The intensity of these struggles seems to have increased throughout the fourteenth century. It was from one such conflict in the fifteenth century that the expansionist imperial state of the Incas emerged.

The contest was with the Chanca polity, near neighbors of the Inca to the north-west; although between the two lay the territory of the another ethnic group, the Quechua. The history of the Chanca is even less clear than the Incas'. There does exist the intriguing possibility that they were the one-time conquerors of a shadowy but undoubtedly large and powerful city, Huari, that several centuries earlier had existed in the Ayacucho valley, some 250 kilometers north-west of Cuzco.[27] By the early fifteenth century the Chanca, it is thought, had become particularly aggressive. They attacked and overcame the Quechua. They then were poised for an assault on the Inca, who were in an anti-Chanca alliance with the Quechua. The attack, aimed at Cuzco, finally came in 1438.

The Inca ruler at the time was Viracocha, a man who had certainly made energetic efforts to defend and expand Inca territory in earlier decades, but who was now in decline. Viracocha, the story goes, withdrew from Cuzco to a nearby fort, taking with him his chosen heir, the son of a secondary wife. This action presented a political opportunity to another aspirant to Inca leadership,

Cusi Yupanqui, who was a son of Viracocha's principal wife. Cusi Yupanqui organized a successful defense of Cuzco, an effort in which he was helped, so Inca oral history told it, by rocks turning into soldiers, and by an encouraging visitation from the Inca sky god.[28] He proceeded quickly to expel the Chanca invaders from Inca domains.

Cusi Yupanqui is without doubt the founder of the Inca imperial state. His military successes established him as the supreme ruler in Cuzco, the Sapa Inca ("Sole Inca"), as the emperors were known. Soon after his victory over the Chanca he changed his name to Pachacutec (or Pachacuti), meaning "cataclysm" or "remaker of the world." In doing so, he may have been imitating leaders of Huari who had also used that name, with possibly the broad aim of legitimizing Inca sovereignty by linking it, if only symbolically, to the power of that ancient place.[29]

Pachacutec led the Inca state for some thirty years, until 1471. In that time he rebuilt and aggrandized Cuzco, turning it from little more than a large village into the imperial capital that was so to impress the Spaniards. The two small rivers flowing through the town, the Tullumayo and Huatanay, were canalized in stone beds to avoid flooding. Clay models were made of the proposed layout of the city, existing buildings destroyed where necessary, and a ceremonial center was built, with open spaces for large assemblies of people. The chief ceremonial addition that Pachacutec made was the new temple of the Sun, *Coricancha* – the "Court of Gold," so called on account of its gold statues and the partial covering of its stone and adobe walls with beaten sheets of gold.[30] This construction was the visible expression of what became increasingly a state and imperial cult of the sun (*Inti* in Quechua), which was conceived of as one aspect of a many-faceted sky god. Inti was now proclaimed to be the founder of the Inca dynasty: Pachacutec and his successors drew legitimacy not merely from martial prowess, not merely from divine support, but from divinity itself.[31]

With Cuzco rebuilt and glorified, Pachacutec embarked on an expansion of Inca territory, dominating in the course of his long reign the highlands over a distance of some 1,000 kilometers north-west and south-east of the capital. The large and rich polities of the Colla and Lupaqa on the western shores of Lake Titicaca, in which Viracocha may have earlier shown a predatory interest, were among the groups now taken. And Inca control was extended west of them down to the Pacific coast.

But it was Pachacutec's successor, Tupac Yupanqui, who was responsible for the greatest extension of Inca dominion. First in the closing years of Pachacutec's reign, and then in his own (1471–93), he brought in a vast area of mountain and coast south from Titicaca down to the Río Maule in central Chile; the highlands up to what is now central Ecuador; and the rest of the Peruvian coast. A mighty capture on the northern coast was the kingdom of Chimor, centered on the city of Chan-Chan, close to the modern Trujillo. This was the largest polity in Peru in the period between Tiahuanacu and the Inca, and the last of a long series of irrigation-based states that over past millennia had arisen in different river valleys in the coastal desert. At its height, the Chimor domain embraced the entire coast from the Gulf of Guayaquil down to central Peru. In overcoming it, the Inca removed their only possible challenger in power and status.

Final additions were made to Inca territory by the next Sapa Inca, Huayna Capac (1493–1525), who pushed a little further north in the Ecuadorian highland, as far in fact as the present border with Colombia; and annexed a relatively small area on the interior slopes of the Andes in northern Peru. He was the last Inca ruler to live out his reign before the Spaniards appeared. The slowing of expansion under Huayna Capac may have been the outcome of natural restraints on imperial growth. The Inca were a highland people, unsuited both physiologically and psychologically to life at low altitudes. The desert coast was less difficult for them than the humid forests of the interior, their intrusions into which tended to end in disaster. Growth was possible, therefore, only north and south, in the highlands. By *c*.1500 it had perhaps gone as far, some 2,000 kilometers above Cuzco and 2,500 kilometers below it, as the available means of administrative and political control allowed.

Of the many remarkable features of the Inca empire, the most striking is the speed of its growth. An explanation of this starts with natural conditions. The Andes are immensely rugged; but the difficulties of north–south movement are far smaller than those of moving east and west, since the mountain valleys run roughly parallel to the coast. The famous roads of the Inca, partly inherited from earlier times and partly their own creation, took advantage of these natural valley routes.[32] The roads were narrow, but unobstructed: they were closed to all but those traveling on the state's business. Along a total of 30,000–50,000 kilometers of road moved *chasquis* – relay runners bearing information and orders – and also, when called for, armies.

Imperial growth, though, was not so much a matter of outright conquest by armies as might be imagined. Rather, it seems to have been achieved by combining traditional practices of Andean reciprocity, now expanded to an imperial scale, with intimidation. The Incas' unexpected success against the Chanca in 1438 gave them a running start. They were suddenly the dominant power of their immediate region. Pachacutec was able to use this authority to draw surrounding, now relatively weaker, *curacas* into alliance with Cuzco. He offered them, in return for tribute and acknowledgment of dominance, gifts of valued items and grand public ceremonies of eating and drinking. Most local leaders in the central Andes, it seems, succumbed to this combination of blandishment and lightly veiled threat.[33] Inca expansion became, in consequence, a rapid and inexpensive affair. The greater the number of polities incorporated in this way, the weightier the pressure the Inca could apply to the next ethnic group they approached. From time to time, of course, they had to fight. But other methods would be tried first. A part of Tupac Yupanqui's successful strategy against the Chimor domain, for example, was to threaten the water supply crucial to that desert polity's existence.

It seems that war became the prime means of enlarging the empire only when the Inca reached cultural areas lacking the ingrained reciprocal practices of the central Andes. This may have been another reason for the empire's limits settling where they did, in central Chile and northern Ecuador. The people of these areas did not use systems of reciprocity, and so were not conditioned to succumb to Inca gifts. Certainly it was in these distant frontier zones that the Inca found the fiercest resistance. Huayna Capac spent many years in combat in the north, for a very small gain of territory.[34]

If the means of Inca expansion are fairly clear, the springs of it are harder to define. Initially, after the disorder caused by the Chanca attack, and the almost miraculous success of Pachacutec's defense against it, simple desire for safety may have driven the Inca to enlarge the area around Cuzco under their control.[35] A momentum of growth may then have been created, with control of new areas becoming a constant necessity as a source of goods to be redistributed among already subservient local leaders. Then again, Inca individuals had an interest in imperial growth, since it yielded rewards for nobles in the form of land, animals, clothing, and other goods. And distinction in combat could mean advance in the governing hierarchy for nobles, and social and status gains also for commoners, who might become provincial *curacas* on the strength of it.[36] The inevitable growth of the apparatus of state and religion also made expansion a temptation, if not a necessity, especially once a certain luxury of splendor became the rule in Cuzco. Part of the tributary labor demanded of newly incorporated regions went to support bureaucracy and cult. And the Inca were not without a sense of religious mission, also. Their very success in expansion seemed to signal the power and rightness of the state's sun cult, and to impose a duty to extend it further.

This assortment of motives for expanding the empire may have been reinforced by the demands of one particular politico-religious practice that the imperial Inca used: the worship of the mummified bodies of former rulers. Ancestor worship was common enough in Andean culture, but it was elaborated to an uncommon degree by the fifteenth-century Inca. The preserved remains of Sapa Incas were symbols of the strength and continuity of Inca power. They were also the most sacred of *huacas*. Each ruler's descendants in the male line – a lineage known as a *panaqa* – were charged with sustaining his cult with proper ceremony. (The sole exception was the ruler's successor, who became the founder of his own *panaqa*.) To enable this to be done in fitting fashion, in Pachacutec's reign lands immediately around Cuzco were taken from their occupants for assignment to the existing *panaqas*. The products of the land should be used to sustain and expand the cult of past kings, so that the record of Inca glory should run far back into time. The mummies occupied palaces in the center of Cuzco, surrounded by the pomp used with living rulers. At times of public celebration and ritual, they were brought out to witness and preside. They were taken to visit each other in their palaces. All this ceremonial was costly. It has been argued that maintaining it was possible only through the passing of each dead ruler's personal holdings to his *panaqa*. The son or other relative who succeeded him as Sapa Inca received the office without its accumulated personal wealth. Therefore he had to extend his realms in order, in due course, to endow his lineage with the means to sustain his own cult. Hence the cult of dead rulers, emphasized after 1438 to reinforce Inca renown and authority while the empire was still in its infancy, in itself became a stimulus to imperial growth.[37]

As the empire expanded, the Inca applied to it an enveloping set of controls. These emanated from Cuzco, always the supreme political and religious center (though in late times Quito, in the far north, became an important secondary place). Through it passed the imaginary lines that divided the empire into its four parts: Chinchasuyu, the north-western quarter, embracing Ecuador and much of northern Peru; Antisuyu, the north-east; Cuntisuyu, the south-west; and Collasuyu, the south-eastern and largest section, comprising the Titicaca basin, highland Bolivia, and northern Argentina and northern Chile. Together these made up Tahuantinsuyu, "Land of the Four Quarters."[38]

The Sapa Inca, quasi-divine supreme ruler, normally resided in Cuzco, though he might, as the case of Huayna Capac shows, go off on long campaigns. Each quarter was governed by a lord (*apo* in Quechua), also usually based in the capital. These governors were generally close relatives of the emperor, members of one of the royal *panaqas*. Below them came a long set of officials, in strict hierarchy, chief among them the *toqricoq*, who were men from Cuzco, though not necessarily *panaqa* members, sent to supervise affairs from various provincial capitals. Beneath them stood the *curacas*, normally the hereditary lords of subjugated polities, and the highest ranking locals in the system. And then followed further ranks of local supervisors, in charge of decimal units of households, from ten thousand down to ten (though the numbers were not always exact). Outside this fixed hierarchy were census takers, who each year did a new count of imperial subjects so as to determine proper tribute levels; and inspectors, who surveyed and reported on the activities of other administrators.[39]

Tribute collection was a major purpose of the imperial enterprise. Tribute was not set directly in goods, but in labor obligations that produced goods. One type of labor tax was the *mit'a*, signifying a set period of service in the imperial armies, in public works of some sort (making roads or public buildings, for example), or in immediate attendance on the Sapa Inca or other high officers of state. Clearly the *mit'a* removed men temporarily, perhaps for quite long periods, from their homes. The other type of labor demand did not; it obliged local populations to work in farming or tending animals in or near their own communities. In each newly incorporated polity, Inca administrators divided productive land into three, not necessarily equal, parts: one each for support of the local population itself, of the state (including the *panaqas* of Cuzco), and of the religious establishment. The labor of the community in question was then applied to each type of land, and the produce (typically potatoes, maize, quinoa, and llamas) distributed accordingly. Some of the food gathered might be placed in local, Inca-built, storehouses as sustenance for passing armies, a reserve against future famines, or simply to provide for people (widows, the elderly, and the sick) who could not feed themselves.

People subjected to these demands for labor were obviously likely to put up some resistance. To minimize it, and indeed generally to promote an acquiescent peace as far as possible, the Inca applied a number of precautionary measures across their expanding domain. One such was to resettle parts of newly taken groups in other areas, so as to break up possible nodes of resistance. These forced migrants were called *mitimaes*. The same word was applied to loyal subjects who were shifted as colonists out to the periphery, there to act as models of good behavior, or perhaps to improve the working of promising farmlands, or to staff a resident frontier garrison.

Another technique of control was to break up potentially dangerous political structures. Generally, existing lineages of *curacas* were left in place – if, as often happened, they had submitted to the Incas' typical combination of wooing and menace. But where fighting had been needed, and the potential enemy remained strong, local leaders were killed, and the polity fractured into smaller pieces. This was done to the large Chimor kingdom, for instance. In such cases, new local leaders would be assigned, and attached to Cuzco with the standard bonds of reciprocity. A further means of keeping *curacas* in line was the removal of their sons and heirs to Cuzco, for education in Quechua and in Inca practices. The children thus became both hostages and trainees for regional administrative offices. The most sacred *huacas* of subjugated peoples were also removed to Cuzco, with their own attendant priests, as another sort of hostage. In a reverse process, the Inca, as might be expected, had temples built in newly taken regions for the installation of their sun cult.[40]

Despite these, and other, stratagems of control, the empire was far from being as peaceful and orderly as has sometimes been thought. Internal revolts against Inca taxation and dominion flared up continually, particularly in the more distant reaches of Tahuantinsuyu, which, being most recently incorporated, were least well indoctrinated and least detached from their pre-imperial orientations and loyalties. Quito (the Ecuadorian provinces), for example, was a constant thorn in the Inca flesh. But even more central regions could be troublesome. The Aymara-speaking groups around Lake Titicaca, for instance, prosperous and powerful before the Incas' ascent, were both hard to conquer and hard to keep down. Pachacutec allegedly had to assault them three times, and they rebelled again in the time of Tupac Yupanqui.[41]

Nor were disturbances limited to the provinces, whether far or near. Rivalries in the governing nobility in Cuzco were endemic. Sapa Incas on occasion grew wary of military leaders whose successes in the field seemed to make them resistant to bidding from the center. Conflict was particularly likely over the succession to the Sapa Inca-ship itself. The Andean tradition, which the Inca followed, was that leadership should go to the most able candidate (meaning, in the imperial Inca case, the man of greatest military promise). This opened the way for all sorts of intrigue, even if the range of contenders was limited to the previous Sapa Inca's sons, since he generally had numerous offspring by a variety of wives. The best-known case of a conflict over succession is precisely the competition between two sons of Huayna Capac, Huascar and Atahualpa, in the late 1520s. This was a particularly long and fierce struggle, and a tragedy for the Inca, since it fatally weakened their state just as the Spanish made their appearance on the South American scene.

Nonetheless, the Inca realm was definitely a state, and the most remarkable political and administrative body produced by the Americas up to its time. The Aztec polity in Middle America was the closest comparable entity, but fell far short of the Inca creation in size and in economic and governmental organization. And nothing else that the Spaniards encountered came close even to Aztec sophistication.

LESSER CULTURES OF SOUTH AMERICA

The largest political systems in South America outside Inca lands, at the time the Europeans arrived, were those of what is now northern Colombia: the Tairona, between the Sierra Nevada de Santa Marta and the coast, the Cenu, a little to the south-west, and the Chibcha (or Muisca), south-east again in the high valleys of the eastern cordillera of the Andes. All three were, by Inca imperial standards, tiny polities, with territories in the range of 10,000–25,000 square kilometers. They were, though, larger than the Inca community before its imperial growth began, and are perhaps most readily comparable in territory and authority to the rich peoples, such as the Lupaqa, who lived autonomously around Lake Titicaca before the Inca overwhelmed them. Like these, the Chibcha and their neighbors were ethnic groups. But despite a feeling of shared origin among the members of each group, considerable social stratification had arisen in them. Hereditary elites provided warrior leaders, administrators of justice, and ruling chiefs whose power came in part from their contact with gods. These societies had a firm economic base in intensive, sometimes irrigated, agriculture, supplemented by hunting and by fishing in the large rivers of northern Colombia. They produced a variety of goods of high skill and art. The Chibcha mined and worked the emeralds found in their territory. The Tairona excelled in elaborating the shells they took from their Caribbean beaches. Chibcha, Tairona, and Cenu all produced excellent cotton textiles, as well as fine work in the gold in which Colombia abounds, and in a gold-copper alloy termed *tumbaga*.[42] This metalwork naturally impressed the Spanish. The first expedition to reach Chibcha territory, in 1536, reported excitedly back to Charles V on the "Bogotá," as they initially called the paramount Chibcha chief (properly termed the Zipa). "This Bogotá is the principal lord of this land, with many other nobles and chiefs subject to him. He is a personage of great wealth, because the natives say he has a house of gold and many rich emerald mines. His vassals honor him exceedingly; in truth, the Indians of this kingdom are very subjugated by their lords. He has conquered and tyrannized over much of the land."[43] Here, aside from the emphasis on wealth, there is the attempt of conquerors of lesser native groups to cry up the political arrangements of their victims. It was important that they should seem as nearly like the Inca and Aztec as possible. The Zipa was certainly no Sapa Inca in embryo. But the Chibcha were locally powerful, which was one of the reasons for the Spaniards choosing the town from the which the Zipa ruled as their own colonial capital, Santa Fe de Bogotá. And that town became in due course the national capital of Colombia.

Apart from the Chibcha, Tairona, and Cenu, the Colombian territory held, of course, many other chiefdoms, less developed than these in governmental practices, social complexity, and technical and artistic achievement. And the rest of what was to become Spanish South America (outside the Inca range) was peopled by a still greater variety of ethnic and cultural groups, ranging from the moderately sophisticated to the primitive. Among the more advanced in centralization of political authority were the Atacama of northern Chile, and the Humahuaca and Calchaquí groups in the highlands of present north-western Argentina. All these were under some degree of Inca control by the early sixteenth century, though their area was not one in which the Inca were strongly active. Their entire region, on either side of the Andes, is dry, rugged, and in general highly challenging to human presence. The Atacama people and their neighbors made a poor living from grazing llamas and related camelids, and from farming, with some use of irrigation. They supplemented their food supply with hunting, and, in the case of the Atacama on the coast, fishing.

Another difficult region was the Chaco, in present north-western Paraguay. Nonetheless, considering the harshness of the climate here, and the poverty of the soils, a surprisingly sophisticated local culture developed, in the form of the Chané (or Guaná) people. These built villages with as many as a thousand inhabitants, living in large communal houses each holding an extended family, under its patriarchal head. The society was ranked socially into nobles, warriors, commoners, and slaves.

Similar in some respects was the better remembered Guaraní culture of present eastern Paraguay, north central Argentina, and southern Brazil, which also built villages consisting of a few large communal houses. In these lived dozens of families making up a kin group. The head of the principal group was also the village leader, though his authority was mainly confined to relations with other villages. Internally, the Guaraní villages were run through agreement among heads of houses and elders. The Guaraní were members of the very large Tupian language group that extended up into Amazonia and eastwards to the coast of present Brazil. They were farmers, growing above all maize and manioc. The products of hunting, gathering, and fishing supplemented the basically vegetarian diet.

Farmers and fishers also were the Mapuche, on the western side of the mountains in the central zones of Chile. These divided into three subgroups: the Picunche in the north, the Araucanians in the center, and the Huilliche to the south of them. The name Araucanian has often been used for all three divisions. They were all tough and hardy people, resistant to both the Inca and the Spaniards after them. The Inca, indeed, called the Picunche "wild wolves" on account of their unwillingness to serve the state and the crudeness of their agriculture.[44] The Picunche used irrigation ditches of Inca design in their dry, middle-northern zone. Further south the Araucanians in the central valley of Chile found enough moisture to support rotation farming of maize, beans and other crops. They bred llamas. Fishing in the Pacific supported coastal dwellers.

To the south of the small-group cultures – Chané, Guaraní, Mapuche – that combined farming and animal raising with hunting, fishing, and perhaps some gathering, lay the vast lands of the true hunter-gatherers, the people of the pampas and Patagonia, on the east of the Andes, and the forests and islands of the west coast. The Tehuelche on the eastern plains and plateaux hunted the guanaco (the wild relative of the llama, alpaca, and vicuña), and the rhea (the wingless, ostrich-like bird native to the region). They lived in tent villages, each village jealously guarding its hunting ground.

West of the mountains in southern Chile, and in Tierra del Fuego, dwelt a large number of different groups, speaking a variety of languages and dialects, generally on the move, but each with a recognized fishing territory. Collectively these peoples have been called "sea nomads." They depended on the mobility provided by hollowed-log canoes for their food supply of fish, sea birds, and shellfish. Of all the peoples of what was to be Spanish South America, these perhaps were the most egalitarian in social and political ranking, with respected elders guiding the affairs of extended families.[45]

BRAZILIAN PEOPLES

In the parts of South America that fell from 1500 onwards to Portugal, the range of native cultures, in social, political, and cultural organization, was far narrower than what the Spaniards were to find. Nowhere in the future territory of Brazil was there anything to match even the polities of northern Colombia, let alone organization on the Incaic scale.

Of the many dozens of tribes in the territory of the future Brazil, possibly the most advanced were the Potiguar, inhabitants of the easternmost section of the north coast. They were skilled in farming, hunting, and fishing. They were also powerful warriors, capable, according to Portuguese reports of the late sixteenth century, of putting 20,000 men into the field. With such forces they blocked Portuguese colonizing movement toward the Amazon.[46] The Potiguar were one of many tribes belonging to the Tupí-speaking group of people who inhabited the Brazilian coast. The name Tupinambá was applied in colonial times to many of the tribes living on the east coast. In the far south of Brazil were the Guaraní, whose culture area ran eastward from Paraguay to the coast. The Guaraní language was a variant of Tupí, and there was little difference, either, between their lifestyle and that of the coast dwellers. The village consisting of several large houses, for instance, was standard from Paraguay to the north coast. Tupí villages had chiefs, and occasionally paramount chiefs could be found, commanding respect in several villages. But chiefs were mainly war leaders; the running of the villages was done by councils made up of the elders of the extended families inhabiting the great houses. Fierce warfare between neighboring Tupí tribes was common, though the Guaraní in this were something of an exception, being conspicuously docile (at least in the face of European colonization). The purpose of fighting may have been in part control of land for farming. But at least as important a motive was the capture of warriors for ritual killing and cannibalism. All the Tupí speakers lived by a combination of hunting, fishing, and farming. Their staple food was manioc, supplemented by peanuts. They also raised cotton. Farming was the work of women; men reserved themselves for hunting and warfare.

If there is uncertainty still about the precise number and names of the coastal Tupí groups, it is nothing in comparison with the confusion surrounding the pre-contact identity of the interior peoples of Brazil. At least for the Tupí, early European explorers and settlers (Portuguese and other) left first-hand descriptions. But by the time Europeans penetrated inland beyond the Tupí range, mainly in the seventeenth century and later, many interior tribes had disappeared, either dissolved by flight or destroyed by disease. Much knowledge of native matters in the interior is, in reality, a hopeful backward projection by anthropologists and historians of the observed behavior of twentieth-century native survivors. In favor of this method it can be said that many forest groups had little or no contact with the outside world until the present century; and, subject as they were to the cultural conservatism of people living with little material margin available for experiment, they probably changed little over the past few centuries.

Lacking though detailed knowledge may be, however, it is clear enough that large geographical zones of the interior were dominated by people of specific language groups. The Brazilian highlands, for example, from the north coast down to the tributaries of the Paraguay River, were peopled by the Gê speakers, possibly the first humans in Brazilian territory. These, partly because the soils of the interior are less fertile than those of the coastal plain, were poorer farmers than the Tupí, and consequently more dependent on hunting and gathering. They were valiant warriors, who strongly resisted Portuguese westward movement in the seventeenth and eighteenth centuries.

Further west still, in the forests of Amazonia, Arawak speakers predominated. Some of them lived in densely settled villages along the banks of the upper Amazon, the Rio Negro, and the headwaters of the Orinoco. Some of them supported themselves, at least in part, by raising turtles in pens beside their huts. But most of the Arawak speakers, away from the rivers, were hunters and gatherers, and at best primitive cultivators of slash-and-burn plots. The poor soils of the forests would not produce well for more than a very few years after being cleared by felling and burning. Forest dwellers were thus condemned to at least a semi-mobile life, as villages had to be kept close to the cultivated plots of the moment.

Finally, along the streams flowing into the lower Amazon from the north, along the upper Orinoco, and in the Guiana highlands, were the speakers of Carib tongues. They were often in conflict with their Arawak neighbors, and apparently indeed pushing south and east against them in late pre-contact times.

THE CARIBBEAN

Arawaks, and to a lesser degree Caribs, provide a human and cultural link between South and North America. The Caribs' name (one given to them by Europeans, it being uncertain what they called themselves) lives on in the form of "Caribbean." Whether in fact this is a good name for that landlocked sea is, however, less clear than previously assumed. It was long accepted that, by the time the Europeans arrived, distinct Carib and Arawak cultures existed in the islands, with the Caribs occupying the Lesser Antilles, and pressing aggressively up against the relatively peaceful Arawak inhabitants of the large islands. Now, though, doubts are raised about the existence of any substantial distinction between the people of the small islands and those of Puerto Rico, Hispaniola, Jamaica, and Cuba. The "island" Carib tongue that the supposed "Caribs" spoke is seen as belonging to the Arawakan group, so the long-assumed linguistic difference disappears. And there seems to have been no fundamental cultural contrast between dwellers in the large and small islands. Even the notorious propensity of the Carib islanders for eating human flesh has been called into question, so that the propriety of the word "cannibal" itself, said to derive from "Carib," is now suspect.[47]

Still, if the presence of "true" Caribs in the sea named after them is now debatable, there is no doubt about that of Arawak-speaking people, and therefore about at least a linguistic continuity between Amazonia and the Antilles, both large and small. Indeed, the Arawak language zone extended further still, to parts of Central America and even Florida.[48]

The Arawak of Puerto Rico, Hispaniola, and eastern Cuba termed themselves Taíno ("noble" or "prudent").[49] This high self-regard reflected their relatively complex political and social behavior. By the late fifteenth century they had organized themselves into chiefdoms, the domains of *caciques* ("headmen") – a term which the Spaniards picked up and carried to the mainland, applying it everywhere to Indian leaders of all levels of importance. Some *caciques* had authority in dozens of settlements, spread out over hundreds of square kilometers.[50] Territorially speaking, Taíno chiefdoms took the basic form of the land bordering a river along its course from a mountain valley to the sea. This arrangement gave access to water, to a variety of land for cultivation, and to the shore and its resources. Fish, shellfish, and turtles figured largely in the diet. Like their distant Amazonian linguistic relatives, the Taíno raised turtles, and fish also, in artificial ponds. Water and land birds were another source of protein. For carbohydrates, they farmed a variety of root crops: manioc, sweet potatoes, peanuts, and others. They grew cotton and tobacco. Slash and burn was the standard method of farming. Sometimes the soil was mounded, a technique yielding particularly bountiful harvests of manioc.

Arawak society in the Greater Antilles was clearly stratified, with chiefs receiving gifts from the newly harvested crops, and enjoying a monopoly of certain foods, among them iguanas (a local delicacy, though the Spaniards were never so persuaded). Chiefs' authority rested typically on such accomplishments as success in war, and possession of a large, seagoing dugout canoe. Their earthly successes were seen as the expression of divine force working in them. They and their relatives lived in separate villages, consisting of large dwellings that housed several related families. Commoners typically inhabited different groups of houses near fields or rivers. Palm thatch was the standard building material. A feature of Arawak society perhaps linking it westward to Middle America was the playing of the ball game (here called *batey*), sometimes, it is thought, to give expression to rivalries between chiefs, and hence, as on the mainland, to those between divine powers as well.

In the southern, smaller, islands – the territory of the "Caribs" – society rested on the same material base, but had not developed so wide a range of status and authority. Here, nonetheless, definite headmen could be found in the typically small villages, drawing authority from prowess in war and possession of a canoe.

FULL CIRCLE, TO MEXICO

Chiefdoms were also the prevailing form of political arrangement, by the time the Europeans arrived, in another large, non-Arawak, Caribbean territory: Yucatan. This, though physically connected to Mexico and Central America, was, in its human affairs, practically as much an island as Cuba or Hispaniola for most of its known past. Here Maya culture had put down its roots many centuries before the beginning of the Christian era, and had flowered into its "classic" form at about the time of Christ. The blossoming lasted for some eight centuries, and had then withered, for reasons not yet fully understood, and perhaps never to be so. Especially in the south of the peninsula, elaborate towns and ceremonial centers were abandoned in the ninth century AD; the complex, allusive, glyphic writing, along with astronomy the pinnacle of Maya mental achievement, decayed; long dynasties of majestic regional lords died away. True enough, in the north of the peninsula, and in parts of its periphery, the collapse was not so complete or sharp.[51] In the north there in fact appeared in the tenth century something that the south had never produced: a Maya empire, of unknown extent, though certainly small in comparison to the Aztecs', and centered on the city of Chichén Itzá. After the decline of Chichén, another, if lesser, regional capital arose, *c.*1200, in the north at Mayapán. But it too subsided in the mid fifteenth century, so that by the time the first Spaniards reached the peninsula, soon after 1500, no larger polities than local chiefdoms remained.[52]

Further west, in southern Mexico proper, a similar cultural and political dissolution took place around AD 1000 among the Mixtec people. For reasons that are again unclear, smaller towns and kingdoms replaced notable city states. These lesser places, in the decades before the arrival of the Spanish in Mexico, were to a degree dominated by the Aztecs. Further west still, and northward, mainly in what is now the state of Michoacán, the Spanish found another major native culture, that of the Tarascans (or Purépecha), that had resisted Aztec attacks with success. This was a polity larger than anything else in Mexico except for the Aztec empire itself. The capital of the Tarascan domains was Tzintzuntzan, a town on the shore of Lake Pátzcuaro in Michoacán. The Tarascans were the most adept metal workers in Mexico, skilled miners, smelters, and beaters of the copper in which their area abounded.

North of central Mexico, as the land grew dryer and less productive toward the *altiplano*, cultural levels fell and political units grew smaller. Many minor native groups occupied this fringe zone, over some of which the Aztecs

correctly placed, along with most of those in the Madeira group, to the north. By 1350, Spaniards from Mallorca and Andalusia, and further Genoese, had visited the Canaries to trade or take slaves from the islands' population.[3] In the mid 1300s, also, the Azores may have been located, though the definitive discovery is usually placed in 1427, when a Portuguese from the Algarve (the southernmost province of the country) put the group on the map. It is impossible, though, to say for sure when these various island clusters were first sighted. Throughout the period so far discussed, and indeed long before it, fisherman from Portugal and the north coast of Spain had been pressing out into the Atlantic. They may have seen much that never entered a written record. It is absolutely certain, however, that they created a fund of experience on which later voyagers drew.

The movement out into the Atlantic coincided with a series of technological advances in ships and navigation that no doubt accelerated it. Some might argue that without these changes the expansion could not have happened; but it is well to remember that the Norsemen had reached North America, via Iceland and Greenland, c.AD 1000, and perhaps maintained a contact for several centuries thereafter, without the benefit of these advances.[4] And the voyages of Iberians and Genoese no doubt themselves forced the pace of change, in an typical example of the mutual influence operating between technology and the historical environment in which it exists.

The importance of the magnetic compass for long-distance sailing needs no emphasis. The compass was possibly a Chinese invention. It was first described in Europe in the late 1100s, and was in use in the Mediterranean by then. The portolan chart, drawn from bearings taken by compass, and allowing plotting of a course between ports over the open sea, came in the compass's train, and was being used by Italians by the start of the fourteenth century.[5] Ships could be more easily kept on course, and more easily maneuvered, if fitted with a rudder hinged to the stern-post. This replacement for the awkward steering sweep is supposed to have had Baltic origins, and had been adopted by Spanish shipbuilders by the 1280s.[6] Agility, and speed also in some wind conditions, were improved as well by adoption of the triangular lateen sail. The lateen had its origins in the eastern Mediterranean. Its use enabled a vessel to "point higher" – that is, to sail more nearly into the wind – than could be managed with the square canvas typical of Atlantic ships of medieval times. When, early in the fifteenth century, south-western Iberian shipwrights mated this sail to a new, shallow-drafted, dhow-like hull, Portuguese and Spanish sailors found themselves equipped with an almost ideal vehicle for exploration: the caravel. This was a nimble, speedy vessel, just as good for crossing oceans as for probing unknown coastlines. A crew of twenty could manage the three big lateens carried by the typical caravel of 30–50 tonnes. The hull was capacious enough to hold many weeks' stores for so small a crew. The caravel, though of cockle shell size, was a long range vessel. It was an efficient tool which opened up the western and southern Atlantic to European access.

Having the right tool is an immense help in doing a job well; but it does not necessarily lead the holder to embark on the task. Motive must be present, and, preferably, propitious circumstances as well. In the late Middle Ages, circumstance and motive converged in the Iberian lands in a way that goes far toward explaining why this rather remote part of Europe became the base from which western expansion began.

First was geographical position. This simple, passive, fact should be given its full weight in accounting for the Iberian lead. First, Iberia stood as the junction between the ancient world of the Mediterranean, and the nascent world of the Atlantic. And if there was a more definite place where those two worlds dovetailed together, it was the part of the south coast of the peninsula that faced the Atlantic: Spain west of Gibraltar, and the Algarve coast of southern Portugal (to which must be added, a little further north, the splendid harbor of Lisbon in the Tagus estuary). Here it was that Mediterranean technology in shipping was adapted to Atlantic conditions, and the resulting caravels were taken to sea by men long accustomed to the greater scale and severer challenges of the great ocean. Here, also, Mediterranean merchant techniques and ambitions, carried westward by the Genoese and others, found an Atlantic home, and did their part to propel the ships of Iberian explorers outwards.

Again, the Iberian peninsula projects south and west into the Atlantic from the main mass of Europe, simply giving explorers departing thence toward Africa or America a head start of 1,000 kilometers or more over men putting out from northern European ports. More important, ships departing on south-western or southern headings from Lisbon, the Algarve, or southern Spain immediately found themselves with following winds and currents to carry them quickly to the Madeira group, the Canaries, and points south and west. Getting back, to be sure, was a slow business, at least until it was discovered that a north-west course from the islands eventually brought ships into the Westerlies of the North Atlantic, which would drive them swiftly to the north of Portugal or Spain. It was supposedly while taking advantage of this wind pattern that Portuguese boats encountered the Azores in 1427.[7] And this circular track anticipated on a smaller scale the transatlantic loop that Columbus was to define at the end of the century.

Iberians, then, were well positioned, geographically and technically, for expansion. What of will and cause? The least complex aim was profit. Late medieval Europe was short of gold. Gold was known to come from Africa. It arrived on the coasts of Morocco, Algeria, and Tunis from unknown sources in the interior. As early as 1291 the two great Spanish kingdoms of Iberia, Castile and Aragon, made a treaty allocating between them rights to conquer and explore in north-west Africa: Castile in Morocco, Aragon in Algeria and Tunis.[8] Though the time was still not ripe for Spanish incursions into northern Africa, and little progress was made on this front for two centuries, the lure of gold remained strong, and was a powerful incentive for the Portuguese voyages of the fifteenth century that finally carried Europeans into the Gulf of Guinea and close to the origins of west African gold.

A more powerful drive for at least southward movement had been, however, deeply seated in the Iberian psyche long before gold began to exercise its draw. In AD 711, in what was perhaps the single most significant event in recorded

Iberian history, Muslims had invaded the peninsula across the Strait of Gibraltar from Africa. Over the following two decades they occupied all but small, isolated areas in the north. For the next five and a half centuries, in the case of Portugal, and for almost the next eight, in the case of the Spanish kingdoms, gradual recovery of territory and re-implantation of Christianity – collectively known now as the *Reconquista*, the Reconquest – were rarely far from Iberians' minds. Progress was intermittent. But in the twelfth century, the example of crusades to the Holy Land took root in Iberia, and helped spur a renewed, and successful, assault on Islam. By 1300, indeed, Portugal was again entirely Christian; and only the Emirate of Granada, in present south-eastern Spain, remained in Moorish hands elsewhere.

The model and spirit of crusade, now reinforced by successes in the peninsula, made Spaniards and Portuguese think of carrying the fight across the water into northern Africa. The freeing of Jerusalem itself came to seem a possible objective. (It remained one until much later; Columbus himself hoped that the wealth he might find would contribute to its liberation.) But, far short of that, any pressure or attack on Muslim North Africa would weaken Islam: direct assault, diversion of trading profits into Christian hands, piracy, plunder – all could be placed under the heading of crusade. The push down the west coast of Africa came to be included in this religious effort, for it held out the ultimate prospect, after an eventual rounding of the southern tip of Africa, of an outflanking of Islam to the south. This would be an especially powerful move if contact could be made with the mythical medieval figure of Prester John, a Christian ruler reputed to hold sway in eastern Africa, or possibly some point still further east.[9]

Southward progress was, however, interrupted for several decades after 1350 or so, as a series of ills that generally afflicted fourteenth-century Europe took their toll also in Iberia: the Black Death, war, and internal social conflict. Castile, by now by far the largest kingdom in the Iberian peninsula, and the Spanish territory that possessed Atlantic shores and experience, suffered severe political and social disruptions for a century. Portugal, already more organized and stable than its Spanish neighbors before the troubles began, recovered sooner. By 1400 it was centered under a powerful and popular monarch, John I (1385–1433), the first of the Avis dynasty. And, although exploration was not to be organized in a large way by the Portuguese state until late in the fifteenth century, nonetheless this absence of internal struggle (and of the disorder and waste it entailed) seems to have enabled the Portuguese to push outward throughout the 1400s with a determination unmatched by the Spaniards or any other European people.

PORTUGAL IN AFRICA AND THE ATLANTIC ISLANDS

A clear statement that the Portuguese had emerged from the doldrums of the late 1300s was their famed attack on the port city of Ceuta, across the strait from Gibraltar, in 1415. This was intended by John and his eldest son, Duarte, as the first step in a crusade-like subjugation of Muslim Morocco. John had in fact first thought of assaulting Islam in Granada, but desisted, apparently under pressure from Castile.[10] North Africa was a closer target, and Ceuta fell quickly, yielded satisfactory loot, and was soon strongly garrisoned. Other Moroccan towns and territories, however, were more stubborn. Despite much effort, focused by another of John's sons, Prince Henry, over the following five decades, the Portuguese managed to do little more than set up a few fortresses on the coast south and west of Ceuta. Tangier, another early Moroccan objective of the Portuguese, did not fall until 1471.

Meanwhile, however, Portuguese seafarers pushed back the limits of knowledge of the African coast. That Cape Bojador, 1,500 kilometers south-west of Ceuta, had been reached in the fourteenth century is clear enough from a Catalan atlas of c.1375.[11] But it still, fifty years later, seems to have marked the boundary between the familiar and the fabulously hazardous zone of the tropical Atlantic. Finally, in 1434 one Gil Eanes, a captain dispatched by Henry ("the Navigator," though in truth his own navigations were minimal), rounded Bojador (after, reportedly, fifteen attempts).

From then on, progress quickened. Although Henry continued to dispatch exploratory ships southward, most of the running was made by private expeditions in which hope of profitable trade was mixed in growing proportions with discovery. In 1444 the Portuguese reached Cape Verde, the westernmost projection of Africa. By the early 1460s, the explorers were almost around the bulge and faced a coastline that stretched before them south-eastward and then eastward. By this time, Africa had long since proved itself a profitable venture. Sources of gold began to be located early in the 1440s; but the Portuguese quickly discovered that for them the richer prospects were in slaving. One Antão Gonçalves in 1441 has the unenviable distinction of being the first Portuguese to ship African slaves back home from the mainland, after taking them in what is now northern Mauritania in 1441. He captured only two; but the example inspired more ambitious imitators, so that by the 1450s the number of slaves entering the European market annually through Lisbon and ports along the southern Portuguese coast had reached 700 to 800.[12] So began the grim story of Portuguese slave shipments from Africa to Europe, and then to America, that over the ensuing four centuries would run into the millions.

To handle the growing trade in slaves, gold, and other items such as red pepper, cotton, and ivory that became available as more of the coast was opened up, the Portuguese set up along it from the late 1440s a chain of fortified trading posts. Only much later, and above all in Mozambique in the south-east of the continent, did Portuguese colonization in Africa take the form of inland movement and occupation of the land. Neither in the fifteenth century nor later did Portugal have the men or the money to conquer, settle, and organize territory in most of its empire. But the trading post mode of colonization owed at least as much to the large Italian, above all Genoese, participation in Portuguese exploration and trade as it did to Portugal's own limitations. Small trading colonies were what the Genoese and Venetians had used in the Black Sea and the eastern Mediterranean to channel Asian goods into European markets. The castle or small fortified city serving to focus and protect exchange was the accustomed Mediterranean form of overseas settlement. The Portuguese, with many Genoese in their midst from the fourteenth century on, adopted it. It was the sort of colony that Columbus, himself a Genoese, still naturally expected to install on the large Caribbean islands, as late as the end of the fifteenth century.

In the Atlantic islands that Portugal reconnoitered at the same time as the African coast, however, things went differently. Here there was no native population – except in the Canaries, where a people often called the Guanches lived. These seem to have descended, rather distantly, from Berber and Black origins in the north-west and west of Africa. They were part-nomadic farmers, arranged in tribes under authoritative lords who proved well able to organize them for fierce resistance to outside interference.[13] The Guanches' fighting abilities, though, were not enough to protect them from Europeans' desire for slaves. In the late 1300s, long before the first west African slaves were shipped to Portugal, Castilians, Frenchmen, and Italians, as well as the Portuguese, had been raiding the Canaries for Guanche slaves. Nonetheless, apart from slaves, the Canaries offered very little in the way of immediately available exports. Nor did Madeira, the Azores, or the Cape Verde Islands (also uninhabited), found by the Portuguese early in the 1450s.[14]

In the Azores, Madeira, and the Cape Verde group, then, the Portuguese had to settle in order to realize the economic possibilities that these territories gradually revealed. (There was no Portuguese settlement of the Canaries, partly because of native resistance, and partly because of Castile's powerful, competing claim to the islands.) Madeira, located before the middle of the fourteenth century, was the first target of Portuguese colonization in the Atlantic. The name means "wood" in Portuguese, and reflects the first impression that the islands left on early visitors. One sort of tree yielded a rich, red dye. Both this and timber were sent back home by the first settlers, who took up residence in the 1420s. In the early days, fish was the basis of the islanders' diet. But, as woodland was cleared, farming began; Madeira's virgin soils, enriched by the ash from burned vegetation, proved excellent ground for wheat. By 1450, half the wheat grown was being exported to Portugal. Water mills had been built by then to provide flour locally. Cattle and grapes thrived similarly. But Madeira hit its full agricultural stride with the introduction of sugar cane, probably from Sicily or Valencia. The first refining mill was set up in 1452. In 1455 sugar production had reached almost 70,000 kilograms, and in the following year, sugar was first exported to England.[15] The creation of sugar estates on Madeira was a sign of things to come for centuries ahead in the Atlantic world (and outside it, in other westernized regions also, for that matter). These were the first plantations – the first demonstration that the tropics and the semi-tropics could provide, cheaply and abundantly, foodstuffs for which Europeans had an immense appetite but could produce locally only with great effort and cost. Further, the sugar plantations in Madeira were the first to be worked by slaves, brought in from Africa and the Canaries in the 1460s to do the hot, heavy sort of work that Europeans shunned away from home.[16] These slaves added to a swelling population in Madeira that passed two thousand in the 1460s.

In other matters, the colonization of the Madeira group was less innovative, but still played an important transitional, or transmitting, role in the broader Atlantic progression. Both the wheat and the sugar trade were run in part by merchants from the Mediterranean (Catalans and Italians), as well as by Portuguese. That immensely important commercial and economic participation of Italians, especially Genoese, in all Portuguese expansion is visible again here. Peninsular Jews also had their part in the sugar trade. When, a century later, the far vaster sugar industry of Portuguese Brazil began to flex its muscles, foreign participation, though now from north-western Europe, would again be central to its growth.

Similarly, in administration, Mediterranean precedents left their mark in Madeira. Most of the responsibility for organizing government fell to Prince Henry of Portugal, after his elder brother, Duarte, by then king, made him in 1433 a lifetime donation of the islands. Henry in turn split them up into three hereditary and perpetual captaincies, to whose lords, the "captains-donatary," he gave great powers, including jurisdiction and monopoly control of productive activities. The model for this system was in the eastern Mediterranean of post-crusading times, when the Italians, Catalans, and French had used similar procedures in creating settlements there.[17] The same system was carried into Brazil once Portuguese settlement started there in the early sixteenth century. Once more, as in technology, commercial practices, and the trading post mode of settlement, currents from the Mediterranean can be seen flowing into the Atlantic, with Portugal providing the conduit.

Things went very much the same way in the Azores, when finally in the 1460s, thirty and more years after the initial discovery, the Portuguese began to settle this group in earnest. Wood and dyes, then cattle and wheat, provided exports and wealth. The cooler, more northerly climate, however, prevented the Azores from imitating Madeira in the sugar business. The close tie between slavery and plantation agriculture, strongly suggested by the early history of Madeira, is confirmed by the almost total absence of slavery in the Azores. Just as in Madeira, however, captains-donatary were named for the Azores, with the same sweeping administrative, judicial, and economic powers.

The Cape Verdes, too, were assigned to captains-donatary after their discovery in the 1450s. Here, though, in contrast to the islands further north, lack of rain hampered farming. Attempts to grow sugar had little success. Other resources were scant, and the islands were far from home. The Portuguese state had, consequently, to step in to some extent to maintain settlement in the late 1400s. The crown, for example, granted settlers a special permit in 1466 to trade in African slaves. The presence of Africans from Guinea, and the relative absence of Portuguese women, led quickly to race mixture. Three of the islands had stable, if small, populations by the beginning of the sixteenth century, with Santiago being by then the best established colony. But no settlers were drawn to the other six islands until two hundred or more years later.[18] The Cape Verdes were a useful way station for Portuguese shipping along the African coast. But their part in the broader Atlantic expansion of Portugal was small.

SPANIARDS IN THE ATLANTIC

Spanish activities in the Atlantic lagged behind Portugal's for a very long time; almost until Columbus's day, in fact. This was not wholly for lack of interest. Spaniards from several parts of the peninsula felt the draw of the south, as the sally of the Catalans c.1300 to the Moroccan coast, and the Aragonese and Castilian interest of the same period in north Africa, show. Alfonso XI of Castile even went so far in 1345 as to declare to the Pope that he had a royal right to acquire the "kingdoms of Africa" by virtue of earlier Castilian rulers' successes against the Moors in the peninsula.[19] The outcomes of such interests and sentiments, however, in the fourteenth century fell far short of Portuguese accomplishments. In part this was because Spain, unlike Portugal, still had not become a political and religious whole. Whereas, after the expulsion of the remaining Moors late in the 1200s, the Portuguese, without distractions at home, could focus their attention on overseas affairs, Spain still lacked any such enabling unity. Politically, it was still split into the two distinct and often contending major kingdoms of Castile and Aragon. And religious division still persisted in fourteenth-century Spain in the form of Islamic Granada. With their house not yet fully in order, Spaniards were not ready to devote themselves to Atlantic ventures on the Portuguese scale. This unreadiness was prolonged, especially in Castile, by the long series of political and social struggles that developed after 1350.

There was one clear exception, nevertheless, to this inward focus: the Canaries. Here fourteenth-century Spaniards, especially again the Catalans, showed a clear interest in what would seem to be the conflicting aims of spreading Christianity, often at Rome's urging, and taking slaves. (As in America later, contemporaries may have seen no contradiction. Slavery after all brought pagans into close contact with Christians, and the gift of the true faith, it could be argued, far outweighed the burden of enslavement.) After several Catalan-directed expeditions of evangelizing friars, the Castilians finally entered the fray in 1393, with an exploratory force to the Canaries dispatched by Henry III. This brought back a profitable cargo of slaves and Canarian products.

The foray of 1393 certainly marks a quantum leap in Castilian attention to the Atlantic, and seems to have been followed up by other expeditions to the Canaries before the end of the century. Still, it is some indication of Castile's persisting tentativeness that when a resolve to settle the islands emerged later in the 1390s, the job was entrusted to Frenchmen, under the rather fitful leadership of one Jean de Bethancourt, a nephew of the French ambassador to Castile. With his expedition of 1402, Bethancourt managed to take and settle some of the lesser islands. In due course Henry III pronounced him king of the Canaries, subordinate to the Castilian monarchy. In reality, he spent little time in the islands, and finally was allowed to sell his rights in 1418 to the Castilian Count of Niebla.[20]

Bethancourt's efforts lacked resolution, but they certainly strengthened Castile's claim to the islands. And this was consonant with a larger claim to Africa that Castile began to enunciate in the fifteenth century, which had far deeper roots in time than the earlier argument of kings' doughty strivings with the Moors. Now it was held that the Visigothic rulers of the peninsula of pre-Islamic times had been lords of the African shores; and that the kings of Castile had inherited these powers.[21] Thus there developed an ever sharper conflict of interests between Castile and Portugal in the eastern Atlantic. Portuguese colonization of Madeira in the 1420s was in part a response to a Castilian expedition to that group in 1417.

Portugal replied in kind with a large expedition to the Canaries in 1424 or 1425, which was an attempt to take Grand Canary; an attempt justified by the contention that the island was not yet occupied by Christians.[22] Exactly how many Castilians there were in the islands in those years in hard to tell. And the titles to the islands granted by Castilian rulers to various of their subjects were overlapping and confused. Still, Castile doubtless had by the mid 1400s the upper hand in Canarian matters in both practice and law. In the end the dispute with Portugal was settled in the Treaty of Alcáçovas of 1479, by which (among many other contested questions) Portugal accepted Castile's claims to the Canaries, and Castile in return recognized Portuguese rights in the Cape Verde group, Madeira, and the Azores – as well as on the African coast south of Cape Bojador. This was a rehearsal for the division of the hemisphere into eastern and western zones of interest, exploration, and conquest that was set up in the more famous Treaty of Tordesillas negotiated between Castile and Portugal fifteen years later.

THE CATHOLIC MONARCHS

The making of treaties about Atlantic (and other) exploration and settlement in the late fifteenth century reflects precisely, of course, the Castilian expansionism that by then was clearly under way, and its inevitable collision with Portuguese achievements and aspirations. It also marks the rise of exploration to the level of prime state business. Before, in both Portugal and Spain, discovery and settlement had generally been something of a sideline for government. But in these final decades of the century there existed, for the first time in the Iberian age of exploration, a powerful and unitary Spanish state that could direct exploratory efforts and negotiate in an authoritative fashion about them.

This was the Spain of Isabella, queen of Castile, and Ferdinand, king of Aragon. The year 1469, in which these two married, ranks second only to AD 711 (and some might reverse the order) in its significance in Spanish history. At the time, neither was on the throne. Ferdinand was unchallenged crown prince of Aragon, and duly succeeded in 1479. But Isabella's claim to Castile was disputed by Princess Juana, daughter (or alleged daughter – and therein lay much cause for contention) of the ruling monarch, Isabella's half-brother, Henry IV. After Henry died, late in 1474, a fiercely contested war of succession broke out. In this, Isabella's party was backed by Aragon. It had been in part to secure such support that Isabella had married Ferdinand. Juana, at first with fewer major Castilian figures behind her than Isabella, nevertheless soon found a champion for her cause in Afonso V, king of Portugal, who hoped to marry her and thus set his line on the throne of Castile.

After four years of contest, Isabella's party emerged victorious. The Treaty of Alcáçovas, of September 1479, was above all a closing of the war. With it Afonso renounced his betrothal to Juana, and agreed that the unfortunate girl, still only seventeen, should be put away in a nunnery so as to destroy any threat she might pose to Isabella's occupation of the Castilian throne. There she remained until her death in 1530. The large concessions in the Atlantic that Castile made to Portugal in the 1479 treaty were, in fact, partly the price paid for the assurance that it gave of Isabella's position.

With, now, undisputed tenure of their respective thrones, Ferdinand and Isabella were able in effect to create a unified Spain. Technically speaking, there was still yet no single "Spanish" monarchy. But the two acted and ruled in such close accord that, to the outside world, Spain was now for the first time one political unit. It was a powerful unit, a rival for any other realm in Europe, and more than a rival for most. Aragon, which embraced Catalonia (and Valencia), under Ferdinand retained and expanded its deeply rooted interest in Mediterranean trade and politics. The Aragonese crown had, during the first half of the fifteenth century, incorporated Naples and Sicily. Already at the time of his marriage, Ferdinand was king of Sicily.[23] During his marriage with Isabella, which ended with her death in 1504, he tended to concentrate on Aragonese affairs, especially his kingdom's long-standing combat with France over border issues and contested territories in northern Italy. But there was little that Isabella did in and for Castile that Ferdinand had no hand in, so that he, while not king of Castile during her lifetime, was very close to being its co-ruler.

Castile, with its larger territory (the whole peninsula except for Portugal, Aragon, the small Moorish remnant of Granada in the south, and the still smaller kingdom of Navarre in the center-north), and its larger population (probably c.4.5 million in 1500, as against Aragon's one million),[24] was the dominant force in the partnership. Late fifteenth-century Castile was also economically more vibrant than Aragon, above all because of its large exports of raw wool to northern Europe. The merchants of its northern cities, especially Burgos and Bilbao, were sophisticated and experienced overseas traders. The Castilian merchant marine was strong. Cantabrian shipbuilders on the north coast were internationally known for their abilities. Basque ironworkers were among the most advanced of the day.

Ferdinand and Isabella, therefore, found themselves facing an opportunity in 1479 that was without precedent in Iberian history: that of creating a unified state, under native government, that would embrace the great majority of the peninsula. This chance they seized eagerly, and with such success that their joint reign is generally seen as the beginning of modern Spain.

They were astute, able, and determined rulers. Ferdinand was taken as a model of the Renaissance prince by Machiavelli, and Isabella yielded little to him in the application of *raison d'état*. Their major aims, duly accomplished, within the peninsula were to concentrate power in the monarchy, and, by various measures, to advance the unification of Spain beyond the mere co-rulership that resulted from their marriage. Here, true enough, they had a firm popular basis from which to work. In the middle ages, inhabitants of many parts of the peninsula, though their strongest loyalty would be to some particular province, carried in their minds a notion of belonging also to a broader "Hispania."[25] It was an identity that Ferdinand and Isabella set about strengthening.

Much of what they did served both their purposes. To increase the authority of the monarchy inevitably meant making it a more palpable presence in their subjects' lives, and so also provided a common point of reference for all "Spaniards." Isabella took care to make court life more splendidly ceremonial and formal than before, in effect to raise the image of monarchy to a higher plane where it would be more remote from, and therefore more impressive to, the mass of the people. The court was still peripatetic, like its counterparts elsewhere in Europe. Many subjects had opportunities to lay eyes on the monarchs as they traveled. But to increase the tangible presence of royal power, Isabella added to the single supreme court of appeal that existed at the start of her reign, the *cancillería* of Valladolid, other high appeal courts: one in Galicia, in the north-west, and another in Ciudad Real, in the center south. This tribunal, created in 1494, was moved to Granada in 1505.[26] Since the provision of justice was held to be the paramount obligation of Castilian rulers, this multiplication of royal tribunals increased not only the visibility of monarchy but also its legitimacy. The series of high courts was soon extended to the Canaries and then to America. In both the tribunals were known as *audiencias*, places were trials were heard.

The monarchs' intrusion into subjects' lives was, of course, sometimes far from welcome. To bring Castilian towns, for long past bases of autonomous regional power, into line, Ferdinand and Isabella greatly increased the number of them to which crown-appointed *corregidores* (literally "co-rulers") were assigned. Rural disorder was tackled by the creation of what amounted to a national police force for Castile, the "Holy Brotherhood" (*Santa Hermandad*), whose organization was set up in the summer of 1476, well before the War of Succession ended. In fact, Isabella's initial purpose with the *Hermandad* was as much to gather fighting men for the war as it was to carry law to the country-side. After her accession, the Brotherhood remained as a sort of rural army, charged with enforcing law in the vast spaces between the local jurisdictions of towns. Members of the *Hermandad* held powers of summary justice. Brigands and thieves could be, and were, executed or mutilated on the spot. Though the *Hermandad*'s range and accomplishments may in the past have been exaggerated, it certainly brought a governmental presence into country areas that had rarely felt it before; it was sometimes used (illegally) to pursue opponents of the monarchy into cities; and it contributed substantially to what was one of the monarchs' main achievements – to give Spain internal peace and order.[27]

The greatest challenge to royal authority in Castile undoubtedly came from the nobility, which over much of the previous two centuries had advanced its own power, status, and wealth at the monarchy's cost. The nobles' power-plays in the dispute over succession had added much fuel to the fire of civil war at the start of Isabella's reign. Historians long tended to exaggerate the crown's success in this prime political contest of the reign, proposing, on insufficient evidence, that Ferdinand and Isabella came close to crushing the Castilian nobility over the twenty years following the War of Succession. But recent reassessment of the question finds that at the end of Isabella's life the nobility had lost nothing in social standing, and little or nothing in wealth. The broad seizures of nobles' vast estates that were once thought to have happened have now been reduced to a return to the crown merely of royal lands alienated since 1464.[28] Indeed, in 1505, nobles' hold over their estates was fortified by a general concession of the previously jealously guarded privilege of *mayorazgo*, or entail, which allowed land owners to protect their holdings from division during inheritance.[29]

Ferdinand and Isabella did manage, however, a severe trimming of the aristocracy's political wings by excluding them to a large degree from central government. New councils of state were created (or old ones substantially reorganized), and were staffed by preference with university-trained lawyers, generically known as *letrados*. High nobles might attend council meetings, and speak; but they had no vote. Thus began the construction of a professionally staffed bureaucracy that would grow over the next century into a vast apparatus of state embracing not only Spain and sundry parts of Europe, but also the American empire. Nobles could certainly find a place for themselves in this apparatus, often occupying prominent positions as viceroys, council presidents and the like. But they could not control it. It was under Ferdinand and Isabella, as one historian remarks, that "the time ended in which nobles made and unmade kings in Castile."[30] Now monarchy and aristocracy were in a mutually useful, if often uneasy and suspicious, alliance. The monarchs controlled central government. Nobles, provided they consented to that, might do as they wished with their great estates, and were free to pursue opportunities to increase their wealth.

If the nobility seemed the most urgent and obvious threat to royal power in the early days of the reign, Ferdinand and Isabella quickly saw that there was another equally potent, but more diffuse, challenge that must be met if Castile – Spain, indeed – were to become truly one, truly whole. This was the problem of religion, or, more precisely, of its variety in the peninsula. As long as Catholicism was not universal in the monarchy, fatal ideological rifts would prevent unity from being achieved. The glaring exception to religious uniformity was, of course, the surviving Islamic presence in the Emirate of Granada. It was obvious enough from the start that only force would bring a solution there; and soon enough, force was applied. But even before that, Isabella moved against the other great variety of heterodoxy in Castile, which was Judaism.

Since at least early Visigothic times, nine centuries past, Jews had lived in the peninsula, and had become an integral part of its social and economic life. They had, indeed, been much better integrated, in both practice and law, than in other parts of Europe. Perhaps this was because, during the Reconquest, settlers were needed to occupy land recovered from the Moors. Jews were welcomed into these retaken territories. It is probably no coincidence that a consistent antisemitism developed in Spain only after the Reconquest had come close to its goal, with the compression of Islam into the single realm of Granada in the thirteenth century. After then, it grew and festered, bursting out in 1391 in pogroms in the Jewish quarters of Seville, Toledo, Valencia, Barcelona, and other towns. Pressures on Jews to convert to Christianity became intense, and the many thousands who submitted to them, the *conversos*, found themselves in the fifteenth century the objects of suspicion by both Jews and Christians. Still, *conversos* continued to play crucial roles in society and economy, working, as their Jewish ancestors had done for centuries, as craftsmen, traders, financiers, doctors, scholars; and also as administrators in church and state. Both Isabella and Ferdinand employed Jewish and *converso* financiers in high posts of government.[31]

However valuable such individuals may have been to the monarchs, though, it was clear that the *conversos* as a whole were a disruptive element in society. To resentments over their continued prominence as craftsmen and professionals was added a popular suspicion, often enough correct, that they secretly continued to practice Judaism. It was to investigate these doubts over genuineness of conversion that Isabella and Ferdinand, in late 1478, applied to Rome for a bull creating in Castile an Inquisition into heresy.[32] It was granted. The first inquisitors began work, in Seville, in 1480. Over the ensuing decade, tribunals of the Inquisition were set up in many other Castilian cities. In 1482–3, Ferdinand revived the long dormant medieval Inquisition of Aragon. The outcome of these efforts was grim. Isabella's secretary, Hernando del Pulgar, estimated that by 1490 two thousand judaizers had been burned, and fifteen thousand others punished in attempts to "reconcile" them with the true faith.[33]

Unconverted Jews (and other non-Christians) were outside the Inquisition's jurisdiction; it existed only to investigate heresy among people supposedly faithful. But the 1480s were a decade just as harsh for Jews as for *conversos*. Popular prejudice found ever greater backing in law. In 1480 Jews were restricted to living in ghettoes. Many were expelled from Andalusia in 1482–3. Finally, in March 1492, came Ferdinand and Isabella's notorious decree ordering all Jews to convert within four months, on pain of expulsion. It may be that the monarchs expected that the great majority would join the Church and remain in Spain. A conversion campaign was waged to that end. But of the 200,000–300,000 Jews then in Castile and Aragon, only 50,000 chose Christianity. The rest left in a great exodus that carried Spanish-speaking Jews to Portugal (a brief haven, since conversion was demanded of them there in 1497), Italy, Turkey, and North Africa.

The Inquisition and the expulsion were more the outcome of a mixture of political and religio-ideological causes than, as has sometimes been suggested, of class conflict between Christian Spaniards (whether workers or nobles) and an incipient "bourgeoisie" of Jews and judaizers. Isabella's piety, sometimes pronounced remarkable, now seems to have been no more than conventional; and Ferdinand's was even less. But both saw religious uniformity as a means, indeed a necessity, for the social and political cohesion of the new state. The forces of dissolution – nobility, towns, local legal privileges, deeply rooted regionalism – were still strong; an all-embracing Catholicism could serve to cement together what so far was joined only through the rulers' marriage. At a more practical level, the Inquisition, by its very structure, was a powerful political tool. Its central body, the *Suprema*, was one of the state councils reporting directly to the crown. Its local agents, or familiars, were numerous. What began as a device for investigating suspected crypto-Jews became a means of checking for any sort of deviation from religious, moral, and political orthodoxy.[34] While there is exaggeration in seeing traits of modern totalitarianism in the Inquisition,[35] its creation (like that of the *Santa Hermandad*) undeniably promoted the centralization of authority that Ferdinand and Isabella consistently pursued.

But whatever fame, or infamy, the Inquisition has conferred on Ferdinand and Isabella's reign, the creation of that Holy Office in Castile seems little more than an administrative maneuver by comparison with the major campaign they waged to restore uniformity of faith to Spain: the Reconquest of Granada. The Emirate had never presented any threat to the Christians' hold over the other Andalusian territories that they had retaken in the 1200s. But it proved a tough nut to crack. The final war of the seven-century Reconquest began in 1481 in a series of frontier skirmishes between the Moors and the Andalusian nobility. The monarchs quickly decided to join in. A dispute over succession in Granada provided them with a weakness that they were able to exploit, specifically through an on-and-off alliance with Boabdil, a leading contender for the throne. Still, the conquest soon became a slow grind of taking the Emirate's towns one by one. Ronda fell in 1485, Málaga in 1487, Almería and Guadix in 1489, to recall only the main places. Finally, in April 1491 began the siege of Granada itself, with the Christians encamped before the city on a site they named, appropriately, *Santa Fe* (Holy Faith). A surrender was signed in November 1491, and the monarchs entered the capital in procession (in whose number went, incidentally, one Christopher Columbus) on January 2, 1492. So ended the territorial Reconquest of Spain; and so began a year that would see Spaniards crossing the Ocean Sea to do unto an enormous and unknown segment of humanity what had been done to them by the Moors almost eight centuries before.

Many motives drew Ferdinand and Isabella into the Granada war. Prime among them, certainly, was the desire to oust an alien creed from the peninsula and replace it with Christianity, for the same reasons as had inspired the assault on *conversos* and Jews. Muslim Granada, however, held threats that Jews did not offer. Over Christendom there loomed in the fifteenth century, ever larger, the shadow of the Ottoman Turks, who, four decades before the conquest of Granada, had taken Constantinople. Islam was again on the rise, and in Spain it had a bridgehead in Granada. The situation was intolerable, not only for religious reasons, but because the Ottoman Empire threatened Aragonese trading and political interests in the Mediterranean.[36]

At home, too, there were material gains to be had from a successful assault on the Emirate. Granada offered rich loot (including slaves) for crown and soldier. It had fertile land that could be, and was, granted to nobles still unrewarded for their support in the Castilian war of succession, or that could simply be added to the crown's domains. As the war progressed and its costs grew severe, such gains for the crown became a motive for pressing on until success was achieved. Again, Granada's silk trade was thriving, and was a tempting object for incorporation into the Castilian economy. Finally, a significant by-product of the war, though hardly a cause for waging it, was the creation, at least temporarily, of a national army. With men coming from noble estates, towns, and the ranks of the *Santa Hermandad*, Ferdinand by the late 1480s commanded a force of 45,000–50,000 foot soldiers and 10,000–13,000 cavalry, an enormous number for the day. This army quickly dissolved once Granada was taken. But from this point on, until well into the seventeenth century, the Spanish monarchy was well known, and feared, in Europe for its ability to put fearsome armies into the field.[37] At home, too, the close link of monarchy with military force that the war created could only contribute to the concentration of power for which Ferdinand and Isabella always aimed.

"Athletes of Christ" the Pope pronounced Ferdinand and Isabella to be after Granada fell, formally giving them the title of "Catholic Monarchs" (*Reyes Católicos*) by which they have been best known ever since. This was recognition as much of the blow struck against Islam in the wider world as it was of the "purification" of Spanish faith.[38] In the event, the monarchs did not at first put as much pressure on the defeated Moors to convert as might have been expected in the year of the expulsion of the Jews. Possibly inspired by the mutual toleration that had marked long stretches of the *Reconquista*, the capitulation terms gave guarantees of the religion, laws, customs, and property of the vanquished. In a foreshadowing of practices used in America a few decades later, local leaders were left in place, though under general Castilian supervision. Despite these concessions, many of the former Emirate's people chose to leave, which may have been the crown's hope. From an initial total of half a million, 200,000 departed, many to North Africa. A further 100,000 had died or been enslaved during the conflict.[39] The 200,000 remaining were subjected to conversion by persuasion: preaching, distribution of Gospels and catechisms in Arabic translation, and the like. The results were promising, but slow. And finally in 1499, Francisco Jiménez de Cisneros, Archbishop of Toledo and head of the Spanish Church, growing impatient, persuaded the crown to order forced conversion. This policy brought a reaction of local revolts. In 1502 there came in Granada a famous burning of Arabic texts. The monarchs had ordered destruction of copies of the Koran; Cisneros may have added other books to the fire, though he saved medical works for his new university foundation at Alcalá de Henares.[40] The same year Isabella resolved that all remaining *mudéjares* (Muslims living among Christians) in Castile should be given the choice offered the Jews ten years before: convert, or go. Most chose to convert.[41] Now, at least in principle, Castile was single in faith as it had in 1492 become single in territory. In Aragon, though, Muslims might still practice their religion. The events following from the Granadan war served to widen contrasts that already existed between Aragon and Castile: the first, to a degree tolerant of political and ideological diversity; the second, showing signs now of the austere rigidity that would make it later in the sixteenth century the temporal champion of the Counter-Reformation.

Amidst their efforts to purge Spain of faiths that challenged Christianity, Ferdinand and Isabella turned to the Spanish church itself with a purifying intent. The aim, as in much else they did in religious matters, was not so much piety for its own sake as for its utility as a tool for national unity. The church in Spain should not only be in partnership, spiritual and political, with the monarchy, but should be a disciplined and well-schooled body, formed to play a unifying part in national affairs. It almost seems that the monarchs wished to charge the spiritual batteries of the country so as to fill it with a crusading Christian energy. If one man may be associated with this effort, it was again Francisco Jiménez de Cisneros. He had entered the Franciscan order at the age of 48. Eight years later, in 1492, Isabella chose him as her confessor. In 1495, the same year as he became primate of Spain, she instructed him to reform the church in Spain. He set about doing so by raising the level of orthodoxy and austerity in its members; especially so among the monastic orders, and, among them, particularly in his own society, the Franciscans. In the last year of his life, 1517, the monasteries of the Conventual, or less strict, branch of the Franciscans were shut in Spain, leaving only the Observants, who closely followed St Francis's vows of poverty.[42] The spiritual dedication of other orders in Spain underwent something of the same renewal. And it was the men of those orders, devout, dedicated, and educated, who formed the vanguard of the mission effort on the Spanish American mainland from *c.*1520 onwards.

COMPLETION AND INNOVATION

As in any treatment of "great" rulers or individuals, there is a danger in the case of the Catholic Monarchs of exaggerating their abilities, originality, and accomplishments. Spain had been in the process of fusion for a very long time. It had been coming together from, indeed, almost the moment of the Islamic invasion. Behind the slowly advancing Christian frontier, principalities had gradually become kingdoms, and kingdoms had drawn together under the rulership of Castilian and Aragonese monarchs. Then again, by the time of Ferdinand and Isabella, the Castilian and Aragonese crowns were already linked. Early in the fifteenth century, a cadet branch of the ruling Trastámara house of Castile had occupied the throne of Aragon. Isabella and Ferdinand had great-grandparents in common.

Similarly, several of the measures most associated with the monarchs were not original to them. An Inquisition had existed in medieval Aragon. Henry IV, Isabella's predecessor on the throne and half-brother, had contemplated creating some special tribunal to watch over the *conversos* in Castile. He, too, had favored setting up new *hermandades* to bring peace and order to the countryside. Again, *corregidores* had long since carried the monarch's authority into some Castilian towns. And if Ferdinand and Isabella were able, as they were, to strengthen the Castilian monarchy by vastly increasing its income,

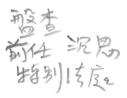

that was in good part thanks to a Castilian economic expansion already in process by 1469. Much of Europe, moreover, shared in that economic growth.

Still, in the emergence of a single Spain that is traditionally, and rightly, located in their time, they played an active part. They were like-minded rulers with complementary abilities and personalities. What might easily, in other hands, have become a jostling for individual power, or a covert contest between Castile and Aragon, was, in theirs, a collaboration, so that the whole became greater than the sum of the parts. By the time Isabella died, in 1504, a genuinely Spanish state existed, and had indeed existed for some years, for all practical purposes. Disputes over the succession held back the fulfillment of its potential for a time. The monarchs' increasingly deranged daughter, Juana, was incapable of ruling Castile. Her husband, Philip of Burgundy, could have done so; but he died in 1506. Ferdinand thereafter governed Castile, though with much internal opposition, until his own death in 1516. Then, finally, with the accession of Juana's son, the sixteen year old Charles I (soon to become, in 1519, Holy Roman Emperor), Spain took the dominant place on the European, and indeed world, stage for which the Catholic Monarchs had prepared it.

Spain's world role began in earnest with the Atlantic voyaging performed by Columbus and various of his associates and imitators in the 1490s. This built on the earlier Castilian probings into the Atlantic, particularly those directed at the Canaries. State to state negotiation between Castile and Portugal at Alcáçovas in 1479 provided Spanish seafarers with a reliable base or stepping stone in the Canaries. It also cleared the way for Spanish exploration westwards, since the same treaty, with its confirmation of Portuguese rights to the African coast, tended to focus Portuguese attention on the south. Exploration in that direction now came under state direction far more than ever before. The Portuguese king, John II, was quick, after Alcáçovas, to send a fleet to build a fortress-cum-trading post, the famous and long-lasting São Jorge da Mina, on what is now the Ghanaian coast. One who went with this fleet of 1482 was Christopher Columbus, then living in Portugal. Then followed a rapid push southward, much of it accomplished by one Diogo Cão at the urging of his king, which took the Portuguese as far in five years as they had come in the previous seventy. Cão's report that he had in 1483 sailed around Africa to the beginning of the Arabian Gulf gave John immense pleasure.[43] The news was premature. But the king's rejoicing reveals what Portugal's aims now were in southern exploration. The allure of African products and African trade had long driven the voyages. But now the view had lengthened to take in direct trade by sea with India and the Orient, by a route around the end of Africa, wherever that might be. Spices, silks, ivory, jade – all the high-priced goods whose entry into Europe the Italian traders had long monopolized – could be had at their source, so the Portuguese thought, once the way to Asia around Africa was opened. They were of course right. And soon another of John's expeditions, led by Bartolomeu Dias, did what Cão thought he had done and rounded the southern tip of Africa, probably in the opening days of 1488. It was not for another decade that the first Portuguese fleet, led by Vasco da Gama, voyaged to India and back. But after Dias, Portugal's attention was firmly directed eastward. An additional attraction there, made more powerful by the resurgent Islamic threat in the eastern Mediterranean, was the improved possibility that circumnavigation of Africa gave of finding Prester John, and other Christian groups and leaders, in Africa or the East. With such contacts made, Islam might be contained, or even attacked in its underside.[44]

Ferdinand and Isabella's attention was fully occupied, while the Portuguese were making these outward leaps in the 1480s, by domestic affairs, among them the war against Granada. It was not by chance that Columbus succeeded in getting their support for his own proposed westward exploration only after Granada had fallen. With that thorn finally, if painfully, plucked from Castile's side, and, indeed, amid the rejoicing following its removal, the Catholic Monarchs at last decided that Columbus's distinctly dubious project was worth backing.

PART II

APPROACHES

CHRONOLOGY OF PART II

1451   Birth of Columbus in Genoa

1492   Columbus's first voyage to America

1493   Columbus's second voyage: settlement of Hispaniola

1496   Foundation of Santo Domingo, as capital of Hispaniola

1498   Columbus's third voyage: first certain European sighting of a South American coast

1500   World map of Juan de la Cosa. Pedro Alvares Cabral lands on Brazilian coast

1501–2   East coast of South America surveyed by Amerigo Vespucci

1502–4   Columbus's fourth voyage: east coast of Central America surveyed

1502–9   Administration of Nicolás de Ovando, "founding" governor of Hispaniola

1503   *Casa de Contratación* founded in Seville

1506   Death of Columbus

1507   World map of Martin Waldseemüller, showing "America"

1508   From Hispaniola, Juan Ponce de León takes Puerto Rico

1509   From Hispaniola, Juan de Esquivel takes Jamaica, and Alonso de Hojeda leads an expedition to the Venezuelan and Colombian coast

1511   First Spanish town on the American mainland: Santa María la Antigua de Darién. Conquest of Cuba, from Hispaniola. *Audiencia* established at Santo Domingo, the first in America. Sermon of Antonio de Montesinos, OP, in Santo Domingo, criticizing colonists' treatment of Indians

1512   Arrival of first bishop (of Caparra, Hispaniola) in America. Laws of Burgos, regulating Spanish treatment of Indians

1513   Juan Ponce de León claims Florida for Spain. Vasco Núñez de Balboa crosses the Isthmus of Panama to the Pacific

1516   Death of Ferdinand of Aragon. Accession to the Spanish throne of Charles I (from 1519, Charles V, Holy Roman Emperor)

1517–18   Spanish reconnaissance from Cuba of eastern Mexican coast

1519   Cities of Panama and Veracruz founded

1519–21   Hernán Cortés conquers the Aztecs for Spain

1519–22   First circumnavigation of globe, by Magellan's expedition

1529   Treaty of Zaragoza: Tordesillas line projected into the Pacific at c.145 degrees east

1532–6   Francisco Pizarro conquers the Incas for Spain

1538   Foundation of Santa Fe de Bogotá

1541   Foundation of Santiago de Chile; permanent Spanish settlement of Chile begins

1542   Permanent foundation of Guadalajara, in western Mexico

1565   Northerly return route from east Asia to America found by Andrés de Urdaneta

FURTHER READING FOR PART II

Still the best reading on Columbus is Samuel H. Morison, *Admiral of the Ocean Sea*. For more modern information, see Felipe Fernández-Armesto, *Columbus*, and William D.

and Carla Rahn Phillips, *The Worlds of Christopher Columbus*. For other Spanish explorers, Louis-André Vigneras, *The Discovery of South America and the Andalusian Voyages*. Francisco Morales Padrón, *Historia del descubrimiento y conquista de América*, is a comprehensive, factual account of both Spanish and Portuguese explorations and conquests in America.

The standard work in English on the early Caribbean is Carl O. Sauer's *The Early Spanish Main*. In his *Conquête et exploitation des nouveaux mondes (XVIe siècle)*, Pierre Chaunu is characteristically interesting and idiosyncratic.

On the military conquests, the tales told by the conquerors themselves are by far the best starting point. For Mexico, see Bernal Díaz del Castillo, *The Conquest of New Spain*, and Hernán Cortés, *Letters from Mexico*. For the Andean conquests, there is no chronicle quite on the same level, but John Hemming, *The Conquest of the Incas* is an excellent modern history, drawing, as it does, directly and deeply on contemporary accounts.

For both the conquests and the sixteenth century generally, great riches are to be found in John H. Parry and Robert G. Keith (eds), *New Iberian World. A Documentary History of the Discovery and Settlement of Latin America to the Early Seventeenth Century*.

[4] COLUMBUS AND OTHERS

COLUMBUS

Columbus had been kept on hold for several years by Ferdinand and Isabella. He had first approached them with a plan for sailing west to the Orient in 1486. Since then he and the monarchs had played a sparring game: he threatening to take his scheme elsewhere if they would not support it, they refusing full backing, but providing occasional subsidies that partially maintained him and kept him hoping for more. Finally he secured the terms he wanted; and the trivial investment that they had made in him before 1492 paid off incalculably in the form of a vast empire in a "new" continent.

Christopher Columbus (Cristoforo Colombo, as he was in Genoa, where he was born in 1451) personified that blending of Mediterranean and Atlantic that, mediated especially through Portugal, contributed so vitally to the early expansion of Europe. Perhaps chief among his many remarkable qualities as a mature man was his seagoing knowledge, gained first in the Mediterranean as a youth, and then in the Atlantic after he began to live in Portugal in the mid-1470s. By 1492 he was as salt-soaked as any earlier explorer of the African coast or any voyager to the Atlantic islands. He had sailed to the east end of the Mediterranean on Genoese trading business; and in Portuguese ships to a variety of Atlantic ports ranging from São Jorge da Mina in Africa to Galway in Ireland (and perhaps, though probably not, to Iceland). In Portugal he married into a rich merchant family, named Perestrelo, of Italian origins. His wife, Felipa Moniz, was the daughter of Bartolomeu Perestrelo, who had been in the 1420s one of the leaders of the expedition that settled the Madeiras, and then the captain-donatary of the island named Porto Santo in that group.[1] Columbus sailed often to the Madeiras on business. His voyaging made him familiar with both colonizing forms that the Portuguese used in the fifteenth century: commerce through trading posts, on the Mediterranean model, on the African coast; and true settlement, for economic development, in the Atlantic island groups.

The notion of sailing west to Asia grew slowly in Columbus. When and where it first came to him is not known. Lisbon, his base after his move to Portugal, bubbled with navigational knowledge, reports, rumors, and ideas, including that of the westward passage. It was not, after all, so surprising a notion, given the prevailing general acknowledgment of the roundness of the earth. One man who contributed much to its currency in Lisbon was a geographer and merchant of Florence named Paolo dal Pozzo Toscanelli, who in 1474 wrote to the king of Portugal pointing out the possibility of sailing westward to China, via the island (soon to be shown as mythical) of Antillia, and Cipangu (Japan). Though this letter produced no immediate outcome in new Portuguese explorations, its content became a commonplace at the Portuguese court, where members of the Perestrelo family were often to be found.[2]

More original to Columbus than the idea of sailing west to Asia was his conception of the distance that would have to be covered. Combining several estimates, both ancient and modern, of the size of the earth and of the linear length of a degree of longitude, in such a way as to minimize distance, Columbus proposed that Cipangu lay roughly where Florida is – some 6,200 kilometers west of the Canaries. Expert opinion of the day held this to be a gross underestimate, as indeed it was (the actual distance being some 19,000 kilometers). And this is one of the reasons for Columbus's long failure to find royal backing. But his calculation was not far off the scale of distances admitted by contemporary opinion. Toscanelli himself had proposed a distance of c.8,000 kilometers from the Canaries to China, and thought Cipangu lay far west of China. And Martin Behaim's respected globe of 1492, summarizing geographical knowledge on the eve of Columbus's first voyage, put Cipangu little farther from Europe than Columbus proposed it was.[3]

Columbus's distortions of geography were probably not, therefore, the only, or even the main, reason for his inability to persuade kings to put up the money for an expedition westward. His first approach seems to have been to John II of Portugal, in 1484. Portugal was the obvious choice, since it was the leader in Atlantic exploration, and voyages of discovery were now definitely seen there as state business. Finding, however, no support in Lisbon, Columbus next, in 1486, tried Ferdinand and Isabella. They, too, remained unconvinced even by his maturing powers of persuasion, though they were intrigued enough to promise to reconsider his proposal once the Granada war was over; and in the meantime supported him with occasional small cash grants. Columbus also made indirect approaches to Henry VII of England, and possibly to the French crown as well. Neither obliged; it is difficult indeed to imagine Columbus pressing these overtures, so much was he a man of the south – though both France and England had ample seafaring experience and interest.

It is worth asking why Columbus insisted on seeking royal support. Many earlier expeditions, larger than anything he proposed, had been funded privately in Spain and Portugal. In fact, an offer of backing does seem to have come c.1487 from the Castilian Duke of Medinaceli, who had, apart from the wealth necessary to provide the ships and crews that Columbus wanted, diverse interests in the Canaries and in Atlantic commerce. Medinaceli later claimed to have maintained Columbus for a time in the late 1480s. But he seems to have withdrawn as a sponsor of any actual expedition because he wished to avoid interfering with whatever plans the Catholic Monarchs might have for Columbus.[4]

In any case, Columbus sought, besides money for ships and men, guarantees that only monarchs could provide. He wanted, in any place he might discover, powers of control and assurances of material gain, whether from riches found or trade that would follow. If these gains were to be secure, his discoveries would need a level of protection available only from kings.[5]

It may well have been, in fact, the extravagance of his ambitions rather than the flaws of his geography that dampened Ferdinand and Isabella's, and other monarchs', interest in him for so long. What he wanted, and finally obtained in 1492, for the proposed voyage itself – three ships, crews, and supplies – was modest enough; the necessary funds were squeezed without difficulty (and certainly without any pawning of Isabella's jewels) from the Castilian treasury. But there was no modesty in his demands for honors, positions, and material rewards if his voyage proved successful. It is still a puzzle to understand why the Catholic Monarchs granted so much to him in the famous Capitulations of Santa Fe, the agreement made at the camp before Granada, in April 1492, and in confirmations given in 1493 before his second voyage. Ferdinand and Isabella conferred on him noble status (something else that only kings could bestow), and made him admiral, viceroy, and governor general, under Castile, of any lands he might find to the west. The admiralty, above all a judicial post, was to pass to his heirs in perpetuity. One-tenth of any net profits from his explorations would go to him (and the rest to the crown). And he might put up an eighth of the cost of any ship trading with his discoveries, and receive an eighth of any profit in that trade.[6]

If Ferdinand and Isabella really believed that Columbus would open a westward route to the Orient, where rich and powerful polities were known to exist, they were, by these agreements, conceding to Columbus not only wealth beyond computation, but also political authority that they could not possibly hope to sustain. Perhaps the celebration and optimism following from the taking of Granada made them reckless, or careless. But it is hard to avoid the suspicion that they did not take him quite seriously; that in the euphoria of victory they simply decided to make what was, compared to the costs of the war, a minor investment, and see what eventuated. The outcome was, of course, totally unexpected. And although the Catholic Monarchs were never faced with the problem of defending claims to Castilian sovereignty in India, China, or Japan, they did, within the decade, have to engineer Columbus's removal from power over the Caribbean islands that he found, and later contest the claims of his heirs.

Possibly, too, the experience of Granada moved Ferdinand and Isabella to back Columbus for another reason. With the Iberian peninsula now unified in religion, they were able to give full attention to repulsing Islam overseas. North Africa was the next obvious battlefield. But the prospect of a new front in the East was still enticing. Columbus himself offered this as a potential outcome of his explorations. He went further, indeed, by holding out the prospect that a combination of an eastern attack on Islam and proper use of the wealth he hoped to find would enable Christians to recover Jerusalem. This connection of old crusading aims with his own scheme had occurred to him by 1492.[7] After then the spiritual aspects of his ventures weighed ever more heavily with him, as he became convinced of his role of contributor, through spreading Christianity, to the approach of the millennium. He was struck by the symbolism of the Latin form of his name: *Christum-ferens*, "Christ-bearing." He bore Christ to the heathen, and, in hastening the advent of the millennium, would contribute to the return of Christ to the entire world. These beliefs coincided with a long tradition of millenarianism at the Aragonese court, predicting conquest of Jerusalem and formation of a world-empire specifically by the Aragonese kings, which may account in part for Ferdinand's interest in him.[8]

Columbus was a powerful mixture of the medieval and the modern, of the mystical and the practical, of the delusive and the persuasive (of both self and others). Convinced at the start that what he would find was Asia, he persisted in trying to fit the Caribbean islands and mainlands that his four voyages revealed into a model of the Orient that he carried in his head – a model that, with each new find, naturally grew more distorted. Till the end of his life, in 1506, he insisted that what other Europeans soon suspected was something quite new to them, was Asia. Sailing along the coast of Venezuela on his third voyage in 1498, he reasoned quite logically that the presence of fresh water far out to sea implied the proximity of a great river. It was, in fact, the Orinoco. He went on to argue that this river must be the fourth stream that descended from the earthly paradise; and that therefore he was within reach of that blessed place. At sea, he was a magnificent intuitive navigator, but a poor handler of the instruments of celestial navigation. Aboard ship, or in royal courts, his persuasive powers could bend seamen and monarchs to his will. But as a governor of colonists in Hispaniola he proved a disastrous incompetent. He was, then, a being of apparent opposites. But for some purposes these contradictions served him well, pulling together in such a way as to set him apart from other great (but mere) navigators of his time. Medieval spirituality drove him to use his practical gifts as a seaman to their utmost extent. Illogic in geography inspired him to persuasive efforts that ultimately won monarchs, captains, and seamen to his side. Sometimes, though, even his rhetorical powers were unequal to the task. During his second expedition he surveyed, in 1494, the south coast of Cuba almost to its western end. This was no mean feat of sailing in treacherous waters. The length of the coastline convinced him that he had found a part of mainland Asia in which civilized people would soon appear; or almost so convinced him. Having announced to his ship's company that Cuba was mainland, he made them swear that what he had said was true, on pain of a large fine, a hundred lashes "for the ship's boys and such people," and having their tongues cut out.[9] Such suspicions that geography was betraying him might intrude once in a while; but they soon evaporated.

SPANISH VOYAGES OF EXPLORATION

The Quincentenary celebrations of 1992 made the events of Columbus's first voyage familiar: the sailing of the *Santa María*, *Niña*, and *Pinta* from Palos in south-western Spain on August 3, 1492; provisioning and refitting in the

1492

Canaries; departure thence on September 6; a swift passage westward before
the north-east trade winds; a light sighted in the early hours of October 12;
Columbus's bestowal, next morning, of the most Christian name San Salvador ("Holy Savior") on an obscure Bahamian island; his claiming of it for the
Catholic Monarchs; his meeting with naked native people; his explorations,
over the next three months, of north-eastern Cuba and the north coast of
Hispaniola; the wrecking of the *Santa María* on Christmas Eve; Columbus's
reading in this accident of a providential sign that he should create a settlement; a fortress, named *Navidad* ("Christmas"), built from the wrecked ship's
timbers, and garrisoned with thirty-nine men; the return to Spain of the *Niña*
and *Pinta* begun on January 16, 1493; westerly winds encountered, but also
great storms; brief haven found in the Azores; more storms before landfall off
the Tagus on March 3; return, after repairs, to Palos; triumphal reception of
Columbus, now truly Admiral of the Ocean Sea, by Ferdinand and Isabella in
Barcelona.

Columbus's three later voyages, begun in 1493, 1498, and 1502, are less
known, for reasons obvious enough; but each of them added immensely to
European knowledge, and ultimately settlement, of America. The second was
the largest of all his ventures, and was in fact planned as a colonizing enterprise.
Columbus, now at what was to prove the apex of his career, found Ferdinand
and Isabella eager, indeed anxious, to dispatch another expedition. Settlement
would cement Castile's claim to what Columbus had found. Some 1,200 men
sailed in seventeen ships from Cadiz on September 25, 1493: adventurers,
artisans, farmers, soldiers, and (of particular concern to the monarchs) priests
to turn the islanders to the path of salvation. Columbus dropped south of his
first route, and entered the Caribbean through the Lesser Antilles. Heading
north-west back to Hispaniola, he surveyed the south coast of Puerto Rico.
Another new land was added to the European map. But then, successfully
returned to Hispaniola, he found his fortress at Navidad destroyed, and all
those he had left behind eleven months earlier killed. Though he had judged the
Arawaks of Hispaniola docile and pliable, even they had been driven to violence
by the demands, for gold and women, of those first European residents of the
Caribbean. The immediately urgent business, though, was to find a site for a
larger settlement; and this Columbus chose to place some 110 kilometers
eastward along the north coast, naming this first Euro-American town, in
honor of the queen, Isabela.

The place was unworthy of its name. It was infertile and unhealthy, and had
a bad harbor. Columbus chose it in impatience, partly because it seemed to be
near possible sources of gold.[10] Isabela was a poor start to what became a
calamity of colonial administration. Columbus had no fundamental interest in
being a governor. He still, and always, was in search of the rich, civilized parts
of Asia that he had given as his first object to reach. In April 1494 he sailed
westward from Isabela in their pursuit, feeling his way along the shallows of
the southern Cuban coast, and then, on the return, locating Jamaica. Back at
Isabela, in September 1494, Columbus found illness, hunger, demoralization.
Some colonists had fled back to Spain in ships taken without his leave.
Complaints quickly reached royal ears of the Admiral's deficiencies, more of

omission than commission. He further eroded his standing with the crown by sending native islanders as slaves to Spain, in an attempt to produce some sort of profit from settlement. With remarkable speed a royal agent arrived in October 1495, with orders to look into the complaints made. Columbus decided it was time to state his own case, and left for Spain in March 1496.[11]

So began his long losing battle with the crown to maintain his powers in the lands over which the Capitualations of 1492 had given him charge. As he, and soon others, extended their probings of the transatlantic shores, and it grew ever clearer that whatever this place might be, it was very large, and probably not Asia, the monarchs' impetuous alienation of control to a voluble Genoese visionary seemed increasingly undesirable. The method chosen to sap his position was bureaucracy. Interfering functionaries of increasing rank were dispatched to Hispaniola. His incompetence, or lack of interest, in administration provided a useful justification for this. The sharpest blow came in mid 1500, when a newly arrived royal inspector, Francisco de Bobadilla, put Columbus in irons and sent him back from Hispaniola to Spain. The monarchs of course ordered his shackles struck off as soon as he arrived; but this was a humiliation inconceivable only a brief time before.

By then, Columbus had completed his third expedition, of the summer of 1498. In this crossing from Spain he went even further south than on the second voyage, so that he and his crew became the first recorded Europeans to lay eyes on the South American coast. His landfall was the island of Trinidad. He then passed between it and the Venezuelan coast, finding in the vast discharge of the Orinoco evidence both of a large landmass and of the proximity of Eden. But lacking time to explore upstream, he departed north and west for Hispaniola.

Up to this time, Columbus had persuaded the crown that the agreements of 1492 gave him a monopoly of exploration along the new coasts. But the combination of his South American find, his administrative failings, and perhaps also the swelling strain of prophetic religiosity in his reports, now moved the monarchs to give licenses for exploration to others.[12] Many were anxious to sail, including several who had been with Columbus on his earlier voyages. So began a new rush of European discovery. Four major expeditions in 1499– 1500, led by Andalusian captains, surveyed almost all the north coast of South America.[13] Their findings appeared in a famous world map by Juan de la Cosa, a Spaniard who had sailed with Columbus in 1492 and 1493, and one of the voyagers of 1499. This map, generally accepted as being of 1500, shows the entire northern shore of South America eastward to Cape São Roque (at the north-east tip of Brazil), as well as Hispaniola, Cuba, and a long North American east coast (reconnoitered in part by John Cabot, sailing for and from England in 1497). La Cosa was uncertain of the connection between North and South America; and also, so the map suggests, of the distinction between at least North America and Asia.[14] But his representation of an immense coast of northern South America, and of Cuba as an island, indicates a rising suspicion at the time that what explorers were encountering was something new.

In April of that same year, 1500, the first known European landing on the east coast of Brazil took place. Pedro Alvares Cabral, commander of the second Portuguese fleet bound for India around southern Africa, sailed far west in the Atlantic and made a South American landfall. Not linking what he found with the north coast of South America, he named it the *Ilha da Vera Cruz*, the Island of the True Cross. Cabral sent a ship back to Lisbon to report the find, and the following year the Portuguese crown dispatched three caravels, under the guidance of a Florentine merchant and geographer, Amerigo Vespucci, to survey this new coast. Vespucci – yet another Italian beguiled by navigation, exploration, and the commercial opportunities they might reveal – had earlier, in 1499–1500, sailed on one of the Andalusian voyages to the north coast. Now, in 1501, he continued his efforts in what he called "the Indies" under the flag of Portugal, hoping to find a southerly passage to known Asia around the great land mass that was revealing itself.[15] His survey of the east coast of South America, possibly as far as the La Plata estuary, lasted into early 1502. He reported that he had seen a "new land," a "continent;" but it is not clear whether he yet regarded it as something quite separate from Asia. The combination of his accounts, however, with the knowledge accumulating from other explorations suggested ever more strongly that America stood apart from the Orient. And this notion found its defining statement in a world map published in 1507 by one Martin Waldseemüller, a priest and schoolteacher of Saint Dié in Lorraine. Here a great ocean is set between America and the East. So renowned had Amerigo Vespucci's reports become (though much of what appeared under his name was forgery), and so long were the South American shores that he had coasted, that Waldseemüller, casting round for a name for the new continent, chose America.

Thus Columbus was doubly deprived: he first lost the powers granted to him in 1492, and then the honor, surely deserved however wayward his geographical notions, of having the subcontinent he had been the first European to see named after him. His worthiness in this respect grew with his fourth voyage of 1502–4. Here again he was a pioneer, this time in surveying the Caribbean coast of Central America from Honduras down to Panama. The rigors of this venture, especially a long stranding on Jamaica on the return voyage, sapped his strength. He did not live to know the humiliation of the misnaming of America, dying in Valladolid in the spring of 1506, some eighteen months later than his patroness, Isabella.

After the burst of voyaging at the turn of the century, exploration lagged for a decade or more as the new revelations were digested, and Spaniards, if not yet the Portuguese, found they had plenty to do in adjusting, as settlers on Hispaniola, to New World conditions. The upper coasts of the Caribbean, from Honduras northward, were oddly slow in being reconnoitered. The first contact came in the east, in the spring of 1513, when Juan Ponce de León, a Caribbean settler made rich by his conquest of Puerto Rico in 1508–9, sailed north-west under royal orders to seek the reported islands of Bimini. After threading through the Bahamas, he took possession of the mainland coast in April of 1513, naming it the Flowery (*Florida*) Isle (possibly an allusion to its abundant vegetation).[16] Ponce surveyed the whole of the east coast of Florida, and part of the west, before returning to Puerto Rico.

To the west, it was not until 1517 that a Spanish expedition first examined the Mexican coast (though it may have been cursorily scouted in 1508 for a passage to the Orient). In 1517, Francisco Hernández de Córdoba, another wealthy settler, but this time of Cuba, took a small expedition westward. His three ships progressed as far as the base of Yucatan on its west side. A second exploration, under Juan de Grijalva, was quickly organized in 1518. This expedition followed Hernández's track, and then pushed forward to a point half-way up the east coast of Mexico. In doing so, Grijalva and his men made the first recorded contact between Europeans and Aztecs. News of this encounter spurred the governor of Cuba, Diego Velázquez, to put together a third Mexico-bound expedition, in 1519. This force, led by Hernán Cortés, did nothing to extend coastal exploration; it did, of course, conquer the Aztecs in quite short order. The task of completing coastal exploration in the northern Caribbean between Mexico and Florida fell to one Alonso Alvarez de Pineda, sailing from Jamaica on the orders of its governor, Francisco de Garay, between late 1518 and mid-1519.[17] By the time, then, that Cortés was planning his assault on the Aztec empire in the autumn of 1519, the entire Caribbean coastline from Florida round to Venezuela was known to the Spanish. They knew also the islands, large and small, of what was rapidly becoming their American Mediterranean; likewise the rest of South America's northern shore down to the easternmost point of Brazil.

On the eastern side of South America, below the limits of Portuguese voyaging, Spanish exploration proceeded slowly. Its motive was less knowledge of the shores themselves than pursuit of that elusive goal, an access to the Orient. Late in 1515 an expedition sailed from Spain commanded by Juan Díaz de Solís, an experienced sailor in American waters. He was charged with finding a passage through South America, and exploring the ocean beyond it. But sailing the Pacific was not to be his lot, for after discovering that the Río de la Plata was not a strait but an estuary, Solís was killed on its shores in a skirmish with native people. The remnants of his expedition went back to Spain.

There, two years later, the government of the young king Charles accepted a proposal from a crabby Portuguese mariner, Fernão de Magalhães, to show a way to the Spice Islands of Asia around America. Magellan, to use the anglicized form of his name, seems to have been sure where this passage lay; but he, like Columbus, had not been able to persuade the Portuguese crown to back him, and, perhaps in retaliation, now brought his plan to Spain. He found receptive listeners there, especially since Spain was by now anxious to establish territorial claims in the Orient to offset those being made by Portuguese who had reached Asia by the route around Africa. In August 1519 Magellan's five ships left Seville. There followed one of the epic voyages in the history of navigation: mutinies, storms, desertions, scurvy, sinkings – but as a result of it, the discovery of the Magellan Strait linking the Atlantic with the Pacific in southern South America, the first documented crossing of the Pacific, and, of course, the first circumnavigation of the globe. Any lingering doubts of the earth's sphericity were now exploded. Magellan was killed by native people in the Philippines, after meddling unwisely in local political affairs. Only one ship, the aptly named *Victoria*, carrying eighteen men (of an original 265 in the expedition) finally returned to Spain. It docked at Seville in October 1522, commanded by Juan Sebastián Elcano, a Basque who thereupon became one of the great heroes of Spanish naval history.[18]

Though Magellan had finally found the western passage to the Orient, the discovery was long of little practical use. Whether by way of the intricate and reef-bound Strait, or of Cape Horn, fighting into the Roaring Forties and the great seas they stirred up, rounding the tip of South America was so daunting a venture that the route was little used for many years. Only in the eighteenth century, with technical improvements to ships, did this Atlantic–Pacific passage become a commonplace, if still fearful, piece of navigation.

One outcome of this was that the Pacific shores of America were explored largely from west coast ports. The first of these, and the one from which the most influential voyages departed, was the City of Panama, founded precisely in the year in which Magellan sailed from Spain, 1519. Ten years before, a gold- and slave-seeking expedition had set out from Hispaniola for the coast of what is now Colombia. There it suffered most severely from native resistance. The survivors finally found refuge in 1511 near the base of the Isthmus of Panama, attaching themselves to a settlement of more welcoming Indians. To this place they gave the name of Santa María la Antigua de Darién. It was the first Spanish (if partly native) town on the American mainland. By this time a stowaway of much innate ability had risen to lead the group, by name Vasco Núñez de Balboa. Two years later Balboa took a party across the Isthmus. And it was he, and not (*pace* Keats) "stout Cortez," who then stood upon a peak in Darien and surveyed the Pacific Ocean. Balboa waded out into this Southern Sea, as he pronounced it, and claimed it and its shores for the crown of Spain. In good Spanish legal fashion, the act was notarized, with the members of the party as witnesses. First to put his name on the document, after Balboa himself, was one Francisco Pizarro, who had been a member of the original expedition from Hispaniola in 1509.

Pizarro was already a leading figure among settlers of the Isthmus. By the time the City of Panama was founded, in 1519, he was also growing in wealth. In the 1520s he put his resources into voyages of exploration down the Pacific coast of present Colombia and the shores of Ecuador. These probings, encouraged by rumors of rich people and lands far to the south, eventually, early in 1528, brought him into contact at Túmbez in northern Peru with coastal outposts of the Inca state. And this inspired him to essay, beginning two years later, the conquest of the Incas. During the conquest, and in the years immediately after it, most of the rest of the west coast of South America was reconnoitered.

Coastal exploration of Central America, and inland settlement for that matter, also proceeded northward from the Panama base, running into southward expansion of Spaniards from Mexico in the late 1520s. The west coast of Mexico itself was the object of several expeditions from the early 1530s on. Hernán Cortés himself in 1535 crossed from the mainland to the southern tip of Lower California, which was still thought to be an island. The Gulf of California to this day, in Spanish, bears his name: the Sea of Cortés.

Upper California's coast, almost to the present Oregon line, was surveyed in 1542–3 by Juan Rodríguez Cabrillo and Bartolomé Ferrelo, sailing from western Mexico at the order of the first viceroy of Mexico, Don Antonio de Mendoza.[19] Sixty years later, in 1602, Sebastián Vizcaíno gave that shore a more thorough examination, producing the first maps of it. In these north-bound voyages the motive was not mere curiosity, but also the search for a northern passage between Atlantic and Pacific – the Strait of Anian, as it was generally called in the seventeenth century. Fears that others, particularly the English and the Portuguese, might find this strait first gave the Spaniards an extra incentive to press northward.

Western Mexico also quickly became a point of departure for ships bound for the Orient. Cortés, again, with the sense of potentially global Spanish empire that the Aztec conquest had inspired in him, was an early mover of such ventures. At his urging one Alvaro Saavedra Cerón sailed in 1527 to follow up on the Magellan expedition's exploration of the Spice Islands. One of the three ships reached New Guinea, though none returned to Mexico.[20] The return to America from Asia – the eastward crossing of the Pacific – indeed remained for several decades an obstacle to the westward extension of Spain's empire into the Orient, where Magellan's voyage had given it claims. The westward voyage across the Pacific, though long, was not excessively hazardous. Ruy López de Villalobos managed it again, with a small fleet, in 1542; but none of his ships came home to Mexico. The North Equatorial Current and North-East Trades that favored westward movement between southern Mexico and the Philippines effectively blocked the return at that latitude. Finally, the key to communication between America and Asia was found in 1565, by an Augustinian friar, Andrés de Urdaneta. He, in his youthful, pre-monastic days, had spent several years in the islands of South-East Asia as a survivor of an ill-fated expedition from Spain that had reached the Orient via the Magellan Strait in 1525. In the late 1550s, Urdaneta, now with a strong sense of where the return route should be sought, persuaded the second viceroy of Mexico, Don Luis de Velasco, to support a new transpacific expedition, one of whose main purposes would be to demonstrate the east-ward voyage. Late in 1559 the king, Philip II, ordered Velasco to organize exploration of the Asian islands. The commander of the flotilla formed as a result was Miguel López de Legazpi; the navigator, Urdaneta. Their four ships left Mexico on November 21, 1564, and arrived in the Philippines on Febru-ary 3, 1565. For the return, Urdaneta chose the fastest ship, and provisioned it for eight months. On June 1, 1565 he sailed from Cebu in the Philippines, striking far north of earlier attempts. In doing so, he picked up both the Westerlies of the north Pacific and, doubtless without knowing it, the help of the Japan Current and then the North Pacific Drift. The voyage to Acapulco lasted four months; scurvy took a toll, sixteen of the crew of forty-four dying.[21] But, like Columbus in the Atlantic, Urdaneta had mapped out an oval pattern of Pacific winds and currents that allowed reliable communication between Mexico and South-East Asia. Communication was the essential precondition for political control, if Spain wished to have it. And in fact, while Urdaneta was feeling his way back to America, Legazpi, as he had been instructed, began the Spanish occupation of the Philippines, keeping the Portuguese at bay, and often finding himself gladly enough accepted by native groups as an ally against the recent Muslim Malay invaders of the islands.

By the 1560s, then, Spaniards knew in some detail not only the coasts of the Caribbean, eastern and western South America, and western Central America, Mexico, and North America, but also those of the archipelagos of South-East Asia. They had made themselves familiar with conditions of winds and currents on these coasts, and were learning to move between them with minimum waste of time. In little more than half a century, Europeans' knowledge of the western hemisphere had grown vastly, beyond earlier conception. People alive in 1490 could hardly, in their wildest speculations, have imagined what was to be securely known as geographical reality seventy years later: not only an entire new continent, but one separated from the Orient by an ocean far broader than anything Europeans, even the Portuguese tracking the African coast southwards, had ever encountered. And by the 1560s, not only was this new western geography known, but also to a surprising degree dominated – dominated by the efforts of European navigators of several nations, but chief among them, beyond question, Spain.

SPAIN AND PORTUGAL DIVIDE THE WORLD

While Spaniards circled half the world to the west, the Portuguese did the same to the east. The two movements met in the early 1520s in South-East Asia with Magellan's arrival in the Philippines under Spanish colors. Over the previous twenty years the Portuguese, advancing on Vasco da Gama's path-breaking voyage to India and back of 1497–9, had surveyed great stretches of the Asian coast and the Indian Ocean with astonishing speed: the Seychelles Islands and the Arabian coast in 1503, Sri Lanka in 1505, the Bay of Bengal from that year on, the Persian Gulf from 1507 on, the Malay Peninsula, Sumatra, and Java between 1509 and 1512, and, farthest yet to the east, the Celebes, Timor, and the Moluccas (the "Spice Islands") in 1512.[22] By 1513, when the first European, Núñez de Balboa, looked out over the Pacific from its American shore, the Portuguese were at its western edge in Asia.

Magellan's expedition was the first European presence in the Philippines, immediately north and a little west of the Spice Islands. His appearance in the Orient in 1520 precipitated several years of military and diplomatic friction between the two Iberian states. The roots of the conflict go back to 1494, when Spain and Portugal agreed, in the famous (infamous, no doubt, to other Europeans) Treaty of Tordesillas, that lands lying in the Atlantic beyond a pole-to-pole line 370 leagues west of the Cape Verde Islands should be Spanish, and those east of such a meridian, Portuguese. The line was not randomly chosen. It was far enough to the west, the Portuguese thought, to preserve their access to Africa, while not so far, in the Castilians' view, as to allow the Portuguese into the Caribbean. Both sides knew that this division would be hard to place exactly on land or at sea. But it was precise enough for the purposes of the day; precise enough, for example, for there to be no doubt that the Island of the True Cross encountered in 1500 by Alvares Cabral on his voyage to India was Portugal's. Hence, among much else, Brazil speaks Portuguese.[23]

But if demarcation of Spanish and Portuguese zones might be debatable only on a small scale in the Atlantic, in the Pacific the question was wide open. Though the Tordesillas agreement was drafted, and could have been drafted, with only the Atlantic in view, once the Pacific became known after 1512–13, the notion grew that the line should be projected into the eastern hemisphere. And once Spain made an appearance in the Philippines, with Magellan, and began also to claim rights in the Moluccas, thereby endangering Portugal's monopoly access, among European powers, to the riches offered by cloves and other spices, agreement on a division became essential. Finally, after several years of local skirmishing in the islands, and protracted negotiation at home, by the Treaty of Zaragoza in 1529 Spain and Portugal resolved on a continuation of the Tordesillas line into the Pacific at *c*.145 degrees east. This placed all the disputed territories in the Portuguese zone. But Spain renounced claims to the Spice Islands only in exchange for the very large payment of 350,000 *cruzados* by the Portuguese; and although the Philippines now lay indisputably on the Portuguese side of the line, Spaniards still set much store by prior discovery, so that once Urdaneta made transpacific communication a routine practicality in the 1560s, Spanish colonization from Mexico proceeded apace. Portugal could do little to stop it. Thus the Philippines became Spanish territory; and remained so until 1898.

Although the islands lacked the civilization and wealth of Japan and China, Columbus might have been happy enough with that outcome. For Spanish missionaries soon set to work in the Philippines, evangelizing the population, thereby setting up a barrier to the eastward spread of Islam, and contributing to the worldwide spread of Christianity. And Manila, the Spanish capital in the islands, soon proved to be the source of great wealth as the entrepôt at which oriental fineries, jewels and spices were profitably exchanged for the silver of America.

[5] *EXPERIMENT IN THE CARIBBEAN*

FIRST ROOTS

Though Spanish exploration of American, and other, shores proceeded with impressive swiftness in the sixteenth century, settlement was a slower business, at least in its early stages. For a generation, almost thirty years, after Columbus first crossed the Ocean Sea, Spaniards on its western side chose to live only in the large Caribbean islands, and on the Isthmus of Panama. And Panama, until it became the base for conquest in South America early in the 1530s, might as well have been another large island, so isolated was it from other Spanish American places. Spanish occupation of the American mainland can properly be said to start in 1519, when Hernán Cortés went from Cuba to undertake the conquest of the Aztecs. His encounter with that great culture is almost on a par in its outcomes with Columbus's encounter with America, since it spurred a vast increase in interest in the new continent, a growth of emigration, a leap in expectations of economic gain, and, partly as a result of these, the emergence of the notion that America was truly the stuff of empire for Spain. The conquest of the Incas a decade or so later served, of course, to reinforce all this.

Modest, though, as the Caribbean stage of Spanish occupation of America may have been, it was a period of essential learning – an apprenticeship for Spaniards in living an ocean's width from home, among people of a sort they had never before experienced, in tropical places whose plants, animals, soils, and climates were new. It was equally a period of apprenticeship for those, remaining in Spain, to whom fell the charge of governing these territories so remote in space and time. All rose to this challenge of learning with astounding speed, so that by the time the occupation of the mainland began, many of the practices (administrative, fiscal, legal, economic, social, cultural) that were to characterize the empire over its whole span were in place in at least embryonic form. The process of learning was far from uniformly positive, to be sure; disasters occurred, or were allowed to occur, including the all but total destruction of the native people of the Bahamas and the Greater Antilles. Regarded from certain angles, indeed, this first Caribbean stage of Spanish colonialism is thoroughly deplorable. Nonetheless, for the formation of the empire, the Caribbean experience was crucial. It was a bridgehead into the new.

Spanish settlement was limited to Hispaniola for sixteen years after it began there, at Navidad, in late 1492. That small fortress (in a really elemental sense a European settlement, since it was built partly from the timbers of the wrecked *Santa Maria*)[1] did not survive until Columbus's return on the second voyage, eleven months later. Finding it destroyed, and the forty or so men he had left there killed, Columbus chose to found the first true Spanish town on Hispaniola, 120 kilometers further east, on a barren, if flat, site near a river mouth that offered some protection for ships. This was Isabela. Public buildings, a church, and perhaps even parapets and a moat were soon in place.[2] But the town never prospered. Its surroundings were not fertile. The European crops, on which those first settlers counted, failed. Very soon there came hunger, sickness, and death. Many began to wish themselves back in Spain, and indeed left once an opportunity arose. In part to correct this initial mistake in settlement, Columbus chose another site on the south coast for a new town, 200 kilometers south-east of Isabela. There in mid-1496 his brother, Bartolomé, began the building of Santo Domingo, which has been the capital ever since. The harbour was good, the nearby land rich, well watered by rain, and densely peopled. A promising gold-field had already been found 50–65 kilometers inland, which was another reason for the founding. Survivors from the north coast quickly shifted to this better place, leaving Isabela all but abandoned by 1499.[3] By that time, two or three small fortresses had also been built in the interior, between Isabela and Santo Domingo, to discourage native resistance to Spanish settlement and its growing demands. But European numbers in Hispaniola were still falling. Though Columbus had come with 1,500 men in 1493, and ships had constantly arrived from Spain since then, by the end of the century the Spanish population of the island (still largely male) was down to between 300 and 1,000.[4]

Outward from Hispaniola

Spanish occupation of Hispaniola in reality began almost anew in 1502, when 2,500 colonists arrived with the second royally-appointed governor of the island, Nicolás de Ovando. Among them were the first European families to emigrate to America. Though, once more, many of the newcomers died, a continuing influx led to net growth, so that by 1508 some ten thousand Spaniards were in place, living in fifteen Spanish towns (*villas*) scattered throughout the island.[5] By then, indeed, Hispaniola was beginning to seem crowded; or, at least, the balance between settlers and useful resources was no longer as favorable as new emigrants expected. The resource most sought after was native labor. And by 1509 the Indians had fallen, through the effects of war, maltreatment, social disruption, and disease, to some 62,000.[6] Though the size of Hispaniola's population before October 1492 is still hotly debated, it was undeniably much larger than this: probably between 200,000 and 1,200,000, and just conceivably several millions.[7] So the expectations of immigrants that they could prosper from the surplus of native production were increasingly disappointed; and Spaniards in Hispaniola looked for new places to settle.

Now, therefore, Hispaniola became the center from which Spanish activities in the New World emanated; whereas before, their source had still chiefly been the coast of Andalusia. This American base had been fifteen years in the making; now it had firm foundations. The first major outward movement came in 1508, when Juan Ponce de León, the later explorer of the Florida coast, was charged by the crown with following up on gold discoveries that he had made in an earlier reconnaissance of Puerto Rico. Back on that island, he created towns near the gold deposits in the south-west and north-east, and assigned the native Taino to settlers to wash gold. This resulted in a native revolt that Ponce fiercely suppressed. There followed a repetition of the miserable story already played out in Hispaniola: the disappearance within a few years of almost all the native population of Puerto Rico.

In the following year, 1509, the pace of expansion from Hispaniola accelerated. An expedition went to settle Jamaica, led by one Juan de Esquivel, a man who had taken part in suppressing native resistance in south-east Hispaniola. The island revealed no gold. Its Taino people, however, when distributed among the incoming Spaniards for farming purposes, fared no better than their counterparts in Hispaniola and Puerto Rico who had been put to digging and panning gold. By 1519 the native Jamaicans were almost gone.[8] Jamaica never amounted to much under Spanish rule: a small community of farming settlers, off the beaten track. It is no surprise that it was the first large Spanish island in the Caribbean to fall to a foreign power. In 1655 the English took it, against little resistance.

Far more significant for Spanish imperial history was a second movement outward from Hispaniola in 1509. In December of that year, two expeditions left the island for the mainland, one under Alonso de Hojeda, directed at the coasts of what are today Colombia and western Venezuela, and the other under Diego de Nicuesa, bound for Veragua; that is, the Caribbean coast of Central America from the Gulf of Urabá at the lower end of Panama, northward to Honduras. The purpose, as directed by the crown, was settlement; but settlement with the specific purpose of securing precious metals, of which the crown intended to take its royal share. The expeditions were sizable affairs. Nicuesa took five ships carrying almost 800 men, Hojeda three with 200–300 men. In the end it was the smaller force that had the greater effect. Nicuesa's expedition was a disaster. Few, if any, of his people survived it. Columbus, on this Panama coast on his fourth and final voyage, had found gold, and spun up, through his reports, the notion that here was a zone vastly rich in metal. Nicuesa, in his hurry to find this wealth, split up his ships, ignored the navigational advice of men who had been with Columbus five and six years before, became lost, and exposed his force to native attack, and, even more deadly, starvation. No settlement of Central America resulted from his enterprise.

Settlement was the outcome, on the other hand, of Hojeda's efforts. Preceding the final success was much fierce combat with natives on the Colombian coast, in the course of which the famed navigator and map-maker Juan de la Cosa lost his life, and Hojeda himself suffered wounds and privations that led to his early death after he returned to Hispaniola in the summer of 1510 to gather reinforcements. Poisoned arrows offered the Spaniards a severity of challenge in this territory that they had rarely been faced with before. The expedition was reduced at one point to sixty men. But under the final leadership of Vasco Núñez de Balboa, and also the doughty influence of Francisco Pizarro, the survivors eventually settled, more in exhaustion than triumph, on the fertile and welcoming western side of the Gulf of Urabá. The town of Santa María la Antigua de Darién was the immediate result; and in the longer term came the founding of the city of Panama on the Pacific side of the isthmus in 1519, and the creation of a new Spanish base, beyond Hispaniola, for exploration and conquest. Without this base, the conquest of the Incas would have been a distant, if not impossible, prospect.

The final outward leap from Hispaniola was to Cuba. The conquest and occupation of this largest of the Greater Antilles began in 1511, with a two-pronged attack led by men who had already honed their swords and skills as *conquistadores* elsewhere: Diego Velázquez in south-western Hispaniola, and Pánfilo de Narváez in Jamaica. Neither of them made any pretence about what they wanted for themselves and their followers: native labor for washing gold and growing food. The occupation of Cuba was a work of violence and terrorism, designed to intimidate the local population into submission. In that it was successful before 1511 was out. The best that can be said of Velázquez's and Narváez's vicious seizure of the island is that it had some redeeming effects in the longer term. Accompanying Velázquez, as a minor treasury clerk,[9] was Hernán Cortés, who a decade or so later in Mexico resolved that there should be no repetition in the land he had just conquered of the mindless destruction of native people he had seen in the Caribbean. And with Narváez went one Bartolomé de las Casas, a recently ordained priest, but in most respects still a colonist with the standard ambitions of the time. The destruction wreaked by Narváez as he bludgeoned his way from south-east to north-west across the island – Las Casas later wrote "I do not remember with how much spilling of human blood he marked that road"[10] – led this future and greatest of defenders of the American natives to ponder the morality of conquest.

The invaders soon found gold in the streams descending from the highlands of central Cuba. A gold rush followed in 1512, drawing crowds of prospectors from Hispaniola. By 1515, six Spanish towns were in place. Cuba began to supplant Hispaniola as the prime Spanish base in the Caribbean. Only the western quarter of the island lacked a European settlement. Most of the towns were sited in areas of heavy native population: labor was always the great magnet. Indians sent thence to the gold placers died in large numbers, so that by 1515 workers were already in short supply. Cuba had in any case, by several accounts, been more lightly peopled before the Spanish came than Hispaniola.[11] The rapid erosion of this slighter base was one reason for the relative brevity of the island's role as central Spanish focus in America. Only ten years after conquerors entered Cuba, Mexico became a far greater attraction; and Cuba, along with the other islands, receded into the background of the now genuinely imperial scheme of things Spanish in America.

GOVERNMENT

The Greater Antilles played the essential roles not only of bridgehead and psychological proving ground for that mainland empire, but also of terrain for experiment in distant administration. Here a variety of governing mechanisms were tried; some were transferred to the mainland when the time came, others were discarded. Naturally enough, Iberian practices were the point of departure. One of Columbus's titles was viceroy (of the islands and mainlands he might discover); viceroys had been an essential part of Catalan–Aragonese regional rule in the Mediterranean since the fourteenth century. Then again, Columbus's brother Bartolomé, who tried to govern Hispaniola in the viceroy's absence in Spain between 1496 and 1498, did so as *adelantado* – a term coming from the verb *adelantar*, "to advance." The title was one of frontier governor, with strong military overtones, and had been frequently used in the Reconquest. In the fifteenth century it was bestowed also on the conquerors of the Canaries. Those islands, in fact, saw several peninsular techniques of government tested overseas for the first time.[12] But as the Canaries were relatively close to Spain, and because settlement of them did not begin in earnest until the 1480s, administrative experience there did not teach fundamental lessons that could be applied to the Caribbean. Far off on the other side of the Ocean Sea, America had necessarily to be its own laboratory.

No royal agent sailed with Columbus on his first voyage. But on the second, in 1493, one was present, in the soon-to-be-ubiquitous shape of a treasury official. (The term *real oficial*, or "royal official," quickly came to mean in America specifically an officer of the treasury: the royal interest in taxes was never in doubt.) Columbus had cried up the potential wealth of the islands, and the crown wanted its share. This was the first intrusion of the state into Columbus's domain. Doubtless this interference would have grown with time in any case; but it was accelerated by Columbus's incompetence and lack of interest in governing, and by the effects of natural problems in settlement that the eager fortune hunters of the second voyage had not foreseen. By early 1494, hungry, sick, and dying men at Isabela were already blaming him for failing to prevent food from rotting, when heat and humidity were the main culprits. Columbus, never a man given to subtlety, tried threats and violence to persuade the men, among them many courtiers and gentry, to work for their own salvation. "The outcome was hatred for the Admiral," Las Casas later wrote, "and this is the source of his reputation in Spain as a cruel man hateful to all Spaniards, a man unfit to rule. Columbus's prestige declined steadily from then on, without one day of respite, until in the end nothing was left of it and he fell utterly into disgrace."[13] Some of the gentlemen took their complaints to Spain. In consequence, a royally appointed inspector arrived in October 1495, and began to act as if he were the chief authority in Hispaniola. Columbus returned to Spain in March 1496 to explain himself, leaving his brother Bartolomé, the *Adelantado*, in charge.

Matters, not surprisingly, grew worse. Being another foreigner, and lacking Columbus's titles and his moral stature as discoverer, Bartolomé would have needed almost miraculous governing skills to hold together the fractious Spanish community. Lacking such powers, in 1497 he found himself faced with a revolt led by one Francisco Roldán, whom Columbus had left as local governor (*alcalde mayor*) of Isabela, a town now rapidly nearing extinction. Roldán set up a rival regime in western Hispaniola, drawing into it by 1498 about half the Spaniards. Though Columbus, back on the island in 1498, was able to make peace with the rebels, he did so only through granting concessions, above all of control over native labor. These, though, did little to diminish Roldán's, and others', hostility to the Columbus brothers. Further complaints sent to Spain in 1499, combined with royal concern over the continuing cost to the treasury of the Caribbean venture, and with Isabella's anger at Columbus's granting of native slaves to Spaniards returning to Spain – by what right, she asked, did he give her vassals as slaves? – finally led the monarchs to send out a far more powerful agent in mid-1500. This was Francisco de Bobadilla, a commander (*comendador*) of the military Order of Calatrava, a well-tested servant of the crown. So ended Columbus's, and his family's, independent power in America, and so was revoked, *de facto*, much of the agreement made at Santa Fe in 1492; for Bobadilla held powers to remove Columbus as governor, and promptly proceeded to do just that on his arrival. The departure, in chains, of the admiral and the *Adelantado* for Castile followed soon after. Adding insult to injury, but showing very clearly where royal sympathies now inclined, Bobadilla pardoned Roldán.

After two years of comparatively peaceful administration, Bobadilla was recalled to Spain, perhaps because he had offended the crown by temporarily rescinding mining taxes in an effort to stimulate the production of gold. In this he succeeded. Much of the metal gathered was, however, lost when a hurricane laid waste the fleet carrying it back to Spain in July 1502. Both Bobadilla and Roldán were drowned: a cause, perhaps, for some bitter satisfaction to Columbus, especially since he, approaching Santo Domingo on his fourth and final voyage to America, read the signs of the tempest's approach and warned Bobadilla. Ignoring the advice, Bobadilla set sail, and perished.

In April 1502 had arrived in Santo Domingo Nicolás de Ovando, a knight-commander (*comendador mayor*) of the Order of Alcántara, and the first fully fledged governor of Hispaniola belonging to the royal bureaucracy. He had accepted a term of two years, but stayed seven. In them he made the island a royal domain. With the new emigrants that his fleet carried, the European population of Hispaniola jumped from perhaps as few as 300 to around 3,000. From this reinvigoration, a confident occupation of the island followed. Under Ovando gold production rose, partly in response to cuts ordered from Spain in the royalty charged on it, from the half prevailing until 1502 to the fifth conceded in 1504.[14] Ovando further boosted mining by assigning native labor to it. He did the same for Spanish-directed farming. A growing supply of foods familiar to Spaniards, particularly beef and pork, was still more important to the willing settlement of the island than the prospect of gold. Cattle, pigs, and horses brought in from 1493 onward, and allowed to multiply wild, had by Ovando's time become very numerous. He imported more breeding stock at his own cost. A growing supply of horses was one reason for the rapidity of Spanish conquest of other Caribbean islands from 1508. Hispaniola proved an excellent breeding ground, offering virgin grassland that was free of predators, and still without diseases and parasites to threaten stock. The precipitous fall of the native population released ever more land for grazing. Though large private landholding had not yet begun, the land for the moment being regarded, both popularly and legally, as public domain open to all, nonetheless here in Hispaniola the model of the New World ranch was being created.[15] Meat quickly became more abundant than it was in Spain; its price dropped. Lard, tallow, and particularly hides began to be exported, providing some needed variety, beyond gold, in the island's marketable products. Sugarcane was introduced in Ovando's time, though sugar was not yet exported.[16] True enough, the Spaniards' staple grain, wheat, was never successfully grown in the islands. But the colonists bent sufficiently toward native culture to accept bread made from manioc flour as a basic food.

The rising Spanish population gathered into new towns (*villas*); or, more precisely, was so gathered, since Ovando had come with royal orders to create new settlements and people them with Christians from Spain. Here is an early realization in America of the Spanish conviction (drawing on a long European tradition) that civilization was essentially an urban matter.[17] Spaniards were not, Ovando was urged, to be allowed to live scattered about the countryside.[18] Most of the fifteen towns that existed in Hispaniola by 1509 seem to have been founded in 1504–5. They were concentrated in the eastern half of the island; but five were on or very near its western shores.[19] By the time Ovando left, in 1509, Santo Domingo was becoming a recognizably Spanish town in its physical form, with stone houses (some of them roofed and floored with tiles from Spain) built by drafted native laborers under Spanish artisans' supervision. The first luxuries were beginning to appear by then, reflecting a rising prosperity: imported musical instruments, candles, damask tablecloths, and silverware. Among the first to prosper were lawyers, repeating in America the rise in wealth and status that they had enjoyed in Spain under Ferdinand and Isabella.[20] But wealth also began generally to show the socially elevating power that it exercised throughout colonial times in Spanish America. Distance from Spain weakened the traditional determinants of social standing in effect there, so that colonials found that mere money could bring them a far greater social lift in America than it could in the peninsula.

Santo Domingo and the other towns were not to have just Spanish populations, but married Spanish populations. The family seemed the natural social unit, and marriage was seen as likely to solidify settlement. Anticipating later general policy, Ovando particularly favored (with grants of native labor, for instance) married immigrants, insisting that men who had left wife and family in Spain should bring them out within three years. The better to root unattached Spanish males, he encouraged them to marry native women. His efforts had some success. In 1514 a partial but probably fairly complete count of householders (*vecinos*) in Hispaniola found 392 of them living in the island's fourteen towns. Of these, about a quarter (92) had Castilian wives; and about an eighth (54) native wives.[21] Many others probably lived unmarried with native women. The children born of these unions can only have added a stabilizing weight to the social structure. More important still, for the genetic and cultural future of Spanish America, was specifically the early appearance of children of mixed blood – the first of the mestizos (literally, the "mixed") who have come to form most of the Spanish American population. Intermarriage of Spaniards and natives (nearly always Spanish men with native women) became normal policy later, at least during the founding phase of the mainland empire.[22]

Another of Ovando's tasks was to audit the accounts of Columbus's government of Hispaniola. To improve collection of royal income in the future, a full set of four treasury officials was appointed to the island in 1501.[23] They were the first component installed of what was to become an enormous bureaucratic machine of government in the Spanish Indies. Two years later, in another step in that machine's assembly, these officials became the American agents of the first governmental body set up in Spain to deal specifically with Indies affairs. This was the House of Trade, or *Casa de Contratación*, created in Seville in 1503 to supervise trade with the Caribbean, collect duties, and act as court of first appeal in trade suits. The *Casa* rapidly developed into much more than this, however, becoming not only the channel through which royal orders flowed to Hispaniola, but also the supreme advisory, and even executive, body for America. Its head, the cleric Juan Rodríguez de Fonseca,[24] was immensely influential in early Caribbean affairs, remaining so until a fully fledged royal Council of the Indies (*Consejo de Indias*) came into being in the early 1520s. At that point the *Casa* reverted to its concentration on trade, which, however, embraced communication with America and control over emigration.

The state's crossing of the Atlantic was marked, among other things, by the creation in Ovando's time of a branch of the *Casa* in Santo Domingo, staffed by the treasury officials.[25] Ovando worked in other ways, backed and directed by Ferdinand and Isabella, to impose the weight of government on Hispaniola. The independence of municipalities had long been a thorn in the royal side in Spain. To forestall any such annoyances in America, the crown gave Ovando powers in 1504 to name first-instance magistrates (*alcaldes ordinarios*) and constables (*alguaciles*) for towns on the island. By tradition, these were elected offices; complaints about Ovando's meddling with them went to Spain, but to little avail. Above the municipal level, royal justice was in the hands of two superior magistrates (*alcaldes mayores*). From them, appeals went to Ovando, who judged rigorously.[26] A strict austerity, allied with remoteness and personal morality, formed his hallmark. With it he stamped his efforts, which were successful, to remedy the chaos of the 1490s, impose royal authority on Hispaniola, and make the island productive enough both to attract new settlers and to satisfy the crown's (especially Ferdinand's, after Isabella's death) thirst for new American income.

Ovando was less careful of natives' interests on Hispaniola than he was of the colonists', or, even more, the monarchy's. He asserted Spain's presence by suppressing what remained of native polities. He began with the island of Saona, off the south-east tip of Hispaniola. Here Spaniards had senselessly provoked Indian hostility, which Ovando read, some say with malicious intent, as rebellion. The ensuing campaign destroyed Saona's native population.

A far larger native state survived in the west of Hispaniola, ruled by a queen named Anacaona. Late in 1503, the region's *caciques* (chiefs) assembled to meet Ovando during what seemed to be a friendly Spanish visit. In the midst of festivities and displays of arms, he ordered his men to attack the native leaders. A rumor of native plotting may have been behind this assault.[27] Whether so or not, Ovando took the opportunity to remove the native leadership. By one report, he hanged eighty-four chiefs, and Anacaona too.[28] The following year, 1504, the Higuey peninsula in south-eastern Hispaniola was the object of his attention, and the final large independent chiefdom of the island disappeared. Though there is disagreement about Ovando's motives and procedures in these attacks, they seem to have been examples of what was already, and what was long to be, a prime Spanish tool of conquest: terrorism. Columbus had used it in his time; and in the other large islands and then on a vaster scale on the mainland, succeeding waves of *conquistadores* yielded to its allures. One of these was that it could bring native allies. Those already defeated, and sometimes those still unconquered, sometimes joined the Spanish and "fought strenuously, such was their fear of the Spaniards whom they accompanied and their desire to please them."[29]

Part of Ovando's reason for eliminating native governments was that he was acutely aware of the centrality of native labor in producing wealth, both public and private, from Hispaniola. The persistence of native political systems might well complicate access to that labor. Further, holding the gift of labor added enormously to his own political strength. Although he received directives from Spain about the assignment of Indian workers to colonists, he had, as governor and man on the spot, much discretion in this key matter.

Grants of Indians had first been made by Columbus in 1497–9, for farming land that he also distributed among early colonists.[30] He had quelled the Roldán rising in 1498 partly by making such grants. Indians intended for agriculture soon found themselves gathering gold, a far more burdensome obligation. These early allocations were termed *repartimientos* (from *repartir*, to distribute). Natives in *repartimiento* were not considered slaves, since they were not the property of the Spaniard to whom they were assigned, but continued under the control of their own leaders – who, generally, were made responsible for supplying the decreed number of workers. But they were certainly forced laborers, subject to the whim of their Spanish masters. This quickly made them an object of concern to Isabella, who from the start inclined to see Indians as inherently free. On the other hand, it equally quickly became obvious that Hispaniola would not yield income to the monarchy, nor Spaniards be persuaded to settle the island, unless native people were forced to work. It was a dilemma met with over and over again in the sixteenth century as the Spaniards occupied the mainland, and one that persisted to some extent until the end of the empire.

In 1503 the monarchs, in orders to Ovando, tried to have matters both ways. In March he was told that it was proper, for maximum gold production, that Indians work in mining; but they must do so of their own will, be well treated, and be paid. The crown's ideal from these earliest days was, indeed, voluntary wage labor by Indians. But neither now, nor for several decades on the mainland, did this come about. In December 1503, a far more severe order was issued. Ovando should compel Indians to work for colonists, in building, farming and mining; though they should be compelled "as free people, which they are." He should set wages and see that workers were well treated.[31] Whatever the contradiction here, this command established, for once and for all, the principle of state compulsion of native labor.

Ovando was in fact well primed to implement such arrangements. His order in Spain, Alcántara, had during its participation in the Reconquest received many grants of frontier places and people, with obligations to administer them, and rights to collect taxes and services that otherwise would have gone to the crown. These grants were called *encomiendas* (from *encomendar*, to entrust or commend). They did not give ownership of land.[32] On Hispaniola, once he had undone the large native polities in 1504–5, and following this familiar notion of trusteeship, as well as the 1503 orders from Spain, Ovando assigned Indians to settlers who showed a need for them for mining, farming, and other purposes. Some he allocated also to royal mines and lands. The numbers granted are unclear. Thus the crude distribution (*repartimiento*) of Indians started by Columbus became, in principle at least, the entrustment (*encomienda*) of native workers to deserving settlers, who were expected to pay and care for these Indians. In reality, nothing changed in the laborers' treatment, which was at best harsh by most reports. The continuation in common use of the term *repartimiento*, instead of *encomienda*, suggests how little changed (though the recipients of Indians were known henceforth as *encomenderos*). It was perhaps this, among other things, that prompted Las Casas, the fiercest foe of forced native labor, to describe Ovando as a good governor, "but not of Indians."[33]

Ovando's successor as governor was Columbus's son, Diego, who had for some time been pursuing the rights and powers granted in perpetuity to his father in 1492–3. His case was helped by his marriage to a noblewoman, María de Toledo, a cousin of Ferdinand; and by Ovando's effectiveness in bringing Hispaniola so firmly under state control, which meant that Ferdinand ran little political or economic risk in returning the governorship to the Columbus family. From 1509 to 1511, Don Diego had only the title of governor, not viceroy. Nonetheless, when he arrived in Hispaniola in 1509 with his wife (the first Spanish noblewoman in America) he set up something of a viceregal court in Santo Domingo. It was perhaps an attempt to compensate in pomp and ceremony for what he lacked in authority. For, although he received some of the Indies' income promised to his father, his powers were largely confined to Hispaniola. He contended with Ferdinand particularly about jurisdiction over Panama and Puerto Rico, both of which drew his and the king's attention on account of their high promise of gold. These disputes, exacerbated for Ferdinand by Don Diego's duplicity in failing to report vacant *repartimientos* of Indians and assigning them to settlers without royal knowledge, led to his recall in 1515.[34] He was restored as viceroy and governor of the islands from 1520 to 1523, but again was called home to answer charges about his administration. He died in 1526, aged about 46. His wife continued the battle with the crown over the family's rights in America. Finally, in 1536 a compromise was struck by which Diego Columbus's descendants kept the title and privileges of Admiral of the Indies, but gave up all other claims in return for the titles of Duke of Veragua and Marquis of Jamaica, a small estate in Panama, a fiefdom of the island of Jamaica, and a perpetual annuity of 10,000 ducats.[35]

Though Don Diego had seen the major threat to his authority and rights as coming from autonomous governors in Puerto Rico and Panama, a far more serious challenge, in the long term, to colonial chief executives' authority was the sort of body that appeared in 1511 in Santo Domingo: the *audiencia*. Just as Isabella had used high courts of appeal to carry her authority through Castile and to the Canaries, now Ferdinand created one for the Indies precisely to limit Diego Columbus's freedom of action.[36] The judges were ordered to meet regularly with him and the treasury officers to read and reply to royal letters and to debate local executive questions.[37] Until the late 1520s, when another *audiencia* was created, in Mexico, the court in Santo Domingo was the chief tribunal in Spanish America. It was the first of many such courts, all of them combining judicial, executive, and to a degree legislative functions, and serving in reality as the main conduits for the transmission of royal will to America.

CHURCHMEN IN THE ISLANDS

Another innovation of Diego Columbus's time, with still more profound effects for Spanish America in the long term, was the effective arrival in the Indies of the Catholic Church. Priests there had certainly been in Hispaniola before; five came in 1493 in Columbus's second sailing, and others with Ovando in 1502. But even in his time the church's presence had been slight. The few priests in the island seem to have tended largely the colonists; evangelization of the natives, which was an obligation laid upon the Catholic Monarchs by the papal bulls of 1493–4 conceding them temporal powers in America, languished. In part this was possibly an outcome of Ovando's own formation. His order, Alcántara, while definitely a part of the Church Militant, had not in the Reconquest taken on an evangelizing role. That was the church's business once the unfaithful had been conquered in the field.[38] But a far larger reason was that Ferdinand, before allowing a large clerical apparatus to develop in the Caribbean, was determined to ensure that Spain, not Rome, controlled it. For this purpose, he sought an extension to the Indies of the powers of royal patronage (*real patronato*) that Rome had given the Spanish monarchy in Granada in 1486. A first concession came in 1501. But only with bulls of 1508 and 1511 did the papacy give Ferdinand what he wanted: a very large measure of control over the creation of churches and monasteries, over the appointment of churchmen of all ranks, and over the collection of church taxes.[39] With these powers in hand, Ferdinand presented candidates for bishoprics in Hispaniola. At the same time church building accelerated in the island. By the time Ovando left, in 1509, various churches existed. He himself had also endowed a Franciscan friary in Santo Domingo. By 1509, that central house had developed three branches in the island; a total of twenty Franciscans were present.[40]

In 1512 the first bishop arrived in America to occupy his see at Caparra in Puerto Rico. In 1513 came the second, to Concepción in Hispaniola. Santo Domingo had no resident bishop until 1519. The first prelates, it is true, did not stay long in place. Both were back in Spain, in absentee status, by 1516. Both had found the resources assigned to them, mainly Indians in *repartimiento*, too slim to support their establishments. But if the commanders proved short in resolution, the rank and file, in the form of regular clergy (members of religious orders), were another matter. In 1511, the Franciscan force grew by twenty-three, and more joined it in 1513. Some, at least, of these men were products of the reform currently being applied to the Franciscan order in Spain by Archbishop Jiménez de Cisneros and others; and as such were more educated, disciplined, and evangelical in inclination than many of their fifteenth-century predecessors. Spiritual energy in Hispaniola received another charge in 1510 with the dispatch by Ferdinand of a small group of nine Dominican friars to the island. His alleged purpose was that they should root out reported heresies in the island, a task for which their order's devotion to orthodoxy especially fitted them. The presence of Dominicans, noted for their dedication to preaching and the matters of the intellect, was quickly to add a strong and distinctive tone to the Church's voice in America.[41]

The incoming friars soon moved beyond Hispaniola. Two or more Dominicans were in Cuba the year its conquest began, 1511. By late 1515 a Franciscan and a Dominican mission existed on the coast of Venezuela.[42] Thus, in Diego Columbus's years as governor, though little of it was his doing, the church expanded its base in America as both institution and mission. From that foundation Catholicism spread rapidly in the following decades, so that by the end of the sixteenth century most of the native people in Spanish territories, from Chile in the south to New Mexico in the north, had at least heard its message.

SPANIARDS AND ISLANDERS

There are students of the Spanish American colonial church who would date the start of evangelizing Catholicism in the empire to a precise day, December 21, 1511. On that Sunday before Christmas, Antonio de Montesinos, one of the Dominicans who had come to Hispaniola in 1510, preached in Santo Domingo undoubtedly the most famous sermon in Spanish American history. He, like his brother Dominicans, had been less struck by individuals' heresies in Hispaniola than by the colonists' mistreatment of natives, which to a degree was certainly the outcome of public policy. This "very choleric and most effective" preacher, as Las Casas described him, harangued his congregation, among whom were notables who held Indians in *repartimiento*, in biblical tones.

I am the voice crying in the wilderness . . . the voice of Christ in the desert of this island . . . [saying that] you are all in mortal sin . . . on account of the cruelty and tyranny with which you use these innocent people. Are these not men? Have they not rational souls? Must you not love them as you love yourselves?[43]

The arrival of the Dominicans may not have marked the beginning of liberation theology in America, as one historian would have it.[44] But their protesting was certainly the first resounding shot fired by the pro-native side in a long conflict among Spaniards over the treatment of Indians in the empire. Montesinos's sermon stirred up an angry buzz of complaint in Hispaniola, which soon reached Spain. Ferdinand briefly took against his favored Dominicans, since criticism of colonists' treatment of Indians clearly stood to undermine production and taxation in Hispaniola and other islands. He heeded the friars' warnings from Hispaniola sufficiently, though, to summon a commission, consisting of senior ecclesiastics and lawyers (who lacked, it should be said, personal experience of America), to look into Spanish–Indian relations.

This junta met at Burgos in 1512. Before ruling on the treatment of Indians, it first felt obliged to consider (as did several later bodies confronting the same questions) the basic standing of the American natives. Like Isabella a decade before, and many other authorities in later years, it declared them free. Nevertheless, the junta said, Indians were vassals of Ferdinand, who for that reason might order them to work, provided that laboring did not interfere with their evangelization, and was beneficial to them and to the public interest.[45] In December 1512 the commission drew up a series of regulations in accord with these principles. These Laws of Burgos, as they are known, were the first attempt at a broad code of Spanish–Indian relations; though, reflecting practical reality in the Indies, the central objects of attention were labor and christianization.

The authors of the Burgos regulations saw in the obligatory labor system of *repartimiento* a means of fusing work with conversion. Indians should be removed, forcibly but gently, from their villages and resettled near their *encomenderos*. These should build a church in each new village, and instruct their people in the basics of Christianity. The old villages should be burned, so that natives should not be tempted to return to their traditional places and idolatries. Bishops should ensure a supply of priests for services in the village churches, confessions, baptisms, and the like. Indians were, then, to be gathered together (*congregados* became the standard term for this much-used practice in the sixteenth century) for better evangelization. At the same time, the new villages were to be a source of labor. Indians must mine gold for five months of the year; after which they should have forty days free to cultivate their manioc. No woman more than four months pregnant, or within three years of giving birth, should mine gold or plant manioc, but should be given light tasks in the *encomendero*'s household. *Encomenderos* should feed their people during work periods, supply them with hammocks, pay them a gold peso a year to buy clothes; see that men had only one wife; and send the sons of *caciques* to the local Franciscans for four years of education. Indians should not change masters. No *encomendero* might be granted more than a hundred and fifty Indians, or fewer than forty. Finally, the laws ordered regular official inspections of native villages.[46]

The Laws of Burgos were an ingenious design for combining conversion of the Indians with labor extraction. For the modern observer they also reveal the educated Spaniard's image of the Caribbean native people twenty years after they had first entered the European consciousness. Indians were seen as idle and given to vice (the preamble to the laws says as much); if not supervised they would relapse into idolatry and promiscuity; unless given a hammock and money to buy clothes, they would sleep on the ground and go naked (both signs of lack of civilization). Though soon modified to a degree by contact with the high mainland cultures, this early-established definition as a backsliding, lazy primitive clung to the native henceforth. It was one point of departure for official thinking about Indians; as was also a conviction that the indigenous peoples, however backward, were free, and also the special responsibility of the Spanish monarchy. The tension between these views accounts for some of the contradictory waverings in sixteenth century, and later, policy on native matters.

The Burgos Laws remained largely unenforced. That is, *encomenderos* continued to use native labor, but the provisions for conversion and welfare were ignored. The Dominicans' indignation about native treatment, of which Las Casas, although not yet a Dominican, rapidly became the most vociferous and influential exponent, was not assuaged. In 1515 Montesinos and Las Casas together went to Spain to argue the Indians' case. Las Casas contrived an interview with Ferdinand, who, however, died soon after, on January 23, 1516. Cardinal Cisneros, becoming regent on Ferdinand's death, was Las Casas's next target. He proved remarkably open to persuasion.

Las Casas proposed that *repartimiento* (or *encomienda,* as the practice was now increasingly termed) should be ended, Indians freed, and administration of the Indies given to ecclesiastics. Cisneros immediately adopted the third point, naming an administrative committee for the Indies consisting of three Jeronymite friars. None of them had any American experience. They were to observe without preconceptions, and decide how the Caribbean natives should be managed. Were they capable of living in a satisfactorily civilized way under self-government? Did they need some sort of Spanish supervision, perhaps in newly created villages? Or might the *encomienda* system, suitably modified and properly subject to the Laws of Burgos, be preserved?[47]

The Jeronymites arrived in Santo Domingo in December 1516, and stayed for three years. This was the only period in which the Spanish American empire was governed wholly by priests. (From 1517 to 1520 the *Audiencia* of Santo Domingo was suspended, leaving the friars untrammeled even by the judiciary.) It was a daring and noble experiment, perhaps possible only at a time of political fluidity at home, as the shift took place from the Trastámara dynasty to the Habsburgs.

In the event, though, so set were local conditions that the Jeronymites not only changed little, but finally proposed changing little. They took away the Indians of absentee *encomenderos,* to general applause; but they found it politically impossible to abolish the *encomienda* system. They judged Indians incapable of self-government in the Spanish style. They recommended the import of African slaves to ease the Indians' labor load. They thought that with enough incentive (gifts of animals and seeds, for example) poor Spanish farmers might be encouraged to emigrate. They built some thirty new villages for "congregation" of Indians, in line with their instructions and with the Burgos Laws. But in the end, and with their assent, the *encomienda* and its abuses remained. Las Casas, whom Cisneros had named "Protector of the Indians," raged in disappointment. Even the new Spanish king, Charles, on the friars' return to Spain, disdained to receive them.[48]

In Charles, indeed, Las Casas found a sympathetic audience. At a meeting at Barcelona in 1518, he had propounded before the young king his convictions about American native people: their capacity to receive the faith and live virtuously in self-government, their inherent liberty, their openness to reason. He went on to win many of Charles's advisers to the anti-*encomienda* position. The outcome was that in May 1520 Charles ordered limited trials of native self-government, despite warnings that the suppression of *encomienda* thus implied would drive colonists from the islands. He went further in July, issuing an order (*cédula*) that declared his conviction of the Indians' freedom, and therefore of the wrongness of their being "entrusted" to anyone. Indians allocated to absentee *encomenderos* should immediately be declared free under the administration of their *caciques*. To avoid "difficulties," other natives in *encomienda* should not be freed immediately, but only as they became "vacant" – that is, as their *encomenderos* died.[49] In this way, the *encomienda* would gradually disappear.

In fact, it did not. As Charles gave his orders in 1520, Hernán Cortés was half way through his battle with the Aztecs. A year or so later, to reward his successful conquerors, he began, unaware of Charles's ban, to distribute Mexicans among them in *encomienda*. The same happened a few years later as Spaniards penetrated South America. And the *encomienda* in the vaster frame of the mainland was to give the Spanish authorities far graver political and moral headaches than it had in the islands. Still, Charles's rejection of the institution in 1520 concludes the first Spanish confrontation of the Indian perplexity: that set of questions about the native people's nature, moral and legal status, and rights that so exercised Spaniards in the sixteenth century. The king had concluded that Indians were free and should therefore live only under self-government (though with clerical oversight). The conclusion was admirable, the product perhaps of youthful idealism. Inasmuch, though, as it ignored the question of how the Indies were to be kept settled with Spaniards if colonists were deprived of easy access to cheap native labor, the conclusion was impractical and short sighted.

THE CARIBBEAN BALANCE

The story of the Spaniards' first quarter-century in America lends itself to strong and contradictory judgments. On the one hand, the period was crucial for the making of Spanish America. On the eve of the expansion into Mexico in 1519, Spaniards could claim to occupy in America an area (roughly the size of Castile) of some 300,000 square kilometers, two-thirds of it in the islands, and one third in Tierra Firme (Panama and nearby parts of present-day Colombia and Venezuela).[50] In that area a multitude of experiments, formal and informal, conscious and unconscious, were tried by people of all sections of the nascent colonizing society, from governors and bishops down to artisans and farmers. This Caribbean experimentation was crucial to the formation of the Spanish American empire. The Caribbean, indeed, was never again to play such a large role in Spanish imperial affairs. Much that was tried, failed; as a result, many Spaniards died, or, despairing, went back home. After twenty-five years, however, few doubted that Spaniards should be in the Indies. Indeed, the sense that America was God's gift and revelation to Spain was by then firmly rooted. And some (the persistent, the well-connected, the lucky) had by 1519 discovered that the distance, both physical and psychological, of the Indies from Spain meant freedom: freedom to do as one wanted, freedom to gather wealth and land, freedom to rise, through wealth and deeds, in the social scale with a speed that the conventions of peninsular life made impossible.

On the other hand, much of this freedom came at the expense of the native Caribbean people. The most drastic example of this was the fate of the Lucayos, the inhabitants of the Bahamas, or Lucayas, as the Spanish called them. These people, the first to meet the Europeans in 1492, were the first to be destroyed. At Ferdinand's direction, given in 1509, Ovando began to bring Lucayos to Hispaniola to offset the decline in labor supply there. They were then either sold as outright chattel slaves, or distributed among colonists as servants bound for life, a status for which the local term *naboría* was used. The crown took a most profitable share of this business. By 1513 the Bahamas seem to have been emptied of people.[51] In Hispaniola, the population of 62,000 or so in 1509, already only a fraction of the pre-contact figure, continued to fall thereafter (to c.28,000 in 1514, 15,600 in 1518, and a few hundred, or practical extinction, by 1540).[52] Parallel losses afflicted the other large islands. Some of the smaller islands fared a little better: island Caribs still could be found in the Windwards in the eighteenth century. Reasons for the terrible collapse are not hard to find, but are much less easily ranked. Disease probably played a powerful part. No devastating epidemic to compare with those that later scythed through the mainland peoples can be clearly identified in Hispaniola until 1518, when smallpox struck the island. But waves of severe disease, among them perhaps influenza and typhus, certainly attacked the Spaniards from the earliest years, and the natives can hardly have escaped them.[53] Campaigns of conquest, with their accompanying episodes of terrorism, undoubtedly killed many, also. More still, probably, succumbed to intense Spanish demands for unaccustomed labor, in extracting gold, carrying heavy loads, building in stone, and cultivating new crops. The *repartimiento*, especially in its first and totally unregulated form before 1500, gave Spanish masters complete control over Indians at a time when the supply of labor must have seemed limitless. The resulting treatment of workers can only be surmised. *Repartimiento* under Ovando was more controlled, but largely in the sense of being more efficient in moving native people around Hispaniola, especially to maintain gold production; and hence more disruptive of community and family.[54] Again, as the demand for natives' effort grew, their diet deteriorated. Production of the staple manioc seems to have held up; but natives no longer could hunt or fish as before, and so lacked protein and fat.[55] Work therefore weighed even more heavily on them, and disease found easier entry. Probably, also, children were less likely now to be conceived; a physiologically caused infecundity was added to reluctance to bring offspring into a disrupted world.

Intentionally and unintentionally, then, the Spanish trampled the Caribbean natives into the ground as they strove to gain a foothold in the New World. Some, a few, saw what was happening and called for a halt, or at least for moderation. But the lure of gain was too strong for much to be changed. The state looked to the Indies for territory, income, and the greater weight and power in the world that these would bring. Individuals saw unprecedented chances for wealth, social advance, and the status that fame could confer. All these ambitions would be carried to the mainland, there to repeat their effects on a continental scale. But there most native cultures proved ultimately more resistant to the invasion, and so, although seriously altered and damaged, escaped extinction.

evidently saw themselves faced with a choice from the start between Cortés and Velázquez. Cortés won over enough to give him an operative authority. Opulent gifts of gold, featherwork, and cotton cloth descending on the Spaniards from Tenochtitlan helped him make a case for staying and conquering. There was unimagined wealth to be had here. At one point, he threatened to pull up stakes and go back to Cuba. This brought an uproar among his supporters, in the midst of which he persuaded the party to name him its chief justice and captain-general (and, as such, recipient of a fifth of all booty gathered).

With these powers in hand he resolved to found a town. This was done with full Spanish formality. And once the place, the Villa Rica de la Vera Cruz (Rich Town of the True Cross), was created, and equipped through his appointments with a full complement of urban officials, Cortés pulled off what has always seemed his most blatant piece of chicanery. He resigned his powers to the town council and magistrates – in full confidence that they would immediately pass them back to him, as they duly did after grave and formal debate. Here Cortés drew on Reconquest practice in Castile, by which newly recovered frontiers were politically solidified through the creation of towns. Towns, in such circumstances, also took on an identity of their own that he doubtless aimed to create in the case of Vera Cruz. A chartered town in Mexico was a legal and political body that could at least make pretence to autonomy from the governor of Cuba, and deal directly with the monarchy. Cortés, holding powers given to him by the town, similarly distanced himself from Velázquez and gave himself some defense against charges of rebellion.

From Veracruz (to adopt the modern spelling) Cortés also probed for information about Mexico in general, and in particular, as he became increasingly aware of it, about the Aztec state. Moctezuma II, informed from the start of the aliens' presence, sent envoys to look, converse, and report. Cortés realized quickly that Aztec power was not monolithic. Much resentment festered on the recently incorporated periphery over Tenochtitlan's tribute demands. The Spaniards saw this at first hand among coastal communities near Veracruz, and from these places took their first native allies, promising them support if they resisted the Aztecs.

Encouraged by these evident fissures in the imperial polity, Cortés began a cautious advance inland in mid-August 1519. To mark this new departure, both physical and psychological, and perhaps to stiffen the resolve of remaining waverers, he declared the ships unseaworthy, and beached them. They were not burned, as the story sometimes has it. He left a garrison of 150 or so at Veracruz. The rest of the party, accompanied by local Indians carrying supplies and pulling cannons, began crossing the tropical coastal plain toward the highland escarpment. The direct distance to Tenochtitlan was some 330 kilometers. The Spaniards moved circumspectly, taking three months for the journey, but on the way had notable adventures. The most important was a contest with Tlaxcala, a city-state 90 kilometers east of the Aztec capital that had long resisted imperial domination. The Tlaxcalans engaged Cortés's force several times. He could count himself the victor in the sense of having survived the attacks of vastly greater numbers. The Tlaxcalans were impressed enough by the Spaniards' weapons and doggedness to see in them useful partners against Tenochtitlan. This was the crucial alliance of the conquest for Cortés. Tlaxcala henceforth never failed to offer men, and a base on which he could fall back. Its example persuaded other foes of the Aztecs to join the Spanish against them.

After surviving an attempted Aztec ambush at Cholula, between Tlaxcala and Tenochtitlan, the Spaniards entered the Valley of Mexico, and reached the capital on November 8, 1519. Moctezuma welcomed them into the city and lodged them in one of the palaces of the past Aztec rulers that surrounded the central temple compound. Ten days later, Cortés took Moctezuma captive, confining him to the Spanish quarters. This, obviously enough, was a risky blow to attempt. But Cortés had well enough gauged the emperor's uncertainty about the Spaniards' intentions and nature as to judge the risk acceptable. He may also have calculated that Aztec power was so densely concentrated in the supreme ruler that if this figure were neutralized, the rest of the upper political system would suffer paralysis. This certainly proved to be so, at least for several months after Moctezuma's capture.

During those months of the winter of 1519–20 and the following early spring, Cortés kept his force in Tenochtitlan, where the Aztecs continued to feed it, though with declining good grace. He gathered information about Mexico, partly from the natives and partly through small forays of Spaniards dispatched to explore.[4] Beyond this, Cortés seems now to have been awaiting a royal reaction, presumably approving, to a report on his activities he had sent to Spain the previous July. Unexpected responses to his doings from much closer at hand, however, forced improvisation on him, and changed the pace and course of the campaign. It proved no bad thing for the Spaniards; he was at his most creative when improvising.

The ship sent with the report to Spain had, contrary to Cortés's order, touched on Cuba. News of his venture spread quickly there. Velázquez put together a large force (900 men) under Pánfilo de Narváez, a seasoned campaigner from the Cuban conquest, to bring his errant underling to heel. Narváez arrived off Veracruz in late April 1520. When word of this reached Cortés in the capital, he decided on a forced march to the coast with some of his men; a surprise attack; and then reliance on his persuasive powers to bring the chastisers over to his side. In all this he was brilliantly successful, and so more than doubled the strength he could put against the Aztecs.

And strength he now needed. For the man he had left in charge in Tenochtitlan, a senior lieutenant named Pedro de Alvarado, had been anything but successful in keeping harmony between invaders and natives. By this time (May 1520), to be sure, organized resistance to the Spanish was finally developing among part of the native nobility. The paralysis of Moctezuma's capture was wearing off. A plan was perhaps made to assail the Spanish party during the major religious festival named Toxcatl, held in May. It was a feast of Huitzilopochtli, a particularly fitting time for retaliation since he was the Mexicas' tutelary god. Sensing danger, Alvarado had attacked gathered lords and warriors in the temple compound at the start of the celebration. Many of them were killed, which weakened the Aztecs' ability to resist from then on. But this fight marked a change in the nature of the Spaniards' struggle with the rulers of Tenochtitlan. The time of psychological maneuvering and mutual measuring was over. It was clear that the final outcome would now result only from physical confrontation.

The Aztecs allowed Cortés to re-enter Tenochtitlan with his enlarged army. Their plan, simple and obvious enough, was to trap him. Cortés wished only to unite his force and escape. For several weeks the Spaniards were unsuccessful in attempts to break out. They finally did so one night late in June or early in July, fighting their way, down the shortest causeway, to the western shore of the lake. Many of them died. (Moctezuma died also, possibly at Spanish hands, possibly of a wound suffered earlier as he had tried to dissuade Mexica warriors from attacking the Spanish.) Most of the horses and all the artillery were lost. This was the "Noche Triste," or gloomy night, of the conquest. Cortés's only hope now lay in Tlaxcala. His safest, though not most direct, way to it lay around the north end of Lake Texcoco, where settlement was sparse. On the journey the Aztecs again brought him to battle, at Otumba. It was a fierce fight, but the Spaniards struggled back to Tlaxcala, whose leaders, after some debate, agreed to take them in.

For Cortés, this was the nadir of the assault on the Aztecs: his force diminished, its technological edge (of guns and horses) blunted, hostility still looming at his back in Cuba, his standing in Spain still uncertain. He seemed totally at the mercy of Mexicans, both his Aztec foes and his Tlaxcalan allies. Now, though, he turned with amazing success to diplomacy outside the Valley of Mexico. During the second half of 1520 he used a mixture of military threat (supported by Tlaxcala) and persuasion to prize local communities in south-eastern Mexico loose from Aztec control. Small places were easily intimidated, and success built on success, so that, despite the Spaniards' expulsion from the Valley, they soon again seemed potential victors against Tenochtitlan. An alien ally now also began its grim work. Smallpox, in an extension of the 1518 outbreak in Hispaniola, had reached Mexico with Narváez in April 1520. By the autumn its effects were severe. Many local native leaders died. Cortés found communities coming to him for advice on government.

By January 1521, when Cortés judged the time ripe to approach Tenochtitlan again, the Aztec empire outside the Valley had dissolved. He decided to mount his attack from Texcoco, 25 kilometers east of Tenochtitlan, across the lake. Texcoco had once been part of the Aztec Triple Alliance, but had latterly been alienated by the Mexicas' overbearance. From this base in early 1521 Cortés subdued Aztec subject towns around the lake shores. Then, in May, he began to move in on Tenochtitlan along its causeways; and also by water, using thirteen brigantines assembled near Texcoco from components cut outside the Valley. By now new arrivals of men whom rumors had drawn from the islands had raised the Spanish force to some 900, along with several dozen horses, and new cannon. Much of the final fighting on the causeways, however, was done by the multitude of native allies, whose fury against Tenochtitlan had sometimes to be restrained by the Spanish. Perhaps even deadlier help in this final siege came from smallpox. Many defenders of the city died horribly from it, the toll of the disease being worsened by starvation in the last weeks. The resistance was heroic. Cortés had almost to raze Tenochtitlan in order to take it. But finally the city yielded on August 13, 1521, as the last independent Aztec leader, Cuauhtemoc, was captured.

So ended the military conquest of the Mexican heartland. Never again, indeed, in what Cortés now controlled – essentially the Aztec imperial territory – did the native population pose any martial threat to Spanish presence. The rest of central Mexico also quickly fell to the invaders. The Tarascans of the center-west, who had stoutly held the Aztecs at bay, collapsed before the Spaniards, perhaps overawed by their success against the empire. Northern Mexico was another story. There the mainly nomadic tribes of the plateau, and various small sedentary groups in the western Sierra Madre, resisted the European invasion long and hard. It was not until abut 1600 that Spaniards could move around the *altiplano* without danger of surprise native attack. The subjugation of the north took half a century, and cost the Spanish far more in lives and money than the Aztec episode. And the north-western mountains always remained a breeding ground of native revolt; but those distant risings posed no threat to Spanish control of the whole, and so were no more than passing flurries of concern to the colonial government.

THE ANDES

The same pattern held true in the rest of mainland Spanish America. The major conquest in South America was of the Inca empire. This was a larger and in some ways more forbidding enterprise than overcoming the Aztecs. The Incas were more organized fighters; and their mountain world was more daunting in terrain and climate than central Mexico. Yet in Peru the Spanish in essence repeated the Mexican exercise, twelve years later. Here Francisco Pizarro, another product of Extremadura, was the leader. He, like Cortés, was a veteran of the Indies. He was, in fact, a tougher and more senior veteran, since he had lived and fought through the hazardous reconnaissance and settlement of Tierra Firme from 1509 on, and by the early 1520s was one of the leading *vecinos* of Panama. He was a little older than Cortés, having been born *c*.1478, and was a ruder character, being the illegitimate son of a minor noble of the Extremaduran town of Trujillo, illiterate, and without Cortés's sophistication and legalistic turn of mind. But he was, for all that, a compelling expeditionary leader, and no mean judge of native political affairs.

He was, too, a methodical man. He approached Peru slowly, responding to rumors of rich lands to the south by probing by sea from Panama in the mid 1520s. This was done with the consent of Pedrarias Dávila, the governor of the territory, whose reputation for erratic ferocity perhaps reinforced Pizarro's natural caution. Having finally proved the rumors by reaching an outpost of the Inca state at Túmbez in northern Peru, Pizarro then went to court in Spain to make a contract (*capitulación*) with the crown for the conquest. Such contracts were the legal rule in the Spanish occupation of America; Cortés's impulsive behavior was the exception testing the rule. In July of 1529 Pizarro's agreement was concluded. He undertook to equip an expedition at his own cost; in return he was to be *adelantado*, governor and captain-general of whatever he might take.[5] The titles gave him supreme civil and military powers, subject only to the monarchy.

Having gathered followers from Extremadura, including several of his brothers, Pizarro returned to Panama. From there he departed south with some 180 men at the end of 1530. His three ships reached the equator in thirteen days. But it was not until September 1532 that he began the march up into the Andes that brought him face to face with Inca power. In the interim he surveyed part of the southern Ecuadorean and north Peruvian coasts, gathered information, seized booty (from Túmbez, for example), and created a base and port, San Miguel de Piura, a little further down the coast.

Other Spaniards arrived meantime from Central America. But the party that Pizarro led inland had only 168 in it, 62 of them horsemen. These were quickly to become the most famous of all *conquistadores*; for if Pizarro was more circumspect than Cortés in approaching the center of native power, once there he acted even more urgently. The Spanish party entered Cajamarca, a major town in the northern Peruvian Andes, on November 15, 1532. The next evening, in the enclosed town square, they attacked and captured the Sapa Inca, Atahualpa. Pizarro had invited the ruler, who was camped outside the town with a large army, to this meeting. He planned an ambush. Atahualpa, suspecting nothing, or if suspecting, made careless by the imbalance of numbers between his army and the Spaniards, came. He was offered – briefly, formally, and unintelligibly – a chance to accept Spanish authority and Christianity. This he not surprisingly rejected. The Spaniards hidden around the square attacked. Their handguns and few small artillery pieces sowed panic. Perhaps two thousand of Atahualpa's company died. No Spaniard did, and only one was injured. Atahualpa was captured. The Spaniards held him in Cajamarca before executing him in late July 1533. He had attempted to buy his freedom with a famous promise to fill a large room with gold and silver. The promise, equally famously and to the Spaniards' surprise, was fulfilled. But a Sapa Inca seemed too dangerous a figure to release. Finally, though, by the time the invaders were preparing to move south from Cajamarca to Cuzco, Atahualpa's value as a hostage was clearly falling, and the simplest course was merely to destroy him.

The seizing of Atahualpa in November 1532 was by no means the end of the Peruvian conquest. But although the Spanish had to fight considerably for the territory, against forces led by surviving Inca lords (most notably in 1536, when a brother of Atahualpa named Manco almost succeeded in ejecting them from Cuzco), as in Mexico their permanent presence was never seriously threatened once they had dealt that first heavy blow to the center.

As in Mexico, too, areas close to the imperial center fell quickly and quite easily. Forces spreading from Peru brought what are now highland Ecuador and Bolivia under Spanish control in the late 1530s; and by the early 1540s, central Chile too. Sebastián de Belalcázar led the Quito, or Ecuadorean, campaign; Hernando and Gonzalo Pizarro, younger brothers of Francisco, directed the incorporation of Charcas, the future Bolivia; and Pedro de

Valdivia commanded the expedition that settled central Chile. All these areas had been part of the Inca empire. In some of them, residual Inca resistance persisted, and had to be quelled. Anti-Inca feelings in the local populations sometimes helped the Spanish in this. On occasion, though, those same populations blocked the Spanish advance; but they did not hold out for long.

Curiously enough, at first sight, the areas that took longest to conquer were those beyond the frontiers of the native empires. In part this was because such places were usually poor in soil, hostile in climate, and thinly peopled. The Spaniards tended for obvious reasons to leave such places to last. Generally only late arrivals or men who for some personal or political reason had been squeezed out of the major conquests showed an interest in tackling these fringes, hoping to gain something, if only status. A more telling reason, however, for the peripheries' proving so refractory was simply that they lacked political centers. There was no single head whose removal would paralyze the entire body, as in the Aztec and Inca cases. Small groups, often mobile and able to live off the land as they moved, had to be suppressed one by one. The effort was often not worth the result. Examples are the forests of southern Chile, the plains of Uruguay and Argentina, much of the interior of Venezuela and Colombia, and Yucatan. Northern Mexico would have been one of these lightly attached peripheries had it not proved to be a rich source of silver. The prospect of that reward spurred Spanish incursion, exploration, domination and settlement from the 1540s on.

The mainland conquests, then, expanded from two main foci. From the middle of Mexico, once it was secured by Cortés, lesser leaders went out south to upper Central America (Honduras, Guatemala, and El Salvador), and then Yucatan, in the 1520s and 1530s; others went west to Michoacán and the west coast in the same years; and yet others, in a far more protracted effort, gradually pushed northward, drawn mainly by silver, until, c.1600, New Mexico, the most remote of the provinces of colonial Mexico, came into being. New Mexico has, since 1848, belonged to the USA. Its capital, Santa Fe, founded in 1609, is a very close contemporary of Jamestown in Virginia, and Quebec in Canada. In South America the source of expanding conquest was the Inca heartland taken by Pizarro. Lesser centers of conquest elsewhere were Panama, whose settlers moved upward through southern Central America, eventually to run into the wave descending from Mexico; and the Río de La Plata, from which, after the collapse of an initial attempt to found Buenos Aires in the mid-thirties, settlers moved up-river to begin Spanish colonization of Paraguay.

North-western South America, far from both Peru and Mexico, underwent its own, distinct process of conquest and occupation. The Venezuelan case was the most idiosyncratic. The coast had early attracted attention, both as a source of pearls and as a mission field. But by 1520 or so the pearls were mostly gone and the missions had failed. With no prospective conquerors and settlers in view, Charles V turned to the Welser banking company of Augsburg to undertake exploration and settlement. As Germans, the Welsers were citizens of the Holy Roman Empire, and Charles's subjects. They could legitimately be allowed into Spanish America. Charles, further, owed them money. Thus, in 1528 a contract was made for the Welsers to colonize Venezuela and defend its coast, in return for the profits of trade. In the event the profits were scant. What the Germans most avidly sought was gold, and they found little. Pursuing it, however, they sent six expeditions inland. The great lure was already, as it was long to remain for explorers of north-western South America, the tales of El Dorado, the reputed golden monarch of the interior. These German expeditions made the first European surveys of the interior. Apart from that, though, the Welser experiment produced little and proved mutually unsatisfactory to crown and company. The Germans failed to profit as they had hoped. They also failed to found towns and pay taxes as contracted. They maltreated both natives and such Spaniards as were in Venezuela. In 1548 Charles revoked the 1528 agreement, and a slow, purely Spanish settlement of the land began. Caracas, the colonial and present capital, was founded in 1567.

One of the Welser's expeditions, led in a famously hazardous Andean crossing by Nikolaus Federmann, had strayed in 1539 into what is now Colombia. There in the interior it ran into a Spanish expedition that had come up from the Caribbean coast. In this north-western corner of South America conquest was slow. The only Spanish presence by the mid-1530s consisted of two small towns, Santa Marta and Cartagena, on the Caribbean. Endless rugged ranges, the valleys between them blanketed in equally endless wet forest, discouraged inward exploration. But, about 1535, native tombs not far inland revealed gold almost on the Peruvian scale. Interest and resolve rose enough for substantial expeditions to be organized. Of these, the critical one was an 800-man force led by Gonzalo Jiménez de Quesada in 1536 up the Magdalena valley. That was one of the few possible passages to the highland interior, though one that was hot and unhealthy. After many tribulations, 160 survivors finally clambered up the valley side to the grassy plateau where the Chibcha culture flourished. In 1538, using the well-tried combination of intimidation, warfare, and politics, Jiménez subdued the Chibcha. Hardly had he done so when there appeared not only Federmann and his German-Spanish band from Venezuela, but also another Spanish company from the south, an offshoot of the force that had taken Quito under Belalcázar. Jiménez had best claim, however, to the interior highlands. He bestowed the name New Granada on the region, and founded on the site of the Chibcha center a Spanish city, Santa Fe de Bogotá, that remains capital of Colombia to this day. Though by the late 1530s many South American regions still awaited European exploration, the domination of the Chibcha nevertheless completed a major phase of Iberian conquest. For this was the last area of high culture to succumb in South America; or indeed in any part of Latin America.

EXPLAINING THE CONQUESTS

The period of the major military conquests by the Spanish, roughly 1520–40, must rank as the most tumultuous twenty years in the history of the Americas. Never before or since can so many lives have been so thoroughly shaken. The

Spaniards' actions may be admired or deplored; but those on both sides of that moral question continue to be fascinated by them, and by the manner of their execution. How could so few dispose of so many? Why did such mighty political structures collapse at what, comparatively speaking, was a mere touch?

The answers are many, and no generally accepted ranking exists of their importance. Any list must, though, include the Spaniards' technological advantages. Their steel swords and steel-tipped pikes were more durable and generally more damaging than any hand-held weapon that they faced. Swords and long pikes probably gave them a greater advantage in close combat than even firearms provided. The guns, both the few light cannon and the more numerous arquebuses that they had, were slow to reload. The alarm caused by their noise and smoke may well have been of greater effect than the injuries inflicted by the shot. But even this scare value was transient; after the first few encounters, native warriors grew used to gunfire. More fearsome were clearly the Spaniards' animals of war: large mastiffs, used especially in the islands to pursue and bring down foes; and, of course, horses – "The mighty horse, which, with mounted man, a monstrous beast appeared, six footed."[6] The Mexicans, lacking large domestic animals, were particularly awed by these, and tended to regard them as touched by the divine. Horses gave the invaders the tremendous advantage of height in combat; riders could strike down on the Indians. After battle, horses enabled pursuit at speeds unknown to the native people. (Though hardly martial creatures, pigs should not be omitted here. Live pigs carried aboard ship, then driven along with the conquering bands, provided the Spaniards with protein in a familiar form.) Finally, the invaders had the great advantage over the natives of being able to move themselves and their equipment over water with ease and relatively great speed. Ocean-going ships were fundamental to the expansion of conquest. And in the particular case of the Aztec contest, the ingenious building of brigantines for use on the lake was central to Spanish success.

The Spanish also had the advantage of better battle tactics. Native attacks were mainly mass charges, whereas the Spaniards fought in disciplined ranks, with pikes facing forward. As the first Indians fell before these, the efforts of men behind them were blocked. Again, and more telling, at least in Mexico, the two sides fought with different purposes: the Spaniards to kill, the Aztecs to take prisoners for sacrifice.

Then there were contrasts of strategy. The Spaniards developed in the islands the practice of the knock-out blow; they aimed from the start to destroy whatever central command the opposition might possess. First, of course, it was essential to identify and locate this authority; hence in part Cortés's and Pizarro's long delays on the coast before their inland advances, as they probed as best they could the politics of their targets. Once the goal was in view, the invaders acted with a purposeful directness that the native side usually lacked, or did not develop until it was too late.

Another, connected, political aim was to identify the enemy's internal foes, to find the strains in the political structure. Cortés was possibly the most adept at this of all *conquistadores*; but to play native rivals off against each other was the aim of all Spanish leaders. Even Pedro de Alvarado – not, to judge by his performance in Tenochtitlan in May 1520, the most subtle of political calculators – managed it with great success in 1524 against contending Maya groups in his conquest of Guatemala. In Peru, Pizarro did not receive as much active native aid as Cortés in Mexico. But he benefited greatly from the enmity between Atahualpa and Huascar, contenders for the Inca throne. Huascar's base and support were in Cuzco; Atahualpa's in Quito, far to the north. Pizarro's force came on the scene as Atahualpa, prevailing in the war of succession, was advancing south toward Cuzco. Even after his capture by the Spaniards, Atahualpa was able to order Huascar executed. Consequently, Huascar's followers tended to see Pizarro, if not as a friend, at least as the enemy of their enemy; and did not resist the Spaniards' further advance into Peru. At least two Andean ethnic groups, moreover, did fight with the Spaniards against Inca resistance, avenging, as they saw it, earlier defeat and humiliation by Cuzco. These were the Chachapoyas people of northern Peru, and the Huanca of the center. Again, in 1534, Pizarro's lieutenant Belalcázar, compaigning to subdue Quito, which remnants of Atahualpa's forces still controlled, found an active ally there in the Cañari Indians. These had suffered severely at Atahualpa's hands. Like parallel groups in Mexico resentful of the Aztecs, they fought now for the Spanish "with savage glee."[7]

To these quite concrete advantages of weapons, native supporters, tactics, and strategy enjoyed by the Spanish must be added intangibles of psychology, especially of the Indian perception of the invaders. One of the most tantalizing questions about the Aztec defeat is whether, as some sources report, Moctezuma took the Spanish as agents of the man-god Quetzalcóatl, who, legend had it, had departed eastward from Mexico several centuries before, promising he would return to claim the land as his inheritance. The year of Cortés's arrival was, by some accounts, the appointed date. Similar predictions were made by several other native cultures that the Spanish overcame.[8] It is possible, even likely, that such stories were post-conquest inventions of the vanquished, intended to explain, or explain away, their defeats. Nonetheless, often enough the Spanish were ascribed some degree of divinity when they first appeared. This is no surprise. The native cultures they overcame generally did not make any solid distinction between the earthly and the divine. The Spanish, unfamiliar in appearance and speech, possessing ships, guns, and horses, acting in unconventional and mysterious ways, were good candidates for some measure of deification. This made wariness in treating them still more advisable; hesitation thus plagued native decisions about dealing with the invasions.

Enormous advantages may have come to the Spaniards simply because they acted, unwittingly, so unconventionally. War in Mexico, for instance, was ruled by protocol. Foes announced their coming attacks, sending ambassadors. The Spanish did not. Wars did not begin in the late summer, the time of harvest. Cortés started his march on Tenochtitlan in August. Splendid gifts of the sort that Moctezuma kept sending to Cortés were intended to convey Aztec wealth and power, and hence to dismay the enemy. The

Spaniards were simply drawn onward by them. There was no apparent reason why the Spaniards should attack. Mexicans understood war as a contest between the populations of cities, who fought to gain tribute, and captives to be offered to the gods. The Spanish, men of no city, had no place in such a pattern. They sought not to capture, but to kill; and from there to proceed to absolute domination, a notion alien to Mexicans. For all these reasons, and others, it is possible that Moctezuma made the ultimately fatal mistake of letting the Spanish into Tenochtitlan simply because confusion prevented him from conceiving how dangerous they were. In South America, the Incas suffered from similarly fatal misapprehensions. One was that no serious threat could come from the coast. Atahualpa had no precedent to warn him of the possibility of reinforcement over the sea. The sea, conversely, had always seemed a limit to the possible power of the coast. The Incas' world, the territory of their empire, was the Andes. That, with few exceptions, was where redoubtable enemies were. Pizarro, approaching up the mountain slopes from the Pacific, was not ignored, but tolerated, even seen as entering a trap. But the disaster befell the trappers, not the intended victim.[9]

The conquests, then, give the impression that the native peoples (especially, perhaps, the advanced ones) were at a greater psychological than technological disadvantage. They simply could not comprehend quickly enough the threat that suddenly confronted them. Patterns of behavior and thought – military, religious, political – bound them to an inadequate set of responses to the new, exotic challenge. There were, naturally, some exceptions, especially in more immediately practical matters. The Aztecs learned to avoid cannon fire by running in zig-zags rather than straight lines; they tried, with some success, to destroy horses by digging pits lined with sharp stakes. Going further still, the Inca leader Manco by 1536 had learned to ride a captured horse in battle. But at the deeper, vital level of understanding the invaders, their actions, and their aims, the native leaders largely failed. Their responses to invasion were therefore slow, hesitant, and confused. The Spanish did not understand the native cultures either, of course, in any profound sense – the intricacies of Aztec religion, or of Inca succession, for example. But they had little need to do so. The simplicity of their purpose (kill, take booty, and above all seize the center) gave their efforts a focus that the opposition lacked. Their technological superiority, in weapons, methods of fighting, and transport, enabled them to realize their purpose. The Spanish had the immense advantage of being on new ground. In total contrast to the Indians, they were away from the familiar surroundings that restrained or conditioned action. Here is another of the liberties that Spaniards found in the New World.

Historians have commonly, and properly, seen much that is medieval in the organization and practice of Spanish exploration and conquest. A clear example is Cortés's exploitation in 1519 of the traditional prerogatives of Spanish towns to bolster his own political and legal position. But in a broader sense the leading *conquistadores* seem fully men of the Renaissance, imitating, if unconsciously, the political style of Ferdinand: pragmatic, subordinating means to ends, agile extemporizers rather than servants of tradition. The same contrast between incisive invaders and bemused non-Europeans recurred time and again over the following three or more centuries as the European expansion proceeded. The Spanish were simply the first to bring what proved to be the terrible weapon of empiricism to bear on non-European cultures – the empiricism that was one of the enduring mental products of the late Renaissance.

The conquests, especially those on the mainland, need therefore a many-sided explanation. The native states were certainly populous, but their peoples were not united. The states existed as structures sustained by many counter-acting tensions. If only a few of these strains were altered, the whole edifice tottered. The native people managed to blunt some parts of the Spanish technical edge; but in aggregate that edge remained throughout a crucial advantage. Above all, the invaders brought an advantage in mentality, one that allowed them to apply their technical superiority to maximum effect, and which, more importantly, overtaxed native powers of adaptability. The Spaniards acted and fought in ways that broke the American rules; the Indians could not decipher and absorb the new, alien rules quickly enough to save themselves.

Still, when all the explaining is done, the conquests remain a conundrum. The overwhelming of the Aztecs and the Incas remains an amazing, barely credible, feat; to be wondered at, if not approved. Despite the flaws in native polities, the Spaniards often found themselves fighting vastly larger forces. How could several thousand Tlaxcalans, for instance, fail to crush Cortés's few hundred by simple weight of numbers? Time after time, the Spanish escaped being crushed, though they were sometimes badly bruised. Each escape, each campaign, seems a close-run thing when seen in isolation. Failure seems an imminent possibility in nearly every case. Yet failure never came. And if the period of military conquest is regarded as a whole, an opposing view emerges: one of the inexorability of Spanish advance. On the ceiling of the Hospicio Cabañas in Guadalajara, the modern Mexican muralist José Clemente Orozco shows Cortés as a man-machine, a striding figure of steel with great bolts for its joints. Perhaps he had in mind the post-conquest vision that the Mexica retained of the Spaniards' entry into Tenochtitlan in 1519: "some came all in iron; they came turned into iron; they came gleaming."[10] Certainly, nothing could convey more dramatically than Orozco's picture the relentlessness of Spanish advance through the Indies that the story of the conquests as a whole conveys.

The contrast between looming failure in particular campaigns and broad success in the conquest as a whole is perhaps a false one. Every disaster avoided, and every threat finessed, reinforced in the Spanish an energizing sense of the rightness of their actions, fortified by the belief that God blessed their enterprise; that, indeed, they were enacting divine will. And as among the *conquistadores* this belief in divine justification grew, so among the natives sureness of their cause, of their gods' power, indeed of their understanding of the universe and its workings, dwindled. This shifting balance of confidence was the invaders' final advantage.

PART III

DOMINATION

CHRONOLOGY OF PART III

1484   Birth of Bartolomé de las Casas in Seville

1501–38   Rome grants to the Spanish monarchy patronage and other controls over the Church in America

1503   First sugar mill built in Hispaniola

1511   First American *audiencia* established, at Santo Domingo

1513   See of Darien created

1516   Las Casas named Protector of the Indians

1522   Papal letter *Omnimoda* entrusts evangelization of natives in Spanish America to regular clergy

1523–6   Cortés is official governor of New Spain (i.e. Mexico)

1524   Arrival of first bureaucrats (treasury officials) in Mexico. Foundation of the Council of the Indies

1526   See of Tlaxcala, the first in Mexico, created

1527   First *audiencia* established in Mexico City (refounded with new judges in 1530). See of Mexico City created

1528–30   Cortés in Spain. He is named Marquis of the Valley of Oaxaca

*c.*1529   First sugar mill built in Mexico

*c.*1530   First silver strikes in Mexico

1530s   Treadle looms imported into Mexico

1532   Vasco de Quiroga's first *hospital*, Santa Fe de los Altos, founded near Mexico City

1535   Arrival in Mexico of the first, and founding, viceroy, Don Antonio de Mendoza

1537   First Peruvian see created, at Cuzco

1538   *Audiencia* placed at City of Panama (reestablished 1564)

*c.*1540   First sugar mills built in Peru

1540   Cortés returns to Spain from Mexico

1541   Assassination of Francisco Pizarro in Lima by Almagrists. See of Lima created

1542   Promulgation of the *New Laws*, reforming Spanish government in America, and controlling the *encomienda*

1543   *Audiencias* established in Lima and Guatemala

1544   First viceroy, Blasco Núñez Vela, arrives in Peru. Revolt of Peruvian colonists, under Gonzalo Pizarro, begins

1545–64   Council of Trent

1545   Silver ores found at Potosí

1546   Silver ores found at Zacatecas: start of mining in northern Mexico

1547   Death of Cortés in Spain. *Audiencia* established at Guadalajara. Grammar of Nahuatl, the first of a Mexican language, produced by Andrés de Olmos, OFM

1548   Defeat and execution of Gonzalo Pizarro: end of Peruvian rebellion against royal rule. See of Guadalajara created

1548–50   Government of Peru by Pedro de la Gasca

1549   Royal ban on *servicio personal* by Indians (i.e. the use of Indians in *encomienda* for labor)

1550   Debate between Las Casas and Sepúlveda at Valladolid in Spain

c.1550   Beginning, in Mexico, of state-imposed draft labor by Indians

c.1555   Beginning of silver refining by amalgamation in Mexico

1556   Abdication of Charles V (died 1558). Accession to Spanish throne of Philip II

1559   *Audiencia* established at La Plata

1563   *Audiencia* established at Quito

1566   Death of Las Casas

1568   First Jesuits in Spanish America, at Lima

1569–81   Administration of Don Francisco de Toledo, fifth, but "founding," viceroy of Peru

1570–1   Tribunals of the Inquisition set up in Lima (1570) and Mexico City (1571)

1571   Silver refining by amalgamation begins at Potosí

1573   Ordinances for New Discovery and Settlement

1574   Ordinance of Patronage (*Ordenanza del Patronazgo*)

1583   *Audiencia* established at Manila

1598   Death of Philip II of Spain. Accession of Philip III

FURTHER READING FOR PART III

Volumes 1 and 2 of *The Cambridge History of Latin America* contain numerous chapters on the topics raised here. The two essays in Volume 1 by J. H. Elliott are especially elegant. A classic work is Clarence H. Haring, *The Spanish Empire in America*. Two modern academic texts, distinguished by their intelligence, are James Lockhart and Stuart B. Schwartz, *Early Latin America. A History of Colonial Spanish America and Brazil*; and Lyle N. McAlister, *Spain and Portugal in the New World, 1492–1700*. Also enlightening are Mario Góngora, *Studies in the Colonial History of Spanish America*, and Enrique Semo, *The History of Capitalism in Mexico. Its Origins, 1521–1763*. Good monographs dealing with the aspects of domination discussed here include: Noble David Cook and W. George Lovell (eds), *"Secret Judgments of God." Old World Disease in Colonial Spanish America* (University of Oklahoma Press, Norman and London, 1992); Inga Clendinnen, *Ambivalent Conquests. Maya and Spaniard in Yucatan, 1517–1570*; Sabine MacCormack, *Religion in the Andes. Vision and Imagination in Early Colonial Peru*; John L. Phelan, *The Millennial Kingdom of the Franciscans in the New World*; Peggy K. Liss, *Mexico under Spain, 1521–1556*; Charles Gibson, *The Aztecs under Spanish Rule. A History of the Indians of the Valley of Mexico, 1519–1810* (but mostly concerned with the sixteenth century); Steve J. Stern, *Peru's Indian Peoples and the Challenge of Spanish Conquest. Huamanga to 1640*; James Lockhart, *The Nahuas after the Conquest. A Social and Cultural History of the Indians of Central Mexico, Sixteenth through Eighteenth Centuries*; Anthony Pagden, *The Fall of Natural Man. The American Indian and the Origins of Comparative Ethnology*.

[7] ADMINISTRATION: THE POWER OF PAPER

CONQUERORS AS GOVERNORS

FROM the military conquests of the mainland there followed a bureaucratic domination of the regions seized. This came more quickly in some areas than in others, but with the same feeling of inexorability that the conquests convey.

The shift from the inevitably military commands of the conquest to civil government did not, though, happen easily. The contracts that leaders of conquering expeditions made with the crown typically granted them titles of governor, so that a nominally civilian chief executive was immediately in place once the fighting was over. He was, moreover, the man who probably had the best knowledge of the region under his control; and his military expertise fitted him to direct the mopping-up operations and expansionary efforts that usually followed from the conquest of some major center of native culture. But once all this was over, or even before, tensions often arose between conqueror-governor and the home authority, precisely because the crown feared that it had given away too much power, and too much potential for profit. The richer the region conquered, the more acute such fears would be.

No region promised greater wealth at the time of conquest than Mexico; and in most respects the story of Cortés and his role in governing the new colony is a representative one. It is of course exceptional in that between crown and Cortés no contract existed; he was, as *conquistador*, technically a rebel. But nothing succeeds like success. After what must have been a nerve-racking period of waiting for a royal response to his calculatedly persuasive reports on the conquest, and to his gifts chosen to suggest Mexico's wealth and artistry,[1] Cortés received in September 1523 his appointment as governor, *adelantado*, and captain-general (i.e. military commander) of New Spain, as he named the conquered Mexico. It had been issued in October 1522. Both Diego Velázquez and his influential backer, Juan Rodríguez de Fonseca, long the chief of American administration at the Spanish end, died in 1524. Chagrin over Cortés's success is said to have hurried them to the grave. Certainly both departed under a cloud of disgrace, having been found guilty of grave distortion of Cortés's record in Mexico, and Fonseca of having accepted payments from Velázquez.[2]

Briefly, now, Cortés was officially in sole charge of New Spain. He showed himself, for the time, an enlightened governor. True enough, he distributed native Mexicans in *encomiendas*. He began to do so before he knew of his appointment as governor, and in ignorance of Charles V's suppression of *encomienda* in 1520. When the king duly objected, and ordered cancellation of the grants, Cortés argued that he had had no other resources besides "deposits" of Indians with which to reward many Spaniards who had fought in the latter stages of the attack on Tenochtitlan. And, for the longer term, if settlers were not granted the tribute and labor of Indians through *encomienda*, they would leave. Then New Spain would be lost to Spain, and many souls to God.

These were typical arguments of colonists wanting *encomiendas*. But Cortés believed that *encomienda* had been much to blame for the destruction of the Caribbean islanders, and was determined that New Spain should not suffer the same fate. Many of those settling New Spain, he saw, "expect to do with these lands as was done in the Islands when they were colonized, that is, to harvest, destroy and then abandon them."[3] To avoid repetition of that calamity, he issued rules for the treatment of the Indians he had "entrusted" to the conquerors. These ordinances, given late in 1524, restated many of the main points of the Laws of Burgos of a decade earlier (the obligations, for example, of *encomenderos* to provide evangelization and food for their charges); but they especially stressed the agricultural employment of the Indians. Their use in mining was banned; native slaves were to be assigned to that.[4] This was in great contrast to the Burgos Laws. Cortés was indeed much concerned to develop farming in New Spain, and made efforts to import seeds and livestock from the Caribbean islands to that end. He forbade *encomenderos* to leave New Spain for eight years after being granted their Indians; and, like Ovando in the Caribbean, hoped to fix Spaniards in the land by binding them with family ties. *Encomenderos* should marry within eighteen months, or, if married in Spain, bring their wives over within the same period, "so that the desire which the settlers of these parts have to remain should be made more manifest."[5]

Cortés, then, despite his misgivings about the *encomienda* in the Caribbean, clearly saw it as at bottom a useful and practicable means of promoting settlement and creating wealth in his new colony. He also had a strong personal interest in the existence of *encomiendas* in New Spain; he may have hoped to make the people of Tenochtitlan itself his own holding, and certainly assigned to himself the populations of Texcoco, Chalco, Otumba and Coyoacán, all of them major towns close to the capital in the Valley of Mexico.[6] Cortés, indeed, rapidly became the richest man in the Indies in the years following the Aztec conquest, and, as governor and conqueror of the colony, was undoubtedly the most powerful. The more the crown learned of New Spain, the more evident and troubling the extent of this power seemed. Equally fraught with potential problems seemed Cortés's creation of a seigneurial group of some 350 figures[7] – the *encomenderos* who were all in their varying degrees Cortéses in miniature, men with the pride of the conquest to swell their egos, and with Indians to rule and make them rich. In the wake of recent regional insurrections in Castile (the revolt of the *comuneros* in 1520–1, when many towns, with some initial noble backing, had challenged royal power), not to mention the long contest the Catholic Monarchs had waged with the Castilian aristocracy, the rise of such power and wealth far away across the western sea was worrying.

Cortés, therefore, was not long left without trammels. These took the form of series of governmental officials, of ever greater seniority. The first to be sent, as in the islands, were *reales oficiales*, officers of the treasury. Four arrived early in 1524. At first they jockeyed for the governor's favor, looking as much for their own profit as for the crown's. But then an unexpected opportunity for influence presented itself to them. In October 1524 Cortés decided to leave the capital, México-Tenochtitlan as it was now called, to make an overland journey to Honduras. His ostensible purpose was to subdue a rebellion by a man who had been one of his major commanders in the Aztec conquest, Cristóbal de Olid. Cortés had sent Olid to take Honduras and seek a strait to the Pacific; but en route he had succumbed to the temptation, perhaps encouraged by Diego Velázquez, who sniped at Cortés from Cuba to the end of his days in June 1524, to try Cortés's own trick and become the independent conqueror of Honduras. But quashing Olid was certainly not the whole purpose of the exercise, for the force of several hundred that departed southward contained not only Spanish and native armed men, but pages, musicians, jugglers, falconers, and cooks. Several high Aztecs dignitaries were also forced to join the party, among them Cuauhtemoc, the last Mexica king, and the pre-conquest rulers of Tacuba and Texcoco. The expedition was, then, akin to a royal progress, designed to exalt the magnificence of Cortés's power.

It was also a disaster. In the mountainous rainforests of southern Mexico there was no food for so large a group. Men and horses died. Cortés suspected plotting among the native nobles; he therefore cruelly executed Cuauhtemoc and several others. When finally he reached Honduras, he found Olid already removed – beheaded – by men loyal to himself. And Honduras (literally the "Depths") proved poor, isolated, and certainly without a strait.

Meanwhile, the cat gone from central Mexico, the four royal mice began to play; or rather, to squabble ferociously among themselves. Latent tensions among the early settlers also broke to the surface, some over grants of Indians, though a more general source of trouble was continued mistrust between supporters of Cortés and those of Velázquez. This rivalry, which had its roots in Cortés's break from the governor of Cuba in 1519, bedeviled New Spain throughout the 1520s. Rumors of Cortés's death on the expedition undermined order still further, since those loyal to him could now no longer appeal to his distant authority, or threaten consequences on his return. Spaniards died in something approaching civil war, and others in an Indian rebellion in the south.[8] The governor's orders on the treatment of natives were disregarded. Enslavement and other maltreatment of Indians grew. Of this chaos Cortés was duly warned in Honduras; but he seemed peculiarly hesitant to return to quell it.

If his purpose in that was to show his indispensability, the plan backfired. For though he re-entered New Spain from the Gulf coast in late spring, 1526, to general and joyful acclaim, especially from the Indians, who feted him in

México-Tenochtitlan in the manner accorded to Aztec emperors, disorder in his territory was the best of reasons for the crown to seek increased control. In the midsummer of 1526 there came from Spain a young magistrate named Luis Ponce de León to conduct an investigation (*residencia*) into Cortés's administration since the conquest, and look into various specific accusations, among them assumption of regal privileges, an intention to withdraw the colony from the monarchy, and the possession of excessive rents. Ponce was also to enquire into the doings of the treasury officers; and, finally, to compile a full account of New Spain's people, features and resources (with particular attention to mines). While doing all this, he was to be acting governor. A re-enactment seemed imminent of Bobadilla's confrontation with Columbus in Hispaniola in 1500.

It was not quite that, for Ponce died within a fortnight of reaching México-Tenochtitlan. Rumors flew that Cortés had poisoned him; but many others fell to the same fever. Cortés did not now regain power, however. Ponce had appointed an ancient and fragile lawyer, Marcos de Aguilar, to assume the governorship and the task of investigating Cortés. After Aguilar in due course expired, in February 1527, the only one of the miscreant treasury officers still in office became chief executive. Some of Cortés's supporters, including the ever-faithful native leaders of Tlaxcala, urged him to seize power; and even, by Bernal Díaz's report, to declare himself king of New Spain.[9] But he, now recovering the political acuity that had apparently been eclipsed by arrogance in 1524, decided his best course was a personal appearance before the Emperor in Spain. He sailed from Mexico early in 1528, with, once more, a number of senior native nobles in train.

It was a shrewd move. As he left, an order summoning him back to Spain was issued. His unexpectedly early arrival, and his voluntary "surrender" to royal authority, seem to have produced a good effect. His foes were thrown off balance. His reception at court was splendid. An order went out that his properties in New Spain were not to be disturbed. But there were limits to the crown's practical favors. Cortés hoped for restoration of his governorship; he had still not secured that at his death, in 1547. What he did get was reinstatement as captain-general of New Spain, and ennoblement as Marquis of the Valley of Oaxaca. As physical expression of this title, the Emperor gave Cortés what was undoubtedly the largest *encomienda* of all time, and moreover one that was unique in that it included land as well as people. The grant consisted, formally, of twenty-two Mexican towns, containing 23,000 tributary Indians (that is, adult males). In reality, the towns were far more numerous, their tributaries perhaps close to 100,000, and the associated lands covering more than 65,000 square kilometers.[10] The towns were not only, or even mainly, in the Oaxaca valley, but scattered over a large area stretching from the Valley of Mexico, down through present Morelos, to both the Gulf and Pacific coasts.[11] The grant was perpetual, and was made an entail (a *mayorazgo*) in what was, at the time, a rare concession of that privilege. While in Spain Cortés re-married. His first wife had died late in 1522, shortly after her move from Cuba to Mexico. His new bride, as befitted an empire-building Marquis, belonged to a noble family, the Zúñigas, of the highest rank and distinction. Her uncle, the Duke of Béjar, was a member of Charles V's Council of State.[12] He was also one of Cortés's keenest backers at court.

With wife, title, and grant, the captain-general returned to New Spain in the summer of 1530. The enthusiastic welcome given by Indians and some Spaniards was doubtless gratifying. But Cortés soon realized how far he had been displaced from the center of the colony's affairs. A material mark of this was that the Marquisate's lands did not include most of the leading towns in the Valley of Mexico, the heart of the Mexican heartland, that he had held before 1528. Far more serious, though, was that during his absence an *audiencia* had been installed in México-Tenochtitlan, its president endowed with full governing authority. Though this court had shown itself miserably corrupt and inefficient, still Cortés could not wrest executive power back from it. When, in 1531, the *audiencia* was refounded with far more able and honorable men, the power to govern became even more remote, and Cortés moved his household south from the capital to Cuernavaca, close to his largest and richest land holdings, on which he raised sugar cane. The palace he built for himself there stands to this day. In Cuernavaca he lived out his remaining decade in New Spain, immensely wealthy, but increasingly a mere symbol of the conquest's triumph, ever more distant from power. Even his military role was eroded when the first viceroy of New Spain took office in 1535, for viceroys were *ex officio* supreme military commanders. In 1540 Cortés returned for a second time to Spain, again to make his case to Charles V. In 1541 he sought to prove his continued worth by taking part in a large Spanish attack on Algiers; but his status in Spanish government by this time was shown by his exclusion from the council of war directing this campaign.[13] After that, he pursued the court, seizing chances to attack the current authorities in New Spain, but gaining nothing. In 1544 he presented himself to the Emperor as a man now "old, infirm and encumbered with debt," who had passed forty years of his life "with little sleep, bad food, and with his arms constantly by his side:" an embarrassing set of exaggerations. Finally he yielded, and prepared to go back to Mexico to die. But death took him, ignobly, of dysentery, as he awaited ship in late 1547 at Castilleja de la Cuesta, a small town outside Seville.

For two decades, then, Cortés had remained something of a thorn in the crown's side, as he struggled, if ever more feebly, against the bureaucratizing of colonial government. He had certainly promoted that process, however, by in effect abdicating his power in 1524–5 during his absence on the futile expedition to Honduras. Even the disreputable and self-seeking officials to whom Mexican government was given in those, and immediately succeeding, years managed to prevent his resurgence. To a certain degree the leading *conquistadores* of the other great mainland prize, Peru, also unintentionally simplified the installation of the machinery of royal government; though they did it differently, by killing each other in factional conflict.

Civil wars among the Spaniards are, indeed, the salient feature of colonial Peru's early political history. They happened because divisions in the conquering forces were deep, far more severe than the Cortés–Velázquez split in Mexico. The Peruvian conquest had two major leaders: Francisco Pizarro and Diego de Almagro. Almagro was the junior partner; in Panama he had been the manager of Pizarro's lands and business. He was an expert and natural man of business; Pizarro was not. The abilities of both men combined well to carry off the Pacific coast explorations opening the way to Peru in the 1520s. But Pizarro, when in Spain in 1529 arranging the contract for the conquest, reserved all the important titles and potential reward for himself, very largely ignoring Almagro's interests and earlier services. This was the seed of future hatred. For the moment, however, though angry, Almagro remained in the enterprise. Then, when the conquering force left Panama in late 1530, he stayed behind to attend to business matters and organize reinforcements. When he, with some 200 men, finally caught up with Pizarro at Cajamarca in April 1533, he found that he and his party were excluded from sharing in Atahualpa's gold and silver ransom, since they had had no part in the Sapa Inca's capture the previous November. Now the discontent was not Almagro's alone, but spread and festered among a large group of Spaniards.

Still no open conflict erupted, because Almagro and his followers hoped to find some other prize in South America to equal Incaic Peru. Seeking it, in July 1535 he set off, in one of the epic marches of the conquest, with a force of some 570 Spaniards and a multitude of native carriers southward past Lake Titicaca, across the Bolivian *altiplano*, over the coastal Andean ranges, and down to central Chile. Though the land was fertile there, and the climate good for living and farming, Chile presented no advanced native culture, no cities, no high artisanry. Almagro, disappointed, but also animated now by news that he had been granted the governorship of part of Peru, returned thither up the Chilean coast, in the first crossing by Europeans of the Atacama desert. If, on the way, he had become aware of the large gold deposits of northern Chile, the history of Spanish Peru might have been happier. As it was, he reached Arequipa early in 1537, and then marched up into the mountains. There open conflict between Pizarrists and Almagrists at last broke out. Almagro took Cuzco and held it for a year. Finally, however, in the battle of Las Salinas just outside Cuzco in April 1538, Almagro was beaten and captured. In July he was garrotted.

The Almagrists now rallied around Almagro's young mestizo son, Don Diego *el mozo* ("the lad"). In June 1541, they plotted, and successfully carried out in Lima, the assassination of Francisco Pizarro, still governor and now also ennobled, like Cortés, as a marquis. Young Diego's followers then pronounced him governor of Peru. But the time of unfettered exercise of authority by the original *conquistadores* was coming to a close. The earlier ructions had induced the authorities in Spain to send to Peru as aide (and bridle) to Pizarro a judge of the *audiencia* of Valladolid, Cristóbal Vaca de Castro.[14] At the time of the assassination, Vaca had already reached southern New Granada. The Pizarrists in the central Andes quickly rallied to him; the Almagrists fell back on Cuzco. Royalists and rebels came to battle on September 18, 1542 near Huamanga (present Ayacucho), a large mountain town half-way between Lima and Cuzco. *El mozo* was soon after captured near Cuzco, and beheaded. Vaca de Castro assumed full governing powers.

With the prime leaders dead, struggle between the original factions abated at this point; but conflict, often violent, soon resumed in Peru, now in a struggle between settlers and royal government that lasted well into the 1550s. Its general cause was an aversion to royal interference, very evident now with the presence of a governor (and soon an *audiencia* and viceroy also), among settlers who for a decade had done much as they pleased. The immediate reason was restriction of access to native tribute and labor. Like Cortés, and in what became after Mexico standard practice on the mainland, Pizarro had distributed Indians in *encomienda* to his followers. Little, if any, control had been placed on the treatment and use of the natives so "entrusted." In 1542 the crown, inspired partly by anxiety about the well-being of its native American subjects, partly by fears that *encomenderos* were becoming a menacingly rich and powerful colonial elite, tried once more to regulate the *encomienda*. The new rules were part of what is probably the most famous piece of Spanish colonial legislation, the *New Laws and Ordinances for the Government of the Indies*.[15] Clause 30 of this code forbade the issue of new *encomiendas* by royal administrators in America, and ordered that when present *encomenderos* died, their Indians should come under royal administration. This was a stunning blow for the holders, who generally saw their Indians as the economic basis of enduring family dynasties; and as recently as 1536 they had been told that the holdings were hereditary. The ire and alarm of Peruvian *encomenderos* were particularly provoked by another clause, no. 29, which ordered that anyone found notably culpable in the Pizarro–Almagro conflict should lose his Indians. This was a severe threat, since almost all *encomenderos* had been involved to some degree in that struggle.

The New Laws had also called for a regularizing of the government of Peru, which was hardly surprising given the infighting of the late 1530s, and growing awareness in Spain of the new colony's size and wealth. A viceroy should be installed in Lima, and preside there over an *audiencia*. Chosen for this task was Blasco Núñez Vela, an experienced naval commander and town governor in Spain, but a man, it quickly proved, quite bereft of political skill and remarkable mostly for his inflexibility. He sailed in 1543 with the first three *oidores* of the *audiencia*. After landing in northern Peru in March 1544, he immediately proclaimed the New Laws, incensing *encomenderos* and their many dependants. When he reached Lima, the *cabildo* appealed to him to withhold the Laws. But he refused, "saying he was merely their executor, and that although he might be boiled in a vat of oil, he could do nothing but implement the said ordinances as they were written, to the letter."[16] The outcome was an armed rising of many colonists, led by Francisco Pizarro's youngest half-brother, Gonzalo. He was a brave and personally attractive man, but of the several Pizarros active in the early colony, the most obtuse.[17] The new *audiencia* in Lima, already at odds with the viceroy after quarrels on the journey, inclined to sympathize with the *encomenderos'* protests over the New Laws. Their sympathy increased, perhaps, as Gonzalo Pizarro's army drew nearer to Lima. In September 1544 the judges arrested Núñez Vela on the grounds that he was a danger to government, and put him on a ship for Panama (and Spain). He, however, managed to get ashore in northern Peru, and gathered a royalist force in the Quito highlands. There, finally, in January 1546 a show-down came between viceroy and Gonzalo Pizarro. At the battle of Añaquito, the rebels defeated and captured Núñez Vela. Soon after, they beheaded him. It was the only instance of the killing of a viceroy by colonists (or anyone else, for that matter) in the history of the Spanish American empire.

From the viceroy's departure from Lima until early 1548, Gonzalo Pizarro was the effective ruler of Peru. The *Audiencia* of Lima needed little persuasion to name him governor and captain-general in October 1544. After defeating the viceroy in Quito, and placing agents in Panama, Pizarro nominally controlled the whole west coast of South America. His more ardent supporters, like Cortés's in New Spain twenty years before, wanted to see him as king of Peru, and titled his illegitimate mestizo son "prince." But most colonists balked at such extreme measures.

In reality, Pizarro's hold on the Peruvian colonists was increasingly tenuous. His keenest supporters were impetuous men whose loyalty, for that very reason, was unreliable. He tried to buy support by granting *encomiendas*, but the claimants were so many that some of the allocations were very small, leaving the recipients resentful, and the Indians harshly burdened. He was driven to threats, violence, and executions to maintain his position, so that the last year of his regime was a reign of terror as he and his grim henchman, Francisco de Carvajal, sought to root out disloyalty.

That is part of the reason why Gonzalo Pizarro's rebellion, like March, went out like a lamb after entering like a lion. Still, the events themselves did not lack surprise and drama. Realizing, perhaps, the limits of the practicable, the home government made no attempt to send an army across the sea against the rebels. Rather, in 1546, it dispatched to Panama a single lawyer, the Licenciate Pedro de la Gasca, arming him with wide powers to pardon and reward those who rallied to the royal cause. He also brought news that Charles V had revoked the offensive clauses 29 and 30 of the New Laws. Slowly La Gasca moved southward in 1547 toward Peru, playing on the underlying loyalties and self-identification of settlers with Spanish values[18] that had enabled the viceroy to assemble a royalist force in Quito in 1545–6. Pardons, and redistribution of the Indians from *encomiendas* taken from rebels, gradually brought people over to the king's side. When La Gasca's force finally confronted Pizarro's army in April 1548 at Xaquixaguana, near Cuzco (always Cuzco, the node of highland affairs), that process of absorption reached its climax. There was no fight; the Pizarrists simply deserted to the king. Gonzalo was taken and beheaded. He was buried in Cuzco, in a chapel of the Mercedarian monastery where the bodies of the two Almagros also lay.[19] Thus the factions were united in death.

BUREAUCRACY ASCENDANT

So ended the age of the *conquistador* in Peru. It had persisted far longer than in New Spain, where Cortés's departure for Honduras late in 1524 cut it perhaps prematurely short. In Peru, the conquerors had almost uninterrupted dominion for fifteen years. The difference comes in part from the greater remoteness of Peru. Authorities in Spain were slower to know Peru, slower to learn of events there, and hence slower to provide remedies for them. Equally telling, probably, was the contractual, legal nature of the Peruvian conquest, dissuading the crown from interference in Francisco Pizarro's domain. Cortés, though soon granted the governorship of New Spain after his success in conquest, always remained suspect.

After Gonzalo Pizarro, royal officers of one rank or another governed Peru. First, briefly, was La Gasca, as President of the *Audiencia* of Lima. After his return to Spain in 1550 there followed almost two decades in which either viceroys or the *audiencia* held executive power. The quality of government in these years was uneven, to be sure; but never again did the crown lose control. A briefly threatening flurry did occur in 1553–4 when a group of highland *encomenderos* led by one Francisco Hernández Girón rose to protest against a law of 1549 forbidding use of *encomienda* Indians as laborers. (Only tribute in cash or kind might now be taken.) Suspension of the law by the *audiencia* quickly defused this rising. Finally, the arrival of Don Francisco de Toledo, fifth viceroy of Peru, in 1569 initiated the run of viceregal administration that continued almost uninterrupted until Independence, two and a half centuries later.

In other parts of the empire, with, of course, variations of circumstance and pace, the shift from *conquistador* to bureaucrat, from military to civil government, followed the patterns seen in New Spain and Peru. Naturally, outside those great central regions of the empire, where native population and potential wealth were concentrated, the issues and contests of control were less urgent. Or, at least, they were so for the crown, which was relatively little concerned if conquerors and their *encomendero* descendants took a large portion of the slight product of, say, Paraguay or Yucatan.

There was one particular circumstance, however, that made the military-to-civil transition less complete in some outlying regions of empire than in the centers. That was the persistence of native opposition. In New Mexico, raiding by Navajos, Apaches, and, in the eighteenth century, Comanches was a constant threat.[20] In Yucatan, until the late seventeenth century, the possibility of native resistance from the deep interior hung over the towns and estates clustered in the north and west of the peninsula. The sedentary Paraguay of Spaniards and Guaraní was menaced by the people of the Chaco.[21] But the exemplary case is southern Chile, whose Araucanians constantly fought Spanish advance to a standstill until the early eighteenth century. Then the Spaniards stopped trying to push southward, and relinquished the half of Chile below the River Bío Bío to the natives, who were not finally defeated until the late nineteenth century. In the sixteenth, they killed Pedro de Valdivia, the colony's founding governor, in 1553; after several decades of successful guerrilla fighting, they killed another governor, García Oñez de Loyola, in 1598; and then, in a broad rising lasting several years, they destroyed or forced the abandonment of all Spanish towns south of the Bío Bío. From 1541 to 1664 the fighting killed some 20,000–30,000 soldiers and settlers on the Spanish side, and probably far more Araucanians.[22] In an effort to punish the Indians, encourage settlers, and maintain Chile's labor supply, the crown reversed its quite definite sixteenth-century policy trend on Indian slavery, by, in 1608, specifically permitting enslavement of "rebellious" Chilean natives. This, not surprisingly, aggravated the conflict.

Frontier hostilities are not of merely incidental interest. The Spanish American empire was a large area that, during its three centuries of existence, was strikingly free of war. Once the military conquests were over, most of its people never felt the direct or indirect effects of conflict that plagued much of the Old World: no sieges, no invasions, no blockades, no armies living off the land. So peaceful, indeed, was most of colonial life that it is hard to find in it any roots of the militarism so visible in post-independence Spanish America. One such root, however, clearly enough was the martial culture of various imperial frontiers, where European settlement was in constant friction with nomadic or at least mobile native peoples. Here the mentality of the conquest, even of the Iberian Reconquest, found an environment to sustain it.

Peripheries apart, however, by the 1550s order was beginning to descend on Spanish America. The main conquests were long over; and the contests that *conquistadores* and early settlers had waged among themselves – no happy bands of brothers, these, but fierce and treacherous competitors for booty, Indians, and land – were yielding to the relentless bureaucratization that emanated from Spain.

The administrative system of the mainland drew on experience in the Caribbean. There, the authority of the second viceroy, Diego Columbus, had been curbed in 1511 by the creation of the *Audiencia* of Santo Domingo. Although that court did not play a strong role in the islands' government, and was eclipsed by the Jeronymite troika of 1516–19, *audiencias* were the governing instruments that in due course the crown found most useful for the mainland. As, in their origins, high courts of law, they provided, first, a unity of judicial and executive functions that mirrored the nature of Spanish monarchy itself. They also offered rule by committee. The court's president generally acted in consultation with the *oidores*, or judges, and all were assisted by staff lawyers. Thus the risks of an individual holding full executive power were reduced. And, again, the precedent of government at home, where councils of state advised the monarch and in effect made both policy and executive decisions, was followed.

The first mainland *audiencia*, that of New Spain, was created late in 1527, as part of what was by then a clearly necessary effort to bring order and royal authority to that rich new colony. Like sixteenth-century *audiencias* in America generally, this one had four judges. Its president, named early in 1528, was a man then serving as governor of the province of Pánuco, a coastal region in north-eastern Mexico which had by this time become considered distinct from Cortés's jurisdiction. This was Beltrán Nuño de Guzmán. He was chosen as president because of his familiarity with Mexico, and because he was a known foe of Cortés, having in the past been an ally of Diego Velázquez in Caribbean affairs. Authorities at home hoped he would therefore dig deeply into Cortés's alleged misdemeanors. He proved, however, a dreadful choice, "a natural gangster" whose "demonic energy... enabled him to command and hold together whole armies of lesser scoundrels."[23] Two of the *oidores* died soon after reaching New Spain. The other two seem to have joined their president in the sack of Mexico that he immediately began. More than investigating Cortés's conduct, Guzmán simply seized his property and Indians, and those of known Cortés supporters, and distributed them among his own backers. Generally the native population suffered greatly under the rule of what is generally called the "first *audiencia*" of New Spain, although it was really the dictatorship of the president. Guzmán encouraged slaving of Indians. Those allotted in *encomienda* to his allies found themselves burdened with vast tribute demands. Guzmán tried to stop news of all this from reaching Spain by censoring outgoing mail. Finally, though, a protest by the first bishop of New Spain, the Franciscan Juan de Zumárraga, was smuggled out, and in 1530 Guzmán was removed from his presidency. The two surviving *oidores* were also removed, sent to Spain, tried, and put in jail, where they died. Guzmán, however, seeing the direction of the wind, had in 1529 left México-Tenochtitlan with an expedition to extend Spanish conquest in western Mexico. This he did successfully, roughly from Lake Chapala up to Culiacán, though again with an unconscionable cruelty to the west coast peoples that caused a lasting hostility to the Spanish there. After ruling for several years what was in effect a personal satrapy in the west, to which he gave the name New Galicia, Guzmán was finally returned to Spain in 1538. He died in prison in 1544.

In 1530 the *Audiencia* of New Spain was reconstituted with a new staff. The president was Sebastián Ramírez de Fuenleal, previously bishop of Santo Domingo. The four *oidores* were serious and distinguished administrators and churchmen. This court is recorded to have remedied its predecessor's misdeeds toward the native population, punished colonists who had mistreated Indians assigned to them or otherwise acted against the royal interest, and begun strengthening royal authority across New Spain by appointing local administrators. From now on, until independence in 1821, the *audiencia* was a fixture of the Mexican capital, its judges and other officers being replaced as they were moved, retired, or died. Gradually, as its business expanded, the court grew in size. In the eighteenth century, the *oidores* numbered ten. The other American *audiencias* underwent a similar expansion.

Nine more high courts were created in the sixteenth century. Next after New Spain came Panama (1538), where an *audiencia* was seen as needed to hear cases from the rapidly growing number of settlers of Tierra Firme (the Spanish Main; that is, the Caribbean coast from Venezuela west and north to Nicaragua). The intent at this point was also that appeals from the entire west coast of South America should go to Panama.[24] But then, four years later, the New Laws called for a separate *audiencia* in Peru, at Lima, and another to attend to cases from Guatemala and Nicaragua.[25] The court at Panama was therefore abolished in 1543; but then reinstated in 1564, in recognition of Panama's immense strategic and commercial importance as the crossing point for people and goods between the Atlantic and the Pacific.

Peru and Guatemala received their *audiencias* in 1543. Next came the high court of New Galicia, or Guadalajara, in 1547, to deal with litigation and affairs particularly from the silver mining settlements that were appearing in western Mexico. In the same year, an *audiencia* was created for Santa Fe de Bogotá, to attend to the growing settlement of New Granada. Then, in 1559, came that of La Plata, or Charcas (modern Bolivia), again largely in response to the local rise of silver mining and its associated population, specifically at Potosí. Quito became the seat of a high court in 1563. Two years later one was ordered for Chile, at Concepción on the Indian frontier. It was, however, disbanded in 1575, because the undiluted authority of a military governor was thought necessary to deal with the Araucanian threat. The Chilean court was reinstated, permanently, in Santiago in 1603. The final *audiencia* created in the sixteenth century was at Manila, in the Philippines. The placing of a court there in 1583 reflected the rapid growth of the city's importance as Spain's outpost in the Orient, and its crucial commercial role after the opening of the transpacific trade to New Spain in the 1570s. Only three more *audiencias* were added to the eleven set up in the sixteenth century: Buenos Aires, briefly from 1661 to 1672, then permanently in 1783; Venezuela, at Caracas, in 1786; and Cuzco, in 1787.

The *audiencias* were all founded in response to a need perceived by the monarchy for a strong judicial and executive authority in particular regions. Aside from that, as in Spain under the Catholic Monarchs, *audiencias* had the broader function of representing royal power. The regions in which they were installed were ones in which there was a concentration of population, both European and native, or a concentration of wealth. Usually population and wealth coincided. Some *audiencias* were erected in places that had long been native power centers, and in which the conquerors thought that the same function could be usefully preserved: México-Tenochtitlan, Santa Fe de Bogotá, Quito. Others were in towns of essentially Spanish making, such as Guadalajara, Panama, Lima, or La Plata, that had some new, post-conquest, political or economic reason for being. The territorial limits of the courts were at first vaguely defined. Jurisdictional disputes were the frequent outcome. But over time these, and simple matters of practicability, fixed the boundaries. In several cases, the jurisdictions were the close origins of the territories of the independent nations of the nineteenth century. The *Audiencia* of Lima, for instance, became Peru; that of Charcas, Bolivia. The territories of the courts in Quito and Santa Fe underlay those of present-day Ecuador and Colombia; and since these *audiencias* were sited in important pre-conquest centers, a direct line can be drawn in these cases from native polities to present states.

After the energetic burst of *audiencia*-founding between 1538 and 1563, most people in Mexico, Central America, and the colonies in western South America were within possible, if not easy, reach of a high court. South Americans away from the west coast had further to go. Venezuela remained in the jurisdiction of the Santo Domingo court, and the Río de la Plata and Paraguay in that of Charcas. But whatever the distance, as political bodies the courts functioned to a notable degree as intended. For most people in the empire the local *audiencia* was the highest representation they would ever see of Spanish power. People of all ranks and ethnic origins had access to the *audiencia* as court of law, though, unsurprisingly, it was mainly white colonists' legal business that ended up there. Still, the ceremonial surrounding the courts' workings, and the public presence of robed judges and crown attorneys, worked continuously to remind colonial society of the distant existence of the royal court and the authority attached to it. Nor was this reminder limited to the *audiencia* cities, for individual *oidores* constantly went on tour – not to try cases, but to investigate administrative problems, and to suggest and implement new regulations.

As law tribunals, *audiencias* were primarily courts of appeal, hearing cases previously tried by lesser justices, and various administrative courts, such as those of the merchant guilds (*consulados*) or the mints. In criminal cases the decisions of *audiencias* were final. Civil cases, if large enough (over 10,000 pesos, after 1542), could be referred to the Council of the Indies, in Spain.

Much of a court's time went to hearing litigation. Two days a week, for instance, were usually given over to suits between Indians, or between Indians and Spaniards.[26] But the administrative function of the body was still more crucial than the judicial to the running of the empire. Broadly speaking, the further an *audiencia* was sited from a viceroy (and until well into the eighteenth century, only two viceroyalties existed, based in Lima and Mexico City), the greater was the executive and administrative authority that it possessed. The precise division of authority between *audiencia* and viceroy, and the degree of administrative independence with which a court could act, varied over time, and from place to place, often enough in accordance with the strength of will of the officials involved. But generally speaking, the president of a remote *audiencia*, such as Charcas or Quito, was an immensely influential figure in his own territory, with a range of executive, military, and legislative powers akin to those of a viceroy. This was inevitable. Slowness of communications between viceroy and provinces meant that some local officer must hold independent power to make urgent decisions. The obvious candidates were the heads of the *audiencias*.

The *audiencia*, then, whose potential as a tool for extending royal authority was clearly seen by the Catholic Monarchs in Castile, fully realized that promise in the Indies. It became there the prime conduit of the Spanish monarchy's force, of that distinctive intertwining of dominion with law. For the longer term, most *audiencias* generated around themselves in their provinces a political geography (in some cases reinforcing what had existed in native times) that over the centuries of colonial rule solidified, and then endured after Spain was gone. Thus, in the early independence years, it was barely conceivable that any city beside La Plata should be capital of Bolivia, or Quito of Ecuador. It is still so. Nearly all *audiencia* seats, of the sixteenth century and later, are present national capitals.

The sole administrative superior to the *audiencia* in the Indies was the viceroy: literally, the man in place of the king. The office had long been used by Aragon to govern its Mediterranean possessions in medieval times; and in the unitary Spain of the sixteenth century, Aragon, Catalonia, and Valencia themselves were run by viceroys. Once viceroyalties were created for New Spain and Peru, the total of these units in Spanish realms became nine: the five just mentioned, and Navarre, Sardinia, Sicily, and Naples besides.[27]

The decision to raise New Spain to a viceroyalty was taken late in 1529, while Cortés was still in Spain, by a special junta convened by Charles V to advise him on government, and particularly on Indian policy, in Mexico. The chosen candidate was Don Antonio de Mendoza, a member of one of Castile's most distinguished noble families. But a series of delays meant that he did not reach New Spain until 1535. In the interim the restaffed *audiencia* did valuable preparatory work, calming and ordering a population that Guzmán's depredatory antics had agitated. Mendoza remained in Mexico until 1551. A sixteen-year tenure was extraordinary in later colonial times. But Mendoza was seen at home as the "founding" viceroy of what soon became known as the "realm" (*reino*) of New Spain; and his conduct in office argued for his being kept there as long as possible. Indeed, in 1551 he went not back to Spain, but to Peru as second viceroy there, charged with the same settling of affairs there, in the wake of Núñez Vela's blunders and the Pizarro rebellion, as he had managed in New Spain. What he could have done will never be known, for he died in Lima less than a year after his arrival.[28]

Mendoza's prime accomplishment in New Spain was precisely to have averted violent reaction to those of the New Laws that attacked the *encomienda*. He himself took a practical attitude toward the *encomienda*, seeing it, rather like Cortés, as a political and economic necessity if Spaniards were to settle in America, but as a system wide open to abuse, and therefore in need of careful vigilance. Though he had no particular esteem for Indians, he took his duty to guard their interests seriously, and they came to regard him, again like Cortés, as their protector.

Word of the New Laws' ban on the inheritance of *encomiendas* and on the issue of new grants of Indians went ahead of the promulgation of the code in New Spain. When a royal agent, Tello de Sandoval, arrived there in 1544 to enact the laws, he was met with howls of protest. But no violence followed, thanks to Mendoza's prevailing on Sandoval to suspend application of the clauses the settlers most disliked, while an appeal on them went to the Council of the Indies. Mendoza was supported in this temporizing by the heads of the three religious orders present in New Spain at the time, the Franciscans, Dominicans, and Augustinians. The Council, and the Emperor, bowed to the advice of the men on the spot, and in October 1545 removed the offending regulations. Thus tensions were kept in check in New Spain, and the foundation was laid for the crown's recuperation of Peru.

That was the most dramatic challenge that Mendoza faced. But his many other actions in New Spain may have had a more formative effect in the colony. He ousted incompetent officials from the lower reaches of the *audiencia*; improved tax collection, and account keeping in the treasury; founded a mint in México-Tenochtitlan in 1536 so as to promote trade through the provision of a reliable medium of exchange; promoted the production of raw silk, and from it the weaving of cloth; and imported, once more like Cortés, seeds and stock so as to expand European-style agriculture in New Spain. Mendoza himself acquired several large landed properties on which he bred the Spanish merino sheep, in the traditional style of the Spanish nobility from which he came. (Engaging in profitable enterprises was a concession to these early, founding, administrators that later officials were denied, at least in principle.) He directed the building of roads for carts and mule trains, fanning out in all directions from the Valley of Mexico to Taxco and Oaxaca southward, Michoacán and Jalisco westward, and Pánuco and Veracruz eastward. In his time, also, began the Spanish expansion into the north that ultimately yielded one of the most radical changes in Mexico resulting from the Spanish conquest: the "civilization" of the *altiplano*, and its incorporation into the political and economic life of the center. The start of northward movement was linked to a native rebellion that began in New Galicia in 1540, a rising known as the Mixton War that briefly seemed a serious threat to the Spanish hold on New Spain in general. The rebellious Indians were dwellers in the canyons north of Guadalajara, and on the west coast at the same latitude. They belonged to several distinct groups, but had in common that they lived on the margin between the developed sedentarism of central Mexico and the simpler, sometimes nomadic, cultures of the north. Their attack on the Spanish was, then, a transient example of the frontier refractoriness that the colonizers encountered in Chile or the far Mexican north. It was also a delayed reaction to the spoliations of Nuño de Guzmán and followers in this region in the early 1530s. The rebellion began with Indian attacks on *encomenderos* and mission friars. With much effort, the infant city of Guadalajara was defended. The viceroy arrived, responding to appeals for help from the acting governor of New Galicia, Cristóbal de Oñate, with 450 Spaniards and, reportedly, 30,000 Aztec auxiliaries.[29] The rising could not long resist such force, and subsided in 1542. In its aftermath, Spanish expeditions, despatched by Oñate and others, pressed further than before up the canyons. The critical outcome was that in 1546 they found the silver ores of Zacatecas. This strike was the first of many made on the *altiplano* over the following century, which turned Mexico into one of the world's prime sources of silver; as it still is.

Mendoza did not live long enough to see the mining potential of the north fully revealed. But New Spain's promise as a silver producer was clear to him from the start. In 1536 he issued his first mining regulations. These emerged finally in 1550 as a considerable mining code, which remained in force until 1577. In general he gives the impression of having achieved a mental mastery of Mexico – of its geography, its developing colonial economy, its politics, and, at least, the European part of its population. He remarked, in the memorandum to his successor that all outgoing viceroys were expected to write, that he had found the Spaniards of Mexico easier to govern than any he had encountered in his career. But they had respect for neither wealth nor rank if not treated as *caballeros*, gentlemen, that is, of noble quality.[30] Here is a glimpse of colonials' touchy pride, founded in the achievement of conquest, or, for newcomers, in the status that they thought they had gained in merely risking the Atlantic crossing. Do little, Mendoza recommended, and do it slowly. He had not, in fact, done little himself; quite the opposite. But for all his activism, he had certainly applied, as one notable student of Spanish colonial government observes, "a policy based on prudence, tenacity, concessions on points of detail and occasional rigour" to draw the conquerors under bureaucratic control.[31]

Mendoza's particular deeds suggest what a viceroy's broad powers were. He was first the chief executive officer in his region. As such he could issue regulations for it, though for these to become permanent law they had to receive final royal approval. He was military commander of his territory, normally bearing the title of "captain-general." He was also *ex officio* president of the *audiencia* in his capital city, and might sit as president of other *audiencias* in his jurisdiction; though, unless a lawyer, which was rare, he could not participate in judging in the court. Nonetheless, he could exercise, if he wished, much influence over the operation of the high courts. In addition, he was vice-patron of the church in his realm, just as the monarch was its patron throughout Spanish territories. This gave his opinions on church matters weight with even archbishops and heads of orders in the Indies. Also, and no less telling, vice-patronage gave him power to present candidates for posts in the lower priesthood. Beyond all this, the viceroy, as chief executive, was *ipso facto* head of the treasury system in his jurisdiction. He was also in principle the chief defender of natives' interest, since he was particularly charged to "have special care for the good treatment, conservation, and increase of the Indians," and might hear cases between Indians as first-instance magistrate.[32]

For all that viceroys could, and often did, do, they remained remote figures for most of those they governed. This was in part intentional policy, for viceroys, like monarchs themselves, should gain authority in aloofness. They occupied large and splendid palaces on the main plazas of the colonial capitals. In these the ceremonial of the royal court was reproduced as far as possible, so that the aura of monarchy should surround the viceroy. For the same reason, most viceroys were chosen from the upper ranks of the nobility; and if they were related to the royal family, so much the better. Their arrivals and departures in America were occasions for elaborate ritual, as were their rare travels within their viceroyalties.[33] Most of a viceroy's time was spent in his capital.

The outstanding exception to this normal immobility was Don Francisco de Toledo, fifth viceroy of Peru. In his long tenure (1569–81) he played the "founding" role in South America that Mendoza had performed in New Spain. Though some of his success derived from his intelligence and personality (he was an energetic, impatient, and authoritarian man), it was also the outcome of his intimate knowledge of at least the heartland of Spanish South America: Peru and Charcas. And this he gained by inspecting the territory in person, in a five-year journey that took him and a retinue of aides through Huamanga, Cuzco, Potosí, La Plata, Arequipa, and back to Lima. In the course of this *visita general*, Toledo wrought a number of socio-economic changes in the interior that impinged especially on the native people. He continued and expanded the process of resettlement, or *reducción*, of Indians into new towns that had started in Peru in the mid-1560s. The aim was greater efficiency in the government of natives, in their evangelization, and in extraction of their labor. He enlarged and formalized the *mita*, or draft labor system, that supplied Indian workers to Spanish mercury and silver mines at Huancavelica and Potosí. And he hastened the adoption by Peruvian miners of amalgamation, a new and economical method of refining silver ores developed in New Spain in the 1550s. One broad effect of these and other measures was to add to the Indians' burden of labor and tribute. Toledo has therefore often been seen as a scourge of the central Andean Indians, and with some justification. He was probably less careful of native interests than Mendoza had been in New Spain. But he governed in a different time, one in which Spain's fiscal needs were far more urgent than they had been before 1550. The ruling monarch, Philip II, had dedicated his empire to defending the true faith against insurgent Protestantism; and, in so doing, plunged Spain into endless European wars. Potosí seemed divinely revealed to fund these contests; and Toledo knew that he must make Potosí yield. The well-being of Indians was secondary.[34]

For the breadth of change that he wrought, Toledo has been called the Solon of Peru. He was a legislative dynamo, throwing off code after code of regulations as he traveled. His mining ordinances superseded Mendoza's for the whole empire, and remained in effect well into the eighteenth century. He was voluminous on the *mita*. He ordained on Indian government, on the organization of hospitals, on the sale (forbidden) of wine to Indians, Blacks and Mulattoes, on the public fountains of Lima, on the sale of adobes, on the inns of Charcas, on coca, and on more else than can easily be imagined. A recent collection of his regulations runs to 950 pages of fine print.[35]

This, of course, was exceptional, indeed unique, and was the result of Toledo's being particularly charged to set Peru straight after what seemed, from Spain, two decades of timid administrative shilly-shallying. The usual source of legislation for the Indies was not viceroys, or any authority in America, but the Royal and Supreme Council of the Indies, a body firmly resident in Spain, and closely attendant on the monarch. The Council came into existence in 1524, partly as a response to the rapid expansion of the American territories produced by Cortés, partly in a broad upgrading of Spanish central administration by Charles V's Grand Chancellor, Mercurino Gattinara.[36] Before then, Juan Rodríguez de Fonseca, once Isabella's chaplain, and later Bishop of Burgos, had long held the reins of the Indies in his hands; though from 1516 on members of the Council of Castile had also taken up American business.

Short of the king, the Council of the Indies was, from its founding to the early eighteenth century, the ultimate authority in the government of America. As the Indies' importance to Spain grew more obvious, the Council became one of the most senior of the state councils that the Spanish Habsburgs used to rule their wide possessions. At the start it had a president and four or five councillors (normally lawyers and clergymen), and a small staff of lawyers, accountants, scribes, and the like. In the seventeenth century the number of councillors rose to ten. Oddly enough, at first sight, few councillors – only a dozen or so before 1700 – were men with American experience.[37] Disinterested detachment was held to outweigh the possible advantage of personal experience.

Nothing in American administration fell outside the Council's purview. It was the final court of appeal from *audiencias*' verdicts. It was the central executive and law-making entity in the empire. Its authority extended to military matters, trade, finance, and, via the royal patronage, to the church. It was the destination of nearly all official, and many private, communications from the Indies. Reports and letters might be addressed to the monarch; but with rare exceptions the Council read and screened them. If they conveyed a substantial problem or bore on some question of policy, the councillors and their staff would send their own, generally succinct, memorandum – a *consulta* – to the monarch, often with suggested courses of action. Back it would come with the royal preference indicated in marginal notes or a separate written statement. The conciliar staff then drafted a suitable royal order, to be signed by the monarch (not with a name, but simply "yo el rey," or "yo la reina" – "I the King," "I the Queen"), and dispatched to the proper person or body in America. This system functioned most energetically in the time (1556–98) of Philip II, the most dedicated royal servant of the bureaucratic system that Spain had necessarily created to manage its broadly scattered realms. He, at the apex of this new "government by paper,"[38] spent countless hours awash in the river of documents flowing to him from a dozen state councils. His hurried marginal scrawlings have been the despair of researchers of his reign's history.

The Council of the Indies received correspondence not only from viceroys and *audiencias*, its immediate subordinates in the American bureaucracy, but from all lower levels of government (and indeed from private citizens who had some case to make or some favor to seek). Beneath *audiencias* were two more ranks of general administrators. The more senior was the governor. Governorships lay physically within the bounds of viceroyalties and *audiencias*, but were generally frontier areas whose combination of remoteness and need for defense made the presence of a senior figure useful. The typical *gobernador*, therefore, was a well-tried military man, able to command in the field. He might carry the extra title of captain-general. He was also, however, chief civil administrator for his region, and its senior judge. Examples of governorships in the mature empire are New Mexico (capital Santa Fe), New León, in northeast Mexico (Monterrey), Santa Cruz de la Sierra, in eastern, lowland Charcas (Santa Cruz), Paraguay (Asunción), and the Río de la Plata (Buenos Aires).

Smaller than governorships, and far more numerous, were *alcaldias mayores* and *corregimientos*. The heads of these areas, *alcaldes mayores* and *corregidores*, were the district officers of the colonies, and as such the crown agents most directly in touch with the people, of whatever rank or color. (The offices of *alcalde mayor* and *corregidor* seem to have been practically identical. The first title was more commonly used in New Spain, and the second in South America. Here, for economy, *corregidor* will be used to stand for both.)

It took time to create and staff this lower end of the colonial bureaucracy. The first district officers of the empire were, in effect, the *encomenderos*. An overlooked function of the *encomienda*, and one of the reasons why the home administration tolerated it long after its dangers to native well-being were clear, was to spread Spaniards across mainland America, and so provide a rudimentary rural administration at a time when money, men, and knowledge were still lacking for the creation of an official system. This, though, gave powers and opportunities for gain to *encomenderos* that in the longer term were intolerable. On the mainland, it was in New Spain that their replacement by local functionaries began most swiftly. The crown told the reformed *audiencia* to proceed with this task. The court went at it eagerly, shifting fifty-three *encomiendas*, from a total of possibly 300, to the control of *corregidores* between 1531 and 1533.[39] Some of these new local officials, it is true, were ex-*encomenderos*, or even current *encomenderos*. But the *audiencia* preferred to appoint men who did not hold Indians, and often named as *corregidores* recent arrivals from Spain. *Conquistadores* and earlier settlers muttered about their exclusion in favor of newcomers lacking status, accomplishment, and wealth. But marginalization of the men who had dominated New Spain in the 1520s, whether under Cortés or Guzmán, was precisely the official intent by this time.

By the mid-1540s, just as northward expansion was beginning, New Spain had some 150 *corregimientos*. By the early seventeenth century, the number had risen to about 200. Peru, at the same date, was divided into eighty-eight of these jurisdictions. There the introduction of *corregidores* had begun only in the 1560s, delayed by the wars, and by the prolongation of *encomienda* that had been necessary to appease restive colonists. Viceroy Toledo carried the reform forward vigorously in the 1570s, seeking, as had been the aim in New Spain, to replace private with public interest at this most local level of administration.[40]

Corregidores were rarely, of course, the ideal and disinterested local governors that policy called for. Like greater administrators above them, they were not only executives, but also magistrates and legislators for their areas; and few of them resisted the temptations that this combination of powers made available. Nearly all *corregidores* were administrators of Indian districts. In these some battened on their charges just as harmfully as *encomenderos* had done before them. In remote districts of, say, Central America or the Andes, they governed almost unsupervised. The only nearby resident European to keep watch over them was the parish priest, and often enough priest and *corregidor* collaborated for their own advantage. *Corregidores* were, moreover, often the dependants or relatives of viceroys. They held office, by gift of their master, only for as long as his term of office. Many saw the position as a transient opportunity to enrich themselves. They seized it, and administration suffered accordingly.

A small minority of *corregidores* and *alcaldes mayores* were governors of Spanish towns in America – mayors, roughly speaking, although the term falls short, since these officials, once again, were a combination of executive, law-maker, and magistrate. Normally, and particularly if the town were a provincial capital or a prosperous port or mining center, these men were carefully chosen royal appointees (as *corregidores* of peninsula cities had been in Isabella's time). They ranked with provincial *gobernadores*, and might well, like them, have a military background.

One of the tasks of such a *corregidor* was to preside over meetings of the *cabildo*, or town council. In doing so, he became the point of contact between bureaucracy and the sole administrative entity dominated from the start by the colonists themselves. All substantial Spanish American towns had *cabildos*, consisting fundamentally of six or more aldermen (*regidores*), and two first-instance magistrates (*alcaldes ordinares*). To these were usually added a variety of constables, jailers, standard bearers, clerks of the works, legal representatives, and inspectors (of weights and measures, and prices, for example). All were local men, and none received any wage from the crown. They were not, then, colonial bureaucrats, though they certainly had an administrative function.

Efforts have sometimes been made to present the colonial *cabildo* as a source of democratic practice in Spanish America; but the argument is sorely strained. Next to no record exists of the election by householders (much less by the whole city population) of aldermen. They were usually appointed by the viceroy or monarch; or, from the later sixteenth century on, tended to have bought their positions from the crown. *Alcaldes ordinarios* were co-opted annually from among householders (*vecinos*) by the aldermen; again there was no hint of popular election. Generally speaking, members of the council came from rich families with standing in local society. Its composition would change largely as distribution of wealth and status shifted.

To the extent that leading families' interests coincided with those of the whole, *cabildos* can be said to have represented their towns. Certainly they protested – to all levels of government, from the Council of the Indies to the local *corregidor* – against anything seen as bureaucratic interference, from the imposition of new taxes to the sending of inspectors to look into local government. Sometimes, by adroit politicking, they won their point. That apart, *cabildos* spent most of their time on internal matters: protecting town commons from incursions by neighboring communities, regulating prices, inspecting goods and food for quality, checking on sellers' weights and measures, maintaining streets, bridges, and public buildings (town hall, jail, parish church). Their scope was limited because generally they were poor. Their fund-raising capacity, from local fees and taxes, was limited by law. And much of their slight income tended to go on public acts, celebrating, for instance, the birth of a prince or the winning of a great victory. Ceremonial was a valued function of a *cabildo*. The office of standard bearer (*alférez real*) tended to command one of the highest prices once posts came to be sold.[41]

Finally, to the administrators of America (in descending order, monarch, councillor of the Indies, viceroy, *oidor, gobernador, corregidor, cabildo* member) must be added the taxman. The treasury official was generally the first royal agent to appear on the scene of any conquest, and thereafter remained ubiquitous. By 1600, at least forty-seven treasury offices were functioning in Spanish America,[42] placed in any major town where tax income was enough to warrant the bureaucratic expense. The royal fisc, or *real hacienda*, was therefore a large structure. It stood aside from the general administration, but was linked to it through the viceroy, who had a special charge to enforce revenue collection. A viceroy's performance, indeed, was measured partly by the size of remittances to Spain during his tenure.

Obvious candidates for a treasury office were ports (for customs duties and sales taxes), mining centers (for royalties on gold and silver), towns amid large native populations (for tribute), and capitals both provincial and viceregal (for assorted taxes). Each office had its *caja*, or strongbox, fitted with three locks. Each of the three principal officers at any branch (treasurer, accountant, and business manager) held a key to one of the locks. Many in the colonies experienced the personal attention of these *reales oficiales*, who were not men to be taken lightly, for they had the force of much law behind them, and their bureaucratic status was not far below that of high court judges. And few escaped indirect contact with them, for almost all were taxed in one way or another. Indians were liable for tribute; most purchases were subject to sales tax; imports and exports paid tariffs.

IMPERIAL MACHINERY IN MOTION

The Spanish American administration of the sixteenth century was a remarkable accomplishment. It had flaws, to be sure, some of which later became serious weaknesses. But, like the military conquests, though government's workings can be explained, its very achievement seems in the end little less than astonishing. By the late 1500s, the Spanish Indies were the largest overseas empire that Europeans had ever possessed. The entire area was governed by a salaried bureaucracy, in America and the Philippines, that cannot have numbered much over a thousand: viceroys, *oidores, gobernadores, reales oficiales, corregidores*, and supporting staff. Sceptics might well object that the intensity and effectiveness of that government were low; and that is quite true by the standards of today's advanced countries. But codes of law were in place and to some extent enforced. Crown prosecutors brought some offenders to trial. Awareness of the laws and the penalties for infringing them was widespread. Many native people had access to high courts, where salaried defenders of Indians sometimes represented them. Taxes and tariffs were collected; though, as anywhere and at any time, evasion was common. Roads and ports were built; coin was struck. As a result, trade flourished, linking regions economically that had been mutually unknown before. Information, as well as goods, flowed regularly and predictably from most of the Indies to Spain, and back again.

Above all, what impresses is that a continent-wide governing structure came into being where nothing comparable had ever existed before. To a degree, the offices and procedures used to create the structure drew on well-tried antecedents at home and in the Mediterranean. But much had to be adapted and invented to meet American challenges: unprecedented distances from Spain, and the resulting slowness of communication; vast and puzzling native populations, of widely varying cultural levels, not to mention languages; new seas, terrains, climates, soils, products. Whatever criticisms may be made of the administration's performance, great energy and creativity in setting it up must be granted to sixteenth-century Spain.

For such a system to function, a ranking of authorities and a clear chain of command were needed. The account given here of the administrative structure suggests that it was rigidly hierarchical; and so it was in some respects. Movement of personnel between ranks, for example, was rare. Because viceroys were generally nobles and men of worldly action ("of cape and sword," as the standard phrase had it), while *oidores* were mostly commoners and by definition lawyers, *oidores* did not become viceroys; the limit of their movement was promotion to an *audiencia* presidency, or to a more senior and central court. Similarly, *corregidores*, not generally being lawyers, did not become *oidores*.

But in its working, the system was far more flexible and adaptable than its fixity of structure might suggest. Communications did not have to pass upward, or downward, level by level. Town councils, for example, indeed private individuals, could and constantly did send their petitions and complaints to viceroys and even the monarch (meaning, in practice, the Council of the Indies). Beyond this, and more important, the governing structure was from the start a political as well as an administrative system. The play of rivalries between governmental entities, viceroys and *audiencias*, for instance, and even between individual bureaucrats, meant that issues were not always resolved in ways predictable by law, and that skilful players, both inside and outside the system, could manipulate government to their advantage.

It is hard to tell how far this politicking was intentionally built into government. Certainly, jurisdictions were often left imprecise: physical ones, such as the boundaries between *audiencias*; or operational ones, such as whether, in a provincial *audiencia*'s territory, the viceroy or the court's president held military authority. In some cases, such blurring resulted from ignorance in the Council of the Indies, the body that set these various limits in America. But the imprecisions were tolerated and often went unresolved for decades because they generated tensions in the machinery of American government that, while sometimes the cause of inefficiency, also made administrators mutually vigilant. The outcome was streams of reports back to Spain from contenders in these jurisdictional combats; they were often indignant and strident reports that overflowed the issue at stake to give other information useful to the Council. Officials at all levels knew, indeed, that they were expected to spy on their fellows, and should expect to be spied on. Private citizens of the colonies were quick, naturally enough, to turn this inbuilt rivalry to their own ends by allying themselves in various ways with the dominant bureaucrats of a particular moment, while sending back to Spain criticisms of others.

This spontaneous informing may well have been more valuable to the powers at court than the formal mechanisms ordained for checking on officials' performance and on broader conditions in America. For evaluating individuals, the *residencia* was the standard tool. It consisted of an inquiry by an incoming official into his predecessor's conduct. Criticisms were gathered from people subject to the man in question; he could then defend himself against charges lodged. Both sides could call witnesses, whose evidence was written down. In principle, all this created a continuous record of the performance of a particular office. In reality, not surprisingly, collusion between arriving and departing officials was often an irresistible temptation; and many *residencias* were simply never taken. Similarly, the *visita*, or inspection of general conditions in some region or institution, had inherent flaws that sapped its value. The inspectors, or *visitadores*, were generally named by the Council of the Indies. They were typically senior men, given powers to assume the functions of any officials they evaluated. The double task, of running normal administration while conducting a major inquiry, was too demanding in many cases, so that administration often became paralyzed, while the inspection was half-baked. The cure was thus sometimes worse than the sickness.

The informality and flexibility apparent in these methods of information gathering and internal regulation extended to other aspects of government. Though the councillors in Spain rained reams of precise rulings down on colonial governors, sometimes wasting time on absurd minutiae – a ban on the raising of chickens in coastal fortresses even made its way into the great summation, or *Recopilación*, of Indies law of 1681[43] – men on the ground in America had in reality much discretion to modify or ignore these orders. This is illustrated by the invariably quoted (though in fact rarely formally invoked) declaration available to viceroys faced with an impractical or unwelcome order: "Obedezco pero no cumplo" – "I obey but do not implement." This was, first, the system's acknowledgment that, given the immense space and time separating Spain·from America, home authorities simply could not always issue apposite orders. A deeper principle revealed here is that the monarch, whose prime task was to make justice available to all, could not be conceived to have intended an injustice; therefore any order likely to produce injustice must be modified, postponed, or ignored. The whole administration was shot through with a similar pliancy, inevitably so given the size of the empire, but not, obviously, without dangers of abuse.

Informality extended also to the naming of officials. It was often done by patronage. Many district *corregidores* were the friends or relations of viceroys, part of a retinue of dependants embarking with the great man on his journey to America and hoping to recoup costs and make profits in the few years of his tenure. Presidents and judges of *audiencias* had their lesser influence in placing dependants in their own courts and localities. Treasury officials and even *corregidores* could in practice select their assistants. Office holding was to a degree regarded precisely as a chance to reward or support dependants; and, of course, to benefit oneself. Officials, particularly the humbler ones, still tended in medieval fashion to see their positions as property, to be used first for their own gain. At the same time, though, with the sixteenth-century burgeoning of bureaucracy in Spain there came also a definite professionalization of the upper officialdom.[44] It is little surprise that viceroys such as Toledo and his contemporary in New Spain, Don Martín Enríquez, took their duties so seriously; they were, after all, noblemen with a sense of public responsibility, and resources of their own to boot. But it is impressive to see with what energy, interest, and initiative many *oidores* of the late 1500s attacked their judicial and administrative tasks.

This is one sign of the maturing of colonial administration in Spanish America. Indeed, the growth of the quality and quantity of officials in the middle decades of the sixteenth century signals the appearance of a genuine apparatus of state in the colonies: a machinery of government capable of imposing policies decided in Spain with a high (though never complete) effectiveness. Its largest and most obvious units were the two viceroyalties: New Spain, embracing Mexico, Central America (less Panama), the Caribbean (including Venezuela), and the Philippines; and Peru, covering all of

South America (less Venezuela, and Brazil, of course a Portuguese territory), and Panama.

The most authoritative expression of Spanish dominion in America and the Philippines, however, lay not in the viceroyalties but in the eleven *audiencias* created over the course of the century, most of them in the middle years. The close union in these courts of judicial and governing functions made them particularly good conductors of the monarchy's power. And the lesser size of the *audiencias'* territories, in comparison with the viceroyalties, made them the natural units of administration and law to which colonizers and colonized turned, and with which they identified themselves. The various *audiencias'* territories were, indeed, in the Habsburg polity, seen as separate realms – the "kingdom" of Quito, or of New Spain, for example – whose unity came not from being part of an empire or even of a viceroyalty, but solely from their subjection to the monarch. The monarch was the post to which all Spanish territories, whether in Spain, other parts of Europe, or elsewhere in the world, were moored. Only in their common connection to that mooring were they united. This discreteness increased the likelihood that colonizers of Chile, for example, would come to see themselves as Chileans first, and only second as citizens of the Viceroyalty of Peru or of an even larger and less tangible Spanish Empire in America.

Although some of them would soon work their way into the state machinery, the inhabitants of the American realms found it largely closed to them in the late 1500s. The only level of government open to them was the lowly one of the town councils, whose powers were small and local. Council members, further, were technically outside the state bureaucracy, since the treasury paid them no salary. This scanty role in administration for colonizers and colonized was matched by a similar lack of political representation. All, it is true, could, and a surprising number did, send petitions directly to *audiencias*, viceroys, or even the Council of the Indies. But no channel existed for sounding a collective voice. Spanish Americans had no place in the Cortes, or parliaments, of the peninsula (except for the briefest moment early in the nineteenth century); much less any formal assemblies of their own.

On balance, in fact, the first century of Spanish government in America is striking for its success in excluding dwellers in the colonies from administrative and political influence; particularly so when the immense powers and potential wealth given Columbus and later explorers and conquerors are recalled, along with the large part played by individual, rather than state, enterprise in the winning of Spanish America. The crown's path to control was far from even or straight. But by the use and exacerbation of factionalism among conquerors, by the relentless showering of law on to the new realms, by the gradual adaptation of known administrative forms to new places and conditions, by the creation of a new, paper-based, bureaucracy, the monarchy's will was made to prevail by the 1560s, at least in the rich, populous and hence important areas. The resultant governing system was markedly authoritarian in design. Most of the early flickerings that can be glimpsed of representative process were doused.[45] Especially telling for Spanish American politics in the long term was the intentional combining in all levels of officialdom of executive, legislative, and judicial powers. Not all officials held equal balances of these powers, of course; viceroys were rarely fully qualified judges; *corregidores* could legislate only locally. But minimal effort was made to separate powers. Indeed, to do so would have been foolish given the need to create order. And beyond, or beneath, this practical aim lay perhaps a deeper concept of the nature and purpose of government – one deriving from Aquinas's view that the key purpose of kingship was to maximize the common good of the multitude.[46] This implied both a downplaying of individuals' rights and a concentrating of authority for a good and beneficent ordering of the whole.

Whatever the motives, theoretical or practical, for bringing together governing powers, a good case can be made for saying that success in that process made Spanish America more closely and intensively administered in the late sixteenth century than at any other time in the colonial centuries, with the possible exception of the late 1700s. (During a long middle period of the empire, government's hold loosened, for a variety of reasons to be seen.) Bureaucratic domination was one remarkable achievement of Spain's first century in America. But bureaucracy, of course, played mostly on the practical surface of the lives of colonists and colonized. A more subtle, more profound attempt at domination proceeded in mutual reinforcement with administration: that of religious belief. The story of Spanish Catholicism's implantation in America cannot properly be separated from that of colonial government's beginnings.

[8] CHURCH: FRIARS, BISHOPS, AND THE STATE

CHURCH AND STATE

Columbus's three ships of 1492 carried no priest. It was a curious omission even for a voyage of pure exploration, given the admiral's already apparent religiosity. There can, however, scarcely have been a later Spanish fleet or flotilla bound for America that lacked a cleric. Certainly the colonizing expedition of 1493 had its ecclesiastical complement: a Benedictine, a Jeronymite, and three Franciscans.[1] Nonetheless, in the first, turbulent decade or more of colonization in the islands, the church remained unremarkable for its numbers or its actions. Then in 1510–11, with the arrival in Hispaniola of Dominicans and a new group of Franciscans, it began to stir busily. The evangelizing of America by mendicant friars, the noblest aspect of Spain's entire imperial exercise, suddenly sprang into motion. If there was an awakening call, it was the Dominican Montesinos's excoriation of the citizens of Santo Domingo in his Advent sermon of 1511.

Though many friars saw the task of christianizing America as a personal challenge, and set about it as zealous individuals, in their labors they were inevitably agents of the Spanish state, collaborators with the rising bureaucracy in bringing the Indies into Spanish control. Though particular instances of conflict between church and state were legion, broadly speaking the two were linked in America in purpose, organization, and operation to a degree rarely matched in Christian history. The prime reason for this was the existence of royal patronage, or *real patronato*, of the Spanish American church.

Ferdinand's reluctance to see the church expand in the Caribbean before Rome had given him wide powers over it was one reason for its early feebleness. To his gratification, the concessions soon came. They extended a series of papal pronouncements inspired by earlier Spanish and Portuguese expansion, starting with bulls in the 1450s that granted legitimacy of occupation of Atlantic island groups, while raising questions about the conversion of the islanders.[2] Best known of all, and basic to Spain's entire imperial scheme, was *Inter caetera*, issued in May 1493, very soon after Columbus's return from the first voyage. In it Alexander VI in essence ceded the crown full and perpetual dominion in America in return for an undertaking to bring its peoples into the faith: a bargain of which Spanish monarchs remained long, if intermittently, conscious. Rome soon followed with grants of control over the ecclesiastical forces needed to achieve this conversion. In 1501 Alexander bestowed on the crown the church tithes from America, so that there should be money to fund evangelization. Then, in 1508, Julius II, in *Universalis ecclesiae*, gave Ferdinand and his successors the right to present to Rome candidates, from archbishops downward, for church posts in the Indies (with the understanding that one of the monarch's nominees would be chosen). Further, the crown was to have control over the building and endowment of cathedrals, churches, monasteries, and hospitals; tithe income was to be used for that purpose. Yet again, it might control the movement of all churchmen to America. (Those approved had their passages paid by the royal treasury.) Finally, in 1538, the crown successfully claimed the right of inspection, with power of veto (the *pase regio*), of all papal dispatches to America.[3] In practice, the Council of the Indies exercised this vigilance, and from its creation in 1524 ran the entire machinery of the *patronato*.

Rome's concession of powers was phenomenal, approached elsewhere only in a grant of patronage made to Ferdinand and Isabella for Granada and the Canaries in 1486. In Spain (except for Granada) Rome retained much influence in the appointment of clergy until the mid-eighteenth century. Part of the reason for its delivery of the American church to the Spanish crown was precisely that the Indies were a challenge of evangelization on a scale that Rome could not itself meet. The task had to be delegated; *patronato* was the cost of doing so. Again, Alexander VI owed political debts to Ferdinand and Isabella; and he and later popes could scarcely ignore Spain's political power in Italy, made absolutely clear in the sack of Rome in 1526.

The *real patronato* bound state and church in the Indies into a single entity. Notions of church–state separation, of course, were scarcely conceivable in the Spain of the time; but the intertwining of the two (with the state always having the upper hand) was truly something original and unique to Spanish America. Once the crown gained its powers of nomination (in reality, of appointment), the American church establishment grew fast. Ferdinand sent Dominicans to Hispaniola in 1510; the number of Franciscans there rose rapidly soon after; and friars of both orders began to spread across the Caribbean. Cortés had priests with him in the Aztec conquest, both regulars (members of orders) and seculars (those not belonging to orders, but subject to bishops). And in the immediately following years others, mainly Franciscans, came to New Spain. Cortés, suspecting a potential for ostentation and wealth-seeking in the secular church, sought as governor to attract friars to evangelize his domain.[4] Particularly remembered among these are the band of Franciscans who came at his invitation in 1524. In imitation of the Apostles, they were twelve in number, as were other and later groups of missionaries, and as had been also St Francis's first band of followers. It is related that after these men had walked up from the Gulf coast, Cortés, kneeling, greeted them at their entrance to México-Tenochtitlan by kissing the robe of their leader, Fray Martín de Valencia. The gesture reflected, perhaps, his own piety; but it also directly signaled to onlooking Spaniards and Indians with what respect he intended the church to be regarded in New Spain. If the conqueror and governor abased himself before barefooted and dusty clerics, how much more should lesser men heed them.

Cortés's objections to church hierarchy notwithstanding, New Spain soon had bishops. In 1520, even before the Aztec conquest was done, Charles V had decided that the territory merited a bishopric. He named it, presumably for lack of information about Mexican places, simply "Carola."[5] In the event, the first see was not formally created until 1526, and was placed at Tlaxcala. But México-Tenochtitlan clearly could not be left long without a bishop. In 1527, Charles V presented to Rome his nomination for that prelacy, a Franciscan named Fray Juan de Zumárraga. Such was the *patronato*'s authority that Zumárraga was in place in New Spain and taking energetic action against the malfeasances of the first *audiencia* at least a year before his diocese was formally created, in 1530. The crown quickly set up other sees as the Spaniards occupied Mexico: Oaxaca (1534), Michoacán (1536), and Guadalajara, or New Galicia (1548). Late in 1547, México-Tenochtitlan was declared a metropolitan diocese, so that Zumárraga was briefly archbishop before his death in 1548.

Elsewhere on the mainland, bishoprics were created with similar alacrity, following closely on Spanish movement into particular regions and the first budding of bureaucracy in them. The very first mainland see was not in Mexico but on the Isthmus of Panama, at Darien in 1513. Then came the first two Mexican foundations; and soon after them Guatemala, Nicaragua, and Honduras in 1530–1. Cuzco was the earliest Peruvian diocese (1537). Lima followed (1541, then raised to metropolitan status, like México-Tenochtitlan, in 1547). Cities with *audiencias* rapidly became the seats of bishops; and so did various lesser provincial capitals. Of the forty-five dioceses created in the entire colonial era, twenty-two were set up before 1550, and only fourteen after 1600; and among those fourteen, only one (Buenos Aires, a see from 1620) was a notable administrative center of the church.[6] As with other sorts of organization of Spanish America, the sixteenth century saw the structure of the colonial church definitively assembled; and much of it was in place before 1550.

Bishops must have their cathedrals, built in the Spanish colonies with the tithe income that the *patronato* conveyed to the monarchy. They were, initially, small and simple buildings, though by mid-century the foundations of imposing edifices still standing today were being laid. Cathedrals necessarily had their clerical staffs of deans, archdeacons, canons, and lesser prebendaries. These, like other bureaucracies, started small but grew irresistibly. Evangelization, however, which was the prime task of the church in America, and one of the central purposes of Spanish colonizing, was rarely undertaken by cathedral chapters. It was mainly the work of the front-line troops of the ecclesiastical army: the priests in the *doctrinas*, or rural parishes.

REGULARS AS MISSIONARIES

Parish priests, in Spain and elsewhere in Europe, were usually secular clergymen. And given the Spanish crown's obvious keenness to set up an episcopal church in America – a well-tried hierarchical chain of command of archbishops, bishops, cathedral chapters, and local priests – seculars might well have been chosen as the true faith's trench warriors to battle America's indigenous paganism. But the young Charles V found his new kingdom's secular clergy slack in behavior and intellect. By contrast, at least portions of Spain's regular priesthood had been energized in mind and spirit by the reforms of the Catholic Monarchs and their indefatigable minister, Archbishop Jiménez de Cisneros. Hence Charles applied to Pope Adrian VI, earlier his adviser and then regent in Castile, to allow regulars, and above all Franciscans from the Observant, or stricter, part of the order, to form the evangelizing force that mainland America demanded. Permission came in the papal letter *Omnimoda* of May 1522. There Adrian also gave the regulars' leaders in America great independence of existing and future bishops, and authority in their mission regions even over the secular clerics.[7]

Thus in the early 1520s not only was the somewhat *ad hoc* evangelizing that friars had earlier performed in and around the Caribbean given Rome's formal blessing, but the door to the mission stage was flung open and mendicant brothers were urged to pass through it. So came to New Spain in 1524 the apostolic Franciscan twelve, soon to be followed by others of their order, then by Dominicans (from 1526 on) and Augustinians (from 1533). Franciscans reached Peru with the conquest, expanding from there to Quito (1535) and to other parts of South America in the mid-century. Dominicans and Augustinians followed close on their tracks. A group of twelve Mercedarians entered New Spain in 1530; but friars of this order found greater space for evangelization in South America. The last major order to send men to Spanish America in the sixteenth century was the Society of Jesus, founded by the Spanish saint, Ignatius of Loyola, in 1534. The first Jesuits reached Lima in 1568 and New Spain in 1572. Most of their highly distinctive missions in remote parts of the Indies were, however, seventeenth-century creations.[8]

The friars were thinly spread over the immense task of conversion they had undertaken. In 1559 there resided in New Spain, for example, only 380 Franciscans, 212 Augustinians, and 210 Dominicans; and among these were many (lay brethren, novices, administrators, the infirm) not active in the field.[9] By the early eighteenth century, the number of Friars Minor in the entire American empire stood at some 5,000. A century later it had risen to about 6,000, roughly a half of all regulars in Spanish America.[10] The Franciscans were always the largest contingent of regulars in the colonies, as they were in Spain itself in the sixteenth century.

The Franciscans of the conquest period were impelled not solely by some charitable desire to convert the pagan, but also by the urgent biddings of a millenarian utopianism they had inherited from the middle ages.[11] They saw themselves as central actors in the final conversion of the Gentiles to Christ. Once that task (and the conversion of Jews and Muslims also) was accomplished, so apocalyptic tradition rooted in the Book of Revelations proclaimed, there would begin a thousand-year period of blessedness on earth, preceded, or perhaps followed, by the second coming of Christ. To this line of belief many Franciscans were drawn from the very foundation of their order in the early thirteenth century. Among those who later found it compelling were some of the dozen Franciscans who arrived in New Spain in 1524. Their order had been the subject of most intense spiritualizing reform in early sixteenth-century Spain, and they were among the products of that effort. One of the twelve, Fray Toribio de Benavente, recorded that their leader, Fray Martín de Valencia, on contemplating the question of converting the heathen, asked himself: "When will this be? When will this prophecy be fulfilled? Shall I perhaps be worthy to witness this conversion? For we are now at the evening and the end of our days and in the last age of the world."[12]

Driven by this sense of the end's imminence, and of their role in bringing it to pass, the Franciscans in New Spain set furiously about the work of conversion. They gave themselves to learning native languages in order to preach, studying native religion so as to know what was to be overcome, enquiring into native history in an effort to place their charges on the cultural map of humankind, founding schools to impress faith and European civility on the sons of native leaders (in the hope that the lessons would filter down to their subjects), designing and building churches, traveling, catechizing, baptizing. By 1533, the Franciscans estimated that they had baptized 1,200,000 native people in New Spain; and 5,000,000 by 1536, when they themselves numbered perhaps sixty. Clearly, little teaching preceded baptism. Dominicans and Augustinians objected strongly to the Franciscans' wholesale approach to baptism – holy water applied from a jar to thousands of heads per day.[13] But baptism was the sacrament that brought admittance to the church; and that was the urgent and overriding goal.

The effort truly verged on the superhuman. The Franciscan who late in the sixteenth century recorded the deeds of his brethren in New Spain, Fray Gerónimo de Mendieta, wrote

> In Spain we know it for a common thing that when priests have to preach a sermon they are so tired and in such a sweat that they have to change their clothes . . . And if after he had preached, a priest were told to sing a Mass or comfort a sick man or bury a dead one, he would think it the same as digging his own grave. But in this land it happened every day that one lone friar would count the people in the morning, then preach to them and sing Mass, and after that baptize both children and adults, confess the sick no matter how many, and then bury any dead there might be. And so it was for thirty or forty years, and in some places so it is still.[14]

Singly, or more typically in pairs, Franciscans fanned out over central Mexico, then the west, and the north, where late in the sixteenth century they contributed much to the pacification of the Chichimeca, and in the seventeenth became the sole order active in New Mexico. But towns offered challenges of conversion, too; and in them, above all in México-Tenochtitlan, Franciscans distinguished themselves in native education. In this the model was Fray Pedro de Gante, a highly educated product of the Flemish Renaissance who arrived in New Spain as a Franciscan lay-brother in 1523. He immediately set up a school, though not in Tenochtitlan, which was being rebuilt after its razing in 1521, but east across the lake at Texcoco. Its first pupils were the Texcocan nobility, many of whom were baptized once the twelve friars of 1524 had arrived. In 1526 Gante moved his school to the resurgent capital, opening it now to native boys of all social ranks; as it remained, under his direction, till his death in 1572. His aim was primary education in the catechism, reading, writing, numbers, and singing. All teaching was in Nahuatl, which Gante quickly learned to speak, and then, among the first to do so, wrote down in Latin letters. He used plays, pageants and music to convey Christian teachings. Thus, European music and musical instruments of the time were grafted on to the native musical tradition. Later a craft school was added to the establishment, where, again, European practice came to blend with native skill in, for example, stoneworking and tailoring.

Gante's school demonstrated and confirmed the Franciscans' early confidence, soon to be shared by the other orders, in native Mexicans' intellectual and artistic capacities. This assurance appeared again in their foundation of a college of secondary and higher learning for Indians in Tlatelolco, the northern section of the capital. It was opened on January 6, 1536, the feast of the Epiphany, and a day traditionally linked to the manifestation of Christ to the Gentiles (personified in the Magi). Over this symbolic ceremony presided Viceroy Mendoza, attended by Bishop Zumárraga and the President of the *Audiencia* of New Spain.[15]

The Tlatelolco college was designed for sons of the native nobility from all parts of New Spain. In it the Franciscans hoped to form a Europeanized native leadership capable of serving as a wedge between Indian society as a whole and the colonizing Spaniards. Only in such separation did the friars see a chance of preserving the native population in physical and spiritual safety. Other orders shared this view. The regime imposed on the boys in the college must have had the friars' own training as its model: sleeping in a large dormitory, rising at dawn, communal eating, regular church attendance, a curriculum of reading, writing, music, Latin, rhetoric, logic, philosophy, and – here a New World innovation – native medicine. No Spanish was spoken; only Latin and Nahuatl. From all this at least some remarkable native scholars emerged, skilled Latinists and translators of Nahuatl who collaborated crucially with the friars in putting Christianity into native terms, and in creating the great compilations on Mexican history and culture that are the most enduring legacy of the early Franciscans in New Spain.

The Tlatelolco college flourished, however, for only a decade or two. It was worn away by a strengthening current of anti-native sentiment among colonials, a current combining several streams: fears that Indians were incorrigible heretics, that to educate them would simply make their heresy more dangerous, and that it would also lift them out of the servile position to which ever more settlers wished to consign them. More telling, though, than even these misgivings was the objection to indigenous Christian priests, whom the Franciscans had particularly hoped to train at Tlatelolco. Rome was not against a native Catholic priesthood; but it was a notion that most of the colonial church and population could not stomach. Until very late in colonial times no Indian priests were to appear in New Spain, or, indeed, anywhere else in Spanish America. And underlying all specific objections to the Franciscans' efforts at Tlatelolco, and similar efforts by them and other orders elsewhere, was doubtless, by the mid-sixteenth century, the growing disdain of Indians felt by a colonial society that contained ever fewer members who had seen native culture in something like its pre-conquest splendour. As that vision faded, native survivors of the conquest found the horizons of their existence – social, political, economic – relentlessly shrinking.

The other orders early established in New Spain rivalled, if they did not quite match, the Franciscans in efforts of evangelization and Indian education. Schools were often attached to the monasteries that sprung up as the friars spread out in all directions from the center of the colony. In the South American colonies the Franciscan primacy is less clear. There were Franciscans, Dominicans, and Mercedarians in Peru in the opening year of the conquest, 1532; after then, the Dominicans were perhaps the quickest to increase numbers and extend their ministry.[16] The Jesuits, once they arrived in Spanish America *c.*1570, entered the fray with an energy befitting the youth of their society. Seeing, though, that primary teaching was already well attended to, they immediately applied themselves to higher education; and, similarly, finding no lack of missionaries and parish priests in the colonial heartlands, decided to take the word to the frontiers. In the western Sierra Madre in Mexico, the inner slopes of the Andes, the western fringes of Amazonia, and Paraguay, they became the prime evangelists, and so remained for two centuries.

THE REGULARS RESTRAINED

Not all was sweetness and light on the mission front, of course. Zeal could easily tilt into fanaticism, especially in men isolated from their religious brethren, not to mention from settler society as a whole. In 1562 the small band of Franciscans working to convert the Maya of northern Yucatan fell into the rage of disappointment when they discovered idol-worship among those they thought they had christianized. In an effort to eliminate all such backsliding, they hoisted suspects up with cords around their wrists to extract confessions about the numbers and sites of idols. Such use of torture was not merely immoral, but illegal; only secular government could apply it.[17] There was, alas, ample precedent in earlier church behavior in the Valley of Mexico. There had occurred, for example, the notorious case of Don Carlos Chichimecatecuhtli. He, a nobleman of Texcoco and a product of Franciscan education, had been found guilty of keeping idols in his house and publicly defaming Christianity. After an investigation led by Bishop Zumárraga, himself a Franciscan and on that account doubly incensed, Don Carlos was garrotted and burned in 1539.[18] This was extraordinary punishment. An offender of Don Carlos's rank must be made an example. To apostates of lesser social and political prominence in the Valley, the Franciscans meted out beatings and perhaps a spell in private jails that the order had built.[19]

If the friars could slip from their ideals in their treatment of their converts, they were prey also to conflicts among themselves. The orders squabbled over mission territory, over methods of proselytism, and over matters of public policy, such as the pros and cons of the *encomienda*. They were subject, also, to a creeping worldliness; it would have been miraculous if they had not been. By the mid-sixteenth century they were beginning to own property, in the form of land and houses, notably in New Spain. This was not through conscious acquisitiveness, for poverty and asceticism were still firmly rooted in most mendicants' minds, but more the outcome of gifts and bequests, some from conquerors and early settlers anxious to salve their consciences as they aged and died. Not that wealth was without its proper uses; it allowed, for instance, for more ambitious building of churches, and for some incipient richness of interior decoration. The Augustinians, in particular, thought it fitting to glorify the Lord with gold and plasterwork in the roofs of their mission churches. Late in the century, lofty and elaborate altarpieces appeared in churches even in native towns. Indeed, it was particularly fitting that they should be in those churches, for such reredoses, often incorporating statues of saints and church Fathers, along with paintings of biblical scenes, were not mere decoration, but illustrations on which preachers could draw.

Wealth, then, the friars could find good use for, even though they might not pursue it. What they did pursue, and what eventually brought charges of worldliness heavily down on them, was a political role in America. Their concern with Indians' well-being put them in the thick of politics almost from the start; again, Montesinos's sermon of 1511 was the signal event. The separation they aimed to create between natives and secular settlers was a threat to labor supply, and hence a threat also to both individuals' income and the state's taxes.

Nonetheless, for several decades the friars had the monarchy's backing. Christianization was at the heart of Spain's purpose in America; and, at a more practical level, the orders provided a useful counterweight to the *encomenderos*, who were, until the mid-century, a far more potent political challenge to the crown than a thin scattering of mendicants. Then, however, the royal view of them grew slowly jaundiced. With the *encomenderos* weakened by legislation and events of the 1540s, and the American bureaucracy gaining strength and reach, the friars' ministry to the Indians began to seem a usurpation of royal powers. Especially irritating was their assumption of jurisdiction (the right to try, judge, and punish Indians for civil as well as religious offences) in their *doctrinas*. This was an intolerable intrusion into the Spanish monarchy's supreme function. The growth of royal disillusion coincided with the deliberating of the Council of Trent (1545–64), one of whose central themes, within its broad effort to stiffen Catholicism's resistance to the encroaching Protestant Reformation, was the subjection of the entire priesthood to the authority of bishops. This aim of reinforcing the church's backbone – that is, the hierarchy extending down from Pope, through bishops, to parish priests – found a welcome in the Spain of the young Philip II. Although the *Patronato* in principle gave Spanish rulers authority over the regular as well as the secular clergy, the regulars' traditional autonomy as self-contained bodies within the church made them in practice less easy to influence. The prospect of their now being placed squarely under the episcopal thumb was a heartening one for a Spanish monarchy irritated, if not alarmed, by the growth of friars' influence over its native American subjects.

Philip II and his advisers were, then, in the 1560s distinctly inclined to rein in the regulars. The king's concerns and intentions were clearly expressed in the instructions given late in 1568 to the newly appointed viceroy of Peru, Don Francisco de Toledo. Philip wished the orders (Franciscans, Dominicans, and Augustinians) to be favored: they had, he said, been of great effect in the evangelization and conversion of the Indians. They had, though, resisted the authority of the bishops in Peru. Some of them, as individuals, had gathered personal property, and had even returned to Spain with money. Such acquisitiveness contravened canon law, the constitutions of their orders, and their own vows. They had tended to build their monasteries in fertile and comfortable places, leaving less appealing areas unevangelized. They were reported to have claimed secular jurisdiction in civil and criminal cases in the districts of their monasteries. They had, further, under the pretext of defending the Indians, interfered in matters of justice and executive government (*gobierno*), "seeking to meddle in [affairs of] law and sovereignty of the Indies, and other things that lead to much commotion, especially when they speak of these things from pulpits and in other congregations and pronouncements."[20]

The regulars, then, had done a good job; but not as good or as complete as it should have been. More parishes, the king pronounced, were needed in Peru. Toledo should create them, in consultation with the bishops and with the archbishop of Lima. These parishes would need curates; but there were too few secular priests available to man them. Since, therefore, the regulars were well used to parish work, they might continue to serve as parish priests. But they should no longer be appointed by their order or monastery, but be nominated by the bishops, for later presentation (to Rome) by the king. Once in place in their parishes, the friars should be subject to visitation and discipline by the bishops (something the orders had adamantly rejected before).

The king proposed also a concentration of the regulars in the major towns, in the sense that large, central monasteries should be set up there, to function partly as training schools in native affairs and languages. From these urban bases, friars should go out as parish priests to small houses in the country. Toledo was to consider reducing the existing number of big provincial monasteries, which were the cause of "certain disadvantages of much consideration."[21] Philip's discomfort here was probably the thought of large bodies of friars living far from the viceregal eye.

Regulars, then, might continue to do what they had done since the conquest: instruct and convert Indians in their villages across Peru. The monarchy was grateful for past efforts. But their freedom to convert where, when, and how they pleased was now curbed by a king who found their autonomy threatening, presumptuous, and conducive to slackness. They must now submit to the king's will. Regulars in parishes were, in effect, to be appointed by him (or, in practice, by his viceroy), since the bishops who were to nominate them were themselves, through the operation of the *Patronato*, the king's men. The bishops would, likewise, be well placed to oversee the friars' new and enlarged houses in the principal towns. One prominent strand running through Philip's orders to Toledo on these church matters, in fact, is a reinforcement of the bishops' authority. In making that emphasis, the king both heeded Trent's resolutions and strengthened their implementation. He strengthened also, of course, his own directive role in the church's life in America.

The changes that Philip entrusted to Toledo for Peru in 1568 were generalized over the Indies by the *Ordenanza del Patronazgo*, or Ordinance of Patronage, of 1574. Here the king drew into one code many earlier orders bearing on royal control of the American church, with the aim of reinforcing his authority. Again, subjection of regulars to the bishops, and their replacement in parish work by seculars, were two of the main means chosen for achieving that end. Still, the secular-versus-regular issue was by no means closed in 1574. Such was the moral and political weight of the orders in Rome, Spain, and America, and such the momentum of their evangelizing in the Indies, that they managed to sustain their pastoral role for many a year. Even so late as the mid-eighteenth century, in so central an area as the Valley of Mexico, friars tended to a large majority (fifty-nine of seventy-two) of parishes.[22] The final ousting of the regulars from these, and their replacement by seculars, came only *c*.1770, as the effect of a far deeper sort of secularization than anything the Spanish world had previously felt. That was the reformism of the Spanish Bourbons, inspired by a centralizing regalism typical of the eighteenth century. Driven by that modern impulse, the monarchy took a degree of control over the entire American church that exceeded Philip II's fondest imaginings.

Nonetheless, Philip's campaign against the orders in the 1560s and 1570s, though it left friars in parishes, had had its intended effect. It had changed the terms on which the regulars worked and existed in the Indies, just as the anti-*encomienda* laws of the 1540s, though finally allowing *encomenderos* to stay in place, had changed the conditions of their existence by denying them free access to Indian labor and subjecting them to the crown's goodwill for extension of the grants. Both groups lost the immense freedom of action they had enjoyed in the early decades; both found themselves far more dependent than before, for their continued activity, on royal benevolence. This said, it might seem contradictory that, even after the 1570s, many regulars appeared as bishops in the Indies. In the first half of the seventeenth century, indeed, slightly more than half (146 of 257) of the men named to and holding bishoprics in America and the Philippines were regular priests.[23] But since, through the *Patronato*, Spanish rulers completely controlled the appointment of bishops, the placing of friars (mostly Dominicans and Augustinians) in sees both indebted the orders to the crown and gave the government a direct access to the regulars' affairs in America that otherwise it would have lacked. By making friars senior members of the episcopal hierarchy in the Indies, the crown thus tied the American church closer to government. And in reality the entire process of the curbing of the orders' independence in the 1560s and 1570s was another part of that solidifying of the Spanish state in America pursued for two or three decades past. The change was a part of what led

Gerónimo de Mendieta, an apocalyptical Franciscan historian of his order's deeds in sixteenth-century New Spain, to pronounce the reign of Philip II to be the Silver Age of the American church, in contrast to the Golden Age of Charles V.[24]

Another block laid in place in the state-building process of these years in America was the Inquisition. Bishops had in fact been energetically active as inquisitors in the Indies since shortly before 1520, and special papal dispensation had been given to regulars, as with parish work, to carry out inquisitorial functions. These generally aimed to promote religious orthodoxy. Indians being converted were an obvious source of concern, and indeed many were investigated and some even executed for backsliding into paganism. Blasphemy among Spaniards was another worry. The contention popular in Spain, for example, that frequenting prostitutes was a venial, not a mortal, sin (especially if one paid), had its adherents in America, and for such errors the early Inquisition pulled people in. But there were as yet in America few suspected judaizers, or foreigners perhaps carrying some virus of Protestantism; so the episcopal inquisition was an *ad hoc*, erratic affair.

As the Counter-Reformation gathered force, however, and the call for church discipline came loudly from Trent, and as the American administrative bureaucracy grew and strengthened, a parallel extension to the colonies of the inquisitorial machinery of Spain seemed useful. In 1565 Philip II ordered tribunals of the Holy Office to be set up in America; the personnel were in place in Lima in 1570 and in Mexico City in 1571. Indians were now exempted from the Inquisition's attentions. Vigilance over their faith was left to the bishops, who were, however, no longer inquisitors. But the rest of the colonial population, Spanish or mixed-blooded, and, of course, any of the Protestant corsairs and privateers now prowling the Spanish American coasts in growing numbers who happened to fall into Spanish hands, were grist to the inquisitorial mill. The political effect of the system, though, was just as important as its doctrinal role. For the king controlled the appointment of inquisitors in America, just as in Spain, and the Supreme Council of the Inquisition sat at court, under the royal eye. Thus this new American bureaucracy, on the borderline between church and state, gave the monarchy another conduit by which to send commands to the colonies and gather information from them. Inquisitors, prosecutors, and scribes were in the viceregal capitals, close to viceroys, *audiencias*, treasury officers, and the upper church hierarchy. The Inquisition's local agents, or familiars, were scattered through provincial towns. They were on the look out for not only religious, but also political, heresy.[25]

EVANGELIZERS AND OBSERVERS OF INDIANS

The christianizing of Spanish America clearly required an organized evangelical force; and this, despite contention among regulars, seculars, and monarchy, was what Spain provided. All saw, however, that conversion would be surer and quicker the better the targets of the campaign were known. Thus Indians became the objects of close study of a broadly anthropological sort.

The best placed to carry this out were the missionary friars, as the largest group of Europeans in close contact with Indians. The friars were also the majority of educated Europeans in America. Many of them had had university training in ancient languages and philosophy. Some were humanists in the best and full Renaissance sense of the term: men keen to recover and update the wisdom of classical European culture, integrating it with Christian belief. For some such men, study of native culture and language became something to be pursued not only to promote conversion, but for its intrinsic fascination.

So many were the missionaries who strove to understand and record native affairs that a sampling of the more remarkable of them must suffice here. Brief recognition should first go again to Antonio de Montesinos, not because he is the source of much information about the Caribbean peoples, but because in his sermon of December 1511 he raised a crucial question about native Americans that became the topic of stormy argument for decades after. "Are these not men?" he asked his indignant congregation in Santo Domingo. "Have they not rational souls?" The degree of Indians' rationality – or, conversely, the degree and nature of their barbarism – soon became of intense concern not only to ecclesiastics seeking the most effective methods of conversion, but also to administrators and political theorists trying to decide how native people should be treated, and even what rights Spain had in America to occupy land, seize property, and dispose of its peoples' lives.

Settlement of the mainland raised such questions to new levels of dispute, since, while the size and complexity of political organization of the great states, their elegant cities, their high craftsmanship, and so forth argued for rationality and civility, proponents of barbarism could support their view with such contradictions of advance as absence of writing, and Aztec predilection for human sacrifice. One who clearly never much doubted the rationality of central Mexicans was Pedro de Gante. His schools in Texcoco and Tenochtitlan showed from earliest post-conquest times, through the most practical of demonstrations, that young native children could learn precisely as Europeans did. Later Franciscan schooling at Tlatelolco and elsewhere simply confirmed this.

A similar confidence in native Mexicans' capacities, though not precisely in their rationality, appears in Vasco de Quiroga, one the most effective pro-Indian activists of the sixteenth century. He came to New Spain as a judge in the reforming second *audiencia* created in 1530. The first and deepest impression that the Indians left on him was of their poverty and their defenselessness against the demands and maltreatment of Spanish settlers. Quiroga, who was a remarkable blend of idealism and practicality (the first energizing the second), decided quickly that a new type of native township was needed for the Indians' economic and general protection. This he called an *hospital*. The term implied refuge, broadly speaking; though a place for treating the sick was certainly a part of it. Workshops for native craftsmen were also to be a part of the community, as well as common land for communal farming. Government should be by native leaders elected by the families making up the population, under the supervision of a Spanish official. A Christian priest should oversee the religious life of the village. Particularly striking about Quiroga's *hospital* plans was that they were consciously modeled on Sir Thomas More's *Utopia*. That work, of 1516, had itself been inspired by the American discoveries of the early sixteenth century.[26]

Quiroga founded his first *hospital* near Mexico City in 1532, naming it Santa Fe de los Altos. A second, Santa Fe de la Laguna, followed in Michoacán after Quiroga completed an inspection of that western region in 1533. In 1538 he became the first occupant of the see of Michoacán, receiving simultaneous ordination and consecration from Bishop Zumárraga of México-Tenochtitlan. From then until his death at a great age in 1565 he strove to protect the bodies and souls of the Indians of Michoacán, where, it is said, his memory lives on. He created his most ambitious *hospital* town on the southern shore of Lake Pátzcuaro, intending it to become the City of Michoacán, the capital of the region, and the site of a great five-naved, star-shaped cathedral.[27] But the church was too large to be made; and the hostility aroused in settlers and also in Viceroy Mendoza by his strategy of protecting Indians through segregation brought the choice of Valladolid (now Morelia) as capital. Quiroga also set up in existing native towns of his bishopric eighty-eight hospitals of a lesser sort: single buildings comprising a chapel, a space for treatment of the sick, and another for the use of the town's native government.[28] These hospitals were to be run wholly by Indians, and so conformed to Quiroga's intent to strengthen native defenses against Spanish inroads of all sorts.

Quiroga clearly saw central Mexicans as rational enough to run their own local government, in a colonial setting, under broad supervision from Spanish officials and priests. It was not, though, so much their intellect that drew him as their psyche. They seemed to him simple, humble, malleable; and perfectible. In 1535 he compared their pre-conquest existence to life in the mythical Golden Age of the Kingdom of Saturn. In both he found "the same customs and manners, the same equality, simplicity, goodness, obedience, humility, festivities, games, pleasures, drinking, idling, pastimes, nudity and lack of any but the poorest of household goods and of any desire for better."[29] (Quiroga limited his attention to the common people; neither Aztec nobles nor the many local *caciques* who survived the Conquest could possibly have inspired such an assessment.) The Spaniards' restlessness, ambition, and cupidity left Indians astonished. In the right surroundings, which Quiroga thought would be native towns of 6,000 families, Indians would govern themselves well and convert easily to Christianity. He hoped that, in the New World, mass conversion of native people could recreate the early Christian church in its pristine purity.[30] No such thing was possible. But Vasco de Quiroga, with his potent blend of idealism, practicality, political skill, and determination, came closer to replicating it, in his diocese of Michoacán, than any other sixteenth-century reformer in Spanish America.

In the 1530s, when Quiroga began his work in Mexico, debate about the nature of Indians and related political questions reached new levels of intensity and sophistication in Spain itself. Few years had passed without dispute of this sort since serious consideration began of Indian treatment with the drafting of the Burgos Laws in 1512. One continuous thread in the discussion was the notion that Indians were "natural" slaves. An early and influential exponent of this view was Juan López de Palacios Rubios, a lawyer but not a cleric, who in 1513 wrote of the Caribbean natives as simple primitives, living as gentle barbarians in harmony with nature. In this he seems to prefigure Quiroga. But the conclusions he drew from that diagnosis were very different. Caribbean people were free while they were isolated. But contact with civilized men, such as the Spanish, revealed a disparity of human status that relegated Indians to the service of their "natural" masters.[31]

These notions of "natural" slavery and mastery came from Aristotle. They received their closest examination, in relation to native Americans, in lectures given in the 1530s at the University of Salamanca by the Spanish Dominican, Francisco de Vitoria. Vitoria, assuredly among the finest intellects of sixteenth-century Spain, was a founder of the intellectual movement known as the School of Salamanca, which made that university into the chief authority on scholasticism of its time. At Salamanca, Vitoria introduced Aquinas's *Summa Theologica* as the central theological text; and in so doing, intensified study in Spain of Aristotle, whose thought Aquinas had had much part in re-establishing in Europe.

It is no wonder, then, that the fraught and interconnected questions of the Indians' human standing, their freedom, their treatment by Spaniards, and indeed Spain's right to dominion over them and their territories, received their most thorough analysis in Aristotelian terms. Aristotle had pronounced that in humanity, as in the rest of the universe, there existed a duality, between those in whom reason dominated and those in whom passions prevailed. Human groups in which intellect failed to rule passions were naturally subservient to others in which reason was in command. These natural slaves were not without reason; but for some cause it was weak in them. The relationship between natural slave and master should not, though, be exploitative, but mutually beneficial: the slave should work for the master, and in doing so improve his or her exercise of reason.[32]

Identifying the natural slave, however, was not simple. Aristotle had proposed barbarity as a broad category. Spaniards looking at native Americans, therefore, debated furiously whether Indians were barbarians. But this, naturally, drew them into further problems of categorization; and the theoretical exegesis of Aristotle could be drawn to so complex a fineness that almost any parti pris or conclusion could substantiated. Vitoria found the high American cultures deficient in reason – and hence barbaric – because, among much else, of their practice of human sacrifice and ritual cannibalism. Eating human flesh he regarded not so much as sinful in a Christian sense, but reprehensible, by Aristotelian criteria, because it showed unawareness of natural hierarchies. Human flesh was not proper food for civilized beings; no more were the insects that Aztecs were reported to eat. Animal flesh was the fitting food for the civilized. The Aztecs ate little of it. On the other hand, their highly organized city life, social hierarchy, and sophisticated trade suggested a well-developed humanity.

The contradictions proved almost endless. They also proved, when confronted by as powerful a mind as Vitoria's, the means for breaking the molds that Aristotle had cast for humanity. For Vitoria finally resolved the puzzle by arguing that the Indians occupied some middle ground between "natural" masters and slaves. Their rationality could not be denied; but it was still not fully developed, its potential still not realized. But, having rationality, Indians were essentially human. Their failings, like those of European peasants, were to be attributed to inadequate education; and, by that token, were remediable. Or they were like children, whom Aristotle had seen as only potential humans, as yet quasi-animal, while their rational faculties were still growing. Applying this assessment to the matter of Spanish rights to America, Vitoria held that, until their raising to full rationality were complete, Indians must stay under Spanish control, as children under parents' formative guidance. One basis of Spain's title to America was therefore a duty to provide this guidance. On the other hand, the Salamanca School's opinion logically became that once the tutorial task was done, that claim to title lapsed; for Indians, as essentially rational, were essentially free.[33]

Vitoria's categorization of American natives coincided nicely with the ruling of Pope Paul III, in *Sublimis Deus* of 1537, that they were fully fit to receive the faith; and that those who denied this, proclaiming Indians to be "dumb brutes created for our service," were simply "satellites" of the Devil. It is no surprise that it was another Spanish Dominican, Bernardino de Minaya, who moved Paul to issue this and other pro-Indian bulls in 1537.[34] Equally unsurprising is that Vitoria's views were not welcomed by the crown, particularly as another of his radical notions was to challenge the long-established doctrine giving universal temporal powers to the Papacy. Christ had not claimed such powers. How, then, could His vicars, the popes, hold them?[35] If they did not, Alexander VI's 1493 grant of general dominion in America to Spain was worthless; and Spain's first and strongest title to the Indies was undermined. Small wonder that in 1539 Charles V banned further debate on titles to America.[36] Nevertheless, the tiresome academics of Salamanca continued to think of the matters Vitoria had raised, and their school became broadly anti-imperialist.

By the 1540s, of course, the question of titles was, literally, academic. There was no practical prospect that Spain would abandon the Indies. Certainly few even of the missionaries in America would have welcomed such a move, however much they wished that secular settlers would leave Indians alone, the better to be guided to true faith and civility by the priesthood. In particular, the Franciscans' longstanding millenarianism had been reinvigorated by Spain's transatlantic expansion; at the same time, once in the Indies and striving to maximize both numbers and speed in conversion, they saw secular settlers as a clear hindrance to their purpose.

One means by which Franciscans sought to separate their charges from the run of settlers and broad European contamination was the preservation of native language. If Indians did not learn Spanish, colonists could less easily influence and command them. This, as much as the desire to promote conversion, was the motive for the friars' monumental linguistic efforts in sixteenth-century Mexico. In the 1520s, forty languages were spoken in the parts of New Spain recently conquered; though, under Aztec influence and policy, Nahuatl had become a lingua franca in much of that area. In the sixteenth century, 109 works were published on or in native Mexican tongues; of these, the Franciscans were responsible for eighty.[37] The first grammar of a

Mexican language, one of Nahuatl, was produced in 1547 by the greatest of the Franciscan linguists in New Spain, Andrés de Olmos, who was possibly the man whom Gerónimo de Mendieta had in mind when he later wrote of a Franciscan able to preach and write catechisms in ten or more Indian languages.[38] The friars' learning of languages, then duly set down in grammars and dictionaries, provided incidentally in some cases a record of tongues that have long since disappeared.

Language was, though, only one part of native culture that the missionaries preserved on paper. Olmos, for example, while evidently a supreme linguist, was also a student of native Mexican affairs in general, and in the 1530s wrote a *Treatise on Mexican Antiquities*; alas, a lost work.[39] An abundance of similar work by other Franciscans in Mexico survives, however. Prime among it is the great compilation of Fray Bernardino de Sahagún, the *General History of the Things of New Spain*. It, too, suffered initial perils, but survived to provide a window of unmatched breadth on Aztec and sixteenth-century native Mexico.

A student at Salamanca in the 1520s, Sahagún came to New Spain in 1529. Learning Nahuatl, he decided to produce an illustrated dictionary of the language.[40] This plan expanded as he turned to parish work, observed his surroundings, and began interviewing surviving native nobles. He taught at times in the Franciscan school in Tlatelolco. His pupils there added information to what he had gathered, and helped him write it down. Gradually his *Historia* was drafted, in Nahuatl; it reached its first stage of completion in 1569. A bilingual text followed, with Spanish and Nahuatl in parallel columns, and illustrations by Indian artists. This is now known as the *Codex Florentino*. Though Sahagún gathered much information himself, and recorded it in Nahuatl, much else came from his native collaborators. The *Historia*, then, because of both its sources and its initial compilation in the native language, gives a markedly "inside" view of Indian life, before, during, and after the conquest. Its twelfth and final book is the fullest available native account of the conquest of the Aztecs, written in the highly charged rhetoric of native formal speech. The sufferings of the dwellers in Tenochtitlan in 1520–1, first from smallpox and then from the Spanish onslaught, are, for example, harrowingly portrayed: "Sores erupted on our faces, our breasts, our bellies; we were covered with agonizing sores from head to foot . . . The sick were so utterly helpless that they could only lie on their beds like corpses . . . If they did move their bodies, they screamed with pain."[41] This last book of the *Historia* is the most historical in content; the earlier sections form a great linguistic-cum-ethnographic compendium on Mexican religion, thought, and society.

Sahagún had no doubts about Indians' intellectual potential. His native collaborators on the *Historia* from the Tlatelolco school were men to whom the Franciscans had so successfully given an education in the European mold. But, by the time his great work was nearing completion, he, like other evangelizers of the later sixteenth century, was growing gloomy about the natives' moral resilience, and hence about the depth of their conversion. There were no Indians in the priesthood, in his view, because they were incapable of celibacy. The climate, abundance, and constellations of New Spain were conducive to vice and sensuality. Conquest, too, had broken the previously rigid moral backbone of Aztec society; now drunkenness and dissolution prevailed. Native religious belief persisted strongly, close to the surface. The Spanish occupation of New Spain might be best seen simply as a step on the way to conversion of China, where Christianity might sink deeper roots.[42]

Two practical realities of the 1570s also served to depress Sahagún's spirits. One was the continued shrinking of the native population, made all too obvious by severe, if still unidentified, epidemics after 1576. Another, more personal, source of distress was growing official hostility to the sort of work to which he had given much of his life. In 1577 Philip II forbade research on Indian history and religion. Most of what Sahagún had written was confiscated (and did not again come into public view until the nineteenth century). This reversal of earlier governmental encouragement of inquiry into Indian matters had several sources. One was the urge to centralized conformity in the church expressed at the Council of Trent, the cleaving to a single line as a means of throwing back the Reformation. An outcome of this was Trent's ban on translation of the scriptures into vernacular tongues. The Bible, for instance, might be used only in its Latin Vulgate version. This led to the Inquisition's seizure in America, in 1576, of translations of sacred texts into native languages. In New Spain, the houses of the Franciscans, the most active translators, were inspected and religious works in Mexican languages impounded. The friars objected that evangelization would suffer; but the new orthodoxy prevailed.[43] The king's order fitted, also, with the official mistrust of the regulars in America that had arisen in the 1560s. The orders were in every way, including intellectual inquiry, too close to the Indians. The Franciscans in New Spain were particularly suspect for their Indian sympathies. More generally, Philip's banning of study of Indians reflects the relegation of native people to a fixed and lowly place in colonial society that was largely complete by the 1570s. (What need was there to know more about common workers and tribute payers?) And, more broadly still, it connects with the Spannish mind's closing to the alien and the unorthodox that had begun c.1530 and had become more obvious with each passing decade.[44]

A man who did more than any other, including Sahagún, to keep American natives in the Spanish government's view, especially when it would rather have forgotten them, was the Dominican, Bartolomé de las Casas. He was a historian of early Spanish America, missionary, ethnographer, but above all else polemicist and propagandist on the Indians' behalf. Las Casas was born in Seville in 1484, saw Columbus there in April 1493 on his return from the first voyage, heard first-hand of Hispaniola from his father (who sailed with Columbus on the settlement expedition of 1493, and returned to Spain in 1498), went himself to the island in 1502 in Nicolás de Ovando's fleet, and there in due course became an *encomendero* who sent his Indians to till fields and mine for gold; nothing remarkable, except inasmuch as being one of those early Caribbean settlers was itself remarkable. Soon, however, he became unusual, and his life (a long one, since it was 1566 before he died) took a new direction. For, it seems, in 1510 he became the first Christian priest to be ordained in America. Why he took this step he does not explain. Nor is it clear who ordained him. Perhaps it was one of the Dominicans who arrived in

Hispaniola in 1510.[45] Certainly the pro-Indian campaign that those Dominicans soon launched impressed him; as did, negatively, the suffering he saw inflicted on the natives of Cuba as Spaniards took that island from 1511 onward. Nonetheless, he was on good terms with the governor of Cuba, Diego Velázquez, and received from him a share in a large *repartimiento* of Indians, whom he put, as in Hispaniola, to farming and washing gold. Then, early in 1514, meditating on biblical texts and his own earlier sermons, he was struck by a passage from the apocryphal book, Ecclesiasticus (chapter 34), beginning "Tainted his gifts who offers in sacrifice ill-gotten goods..." He recalled also once being denied confession in Hispaniola by the Dominicans, who refused to absolve men who held Indians. Further reflection led him quickly to the conclusion "that everything done to the Indians in these Indies was unjust and tyrannical."[46] It was a conviction that directed the rest of his life's activity.

The next half-century saw him cross the Atlantic several times. In Spain he argued the Indians' case with officials, recruited missionaries, and, in his latter years, wrote sprawling tracts and histories. In America he supervised schemes of peaceful colonization and conversion, wrangled with administrators and settlers (for whom he became "one of the most hated men who had ever been in the Indies"),[47] and exercised two offices: Protector of the Indians, which title he received from Cardinal Cisneros in Spain in 1516, and Bishop of Chiapas, in southern Mexico (1544–50). In Spain, he had striking initial successes in influencing the decision to experiment with theocratic rule, under the three Jeronymites, in the Caribbean (1516–19), and Charles V's condemnation of the *encomienda* in 1520. But his own experiment in peaceful settlement, limited to priests and Spanish farmers, on the Venezuelan coast failed in the early 1520s. In disappointment he entered a Dominican house in Santo Domingo in 1522, took his vows as a Dominican the next year, and for the next decade retired from active life, while informing himself about theology, law, and the early history of the Indies – of which he began to write in what was to become his massive *Historia de las Indias*. Late in the 1530s, with other Dominicans, he attempted an innovative peaceful conversion of particularly refractory Indians in the province of Tuzulutlan, in north-east Guatemala. By agreement with the regional governor, secular Spaniards were to be excluded for five years, and no *encomiendas* granted in the area. Here Las Casas tried principles recently offered in his tract *The Only Method of Attracting All People to the True Faith*, in which he argued against the use of war against Indians, and for conversion solely by appeal to reason and will. The experiment of Tuzulutlan (or, as Las Casas came to call it, the land of Verapaz, or True Peace) succeeded during the 1540s, in part because it incorporated maintenance of the powers of native leaders; with them, consequently, Las Casas was able to negotiate to allow undisturbed preaching by the Dominicans.[48] After 1550, however, for reasons unclear, revolts erupted.

Meanwhile, back in Spain in 1539 to recruit Dominican missionaries for his scheme, Las Casas was able to give added impetus to a pro-Indian current already strongly running, shocking the court with the outright propaganda of his *Very Brief Account of the Destruction of the Indies* (by Spanish settlers and officials, of course), and contributing powerfully to the opinion in imperial government from which the New Laws of 1542 emerged. He was, though, an uncomfortable presence at court. An offer was made to him of the see of Cuzco, which he rejected. But in 1544 he accepted the bishopric of Chiapas, since Verapaz lay on its southern side. In Chiapas – where, perhaps remembering his own experience long before with the Dominicans in Hispaniola, he proposed to refuse absolution to Spaniards who held Indian slaves or did not repay gains made from *encomiendas* – he was met with hostility, threats, and even riot among the settlers.[49] The Indians of Verapaz, conversely, gave him a warm welcome. But the recently founded *Audiencia* of Guatemala sided with the *encomenderos* and settlers, leaving him without governmental support.

It was not so much these setbacks, however, as the revocation of clause 30 of the New Laws, banning inheritance of *encomiendas*, that made Las Casas hurry back to Spain in 1546. He found that the court had undergone one of its periodic swings on the question of Indian treatment, alarmed by, among other things, the current revolt of colonists in Peru. And by now Las Casas, through insisting that restitution must be made to Indians for what the conquerors, *encomenderos*, slaveholders, and other Spaniards had taken or earned from them, seemed to be challenging not only Spain's use of the Indies, but also its right to be there at all. For his reason for calling for restitution was that the entire conquest and exploitation of native Americans had been unlawful.[50] Conquerors were *ipso facto* thieves. If he was made to explain himself in Spain, he can hardly have been surprised.

His influence at court, however, was still powerful, and was certainly instrumental in persuading Charles V, via the Council of the Indies, to order in 1550 a suspension of conquests in America until lawyers and theologians had ruled how they could be justly made. This led to what is undoubtedly Las Casas's most famous public appearance, arguing before an august council of fourteen in the summer of 1550, at Valladolid, not simply for conquest without force, but one entrusted to missionaries alone (at least in areas safe from danger). Underlying this was his belief that the Spanish monarchs' title to the Indies rested solely on "the extension of the Gospel in the New World, and their good government of the Indian nations."[51] He was, indeed, now approaching his late and extreme position that Spain's only purpose in America was to convert; and even that if conversion could not be managed without force, it was better that Indians not be converted, and that Spain lose dominion in America, than that the native peoples be destroyed. Opposing Las Casas before the council was one Juan Ginés de Sepúlveda, a translator and humanist writer whose defense of conquest by war, entitled *Democrates Alter*, Las Casas had blocked from publication in 1548. Sepúlveda argued, using Aquinas's arguments, that war against Indians was just, on account of their evident sins and vices, for better spreading of the Word, and because they were clearly slaves by nature, who would benefit in serving superior men, such as Spaniards. Aristotle's natural slave thus resurfaced at Valladolid, despite Vitoria's lifting of native Americans from that category of humans a decade before. He did not survive, however. Although no formal decisions emerged from the Valladolid meeting, Las Casas's views apparently won the greater support.

And certainly, after then, conquest without force became the prevailing policy, if not always the reality, being formalized in a set of ordinances that the Council of the Indies drafted in 1573 after consulting Las Casas's manuscripts.[52]

America saw no more of Las Casas after 1550. In that year he resigned his bishopric in Chiapas, and took up residence in Dominican houses, first in Valladolid and then in Madrid, which became the fixed seat of government in 1561. From these bases, until his death in 1566, he applied himself to the role of Protector of the Indians before the court, with all the effect that his abilities, experience, and relentless vitality gave him. He recruited Dominicans to continue the work in America. And he wrote voluminously, finishing his *Historia de las Indias*, and also producing, among much else, an *Apologética Historia (Apologetic History)*, an ethnographic study of American native culture intended to refute the criticisms made of Indians since the first contact.

In his will, of 1564, Las Casas stated that "God...saw fit to choose me as his minister...to plead for all those people of the Indies...against unheard of and unimagined oppressions and evils and injuries received from our Spaniards...and to restore them to the primitive liberty unjustly taken from them."[53] Oppressed but fundamentally free: these are two certainties about Indians that Las Casas had striven to inject into policy-making for half a century. They were free because God had created all men free. But anyone who observed them could see their oppression.

A third quality of Indians of which Las Casas was convinced demanded more elaborate proof: full rationality. He argued for this lengthily and intricately, drawing on whatever arguments, classical or Christian, came to hand. The fundamental reasoning of the case was Aristotelian, and consisted of showing that Indians did not fit Aristotle's definitions of barbarity. There were awkward corners to negotiate: for example, lack of true writing, and human sacrifice. But outweighing these defects were the positive qualities of "excellent, subtle, and very capable minds." Most Indians were

> likewise prudent, and endowed by nature with the three kinds of prudence named by the Philosopher: monastic, economic, and political. Political prudence includes the six parts which, according to Aristotle, make any republic self-sufficient and prosperous: farmers; craftsmen; warriors; men of wealth; priests...and sixth, judges or ministers of justice who govern well.[54]

In their government, indeed, and in observing "natural reason," Indians had even surpassed those most prudent of past peoples, the Greeks and Romans.

In comparing native American cultures to those of the past, and in trying to untangle the problem of the presence in any of them of contradictory behaviors (in the case of Mexico, for example, the building of large and elaborate cities in which human sacrifice was practiced), Las Casas concluded that human conduct was not the product of a particular people's fixed psychology, but rather a function of its progress along a path of development. Native Americans were generally not far along this track. Elements of ruder behavior persisted in them. (Human sacrifice, he noted, had once been widely practiced among peoples who now condemned it.) But – and here he came close to Vitoria's diagnosis of Indians as children, but educable children – progress was probable, even inevitable.

> We all have the need, from the beginning, to be guided and helped by those who have been born earlier. Thus, when some very rustic peoples are found in the world, they are like untilled land, which easily produces worthless weeds and thorns, but has within itself so much natural power that when it is ploughed and cultivated its gives useful and wholesome fruits.[55]

Las Casas, then, from his effort to characterize native Americans in order to save them from exploitation, emerged with an evolutionary notion of human development of which only the seeds existed before.[56] This was a large conceptual contribution to the nascent art of anthropology that the European encounter with the American populations inspired.

Las Casas is Latin America's most renowned churchman, Vitoria the leading legal theorist on issues raised by Spanish overseas expansion, Sahagún the founding ethnographer of native American cultures. But many others, mainly missionary friars, thought and wrote on the matters that occupied these three in the early post-conquest decades. In New Spain there was Fray Toribio de Benavente, nicknamed "Motolinía" ("poor man") by the Indians for his extreme dedication to the Franciscan vows of poverty. No less did he adhere to Franciscan millenarian beliefs, and so took a leading part in his order's early efforts in mass baptism. Though critical of Aztec cruelty, which was, he thought, clearly the Devil's work, in his *History of the Indians of New Spain* (1541) he generally praised, like Quiroga, the Mexicans' gentleness and receptivity to the faith.[57] In South America there were fewer towering figures, in part because New Spain, being earlier conquered, had taken the best of the outstanding crop of Spanish regulars trained early in the sixteenth century. Much of the recording of Indian culture done in Mexico by friars was, in the Andes, the work of laymen. One was Juan de Betanzos, an official interpreter in Quechua who married a woman of royal line from Cuzco. Another was Pedro de Cieza de León, a young Spaniard who observed and recorded acutely as he moved through the Andes in the late 1530s and 1540s. The leading clerical student of the Andeans was the Dominican, Domingo de Santo Tomás, who arrived in Peru in 1540, and soon took up cudgels for the Indians in a distinctly polemical, Lascasian style. His long journeys through the central Andes gave him a first-hand knowledge of the mountains and their people. In 1560 he published the first grammar of Quechua. His major political campaign, waged in the 1550s, aimed to free the native Peruvians of the *encomienda*'s burdens. He had only limited success. He was bishop of La Plata, or Charcas, from 1562 till his death in 1570.

The efforts of this variety of men had created by 1570 or so an immense knowledge of the native cultures conquered or encountered by the Spaniards in America. Whatever the motive for gathering information – surprise, simple admiration, intellectual curiosity sharpened by humanistic training, a desire to know native religion the better to attack it (and the Devil presumably behind it), a moral urgency to defend Indians from the ravages of conquest, or some political agenda aiming to change the entire form of colonization – the outcome was an intellectual incorporation of the Indian into the Spanish mental world that paralleled the physical and legal incorporation of American territory into the monarchy. It was, effectively, a mental domination of the Indian, a campaign in which ancient weapons of analysis taken from the arsenals of Greek and Roman thinkers, and of medieval churchmen, were found still indispensable; though they were unalterably modified by the novel use to which they were now put.[58] Few Spaniards, of course, were fully aware of all that had been learned of Indians in that half-century after conquest. It was of concern mainly to administrators and clerics. Colonists, on the whole, formed their own views of Indians from practical experience. These in some respects coincided with the intellectuals' conclusions. Both groups found Indians generally to be simple people, docile, childlike, not yet fully formed in mind or morality. For the rank and file of settlers, this diagnosis provided both reason and opportunity for misuse and exploitation. For at least some leaders in both church and state, long into the colonial era, it was reason to work for the defense of Indians against those abuses; though difficulties of enforcement, and the press of circumstance, often negated these protective efforts.

Understanding, and protection, of Indians carried, however, a deep irony. For the more the church sought to defend and even separate native Americans from settlers and the state, the more its efforts contributed to their domination by the invading culture, of which it was an elemental part. Orders and state may have had their conflicts in the post-conquest years over mission methods and sharing of authority over Indians. But as friars moved across the colonies, and their great mission churches, often fortress-like and assertively European in style,[59] rose to dominate the landscape, the message to the conquered was obvious enough: it was all invasion, no matter whether the outsiders wore chain mail or woolen robes, whether they bore swords or crosses.

[9] SOCIETY: OLD ORDERS CHANGED

POPULATION

It is arguable that nothing has marked the social history, indeed the entire history, of Middle and South America since 1492 more than the enormous loss of native population that followed the Europeans' arrival. That the loss was enormous, there is hardly any doubt; although its exact proportion is impossible to calculate because the number of native inhabitants at the moment of contact is unknown, and will probably always remain so unless unimagined new sources of information appear.

Seriously intended estimates of the population of the whole American continent just before 1492 run from 8.4 to 112 million.[1] For individual regions, the range is similarly wide: for example, Peru (as it now is), 4 to 15 million;[2] central Mexico, 5 to 25 million; and Central America, 2.25 to 5.45 million.[3] These are the areas for which knowledge is most "precise." The enormous variability is partly the outcome of differences in methods of calculation. A common technique has been the backward extension of rates of decline from later periods (1550–1650, for example) for which more, though far from wholly, reliable data are available. This is a simple mathematical operation; but there can be no certainty that the loss rate before a certain date in a particular area prevailed after that date. Other researchers have begun from the counts made by European explorers and conquerors. But these were inevitably rough and impressionistic. For central Mexico, late Aztec tribute assessments provide some guide, though presenting problems of completeness and interpretation. And then, beyond and perhaps more influential than these technical problems, are the effects of politics in the estimates, both old and new. Las Casas was the first of the determined "high counters," as they are now called,[4] with, for example, his notorious assertion that pre-Columbian Hispaniola held 3–4 million people.[5] It suited his political purposes to make the post-conquest loss seem high. Conquerors' glory, and prospects of reward, were similarly enhanced by high estimates of the size of the forces they had vanquished. Today, high counters tend (though there are honorable exceptions) to be nativists, or nationalists whose political or ideological ends are served by claims of high loss (and therefore of high initial numbers). Conversely, those who prefer to see European expansion in a positive light incline to play down its negative demographic outcome.

Loss rates after contact, then, are disputed, just as are the initial numbers from which the losses began. But no one disputes that some degree of decline took place; and, indeed, those who argue for small declines have the more difficult case to make. From the mid-sixteenth century onward, the growing Spanish bureaucracy in America counted tributaries in the colonies: adult Indian males on whom a head tax was imposed (as it was on commoners in Castile). These counts were not made at regular intervals across the colonies, nor with equal care in all places; and they are replete with problems of interpretation (for example, by what factor to multiply the number of tributaries to arrive at a total population). But they do provide periodic tallies of the same category of people, which should reflect variations in the whole fairly consistently.

Calculating mainly from these tribute records, historians have posited native populations for central Mexico (roughly speaking, Mexico south of the *altiplano*, less Yucatan) thus: 1548, 3.6–6.3 million; 1568, 2.65 million; 1595, 1.375 million; 1620–5, 730,000.[6] By this estimate, the Indian population in the mid-1620s was 11.6–20.3 percent of what it had been some eighty years earlier. Since some decline had certainly taken place between 1519 and 1548, it is beyond reasonable dispute that the native population of central Mexico fell by over 85 percent in the century after the military conquest. The 1620s seem to have marked the low point in Indian numbers. A slow, but accelerating, recovery began soon after then.

The story was similar in Peru, the other large area for which thorough demographic research has been done for the early colony. The first broad count of natives there was supervised by Viceroy Toledo in the early 1570s. It suggests an Indian population of about 1.3 million in 1570. By 1620 the number had fallen to *c*.700,000: a decline of 48.5 percent in half a century (and one of 83 percent from even the low 4,000,000 estimate of the precontact total).[7] Thus, to the 1620s, the Peruvian decline may have been slightly less severe than New Spain's. But Peru had not yet reached its low point. This seems to have come in the mid to late seventeenth century; though estimating the true number of Indians in seventeenth-century Peru is complicated by their clearly large migrations. The Andes offered more refuges from Spanish reach than New Spain did; and many natives took advantage of a loophole in the law that made people who moved away from their birth places to another community exempt from tribute and forced labor. Not surprisingly, there arose a multitude of these *forasteros*, as they were called; and officials did not count them until the late 1600s. But despite this omission, there is little doubt about the downward trend of Peruvian native numbers over much of the seventeenth century.[8]

A growing number of local studies show that great losses of native people, of three-quarters or more of the pre-contact figure, seem to have been the rule across Spanish America in the aftermath of conquest.[9] No large mainland area, it is true, saw the extinction of its pre-contact population that the Greater Antilles and the Bahamas suffered in the sixteenth century. (It is worth recalling, though, that the nomadic tribes of the Mexican *altiplano* had disappeared, first through warfare and then by cultural absorption, by the mid-seventeenth century.) The only possible exception to this terrible trend is Quito, or present highland Ecuador, where research has indicated a strong recovery in the seventeenth century after grave losses in the sixteenth. But even this may be an illusion, the result simply of more complete counting by Spanish officials after 1600.[10]

The consensus is that only disease could have produced this demographic collapse. Great waves of sickness are known to have swept across the mainlands decade after decade in the sixteenth century, and thereafter less often, but still wreaking havoc when they came.[11] Smallpox was probably the worst killer of Indians. It and the plague can be clearly identified from contemporary descriptions. Less surely present, but quite likely to have been so, were typhus, measles, mumps, and influenza.

These ills were devastating, nearly all now agree, because they were new in America. If the American natives' ancestors in Asia had been subject to the pathogens causing these diseases, they had not carried them along in the migration to America. Or, perhaps, the microbes had evolved in the Eurasian Old World after the departure of those who were to become native Americans, and had produced new strains of the sicknesses. In any case, the diseases that the Europeans inevitably brought to America after 1492 were novel there, and Indians seem consequently to have had little or no resistance to them. In the first attacks of each disease, at least, it is likely that all age groups in the infected population suffered severely. Children who survived an illness would acquire an immunity to it, so that subsequent episodes of the same disease would result in higher death rates among those not infected before. These would mainly be children born since the previous attack. But the destruction across age groups caused by initial assaults meant the disappearance of many people of reproductive age, and hence fewer children. This drop in births, added to mortality from the diseases themselves, suggests that the decline in total numbers was particularly steep in the early years after the conquests, when newly imported ills were constantly appearing. Experience elsewhere in the world, though fortunately never again on so vast a scale, with these so-called "virgin-soil" epidemics shows that the exposed population takes three or four generations to develop a collective resistance to them. This finding fits with the slowing, and eventual reversal, of decline among American natives observable a hundred years or more after first contact with Old World outsiders.

The Americas were not Edenically free of disease before the Europeans came, of course, though the number of serious epidemic ailments seems to have been much smaller than in the land mass of Europe, Asia, and Africa.[12] Internal parasites, bacterial pneumonia, and tuberculosis were present; as perhaps were yellow fever, malaria, typhus, and just possibly typhoid. America held no pathogen, however, capable of exacting revenge on the Old World for what its bacteria and viruses did to the New. Indians saw that Spaniards did not die in epidemics, and raged. The one noteworthy exception may be syphilis. A virulent, quick-killing, form of it appeared in Europe directly after Columbus's first return. Whether it was caused by a new pathogen brought back from Hispaniola by his men, or by a coincidental mutation of the related yaws treponema already existing in Europe, has been the topic of lively, but inconclusive, debate for several decades past.

Epidemics were not the only destroyer of Indians in the sixteenth century. The case of the large Caribbean islands shows that Spanish arms could kill many. Intentional massacre of entire villages as a terrorist tool of conquest was used both there and later in the mainland campaigns. The "Black Legend" – the proposition that Spaniards were unusually cruel and destructive in their treatment of non-Europeans – had part of its origin in such episodes, publicized, it might be added, by Las Casas above all others. Early Spanish presence in Hispaniola, Puerto Rico, Jamaica, and Cuba also showed how disruptive to native culture and survival the settlers' post-conquest demands could be: Indian men and women put to unbearably heavy work, families split up by labor drafts for long periods, tribute taken in foods that the people themselves needed, land overrun and crops eaten by Spanish domestic animals. Of all this there is incontrovertible evidence, not only for the islands but for the mainland, too. Less easily shown, though highly likely, was the psychological damage done to American natives by the experience of conquest and domination: the revelation of gods' powerlessness, the invalidation of world-view. Early friars and chroniclers give anecdotal reports of suicides, abortions, and infanticide. Some evidence exists that disinclination to reproduce was a cause of falling birthrates after the conquest; though that is not the finding for sixteenth-century Peru, where birth rates seem to have risen after epidemics, as if communities were trying to make up their losses.[13]

There was, therefore, a variety of downward pressures on native numbers. But those just proposed do not seem enough to account for the vast losses suffered by the mainland peoples for so long after the military conquests. Spanish ignorance, carelessness, maltreatment, and cruelty were probably mostly to blame for the destruction of the Caribbean peoples. But administrators, and to a lesser extent colonists, learned from that experience, so that from the 1520s protective laws and practices began to have some effect. True enough, the mainland populations at first seemed so huge that, for many settlers, squandering the Indians granted to them in *encomienda* posed no practical danger. This led, for example, to the ill-treatment of Indians in New Spain in the late 1520s, when the grasping regime of Nuño de Guzmán had replaced Cortés's more protective rule. But laws had some effect; if they had not, the colonists' reaction to the New Laws in 1542, and to the ban in 1549 on the use of *encomienda* Indians for labor, would have been less clamorous. Finally, however, once the process of domination was in train and the danger of native resistance receding, Spaniards had no interest in destroying Indians. Quite the reverse: Indians, as workers and tribute payers, were the root of the wealth that both state and settlers looked for in America. This was particularly clear in the high-culture regions. Their peoples had many skills immediately useful to the Spanish, and were used, from pre-conquest times, to being organized into labor forces by government. It is a speculative thought – but perhaps the Caribbean people, had they seemed as full of economic promise as the Mexicans and Andeans later did, might have been spared the intolerable pressures that quickly destroyed them.

There will always be some doubt about allocating blame among causes for the deaths of those many millions on the mainland of sixteenth-century Spanish America; in part because crucial data do not exist (Spaniards did not, and probably could not, record how many succumbed to this or that epidemic), in part because the debate will probably long remain as much political as historical. The most sophisticated inquiry to date, however (though it deals only with the Valley of Mexico), concludes:

> The catastrophic decline in the [Valley's] Amerindian population was due to the combined effect of a series of epidemic crises, each of which reduced the population significantly.
> By far the most important factor in these crises were the profound short-term increases in mortality engendered by the "virgin soil" epidemics. No reliance need be made on the so-called Leyenda Negra [Black Legend] of Spanish cruelty to explain the holocaust.[14]

This confirms earlier and more impressionistic conclusions for New Spain and other areas of high culture. It will not be the last word.

As natives disappeared, Spanish numbers (once the late 1490s were past) grew constantly. The actual total of Spaniards in the early colonies is, though, hardly clearer than the Indians' numbers. No head tax was applied to them, so there was no need to count them for that reason. And though licenses were legally required for traveling to America, many people clearly sailed without them; so the number of emigrants is uncertain. By about 1570 the total number of Spaniards in the Indies was probably between 125,000 and 150,000. They lived in some 225 towns.[15]

In the conquest decades, most emigrants had been young, single men (though families had begun to arrive in Hispaniola in 1502); some of these married or cohabited with native women, engendering the beginnings of the mestizo population that in the end was to become so central a demographic and cultural feature of Spanish America. Then, after the conquests, Spanish families became more frequent, as a broader socio-economic range of men began to cross the ocean – artisans, lawyers, administrators – some of them with wives and children.[16] At the same time single Spanish women began to move to the Indies in growing numbers. The official emigration licenses suggest, in fact, that between 1509 and 1538 rather more adult single women than married women crossed the ocean. There was occasional official concern about the morals of some of these; and certainly among them were adventurous camp followers. But many were women who saw in the Indies the possibility of marriage, at a time when there was an excess of marriageable women at home.[17] Marriage also offered a chance to tap into America's economic promise. A story from Guatemala, about 1530, has a group of young Spanish women brought from Spain by the governor of the province, and ex-conqueror of the Aztecs, Pedro de Alvarado, discussing the prospect of marriage to unattached conquerors. To the objection that these were aging men, many of them maimed, or uglified by wounds, one of the group retorted:

"We're not going to marry them for their looks, but to inherit their Indians. They're so old and worn out, they're certain to die soon, and then we can choose whatever young men we please instead of these dotards like changing an old broken pot for a new whole one."[18] The tale may be apocryphal; but the young, wealthy widow of a *conquistador* or *encomendero* was not a rare figure in the sixteenth-century colonies.

Up to 1560 about a tenth of emigration licenses went to women. This was an average. The proportion was certainly smaller early in the century, and higher by the middle decades. In the 1560s women were a quarter or more of emigrants from Spain. The actual populations may have held more women than the licenses suggest. In Peru, by the 1540s, the male–female ratio among Spaniards was seven or eight to one. In 1550 a thousand Spanish women were in Peru, scattered through all the major coastal and highland towns. At the start of the seventeenth century, Lima alone is said to have had 5,359 Spanish women, giving them a slight edge over men (5,258), in a total population of 26,441.[19] The proportion was probably similar in other large Spanish centers. By that time, although emigration from Spain was still rising, many "Spaniards" in the colonies were in fact locally born, in, presumably, almost equal numbers of females and males. Among Spaniards, what might be called the "demographics of conquest" – a large male preponderance – had given way to the gender balance of a normal population, with all that that implied for family formation and the decline of stable unions between Spanish men and non-Spanish women.

Most of those women were Indians. But, almost from the beginning, Spaniards had taken African women as consorts as well. Africans, mostly slaves, but some free, became a prominent feature on the social landscape of early Spanish America. There were Blacks in the expeditions of conquest. They fought alongside the Spanish, and so were seen by Indians from the start as part of the invading culture. The Black conquerors arrived with their masters from Spain. Soon, though, a flow of slaves began directly from Africa. By the best estimate, it brought to the Spanish colonies between 1526 and 1600 at least 75,000 slaves. About a half of them went to New Spain, where they numbered, by 1570, some 20,000.[20] At most, a third of those imported were women, since males were in greater demand, and hence more profitable to traders. Consequently the slave community produced few children. And that, added to high mortality, meant that new slaves had constantly to be imported from Africa. Though few African offspring were born, partly Black children certainly made an appearance in the sixteenth century. There were *mulatos* (Black and Spanish) and *zambos* (Black and Indian). Since a child took its mother's status, black men had reason to produce offspring with Indian women, who were free by law. Conversely, the children of a White father and Black mother were slaves if she was a slave. But White fathers were often in a social and financial position to free their children.[21] Both circumstances reinforced the other obstacles to natural increase in the Black slave population, while adding new dimensions to Spanish American ethnic blending, which had first consisted of only the White–native mixture. And as the numbers of mestizos, *mulatos*, and *zambos* grew, so the

possibilities of mixes of mixes also rose, accelerating and complicating miscegenation.

SOCIAL HIERARCHY

These various elements shook down into a structured society by the late
1500s. Though the structure that emerged was by no means rigid or compart-
mentalized, it was shaped by an innate notion of hierarchy. A passage from a
memorandum of the Council of the Indies to Charles IV in 1806 shows how
long this idea stayed embedded in the official Spanish mind.

> If it is undeniable that, for the maintenance and good order of a monarchical
> state, diverse hierarchies and spheres are of supreme importance, since their
> ranked and interlinked dependency and subordination produce and sustain the
> lowest vassal's obedience to, and respect for, the sovereign's authority; how
> much more necessary is such a system in America, on account of both the greater
> distance from the throne, and the great number of those sorts of people who,
> owing to their wicked origins and nature, constitute a very inferior species, not to
> be compared with the common people of Spain; it even occurring that the known
> children or descendants of slaves sit down and fraternize with those who derive
> from the first conquerors or from families that are noble, legitimate, white, and
> free of all taint.[22]

Here is a splendid concatenation, indeed, of prejudice and ignorance from
these mandarins of the late empire: the American population dichotomized
into noble Whites and a perverted remainder; the Whites all pure-blooded and
legitimate; the rest perpetually contaminated by an assumed bastardy somewhere in their origins. But overriding this distortion by far in historical
significance was the assumption that such a population can be kept orderly
only through hierarchical organization. People must have, and know, their
place in society. They know it through their links of "dependency and subordination" with those above them. Those links also extend downward to locate
people lower on the scale.

The use of the image of link (*eslabón* in the original Spanish) in describing
the needed social structure brings to mind the classical chain of being, along
which all parts of creation were located, in proper and immutable order. This
notion of society indeed had its origins in ancient thought. It also drew –
hardly surprisingly, since he was the great restorer of Aristotle, prime among
the ancients – on Aquinas's concept of society as "first ... a hierarchical
system in which each person or group serves a purpose larger than any one of
them can encompass."[23] Inequalities are an intrinsic part of this hierarchy, to
be corrected only when Christian justice is threatened. The society's members
should accept them as inevitable attachments to each rank and its role. These
European notions of what a proper society should be were reinforced in the
Indies, at least in the high-culture areas, by native precedent. Aztec and Inca
societies were not one whit less hierarchical than Spain's in the conquest
period; perhaps, indeed, considerably more so. In applying their assumptions

about the natural working of a society to America, the Spanish found among the most valued of those they colonized, the peoples of the high-culture areas, no resistance of principle. Only the less developed cultures tended to egalitarianism; that was, in part, why the Spaniards found them hard to overcome.

Notions of hierarchy and inequality applied not only to individuals, but also to groups within society. Indeed, society's basic units were not, in the Spanish view, individuals, but groups of various sizes, each with its particular part to play in consonance with the others. It was a notion of social composition typical of medieval Europe. Equally medieval was the concept that secular society divided first into two large and firmly separated segments: the noble and the plebeian estate.[24]

The society of estates persisted strongly in sixteenth- and seventeenth-century Spain. But only the expectation that that was how a society should be, rather than the specific forms it took in Spain, transferred across the Atlantic. There were, for example, hardly any titled noblemen in America for almost two hundred years. Until late in the seventeenth century, almost the only title holders in the colonies were the viceroys, who were transitory figures. On the other hand, nobility as a concept was abundantly present in America. Colonists as a whole, indeed, thought of themselves as a nobility, in the sense that they made up the upper section of society that was occupied by the nobility at home. For some, also, braving the hazards of the ocean crossing was an experience that in itself seemed to demand heroic qualities; and heroism was a noble trait. There was also a legal reason for the assumed noble status of Whites in America. In Spain, commoners paid a head tax, or *pecho*. But in America all people considered white were free of such levies. Thus the peasant, carpenter, or tailor arriving in the colonies suddenly possessed one of the most cherished privileges of the Spanish noble, and felt himself ennobled by that gain.

Thus in some measure an estate simply of "Spaniards," whether immigrants, *criollos*, or even mestizos who looked like Europeans, took the place in America of the noble estate in Spain. And the native population became the equivalent of a European common estate. The term "estate" (*estamento* in Spanish) was not used, however, for these groupings, but rather *república*. A colonial society consisting of two such republics, one Indian and the other Spanish, was, by the time of the mainland conquests, what administrators in Spain hoped to produce in America. The intent was that such a division would help to protect natives from predatory Spaniards, promote their conversion, and simplify extraction from them of tribute and labor. It would also further the crown's political aims in America by blocking colonists' access to native possessions and labor, and so slow the growth of their political and economic power.

In certain practical respects, the policy of two republics failed from the start. It was undermined by race mixture. The crown itself, holding to the canonical principle that people should be free to wed whom they chose, did not ban Spanish–Indian marriages. These, it is true, were few, and did not produce many children. But outside marriage, mestizo infants appeared, after the requisite number of months, wherever Spaniards went. The clear waters of the bipartite society were instantly muddied. Then the crown itself mortally wounded the policy of separate republics by allowing expansion of the *encomienda* to the mainland. Spaniards and Indians were thereby thrust together, rather than apart. Policy-makers were perfectly aware of this, but had to yield to the urgent need to fix settlers in the vastness of America. For a time, the *encomienda* seemed the best way of doing that. Then again, the presence of Blacks in the colonies, and soon enough of *mulatos* and *zambos* as well, meant that the two-republic model simply did not fit the developing social reality.

Nevertheless, true to the principle of estates, Indians and Spaniards did always remain legally and functionally distinct populations in the Spanish colonies. Though historians in recent years have discovered how widely and ingeniously Indians adapted to and resisted Spanish pressures, there is no denying that throughout colonial times they were the dominated, and that the Spanish, whether as state or individuals, were the dominators. Most adult Indian men paid tribute, as the law required; and Indians supplied most of the physical labor consumed in the colonies, as law or economic conditions dictated. The broad assessment of American natives reached by Spaniards by the mid-1500s – that they were free, fully human in potential, but still childlike in intellectual and moral development – was expressed in laws that treated them as minors, needing legal protection.[25] For example, they might not, except under the supervision of a Spanish justice, sell fixed or movable goods worth more than thirty pesos (the price of 40–50 bushels of maize in the Valley of Mexico *c*.1580, or of three or four llamas in Potosí *c*.1590).[26] They were excused from paying sales tax (*alcabala*) except when trading Spanish goods. A system of legal defense was created, consisting of lawyers on the *audiencia* staffs specializing in native cases, and, in New Spain, a general Indian court in Mexico City.[27] Countless other regulations and practices could be cited to show that Spaniards, in Spain and America, saw the American natives, within the colonial regime, as being radically distinct, in social, economic, cultural, and legal senses, from themselves. They were certainly an integral part of society, but one whose function, like that of European commoners, was to sustain, through work and taxes, the higher components of society and the existence of the state itself.

The Spanish section of the American population inherited the role of defense that had belonged to the noble estate of medieval Europe, and briefly played it well enough. Defense of the realm was, in fact, a duty that *encomenderos* owed the crown in return for their grants of native services and tribute. They and other early settlers certainly took up arms against native insurgency in the sixteenth century. The Mixton war in western New Spain in the early 1540s was one example; Chichimeca raids on early Spanish settlement of the Mexican *altiplano*, another (though that was as much conquering as suppressing revolt). But as the age of conquest passed, and as changes in the law undercut the *encomienda* as the basis of a proto-seigneurial class in American society, settlers' martial inclinations atrophied. In truth, there was little to keep them exercised, except in the frontier zones where Indian raiding was constant, or on coasts, mainly in the Caribbean, where piratical attacks often fell. The prime function of settlers became, then, one of occupying, operating, and supervising (beyond the activities of government) the colonies. This function had a large economic component. It included working land and mines; trading, at every level from retail shops to transoceanic exchange; setting up communications and transport, over both land and sea; establishing manufacture, from small craft shops to sizable cloth works. Some of this had been done by nobles in Spain. Raising sheep and cattle on large estates was the most characteristic productive activity of the upper nobility of the Castilian highlands and Andalusia. And holders of high titles were not above profitable participation in the Indies trade. But the settlers in America certainly went beyond what even the neediest Castilian *hidalgo* would stoop to when they dirtied their clothes, if not their hands, in supervising ore-cutting in a mine, or in running a blacksmith's forge. And there were many, as Spanish numbers rose in America, who actually put their hands to tools. Thus the analogy between the noble estate in Spain and a colonists' "estate" in America, while broadly valid, stops short of the bottom end of the settlers' group.

The notion of society as an assemblage of groups rather than individuals extended downward below the level of estates or republics. Function generally identified these groups, though function was always linked to some degree with status. Churchmen were the most obvious such unit. They were not considered a separate estate, as in medieval Europe, perhaps because of the exceptionally close binding of the colonial church to the state. But they were certainly a corporate body, unified by function, and possessing distinct legal privileges, such as their own courts. Other groups – merchants and miners, for example – saw themselves as similarly distinct, and deserving. They, also, in time, gained their formal legal identity and privileges. So, too, did the military, once it was formally created late in the colonial era.

Neither native nor Spanish society in America remained fixed in its form or workings after the conquest. The sixteenth century brought profound developments in both groups that set Spanish American social history on a course that it long pursued. Broadly speaking, native society became simpler in structure, and Spanish society more complex. Neither change is particularly surprising, given, for example, the enormous decline in numbers on the one side, and their growth on the other. But the processes are worth comment and illustration.

The most obvious, and dramatic, simplification of the high Indian cultures came during the military conquest, with the removal of their supreme rulers and their accompanying administrative and religious bureaucracies, staffed by their relatives and other high nobles. This decapitation of native states by the Spanish is a commonplace of the conquest, as is the broadly successful installation of new European heads on the American bodies in the form of triumphant conquering captains and their lieutenants and advisers. Left relatively undisturbed, however, at least politically, by the defeat of native states were the local lords of units that had been incorporated into the large polities quite recently – generally no more than a few decades before the Spaniards came. These men often welcomed the demise of the state structures; some, indeed, contributed to their downfall by helping the Spanish.[28]

The Spanish, extending a Caribbean term to the mainland, generally called these local lords *caciques*; or sometimes in the Andes, using a proper regional name, *curacas*. There was actually, as might be imagined, a wide range of local authorities in various regions and cultures; but to most settlers, they were all *caciques*. Whether or not these men had aided the conquerors, they and their family lines tended to do well in the succeeding decades. The main reason was that the Spanish needed them. While knowledge of mainland Indians (of their productive capacity, tribute systems, administration, and psychology) was still being gathered, *caciques* were essential go-betweens. They, in turn, could profit from the new conditions. Free now from Inca, Aztec, or other comparable controls, they could act more independently than before, for their own and their communities' benefit. In the very early years, when tribute rates were unregulated, they could negotiate favorable payments with the *encomendero* to whom their people had been assigned. If *encomenderos* wanted native workers, it was largely through the *caciques* that they must get them, on mutually satisfactory terms. There were instances, certainly, in which *encomendero* and *cacique* conspired for their own gain against the interests of the mass of the people. Or *caciques* might use their restored autonomy for private advantage, declaring, for example, communal land to be their own property. Generally, though, they worked to protect their people from both Spaniards and competing native neighbors (for the downfall of the overarching native states had led to resurgence of local rivalries).

For some years after the conquest, then, these local lords did well socially and economically; better, perhaps, than most had done before it. The Spaniards generally regarded them as *hidalgos*, and used the honorific "don" with the more eminent of them. *Caciques* were usually able to keep the various slave-like and serf-like dependents they had held in the past, and in some cases may have added more. These servants were often exempt from tribute to the Spanish. But in the middle decades of the century the lords' situation began to deteriorate. Their intermediary role became less important as the Spanish bureaucracy grew in numbers and knowledge. Their subjects and dependants fell victim to epidemics. And, because the Spaniards' tribute income went down as the population shrank, the administration abolished exemptions, making almost all grown native males, except *caciques* and officers of town government, into tribute payers. Thus native lords lost many of the personal servants who had given them labor, income, and status. Indian *caciques* there still were, nonetheless, until the end of colonial times. But their numbers fell, and some longstanding lineages disappeared. Some survived by adopting European-style economic behavior, going into some kind of market-oriented business to replace the material support they had once had from personal dependants.[29] *Caciques* sought to straddle the cultural gap between their own and the European world by dressing in Spanish style, riding horses, drinking wine instead of a native potion. But increasingly, from the mid-sixteenth century on, these men found themselves sliding, willy-nilly, into the function that the Spanish ever more insistently thrust on them: that of agents charged with making their people produce goods or labor, and with siphoning off a large part of that production to colonists and the colonizing state. They themselves lost materially and culturally in the process. "The curaca became, in the eyes of his people, only a dim shadow of his former institutional self."[30] This comment refers specifically to the north coast of Peru in the mid-1500s. But it is valid to some degree for all the core regions of Spanish settlement, which coincided with the pre-conquest areas of high culture. Elsewhere, the less developed native culture had been, and accordingly the less dense Spanish settlement, the lighter the pressures on local rulers were, and the smaller the changes in their status. But the more peripheral places tended to have more egalitarian social arrangements in the first place; and so local leaders there had less to lose.

In sum, then, by the late sixteenth century native societies had not only vastly fewer people than immediately after the conquest, but local leaders whom depopulation and Spanish pressures had broadly laid low, both materially and culturally. Along with that depression of the upper reaches of surviving Indian society had come a raising of its lower levels to what was now an almost universal category of tribute payers. What had been, in the regions of high culture, a broad, multi-striped band of social functions and privileges was now a narrow ribbon of what Spaniards, at least, increasingly saw simply as "Indians" or "natives" (*naturales*). Between the edges of that ribbon there survived, to be sure, though often outside Spanish view, an impressive range of genuinely native behavior; but it survived in a drastically compressed social structure.

Spanish society in America after the conquest took a course that was the reverse of the native pattern. It grew more complex and more stratified. The conquering bands had certainly had their social rankings, some originating in Spain and some in America. Perhaps a quarter (38 of 168) of the men who took part in the capture of Atahualpa at Cajamarca in 1532 were *hidalgos*, though mostly from the lowest margin of that category in Spain ("very small gentry," none using "don").[31] But length of experience in conquering and settling could override such imported status. By the time of the mainland conquests, then, America was starting to supply its own determinants of social standing. On the whole, though, the conquerors fell within a narrow social range, most being commoners from the manual trades or lower professions.[32]

Taking part in a major conquest, such as those of the Incas and Aztecs, and, to a lesser extent, of such areas as Guatemala, New Granada, and Quito, catapulted even the humblest commoner to high standing in the Indies. Such men became the senior mainland *encomenderos*. Their fame was, therefore, buttressed, at least for two or three decades, by abundant tribute from large numbers of Indians. Though these men, with the exception of the greatest leaders, did not gain noble titles or even the use of "don," they became, functionally, an incipient American aristocracy. Early, but post-conquest, settlers – the *primeros pobladores* – also ranked high in the Indies, though below conquerors, for most of the sixteenth century. Many of them, too, became *encomenderos*, with wealth to back their status as, if not heroes, at least pioneers. If they could not have titles, *encomenderos* tried to surround themselves with the material trappings of nobles: large houses set on broad lands, and filled with a retinue of relatives and dependants.[33]

Soon after the conquests the social range of immigrants widened. The expanding clergy added a new dimension of educated men. There came administrators, most of them university-trained lawyers, to form a new professional segment of the top of society. Viceroys soon arrived to become, among other things, the pinnacle of the social structure; that was one large reason for their selection from the high aristocracy. Larger numbers of fortune-seeking lesser nobles – untitled dons – also appeared in the colonies once reports of wealth crossed the ocean eastward. Most of them, however, hoped to fill their pockets and then return to Spain better equipped than before to enjoy civilized life there. They were helped in this by the preference given to them in the distribution of *encomiendas*.[34] Many of them did go back, so that the social dominance enjoyed by this group endowed with a traditional sort of Spanish status did not last long. And, of course, besides these higher-ranking figures, the Indies-bound exodus of common people – men, and increasingly women also – continued and grew as the years passed. There sailed artisans, agricultural workers, merchants petty and not so petty, muleteers, the odd miner or man of arms. Once across the Ocean Sea, all jostled to find a place to live, a means of support, and a niche in the ranks of the developing society.

Broadly speaking, Spaniards in the Indies in the sixteenth century arranged themselves socially less and less by Iberian criteria of rank, and increasingly by new American standards. Besides the fame and fortune accruing from participation in exploration, conquest, and early settlement, simple wealth gained from using America's human and natural resources soon became a strong influence on social standing. As the native population fell, and the number of Spaniards rose, ever fewer immigrants could aspire to the seigneurial life that *encomenderos* had tried to recreate in the colonies. What America then offered, and much more liberally than Spain, was the chance to make money through personal effort. Engaging in commerce, farming, mining, or some trade then became not merely socially acceptable, but desirable. This was true to an extent from the start. There were early *encomenderos* who were not content simply to lie back and accept tribute, but who used the native workers granted to them to work land to produce food for markets, or mines to yield bullion that even in an uncoined state was money. But the emphasis shifted as the first century progressed. The prospect of tribute-based colonization faded, while active creation of wealth through entrepreneurship, whether at a high or low level, became both necessary and more appealing. A Spanish immigrant in Lima remarked in 1587, "People never ask [here] in what occupation a man has made money, but how much he has; and when they are told that he has something, they shut their mouths and are silent."[35] Those who succeeded rose in public esteem. The process was to be repeated often in later European emigrations. The migrants, probably above average in enterprise to begin with, found, in their new overseas freedom from the social constraints of home, a welcome chance to better themselves economically, and often enough socially as well.

MESTIZOS, AFRICANS, AND OTHERS

One of the novelties that America offered to arriving migrants was people of mixed blood. Though the presence of these was increasingly obvious as the sixteenth century advanced, precise numbers are still harder to measure than those of Spaniards or Indians. One historian's guess "that the Spaniards commonly left more pregnancies in their camps than they did casualties on the field of battle," and that "Biologically speaking, it was neither microbe nor sword nor mailed fist that conquered Mexico. It was the *membrum febrilis*,"[36] is supported by much anecdotal evidence; but no one counted the outcome. The most reliable estimate of these Spanish–Indian mestizos for any region of the sixteenth-century empire puts their number in central, southern, and western New Spain *c.*1568 at some 2,400. The total population of the same area at the time was of the order of 2.7 million (besides the mestizos, about 2.65 million Indians, 63,000 Spaniards, and 23,000 *pardos*, or people wholly or partly Black).[37] Only 0.09 percent of the whole would seem, therefore, to have been mestizo. But this is perhaps a severe understatement of the biological, if not the cultural, reality. Many of the mixed-blooded children born early in colonial times, especially those more European in appearance, were raised by their Spanish fathers. These "euromestizos" are included here in the Spanish category. The mestizos shown, then, are the remainder, or "indomestizos." And undoubtedly other people who were genetically mestizo are hidden in the Indian total.

Though the mestizos (or the proportion of them here enumerated) were such a small part of the central Mexican population in the 1560s, they seem to have increased more rapidly than any other of its components thereafter. By 1646 they (that is, again, "indomestizos") had multiplied seven times, to some 17,000, or 1.1 percent of the total; whereas the number of *pardos* had grown by a factor of 2.3 (to some 62,000) and that of Spaniards (both European- and American-born) had only doubled (to about 125,000).[38] The higher rate of mestizo increase persisted thenceforth, as would be expected as the absolute number of mixed-bloods increased.

New Spain probably led the way among large regions of the empire in Spanish–Indian genetic mixing, for at least two reasons. First, the process started earlier there than anywhere else on the mainland, except lower Central America. Second, the balance of the two ethnic components also tended to equality earlier in New Spain than elsewhere, which should, other things being equal, have maximized the rate of mixture: the native Mexican population seems to have fallen particularly fast, while the colony drew more immigrants from Spain (a third or more of the total) than any other in the 1500s.[39] Conclusive comparisons with other regions of the empire are impossible to make, however, for lack of trustworthy estimates of the non-Indian elements. But the limited example of Lima in 1614 shows that mestizos, as broadly identified, were then only 0.8 percent of that city's population (192 in a total of 24,650).[40]

Numbers of Blacks are clearer, since they were a more distinct element of the population than mestizos; though the imprecise counting caused by variable defining in the case of mestizos applies also to the mixed-blooded off-spring of Blacks – *mulatos, zambos*, and other mixtures less than half African. What is immediately striking about Africans is how many of them were present by the late sixteenth century in comparison with all other groups except Indians. This was clearest in New Spain, as would be expected, since it had received the largest number of slaves. According to a census of 1570, eight large towns in the centre and south of the colony, including Mexico City, then held 9,370 Black slaves and 1,160 mulattoes, as against 9,720 Spaniards. The capital contained the vast majority of the African element – 8,000 Black slaves and 1,000 mulattoes, among 8,000 Spaniards – probably because the wealth concentrated there made for common use of slaves in domestic service. By 1612, Whites were heavily outnumbered by Blacks in Mexico City: 15,000 Spaniards as against 50,000 Blacks and mulattoes (and 80,000 Indians).[41] Another count, this time of Blacks together with people partly black, puts some 22,600 of them in central Mexico *c.*1568 and 62,400 in 1646 (respect-ively 0.8 and 4.24 percent of the total population).[42]

Spaniards took Blacks with them wherever they went in the Americas in the sixteenth century. But it was Peru, as the second main focus of Spanish settlement after New Spain, that was the other large market for African slaves. The result, as in Mexico, was that towns there quickly came to have a large proportion of Blacks and part-Blacks in their populations. In the mid-1550s Lima had perhaps 1,500 such in its citizenry – half of all those in Peru, and perhaps a number equal to the Spanish population of the town. By the 1590s the count had risen to some 7,000. The Lima census of 1614 shows 10,386 Blacks and 744 mulattoes (41.9 and 3.0 percent of the total population of 24,650). Lima was, in fact, genetically almost half African (or part African) from the 1590s to the end of the seventeenth century; and the same can be said generally of both coastal and highland towns in northern and central Peru.[43]

It was perfectly obvious, then, by the late decades of the sixteenth century that Spanish American society did not consist of Europeans and native Americans alone, and never more would do so. A third element, partly Black and partly a mixture of Indian, Spanish, and Black, was rising in numbers to occupy, or better, perhaps, to create a social space between Europeans and natives. This element, genetically and culturally varied as it was, came to be seen as a third major grouping of American society. It is tempting to dub it an American estate. But it had no unifying legal definition. Rather the reverse was the case, in fact, since Blacks, for example, were treated separately in law from others, and slaves differently from free men. On the other hand, people in this third group were legally distinct from Indians, and Spaniards, in being exempt from the state's forced labor systems, and also in practice from tribute payment. But, above all, mestizos, Blacks, mulattoes, and all the other more complex intermixtures that appeared as time passed were lumped together because they were neither native American nor Euro-pean. The generic term applied to them was *castas*. The word does not translate as "caste" in the usual English sense. Fluidity, rather than rigidity, of social and economic position, within certain limits, was the essence of being a Black or mixed-blooded *casta* in colonial Spanish America.

That fluidity could, though, make for discomfort. The clear emergence of the mestizo on to the social scene in the mid-sixteenth century was met with suspicion, both official and private. Up to then Spaniards had been few enough for mestizos to be seen as allies, as part-Europeans collaborating in the domination of America. But as the white population grew, from immigration and natural increase, mestizos slipped in esteem. Ever fewer of them were the products of marriage. Spaniards, made acutely, even pathologically, conscious of legitimacy and "purity of blood" by long coexistence with Jews and Muslims, increasingly tended to disdain mestizos for their irregular origins. Despite this, of course, Spanish males continued to sire children in casual or even lasting unions with Indian or mestiza women. And the more European-like of the offspring might still be raised in Spanish households, or at least would have some advantage in finding economic and social openings. But those who looked more Indian, but not enough so to enter the native world fully, were the objects of both native and Spanish suspicion, and of Spanish scorn. "You are to expel mestizos from Indian villages and send them to the nearest Spanish towns, where they can learn trades and seek employment, instead of living as vagabonds and setting a bad example to the Indians, as they do" – so ordered the governor of Peru, Lope García de Castro, in his instructions of 1565 for newly created *corregidores de indios*.[44] This became the lasting and standard official view of mestizos: idle and drifting troublemakers, irritating misfits for whom the simple Spanish–Indian model of early American society had no clear place. Their Indian-ness, transmitted not only through their gestation by a native mother, but also through her milk, was also cause for alarm. Might they not, resentful and often skilled in arms as they were, lead Indians against the Spanish?[45] They did, indeed; but not until the eighteenth century.

Despite the nervousness they inspired, as their numbers grew mestizos inevitably took a wider role in society. Though some, the more Indian, found few openings outside manual and menial labor, and others, the more European, managed to insinuate themselves into the lower reaches of the secular priesthood and the bureaucracy, most gravitated to a middle range of occupations. They might become, for instance, supervisors on farms and in mines, perhaps small farmers themselves, muleteers, petty merchants, or artisans. How mestizos ranked in the popular view is suggested by their treatment by guilds in sixteenth- and early seventeenth-century Mexico City. The trades that considered themselves most elevated (armorers and sword-smiths, for example) clumped mestizos with free Blacks and mulattoes, denying them any advance in rank. Less exalted crafts allowed mestizos to become masters, while limiting other non-Whites to journeyman status. The least pretentious – candle-makers and cobblers – gave mestizos, free Blacks and mulattoes alike access to all ranks.[46] Thus Spaniards certainly consigned mestizos to the *casta* mass; but they gave them a slight, though not definitive, preference of status within it.

Blacks and mulattoes were more easily and more precisely placed in society. To begin with, they were more distinctive in appearance than mestizos were. Second, the taint of slavery always clung to them, even if they had been freed or were the descendants of freedmen. Slavery had, at some point, been the mechanism responsible for the arrival of all Blacks in America. Third, Spaniards felt toward Africans none of the lingering sense of responsibility that Indians inspired in them, even if faintly as time advanced, and that, via Indians, attached even more distantly to mestizos. Spain had received no charge to convert and care for Africans. Africans, moreover, came from places associated with Islam. Many, though – or so the belief was – had had the chance to take up Christianity, but refused it. Their spiritual welfare, therefore, was no concern of Spain's. In general, for a combination of these reasons, Spaniards regarded, and legally categorized, Blacks as *gente vil*, or base people; whereas mestizos fell on the margins of *gente de razón*, fully rational people such as Spaniards were.[47]

In fact, nonetheless, Blacks proved so useful to Spaniards in America, from the conquest on, that the real position that many of them occupied in society was higher than their legal definition would suggest. An exception to this is the considerable number of field slaves who were working, by the end of the sixteenth century, on plantations producing sugar on the Peruvian coast or in southern Mexico, for example, or cacao around Guayaquil on the coast of Quito. But, these aside, the sense of alliance, or even fraternity, evident in the conquests between Spaniards and Africans persisted thereafter. Colonists tended to regard Blacks and mulattoes, whether slave or free, as more able and more reliable than Indians, and so gave them tasks and responsibilities that set them higher on the social and economic scales than all Indians, besides *caciques*. Further reason for this is not hard to find. Many of the Blacks in America in the 1500s came from regions of West Africa in which iron-working and cattle-tending were part of material culture. These people had abilities immediately useful to Spaniards, and not possessed by most Indians. Again, Africans in America were cut off from their cultural origins. For their own well-being, psychological comfort, even safety, they had no choice but to identify with Spaniards.

It is no surprise, then, to find many Blacks as personal and domestic servants of Spaniards after the conquests. Having as many such servants as possible was also, of course, an important mark of prestige for the settler. *Encomenderos* often kept a large retinue of them. Colonists might also set up their slaves in craft shops; African blacksmiths were particularly common in early post-conquest Peru.[48] There are known cases in which a slave master craftsman was sent off by his master to another city to set up an independent artisan shop there; the profits to be remitted to the slave owner. Broadly speaking, Spaniards used Blacks to supervise native workers. The lesson that Indians had learned during the conquests, that the African was part of the invading culture, was reinforced after the fighting was done. Occasional Spanish fears that Indians and Blacks would unite against them proved almost entirely unfounded.

The rising presence of Blacks, though, made many Spaniards nervous, especially as, after 1550 or so, the numbers of Africans in the main colonial towns equaled and then passed the numbers of Europeans. A law of 1551 forbade them to bear arms.[49] As with the perceived mestizo threat, these fears were exaggerated. But they were not groundless, for, although no serious danger to Spanish settlement ever came from Blacks, protests there were aplenty in the form of runaway slaves and their communities. Panama had the largest black population after New Spain and Peru in the sixteenth century, brought in to work in the carriage of goods across the Isthmus between the Atlantic and Pacific fleets. Slaves drove mule trains, loaded cargoes, built ships and storehouses, and, as everywhere, served as domestics.[50] Some of them fled into the forests. Francis Drake, leading his first assault on the Spanish Caribbean in 1572, found these maroons (cimarrones) a useful ally. After the failure of an initial attack on Nombre de Dios, the Spanish port on the Caribbean side of the Isthmus, he

> came to the sound of Darién and having conference with certain Negroes which were fled from their masters at Panama and Nombre de Dios, the Negroes did tell him that certain mules came laden with gold and silver from Panama to Nombre de Dios. Who in company of these Negroes went thereupon on land and stayed in the way where the treasure should come, with a hundred shot, and so took two companies of mules . . . and he carried away the gold only, for they were not able to carry the silver through the mountains.[51]

Nowhere else in the empire offered runaway slaves such power to damage Spanish interests; Panama was a peculiarly tender spot, since South American silver on its way to Spain there crossed from Pacific to Atlantic. Maroons elsewhere were a nuisance, a disruption of order, but a thorn rather than a sword in the side of the body politic. One group in Esmeraldas, on the northern coast of Quito, originated c.1570 in the wreck of a slave ship. The Blacks blended with the local natives, creating a large zambo population that never succumbed to the feeble Spanish efforts to subdue it. The region was isolated and of small economic importance.[52] Another outlying area in which a largely autonomous local Black culture took root was the south-western coast of New Spain around Acapulco. The Spanish regarded more seriously an African separatist presence that developed in central Mexico. Maroons, by the early 1600s, regularly threatened the crucial road between Veracruz, the main port on the Caribbean coast, and the interior. In 1609 these renegades were reported to have chosen a king, named Yanga. Rumors circulated of a plot to kill all Spaniards in Mexico City. The viceroy immediately put together a militia force of six hundred to subdue the rebels. But their guerrilla tactics proved hard to overcome, and the authorities finally had to strike a bargain with Yanga whereby he and his people might live unmolested in the mountains so long as they stopped raiding. Two years later another, perhaps more substantial, plot was discovered for the killing of the white inhabitants of Mexico City. This was put down in 1612 with the execution of thirty-six supposed Black leaders. There was more trouble in 1617, when maroons started raiding in the countryside again. They were easily suppressed by force this time; but the offenders were allowed to stay at large in a town of their own named San Lorenzo de los Negros.[53]

These episodes in central New Spain suggest the ambiguity of Spanish attitudes toward Blacks in America. On the one hand was a feeling of the need to treat them cautiously, inspired by fear, certainly, but perhaps also by a lasting sense that Europeans and Blacks were essentially on the same side, collaborating to control Indians and America itself. On the other hand was disdain, and even scorn, for a category of people long associated with slavery and heathenism. Spaniards' equivocation was reinforced by the economic and social desirability of owning Black slaves. In the Spanish view, they did some sorts of work better than Indians could; and there was no question that possessing Blacks conferred far more social prestige on an individual than employing Indian servants, even Indian slaves. A classic comment on the topic came from Bishop Mota y Escobar, of Guadalajara, visiting the silver mining town of Zacatecas in the opening years of the seventeenth century. He found there some eight hundred Black and mulatto slaves, men and women; and also a number of free Blacks, "who come and go, and hire themselves out for work in cattle-raising, farming, and mining. And generally both slaves and freemen are bad and pernicious. But it is as they say here: 'Bad to have them, but much worse not to have them'."[54]

The ambiguity of Spanish attitudes is also suggested by the clear presence of free Blacks and mulattoes in the colonies from the start. Spaniards wanted slaves, but, it would seem, were unwilling to bar them rigidly from freedom. Slaves who were put to craft work, for instance, might be allowed to keep some of the shop's income and slowly accumulate funds with which to buy their own liberty. Owners might free mulatto children they had themselves produced. They also sometimes freed slaves in their wills. They showed, perhaps, a tendency to prefer women in these bequests of liberty; and that promoted freedom further, since subsequent children took their status from their mothers. It is true that owners gave up less in freeing women; male slaves had a greater economic value. And the males who were freed tended to be older and hence less valuable. But a long medieval tradition existed in Spanish law providing openings to freedom for slaves. One student of slavery in New Spain offers an apt assessment. "The distinctiveness of colonial Mexico, and perhaps that of other Spanish colonies, rests not on the ease and frequency of manumission but rather on the absence of an environment which frowned upon freedom for black slaves. The Spaniards in Mexico never quite rejected the idea that slavery was contrary to natural law and reason and never quite embraced the view that Africans were created to be slaves in perpetuity." But freedom was always more likely to go to those who were less economically useful: children, women, the elderly.[55]

TOWNS

The physical framework in which Spaniards and *castas* arranged themselves socially was above all the city. In Spanish America today, and indeed in Spain too, the notion persists strongly that cities are the proper place for the development and exercise of civilization. The country may be briefly visited for purposes of restoration or refuge, or, in the case of landowners, of supervision and the pleasures of proprietorship. But rare still is the educated person who would choose the country life over the urban, out of fascination with flora and fauna, or enjoyment of undisturbed natural rhythms.

This preference for city life doubtless has many sources. But one of them is the ancient Greek notion that true, civil, people must inhabit a city, for a city is the only possible environment for developed political and moral existence. Those who live elsewhere are probably barbarians, lacking the political order for which the city provides a setting, and which indeed is the essence of city.[56] At the other, pragmatic, extreme from this principle it is easy to imagine why early Spaniards in America (and, for that matter, Christians pressing back the Moors over the centuries of reconquest in Iberia) would gather in cities. Such places offered physical and psychological strength in their concentrated numbers, and served as defensible bridgeheads in new (and in the American case, alien) territory. Further, medieval experience in Spain had given the city a corporate identity firmly defined in law. A town had legal rights (for instance, to choose its administrators and justices, and to allocate land for building and agriculture) from which its citizens could benefit, and which far exceeded any privileges they might exercise as individuals. This became so once it had been legally founded, and even before it had any physical identity beyond its site. Thus, in the notorious example, Cortés founded Veracruz at the start of his Mexican campaign, naming aldermen and magistrates, and renouncing his authority in the expedition to them. They, then, as representatives of the corporation, quite legitimately appointed him governor of the town. He thereby became in fact and law the supreme Spanish official in Mexico, head of an autonomous corporation; and as such was able to take independent command of the party that he had brought from Cuba at Diego Velázquez's order, and redirect it to the purpose of conquest.[57]

The typical Spanish American town was built on a grid pattern, with eight major streets running outward from the corners of a central plaza. Around the square were ranged the major municipal structures (town hall, or *casas de cabildo*, jail, a treasury building if the *Real Hacienda* had a branch in the town), the parish church, and possibly, if space remained, houses of pre-eminent citizens. Generally speaking, the more important a family, the closer its house stood to the plaza. Many sources have been proposed for this distinctive chessboard design: native cities such as Tenochtitlan, medieval fortress towns of southern France and north-eastern Spain, the influence of the Italian Renaissance, and, behind that, Vitruvius, the Roman author of *De Architectura* of the first century BC. His precepts appear clearly in parts of the Philip II's *Ordinances for New Discovery and Settlement* of 1573. But the oddity is that many towns had been built on the grid pattern long before those rules were issued. From the first, indeed, it seems that Spaniards, whether conquerors, settlers, or officials, carried to America the notion that that was the proper form for a settlement, even though most of them came from parts of Spain in which medieval towns with narrow, winding streets were the norm. Some "collective intuition" seems to have been at work.[58] Certainly the grid was a simple, even obvious, design on which to lay out a new place, especially if the site chosen was more or less flat, as many were. Division of square or rectangular blocks into house lots was simply done. But some attempt seems to have been made to impose the grid model also on irregular sites, such as the narrow valleys in which some mining towns were founded.

Whatever its source, the grid plan was well fixed in the minds of explorers and conquerors; and, it has been suggested, not simply as a practical convenience, but as a physical metaphor of the orderliness and civility that cities ideally embodied. It is as if the Spanish sought to declare the civilization they believed they were carrying to America in laying out everywhere they went that urban pattern of central square, straight streets, and rectangular blocks. Naturally they tried to impose this same design on native communities, into which they hoped also to inject their version of civility.[59] The new communities into which many Indians were "reduced" from the mid-1500s onward were planned in this way, in the hope that urban surroundings would foment in the native people the *policía* – good, legal order and behavior – that Spain sought to inculcate in them. In reality, even the newly created native towns resisted this imposed geometry; as did the native *barrios* that generally grew up around the central grid of Spanish cities. In the "reductions," the plaza tended to be simply an open space in which the parish church was the sole marker of authority; while the correspondence between social position and distance from the plaza, so rigidly set in Spanish towns, was weak in native places.[60] In Indian *barrios*, the straight streets of the town centre tended to give way to wandering alleys and randomly placed houses.

It seems no chance that the greatest symbol of Spanish imperial power, Philip II's monastery-palace of San Lorenzo del Escorial, should also have been built on the gridiron plan. (Is it, though, some hint of uncertainty, humility, or irony in the king that he should have chosen a place named "The Slag-Heap," the literal meaning of *escorial*, for this massive expression of the state?) Certainly, in America, Spanish towns were the symbols and the foci of colonizing power. The central cities were the seats of viceroys, archbishops, *audiencias*, the treasury, the Inquisition. In smaller towns the monarchy was represented directly by a *corregidor* or *alcalde mayor*. But the *cabildo*, the town council of aldermen and magistrates of first instance, while defending the municipality's interests before outside authorities, was also a part of colonial government. Most aldermen, after the early decades, indeed received their positions through royal grant or by purchase from the state. As long as it was in their interest to do so, they played their part in imposing the official will on America and its native people. And as, in general, powerful private settlers pursuing economic interests in and around their towns, they certainly contributed in the wider sense to Spanish domination of American territory. Other powerful men, too – landowners, merchants, miners – even if they were not council members, along with the lawyers, notaries, and clerks who organized their activities, clustered in towns; making these, in a graphic phrase, "centrifugal points of assault on the land and its resources."[61]

FAMILY AND FRIENDS

If the city was a crucial socio-political unit on the large scale in the success of Spanish colonization, so was the family on a smaller scale. Official policy favored the formation of Spanish families in America from the start, and for that reason encouraged women to emigrate. At the behest of the Catholic Monarchs in 1498, thirty females were among Columbus's party of 330 on his third voyage to the Caribbean. In 1505 Ferdinand issued the first example of an oft-repeated command that married men in the Indies (Hispaniola alone, at the time) whose wives were still in Spain should go and fetch them, or arrange their passage across the Atlantic. The aim was to set a good example for Indians, to reinforce the Spanish colonial hold through population increase, and to strengthen the will of settlers to "reside and remain in these parts" – to use the words of Hernán Cortés, who in 1524 disposed that the *encomenderos* whom he governed in New Spain should bring over their wives in eighteen months, or lose their Indians. A true *vecino*, or householder, another royal decree of 1544 stated, lived with wife and children. Men separated from their wives were not established in America: "they never perpetuate themselves, nor attend to building, to planting, to raising animals, to sowing, to doing the things that good settlers accustom to do."[62]

Despite the implication of these constant urgings, it seems that in fact many married men moving to America did take wives and children with them. And family in a wider sense was central to individuals' efforts to set themselves up, survive, and prosper in America. The Pizarros are a prime early example. Francisco Pizarro recruited three brothers (Hernando, Gonzalo, and Juan) and other relatives as assistants in the conquest of Peru. This turning to relatives is scarcely surprising. The conquest years and their immediate aftermath were a time of fierce rivalries and hence great temptations to betrayal. Kin were likely to be the most reliable subordinates. The principle endured once settlement was established. Who could be more trusted than a brother, a cousin, an uncle, or a nephew as a business partner, or as an agent to carry cash to Spain and do business there? Extended families, moreover, were likely to straddle various occupations and social levels in Spain; and, in time, in America also. They became, then, networks on which their members could draw, for the particular expertise of a merchant or a lawyer, perhaps, or the influence of a well-placed official. A family connection might be useful simply for the status associated with it. A quite local reputation in Spain could carry across the Atlantic. One Alvaro de Paredes Espadero, for instance, son of an *hidalgo* family in Cáceres in Extremadura, and a relative of a member of the Council of the Indies, found his family's name the key to bringing off an unexpectedly good marriage in Mexico City in 1590. His bride was the sister of an official in the *audiencia*, and brought with her not only a dowry of 8,000 pesos, no small sum, but political and social connections.[63]

The trust a settler placed in family members extended out in diminishing measure to friends, people from the same home town, and finally those from the same region of origin in Spain. Again, this was very clear in the conquests and early settlements. Nicolás de Ovando, another native of Cáceres, while en route to Hispaniola in 1502 gathered fellow Extremadurans as members of his large refounding party. One of them was Francisco Pizarro, a native of Trujillo, a town some 45 kilometers east of Cáceres. Twenty-five or so years later, Pizarro himself went back to Trujillo and Extremadura to collect not only relatives but local compatriots for the conquering expedition to Peru. The ties of Spanish city and region long remained strong in the Indies. For instance, a Galician from north-west Spain arriving in America would find a welcome, lodging, perhaps even work among fellow *gallegos* already established there. The most distinct of Spanish regional groups in the Indies were the Basques, who clustered together to become prominent in, among other things, commerce and mining. Galicians and Basques had a strong defining identity in their languages. This must have been particularly so with the Basques, whose language, quite unrelated to the Romance tongues of the rest of Iberia, can only have seemed an exclusive code to other colonists. Certainly Basques were a frequent source of suspicion and annoyance to other Spaniards in America.

So, in a series of physical and notional frameworks, the Spanish disposed themselves across America in the sixteenth century, creating a society that reproduced a good part of what they had come from, but added new elements to it that the American experience produced. The European noble estate became, *mutatis mutandis*, the republic of Spaniards. The Spanish medieval town of narrow, sinuous streets became the rectilinear and rectangular American city – except on its Indian outskirts, where, perhaps symbolically, the older pattern re-emerged. To the trusties of family, home town, or home province were added in some degree black slaves and freemen, bound to their owners and masters by the shared rigors of exploration and conquest. In the single American republic of Spaniards, colonists moved up the social scale, and probably down as well, more freely than in Spain, with wealth becoming a more powerful influence on standing. The Spanish common estate found its American counterpart in an Indian republic in which, long before the end of the century, both the numbers and the social range of pre-conquest times were severely narrowed. Then, to these familiar or partly familiar features of society were added, increasingly obvious as time passed, the uniquely American products of a three-way racial and cultural mixture – mestizos, *mulatos*, *zambos*, and, in time, other intermediate *castas*. Their growing presence was to do more than anything else to move the society of the Indies away from its European, and native, origins, and make it, over the balance of the colonial era and beyond, distinctively Spanish American.

[10] *Economy: Ships and Silver*

We order and command the viceroys, presidents, governors, and ministers of Our royal treasury to take the greatest care in seeking the profit and increase of all that belongs to Us in the provinces under their administration, and to apply their entire attention and diligence to the exploitation and working of the mines, to the collection of Our royal imposts and to the remittance to these realms of what is gathered; proceeding with great diligence, not allowing withholdings or delays in any sum from one year to another... The good administration and lawful growth of Our royal income (which will be most pleasant to Us) is fitting to the service of God, our Lord, and to the preservation of these realms. And we charge Our viceroys and presidents, that, considering that this is the nerve and spirit that gives vigour and being to the Royal Estate, they gather with Auditors, Royal Officials, Ministers and other persons who may seem most fitting to achieve this end, and that they discuss and treat these matters, and the reduction of expenses in so far as possible, so that by this means, and others that they may arrive at, Our Royal income is increased, so that We may use it to attend to the needs of Our Monarchy...[1]

This exhortation from Philip III, directed in 1617 to his senior administrators in the Indies, suggests how crucial American income had become to the Spanish crown in the sixteenth century. The "service of God" was no mere rhetorical flourish, for American wealth, particularly in the form of surging silver production from the 1560s, had been part of the inspiration for Philip II's commitment of Spain to the militant defense of Catholicism in Europe.[2] And, indeed, the appearance of that wealth seemed providential, a sign that Spain should assume the role of temporal leader of the effort against expanding Protestantism in northern Europe. By some measures, American wealth was astonishing. Silver production from Potosí alone in 1592, worth about 5.6 million ducats, amounted to some 44 percent of the Spanish crown's average yearly spending on state business in Europe between 1593 and 1597.[3] That, though, was Potosí's best year ever. And the crown did not receive the entire output, of course, but only the royalty on it of about 21 percent. The total revenue of the crown from America, including mining royalties, sales taxes, customs duties and other levies, amounted, in years of high remittances from the Indies, to about a fifth of the total royal income during Philip II's reign (1556–98). The fact, however, that a large shipment of bullion could reliably be expected every year, and that the trend of these arrivals was upward until 1600, made American "treasure" especially valuable to Philip II as a source of financial leverage. With it as security he could raise loans to fund his political and military efforts in Europe.[4]

Though the full extent of America's mineral wealth was not apparent until the second half of the sixteenth century, the royal and individual hopes for bullion before then that grew from Columbus's initial reports on Hispaniola and Central America were not disappointed. The Greater Antilles, though the scene of much washing for gold in the first two decades of the century, do not seem to have yielded abundantly. But spoils from the mainland conquests were a different matter. Cortés's initial party in Tenochtitlan seized plentiful gold; but lost most of it in the lake during their flight from the city in mid-1520. Atahualpa's famous ransom in Cajamarca of the amount of gold and silver needed to fill a large room to the height of a raised arm was an even greater haul. Together with other booty it came to about 1.5 million pesos, the equivalent, perhaps, of 1.5 million ounces of silver. The king's fifth of this reached Spain.[5] Other regions that proved rich in loot of worked gold were the Peruvian coast and highland Colombia.

In the early years after the conquests, the looting mentality expanded into one of extracting wealth through tribute collection. The ideal, perhaps, of most early *encomenderos* was to preside over lordly households and lands while being sustained by the tribute, in gold, food, cloth and other products, of the native communities granted to them. But not all *encomenderos* found their tribute receipts sufficient in quantity and variety, and far from all were content in a role of passive receipt of their Indians' products. Given the obviously widespread presence of gold (and, it was soon clear, silver also) in the mainland subsoils, it is no surprise that mining was one of the first enterprises to which they turned. The crown, too, was deeply interested in the mining of precious metals. Bullion was money. For the monarchy, indeed, even more than for colonists, American wealth always meant mining more than any other sort of production.

MINING

Mining in New Spain began within a decade of the conquest. Although some gold was extracted, chiefly in the south, it was soon clear that Mexico was richer in silver ores than in gold. The first silver strikes came *c.*1530, at Zumpango and Sultepec. Taxco and Tlalpujahua followed *c.*1534. All these were in central Mexico, within 150 kilometers or so of the capital. They produced encouragingly, especially as there was still no more ambitious standard against which to set them. But the full extent of Mexico's silver wealth was not revealed until the mid-1540s, when Spanish exploration reached the first of the great ore deposits of the northern plateau. This was at Zacatecas (1546); and from there other northern discoveries were made, at, for example, Santa Bárbara in 1567 and San Luis Potosí *c.*1592. At Guanajuato, on the border between central Mexico and the arid north, and well south of Zacatecas, silver ore seems to have been found *c*.1550. Guanajuato was overshadowed by other districts for almost two centuries, but finally rose to become the new Potosí of the empire, outstripping any other silver center in New Spain or South America by a wide margin after 1740.

The ores of Potosí itself, long the token of Spanish American wealth for Spaniards and other Europeans alike, came to light in 1545. The Spanish, with the Pizarro brothers in the forefront, had worked the nearby mines of Porco, itself a major pre-conquest source of silver, from 1538. The discovery of the Rich Hill of Potosí was an offshoot of that effort; and the scion very soon outgrew its parent. In the century after 1550, the Potosí district, with the Rich Hill always its main source of ore, produced about a half of Spanish America's silver.

The Andes proved richer in gold than New Spain, with major mining centers developing at Carabaya (1542) in south-eastern Peru, Chachapoyas and Valdivia (*c*.1550) in northern Peru and central Chile respectively, and Zaruma (*c*.1560) in southern Quito. But it was New Granada that dominated gold production in the Andes, and everywhere in the empire, in the sixteenth century and later. Production began at Popayán, in the south, before 1540, and at Antioquia, in the north, in 1546. New Granadan gold output seems to have passed through a deep slump late in the seventeenth century, while still exceeding that of any other region; and then climbed strongly throughout the eighteenth.

At the beginning, Spaniards drew on native mining and refining techniques wherever they existed. In New Spain native knowledge of metallurgy was slight, except among the Tarascans in the center-west, who were skilled producers and workers of copper. From them early Spanish silver miners may have learned something. In the Andes they certainly took much from a long and developed tradition of underground mining, smelting, and elaboration of refined metals. The Andeans were familiar with gold, silver, copper, and tin; and from the latter two, they alloyed bronze. Silver was the Spaniards' main interest. Such was the native skill in producing it in the Andes that until almost 1570, Spanish mine owners in effect rented their mines to Indian managers, who in turn hired workers to cut and refine the ore. Spanish iron and steel tools probably were an advance over native implements in work below ground. But refining of silver in the central Andes, predominantly at Porco and Potosí, was done in longstanding native fashion using small furnaces of stone or clay named *guayras*. The Quechua word means "air," and the furnaces were so named because the fire inside them was fanned simply by the mountain winds rather than by bellows. The fuel used was either *ichu*, the rough grass of the highlands, or llama dung. This simple smelting method was cheap, and efficient enough when applied to high grade ores to yield a profit for both native workers and Spanish mine owners.

In New Spain, silver was also produced by smelting for some years after mines were first opened. The technology here, though, was European, consisting essentially of a small furnace in the form of a hollow, square column of stone, 1.5 to 2 meters high. The charcoal fire within was blown by bellows. It was a cheap and simple apparatus. Even where powered bellows were used, with the energy coming from a water wheel or animals, the necessary machinery could be built of wood on patterns familiar from mills for fulling wool or grinding grain. Some early colonists, at least, would have known of these designs, even if, as seems likely, there were few experienced miners among them. Almost certainly there was as well some early flow of mining and refining knowledge to New Spain from Germany, the European region most advanced in metallurgy in the sixteenth century. Miners from Silesia crossed the Atlantic to Santo Domingo in 1528 as part of the Welsers' colonizing effort in Venezuela. But they never reached Venezuela. Some went back to Europe, but fifty or so seem to have remained in the New World, and quite possibly moved on to Mexico. In the mid-1530s the factors in Seville of the other great German banking house of the day, the Fuggers of Augsburg, definitely sent German smelters to New Spain to give help with difficulties in smelting silver.

Germans possibly had a part in bringing about a radical advance beyond smelting that was achieved in New Spain in the mid-1550s. This was the introduction of amalgamation of silver ores, a refining process that revolutionized silver production in Spanish America and that may rank, in its worldwide effects, as high as any other technical innovation made in the Americas since Europeans first went there. The principle of amalgamation – the curious capacity of mercury to bind to certain other metals, even when they are in the form of ores – had been known in the Old World at least since Roman times. It had been long used on a small scale, as, for example, in the recovery of gold and silver filings from the sweepings from a silversmith's floor. It probably passed early to America, since mercury has been found in the remains of the first Spanish town on Hispaniola, at Isabela, which suggests that gold may have been extracted there from alluvial sand or crushed rock by amalgamation. But it was in New Spain that mercury was first used to draw silver from its ores on what could be called an industrial scale. One Bartolomé de Medina, a Spanish cloth merchant from Seville, is given main credit for the invention. In 1555 the viceroy granted him monopoly rights in the process in Mexico for ten years. Clearly associated with Medina, however, perhaps particularly in developing the machinery for crushing ore to the fineness that effective amalgamation required, was a German named Gaspar Lohmann. Both were active in Sultepec and the newly opened deposits at Pachuca in the mid-1550s.

Large-scale amalgamation appeared in New Spain not simply as the outcome of Medina's and Lohmann's inventiveness, but clearly as a response to changing local conditions. By the 1550s ores rich enough to be smelted at a profit were becoming scarce. They had mainly been surface deposits enriched by weathering, and were soon skimmed off. Enormous quantities of ore remained, obviously enough; but they were of lower grade, and furthermore had to be brought up from increasing depths. The ores' yield, therefore, dropped, as their cost rose. Medina and Lohmann's amalgamation process, with its capacity to refine great volumes of poor ores quite cheaply, was the answer. How eagerly the process was seized on is shown by that fact that over 120 refiners took it up before 1555 was out.[6] In the following years it spread to nearly all Mexican silver centers.

For lack of records, amalgamation's immediate effect on Mexican production cannot be seen. But in Potosí it had demonstrably dramatic results. The same problems of declining ore yields and rising costs as had earlier afflicted Mexico were depressing output there by the late 1560s. Viceroy Toledo arrived from Spain in 1569 with orders to install the mercury process in Potosí. He indeed played an active part in its adoption there, but the miners of Potosí would doubtless soon have used it in any case. The first mills for refining by amalgamation were built in the town in 1572. That was also the year of lowest production since records begin, in 1549. Between 1572 and 1582 output grew 6.7 times (from 26,000 to 174,000 kilograms). By 1592, the peak year in Potosí's history, it had risen to almost 202,000 kilograms. Amalgamation, it is true, was not solely responsible for this boom. In the 1570s, Toledo had also increased the labor supply, reorganizing the forced drafting of native workers to miners and refiners in Potosí. But without amalgamation those reforms would have served little. The extra workers might have mined much ore at low cost. But it could not have been refined profitably with either Andean or European smelting techniques.

Amalgamation processing was itself far from cheap to set up; but the large initial investment required paid off quickly. The fundamental need was for a means of crushing the ore finely, so that the mercury, when added, could come into close contact with as much of the mineral as possible. This was done everywhere with a mill consisting of four to twelve vertical, iron-shod stamps, which were lifted in turn by cams rotating on a heavy shaft. The motive power was a water wheel, where sufficient flow and head were available, or teams of mules in dry areas, such as northern Mexico. Once milled, the ore was mixed with water and mercury, and sometimes other reagents, such as salt, iron filings, and copper sulphate, that empirical testing proved useful. In the Andes, the mixing was done in large tanks holding some 2,300 kilograms of ore. Sometimes these were heated from below to speed the reaction. In New Spain, wooden troughs served the same purpose in the sixteenth century. After then the common method was to spread the blended ore out on a paved court, a practice that led to the use of the term *beneficio de patio*, or "patio processing," for amalgamation in New Spain. After some weeks (the actual time depending on the ambient temperature and other, lesser variables) the refiner would decide, from experience, that the combining of mercury with silver was complete. The entire mixture was then washed, usually in wooden vats, sometimes fitted with powered rotating paddles. The mercury–silver amalgam sank to the bottom, whence it was gathered up, and excess mercury physically squeezed from it. Heating the amalgam then made the remaining mercury evaporate off; a honeycomb of pure silver remained. Once amalgamation became commonplace, refiners tried with some success to minimize the loss of mercury in the process. They found it possible to recover some of it by carrying out the heating of the amalgam beneath a metal or clay hood. The mercury vapor condensed on the inside of the hood into the metal's familiar liquid form, which could then be collected. The practice also had the advantage of reducing somewhat the risk of poisoning from mercury vapor, which is notably toxic.

Amalgamation was a long, many-staged process, and in its complexity a far cry from earlier refining by smelting. The amalgamation plant, known in the Andes as an *ingenio* and in New Spain as an *hacienda de minas*, was a large and expensive affair, with its crushing mill and associate driving mechanism, tanks or patio, washing vats, store rooms, living quarters for workers and supervisor, and often enough a small chapel. The water-powered *ingenios* built in Potosí in the 1570s cost on average 50,000 pesos each, the price of fifty modest houses, or five thousand llamas. Such installations were, along with mine workings themselves, and ocean-going trading vessels, the largest capital investments made by colonists in Spanish America.

This need for heavy investment made amalgamation the almost exclusive domain of the white portion of the population. In New Spain, where the native role in silver production was from the start limited to laboring, the coming of the new technique brought little change for Indians. But in the central Andes it meant an end to the control of extraction and refining of ores that many skilled native miners had enjoyed, along with some share of the profit, from the 1540s to the 1560s. These men did not have access to the cash needed to build *ingenios*. Further, the technology of water wheels, geared machinery, and iron and steel was an import, and alien to them. Indians in Potosí and elsewhere, then, did not become *azogueros*, the owners of refining mills and the dominant force in silver production after the 1570s. Native production of silver, on the other hand, did not stop at that point. *Guayras* long continued to burn on Andean mountainsides, smelting small pieces of rich ore that indigenous men, and women, picked out from mine tailings, or that underground workers took from the mines as part of their wages. In aggregate this smelted production may have been considerable, though it is impossible to estimate its amount. The same happened in Mexico, where Indians and mestizos were always to be found operating small smelting furnaces in and around Spanish-dominated mining towns.

By Spanish law, subsoil rights in America remained with the crown. Private possession of land included only the surface. But individuals might claim mines, and then work them for their own profit so long as they paid a royalty to the treasury. The basic rate in the sixteenth century was a fifth of the metal produced, the *quinto real*. Reductions in the tax were granted from the mid-century onward to stimulate mining. New Spain was seen as particularly needing this help, so that in the second half of the century (and later) the prevailing rate there was a tenth. It is mainly from these royalty records, which become more complete as the century progresses, that mining production has been calculated. The best such estimate to date places Spanish American silver output from its start until 1600 or 1610 at 375–400 million pesos, or 10.6–11.3 million kilograms.[7] By far the greater part of this amount was produced after 1550, as Potosí and the north Mexican mines began to yield. The rate of increase of total Spanish American production in the period 1560 to 1620–30 was the highest of any long period in the colonial era, at about 2.3 percent annually. Potosí, once amalgamation was adopted there, was mainly responsible for the high volume of output, and for a time for its growth also. Production at Potosí leveled off, however, in the 1590s and then began to fall in the new century, as ore quality declined and the costs of extraction rose with the increasing depth of the mines. But it was still the largest silver producer in the Indies, and its output did not subside to 1572 levels until the early eighteenth century. Production in New Spain continued to rise until the 1620s, before dropping slightly for perhaps forty years. There, several substantial mining districts were always in operation, and a decline in one or two of them did not much affect aggregate output.

Gold output grew also in the 1550–1620 period, but less quickly. The most complete estimate to date shows the following decadal totals, converted to an equivalent value in millions of silver pesos, for New Granada, New Spain, and Peru combined. Of the 33.11 million total for the whole period, New Granada produced 22.36 million, or 67.5 percent.[8]

1551–60	6.67
1561–70	2.75
1571–80	2.78
1581–90	2.28
1591–1600	4.77
1601–10	6.88
1611–20	6.98
Total	33.11

Not only did gold output grow less quickly than silver's in the second half of the sixteenth century, but its value was far less. That remains true even if the earlier gold booty of the conquests is taken into account. The total amount of gold gathered by the Spanish in New Granada, New Spain, and Peru from 1521 to 1610 has been estimated at the equivalent of 48.46 million silver pesos.[9] That is but 12 percent of the proposed c.400 million peso silver production of Spanish America to 1610. It was probably at some point in the 1540s, when little gold was left to loot, that the value of silver mined passed that of gold acquired. The lure of gold may first have drawn Spain and Spaniards to America; but it was the reality of silver that kept them there.

The third economically important metal mined in the colonies was mercury, obviously a strategic material once amalgamation became the normal method of refining silver ores. Constant searches for mercury deposits in New Spain revealed no useful source there. But Peru was a different matter. From Huancavelica, in the mountains 240 kilometers south-east of Lima, native people had long taken cinnabar (red mercuric sulphide) for cosmetic uses; and the Spanish subsequently found it a deposit large enough to supply the mercury demands of Potosí and other Andean mines for most of the colonial era. Its output was not, though, sufficient to cover Mexico's needs as well. Fortunately, Spain itself held one of the world's largest mercury sources, at Almadén, north of Córdoba. Mining there went back to Roman times, but much ore remained to be extracted. For most of the span of the empire, Almadén supplied Mexican silver producers with the mercury they needed. As the sources of a material of vital interest to Spain, the mines of both Almadén and Huancavelica were placed under state administration, although contractors from whom the crown bought mercury at negotiated prices actually worked them for many years (Almadén until 1645, and Huancavelica until 1782). The mercury produced was distributed through the royal treasury system, and sold at prices fixed by the government. This royal monopoly of mercury was created partly to ensure supply, partly to produce a profit, and partly to force silver miners to pay the royalty due on silver – since, in law, a treasury office would sell them no more mercury until they had paid the fifth or tenth they owed on silver previously refined. In practice this system was less than wholly effective. Some silver escaped taxation, though no one knew, or knows, how much; and some mercury escaped the monopoly into private trading channels.

By the end of the sixteenth century, silver mining was clearly the most heavily capitalized productive activity in Spanish America, the one showing most pronounced specialization and division of labor, and the one in which imported technology played the largest part. (Amalgamation, though developed industrially in New Spain, is taken here as an imported technology, since it had no native American roots.) The large mining towns would be instantly recognizable to a time-traveler from the present as industrial centers: smoke, smells, polluted water, noise, bustle, contrasting opulence and poverty, sheer size. By 1600, Potosí had some eighty thudding refining mills in operation, spread along several kilometers of the small river flowing through the town. To prolong milling beyond the rainy summer months, a series of interconnected dams had by then been built in a massif to the east of the town: another large investment. In New Spain, Pachuca had forty-nine operating mills c.1597; Taxco, forty-seven; Zacatecas, twenty. The entire colony had 372 active *haciendas de minas*, in which were installed 399 animal-driven stamp mills and 205 powered by water. Almost all the *haciendas* with water wheels were in the center and west, where substantial rain falls, at least in the summer.[10]

CLOTH

Among other productive activities in the sixteenth-century Indies, those closest to mining in their degree of technical innovation and their reliance on the formation of fixed capital were cloth and sugar making. In textiles, there was of course a native tradition to draw on almost everywhere. And some regions, such as central Mexico and coastal Peru, had for many centuries past produced cloth of outstanding fineness and design. The Mexicans spun and wove cotton, lacking any wool-bearing animal. The Peruvians also used cotton; but their most remarkable weaving was of llama, alpaca and vicuña wool, which they first spun to an astonishing fineness, a quality all the more remarkable in that it was achieved on simple, hand-held spindles. For weaving there was the backstrap loom, and an even simpler arrangement in which the warp is simply stretched between pegs set in the ground.

These looms, and the elemental spindle, remained in use after the conquest, and indeed can still be seen in the Andes; men driving llama trains, for instance, spin as they walk along. But the Spanish saw prospects of profit in quicker production, and soon imported European apparatus to that end, notably spinning wheels and treadle looms. These were devices of thirteenth-century origin, and in Spanish America continued in use until the nineteenth, finally succumbing to the power-driven machinery typical of the industrial revolution. But in sixteenth-century America they were radically new, and led to greater division of labor and much increased output.[11] They first came to Mexico in the 1530s, and followed on the conquerors' heels to South America. Complementing this technical advance, and accentuating its alien quality, was the arrival of two new fibers, of which sheep's wool was the more important in the long term. Its availability was a radical departure everywhere except in the central Andean natural range of the American camelids. Viceroy Mendoza himself brought the renowned Spanish merino sheep to New Spain, and ran flocks for his own profit. The more coarsely fleeced churro sheep had arrived sooner, via the Caribbean islands, where it had been introduced early, though it did not thrive.[12] Indians in both Mexico and South America quickly took to raising the animals themselves. Mendoza also sought to create a silk raising and weaving industry in New Spain, drawing on the great silk working tradition of Moorish Spain. In this effort, Cortés was another keen participant. Silk worms were imported and mulberry plantations created to feed them. For much of the sixteenth century the production of silk thread prospered, especially in the south, and weaving throve in Mexico City and Puebla. Finally, though, with the rise of the transpacific trade in the 1570s, competition from oriental silks overcame the Mexican effort.[13]

The production of thread and cloth with the new Spanish machines tended early to concentrate in workshops, commonly termed *obrajes*. These were generally premises in which carding, spinning, and weaving were carried out under a single roof. *Obrajes* are mentioned at Puebla as early as 1539, less than a decade after the town was founded. The inventory of Cortés's estate, drawn up in 1549, shows that he had built one near Cuernavaca, his seat from the early 1530s. This establishment contained a water-powered fulling mill, four functioning looms, and twenty-one spinning wheels. The labor force of carders, spinners, weavers, and fullers is estimated at forty to fifty. They worked both merino and coarser wool.[14] Fifty years or so later, mechanized textile production was a salient feature of the Mexican economy. In 1604, between 98 and 130 *obrajes* and smaller workshops called *trapiches* were producing cloth. They were widely distributed across the center and west of New Spain, with large clusters in and around Puebla, Mexico City, Texcoco and Tlaxcala. The workforce in each is thought to have averaged about fifty, so that the total number making cloth by these imported methods was perhaps six thousand. This was two-thirds of the number of workers in Mexican silver mining in the same years.[15] How much cloth was produced, both in absolute quantity and in relation to native production by traditional methods, it is impossible to say; but clearly spinning and weaving in *obrajes* had become, by the late sixteenth century, a major component of the European side of the colonial economy. It had grown with backing from the crown, which was broadly keen to ensure an adequate supply of affordable cloth in the colony.[16] Late in the century qualms arose about competition with producers in Spain, but not to the point where effective restrictions were applied to Mexican production.

Obrajes appeared in Peru soon after the conquest and multiplied there, again with royal support, in the mid-1500s. The emigration of Spanish master weavers and accompanying carders, fullers and so on was encouraged; most major towns soon had their *obrajes*, where cloth continued to be made for the rest of the colonial period.[17] Still, it was not Peru but Quito that became the leading textile region of South America. The province's central highlands offered great expanses of good grazing for sheep. And once local gold production began to decline, from about 1560, cloth making seemed to leading settlers (most of them *encomenderos* still, in this rather isolated region) a promising means of acquiring cash. Fabric was a product compact and valuable enough to bear the high freight cost of export from Quito. Quito, indeed, for the rest of the colonial period depended on external textile sales to earn the money it needed to buy goods from elsewhere, and particularly from Europe; without cash it had no entry into the transatlantic trade. Its textile makers found they could sell cloth northward to New Granada, for gold; and southward to Peru and Charcas, for silver. The opulent age of *quiteño* cloth production was the seventeenth century. But the first *obrajes* probably date from the 1560s, when *encomenderos* and *caciques* joined forces to set up the workshops in native villages. The Spaniards looked for cash gains from sales. The native leaders, in return for organizing labor, took a salary from the *obraje*. But equally attractive to them was the fact that some of the profit went to pay their subjects' tributes, for which they were personally responsible. Thus native "community *obrajes*" came into being in Quito. By the opening of the seventeenth century, fourteen of them existed in the highlands. Some of them had been founded, at least, on a notably large scale, with two hundred or more workers. They remained one major base of textile production in Quito until the early eighteenth century. The other consisted of shops owned privately, as in Mexico or Peru, that land owners set up on large rural estates where the primary raw material, sheep's wool, was produced. Between 1601 and 1628 the crown granted thirty-eight permits for the building of such *obrajes* in Quito.[18]

SUGAR

If cloth manufacture was often sited in cool highland areas suited to running sheep, the warmth needed for growing cane meant that sugar production was generally a lowland affair. The Atlantic islands settled by Portugal and Spain in the 1400s had generally proven welcoming to cane, and sale of sugar to the mainland had become good business, as Columbus learned in visits to Madeira before 1480. Planting cane, then, was logically among the first ventures in commerical farming tried in Hispaniola. The first mill was built there, at Concepción, in 1503. It was only after 1515, however, that, with the yield of gold placers declining, and the sugar price in Europe rising, settlers on Hispaniola gave serious attention to sugar. A strip of coast immediately west of Santo Domingo was planted with cane. The first sugar refined emerged from a small, animal-powered mill, or *trapiche*. In 1517 the first water-driven mill (*ingenio*) came into action. The design of its essential component, the cane-crushing rollers, had its origins in Sicily. It had been used in the Canaries, from where men were now brought to build and run mills in Hispaniola. Two vertical wooden rollers, geared together in counter-rotation, were the crux of the design. The cane was drawn between them, and its juice squeezed out as it went.[19] This device passed to the mainland, although there a three-roller pattern seems to have been used from the beginning, with the central roller driving, through gears mounted above, two others on each side. This arrangement gave the outer rollers opposing rotations, so that a piece of cane could be passed through in one direction, and then immediately back in the other to press more juice from it.

Hispaniola thus became the first American colony exporting (to Spain) a plantation product. The other large islands followed suit in due course. Sugar production in New Spain, conversely, was largely for local consumption. Cane and milling technology had been carried there by 1530 from the Caribbean. The lower valleys around Cuernavaca and the coastal lowlands near Veracruz were the first good territory found for the crop. Then, as the century progressed, sugar planting extended westward into Michoacán, and Colima on the Pacific coast. Cortés, again, is the most famous of the early Mexican sugar raisers. His first mill (*c*.1529) at Tuxtla, on the Gulf coast, was probably the first in the colony. He built another, with accompanying plantation, near Cuernavaca in the thirties. The area around Cuernavaca became the major producing region, from a combination of climate, fertility, and above all closeness to the great market provided by Mexico City. The sweet tooth that New Spain – and the rest of Spanish America – developed in the sixteenth century constantly amazed newcomers and visitors from Europe; though it was a time in which the demand for sugar in Europe itself was apparently insatiable, as the largest American exporters of all, the planters in Brazil, found to their benefit. Indians as well as settlers took eagerly to sugar in New Spain, the natives probably consuming the less refined forms and the by-products such as molasses, while the clayed, whiter end-product went to colonists who could afford its higher price. By the early seventeenth century, fifty or sixty large *ingenios* and *trapiches* were at work in Mexico, producing perhaps 3.5–5.0 million kilograms a year; and many smaller mills besides.[20]

Some early Mexican sugar also went to Peru, though this trade had subsided by 1560 as a result of rising local output and a consequent drop in price. The first small sugar *trapiches* in Peru date from *c*.1540. A reliable source, Pedro de la Gasca, states that four were running in 1549. From then on production rose to meet a local demand as impressive as Mexico's. (In 1542 the city council of Lima had banned the making of candied fruit because it caused harm to the republic and turned men into idle vagabonds. Underlying, perhaps, what seems a curious puritanism were the facts that sugar was dear, was valued as a medicine, and that importing it from Mexico drained scarce specie from Peru.)[21] From the start, Peruvian cane growing was concentrated in the irrigated river valleys crossing the north and central coast.

The great age of the plantations that grew up in those green patches amidst the desert was the seventeenth century, when the Peruvian mills supplied sugar to much of the west coast of South America and the central Andean highlands also.

The sugar refinery was a plant as complex and expensive as a silver-refining mill. The roller mechanism for expressing juice from the cane was a simpler device than the stamp mill; but the drive trains needed to carry energy from the water wheel or animal team to the crushing machinery were similar in both cases. In place of the patio or refining tanks, the sugar mill had a boiling house, equipped with large copper vats, and a purging house, with possibly hundreds of molds, where the boiled-down juice was formed into loaves. (The process is described in some detail in chapter 13, below, on colonial Brazil.) The apparatus, the buildings needed to hold it, and attached storerooms and living quarters were a costly proposition. In sixteenth-century Mexico a sugar mill cost 50,000 pesos; in the mid-seventeenth, refineries owned there by the regular clergy sold for up to twice that sum.[22]

DYES

Sixteenth-century sugar making in New Spain has been described as Mexico's "first agro-industry,"[23] and the same may be said of it for Peru. It was not the only such industry, though certainly the largest. From the early 1560s New Spain also produced indigo, a rich blue dye extracted from leguminous plants of the genus *Indigofera*. Production began near Cuernavaca, but soon spread southward into warm southern areas and Yucatan. To extract the dye, the leaves had to be cooked and mashed. Preparing indigo on a large scale thus required boilers and crushing machinery, sometimes driven by a water wheel. The mills, of which more than 48 existed in Yucatan by the late 1570s, were therefore substantial pieces of fixed capital, though an order of magnitude smaller than sugar refineries in cost. Mexico sent almost 7,000 kilograms of indigo to Spain in 1576. In 1609 the export was 132,000 kilograms, worth almost 550,000 pesos, a very large sum indeed.[24]

Another dye was a still more valuable export of New Spain from the early years. This was cochineal, a red powder made by crushing the dried bodies of a small insect living on the nopal cactus. The preparation of cochineal differed, however, from indigo extraction in that it used no mechanical processing, or indeed any imported technology at all. Pre-conquest practices persisted throughout the colonial period, with Indians tending, collecting, drying, and pulverizing the insects. Southern Mexico, particularly the Oaxaca region, was the producing region. Spaniards bought the finished dye, mainly for sale across the Atlantic. The first export to Spain was in 1526; the first Mexican cochineal reached Antwerp in 1552, and London by 1569. By 1600 or so, Spain received perhaps 113,000–136,000 kilograms of Mexican cochineal yearly, worth some 600,000 pesos.[25] The dye remained throughout colonial times New Spain's second export in value, behind (though far behind) silver.

SHIPBUILDING

A very different product of southern Mexico, and one relying on, indeed embodying, imported technology, was ships. From 1522 to the late 1530s, Cortés organized shipbuilding at different places on the Pacific coast – primarily Tehuantepec and Acapulco – for projected explorations. That he could have found the necessary carpentry skills among his men so early might seem odd. But that simply indicates how far bands of *conquistadores* were samples of the general Spanish population rather than professional soldiers. In 1521, Cortés had made excellent use of one carpenter-conqueror, Martín López, to build the brigantines that gave him control of the lake during the final siege of Tenochtitlan. It was not so much Mexico, however, as Central America that developed as the main shipbuilding area on the American west coast for most of the sixteenth century. The first vessels were made in Panama in 1517, at Balboa's order, for exploration. Others followed in the 1520s, including those that Pizarro used for southward exploration toward Peru. Then the pace of building rose *c.*1530 to supply the needs of a new trade in Indian slaves from Nicaragua to Panama. By 1533 over thirty ships were sailing the Pacific, half of them, or more, slavers. Nicaragua's being the source of the slaves was certainly the prime reason for shipbuilding's rise there; but the region also had abundant wood for hulls and masts, fibers for ropes, and pitch.[26] Wealth of raw material, particularly of wood, later underlay also the development of Guayaquil, in southern Quito, as a shipbuilding center. By the late sixteenth century it was a major producer of shipping. Since passage of Cape Horn was a fearful obstacle to the movement of Atlantic shipping into the Pacific until the eighteenth century, Guayaquil and Central America were long almost the sole suppliers of vessels for the considerable trade that developed up and down the west coast with the settlement of Quito, Peru, and Chile.

CRAFTS

Ocean-going ships were the among the most striking examples of European technical innovation in sixteenth-century America, far exceeding the canoes of the native Caribbean or the large rafts of pre-conquest north-west South America in their ability to move cargoes and use the sea as a relatively rapid, multi-directional highway. They were also the most obvious and imposing products of Spanish artisanry. But artisanry on a smaller scale had just as profound an aggregate effect on the lives of colonizers and colonized. The speed with which Spanish craftsmen appeared in America and went to work might at first seem surprising; but given the opportunities for gain that the inevitable demand for familiar goods from *encomenderos* and other wealthy settlers offered, it is less so. Probably at least a tenth of Spanish settlers in Peru up to 1560 were active craftsmen, eight hundred or more of them.[27] In order of descending numbers, the following were present: tailors and shoemakers; ironsmiths; builders; then lesser numbers of silversmiths, barber-surgeons, muleteers, pharmacists, confectioners, arms makers, candlemakers, musicians; and even a bookbinder.[28] Some specialization and subdivision of trades was initially lost in the transfer from Spain; but by mid-century there was little available there by way of craft products that could not be had made locally, if a little more roughly, in Lima, Mexico City, or other provincial cities. This was quite clear in the Peruvian civil wars of the 1540s. Most of the muskets, armor, swords, horseshoes, and pikes used by all sides were locally made. Builders and carpenters soon imposed a familiar and enduring appearance on towns. "By 1545 the outward aspect of Lima was already what it was to remain for centuries, long lines of bare adobe walls broken by splendid wooden doors."[29] Gonzalo Pizarro, during his rebel leadership of Peru in the 1540s, kept a band of players capable of performing Renaissance part music. Musicians might double as dance masters. In 1552 a resident organ maker built a substantial instrument for Lima cathedral.

Clearly, most of the goods produced by these immigrant craftsmen went to Spanish settlers. Equally clearly, incoming artisans could and did draw on rich native skills in working stone and cloth, and in the Andean case, metal also; and to that must be added the ironworking abilities of Africans. But still a powerful acculturating influence flowed through Spanish craftsmen in the opposite direction, for many of the apprentices trained by arriving Spanish artisans were Indians and Blacks. And thus Spanish techniques, tastes, and standards were diffused into the new, miscegenizing culture.

FARMING

Most craftsmen worked in towns. And colonial towns, with their imported architecture and layout, and the various representatives of state power that they contained, as well as the new techniques of immigrant artisans, were obvious concentrations of acculturative influence. But signs and forces of change flooded across the countryside, too, as Spanish farming practice expanded. If introduced micro-organisms made themselves felt all too soon in epidemics, far larger fauna were not far behind: hens, goats, sheep, pigs, donkeys, cattle, horses. These animals, in fact, established themselves in most parts of Spanish America before any definite farming began. In the Caribbean islands they ran wild from 1493 on, and multiplied into numbers that not only fed the island settlers, but provided vigorous stock to occupy the mainland. The rangy Spanish pig was as telling an ally of the *conquistador* as the horse – indefatigable, omnivorous, adaptable to almost any climate and vegetation America had to offer, from tropical swamp to highland desert. The rough and tough cattle were equally invasive; though more selective in their feed than pigs, they were better able to range fast and wide in pursuit of the grasses and grains they sought. Horses did likewise. The result was that the natural pastures of the mainlands, notably in northern Mexico and the plains of the Río de la Plata, but in many smaller areas elsewhere, saw enormous herds of feral animals appear with astonishing speed. The grasslands, never grazed before, and free, like those earlier in the Caribbean, of natural foes of the new animals, whether microbes, insects, or large predators, offered conditions in which numbers could grow tenfold in three or four years.[30] This bovine and equine paradise was fleeting, to be sure; damage from overgrazing was apparent in northern Mexico in the closing decades of the sixteenth century. But the numbers, if no longer explosively increasing, remained high. In 1586, two cattlemen in the Zacatecas region branded 75,000 young steers on the large estates they had by then created to supply the mines with meat and leather, and to send stock south for sale in central Mexico.[31]

Some of that northern beef ended up in the diet of Indians in the center. As cattle multiplied, and the price of beef fell, meat protein became widely available to the mass of the native people for the first time in their history. It was never cheaper, perhaps, than in the mid-sixteenth century. That, too, was perhaps the time when milk, cream, and cheese began to assume the large part they now play in the Mexican diet, a part surprisingly larger than in the Spanish. Again, though Indians themselves rarely raised the large imported animals, they took quickly to keeping pigs, sheep, and chickens, so that beef was not the only flesh now available to them. In sum, then, for native Mexicans the arrival of European domestic creatures brought a distinct modification of diet, and some change in the manner of producing at least its protein content, from cultivation of beans to raising of small animals. The same goes, with regional variations, for American natives elsewhere.

The dietary gain (if gain it was) came, however, at a cost. Indians had never had any need to fence crops in New Spain, since there were no large herbivora to eat them. That changed with the arrival of cattle. By the 1540s destruction of maize plots was a severe problem in central and southern Mexico. Viceroy Mendoza went so far as to ban cattle ranches (*estancias*) in the valleys around Oaxaca; and commented to Don Luis de Velasco, his successor, "The Spaniards cry that I have ruined them, and they are right...But...if cattle are allowed, the Indians will be destroyed."[32] The difficulty was not just that cattle trampled and ate the maize, but that aspiring Spanish stockraisers had strong motive to push Indians off their communal lands to secure grazing. This was a conflict wherever in America Indians farmed land that could feed cattle. In New Spain, Mendoza and Velasco, with crown backing, sought to mitigate it by urging the use of the northern plains for stockraising. To that end, Velasco issued land grants in the north during the 1550s. There was by then in any case the added attraction of the rising market for meat and hides in the northern mines; besides which, it suited all Spaniards if cattle in any way disrupted the nomadic Chichimeca of the *altiplano*, who clearly posed a potential threat to the Spanish presence there. This was not the only case in which cattle were explorers and conquerors alongside men.

Sheep could pose similar problems, especially since, in contrast to cattle, their main grazing areas remained in central and southern Mexico. Following the Iberian pattern, sheep breeders soon began to practice seasonal transhumance. By the late 1570s flocks totalling 200,000 or so moved for the winter from the surroundings of Querétaro to Michoacán; there was a similar movement from Puebla to the Gulf coast. Villages along these sheep runs suffered crop damage. Goats, too, with their predilection for eating plants right down to their roots, were a mixed blessing. They could thrive where no other useful animal would, yielding meat and milk; but often at the cost of soil erosion.

In general, indeed, it is hard to strike the balance of the pros and cons for the land and native people of the Spanish American empire of the introduction of European livestock. The equation inevitably contains too many imponderables for a clear answer to be evident. The gain of a new source of protein was offset by loss of crops and probably of some farming land (though some of the land occupied by grazing animals had clearly fallen largely or wholly vacant with the collapse of native numbers). Oxen, horses, donkeys, and then mules complemented the sole American beast of burden, the llama of the central Andes. Elsewhere, they relieved humans of the age-old task of carrying freight, but again at a cost in land. The same was true of their provision of useful materials beside food. Leather for clothing, shoes, and general use became cheap and plentiful, where it had largely been unavailable before. Wool there had never been before, except in the natural range of the Andean camelids, from Chile to southern Ecuador. The existence of some native groups was changed radically by the arrival of the new creatures. The nomads of the South American pampas became horsemen hunting the wild cattle that multiplied endlessly on those plains.[33] The Navajo of New Mexico and Arizona turned from raiding their farming Pueblo neighbors for a living, to tending the churro sheep and weaving its wool. In the more central areas of complex culture, the changes were perhaps less profound, more a matter of adding what was useful in the new than of radically changing the old. Nonetheless, a world with the European domestic animals present must have seemed quite distinct from a previous one without them; as distinct, perhaps, as the times in Europe before and after the arrival of mechanical means of transport.

Less dramatically obvious than introduced fauna, but equally pervasive, were the new food-yielding flora that the Spaniards imported: citrus fruits, peaches, pears, apples, grapes, melons, bananas; onions, olives, radishes; sugar cane; rice; and the standard European grains, with wheat pre-eminent among them for the Spaniards. These were not a fair exchange for what America gave the world by way of new foods, beginning with maize and potatoes. But they made their mark on the American landscape; and Indians, if they did not eat many of these new vegetable foods, assuredly were soon familiar with them as the colonists, beginning with the *encomenderos*, demanded that they grow them. It must have been a great relief to the Spanish to discover in Mexico so much good land for wheat. The Caribbean islands and Panama had been a disappointment in that respect, and there was little a Spaniard hankered after more than fine wheaten bread. Highland New Spain proved ideal for the crop. The first major area put to wheat, in the 1530s, was the vicinity of Puebla, and the nearby Atlixco valley. Then, as the northward mining movement started late in the next decade, wheat followed, and so, gradually, "the former wastelands of the Bajío [became] converted into the most important, prosperous, and modern agricultural area of New Spain."[34] Travelers from Europe were amazed by the high yields that wheat farmers extracted from the Bajío. Its farming for wheat, and maize also, was another aspect of that inclusion of the north into the mainstream of Mexican life for which silver mining was the prime motor. In the more distant north, wheat and maize growing appeared near mining centers wherever suitable soil, and water for irrigation, could be found. Other, smaller wheat areas developed in Michoacán and elsewhere in the west. By the end of the sixteenth century, colonists generally had all the white bread they wanted; and newcomers commented on its quality. More indicative of long trends in Mexican history, though, was the appearance in the north of the *tortilla de harina*, the tortilla made from wheat flour. Here was symbolized in food the distinctively mestizo culture of northern New Spain: the alien grain prepared in the thin, flat form of the traditional Mexican maize bread.

In South America, too, land for wheat was abundant, although what was to become the largest and most famous area of all, the wet pampa of Argentina, was not planted with it until the nineteenth century, for lack of demand. On the western side of the subcontinent that the Spanish mainly occupied, they were able to take advantage, like the native cultures before them, of the effect of varying altitude on local climate to create niches for wheat growing. The coastal valleys of central Peru yielded enough of it, under irrigation, to supply the coastal towns in the sixteenth and seventeenth centuries. Cochabamba and other mid-altitude basins sent wheat to Potosí and other highland mining centers in Charcas. Central Chile, with its Mediterranean climate, proved ideal wheat territory, and dispatched large exports of it to Peru in the eighteenth century. In the north, the elevated plains around Bogotá and Caracas gave the wheat that was locally needed. Colonists everywhere, of course, and increasingly so as the proportion of American-born settlers grew, ate New World foods as well as the crops of European origin. Maize became almost as basic for them as it was for natives; and in fact crossed the Atlantic to become a staple in north-western Spain in the seventeenth century. The potato was another American vegetable that Spaniards and colonists took to, after initial suspicion. Indeed, it was the Spaniards who carried the potato from the Andes to Middle America, and also to Europe. Potato growing began in the Spanish Basque country before 1600.[35] Other examples of American foods adopted more or less eagerly by colonials – chocolate, tomatoes, avocados, chili, and so on – are legion.

Nonetheless, it was the settlers' insistence on having their familiar European foods available, rather than their consumption of American crops, that proved disruptive to Indians. And the disruption was magnified by their importing, also, of alien notions about the tenure of land on which crops and animals were raised. The concept of private landholding had scarcely appeared in native American cultures. Only in the Inca and Aztec polities, at the pinnacle of the nobility, was there any trace of it; and that was a late pre-conquest development. The prevailing concept of land was that it was communal property, whose use could be allocated to individuals or families as long as they worked it. The Spanish, by contrast, though expecting to find some land attached to towns for communal uses such as grazing and charcoal making, thought of it first as something to be possessed individually and exclusively.

Legal possession came from the monarch, since, as in the Reconquest, all areas newly conquered were defined as *tierras de realengo*, or royal territory.

The crown might itself grant the land away, or, as more commonly happened in America, for reasons of distance, delegate the granting to some colonial authority – conqueror, governor, viceroy, and often, in the early days, town councils. Generally these locally made grants became permanent only when the crown confirmed them.[36] Many Spaniards in sixteenth-century America asked for and received land in this way, from urban plots for a house to great swathes of countryside for grazing. *Encomenderos* were among the earliest applicants, since their allocations of Indians did not include land. Far from all the land that Spaniards acquired in the 1500s, however, came to them in this state-regularized way. Some was bought from Indians, generally from *caciques* wrongfully alienating communal territory for personal gain or to secure cash with which to pay their people's tribute. And some was simply occupied (as when, for example, cattle strayed on to unassigned land), or seized. Doubtless, *de facto* occupation became more tempting and simpler as land fell vacant through population loss. But how much of the native community land coming under Spanish control was already unused for that reason, and how much was torn from active cultivators, is impossible to say. The proportion certainly varied by region. On the coasts of Peru and New Spain, for instance, where population losses were particularly severe, a larger proportion of the land taken by Spaniards had fallen into disuse than in the highlands of either area.

In the 1590s the crown began to accept payments to regularize deficient or absent titles, in a programme of "composition" that went along with a new policy introduced under Philip II of auctioning off, rather than granting, new land titles.[37] The change reflects not only Philip's always desperate need of funds, but also a growing demand for land in the Indies after the mid-century. Spaniards' interest in agriculture had risen slowly from a slender start in the immediate post-conquest years. At that time it seemed likely that Indians, working their own land, would supply as tribute most of what the colonists wanted by way of food. Some *encomenderos*, it is true, there were even then who wanted land to produce food for sale; and more, perhaps, for a mixture of commercial and psychological motives, since landowning was part of the lordly lifestyle they aspired to create for themselves. But still, it was only when a blend of demographic decline and rising Spanish numbers made the notion of a tribute-based existence for settlers increasingly dubious that land-owning became a general ambition grounded in economic reality.[38] This realization, in the middle decades of the century, coincided, furthermore, with the rise of the silver mining centers in Charcas and northern New Spain. It was not hard to see in that development good possibilities for profitable sales of farm products.

And so there appeared in the latter part of the century a multiplicity of private farms, of varying sizes, owned mainly by Spaniards and *criollos* (American-born Whites), but some also by Blacks, *castas* (mixed-blooded people), and undoubtedly some Indian leaders. In New Spain, the term *labor* was generally used for a small farm producing wheat and other crops for a local market. In the Andes, *chácara* (Quechua for sown land) had the same sense. In both areas, *estancia* meant land held for grazing. On many of these, the owner might have been found physically laboring; though, if he were white, he would certainly rather not have done so. By the end of the century, the size of the farms varied enormously, from a few dozen hectares of good arable land in a valley floor up to many thousands of hectares of sparse grazing on some arid plain. There was much buying and selling of land, so that farms' size and boundaries shifted often. With time, some of the larger holdings began to take on the look of the classic Spanish American rural estate, the *hacienda de campo*. But that term, and the institution itself – a sizable piece of land with a large house, laborers' accommodations, barns, stables, work rooms, and so on at its center, often self-supplying in foodstuffs and basic craft goods, indeed a rounded and self-contained community – belongs to the seventeenth century and later. The first colonial century saw the bases of the rural *hacienda* laid down in smallholdings. And in fact smallholdings remained an important social and economic element of the country scene of the colonies until the end.

Even the smallest private farm was likely to use European iron and steel tools to prepare the land for sowing, rather than the wooden digging sticks that were the most advanced native tilling tools. Larger places might well have steel-bladed ploughs (over twelve thousand ploughshares were sent from Spain to Mexico alone in 1597)[39] and oxen or mules to draw them, though clearly there were many steep fields in the Andes and elsewhere where they would not serve. Still, the great grain lands opened up by the Spanish in the first century, particularly those of New Spain, were worked extensively, as in Europe, rather than in the intensive American fashion. Yields per hectare were undoubtedly lower than the amazing levels sometimes achieved by native methods (with maize around the lakes in the Valley of Mexico, for example); but the use of animal-drawn tools raised the yield per unit of human labor expended on cultivation. The outcome was that European-style farming made inroads into even the supply of traditionally native foods. By 1630, for example, Mexico City's maize came largely from colonists' farms around it rather than from Indian communities. This rise of commercial agriculture was promoted still more by the use of animal-drawn carts. It was simple and relatively cheap to move farm products to market over considerable distances – tens, even hundreds, of kilometers – where the terrain allowed carting roads to be made. If it had not been so, the existence of the mining towns on the Mexican *altiplano*, for example, would have been distinctly more tenuous than it was. But where carts could not go, mule trains generally could.

By 1600, then, many fertile regions of Spanish America, and some regions that were not so fertile, were well scattered with privately held smallholdings, farms, and nascent estates. Few of the owners were native people. These lands were worked by predominantly alien techniques to produce predominantly alien crops; though with time those methods were applied also to some native crops. Large, imported animals were a key part of the new agricultural method, putting non-human power for the first time at the service of American agriculture. Large tracts of private land, particularly those unsuited by climate, terrain, or fertility to tillage, served as grazing for these exotic beasts – not merely those used for draught, but a far larger number raised to give meat and raw materials, particularly wool and hides. Meat in the amounts now available was an innovation in the American diet. Similarly, wool and leather became unprecedentedly common. The animals' numbers multiplied prodigiously in the new environment (almost 1.3 million cattle in New Spain by 1620, by one estimate, and 8 million sheep and goats combined).[40] In among the private landholdings, to be sure, native communities survived, each with its communal lands, safeguarded by Spanish law, that its people still worked by prehispanic methods. Native farmers grew crops for their own subsistence, and certainly also for cash sale, where marketing opportunities existed (as, for instance, in nearby colonial towns). But Indian towns and villages had lost at least some of their best land to Spanish purchase, theft, and incursion. They were also fewer than a century before, inevitably so as a result of demographic contraction, and of Spanish policies, enacted from the mid-1500s on, of gathering Indians into new "congregations."

NATIVE LABOR

One purpose of creating those congregations had been easier access to native labor. Indians were brought together so that they could then be more easily removed to work in tasks profitable to both colonists and the colonial state. This was one in a whole progression of schemes devised to exploit native labor. In fact, questions of how, and how much, Indians should work for Spaniards were among the most hotly debated issues of imperial governance in the sixteenth century. The questions were not merely the practical ones of how to use a rapidly shrinking resource, but also the moral ones of how to reconcile the required conversion, civilization, and good treatment of native Americans with the soon-evident need to compel them to work if the colonies were to produce gain.

On the mainland, *encomienda* was the first solution tried. *Encomenderos* were supposed to look to the spiritual and material well-being of the Indians granted to them in return for tribute received. That tribute, for several decades, might take the form of labor ("personal service" was the term used) as well as offerings in bullion or goods. The outcome, though, tended to be as in the Caribbean islands: excessive and uncontrollable demands from the *encomenderos*, and rare meeting with the obligation to enlighten and improve the Indians. That imbalance, among other causes, led to the crown's attack on the *encomienda* in the New Laws of 1542; and, seven years later, to a ban on personal service from Indians in *encomienda*. Though neither the *encomienda* nor labor exactions in it disappeared at this point, nor in some places for long afterward, the 1549 order does mark the beginning of the end of *encomienda* as the prime source of native workers in the central colonial areas.

It was replaced in those regions by state-directed systems of draft labor, in which native communities were ordered to supply a small proportion of their grown men at fixed intervals for assignment to particular tasks. In the central Andes the mechanism was called *mita* (Quechua for "time" or "turn"), the term used by the Incas for their own system of obligatory state labor; and the Indians caught up in the Spanish scheme clearly saw in it a link with preconquest practice. Elsewhere the Spanish word *repartimiento* ("distribution") covered the draft system (one of several official uses to which that word was put in the colonies). In New Spain a parallel existed in the native institution of compulsory public work, *coatequitl*, which continued to operate in surviving Indian polities after the conquest, though the name was not applied to the Spanish draft system.

Examples of *ad hoc* drafts can be found in the mid-century. In 1550, for example, Viceroy Mendoza drafted Indians to work on Spanish wheat farms around the capital, to relieve a grain shortage. Again, after severe flooding in 1555, Viceroy Velasco put some six thousand Indians to building dikes and diverting streams to protect Mexico City.[41] Similar cases occur in the Andes also in the 1550s and 1560s. But in both regions it was the 1570s that saw draft labor generally and uniformly set up, through the efforts of Viceroys Toledo, in Peru, and Enríquez, in New Spain.

At first the drafts were not overwhelmingly onerous. In the Valley of Mexico, the "take" in the *repartimiento* set up for farming was 2 percent of adult men during the growing season, and 1 percent in the rest of the year.[42] In the most notorious draft of all, the *mita* organized by Toledo for Potosí in the mid-1570s, some 16 percent of grown men from most native communities lying between Cuzco and Potosí were ordered to move to the mines and stay there for a year. The total number was some 13,500; but each man had to work only one week in three, so that some 4,500, or slightly over 5 percent, were actively laboring in mining or refining at any moment.

In their initial organized forms, these drafts may actually have spread the labor burden more evenly among the native population than the *encomienda* had done; for some *encomenderos* worked their people pitilessly, and others lightly. Another gain over earlier "personal service" was that draftees received a statutory wage. It was probably not a living wage for a family; but in the *encomienda*, with the rarest exceptions, no wage had been paid at all – the intended rewards were intangible, and rarely delivered. In principle, also, draft labor should have given Indians some protection from abusive employers, since the state, represented by an allocating official, stood between employer and worker. But the benefit in practice may have been small. From the administration's standpoint, drafts offered two economic gains. One was that the shrinking labor supply could be channeled to what was considered essential production, defined as "public works." These included, certainly, building of roads, bridges, drainage works, churches, and other public edifices; but, more crucial to both state and individuals, agriculture and mining. Second, drafts broke the close control over labor that *encomenderos* had held; now workers could be given to incoming Spaniards who might well be more entrepreneurial than aging *conquistadores* and their socially pretentious offspring.

In the areas of intense economic activity by the Spanish, *mita* and *repartimiento* were, though, inadequate almost as soon as put in place. In New Spain, severe epidemics, possibly of typhus, shrank the remaining Indians' numbers drastically in the late 1570s. In the central Andes, also, the native population continued to fall while the demand for workers at Potosí and other silver mines, at Huancavelica (the source of the indispensable mercury), and generally for farming (to feed the booming mining towns), leaped upward. Constant immigration from Spain created further imbalance between supply and demand in labor. One outcome was that the draft quotas increased in the closing years of the century; by 1600 some draftees were working every other year at Potosí, instead of one in seven. A parallel result, clear in its economic logic, was that Spaniards needing workers hired them individually wherever they could find them. Since almost all adult native men were liable for drafting, such private hiring cut into the numbers available for forced work – from which Indians were ever more anxious to escape, of course, as the "take" increased. By about 1600, then, working for wages was well ensconced in regions and activities of high demand for labor. The numbers are clearest in silver mining. In New Spain the total workforce was counted *c.*1597 at 9,143, of whom 6,261 were waged (68.5 percent), 1,619 *repartimiento* men (17.7 percent), and 1,263 black slaves (13.8 percent). In Potosí, a few years later, the total daily workforce was about 9,900, of whom some 55 percent were waged. If other mines by then active in the Potosí district are taken into reckoning, the proportion of wage workers rises, since those mines received no draft. Miners and refiners in the central Andes used hardly any black slaves; they reportedly succumbed too soon to disease in the high altitude chill to make buying them a good investment.

Hiring of Indians for wages spread across productive activities controlled by colonials. Some native workers in textile shops, some on estates, some in artisanry, received negotiated cash sums for their labors. The evidence, though thin and scattered, is also that such workers' wages rose in the late 1500s, and rose indeed faster than prices, so that their real income grew.[43] The relative price of labor should certainly have increased as workers became a scarcer commodity, and as, under more or less permanent contract, they acquired skills valuable to their employers. So desirable did skilled workers become that employers competed for them, luring them away with offers of higher wages. And in some cases advances on wages were given, not so much to tie a worker through debt to a workplace, as to attract him to it in the first place.

Thus, in the regions most heavily developed economically by colonists (which corresponded generally with the areas of prior high native culture, but expanded now by silver discoveries), employment of Indians moved in the sixteenth century from the retainer-like relationship of the *encomienda*, to the state-run (but salaried) draft of *mita* and *repartimiento*, to the private and individual contracts of wage labor. A variety of causes drove this progression: the crown's reliance on, then rejection of, *encomienda* as a method of settlement; rising immigration from Spain; and, most powerful of all, the effects of native depopulation in, first, shrinking the pool of available workers, and, second, forcing the colonists to start organizing essential production themselves.

Even in the central areas, however, the advent of a new stage did not necessarily mean the disappearance of a previous one. *Mita* labor was crucial to Andean silver mining to the end of colonial times, because it provided a cheap and reliable supplement to wage labor. Similarly, in New Spain, although the then viceroy ended drafts for agriculture in 1632 because they had become unnecessary, *repartimiento* for silver mining remained active, at least for mines in the center and south.

And in peripheral regions, where Whites and their enterprises were fewer and less dominant, use of native labor took a variety of courses. A common feature was survival of the *encomienda* as a source of labor, despite the decree halting personal service in 1549.[44] In outlying parts of New Spain, such as New Mexico and Yucatan, as well as in remoter regions of South America, such as Venezuela, New Granada, Paraguay, and Chile, it little concerned the crown if the *encomienda* persisted in its initial form, since there was little to be lost there, politically or economically, to a well-rooted seigneurial elite in society. In fact, it suited the crown's purpose that the *encomienda* should continue to play its anchoring role in those more or less marginal places, holding settlers usefully in place on the land. It was typical of the peripheries, also, that unless some new economic resource or new export opportunity appeared, competition for labor was slight; hence the economic need to move from *encomienda* to draft was small, or arrived much later than in Peru and New Spain. Again, the marginal areas had had small or weak state structures before the conquest, and little in the way of state-organized labor; so there was no precedent in them to help the Spanish to set up their own drafts.

A blend of *encomienda* and *repartimiento*, whereby *encomenderos* were the main recipients of draft labor, emerged in Paraguay and New Granada. In Chile, by contrast, while *encomienda* continued to provide laborers until the late eighteenth century, drafts were not used. Colonists not holding *encomiendas* rented workers from those who did, in a practice suggesting the relegation of *encomienda* Indians almost to chattel status. It was, in fact, precisely in Chile that outright enslavement of Indians persisted most strongly. After the great native revolt in the south beginning in 1598, it was specifically permitted; and until abolition in 1674, Indians taken in war were legally put to work as slaves. Indian slavery had generally been ended in the empire c.1550 because of its blatant contradiction of the principle, by then well established, that Indians were intrinsically free; and also, perhaps, because slavery was a labor system afflicted with the same rigidities as *encomienda*, when what was needed was the flexibility in allocating workers that the draft provided. But an old policy persisted that Indians who rebelled against Spanish rule could legitimately be enslaved. This meant continued Indian slaving not only in the southern extreme of the empire but in the far north as well, when Comanches and Apaches raided New Mexico. Calling this "rebellion" bordered on sophistry, since those peoples had never been under Spanish control. But it was a convenient fiction, for it provided a steady, if small, supply of slaves to northern New Spain on into the seventeenth century; while also helping to sustain settlement in the distant north, since colonists profited from selling the slaves they took.

BLACK SLAVERY

In aggregate, Indians were far outnumbered as slaves by Blacks in the sixteenth century, as slave imports from Africa rose with the passing years. And those Blacks were an increasingly large supplement to native labor in its various forms, as the indigenous numbers fell. Their participation in higher-level occupations, such as management and artisanry, was important as a social as well as economic phenomenon. But where they became all but essential to the colonial economy was in providing labor that native people could not, for whatever reason, supply. The extreme example is agricultural work, particularly in sugar, on the large Caribbean islands, where literally no indigenous people remained after the mid-sixteenth century. Sugar was in general the province of black slaves everywhere, for at least two reasons. The warmer, lowland areas in which the cane thrived, such as the Mexican and Peruvian coasts, had suffered more severe losses of Indians than the highlands; and, at least in the Spaniards' stereotypical view, Africans withstood hot, heavy work better than Indians. That same opinion, added to the generally low level of prior native political, and hence labor, organization in tropical areas, led also to Black slaves often being used to pan gold – since alluvial gold tended to accumulate in the lower reaches of rivers. Hence gold extraction in New Granada, the metal's main Spanish American source, became largely the work of Blacks. So was the cultivation of cacao in southern lowland Quito and in Venezuela.[45]

TRADE IN THE COLONIES

The products of the variety of workers and of working arrangements found in sixteenth-century Spanish America reached a wide range of consumers. Indians farming their community's lands produced largely for their own subsistence. But when impressed for service in *repartimiento* those same men might find themselves on a colonist's estate ploughing land for wheat that would be sent to a market a few, or a few hundred, kilometres away. One further profound difference between economic practice in 1500 and, say, 1600 (besides technology, forms of land tenure, labor systems, and the like) was an immense growth in exchange over distance. Such exchange was not unknown in native times, of course. Columbus met coastal trading canoes off the Honduras coast in 1502; Aztec *pochteca* brought the products of northern Central America to Tenochtitlan; the Inca state directed movement of goods up and down the Andes. But the distances, as well as the size and variety of trade, grew vastly once the Spanish came. Peru had never before dealt directly with Central America and Mexico; nor Charcas with the Río de la Plata; nor the Greater Antilles with Panama. Clearly ships, carts, oxen, horses, and mules were the key to this immense expansion of interchange, offering swift and relatively cheap carriage of large volumes. Also propelling it, of course, was the belief, grounded in much European experience, that trade was the surest source of profit. Spanish American colonial experience validated that belief from the earliest days until the last. Then again, trade over distance grew and thrived precisely because the possibility of moving goods encouraged settlers to look for places where this or that item could easily be grown or made. Thus they found and developed large areas enjoying comparative advantages for some particular purpose. The Bajío proved ideal in soil and climate for wheat and maize; and the grain could be moved cheaply enough by cart to central Mexico or the northern mines to allow for profitable sale there. Southern Peru offered excellent conditions for grapes; wine produced there could be cheaply sent northward by ship to Lima and beyond (even to New Spain), and by mule to the Andean mines, where it competed successfully by the late sixteenth century with Spanish wine that carried a still higher freight cost. Large and specialized zones of production were in clear evidence across the empire before 1600: the two just mentioned; the cattle lands of northern New Spain; the sheeplands of Puebla, and of Quito in South America; the sugar areas of the Antilles, southern New Spain, and northern Peru; the developing mule and cattle lands of Tucumán in present northern Argentina. In an impressive realization of the potential of economic geography, production fed trade and trade stimulated production in these naturally favored areas.

Most of the exchange of these agricultural products, and manufactures made from them, was within the colonies, either within single *audiencia* territories, or between them. The most powerful magnets of trade were the administrative cities, and the mining towns – and especially the latter, because they both tended to have large populations and were the source of the most desirable commodity exchangeable for goods: silver (whether in unminted or coined form). By one historian's rough estimate, a little over half the silver refined in Spanish America went to buy goods produced in the colonies; and these regional purchases by mining centers amounted to 60 or 70 percent of the value of transoceanic trade to and from the mining areas.[46] If these calculations are right (and much descriptive evidence argues for them), bullion produced in America did not, as often assumed, flood directly out to foreign destinations in Europe and the Orient, but instead passed through and energized internal trade circuits before it left America; and far from all of it did leave, though the fraction remaining undoubtedly varied with time.

OCEANIC TRADE

What sixteenth-century Europeans saw, however, and East Asians soon after them also, as they looked toward Spanish America, was not a developing structure of internal exchange, but shiploads of gold and silver crossing the oceans toward them. The transatlantic trading system of Spain, and then the transpacific commerce, have likewise long captured the attention of historians; and with good reason, since these were maritime operations to rival in scale and pomp anything before or since, and economic movements that wrought irreversible effects on Europe and the wider world.

The small groups of ships used by explorers gradually expanded with discoveries and conquests into flotillas, then into fleets, and finally, in the second half of the century into great armadas carrying people and European cloth, tools, wine, foods, and other exports to America, and silver, dyes, leather, sugar, and medicinal plants back to Spain. In 1526 sailings of single merchant ships to and from the Indies were forbidden. Convoys, for safety from enemy attack and for best use of the limited number of pilots capable of mathematically based navigation, were the rule thenceforth. By the best estimate, at least 85 percent of Spanish transatlantic sailing from 1500 to 1650 was done in convoy.[47] Security increased from *c*.1540 with the entry into service of galleons, ships initially of perhaps 250 tonnes (though they reached 800 by the end of the century) in which some of the fine line of Mediterranean galleys was combined with the seagoing ability of Atlantic trading vessels to produce a relatively fast and handy fighting ship that could also carry cargo.

By the mid-1560s the classic Spanish American "fleet system" was in place, undertaking the *Carrera de Indias*, the "Indies run," each year. Two fleets were the backbone of the communication structure between Spain and America: the *flota* (simply "fleet") sailing to and from New Spain, and the *galeones* (galleons), whose destination was the Caribbean side of the Isthmus of Panama. Both fleets might consist of several dozen ships, though as important as the number was the growing size of the vessels as the century wore on. And both fleets included galleons, for defense and for freight of the main return cargo, silver. The Isthmian-bound *galeones* were so called because that fleet had a larger complement of galleons, to bring back the larger fraction of American silver that South America produced.

The standard rhythm of the *Carrera* was, broadly, thus: the fleets should leave Spain in the early to mid summer; cross the Atlantic via the Canaries, following Columbus's route; enter the Caribbean in late summer through the Lesser Antilles; proceed to their appointed destinations on the Isthmus or the Gulf coast of Mexico (with some ships dropping away to the Greater Antilles and Venezuela); discharge cargoes and load homebound goods; winter in the Caribbean; combine at Havana in the late winter or early spring; and make the eastward crossing, via the Florida Strait and perhaps the Azores, and again following Columbus's pattern, in the spring and early summer. If they adhered to this timetable, the fleets avoided the late summer and early autumn hurricanes of the Caribbean and western Atlantic, as well as the winter storms further north. As the goodly number of wrecks off Florida and Bermuda suggests, however, the schedule was not easily followed. Delays in leaving Spain, enemy presence, slow arrival of cargoes (especially silver) for the return voyage, mere logistical complexity – all could and did interrupt the rhythm of the *Carrera*. Nonetheless, *grosso modo* the design functioned as intended, transporting hundreds of thousands of people, animals, goods, bullion, and, not least, information and administrative orders across the Atlantic in the sixteenth century.

If all went exactly as planned, the combined returning fleet reached Spain at around the departure date of the next sailing. The same ships, however, could not possibly be refitted and reloaded in time to sail again that same summer.

So shipping was needed for four distinct fleets if the annual round were to be sustained. This meant much time spent lying in port; ships in the *flota* to Mexico spent only a quarter of their time at sea,[48] and the proportion for the *galeones* must have been similar. The cost in idle capital locked in motionless ships and their cargoes was high. But that was the price of safety. Single-ship and small-group sailings were simply seen as too risky.

It was also the price of the monopoly structure of the trade. After the creation of the *Casa de Contratación* in Seville in 1503 to regulate communication with the Indies, that city gradually became, in law and fact, the sole conduit for all Spanish contact with America. It was already a great trading center, with a powerful merchant guild, and branches of many European trading houses, especially those of Italy, the Genoese prominent among them. The merchants of Seville seized on the American trade as their own province. It suited them that fleets should sail only at long, predictable intervals, and that no other legal channel of trade with America should exist; for that enabled them to drive up prices by withholding goods from the transatlantic market. It suited them also that there should be only a few legal points of entry to the Indies, for that also helped them to control supply. All goods entering New Spain had to be unloaded at Veracruz, the sole destination of the *flota*; and all goods destined for Peru and elsewhere on the west coast of South America had to go in the *galeones* to the Isthmus, for freighting across to the City of Panama, and loading there into a legally regulated Pacific fleet. Crown and merchants were in full accord in these matters. What concerned the government above all was that its silver – the royal fifth and other taxes – should not escape from its grasp, and that customs duties on the American trade should be collected. Both aims were more easily achieved if contact with the Indies were concentrated into a few sailings, and funneled through a minimum of access points. If the crown should by chance lean toward a loosening of the fleet system, it would increasingly find itself reminded, as the years advanced, that the merchants of Seville were a valuable source of credit to the state, and that a weakening of the Seville monopoly would benefit neither them nor the treasury.

The closed structure of the *Carrera* in fact served crown and merchants well in the sixteenth century, better than in any later period. The trade grew in volume and value almost without interruption from 1505 to 1610 (*c.*23,000 tonnes of outward- and homeward-bound shipping from 1505 to 1509, and *c.*228,000 tonnes from 1605 to 1609).[49] The causes of the growth were several: growing demand in America for Spanish and other European goods as a result of emigration and natural increase of the colonizing population; rising bullion production, giving colonists the means of paying for imports; colonists' growing engagement in economic activities as time passed, creating a demand for European tools and materials, such as metals; rising and spreading wealth among settlers, spent partly on European luxury goods; and underlying the whole transatlantic exchange, of course, Spain's domination of the sea. Pirates and semi-official raiders might slip into the Caribbean, as Frenchmen and Englishmen did before 1600, and snatch substantial prizes, to the Spaniards' irritation and alarm. But no nation could yet seriously threaten the great trading fleets at sea. The failure of the Armada sent against England in 1588 was a warning of things to come; but the lesson was not clear until the new century was well begun.

Possibly the most serious threat to the transatlantic trade in the late sixteenth century was not a military one from Spain's growing number of European enemies, but a commercial one from colonials' enterprises in the Pacific. After the discovery of a practicable route between New Spain and the Philippines in the mid-1560s, venturesome traders in Mexico City soon decided to try their fortune in the Orient. The mercantile gateway to the east was Manila, founded on Luzon in 1571 as the Spanish capital in the Philippines. Oriental goods reached Mexico from Manila in 1573, carried by the first of the Manila galleons. Those were great sturdy vessels that were soon being built in the Philippines from local teak. What above all energized this transpacific trade was the relative shortage, and hence high valuation, of silver in the East. The Chinese valuation of silver in terms of gold in 1572, for instance, was 150 percent of the Spanish American valuation (8:1 versus 12:1).[50] A broad range of goods bought in the Orient seemed extraordinarily cheap to those buying them with silver. And since the largest source of silver at the time was Peru, where Potosí was precisely in the 1570s experiencing its most spectacular boom of all time, the Mexico City merchants who started the Manila trade soon found themselves acting not so much as importers into New Spain as negotiants of the exchange between Peru and Asia. Peruvian silver, transshipped into the galleons at Acapulco, spread from Manila throughout eastern Asia. Some of it was carried by Portuguese merchants working from their base at Macao, set up on the south China coast in the mid-1550s. The Portuguese bought silks at Canton nearby. These, together with porcelain, perfumes, ivory, gems, spices, and even iron and copper, arrived back in Acapulco after the arduous four-to-seven month arching traverse of the north Pacific; and thence much passed southward to Peru.

The trade grew with startling speed; indeed, for the authorities and the merchants in Seville, with thoroughly alarming speed. In 1597 the amount of silver leaving Acapulco was greater than the value of New Spain's trade with Spain. In 1602 the town council of Mexico City judged that 5 million pesos passed annually through Acapulco to the Philippines, 3 million of which came from Peru. (Potosí's production was some 6.9 million pesos a year at the time.) Various restrictions were tried: only two ships might ply between Acapulco and Manila, carrying westward a maximum of 500,000 pesos (1593); the two ships might not be larger than 200 tonnes (1604); only three ships, of 300 tonnes or less, might trade yearly between Peru and Mexico, and carry no silver (1604). Finally, in a desperate effort to stop the hemorrhage of South American silver across the Pacific, and at the insistence of the Seville merchant guild, the crown in 1631 banned trade between Peru and New Spain altogether. None of this had much effect, so powerful was the lure of profit in exporting silver. Trade was still allowed between Peru and Central America; transshipment of goods and silver thence to Mexico was simple.[51] The Manila galleon of 1646 proved, on investigation, to be carrying from six to fourteen times the amounts of silver that the consigning merchants had registered for export.[52]

The great sums committed to the Philippine trade show how much silver the substantial merchants of Mexico City, and Lima too, had at their disposal. Much of the profit of the colonies' productive activities came to rest in the coffers of the import–export merchants, above all because they, acting in concert among themselves and also with exporters in Seville, could to a considerable degree set the price of goods from Europe, as well as those from Asia. No producers in America had a comparable power to fix the price of their wares, whether food, cloth, craft items, or anything else. They certainly tried to do so; some estate owners, for instance, sought to extend their lands not so much to grow more as to prevent others from raising competing crops. But generally the market structures of the colonies, small and inefficient as they mostly were, provided in all but the short term some regulation of prices.

The profitability of the import business was clear from the earliest years. In 1529 the *alcalde mayor* of Oaxaca, and *encomendero* to boot, Juan Peláez de Berrío, wrote to Spain: "It seems to me that one of the good and most important businesses in this land is merchandise, for in that are the true mines, beyond what one can believe... The profit is so sure and so large that a well stocked shop here is the richest thing in the world, alchemy itself... Would to God I had brought a thousand ducats' worth of clothing, for, as things are here, I could easily send back four, or even five, thousand from it, such is the need of Castilian clothes."[53] With time, local production of course expanded to cover everyday needs such as clothes; but even then importing merchants could still charge premium prices for luxuries not made in the Indies (or, even if made there, lacking the European or Oriental cachet) – silks, taffeta, satin, velvet, damask, linen from Holland, Rouen cloth, Spanish paper, Spanish wine, passementerie of silk, silver, and gold, kid gloves, hose, laced buskins, saffron, spices...[54]

INVESTMENT

Their profits made merchants a leading source of credit in the colonies. They lent overtly at the legally approved annual rate of 5 percent, but in reality often at far higher interest if the risk seemed greater, to investors in property, mining, and all other lines of production. While this credit-supplying role of merchants is broadly clear, however, precisely how they performed it in the sixteenth century is far less so; and indeed the general topic of investment and capital formation in the early colonies is the least known, because least visible, aspect of their economic history.

It is, though, certain enough that most investment in the Spanish Indies in the sixteenth century was generated in America. The main exception was the period of Caribbean settlement, when funds came from Castilian, Italian, German, and Flemish sources.[55] Even then, however, gold mining and agriculture could provide sizable accumulations, as Pizarro's funding of the Peruvian explorations and campaign from his landholdings in Panama shows. Loot from the mainland conquests then gave the fortunate and the careful an opportunity to gather large quantities of gold, though their full potential as investment funds depended on their being hoarded until the extreme inflation of prices (enormous amounts of gold pursuing rare European goods) of the immediate conquest had passed. Once *encomienda* was in place on the mainland, Indian labor became the major source in the creation of fixed capital. Houses, storage buildings, irrigation works, early smelting apparatus, local roads – all these could be built with *encomienda* labor with little or no cash outlay by the *encomendero*. Canny *encomenderos* could also amass liquid capital in the form of bullion by sending their Indians to mine gold or silver, or by selling other tribute paid in kind in local markets. Evidently enough, the growth of mining was central to any gathering of funds for investment, with silver even in an unminted form becoming from the 1530s in New Spain, and from the 1540s in Peru, a convenient vehicle for accumulating value as well as for enabling exchange. Coined silver, of more reliable value than the motley bits of metal that first served as money, became increasingly common with the foundation of a mint in Mexico City in 1536. Another was set up in Lima in 1565; but Viceroy Toledo moved its operations to Potosí, where striking of coin began in 1574.

Mining seems to have produced its own start-up capital (in addition to the stimulus given it by *encomienda* labor). Weathering had often raised the silver content of the surface ores that were usually the first to be worked. Not only, therefore, was their extraction cost minimal, but the early smelting was of mineral with a very high silver content, up to 50 percent on occasion by some reports. Initial profits could therefore be high, even if, as in the Andes, native workers received a large share of the product. Something similar happened when amalgamation began. Here the capital cost in milling machines and other apparatus was large. Typically, however, amalgamation processing was installed in places that possessed accumulations of already-mined ore that had proved too poor for smelting. Much of this material could be worked profitably with mercury. Thus the early amalgamators were spared the cost of extraction while they were building their refining mills, and ploughed much of what they refined back into the producing apparatus. In the first five years of amalgamation in Potosí, 1571–5, records indicate that the miners reinvested some 42 percent of their after-tax production in refining plant. Refiners using amalgamation received help and, in effect, encouragement from the crown in the form of credit on their mercury purchases. The treasury tolerated substantial debts on this account until well into the next century; they were, in reality, interest-free loans.

Rising silver output after the mid-century generally stimulated trade. In isolated regions far from mining centers and off the economic highways of the empire, barter persisted, and perhaps also the use of some non-metallic medium of exchange, such as cacao beans in southern Mexico. But broadly speaking, the second half of the sixteenth century brought a monetization, if uneven, of the Spanish Indies. From growing commerce, merchants, especially those in long-distance trade, extracted handsome profits. By one report there were in Lima soon after 1600 some with million-peso fortunes, many with 500,000, and very many with 100,000.[56] Merchants lent from these hoards, becoming one major group of creditors in the colonies. The other large lender by that time was the church, and particularly the orders of regulars. They, in the second half of the sixteenth century, had had grown stout, if not yet fat, on gifts and bequests in silver or property. Lending from these resources became a standard practice until the mid-nineteenth century. Merchants and priests were, then, the closest approximation to bankers to emerge in the Indies. No true banks ever appeared in colonial times, though some of the large merchant houses in eighteenth-century Mexico performed many banking functions.

DOMINATION SURVEYED

The identification of resources, the introduction of alien crops and animals, the application of new productive tools and techniques, organization of labor, the mapping and plying of trade routes on land and sea, the opening of economic circuits through which flowed increasing charges of silver coin: all constituted a striking economic domination, even an economic reformation, of Middle and South America in the sixteenth century. The economic was linked, of course, with every other aspect of Spanish treatment of America and its native peoples in that first century. The church, while some of its members strove to protect Indians from labor exactions and the maltreatment they often entailed, served broadly to bring native peoples into the Spanish physical and mental orbit. A parish priest might criticize *encomenderos* or the *mita*; but, paradoxically, the more his effort to protect Indians attached them to him, the more powerful an agent of Spanish presence he became. The state, too, was naturally and inextricably bound up with economic matters. America's wealth, once identified in present and potential forms, became a central part of Spain's fiscal being. The government logically worked to raise its income from the Indies, as it gained the administrative means to do so, by modifying systems of production (in suppressing the *encomienda*, for example), maximizing the use of a dwindling labor supply (through setting up drafts), and adjusting taxes (lowering the silver royalty to a tenth in Mexico, for instance, to encourage there what seemed a frailer mining industry than the central Andean enterprise).

But Spanish domination was not by any means a simple imposition on America of alien methods and solutions. It was equally an adjustment and adaptation of the European to New World conditions that sometimes came close to new invention. The American *audiencia* by the late sixteenth century had moved far from its Iberian source in becoming as much an executive as a juridical body. The estate structure of Spanish society shifted across the Atlantic, but the occupants of the estates changed, with ethnicity rather than function now becoming the determinant in placement. Spaniards' partiality for wheat resulted in the location of excellent wheat lands in New Spain and elsewhere; but colonists ate maize (and potatoes and manioc too) soon enough as well. The interesting, but unexploited, qualities of mercury long known in Europe were developed, in mid-sixteenth-century Mexico, into the basis of a silver-refining industry whose product had worldwide economic effects. Even long-accepted European notions of what constituted humanity necessarily expanded when Spaniards met people whose qualities contradicted the old patterns. In sum, the same capacity to learn, to improvise, to respond creatively to the unknown and the uncertain that had given the *conquistadores* a crucial edge over the native states, persisted among early residents of the Indies, both officials and settlers, advancing the processes of domination that are the essence of Spanish American history between the conquests and the end of the sixteenth century.

PART IV

MATURE COLONIES

CHRONOLOGY OF PART IV

1559 Beginning of royally approved sale of office (notarial posts) in Spanish America

1566 Beginning of Dutch revolt against Spanish rule

1586–1617 Life of Isabel Flores de Oliva (Santa Rosa de Lima)

1588 Defeat of the Spanish Armada sent against England

1590s Rise of foreign incursions into the Caribbean

Late 1590s First Dutch settlers on Guiana coast of South America

1606 Royal decree permitting purchase of almost all local offices. Beginning of silver boom at Oruro (lasting until c.1630)

1609–21 Truce between Spain and the Dutch

1610 First Jesuits reductions (missions) among Guaraní in Paraguay

c.1611–c.1681 Life of Diego Quispe Tito, prime early painter of the Cuzco school

1621 Death of Philip III of Spain. Accession of Philip IV. Foundation of Dutch West India Company

1624 English seize St Kitt's in Leeward Islands

1628 Piet Heyn captures a Spanish treasure fleet off Cape Matanzas (Cuba)

1633 Beginning of sale of fiscal offices in Spanish America

1634 Dutch seize Curaçao

1635 French seize Martinique and Guadeloupe

1648?–95 Life of Juana Ramírez de Asbaje (Sor Juana Inés de la Cruz)

1655 English seize Jamaica

1660s English settlement of mouth of Belize river

1665 Death of Philip IV of Spain. Accession of Charles II. France sends official governor to Tortuga: beginning of colony of St. Domingue, later Haiti

1677 Sale of *corregimientos* and *alcaldías mayores* permitted

1680–93 Revolt of Pueblo Indians in New Mexico

1687 *Audiencia* offices put up for sale

1700 Death of Charles II, final Habsburg ruler of Spain

1701 Accession of Philip V, first Bourbon king of Spain

1701–14 War of the Spanish Succession

1712–13 Peace of Utrecht

c.1710 Zacatecas overtakes Potosí in silver production

1714 Ministry of the Indies created by Philip V

1717 *Casa de Contratación* moved from Seville to Cadiz

1728 Caracas (or Guipúzcoa) Company founded in Spain

1730 Mestizo-led rising at Cochabamba

1739 Viceroyalty of New Granada established

1739 Rising at Oruro, opposing tax increases

1739–48 Wars of Jenkins's Ear and of Austrian Succession

1742 Beginning of Juan Santos Atahualpa's rising in Peruvian Andes

1743 *New System of Economic Government of America*, by José del Campillo y Cossío

1746   Our Lady of Guadalupe proclaimed patroness of New Spain. Death of Philip V. Accession of Ferdinand VI.

1748   Last sailing of *galeones* to Isthmus of Panama

1756–63   Seven Years War

1759   Death of Ferdinand VI. Accession of Charles III

1763   Peace of Paris

1764   First American ports opened to single ship trade. First intendant placed in America (Cuba)

1765   Rising in Quito against growing fiscal pressure

1765–71   Gálvez's inspection of New Spain

1767   Expulsion of the Jesuits from Spanish territories

1776   Last *flota* sails to New Spain. Viceroyalty of the Río de la Plata established

1777   Arrival in Peru of José Antonio de Areche as general inspector

1778   "Regulations and Royal Tariffs for Free Trade between Spain and America" promulgated

1780–81   Revolt led by Túpac Amaru II in Peruvian Andes. Clavijero's *Ancient History of Mexico*

1781   Siege of La Paz (Bolivia) by Túpac Katari. *Comunero* revolt in New Granada

1785   Foundation of the Academia de San Carlos (of fine arts) in Mexico City

1787–8   *Audiencia* established at Cuzco

1788   Death of Charles III. Accession of Charles IV

1804   Seizure by the crown of the church's *obras pías* in America

1808   Abdication of Charles IV. Accession, and exile, of Ferdinand VII

FURTHER READING FOR PART IV

General works on the seventeenth century in Spanish America are few. A recent exception is Ruggiero Romano, *Coyunturas opuestas. La crisis del siglo XVII en Europa e Hispanoamérica* (El Colegio de México/Fondo de Cultura Económica, Mexico City, 1993). Again, the first two volumes of *The Cambridge History of Latin America* contain fundamental readings. D. A. Brading, *The First America. The Spanish Monarchy, Creole Patriots, and the Liberal State, 1492–1867*, offers a wealth of insight into seventeenth- and eighteenth-century attitudes. Louisa S. Hoberman, *Mexico's Merchant Elite, 1590–1660. Silver, State, and Society*, is the most complete treatment of New Spain for the seventeenth century. Consult also J. I. Israel, *Race, Class and Politics in Colonial Mexico, 1610–1670*. For both the seventeenth and the eighteenth centuries, William B. Taylor, *Landlord and Peasant in Colonial Oaxaca*, and *Drinking, Homicide and Rebellion in Colonial Mexican Villages*, say much about the interactions of Indians and Spaniards.

For Peru, Kenneth J. Andrien, *Crisis and Decline. The Viceroyalty of Peru in the Seventeenth Century*, Karen Spalding, *Huarochirí. An Andean Society under Inca and Spanish Rule*, and Kenneth Mills, *Idolatry and its Enemies. Colonial Andean Religion and Extirpation, 1640–1750*, are all full of interest. See also John L. Phelan, *The Kingdom of Quito in the Seventeenth Century. Bureaucratic Politics in the Seventeenth Century*. For New Granada, Anthony McFarlane, *Colombia before Independence. Economy, Society, and Politics under Bourbon Rule*, is a valuable contribution; as, for colonial Ecuador, is Kenneth J. Andrien, *The Kingdom of Quito, 1690–1830. The State and Regional*

Development. Susan M. Socolow, *The Women of Colonial Latin America* (Cambridge University Press, Cambridge, 2000) is a general account. Many of the essays in *Sexuality and Marriage in Colonial Latin America* (Asunción Lavrin, ed., University of Nebraska Press, Lincoln, 1989) deal with the seventeenth and eighteenth centuries; as does Patricia Seed, *To Love, Honor, and Obey in Colonial Mexico. Conflicts over Marriage Choices, 1574–1821*, a study which has as much to say about social history as it does about marriage.

For the eighteenth century, Nils Jacobsen and Hans-Jürgen Puhle (eds), *The Economies of Mexico and Peru during the Late Colonial Period, 1760–1810*, ranges widely. Richard Garner's *Economic Growth and Change in Bourbon Mexico* is the most thorough economic study made of any region of colonial Spanish America. For Indian risings, see Scarlett O'Phelan Godoy's notable *Rebellions and Revolts in Eighteenth Century Peru and Upper Peru*, and Steve J. Stern (ed.), *Resistance, Rebellion, and Consciousness in the Andean Peasant World* (as well as Taylor, *Drinking* . . . , above). For Bourbon innovations, Colin M. MacLachlan, *Spain's Empire in the New World. The Role of Ideas in Institutional and Social Change*. John Lynch, in *Bourbon Spain, 1700–1808*, says much about Spanish America and its relationship with the metropolis. *Reform and Insurrection in Bourbon New Granada and Peru* (John R. Fisher, Allan J. Kuethe, and Anthony McFarlane, eds), conveys the rise of tensions in the eighteenth century in the Andean parts of the empire.

[11] *THE SEVENTEENTH CENTURY: A SLACKER GRIP*

CHALLENGES TO SPAIN

For political and military achievement the sixteenth century has no rival in Spanish history: the New World brought to heel in the west; the Turks kept at bay in the east; heresy assaulted in the north; an empire created spanning two-thirds of the world's circumference, from Manila at 120 degrees east to Lower California at 120 degrees west. Spain's feats seemed superhuman, and so indeed Spaniards sometimes thought them to be, seeing divine inspiration and appointment in their nation's acts. The cost, though, was great; and what was built was not as sturdy as it seemed to other Europeans awed throughout the 1500s by Spanish power. By the end of that century of imperial explosion, those at its center began to feel a hollowness around them. That sensation, strengthened increasingly by tangible reality, was to dominate the new century.

PROBLEMS AT HOME

The reasons for Spanish gloom and disillusion, and for real decline that accompanied it, are as varied as they are numerous, and almost as debatable now as they were then. Was the fault in part America's? Clearly, colonizing did not drain Spain of money; the flow was overwhelmingly in the other direction. But did, perhaps, the American enterprise deplete Spain's reserves of men of energy and initiative? Did it reinforce in Spain medieval notions of glory won through feats of arms, at the expense of the adoption of the idea arising elsewhere in Europe that strength resided in humdrum and steady pursuit of trade and industry? Neither point can be proved; but neither can be dismissed out of hand.

What is clear, however, is that Spain's possession of America and the receipt of American wealth encouraged a depth of engagement in European affairs that soon left the country overextended. This was particularly so in Philip II's reign (1556–98), four decades in which American silver production, propelled by amalgamation, boomed. If Philip had been content to scale his European plans to the rising current of silver crossing the ocean to Spain, all might have been well. But instead he used it as the basis of still larger enterprises, borrowing heavily at home and abroad to finance them on the security of silver receipts to come. Among the outcomes was a series of state bankruptcies, or repudiations of debt, in 1557, 1575, 1596, and then, early in the reign of his son, in 1607. The first, it is true, was not of Philip II's making. But the others reflect his overcommitment of Spain's resources, not so much despite as because of the American cornucopia. It seemed that this wealth had been divinely delivered to Spain to enable it to become the leader in containing Protestantism. Philip, from duty but with misgivings, took command of what proved a Canute-like venture.

The main foes were the Dutch, in a revolt from 1566 against their Spanish rulers inspired by religion and national feeling. It was for Spain an endless, sapping war. Philip's efforts to draw in French Catholic help against the Netherlands embroiled him in France's civil wars to no good final effect. His attempts to eliminate English support for the rebels and more broadly to nip the burgeoning growth of Elizabeth's Protestant England were outright and costly failures. The first and most telling of these was the disaster of the Armada of 1588, when forty to fifty of 130 ships were lost, along with some 15,000 men. Spain soon made up the lost vessels. But the defeat by a combination of arms and weather was an arresting psychological blow.[1] The great charger of state, thunderously advancing for so long past, seemed suddenly to have crashed to the ground. Spain's foes were heartened, and the Protestant cause advanced.

Philip's final decade was therefore one in which Spain lost its earlier certainties of rightness. Not only were there more blows in the external world – England's brief holding and sacking of Cadiz in 1596, the failure of another fleet sent against England in 1597, ineluctable granting of secession to the Netherlands in 1598, a peace, from weariness, with France at Vervins in May of that same year, five months before Philip's death – but growing evidence of strain and decay within. Royal impecuniousness led in 1590 to the imposition of a new tax, the *millones*, on a Castilian peasantry already heavily burdened by increases earlier in the reign. Despite this, in 1596 the repayment of crown debts was suspended. This further weakened a Spanish economy that was now visibly in difficulties. The market and industrial towns of northern Castile, prosperous early in the century, were in decline, and their population drifting southward. More general, still, than this was a shift of population from the country to towns, not so much, it seems, because of attractive economic opportunity in them but because of the intolerable cost of staying on the land. Taxes, tithes, and rents took more than half the value of a peasant's product.[2] Most Castilian peasants were tenants, and more became so during Philip II's reign, as he, again to raise money, sold not only communal lands but also, with papal permission, some of the church's as well. Hence, curiously in a reign often thought of as prematurely absolutist, control of land tended to pass from the crown to rising and existing nobles. Great estates grew up, especially in the south.[3] More and more peasants of Philip's time, therefore, fell under the private jurisdiction of lords, and subject to whatever demands for rent and labor services their masters might make. The social outcome was exodus from the land; and the economic one a rising shortage, and price, of food. The absurdity arose, then, in the late years of the sixteenth century, of the country's importing staple grains that it had all that was necessary – soil, climate, land, and labor – to produce in abundance. It was an early example of the economic nonsenses, inspired by idiosyncratic social and cultural norms, that were increasingly to puzzle outside observers of Spain over the next several centuries. That this economic irrationality could have clear practical effects was soon demonstrated. Malnutrition and urban crowding made Spain a fertile ground for epidemic disease, as the country's seventeenth-century history repeatedly shows. Now there is no doubt that the population was falling, rather than simply migrating. The first attack came in 1596, when bubonic plague entered at the northern port of Santander. Over the next four years, perhaps half a million Spaniards succumbed to the disease.[4]

FOREIGN INCURSIONS IN AMERICA

Across the Atlantic, too, the 1590s brought disquieting signs that past certainties might not last. That was the decade in which foreigners began to show ominous naval and commercial strength in the Caribbean, which the Spanish had taken for their own lake. Before, to be sure, there had been pirates and privateers: LeClerc and other Frenchmen before the Treaty of Cateau-Cambrésis in 1559, and more notoriously Francis Drake in the 1570s and 1580s. But in the 1590s foreigners began to look for a more regular, though of course contraband, trade with the Spanish colonies. Particularly interested were the arch-enemies, the Dutch, whose herring industry at home needed a reliable supply of salt. Their earlier source, Setúbal, just south of Lisbon, had been closed to them by Philip II. Another source of supply was the Cape Verde islands. But Araya on the eastern coast of Venezuela, though further off, was more attractive. A ship sent there could not merely load salt, but trade with settlers on the Main and in the islands, attack intercolonial trade, and even possibly pick off a ship separated from a transatlantic fleet. The venture had its risks; in 1593 the Spanish captured ten Dutch ships carrying Caribbean dye-wood and other goods off eastern Venezuela.[5] But the prospect of profit combined with sapping Spanish trade and confidence was something a Dutch-man could hardly resist. Besides the primary business of salt digging, trade of Holland and English cloth for pearls and tobacco from Venezuela grew. Turning north, the Dutch soon also found Hispaniola and Cuba to be good sources of hides. Settlers and even Spanish officials were pleased to trade on the generous terms the Dutch offered. So disturbing did this commerce soon become to higher authorities that in 1603 orders came from Spain to hinder it by the desperate measure of removing Spanish settlement from the north coast of Hispaniola. Towns were duly abandoned, though people still keen to buy contraband remained.[6] Worse, northern, and especially north-western, Hispaniola became open territory for alien settlers. Predominant among them were the piratical French boucaniers. Their bases gradually became permanent in the first half of the seventeenth century. Thus the foundation of French-speaking Haiti was laid in north-western Hispaniola: a dismal history originating in Spanish panic.

Among the Dutch, also, rising trade soon brought thought of settlement in its wake. Their first attempts (and some English ones, too) seem to have been made on the "Wild," or Guiana, coast between Venezuela and the Amazon. Raleigh gave an enticing account of this in 1596; but by then the Dutch were already planning trading posts on it, which were in place before 1600. There was hope of precious metals; but gums, oils, and dyes proved to be the more mundane reality. Notwithstanding, Dutch trade in the Caribbean and South America at the turn of the century was highly profitable to them; and highly expensive to the Spanish, who had to divert ever scarcer funds to efforts to thwart the interlopers. They had some success. But so large were Holland's naval reserves by now that small setbacks were taken in stride. And soon the same could be said of France and England also. It was clear, as the seventeenth century opened, that Spaniards could no longer assume, as most had since Columbus, that the Caribbean was exclusively theirs.

It was amid the confusion and rivalries of the Thirty Years War (1618–48), however, and after the end of the Spanish–Dutch truce of 1609–21, that foreigners began to make truly serious inroads into the Spanish hold on the Caribbean. In 1621 the Dutch founded their West India Company, a blend of private and state enterprise, to trade and, if necessary, administer in America, and broadly to harass Spain in the Atlantic. The Company's most spectacular success came early, in 1628, when its squadron, commanded by Piet Heyn, captured a returning Spanish fleet off Cape Matanzas in northern Cuba. It was the first time one of the great Spanish Atlantic fleets had been taken, and another staggering blow to Spanish martial confidence, as well as to the treasury. The resulting haul of six million pesos (170,000 kilograms of silver) went in part to fund a successful Dutch attack on north-east Brazil in the following year.

By the time of Matanzas, Spain had also begun to lose islands in the Caribbean to foreigners. The English, seeking bases for trade with Spanish colonials, and sites for growing the tobacco now in quickly escalating demand, seized San Cristóbal (soon St Kitt's) in the Leeward Islands in 1624, and Barbados in the Windwards in 1627. Despite Spanish attempts at reconquest, sometimes briefly successful, other islands in the Lesser Antilles quickly fell to the English and French (Martinique and Guadeloupe, for example, in 1635). These islands the Spaniards had generally regarded as "useless," and had left unsettled. In 1634, though, the Dutch took a place that was both occupied (if scantily) and far closer to Spanish mainland centers: Curaçao. Losses in the Greater Antilles followed within two decades. An English force sent by Cromwell against Hispaniola in 1655 failed in its attack on Santo Domingo, the capital town. But on the rebound it took Jamaica, where some 150 Spaniards resided. Jamaica remained under English control until 1962. Meanwhile, the *boucaniers* had continued their hunting and smuggling in northern Hispaniola. The island of Tortuga, just off Hispaniola's north-west coast, had become notorious as a base for these French pirates. In 1665, Louis XIV's administration dispatched a governor to Tortuga to impose some order among the raiders; and also to supervise a more peaceful settlement, with farms and ranches, of nearby parts of Hispaniola. This duly followed, and the formal French colony of St Domingue began to extend over the western end of that large island. Less formal, but still more insolent a challenge to the Spanish, was the largely English incursion into the Caribbean coasts of Central America in the mid-century. In 1642 came the capture of Roatán Island in the Bay of Honduras, a good base for piracy and smuggling, and also for dyewood cutters active in what is now Belize. The Spanish built expensive forts to repulse these intruders. But in such thickly forested and thinly peopled areas there was little hope of success against men impelled by a profitable trade. The English woodcutters set up a base at the mouth of the Belize River in the 1660s, the seed of what was until 1981 a British colony. They also came to exercise much, if intermittent, control on the eastern coast of Nicaragua, as the persistence there to this day of English place-names suggests. The first English attempts at settlement of that Mosquito Coast date from the mid-1630s; and only in the 1780s did Spain finally manage to drive the interlopers out.

With the exception of the Guianas, over various pieces of which the Dutch, French, and English haggled throughout the 1600s, creating some small settlements, no part of Spanish South America fell to foreign control in the seventeenth century. That north European trio of scourges of the Spanish contented themselves in South America with piracy and smuggling. The main target for illicit trade was Buenos Aires, a port almost completely closed by law even to Spanish shipping, in an attempt to stop the escape from it of silver produced in the Andean mines. But as with the attempted restrictions on trade between Peru and New Spain, and on transpacific exports, prospect of profit swept the law before it. There was no plugging the drain of silver through the Río de la Plata, exchanged for African slaves and European goods of various sorts bound mainly for the highland mining towns. The west coast of South America was protected by geographical isolation from such constant commercial attention. But European raiders occasionally penetrated the Pacific to attack ports and shipping on the west coast, sowing alarm far disproportionate to their numbers. The Dutch sent powerful, state-dispatched, squadrons around the Horn in 1615, 1624, and 1643. The latter two had among their aims the creation of trading posts on the west coast. But the Spanish prevented that, and damage and losses were on balance slight. There followed almost forty years in which the west coast saw no foreigners. Then came English filibusters across the Isthmus from the Caribbean, seizing small Spanish ships in the Pacific and using them to raid ports and harry shipping, always in pursuit of silver. The first piratical onslaught was in 1680–1; the second, from 1685 to 1689. In these two episodes the Spanish lost over fifty ships and over two hundred men. The greatest damage may have been, though, in disruption of the lively coastal trade. Not only were its ships captured, but in an effort to deter the pirates, ports were closed and goods withdrawn inland. Finally colonists, despairing of the government's ability to defend the coast, subscribed to the purchase of two armed frigates. These turned the tide against the intruders.[7]

The seventeenth century was the great age of piracy in the Caribbean too. Officials in the new foreign settlements there, and their home governments, were for several decades tolerant of it. The main victim was Spain. But as the island colonies became more formal, and their populations grew (which some did with spectacular speed, Barbados's rising from 1,850 to 37,000 Whites between 1628 and 1643, for example);[8] and as they also rose in economic importance to their home countries, especially with the shift from tobacco to sugar and other tropical crops after the mid-century; then the French, Dutch, and English view of corsairs became more critical. The Spanish were able to bargain in some measure with the intruders, offering recognition of the foreigners' island holdings in exchange for help against piracy. This was one reason, though political and military reality was the larger one, for a series of treaties granting territorial titles that began in 1648 with the cession of Curaçao and St Eustatius to Holland, and ended in 1697 with the recognition of French St Domingue. Spain acknowledged all English claims, except that to Belize, in 1670.

So it was that well before the end of the seventeenth century Spain ceased to be mistress of the vestibule to the great edifice of the American empire. Robbers henceforth lurked in the main portal of the Indies. That was of greater import than the loss of Caribbean territory, for in reality not much that Spain valued for its productive capacity had gone. The newcomers, certainly, produced richly where Spain had never tried; but there was land enough for sugar still in Peru, New Spain, and Cuba. Nor, strategically speaking, did the losses to the French and the Dutch much matter for the balance of the colonial period. By 1700 Holland was no longer a major European power. And, through the Bourbon connection set up by the War of Spanish Succession (1700–13), Spain and France were generally allies in eighteenth-century wars. But the English, France's rivals for European and even world power in the eighteenth century, were a different matter. To have them ensconced in the Caribbean was a severe handicap; their already formidable naval power was made still more menacing by the existence of their bases in Jamaica and the Lesser Antilles. Wars in the eighteenth century came to mean for Spain frequent breaks in contact with America, with attendant disruption of trade and governance. The final English insult came in Simón Bolívar's taking refuge in Jamaica in 1815, before starting his slow but finally successful campaign to free northern South America of Spanish rule.

With the rarest of madcap exceptions, such as a Portuguese scheme to seize Potosí from the Atlantic coast in the 1640s,[9] foreign powers did not plan major assaults on the Spanish American mainland in the seventeenth century. It was far less troublesome and costly simply to tap into the Spanish American trade from offshore settlements. Viceroys and *audiencia* presidents, therefore, rarely had to ward off anything more serious than piratical attacks. That was just as well, since the military establishment was small and ill-prepared except on the empire's periphery.

CREOLES ASCENDANT: COLONIALS IMPOSE THEIR WILL

If the external threat to Lima or Mexico City was in reality slight, royal officers were increasingly conscious of a more insidious, and ultimately far more powerful, challenge from within. This came from the ever-rising number of American-born Whites, congregated mainly in the cities and towns of the empire – the creoles (*criollos* in Spanish, from the verb *criar*, to raise or rear). The term *criollo* was often applied in the sixteenth century to American-born Blacks. But it was used early of Whites as well. "There gathered in this city the sons of householders [*vecinos*], who by another name are called *criollos*," reported one of the crown prosecutors in the *Audiencia* of Lima in 1567.[10] From the start administrators regarded these white Americans with suspicion or even trepidation. They seemed footloose, proud (of their ancestors' participation in the conquest), idle, and troublesome. The youthful group in Lima in 1567 had disrupted a religious procession in the nearby port of Callao, tearing down decorative cloths hung out for the occasion, then mocking and injuring a magistrate who tried to stop them. Peninsulars in America remained until the end uneasy about creoles: people who thought themselves equal with Spaniards, but who were not quite Spaniards; perhaps tainted with some Indian or black blood; perhaps made idle, frivolous, irresponsible by the weather or the environment of America; softened mentally and physically by the tropics. The antagonism was mutual. Some creoles, even before the sixteenth century was out, tended to regard incoming Spaniards, whether officials or private immigrants, as usurpers of positions, wealth, and status properly belonging to families gloriously descended from conquerors and first settlers.[11] "O Indies! Mother of strangers, a shelter for thieves and delinquents, a homeland for foreigners, sweet kiss and peace for newcomers. O Indies! Stepmother to your own children and exile for your native sons, a scourge and knife for your own people," exclaimed a Mexican creole apologist for his kind in 1604, perhaps providing too easy confirmation for peninsulars already persuaded of creole foolishness.[12] The sense given here of creoles' strong attachment by this time to their American birthplace is, however, real.

For lack of discriminating censuses, the balance of numbers between peninsulars and creoles in the sixteenth and seventeenth centuries is unclear. One estimate for New Spain gives *c.*6,600 peninsulars against *c.*11,000 creoles in 1570, and *c.*13,800 against *c.*169,000 in 1646.[13] This last figure seems high; but a heavy *criollo* dominance in Mexico, or elsewhere, by 1600 would not be surprising, given the large number of Spanish women present in the Indies since the mid-sixteenth century. By the end of that century, as would be expected, the creole segment of society had acquired its own internal social ranking. This was most developed in Mexico, the earliest of the major mainland colonies. There, at its head as the century turned, stood a sole titled family: the Marquises of the Valley of Oaxaca, the descendants of Cortés. Three other rich, landholding families received titles in the first half of the seventeenth century. Beneath these in status, though not necessarily much in wealth and property, was a larger group of what had become aristocratic creole clans, stemming from conquerors, early *encomenderos*, and sixteenth-century senior administrators. By the early 1620s some fifty of these families in New Spain had created entails (*mayorazgos*) to protect their holdings in urban and rural property, proprietary offices, mortgages, loans, and assorted goods. They had become tightly interlinked by marriage. Some had blood ties to the upper Castilian nobility. They often had close connections also with the colonial administration; it was common enough for senior officials, who had high status without matching income, to marry the daughters of this untitled Mexican nobility in an exchange of influence for money.[14] Below these wealthy and high-ranking families came all manner of creole traders, lawyers, priests, doctors, stockraisers, artisans – shading off into mestizo society, similarly differentiated at its own lower level.

As this sketch of Mexican creole society suggests, many American-born Whites were not content to yield profitable offices and occupations to immigrants. The gripers were mainly from the ranks of the *beneméritos* – the "deserving" grandchildren and later descendants of *conquistadores* and *encomenderos* who came to hold an almost comical belief that their forefathers' heroism entitled them to the monarchy's perpetual support and gratitude. But some even of these, and certainly many of those who lacked such illustrious background, were active enough in pursuing money. Some also pursued political power, for its own sake and for the social and financial returns it could bring.

In the sixteenth century, creoles found political opportunity mainly in town councils. Before the 1590s, most *cabildo* posts were distributed by royal gift, and once adult creole men appeared on the scene, they began to receive positions, in recognition of their services or perhaps of ancestry. While a council's authority was certainly local, it was not negligible. It included levy of local taxes, regulation of the supply and price of grain and meat, and control over building lots and municipal commons. *Cabildos* proved adept at resisting viceregal and even royal orders that seemed harmful to a town's (or, more exactly, the local economic elite's) interests. They could and did send representatives to the viceregal and royal courts. Finally, councils were in practice if not in constitutional intent a distinct force in the application of law, since it was the aldermen who selected annually a town's two *alcaldes ordinarios*, or magistrates of first instance. These were generally drawn from the same social and economic group as the aldermen themselves; so the leading citizens of towns, through the *cabildo*, gained an influence over jurisdiction, the most central and precious of the monarch's functions. An *alcalde ordinario* was not likely to rule consistently against the interests of peers who had chosen him.

In the seventeenth century, creoles added to their domination of *cabildos* some movement into *alcaldías mayores* and *corregimientos*, the local governorships that were the lowest rung of the salaried royal bureaucracy. Viceroys and *audiencia* presidents generally made these appointments, perhaps as a means of placating disgruntled *beneméritos*, perhaps because of personal ties – credit received, children intermarried – with creoles. The positions often gave good opportunity for profit from near-monopoly sale of goods to rural Indians. Local office, however, was by no means the limit of creole bureaucratic advance. Late in the sixteenth century, to take one example, a son of one of the wealthiest and most eminent creole families in Mexico became royal treasurer in the capital. And between 1610 and 1687, creoles received almost a quarter of the senior appointments (as staff attorneys, prosecutors, or judges) made to colonial *audiencias* across the colonies. The availability by then of advanced legal education in American universities, particularly those in Lima and Mexico City, may account in part for this surprisingly high figure.[15] Again, though, local ties between high administrators and high creole society cannot be discounted.

For those without influence or some family claim on royal gratitude, the crown opened another door to office by making an expanding range of positions purchasable. This began in 1559 when, scraping for money after the recent state bankruptcy, Philip II ordered notarial offices sold in the Indies.[16] As fiscal woes deepened, the variety of salable positions grew. Offices in the two mints in New Spain and Peru could be bought after the late 1560s.[17] In 1591, struggling with the cost of the failed Armada of 1588, Philip put up for sale various of the positions in town councils, principally the *regimientos*, or aldermanships. These had in truth been transferable by private sale for decades past, after the monarch's initial bestowal of them.[18] But now the standard way to a *regimiento* became simply to buy it. Then a decree of 1606 made almost every local office purchasable, not simply for a lifetime, but in perpetuity. The holder might, on payment of a tax of half the post's value, pass it to another person; and he to another; and so on. As a result of this ruling, the accounting year 1606–7 brought the largest proceeds ever in colonial Mexico from office sales: the weighty sum of 300,342 pesos.[19] Still, though, fiscal needs pressed. Philip IV's administration took the drastic step of extending sales from municipal to bureaucratic positions. In 1633 appointments in American treasury offices, and in the auditing tribunals (*tribunales de* *cuenta*) created early in the century in Mexico City, Lima, and Santa Fe de Bogotá, were offered. In the 1640s, the infection spread to the Spanish end of the imperial administration, with the offer of lower positions in the Council of the Indies to buyers. Under Charles II the process was completed. First, in 1677, *corregimientos* and *alcaldías mayores*, and then in 1687 posts in *audiencias*, including the judgeships themselves, were put on the market. The crown thus weakened, for cash, its exercise of jurisdiction at the highest American levels. This was an even more striking surrender to fiscal expediency than the sale of the viceroyship itself, which indeed took place soon after. In the mid-nineties the Count of Cañete bought the post of viceroy of Peru.[20]

Creoles took advantage of the sales to enlarge their presence in government. After 1591 their hold on *cabildos* tightened. They dominated the councils of Mexico City and Lima, and certainly almost everywhere else, in the seventeenth century. While, for example, only 19 percent of the *alcaldes ordinarios* of Lima were Peruvian creoles to 1599, the proportion rose to 71 percent in the 1600s, and 81 percent in the 1700s. Again, it was very largely sale that produced a growing creole presence in the fiscal system. Peninsulars heavily dominated both the auditing tribunals and the treasury until selling of posts in them began in 1633. Then creoles began to buy their way into these bodies at every level, so that the collection of royal income was increasingly entrusted to men who had ties of friendship, marriage, and business with the leading families of the empire's major towns. The result was a clear fall in the quality and preparation of fiscal officers. Increasingly a high offer became the main reason for making an appointment. Worse still, future tenure of a position was also put up for sale, so that men bought offices for younger relatives to assume at a later date; and there was no knowing how capable they might be. For the accountant's post in the auditing tribunal at Lima, multiple sales of "futures" led to there being six buyers in line in 1653.[21]

Selling of fiscal, or other bureaucratic, office had other drawbacks. It weakened the viceroy's powers of patronage. It damaged morale and perform-ance by interrupting patterns of promotion; officials who could have expected before that honest and efficient work would take them over the course of a career from provincial to central posts no longer had that incentive. Perhaps most obviously self-defeating of all was that bureaucratic offices were salaried. In seventeenth-century Lima, for instance, the price of treasury posts ranged from 5,375 to 18,750 pesos. The accountant's annual salary there was three thousand pesos in the mid-century.[22] Thus sales meant a brief surge in royal income in exchange for certain future loss; and that in addition to whatever the inefficiency or outright dishonesty of the buyer might cost.

Purchase did not increase the number of creole *alcaldes mayores* and *corre-gidores*. The reverse, in fact: after selling of these local executive posts began in 1677, creoles perhaps received fewer of them than before, possibly because merchants in Spain bought the appointments for peninsulars who, they hoped, would market exported goods profitably among Indians. The same was not true, however, of *audiencia* offices. From a little under 25 percent before 1687, the year the positions were first offered for cash, creole repre-sentation in the high courts rose to 44 percent in the period 1687–1750. Then, with attempts precisely to reduce American influence in the high courts, it dropped back to 24 percent in the second half of the eighteenth century.[23]

American-born colonists thus multiplied their influence over imperial ad-ministration in the seventeenth century, either through pressure informally placed on bureaucrats, or by becoming bureaucrats, through appointment or purchase, themselves. What this meant for the efficiency and honesty of government it is impossible to say exactly. Perhaps there were public-spirited creoles who sought appointments because they felt they could do a better job than peninsular bureaucrats. Far more numerous, though, in all probability were those who saw acquisition of office as a profitable investment, with the return coming in salary, commercial opportunities, possibilities of "borrow-ing" royal funds for personal use, chances to favor family and friends; and, of course, in gain of status, and the simple exercise of power. Not all, by any means, of colonials' assumption of state business was illegal or immoral; though it all tended to be costly to the crown. The treasury, for example, resorted to local farming of taxes as a solution to shortage of staff. Tithes, customs duties (*almojarifazgo*), and the sales tax (*alcabala*) were often col-lected in this way. The gatherers, typically town councils or groups of local merchants, naturally bid less for the contract than they thought they would collect. Clear illegalities, by contrast, resulted from the large involvement, partly through purchase of positions, of private citizens in the minting of coin in both Mexico City and Potosí: the illegal minting of untaxed silver in the first case,[24] and severe adulteration of coins in the mid-century in the second.

An example of a more generalized sort of distortion of government brought about by close association of bureaucrats and local people can be found, again in Mexico City, in 1621. The senior *oidor* and other judges of the *audiencia*, which temporarily held executive power in New Spain in the absence of a viceroy, concocted a scheme with the creole-dominated *cabildo* of the city, and others, to corner the urban market in wheat and maize. They were briefly successful in driving up the prices as planned. The racket was halted by the incoming viceroy, the Marquis of Gelves, who was a man appointed precisely to carry to Mexico the tautening of government, not least of its fiscal aspects, that Philip IV's reforming minister, the Count of Olivares, had begun to apply to Spain itself. The matter of grain sales was, in fact, only the opening round in a two-year battle between the viceroy and the *audiencia*. Into this conflict, all major forces in government, church, and society in Mexico City were drawn, on one side or the other, for a variety of causes. The archbishop at first sided with Gelves, but the two soon split over their divergent view of creoles, whom Gelves lumped together in iniquity with the *audiencia*. Tensions mounted, until finally the viceroy banished the archbishop from New Spain. The archbishop ignored the order and retaliated by excommunicating Gelves and closing all the churches in Mexico City. Finally, in January 1624, riots broke out. The *audiencia* and leading creoles made, it seems, no determined attempt to contain them. The result was a sacking of the viceregal palace, from which Gelves allegedly escaped with his life only by mingling with the mob and joining in its cry of "Kill the viceroy."[25] He was quickly relieved of office; and reform of government lost momentum in New Spain.

Though it was a complicated, many-faceted, affair, the confrontation between Gelves and the *audiencia* of New Spain, and its outcome in the viceroy's humiliation, suggest how firm the link between creoles and bureaucracy had become quite early in the seventeenth century. The time had passed when reforms threatening colonists' interests could simply be imposed by fiat from Madrid. Gelves's style was doubtless abrupt; he was something of a puritan. But his failure showed clearly to anyone willing to observe that government of the Indies was now more than ever before a matter of negotiation rather than command. A new role for governors was that of brokerage between the aims of the monarchy and those of the colonials.[26]

This tendency strengthened as the century progressed, to the point where a new "colonial pact" emerged, expressing the monarchy's weakness in America (as in Spain also) on the one hand, and the rising real power (founded in wealth and political influence) of upper creole society on the other.[27] What the crown wanted from America above all else in the seventeenth century was money (a fact symbolized by the uniting under one president of the Councils of the Treasury and of the Indies in 1678). Since silver production was no longer rising as it had before 1600, and as at least the legal transatlantic trade was declining, with a commensurate fall in silver imports and duties collected, new or higher taxes seemed necessary. But these the creoles would in general not countenance. Therefore, in a forced shift to pragmatism, the crown raised funds by selling what creoles would buy. Offices, of increasing seniority and jurisdictional weight, were their first preference. But there was much else: titles of nobility (notably from the 1670s on), "compositions" remedying missing or defective land titles, extensions of *encomienda* grants, pardons for a variety of transgressions, legitimizations of natural children, and, not least, bonds (*juros*) issued by the home government. These sales at once strengthened the notion that government was something that could be manipulated by money, that wealth was political influence; and also the idea, firmly established in America in the previous century, that wealth underlay social status.

These persuasions were not unique to the colonies, of course. If in America they were in part the outcome of fiscal pressures imposed from Spain, they were all the stronger there, across the Atlantic, where the fiscal strains originated and were most acutely felt. ("A mighty knight is Sir Money" – "*poderoso caballero es don Dinero*" – wrote the satirist Francisco de Quevedo, "for he makes equals of the duke and the drover.") It can be no chance that the seventeenth century saw the addition of "wealthy" to the basic sense of "powerful" that *poderoso* had long carried. Olivares was quick to blame the penury and weakness afflicting Spain by 1630 precisely on the *poderosos*.[28] Spanish politics is marked ever more clearly as the century advances, and central authority atrophies, by the emergence of rich and powerful regional oligarchies.

The term oligarchy has sometimes been applied to leading creole groups in America. But it is too strong. Oligarchies in Spain, full of titled nobles, had a self-assurance, grounded in a deep sense of family and provincial history, that creoles still lacked. Colonials, however strongly attached to place of birth, still finally sought a sense of self-worth, of social validation, in a Spanish framework; hence, in part, their pursuit of senior offices, and of noble titles. They knew also, though perhaps unconsciously in most cases, that their own standing in every way depended on Spain's imperial presence in America. There appear in seventeenth-century America only the faintest glimmerings of separatism – nothing remotely comparable to the sentiments of Catalonia, or any other Iberian region overburdened by Castile's demands and undertakings. Creoles' disloyalty was limited to feathering their nests at the monarchy's expense, to subverting government to their own advantage. And most would have vehemently denied any lack of fealty, regarding their gains as the due of the leaders of colonial society – Spanish colonial society.

PRODUCTION, TAXES, AND TRADE: SPAIN FRAIL, AMERICA STURDY

Sale of office was one means used by the crown to tap into the rising prosperity of at least the central colonial areas. That rise seems to have persisted from the late sixteenth century for several decades into the seventeenth, though the evidence is patchy and somewhat contradictory. The firmest information is on silver mining. Even there there are doubts, certainly, because production has been calculated from royalty records, and some evasion of the tax clearly took place. But, precisely for that reason, the estimates of output are minimum possible amounts, and hence useful indicators.

MINING AND TREASURY INCOME

Royalty receipts by the treasury show, broadly, that in the central Andes and New Spain silver production rose in the early 1600s. Potosí's decline, it is true, began almost with the new century. Never again after 1605 did taxed production there exceed 1,500,000 pesos, as it had done several times since 1592. Potosí's decline in registered output lasted until the 1720s, with only occasional resurgences as important, but always lesser, ore deposits were found and worked at various sites on the Bolivian *altiplano* and in the nearby eastern Andean ranges. It was an initial boom at Oruro, the largest of these places, from 1606 to *c*.1630 that propelled central Andean production upward until about 1620. After then decline at Potosí became the dominant force; and from the 1630s to the 1660s Oruro followed it downward. Potosí's decay seems mainly to have been the reverse side of the coin of its success. What was so extraordinary about its Rich Hill was the dense concentration of rich ores that the peak contained. The great mass was easily worked – and therefore quickly exhausted. Enormous amounts of poorer one remained beneath the peak. Not only, however, did this ore yield less silver, but it also cost more to extract. Deep shafts, and galleries for drainage and ventilation, were expensive undertakings.

In New Spain it now seems, against earlier views, that silver production did not fall in the seventeenth century, except for a dip *c*.1635–65. The seventeenth-century trend of Mexican output is, in fact, quite steeply upward, thanks to strong growth after 1670 that persisted, always of course with interruptions, until 1810.[29] Mexican production was spread among six or more districts and centers, so that local decline had a small effect on the whole. The difficulties of the middle decades were in any case largely external to mining. They were partly the result of a governmental decision to divert the flow of mercury originating in Almadén from Mexico to Peru, which was short of mercury on account of decline at Huancavelica. At the same time, the treasury began collecting Mexican miners' accumulated debts for mercury distributed in the past. The double blow of shortage of money and of the essential reagent for refining ores shook Mexican mining for three decades. But it emerged fitter from the trial, with more discriminating investment than before from large merchants in Mexico City, and also a partial return to the smelting techniques of pre-amalgamation days. This, though its accomplishment still remains puzzling, clearly gave some protection against future shortages of mercury.

By *c*.1700 rising output in Mexico was enough to reverse the generally downward trend of total silver production in the colonies that had begun some seventy years earlier. Around 1710 Potosí yielded its leadership in output to Zacatecas (with taxed totals, respectively, of 1,220,000 and

1,560,000 pesos for 1710–14). By then silver production was rising fast in almost all Mexican districts; but fastest and most consistently in Guanajuato, which overtook Zacatecas c.1730 to become the new Potosí of Spanish America for the rest of colonial times.

In the seventeenth century, however, the original Potosí, even in decline, gave so much more silver than other mines that its waning was enough to produce a falling trend in colonial silver output – taxed output – as a whole, c.1630–1700. What is surprising is that even in Peru this did not bring an immediate drop in treasury income. Receipts in the Lima treasury office, into which the balances from the regional offices in the central Andes flowed, did not reach their seventeenth-century peak until the early 1640s, and remained strong until the mid-1650s. The decadal totals of royal income at Lima (rounded to the nearest thousand pesos) indicate the broad pattern:

1607–10	16,432,000
1611–20	34,377,000
1621–30	33,399,000
1631–40	38,101,000
1641–50	35,809,000
1651–60	37,910,000
1661–70	19,935,000
1671–80	35,893,000
1681–90	24,995,000

There was, it is true, some sleight of hand in these sums. A large and growing part of royal income at Lima from the 1630s on was in "soft" money (gifts and loans to the crown, sales of *juros* and offices) rather than in solid tax revenue. From 1643 to 1649, for example, no less than 22 percent of receipts came from loans.[30] Nonetheless, the fact that colonials, largely creoles, were able to put up such sums suggests an enduring prosperity among them for a long time. Only in the 1660s did receipts from loans in Lima drop, and very markedly. At the same time remittances to Lima from regional treasury offices also fell sharply; and particularly so from Potosí, Oruro, and La Paz (near Oruro), in reflection of the persistent slump in mining.

The trend of income at the Mexico City treasury office, whose accounts included local income as well as the balances of the regional offices of New Spain, has similarities to Lima's in showing an initial rise in the seventeenth century, and then a fall. The fall, beginning perhaps c.1630 was, though, slight.[31]

June 1605 to June 1615	20,784,000
July 1615 to May 1625	22,343,000
(July 1625 to June 1630	9,882,000)
November 1636 to February 1645	19,550,000
February 1645 to June 1655	20,413,000
April 1660 to March 1671	18,882,000
April 1671 to May 1681	24,173,000
June 1681 to June 1690	24,867,000

In general these Mexican figures seem to follow the trend of silver production more closely than do those from Lima. Especially notable is the resurgence of income after the 1660s, a time of revival of registered silver production. The coincidence is probably not fortuitous.

For the penurious Spain of the seventeenth century, rising treasury receipts in the early decades (and the late ones also in New Spain) were helpful. But they were less so than the numbers suggest, because a growing fraction of American fiscal income stayed in the colonies. Some went to payment of loans, interest on *juros*, and salaries of offices sold. But far outstripping these was the great and rising cost of defending the colonies, and transatlantic shipping, from aggressive and intrusive foreigners. Fortresses, arms, garrisons, and naval shipping absorbed huge sums in the seventeenth-century Indies. Between 1607 and 1610, only 16.5 percent of the Lima treasury's spending was on defense, some 2.6 million pesos. From 1611 to 1650, the proportion rose to around 25 percent – an average of 8 or 9 million pesos per decade. In the 1660s and 1670s, a third of expenditure went to defense; and in the 1680s, no less than 43 percent (10.3 million pesos). These, and other, costs reduced Lima's remittance to Spain from 51 percent of outgoings for 1607–10, to 35–40 percent for 1611–60, to 14.9 percent in the 1660s, 16.9 percent in the 1670s, and a paltry 5 percent in the 1680s. In silver, the decade of highest remittance was the 1640s, at almost 15 million pesos. In the 1680s, the Lima treasury sent home only 1.27 million.[32]

It was much the same elsewhere. Having supplied 1.37 million pesos to Spain in the first decade of the century, the treasury in Santa Fe de Bogotá managed only 48,000 from 1685 to 1700, mainly because of the cost of defenses at Cartagena on the Caribbean coast of New Granada. From 1672 Santa Fe was ordered to send annual defense subsidies (*situados*) to that crucial port, where the *galeones* generally wintered after unloading their goods, and collecting Peruvian silver, on the Isthmus. Certainly Santa Fe's remittances to Spain had dwindled constantly for assorted reasons; but it was military expense that finally reduced them to almost nothing.[33]

Mexican treasury remittances to Spain likewise fell drastically through the 1600s, from a high in the first decade of 10 million pesos to a low, in the last, of 2.7 million. The average over the century was some 5.7 million per decade. New Spain carried a very large load of defense charges, not so much for its own coasts or the northern interior, as for the Caribbean and also the Philippines. Between 1618 and 1621, for example, 1.65 million pesos of crown funds were sent to Manila for military purposes (possibly in anticipation of Dutch attacks there), while only 1.14 million (plus a large amount of cochineal on royal account) went to Spain.[34] *Situados* of unknown amount were also dispatched to Havana, Santo Domingo, Puerto Rico, and Florida in those four years, as they were to be repeatedly thenceforth. Exactly how much New Spain spent on defending the eastern approaches to the Empire is hard to say, since many disbursements were recorded under "miscellaneous" account headings. But it seems that after 1640 at least a third of total outgoings from all Mexican treasury offices went for military purposes in the Atlantic and the

Caribbean. Not only did New Spain supply funds for fortresses, arms, and garrisons in the Greater Antilles and Florida, but it also ended up paying much of the bill for naval protection of the transatlantic fleets. The additional cost of supporting administration and defense in the Philippines was extraordinarily high. Between 1581 and 1700 New Spain sent to Manila no less than 23 million pesos in public funds, almost a third of the amount (76.2 million) dispatched to Spain in that same 120-year period.[35]

The monarchy's receipts from America, then, shrank in the 1600s, and particularly after the mid-century. The trend in private shipments of silver to Spain was, however, quite different; or so the weight of evidence, none of it wholly reliable, would suggest. The reports of Dutch merchants, French consuls, and other unofficial sources in seventeenth-century Spain give a very different view of incoming American bullion from what Spanish treasury records show. By these estimates total arrivals (public and private) remained roughly level until the mid-1640s. Then came an abrupt drop until the late 1650s (but the records are incomplete for the entire period 1635–60, so that arrivals may have been higher). There followed in the 1660s and 1670s a sharp upsurge, to sums far higher than any ever received before (171.5 million pesos in the 1670s, for example); and then a leveling off from 1680 to 1699, but still at a very high average (13.8 million annually, a figure never approached before 1670).[36]

Since there is no doubt that crown remittances from America fell drastically in the second half of the century, the high arrivals of bullion reported after 1660 must have been largely private shipments. They were, evidently, mostly sums sent by colonial merchants to buy European goods. They were almost all sums, also, sent undeclared, to avoid duties and defense levies, and also possible confiscation of incoming private cash as forced loans to the crown – an unfortunate practice that had grown rather common after 1600. The unofficial sources reported total bullion arrivals of 665.2 million pesos between 1650 and 1699, of which only 43.6 million (barely 6.6 percent) were registered. Some of this silver never touched Spanish soil. It was transferred from the incoming fleets to foreign ships waiting offshore. Some – much – of it went directly into the coffers of the great number of French, Genoese, English, Dutch, Flemish, and German merchants residing and trading in Seville, Cadiz, and other Spanish towns. The crown was well aware of the fraud, but for lack of means and fear of reprisal for attack on powerful foreign interests did little to stop it. In what became its characteristic seventeenth-century practice across all Spanish territories, the administration, faced with problems beyond its possibility of control, sold pardons for blatant infractions of the law. The merchants willingly paid negotiated amounts, in a form of self-regulated taxation.[37]

The size and pattern of the unofficial bullion receipts throw into doubt the long accepted decline of Spanish American trade after 1610–20. There was certainly a fall in number of ships and total tonnage in the official transatlantic fleets after then, and the decline became steeper as time passed. Between 1600 and 1650, 6,573 ships participated in the *Carrera de Indias*, as against only 1,835 (22 percent of the century's total) from 1650 to 1700.[38] The probable weakness of bullion receipts around the mid-century certainly fits with the drop in the *Carrera*'s volume. But the recovery after then plainly contradicts it. The conclusion must be that the value of the trade did not fall as much as its volume; and that after 1660 its worth actually rose, with a growing fraction of it consisting of high-value, low-volume, non-Spanish products (fine cloths and hardware, for example), exported by either foreigners or Spanish merchants working with them. Decline of total exchange between Spanish America and Europe seems even less unlikely to have happened if contraband in the Caribbean is taken into account. How much this amounted to will never be known for sure. But it can only have grown as the Dutch, English, and French settled into their island bases after the mid-1620s.

The trends in unofficially reported bullion arrivals in Spain fit partially with known patterns of taxed American silver production in the seventeenth century: strong to 1630, weaker in the forties, fifties, and sixties. There is contradiction, though, in the 1630s (arrivals up, production down), and from 1670 onward (arrivals sharply up, production at best in a gradual total decline, though with New Spain resurgent, and Potosí's rate of descent slowed, *c.*1665–90). Some combination of two possibilities seems for the moment most likely to explain the discrepancies. Colonials may have for some reason (war, unfavorable terms of exchange) held back bullion exports for years or even decades. Second, silver production may have been higher than the royalty record shows, and exports of untaxed silver likewise. It is clear, for instance, that untaxed silver from mines flourishing in the south of the Potosí district *c.*1680 escaped through Buenos Aires. Tax evaders did not, though, have to use a back door like Buenos Aires to slip silver out. In 1654 the largest galleon in the South Sea Squadron, the 1,200 ton *Jesús María*, ran aground near Guayaquil. Inspection showed the ship to be carrying at least two million, and possibly up to nine million, pesos in untaxed, unregistered silver.[39] That was the equivalent of 250–800 percent of the Potosí district's annual official output at the time. The Squadron (the *Armada del Mar del Sur*) was a state-funded flotilla created to defend maritime trade and communication between Panama and Peru. Guarding silver exports from the likes of the Dutch was, of course, among its main purposes. But native enemies were now in the heart of the system. Here was a royal vessel being used, necessarily with some collusion from its officers, to defraud the crown of perhaps more than 100,000 pesos in income.

The shrinking volume of the *Carrera de Indias* has often been taken as evidence of economic decline in Spanish America in the 1600s, in parallel with economic contraction in Spain itself and other parts of Europe. The fleet trade dwindled because the colonies produced less to export; so went the argument. By the same reasoning, the strength of bullion receipts in Spain – indeed, over the century, their rising trend – for which there is now persuasive evidence, goes against notions of colonial decline. It is not enough to refute them, since silver was far from being the colonies' only product, and the links between silver production and the broad economic state were many and complex. But it is a noteworthy pointer.

Textiles and farming

The direction of that pointer is confirmed by recent research on a number of productive activities across the American empire. The best known of these, after mining, is cloth making. One of the two major textile areas, highland Quito, saw clear expansion in the seventeenth century, with the number of legally established *obrajes* rising from about 55 *c.*1620 to 117 *c.*1690 (and 57 other unlicensed mills then also). Although actual output is elusive, there seems no doubt that it grew to about 1690, when production probably reached its maximum for the whole colonial period.[40]

Quito was unusual in seventeenth-century South America in having stability, or possibly growth, in its native population, largely as a result of immigration. Part of its textile expansion was a response to rising internal demand for clothing, though it continued to export fabric north to New Granada and south to Peru. In the second important textile region in the Indies, central New Spain, Indian numbers continued their post-conquest fall until the 1620s, and then began a slow increase. Here again, it may be that demographic shifts influenced the fortunes of textiles. Output in Puebla, for example, an active textile center almost from its founding in the 1530s, turned downward in the 1580s, in part precisely because of rising production in the Andes, which had been an export market for Mexican cloth, but also perhaps in response to falling demand locally. By contrast, the Valley of Mexico, above all the towns of Coyoacán and Tacuba, produced strongly, especially in the mid-seventeenth century. A little further north, near the parts of the *altiplano* to which sheep-raising had shifted from more central pastures, the 1600s saw Querétaro become the main wool weaving center of New Spain. In 1640 it had six *obrajes*; in 1718, twelve, and other smaller *trapiches*. Querétaro grew in response to rising demand from Mexico City, and from Zacatecas and other northern towns as mining revived in the late 1600s. Its output in part replaced imports of Spanish woolens.[41]

Agricultural production in the seventeenth century (or any other colonial period) is hard to assess, for lack of firm and continuous information. Tithes would seem the best source. But they were often farmed, so that the amounts collected did not necessarily bear a fixed relation to production. Further, Indians paid no tithe on what they produced on communal lands granted or confirmed to them by the state, so that no record remains of much of the food raised by the largest group in the population. Indians' total production of food certainly fell from earliest colonial times, more or less in line with population decline; fewer people needed less. A positive outcome of that decline would logically be that food raising generally was concentrated on the better land that any community or area held. Hence, other things being equal, a certain quantity of labor put into farming should have produced more food than before. Any such rise in labor productivity would have lifted the living standard of the drastically shrunken population that survived.

Commercial agriculture is easier to observe than subsistence farming, since its transactions are far more likely to have been recorded in writing. An intensive study of the Lambayeque region of coastal Peru, north of Lima, shows it to have been a prosperous source of both sugar and cattle in the seventeenth century.[42] It declined only under the influence of the earthquakes and volcanic eruptions that brought decline to much agriculture on the Peruvian coast after 1687. The main market for Lambayeque's sugar and wheat was Lima. The prosperity of the producing area suggests economic vigor in Lima, to the extent that can be read in its demand for food. Another Peruvian region that suffered in 1687 was Arequipa, in the far south. This was above all an area of wine-making, doing well from sales to Lima and to highland cities such as Cuzco and Potosí from the late 1500s. It was a time when Peruvian wine was displacing Spanish imports in South America. Other southern Peruvian regions suited for growing grapes, such as Tacna, Sama, Moquegua, Pisco, and Nazca, followed Arequipa's example. As a result the price of wine fell in the 1590s. Despite this, and the beginning of competing production in what is now western Argentina soon after 1600, Arequipa remained a major source of wine throughout the seventeenth century. It did not flourish as before, but neither did it fade.[43]

New Spain made little wine in the seventeenth century, but, like Peru, grew much sugar. The plantations set up earlier near Cuernavaca and in Michoacán particularly prospered from about 1620 in response to the demands of the Mexican sweet tooth.[44] In northern Mexico, *haciendas* continued to raise great numbers of cattle and sheep, though they certainly found local demand dropping for meat and hides during the contraction of mining after 1635. This led to sale, whole or piecemeal, of some estates. With the later revival of mining, new owners reassembled them. Individual *haciendas*, as created in the late sixteenth century, might not survive; but the model of the great northern estate emerged intact and strong from the difficulties of the middle decades.

The monopoly in cacao production held by southern Mexico and northern Central America was broken in the seventeenth century with the spread of cultivation to Venezuela and Guayaquil. Both became exporters of the chocolate bean – first Venezuela legally to New Spain in rapidly rising amounts from the 1620s to 1650, and then Guayaquil, through contraband, to the Dutch in the Caribbean after the mid-century.[45] An even more vibrant contraband trade was, however, that of tobacco, grown on plantations developing all along the Venezuelan coast and on some offshore islands, and bought by the Portuguese, Dutch, and English from the early 1600s.

Broadly speaking, then, commercial agriculture is a prominent feature in Spanish American economic life in the seventeenth century. Its impulse was various: local demand in some cases, intercolonial trade in others, and international trade, increasingly through contraband, in yet others. Of the large regions only Central America lacked a profitable commercial crop or animal product. Cacao had played that part there, at least in the north, in the sixteenth century, but its place in the Mexican market was taken after then by Venezuelan chocolate. The Central American provinces, however, do seem to have produced adequate food for their own small markets and subsistence needs after 1600.[46]

Evidence on various sorts of production in seventeenth-century Spanish America is, as these examples show, scattered and partial. It will be a long time, if ever, before production of, say, wheat or sugar is as firmly established as silver output has become (and doubts remain even there because of tax evasion). Still, the weight of available evidence is on the side of increase, or, at the least, stability in output of foods and goods over the span of the century. Subsistence food production, of course, presumably continued to fall in the large regions where losses of Indians persisted; fewer people needed less to eat. But foods that reached consumers through markets seem to have normally been in adequate supply, even as the number of buyers rose with the growth of non-Indian parts of the populations. A combining of this with evidence about silver production, treasury income, bullion exports, and trade (legal and contraband) suggests that at the very least Spanish America avoided the economic gloom that enveloped Spain itself for most of the century. Conditions obviously varied from place to place, and may have become generally harder in the middle decades. But broadly speaking, a Spaniard looking for material comforts would probably have been wise to choose America over Spain after 1600. And it may be that the Indian peasant's lot was easier than that of his or her peninsular counterpart.

TRADING LINKS AND SELF-SUFFICIENCY

Underlying this relative prosperity of the colonies was a continuation of processes begun in the sixteenth century. Trade between colonies, and over long distances within them, seems to have flourished in various instances, despite some official attempts to block it when it threatened Spanish interests (as in, for example, the draining of Peruvian silver to Asia via Mexico). Broadly speaking, then, in the seventeenth century the Spanish American colonies continued to move toward becoming an integrated economic system, in which areas with natural advantages for producing this or that commodity were able, through rising exchange, to capitalize on those advantages. Venezuelan cacao exports to Mexico, trade of Quito cloth to Peru and New Granada, and great cattle-drives from the Río de la Plata up to the Andean mining zone, exemplify this integration. Clearly there were limits to trade. Transport costs, especially on land, worked against exchange of cheap, bulky goods. But where boats could be used – for freighting sugar or wheat to the cities of west-coast South America, for example, or carrying Paraguayan *yerba mate* down the Paraná to the towns of the Río de la Plata – trade was particularly active.

The rise of exchange and of regional specialization of production, each reinforcing the other, contributed to a growing economic self-sufficiency of Spanish America in the seventeenth century. Transoceanic imports, whether from Asia or Europe, increasingly consisted of the luxurious, the novel, the status-conferring. American sources, near or distant, could provide most of the basics. This economic autarky had varied origins. It was the outcome of Spaniards' learning the economic geography of America in the sixteenth century. It was a natural product of time, as numbers of craftsmen and farmers in the European mold grew with immigration and with the training of Blacks and Indians in Spanish methods. It was probably advanced after 1600, though in ways still to be traced, by the growing retention in America of royal income, a change that seems inherently likely to have produced multiplier effects.[47] Some part of the treasury's great disbursements for defense inevitably came back to American merchants, whether importers or local traders; and their profits were a source of credit for colonial investment. The second part of the century certainly offers evidence of colonials' willingness to invest productively. The revival of mining in the Zacatecas district after 1660, for instance, drew more deeply on Mexico City capital than it had before. Profits from wool weaving in Querétaro were reinvested locally in the final decades.[48] Andean miners' clubbing together to buy ships to expel English pirates from the Pacific in the mid-eighties is another form of productive investment.

Again, creoles' rising numbers and self-awareness made for a greater desire to control their economic existence, and to reduce outsiders' gains from it. The classic case here is the rise of the *peruleros*. They were traders and factors from Lima, increasingly creole in origin, who *c.*1600 began to insert themselves into the fleet trade across the Atlantic. Their aim was to shortcircuit the working of the *Carrera de Indias* to their own advantage. To do this, they reduced their purchases of goods brought by the *galeones* to the Isthmus of Panama. The great fairs held there on the ships' arrival had been, during the 1500s, Lima's source of European goods. Now the Lima men started to travel to Seville themselves on the returning fleets, taking large sums in silver to buy there directly from suppliers. In this way they avoided duties charged on the Isthmus and took for themselves the profits of the Seville exporters. These, naturally, complained vociferously at the intrusion. In 1626 they petitioned the king to "remedy the great excess that has come about . . . with ten or twelve barefoot men who come in the *galeones* [bringing] a third of the silver that [the ships] carry" to buy on behalf of Peruvian importing merchants.[49] There was, though, no stopping these crude colonials, who, however bare of foot, were only too sharp of eye in seeing how much the clumsy structure of the official Atlantic trade had been created and adapted to favor crown and Spanish exporters. Such contorted machinery cried out for simplification; and if Spanish officials and merchants would not attempt it, creoles were glad to do it for them. The final simplification of the *Carrera*, of course, was to stop using it altogether, and to buy from, and sell to, contraband traders. This was a step that growing numbers of colonials took in the seventeenth century, and was in itself a form of economic self-determination.

INDIANS IN THE HEARTLANDS: MAKING THEIR OWN SPACE

Indians, too, showed in the seventeenth century a certain probing for self-determination, within, of course, broad limits set by colonial state and society. Those limits were generally, in the 1600s, less well patrolled by the imperial government than they had been earlier, and this gave native people expanding room to discover for themselves as comfortable a place as possible in the colonial scheme. The probing took place mostly in the central zones of the empire, for it was there that native people had most to avoid or adjust to in the way of burdens and imposed changes. On most of the periphery the relative lightness of Spanish presence, both official and private, meant that the Indian–Spanish relationship moved less quickly away from its sixteenth-century beginnings.

Physical movement

Mere movement from one place to another was the Indians' simplest form of self-determination. Though an early decree, of 1536, declared them to be generally free to move, except from places to which they had been "reduced," later regulations restricted that freedom.[50] Certainly, the practical assumption was that Indians would remain in the place on whose tribute list (tasa) they figured. Normally this was their birthplace. There were exceptions, the most obvious of which was that men assigned to forced repartimiento or mita work generally had to travel to do it. If they had to go far, for a long period, wives and children might go with them. Also exceptional were those unattached to any native community, men known as naborías in New Spain and yanaconas in the Quechua-speaking parts of the Andes. These in pre-conquest times had generally been the personal dependants and servants of native lords; and after the conquests they tended to assume a similar connection with leading Spaniards. With time the meaning of the terms grew broader. Naboría came to mean an independent, salaried worker; and yanacona, a permanent employee, sometimes salaried, of a Spaniard. But both were expected to be more mobile than members of native communities.

By 1600 or so, however, many natives besides forced laborers and naborías and yanaconas were showing a resistance to staying where the Spaniards thought they should be. The forced labor systems themselves, in fact, encouraged long-term or even permanent movement of people. Much of the enormous native population inhabiting Potosí by 1600 had originally been brought there by the mining mita, the single largest draft in the empire. After their year in the town, many men, having exhausted whatever supplies of food and clothing they had brought with them, apparently preferred staying on as workers in mining, refining, or something else, to the prospect of a long journey home with family. Others moved out of the town to nearby valleys, apparently as subsistence farmers or workers on chácaras. The boom at Oruro after 1606 was another lure to Indians who had learned mining and refining in Potosí after being taken there by the mita. In fact, Oruro drew off mita men on their way to Potosí. They worked there as contracted wage laborers, since the authorities made hardly any mita allocation to Oruro. The other lesser mining centers that rose and fell in the Potosí district after 1600 were similarly mita-less, and had only the attraction of wages to secure workers – some from Potosí, some from native towns.

Thus those who were first moved by the mechanism of forced labor might then become permanent migrants under the lure of waged work. An initial uprooting by draft was by no means essential, however. At the start of the seventeenth century, Lima's native population of about 3,000 included some 1,730 migrants, 34.5 percent of whom came from northerly regions of Peru, and even in a few cases from Quito and New Granada – places outside the catchment area of the *mita* draft that the city, like many others in the Indies, received for purposes of upkeep. A large attraction for these outsiders was clearly the earnings, in cash and kind, they could secure as craftsmen, domestic servants, laborers on nearby smallholdings, muleteers, and the like.[51] Clearer still was the case of Indian workers in the silver mines of northern Mexico. There, no *repartimiento*, or draft, ever functioned, mainly because the thin local population of nomads could not be organized into a workforce. Instead, from the start around 1550 at Zacatecas, migrant natives from central and western Mexico worked the mines and refineries, for wages. From Zacatecas, as from Potosí, skilled men then spread out as other ore deposits were found, drawn by the high reward that the initial workings usually yielded. San Luis Potosí in the 1590s and Parral in the 1630s were two new major silver centers that drew accomplished Indian workers from Zacatecas. So there arose a permanent, mobile corps of native silver producers in the north. At the same time, though, new native workers continued to move up from the south, especially when new strikes made prospects for earnings seem good. This flow of Indians into northern Mexican mining continued into late colonial times.[52]

The large towns of the empire, all of which came quickly to be focuses of Spanish control and culture, were the first places to offer waged work to Indians. These settlements, most of them administrative or mining centers with substantial white populations, produced the most intense demand for labor; and it was therefore in them that draft labor arrangements were first likely to prove inadequate. Hence the appearance in them of individually contracted, native waged workers well before 1600 is unsurprising. What is striking, however, is the spread of wage labor into the countryside soon after its appearance in towns. Again, rising need for workers is the reason, the outcome of a varying combination of population loss, local demand for food, and the inadequacies of draft systems. The white owners of wheat farms in the Valley of Mexico, for instance, were hiring Indian laborers in the 1580s to grow grain for the capital.[53] The process was self-reinforcing. Even if the native population had not still been contracting, the use of waged workers would have shrunk the pool available for drafting, giving employers further reason to go out and hire (at, of course, a rising real wage). Since native Mexican numbers in fact fell until the 1620s, the negative effect of hiring on the draft was exacerbated. So great, indeed, was the shift to waged labor on the growing number of *haciendas* in New Spain that in 1632 the administration ended the *repartimiento* for agriculture (leaving it in place for mining). The wage system grew so quickly because it suited not only employers, but also Indian villagers. By earning comparatively generous wages on colonials' farms, they could more easily pay tributes. By, in many cases, leaving their communities and taking up residence on those farms, they could do even better – perhaps avoid tribute altogether, and also the demands (until 1632) of the *repartimiento*. Wage-labor thus provoked native migration

FIGURE 11.1 *The Annunciation*, by Cristóbal de Villalpando. (Private collection.)

FIGURE 11.2 *St Matthew*, by Melchor Pérez de Holguín. (Carlos Reyes-Manzo, Andes Press Agency.)

FIGURE 11.3 *Archangel with a Matchlock Gun, Salamiel Paxdei* ("peace of God"): one of many such paintings of military angels, dressed in Spanish aristocratic style, from the central Andes. (Late seventeenth century, Circle of the Master of Calamarca, Lake Titicaca School, Bolivia. New Orleans Museum of Art.)

FIGURE 11.4 *Archangel Michael Triumphant.*
(Seventeenth-century polychromed mahogany sculpture,
by an unknown artist of the Cuzco School. New Orleans
Museum of Art.) 多彩色红木

FIGURE 11.5 *Our Lady of
Pomata.* A painting of the
miracle-working statue of the
Virgin of the Rosary at Pomata,
a small town on the west shore
of Lake Titicaca in Peru.
(1675, Circle of Quispe Tito,
Cuzco School, Peru. Brooklyn
Museum of Art.)

FIGURE 11.6 Saint Augustine, defeating heresy, represented by Martin Luther, held down by the saint's foot. (Early eighteenth century, by unknown artist, Bolivia. New Orleans Museum of Art.)

FIGURE 11.7 The Virgin of the Fifth Seal. The image now lacks the silver spear with which she took part in Heaven's war against Satan. (c.1740, polychromed wood with silver, attributed to Bernardo Legarda, Ecuador. New Orleans Museum of Art.)

FIGURE 11.8 Biblical prophets before the church of Bom Jesus de Matozinhos, at Congonhas do Campo, Brazil, by O Aleijadinho (António Francisco Lisboa), 1800–05. (© South American Pictures.)

FIGURE 11.9 Casa Nacional de la Moneda, Potosí, Bolivia. The severely styled mint of the late eighteenth century is reputedly the largest secular building of the colonial period in South America

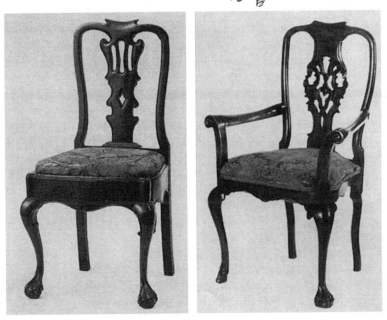

VISTA DE LA PLAZA DE MEXICO NUEVAMENTE ADORNADA PARA LA

CARLOS IV. *que se coloco en ella el 9 de Diciembre de 1796, cumple años de*

por Miguel la Grua, Marques de Branciforte, Virrey de Nueva España, quien

gratitud y consuelo general de todo este Reyno, e hizo grabar esta Estampa, que

ESTATUA EQUESTRE DE NUESTRO AUGUSTO MONARCA REYNANTE

la Reyna Nuestra Señora MARIA LUISA DE BORBON, su amada Esposa y

solicito y logro de la Real Clemencia erigir este Monumento para desahogo de su

dedica à Sus Magestades, en nuevo testimonio de su fidelidad, amor y respeto

FIGURE 11.10 View of the Plaza Mayor of Mexico City, 1797, by José Joaquín Fabregat: neo-classical reordering imposed on Mexico City by the government of Charles IV (mounted, center). The baroque cathedral stands in the background, with the parish church of the Sagrario attached to the right of it. On the extreme right, part of the viceregal (later national) palace. (Benson Latin American Collection, University of Texas at Austin.)

FIGURE 11.11 An early example of the invasion of North European taste: Mexican-made chairs (1750–1800) in the "Mexican Chippendale" style. (Brooklyn Museum of Art.)

FIGURE 11.12 An eighteenth-century Peruvian table, of cedar. Dense baroque decoration was not confined to churches. Note the spiralling Salomonic legs and the lacy carving of leaves and fruits. (Brooklyn Museum of Art.)

FIGURE 11.13 A folk dancer's hat (glass beads and silver on velvet) from eighteenth-century Bolivia, possibly Potosí. (Brooklyn Museum of Art.)

FIGURE 11.14 Early post-independence foreign investment in Mexico: English mine buildings near Bolaños, probably of the 1820s and 1830s, when the English Bolaños Company was active. In both design and stonework, these buildings are strikingly alien to Mexico.

FIGURE 11.15 *El Citlaltépetl*, by José María Velasco (1879). The "Hill of the Star" (also known as the Pico de Orizaba) is the highest peak in Mexico. A train descends the Gulf Coast escarpment on the recently built Mexico City to Veracruz line. (© INBA, Mexico.)

not only to towns, but also to country estates, some of which now began to be village-like themselves, with small dwellings for resident workers added to the basic plan of owner's house, chapel, and storage buildings.

The combination of push and pull causes that led Indians to leave their own communities seems to have operated even more strongly in the central Andes than in New Spain. By 1690 almost half the population of the bishopric of Cuzco, covering much of southern highland Peru, consisted of *forasteros* – Indians who had left their places of origin for other native villages, estates, or larger towns. In the province of Charcas, directly to the south, *forasteros* were similarly numerous.[54] A great initial impetus for this movement had come in the 1570s from Viceroy Toledo's concentration (*reducción*) of natives into new communities for ease of administration, religious instruction, and enforcement of tribute and labor levies. This was a far more swingeing reform, affecting perhaps as many as 1.5 million people, than any relocation programme attempted in New Spain. It seems largely to have failed. The new places were sometimes badly sited for farming, or for access to the people's scattered lands. Indians left the "reductions" to return "home." Others left to become resident workers on colonials' farms and estates. Others simply fled into the Andes' numberless hidden places. All wished to avoid the mining *mita*, the feeding of which had been a prime purpose of the reduction enterprise. And by a quirk of Toledo's legislation, those living away from their own communities (including the reductions) were exempted from *mita* service. Further, those who moved could probably avoid paying tribute as well. Indians had, then, every reason to flee. And colonials who were not miners quickly came to realize that they had equal reason to harbor the fugitives and to resist the attempts made by later viceroys to reinsert them into the *mita*. For, just as in New Spain, a falling native population meant shortage of labor in the highlands. As in New Spain, also, an outcome of shortage was rising employment for wages, both in the urban labor market of Cuzco and out in the country. The degree of penetration of working relations by wage labor, a practice far from the traditional Andean conviction that work was a matter of reciprocal duty in a community, is clearly revealed in a contract of 1666 by which an Indian undertook to work for pay on an estate belonging to his own *curaca*.[55]

As these examples of native migration, and its connection with different lines and forms of work, show, the Indians' response to colonial pressures (demands that they provide labor, pay tribute, submit to relocation) was varied and complex in the late sixteenth and seventeenth centuries. Refusing to be "reduced," some Andeans fled to where Spaniards could not find them. Others took refuge precisely among colonials on rural landholdings or in large towns. Some chose to support themselves by subsistence farming. Others took the opposite course of embracing the aliens' economic world of money-mediated markets for goods and labor, and plunged into sorts of work – crafts, silver refining, domestic service – that were defined by European standards. Clearly the circumstances and proclivities of individuals had much to do with their choices. Clearly, also, what they did might depend more on communal needs than on their own preference. It suited Andean *curacas*, for instance, that some of their people be hidden away in places unknown to the authorities. The tribute demand on the *curaca*'s community would be lessened (because the population would be recorded as smaller than it really was), while he would have subjects to draw on to fulfill *mita* requirements, perhaps, or to put to his own use in some sort of production or trade. But, whatever the course chosen, the overwhelming impression is of the Indians' adaptability and flexible responsiveness. In the sixteenth century, the leaders in the high-culture areas had quickly shown these qualities. In the seventeenth, the people as a whole did likewise. There was little passivity here. "If you can't beat them, join them" might seem the attitude of many Indians; and to a degree it was. But the procedure was in reality more subtle. It consisted of meeting the demands of colonial state and society at some level close to the minimum they would accept; of playing the European economic game to the degree necessary to ensure material survival; of taking on a European disguise the better to defend the native identity. It was, perhaps, a case of taking one step forward (into the colonials' world) in order to safeguard two back (into the native world); of *sauter pour mieux reculer*.

It was, of course, impossible to preserve everything. Voluntary migration further sapped community identity and practices that had already suffered heavy blows before 1600 from depopulation, labor levies, and *reducción*. Working for a wage under conditions set by individual contract pushed people in the direction of personal autonomy, and away from both the collective practices of native communities and the political authority of traditional native rulers. Indians who moved permanently or even temporarily to large towns, especially to new foundations like the mining towns where Spanish ways were so dominant, were likely to become cultural mestizos. To the degree that they absorbed the economic criteria of social standing that Spaniards and colonials adopted, native society, it has been said, began moving away from caste and toward class.[56] That movement was long and slow, and indeed is not yet complete in areas where native peoples are still plentiful. But the change had visibly started by 1600, and grew ever clearer after then.

MENTAL SELF-DEFENSE

Decisions about migration and taking a job for pay were largely a conscious matter, though the individual taking them might not be fully aware of all the forces inclining him or her to make the choice. In less tangible and conscious aspects of life as well, however, incorporation of the Spanish into the native can be seen proceeding fast after 1600. Recent research on the absorption of Spanish into the Nahuatl of central Mexico shows that in the sixteenth century borrowings were nearly all nouns, and that native pronunciation and grammar were barely altered. But then "the dam broke."[57] Indians began bringing Spanish verbs into Nahuatl; and Spanish prepositions too, which is still more striking since Nahuatl did not possess them as discrete parts of speech. Another borrowing was the Spanish (indeed, European) means of showing plural by adding a distinct suffix to a noun. This began to be done not only with borrowed words, but with some Nahuatl nouns also. There is suggestive evidence also that native speakers began to use sounds that Spanish possessed but that Nahuatl did not. Thus, under the influence of spoken and written Spanish, central Mexicans drew into their language not only borrowings that dealing with Spaniards, colonials, and their speech made necessary, but also elements of Spanish (prepositions, for example) that were simply of linguistic use.

More fascinating still as evidence of native mental approach to, and incorporation of, what was Spanish are the idiosyncratic documents from central and southern Mexico called *títulos* (titles), all apparently dating from after 1650, though written in archaizing styles to make them seem from the previous century. Their purpose was, apparently, to bolster communities' claims to land; but they are not land titles of a legal sort, but a blend of local myth and history intended to solidify a community's sense of its lasting individuality and occupation of its land. They draw on popular, oral culture. They give little sense of passing time; they aim precisely to convey timelessness, a deep and constant mythical identity. And in doing so, they blend the indigenous with the Spanish. Spanish authorities as well as native are appealed to indifferently as part of a group's past, with no sense of one being more legitimate or favorable than the other. Indians as well as Spaniards may figure as hostile intruders. Christianity and indigenous beliefs are given equal weight in the people's spiritual identity. "Oh my dear children, you must entirely understand that Cortés don Luis de Velasco Marqués brought us the true faith,"[58] went one writer's exhortation in the late 1690s. Here the blur simply conflates the conqueror of the Aztecs with the second viceroy of New Spain; but elsewhere the melding extends to running together the pre-conquest and the post-conquest into one historical entity. If the *títulos* are really a true reflection of Indian commoners' view of their past and of their present identity, they show a great capacity for synthesizing contrasts and changes in quite recent history, and a truly amazing acceptance of the culture and beliefs of the invaders. It was not, though, a passive or resigned acceptance; but rather an active integration of the imposed culture into a mental world still very reminiscent of the Aztecs' vision of the supernatural as a mesmerizing swirl of spirits and gods.

Incorporation of Spanish into native language has been studied closely only for central Mexico; and *títulos* may be unique to the center and south of New Spain. But both the linguistic borrowings and the historico-cultural blendings shown in these two phenomena fit with a pattern, visible across the areas of high native culture, of creative response to various sorts of invasion and intrusion – of taking from European techniques, practices, and beliefs what could be usefully adapted to native life under colonial rule.

Nowhere is this adaptation clearer than in religion. Indian spirituality remained in the seventeenth century, as it still does, a complicated blend of the native and the imported. Many friars in the early post-conquest evangelizing campaigns had had hopes of displacing native cult with Christianity, inspired perhaps by the view of Las Casas and others that indigenous religious history could be read as an approach to the true faith, a progression that they could now complete. But this optimism was fading by 1600 as the obduracy of Indian belief became clear. And soon, under perhaps the influence of the same Counter-Reformation intolerance now palpable in Spain itself, clerics in Spanish America began arguing for an attack on native "idolatry," as it was often seen. Campaigns of "extirpation" were mounted, particularly in the central Andes, where they lasted, on and off, throughout the century. Special inspectors were sent out to native communities to dig out offending practices and punish their perpetrators.

The inspectors' reports confirmed the church's worst fears. Ancestor worship was still common. If necessary, people went back to the pre-*reducción* sites of their communities to make offerings to mummies still preserved in caves. There was perhaps still some ritual sacrifice of children in the early 1600s. Offerings were still being made to *huacas* (to, for instance, stones believed to be the petrified forms of humans or animals). The extirpating priests might try to suppress such practices by destroying the physical objects of worship; but the people tended simply to replace them, since the spirit of the deity in question persisted even when the "idol" was smashed or burned.[59] The Spanish inquiries uncovered, in fact, a vibrant continuity in native beliefs and practices from the pre-conquest into the sixteenth century, and then on to the seventeenth; and for the Indians this persistence was more a matter of what was natural than a show of defiance.

Into these survivals Christianity had been woven, with an intricacy that was the despair of the investigating Catholic priests. Seasonal festivals of the Andes became entangled with Christian feasts, so that images of saints might be offered the traditional gifts of coca, *chicha*, and guinea pigs. Conversely, sacred objects might be hidden in Christian altars, to be worshipped while people were in church. The old Andean feast of Caruamita (the "time of yellowing" when maize ripened) was blended with the feast of Corpus Christi. Under cover of the Christian celebrations, Andeans made their own, ancient sort of confessions and sacrifices to local deities so that the crops would be protected from the threat of frosts that June brought.[60]

Almost all Indians had been impressed from the start by the evident power of the Christian god – their defeat was clearly in part his doing – and out of fear and also a desire to gain access to that power themselves, had taken up his worship. Evangelizing friars, then, had that great force on their side besides whatever personal powers of persuasion they might be able to deploy. Under the friars' instruction, Indians also came to revere Christ, the Virgin Mary, and what seemed to them the lesser Christian deities, the saints. The saints, indeed, seemed the closest analogy to indigenous local gods, and so it was common for a saint to be the immediate object of worship in small places, each parish church holding an image of its patron figure. Andean churches most certainly had these images, and Andeans certainly revered them and respected their powers. But it may be that the cult of saints, and indeed the hold over Indians that Christianity had gained by the seventeenth century, was still stronger in New Spain. Why this should have been so is unclear: perhaps a longer period of uninterrupted evangelization after the conquest, by more numerous and dedicated friars; perhaps the greater accessibility of native communities in Mexico; or perhaps a greater keenness in those communities to build a church and acquire a patron saint as marks of local identity and status. Whatever the cause, in the final years of the sixteenth century the cult of Spanish saints put down deep and lasting roots in the high-culture areas of New Spain. By the opening of the seventeenth century, Indians clearly regarded their images as the source of miracles, just as Spaniards did.[61]

Yet just as it seems that Indians had accepted some piece of Christianity in a more or less "pure" state, complications intervene. In late sixteenth-century Mexico City, native craftsmen made glazed incense burners in the form of male and female saints. To celebrate St Francis's day in 1593, again in Mexico City, other artisans showed him astride an eagle seated on a cactus[62] – the latter being the defining symbol of native Tenochtitlan, since the Aztecs had reputedly received a divine command to found their city on a site where an eagle was so perched. Repeatedly, then, native myth, history, and cult intertwined with the imported faith. One result is that it is impossible to know exactly what Indians did believe. There is no doubt that they accepted Christianity sincerely; but for almost all of them it was never more than a part of their faith, something to be absorbed into earlier beliefs, just as the deities of native invaders had typically been added to a conquered people's pantheon of gods in pre-Columbian times. As in those earlier days, the Christian invaders' faith may have continued to seem alien, something belonging more to the outsider than to the vanquished. But it was too powerful to be dismissed, too full of potential benefits to be ignored.[63]

A Christian figure with whom natives of Mexico, at least, found it particularly easy to identify, perhaps because she seemed the closest approach to the idea of the mother-goddess so strong in their own beliefs, was the Virgin Mary. The Virgin of Guadalupe has long been taken as the obvious example of this affinity. The time-hallowed story of her appearance to the Mexican Indian Juan Diego in 1531 traditionally made her the protectress of native people from earliest colonial times, and, in due course, of Mexico as a whole. Her tie to the indigenous was strengthened by the fact that the apparition reportedly took place at the Hill of Tepeyac, a site near Mexico City sacred to the goddess Tonantzin, "our mother." Regrettably, though – for the niceness of that linkage and for the tenderness of the story – research shows neither any record of an apparition in 1531, nor any indication that the cult of Guadalupe, which certainly existed by the 1550s, was particularly Indian. Quite to the contrary, in fact: Spaniards were its main adherents, which is not surprising considering the immense devotion they had long given to the image of the Virgin enshrined at Guadalupe in Extremadura. The cult of the Mexican Guadalupe was, further, mainly limited to Mexico City and its close surroundings until the mid-seventeenth century. And though by the early eighteenth century Tepeyac was the prime pilgrimage site in Mexico, it was only after 1746, when the Mexican bishops and cathedral chapters proclaimed Our Lady of Guadalupe to be the patroness of New Spain, that her cult became colony-wide. And only then did a broad Indian linkage with her begin, far more as the result of teaching than of any earlier devotion. It may even be that the eighteenth-century promotion of the Guadalupe cult was the conscious doing of creoles seeking some symbol of proto-national Mexican unity.[64]

But if the idea of the Virgin of Guadalupe as a specifically Indian version of the Madonna no longer holds good, it remains true that Indians found the figure of Mary immensely appealing and comforting. She was, after all, the greatest of Christian saints; and as Indians turned to saints in the late 1500s, they embraced her among them. Like Christians from earliest times, they viewed her above all as intercessor, a loving mother pleading for them before the paternal but stern God. The medieval Spanish mind linked her closely with the land and its fertility; some native female deities had the same association.[65] The Virgin, then, was perhaps the easiest and most attractive of Christian figures for Indians to fuse into their spiritual life. Among the various aspects of Christianity that they made their own, she stood out prominently.

Across the whole breadth of life's activities, then, from the economic to the spiritual, Indians, by or during the seventeenth century, absorbed from the invaders much that was useful for their own gain or comfort, often with the aim, intentional or unconscious, of using the alien as best they could in order to protect themselves from it. Clearly the borrowing was heaviest in the empire's central areas, where Spanish numbers and cultural weight were greatest. Elsewhere it varied, broadly according to the weight of Spanish presence, although colonials' influence on Indians depended not only on numbers but also on the local conditions within which that influence operated.

INDIANS IN THE PERIPHERIES: LESS REGIMENTED, LESS PROTECTED

Seventeenth-century New Granada is a case in point. This was a large area, roughly within present Colombian boundaries. It was strongly regionalized even from before conquest because, first, of a brokenness of terrain unusual even for an Andean territory. Partly because of that array, or rather disarray, of valleys, basins, rivers, and rainforests, the largest pre-Columbian polity (the Chibcha) was tiny by Aztec or Inca standards. The other native groups, largely agricultural and sedentary, were politically as well as geographically separate. The Spanish occupation brought little gain in unity, in part because of these pre-existing diversities, in part because it too was diverse, with competing expeditions coming in from different directions and settling in independent groups. Thus New Granada was born fissile, and so it has stayed. The *Audiencia* of Santa Fe de Bogotá (1547) in reality had little authority outside the center-east. The other two major centers of power were Cartagena on the Caribbean coast in the north, and Popayán, overseeing a vast area in the south. New Granada, then, while peripheral to the empire's heartlands, had its own internal centers and peripheries.

Indians' colonial fortunes varied with this regionalization. Everywhere in New Granada the *encomienda* was the prime relationship before 1600 between settlers and natives. *Servicio personal*, the working of Indians for their *encomenderos*, continued as the standard labor system thirty years or more after its decline began in Peru and New Spain. Only in 1597–8 was *repartimiento* (state-organized draft labor) set up in New Granada, and then only in the central highland zone dominated by Bogotá. By then *encomenderos* were so much in social and economic control of that region, with rural estates established to provide grains and meat for the city, that they managed, through connections with officials, to channel to themselves most of the drafted workers. Others were put to urban building, silver mining, household work, and cloth making in a small number of *obrajes* that began to appear in Bogotá about 1600. The labor burden on Indians in the seventeenth century was heavy, as the native population continued to dwindle after its severe reduction in the 1500s, and as New Granada achieved some measure of the economic diversification, and autonomy, more obvious in the imperial heartlands. But at least in the region controlled from Bogotá there was a degree of oversight by senior officialdom.

THE PERSISTENT *ENCOMIENDA*

Away from the center the lot of seventeenth-century Indians was harder still. In many of these outlying areas *encomienda* persisted after 1600 in its original form, as the prime means of exploitation of native labor, some of it used for gold extraction. New Granada reached its first peak of gold production, from several fields, between 1580 and 1620. The richer miners began importing black slaves before 1600 to meet a need for labor that the shrinking Indian population could not supply. But slaves were expensive, so that those who had access to the remaining natives, above all the *encomenderos*, used them to the fullest. Gold output leveled off or subsided after 1620, and did not revive until about 1700. But metal was still forthcoming in amounts large enough to lubricate internal trade (a mint was created at Bogotá in 1620) and to pay for goods bought from Dutch and other smugglers on the Caribbean coast. Throughout the century, then, *encomienda* Indians found themselves pressed into mining and washing for gold. The *encomenderos* of Popayán put their people to farming as well as to mining, under conditions described as "virtual enslavement" in the late seventeenth century.[66] Treatment was no better in other gold areas further north and west. Indeed, in the 1680s a royal inspector found severe exploitation of Indians in places near Bogotá. By then law on Indian labor was being ignored under the very nose of the *audiencia*, such was the loss of administrative control that the crown had suffered in New Granada.

On the periphery, then, and even more on the edges of the periphery, Indians stood to suffer from weakness or negligence in government. A common trait of these imperial fringes was persistence of the *encomienda*, often with its labor privileges still attached, as in much of New Granada. This might seem the result simply of governmental carelessness about areas deemed both physically and economically marginal. And perhaps it was to some extent a matter of neglect. But continuation of the *encomienda* also served practical ends. For on the edges it still usefully played the role it had had everywhere in the beginning, as a means of anchoring settlers in places where, for reasons of isolation or poverty, they would otherwise not have stayed. As a result, the imperial fringes presented anachronistic social and economic traits in the 1600s. In particular, Indians often found themselves subject to a sort of seigneurial control by settlers that had been weakened elsewhere by the rise of draft and wage labor. Where demand for natives' work was high, as it was in some outlying regions of New Granada, Indians found themselves at the unregulated mercy of their *encomenderos*, especially as these remained the prime economic and social power in the land.

In these respects, Venezuela resembled New Granada in the first half of the seventeenth century, with the difference that the work to which *encomienda* Indians were put was cacao production. The strength with which *encomienda* persisted here as an institution, and a social ideal for colonials, is suggested by the fact that most of the best grants on the coast near Caracas were held, in the mid-1630s, not by descendants of sixteenth-century original settlers, but by recent immigrants who had gained them by marriage. These men, successful entrepreneurs, were the first of the *grandes cacaos*, or lords of chocolate, who in the next century were to dominate Venezuelan society so thoroughly, and ultimately present powerful opposition to Spanish rule in the region. But the earliest of them, before 1650, built their wealth on the basis of *encomienda* in its sixteenth-century, labor-yielding, form. After then, it is true, as cacao production grew, they increasingly replaced natives with black slaves, as a source both of labor and of social standing. The growing numbers of Blacks on the expanding estates of the Caracas coast resulted in a displacement of natives, and their gradual replacement by mixed-blooded *zambos*. In 1691 the crown finally put an end to *servicio personal* in Venezuela, without great protest from the remaining *encomenderos*. Black slavery had proved the more satisfactory source of labor for growing cacao.[67]

FRONTIER MISSIONS: FRANCISCANS AND JESUITS

On the remoter fringes yet another feature of early sixteenth-century colonization tended to persist: a large role for churchmen, particularly mendicants, in what was in reality Indian government. The clerics' formal task may have been simply spiritual care; but since they were often the only outsiders in regular contact with natives, they inevitably came to be seen by their charges, and to see themselves, as agents of imperial power. This was also true, to be sure, of priests ministering to parishes in the central colonial areas. But on the edges, where other officialdom was sparse, the clerics' influence and authority were that much greater.

A classic case was New Mexico. The evangelization of Pueblo people here was entrusted to the Franciscans soon after settlement began around 1600. Conflict between the friars living in the native communities and the crown's governors seated in Santa Fe was at the center of New Mexican history for most of the century. The friars' ideal, never achieved but certainly approached, was sole domain over the Indians. The governors strove to sustain royal authority against this mendicant pretension. *Encomienda* lived on in New Mexico, with holders, as elsewhere on the periphery, dominating local society and such small economic activity as existed, principally farming. *Servicio personal*, it is true, was not part of the New Mexican *encomienda*. But *encomenderos* used their eminence simply to force Indians, quite illegally, to work for them. Naturally the Franciscans opposed them in this, not only for the Indians' well-being, but because they themselves also needed workers for the lands that sustained the missions. Though Spanish secular settlers were few (only 170 able-bodied men in 1679, for example),[68] the resulting pressures on the Indians were heavy. And after the Franciscans began vigorous attempts to stamp out native "idolatry" around the mid-century, the Pueblos' distress slowly rose to breaking point. In 1680 they seized Santa Fe and drove out both settlers and priests from New Mexico. It was the most serious rebellion against colonial rule in seventeenth-century New Spain. The Spanish did not recover Santa Fe until December 1693.

Another outlying area in which the Franciscans' role remained large in mid-colonial times was Yucatan. As late as 1737 they still held twenty-nine of the sixty native parishes in the peninsula.[69] Here, though, the pressures were less intense than in New Mexico. Native numbers were greater, so that the few thousand resident Spaniards and creoles (1,300 heads of household about 1670, for instance, against a native tributary number of some 33,600)[70] were able to realize in modest measure that general early desideratum – an empire sustained by Indian tribute. Draft labor, by *repartimiento*, operated in seventeenth-century Yucatan, but seems to have impinged but lightly on native communities. Colonials, happy enough, apparently, to base their subsistence on the Indians' tribute offerings of maize and beans, showed little economic verve. Small cattle-raising *estancias*, from the 1580s on, and limited to the north and west of the peninsula, were their main attempt at production. And these needed little native labor. Yucatan, then, in the 1600s was among the imperial areas to see least disruption of the native living patterns that had emerged from the previous century. It was a period of respite, for the Mayas' experiences in that earlier time had been far more trying.

The Franciscans might seek complete authority over their wards on the imperial fringes. But the religious who came nearest (very near, indeed) to gaining it were the Jesuits. Because of the Society's late arrival in Spanish America, *c.* 1570 – by which time others were already attending to the central areas – it gave its evangelizing efforts from the start to the frontiers. In the 1600s Jesuits could be found where hardly any other Europeans, clerical or lay, would care or dare to go: in the north-western sierras of New Spain; on the interior slopes of the Andes, from New Granada down to Charcas; and in eastern Paraguay.

The Jesuits' Paraguayan *reducciones* are the most renowned of all evangelizing attempts in Spanish America, precisely because of the extreme degree of organization that the priests managed to impose on the Guaraní whom they gathered into their missionary villages, and the independence with which they worked. The communities lay in a large area between, and on both sides of, the Paraná and Uruguay rivers, south-east of Asunción, and extending into the present Misiones province of northern Argentina, and over into southern Brazil. The first Jesuit reductions among the Guaraní date from 1610.[71] They were new towns, built on the gridiron plan laid down in Spanish colonial law. The central plaza was dominated by a large church, generally made mostly of wood, which was carved and painted in the interior to provide a measure of sumptuousness. Next to the church stood the residence of the two priests who generally attended each reduction. Indians' dwellings lined the streets extending out from the square. In great contrast to past Guaraní practice, but of course in accord with the Jesuits' notions of Christian and civilized propriety, people lived in the reductions in nuclear families, one per house, rather than in the large buildings holding related families of which the traditional native villages had consisted. The priests brought European music and its instruments for use in church services and celebrations. They taught their charges European crafts, even training some as printers to produce religious texts in Guaraní. Reductions were equipped with hospitals offering a blend of European and local medicine. Some land was worked communally, and some as private, family plots. The grains and cotton grown on public land were held in a storehouse to supply the needs of those who could not farm for themselves, to provide seed for the next year, and to ensure some reserve of goods that could be exchanged for European imports. From the common lands came abundant livestock: cattle, horses, mules, sheep, and oxen (for farm work). Tens of thousands of cattle could be found around some missions by the late 1600s. They yielded one major export, hides, which was sent down river to Buenos Aires and shipped thence to Europe. The other product for which there was a large outside demand was *yerba mate*, mostly gathered wild in the seventeenth century, and cultivated thereafter around the missions under Jesuit supervision. The market for *mate* extended over the Río de la Plata basin, and up into the Andean mining settlements. With the cash earnings of such sales the Jesuits paid their Indians' tributes to the crown, and bought tools and materials needed within the reductions.

As far as they could, the Jesuits isolated their mission areas from secular settlements and their administrative authorities. In Paraguay they largely succeeded in this, despite much predictable resentment from colonials in and around the Paraguayan nucleus at Asunción over the removal of large numbers of natives – the population of the reductions probably exceeded 100,000 – from the potential labor pool. In one notable episode, however, the reductions were drawn deep into the state's affairs, and not without the Jesuits' consent. Early in the 1630s their more northerly Guaraní reductions came under attack by roving slave raiders, the *bandeirantes* of the southern Brazilian town of São Paulo. The missionaries took the survivors southward into the Misiones area; and then, in the practical and militant manner of their Society, got leave from the Council of the Indies to arm their Indians. In 1641 a force of some four thousand Guaraní, commanded by the governor of Paraguay, beat back the *paulista* raiders, not only defending the reductions, but in effect blocking one front of Portuguese expansion into Spanish territory. Thus the Jesuit reductions played the part assumed by other outlying missions

– but here with a vigor all of their own – of stabilizing the empire's frontiers. In the 1680s and 1690s, indeed, reductions were re-established in the region abandoned sixty years before.[72]

If the mission relationship between priests and Indians was extraordinary in Paraguay, so was the interplay of Guaraní and secular settlers a little further west. From the start the position of the Europeans in Paraguay had been unusual, since the first to arrive there had been fugitives from the failed settlement of Buenos Aires in the mid-1530s. The 350 or so refugees, among them Portuguese, Germans, and Italians, arrived in Guaraní territory in a peculiarly accommodating frame of mind, found the Indians far less hostile than the plains people who had assaulted Buenos Aires, and set up the town of Asunción in 1537. There was, then, no military conquest of Paraguay; and the domination that certainly did occur was achieved with far less inequality developing between the two sides than anywhere else in the Spanish colonies.

The Guaraní found in the Europeans useful allies against their nomadic enemies in the Chaco to the west. The colonists' gain from this alliance was to receive the status of headmen in native society. As such, they acquired native women; and it was women in that culture who did the agricultural work. Thus the Europeans found themselves well provided with both concubines and farm workers. And with the women came relatives who swelled the foreign-led households. All constituted, quite informally, something between a set of personal dependants, along the lines of *naborías* or *yanaconas*, and an undeclared *encomienda*. In fact, the term *encomienda originaria* was applied to these arrangements. In the 1550s *encomienda* was formally created in Paraguay. The typical practice received the name *encomienda mitaya*. Native communities up to 200 kilometers from Asunción were included in it. They gave tribute less in kind than in labor, again performed largely by women. Although the intent of the *encomienda mitaya* was that workers would come by turn from their villages to work for their *encomenderos*, the earlier pattern of Indians, especially women, becoming attached to a colonist's domestic retinue persisted. As the native population dropped, indeed, through disease and precisely through the removal of women from their communities, colonists in the seventeenth century sought female workers avidly, even exchanging them among themselves for goods such as horses and clothing. Relations between settlers and natives did not sour, however, as much as this chattel-like treatment of women might suggest. One reason, clearly, was that precisely because the Europeans had possessed large female households from the start, miscegenation had progressed unusually quickly in Paraguay. After the founding generation, most "Spaniards" were in fact mestizos. And even though these continued to be the controlling minority in the society, that minority adopted the material culture, the habits, and even the language of the natives far more fully than any parallel group elsewhere in the Indies. There was little Spanish immigration into Paraguay, since the place had little to offer economically, except for modest profits from *yerba mate* exports. Hence the leadership of local society remained mestizo. And, to the present, Paraguay is freer of a sense of divisive contrast between European and native than any other

Spanish American country. Guaraní is an official national language, and is spoken at all social levels, albeit sometimes with a strong Spanish influence.[73]

Indians living on the fringes in the seventeenth century, then, generally found themselves living in social and economic arrangements that had largely disappeared in the imperial centers. These holdovers could be amazingly persistent; some small examples of the *encomienda mitaya*, for instance, still functioned in Paraguay in the 1780s. Where falling Indian numbers and settlers' economic activities combined to place a heavy labor demand on the native population, as they did in parts of New Granada, Venezuela, and New Mexico, Indians could suffer severely under these antiquated systems, especially because the rule of law grew generally feebler with distance from the large administrative centers. In other peripheral places, though – Yucatan and Paraguay are, in their different ways, examples – the position of natives was, with inevitable exceptions, broadly less burdensome (although Paraguay, in both its secular and religious settlements, was *sui generis* to such a degree that it can hardly be included in comparisons).

WOMEN, SECULAR AND RELIGIOUS

NATIVE WOMEN

One Paraguayan parallel that will bear some weight is between Guaraní women's activities among the settlers, and those of native women elsewhere. In the seventeenth century movement of Indian women from rural villages into colonial towns was common across the empire. As men went to towns under the dictates of draft labor or to find waged work, their wives often accompanied them, seeking occupations also that would provide a supplement to the man's income. Domestic service was a common choice, though often a hard one, since once in a household a servant might find it hard to escape. Cases are known of women being held in service for years for non-payment of small debts.[74] Somewhat better off, if not economically at least in independence, were the many native women who took up some sort of petty trade, such as preparing food, or *chicha* or *pulque*, and selling them on the street, or retailing vegetables and fruit from a small shop (*pulpería*). Some, but far fewer, Indian women, usually those of higher standing, perhaps with family links to local native leadership, owned and rented out houses and shops in white-dominated towns. These women are difficult to distinguish from mestizas doing the same thing. Indeed, prospering *indias* might come to be seen as mestizas, as economic definition of ethnicity and status did its typical work in mid-colonial times.

Native women working in large colonial towns were important mediators between native and foreign culture. That role was epitomized by the many who looked after children, and especially by those who worked as wet nurses. In seventeenth-century Cuzco *indias* cared not only for the children of colonists (and of the hispanized descendants of Inca nobility), but also for those of black slaves, and orphans.[75] Such women inevitably gave their charges some familiarity with native language, mentality, beliefs, and, of course, parts of material culture such as food and clothing. They were doing what, in the reverse direction, Spanish women in America have long been seen to have done after the conquest: acting as conduits through which one culture flowed into another.[76]

WHITE WOMEN

With movement and migration so frequent among Indians in central areas in the seventeenth century, producing among other results a growing presence of native women in towns, it may be that *indias* then became more important than white women as cultural intermediaries. For as they entered an expanding range of working roles that put them in constant contact with colonials, it seems that the set of activities open to white (and almost white) women may have narrowed, at least in comparison with conditions soon after the conquest, when the rules and traits of settlers' society were still fluid and in formation. Nonetheless, white women of middling and high social rank were not as devoid of opportunities in mid-colonial times as might be expected. Spain certainly sent to America its assumptions that families were hierarchical units in which ranking males had patriarchal power; and that women were physically, psychologically, and morally fragile, and therefore in need of male supervision and protection.[77] But other parts of the Spanish tradition gave certain categories of women some freedom of action; and as was generally so, American conditions tended to loosen Iberian norms. By Spanish law, women retained control of property they owned before marrying. Dowries, though administered by a husband during his life, reverted to the widow after his death. If a groom made a gift, or *arras*, to his betrothed, that too became hers on his death. Hence "the legal and economic personality of the woman was not absorbed by marriage,"[78] and in reality economically active widows were no rarity, to be found on occasion running estates and farms, and a wide variety of productive and marketing business. Neither were mature, unmarried women barred by law or custom from the same sorts of work, or from other such means of supporting themselves independently as, say, sewing or teaching.

One striking feature of women's existence in the 1600s might be read as evidence of self-determination taken to an extreme, but had in fact other causes. This was the extraordinarily high rate of illegitimate births, above all in the large towns. In Lima, for instance, between 1562 and 1689, the rate for white and mestizo children was never lower than 40 percent; and for Indians, Blacks and mulattoes, between 1618 and 1649, a little over 70 percent. In seventeenth-century Mexican cities illegitimacy stood at over 40 percent. At the end of the century, Guadalajara had rates of 61 percent for mulattoes and 39 percent for *españoles*.[79] These were levels of illegitimacy higher than those in Spain at the time, which were in turn above those elsewhere in Western Europe. The reasons included, in the case of *casta* women, the frequency of informal liaison, often long-lasting (*amancebamiento*), with men of similar origins or with married and unmarried men of higher rank; and, for white women, a relative shortage of men of equal social standing, which allegedly led them to yield sexually to males in the hope of assuring a marriage. Again, Spanish precedent had an effect, since a man who promised a woman marriage, and then had sexual relations with her, became responsible for her honor before both law and church. Amid a shortage of suitable men, many white women evidently thought the concession of sex a risk worth assuming to secure a partner. Given the shortage, however, such women then may have become satisfied with the second-best of a lasting but informal union. The outcome was many illegitimate children. Illegitimacy rates were, conversely, lowest, and rates of marriage highest, in Indian rural communities, where numbers were more evenly balanced, and where, perhaps even more tellingly, adherence to traditions of marriage was stronger than in the socially more tumultuous cities.

NUNS AND *BEATAS*

Another, but very different, outcome of the lack of eligible spouses, especially for the daughters of well-to-do colonial families, was a growing number of nunneries in the seventeenth century. The first religious houses for women had appeared very soon after the mainland conquests. In New Spain, for example, Bishop Zumárraga created a *beaterio* in México-Tenochtitlan to house six Franciscan laywomen whom he had brought in from Spain to teach Indian girls.[80] More *beatas* – pious women who took simple vows under the rules of the third orders of Franciscans and other similar societies[81] – soon followed. And the first fully conventual foundation in New Spain came soon after, in the 1540s, with the creation of Nuestra Señora de la Concepción, again in the capital. The Conceptionist order remained strong in the Indies, though Franciscan, Augustinian, Dominican, and Carmelite houses for women were also soon in place in the major towns.

Although historians have given much attention to the secular side of convent life – the luxury in which some nuns lived, the episodes of eyebrow-raising behavior in the locutory, occasional scalings of the walls, and, more seriously, the considerable part played by nunneries in local economies – there is no questioning the true religiosity of many nuns. The founding period of many of the houses, the second half of the sixteenth century, was also a time in which the value of contemplation, often deeply tinctured with mysticism, was stressed by the church. It was the time, in Spain, of St Teresa of Avila, and of St John of the Cross, both ascetics, and indeed the restorers of the primitive austerity of their order, the Carmelites. Thus the social reasons for the founding and growth of convents should not be overemphasized. It was not simply, or even mainly, lack of suitable husbands that led women to take conventual vows; but rather, for many of them, a genuine vocation.

After 1600 the number of convents in the Indies rose, spreading from central to provincial towns. Their populations grew also, so that in the late 1600s each of the six senior houses in Lima, the *conventos grandes*, may have had a thousand women within its walls. Far from all of these, perhaps a third to a half, were professed nuns, with the balance consisting of servants, novices, and girls temporarily resident for schooling. The thirteen nunneries in Lima are said to have held at one point a fifth of the city's female population. On the other hand, in Mexico City there were only 888 professed nuns *c.*1800, although the number had been falling since 1750 or so.[82] The seventeenth-century convents remained contemplative, at most taking in a number of girls to be educated (mainly in what was needed to run a household). No convents of teaching orders appeared until the mid-eighteenth century. Like the nuns themselves, the pupils in the 1600s were the daughters of creole families prosperous in fame and fortune, of merchants, government officials, landowners, successful miners, lawyers, and doctors. Thanks to the fees paid by pupils' families, to the dowries required of novices, to bequests and to gifts, many convents found themselves growing richer in cash as well as spirit as the seventeenth century advanced. Late in the century some began to make loans from spare funds, mostly to safe borrowers in the monied sector of society. Then they also took to investing in city property, to such effect that toward 1800 eight large convents in Mexico City were worth over seven million pesos in various urban buildings. Nunneries were by then the largest property owners within the church; and the church held almost half of all the city's property.[83]

Although no women's order in the Indies devoted itself wholly to education until the eighteenth century, it is certainly true that before then nunneries offered the best conditions for cultivating the mind available to women interested in doing so, and that nuns were, collectively, the closest approach to a female intellectual community in Spanish America. The outstanding example is Juana Ramírez de Asbaje (?1648–95), better known and celebrated as Sor (Sister) Juana Inés de la Cruz. She was the illegitimate daughter of a woman from a creole family that owned land a little south of Mexico City. Nothing certain is known of her father.[84] As a child she showed great mental precocity, reading from the age of three in the books in her family's collection. Part of her later childhood she spent living in the viceregal palace in the capital, invited there by a vicereine astonished by such a prodigy. Then in 1668 she became a Jeronymite nun; not, it seems, out of any strong calling, but precisely because the convent seemed to her the place most conducive to the life of thought and writing that she had by then decided to make for herself. She wrote voluminously, particularly in poetry and plays (works both of morality and comedy), using with much skill the conventions of the Spanish conceptism of her time, which freighted word and phrase heavily with multiple and often uncertain meanings. She was an able and moving poet in this metaphysical mode, and has been accounted the final luminary in Spain's greatest literary period, the Golden Age of the seventeenth century.[85]

Among her best known poems are those telling of unrequited or misdirected love. One of them begins

> Who thankless flees me, I with love pursue
> Who loving follows me, I thankless flee:

To him who spurns my love I bend the knee,
His love who seeks me, cold I bid him rue...[86]

Such lines very probably do not refer to actual affairs of the heart, given Sor Juana's firmly declared aversion to marriage and her often repeated self-dedication to a life of intellection. They have, rather, been persuasively read as disguised confessions of mental and even psychological conflict within her – of her feeling of being torn between, on the one hand, commitment to the values and learning, if not profoundly to the faith, of the church she belonged to; and, on the other, her love of writing and of mental exploration of a broad range of worldly topics. Her interests included, apparently, the new scientific knowledge and method of the time, in the attenuated form in which they crossed the Atlantic from Europe. She gained some familiarity with them through many conversations, in her convent's locutory, with New Spain's leading male savant of the late 1600s, Don Carlos de Sigüenza y Góngora. He had been a pupil of Fray Diego Rodríguez, the first holder, from 1637 on, of the chair of mathematics at the University of Mexico, and a teacher who had included the findings of Brahe, Copernicus and Kepler in his courses. When, finally, Sor Juana came under criticism from church authorities both for the unwomanly nature of her dedication to writing and intellectual inquiry, and for applying her superior mind to them rather than to matters of faith, she argued for the value of secular subjects, such as history, architecture, geometry, arithmetic, and physics, for a full understanding of theology. But there was no deflecting her critics; nor her self-criticism, for her unorthodoxy clearly inspired guilt in her, not to mention a sense of alienation and even despair. "Let not the head which is the repository of knowledge expect any other crown than that of thorns," she wrote, under attack. Finally, in 1694 she yielded, renouncing all her possessions, including her books and her musical and scientific instruments. She spent the last year of her life, before dying in an epidemic in April 1695, in contrition and self-chastisement; though never, it seems, formally abandoning the study of humane letters.[87]

Sor Juana, it could be said, was broken over the divide between the old and the new in Spanish America, between the baroque, which harboured within it sundry medieval remnants, and the Enlightenment, which in her thirst for worldly knowledge she prefigured. That tension was so damaging to her precisely because she was a woman; a male religious with her interests would have met with less intolerance, if any.

The ideal of creole womanhood, and specifically of religious womanhood, can be found at the opening of the century, and in the other viceregal capital, Lima. There in 1586 was born Isabel Flores de Oliva, on whose infant cheeks appeared one day the images of two perfect roses. The connection with the "rose without thorns," the Virgin Mary, was soon made. In 1597 the child was confirmed under a new name, Rosa de Santa María.

Throughout her short life (she died in 1617) Rosa was at the center of social life and religious cult in Lima. She became a *beata* at an early age, first using the Franciscan habit, and then in 1606 taking the vows of the Dominicans' third order. She continued to live at home, in a cell in the garden, where she sewed and embroidered for the high-society ladies who came often to talk with her. She changed the words of popular love songs to those of divine love, and accompanied herself on the guitar as she sang them. A reputation for working small miracles gathered around her. Then, shortly before her death, a more profound sign of her sanctity appeared, when a portrait of Christ before which she was praying began to sweat – and persisted in doing so even after two Jesuits from their neighboring college twice wiped the moisture from the paint. After her death, adoration of Rosa intensified. People of all ranks regarded her cell as a shrine. And despite some initial concern by the Inquisition over the authenticity of this cult she was beatified in 1668, and, as Santa Rosa de Lima, canonized in 1671 (becoming the first New World saint) and declared patron of America.

Sketched thus, it seems a gentle, simple life, recalling in its sweetness many depictions of Mary by Spanish and Spanish American painters in the seventeenth century. But there was a grimmer side of Rosa, recalling equally those many other works of the time emerging from painters' and sculptors' workshops that exalt the suffering of the saints, not least the Virgin. This was an age of Mariolatry in Spain and the Indies, and Rosa's quick canonization may have resulted from her identification as a revival of the Madonna.[88] Like the Virgin she suffered, though necessarily by self-imposed trials: a diet of bread, water, herbs, juices, and ashes; chili rubbed on her eyelids; fierce self-flagellation; sleeping on a bed of three knotty willow trunks; praying while hanging by her hair from a peg in the wall; bleeding from a crown of thorns pressed into her scalp. The self-discipline perhaps spilled over the line, often difficult to fix, between the devout and the psycho-pathological, and possibly had sexual undertones. That, too, may have been behind the Inquisition's hesitation.

ARTS, FORMAL AND POPULAR

THE BAROQUE

In its tension of light and dark, Rosa's existence seems a good example of the baroque quality that some have ascribed to the seventeenth century in Spanish America.[89] Whether anything useful can be meant by applying the baroque label to a whole culture is debatable, especially since the term is such a capacious and undefinable catch-all. But some of the traits of the baroque in various forms of art – a fascination with the manipulation of shape and space, a celebration of complexity and contrast, a delight in opulence and grandeur, a certain thrilling to the macabre – can be seen, transmuted, by anyone inclined to view things in that way, in such varied phenomena of the seventeenth-century colonies as complexity of social ranking, hot ecclesiastical pursuit of "idolatry," love of ceremony and processions, and savage fights for precedence by both churchmen and bureaucrats in their respective settings.

In the arts, the baroque of course is unmistakably present. It is the dominant tenor from the mid-seventeenth to the late eighteenth century. Sor Juana's poetry and other writing are one example among many in literature. It is even clearer in the productions of the host of painters active in the larger colonial towns, churning out work from their studios in response to orders for personal portraits, portraits of Spanish monarchs, landscapes, and, above all, devotional pictures for private houses, monasteries, convents, and churches. Among the most accomplished were Cristóbal de Villalpando (1645–1714) in New Spain, and Melchor Pérez de Holguín (c.1665–1724) in Potosí, who was perhaps the leading painter of colonial Spanish South America. On both of these the influence of the Seville school was heavy, with Villalpando in the debt of Juan de Valdés Leal, notably the creator of somber still-lifes in the *memento-mori* line, and Holguín aspiring to the level of Francisco Zurbarán, who was certainly a less gloomy spirit, but one immune from frivolity.[90] Equally profuse was the production of formal music, for use above all in the cathedrals, and written by organists and choirmasters either imported from Europe or trained in European canons in America. It was, however, in music that the baroque influence was slowest in appearing. For most of the seventeenth century the older tradition of polyphony persisted.

The most obvious surviving evidence of the baroque is in architecture. From roughly 1650 the eclectic mixture of romanesque, gothic, renaissance (particularly in its Spanish plateresque offshoot), and simply *ad hoc* pragmatic invention that had appeared in civic buildings and monastic and other churches yielded to an American version of the baroque. This tended to simplify its European sources, paying more heed to the modeling of surface than to manipulation of masses and volumes. This modeling could be complex and dramatic, as, for example, in the façade of one of the greatest of Spanish American churches, the cathedral of Mexico City, dedicated in its present design in 1667. In this case there are massive pilasters projecting out from the main plane of the façade, linked to it above by great, curling brackets of stone; and set back from it are the doorways to the nave and the two side aisles. But the addition of smaller decorations, such as spiral columns flanking sculpted panels, detracts from the play of masses, and makes for a slight sense of jumble that saps the undeniable grandeur of the whole. In many lesser churches of the Spanish American baroque, an appliqué of decoration to the exterior is the only claim to distinction. A highly carved façade, and perhaps two decorated belfries flanking it – all striking enough, certainly – may be applied to a building that is otherwise little more than two tall intersecting boxes with a dome over their crossing. It is above all this decoration (together with the massive, intricate, and gilded altarpieces in the interior that reached their full splendour with the eighteenth century) that the term "baroque" has come to mean when applied to Spanish American churches.

POPULAR ARTS

As in architecture, so with other art forms, or at least those of high art: Spanish colonial baroque, broadly speaking, differs from its European models mainly in taking only part of their content and intent. Its originalities are small. But the opposite is true of popular arts in mid-colonial times, where Indians and *castas* made rich additions to the European base. Music was a large element in the evangelizing armory of the early mendicants. They organized native choirs for their churches, and taught Indians to accompany the singing on European instruments – viols, trumpets, sackbuts, fifes and the like. Some traits of native music, especially perhaps rhythms, were woven into the European forms. To this blend of European and American was added in the seventeenth century a large African contribution. Again rhythm was a strong influence. By 1600 African drumming was more often heard in Mexico City than that of Indians. And after that varieties of rhythmic songs known as *guineos*, *negros*, and *negrillas* entered the musical repertory in both Middle and South America. Their texts were in an Africanized Spanish. One *negro* from Cuzco has the title *Bamo, bamo en bona fe* (*Vamos, vamos en buena fe*, "Let us go, let us go in good faith"), and another, *Caia guinea bailamo lo congo* (*Calla, guinea, bailamos el congo*, "Hush, man from Guinea, and we'll dance the congo"). Clearly these songs and dances had currency outside the black community, since Spaniards and creoles wrote words, in dialect, for them. Sor Juana was among those to do so, producing *negros* and *negrillas* for use as *villancicos* (popular songs associated with some religious festival, especially with Christmas).[91] She also wrote Nahuatl words for Indian *villancicos*.

There are parallels to this popular music in painting and architecture. The most obvious in painting is the Cuzco school of the late seventeenth century and onward, generally considered to have originated in the work of the Indian artist Diego Quispe Tito (*c*.1611–*c*.1681). The forthrightness of the Cuzco canvases – there is more to them than a naive charm of primitiveness – has made them the most widely known product of colonial painters outside Spanish America. They typically show archangels dressed in the most sumptuous secular attire of the time, wielding swords or even firearms, and Madonnas viewed face-on, with vast, triangular, gold- and jewel-encrusted robes. The flatness of the style, the simplicity of composition, and the frequent use of decorative gold leaf on the canvases combine in an alluring mixture of simplicity and opulence. But the work is not wholly Indian. The figures are adaptations from European engravings, and, in the case of the angels, specifically from French military manuals.[92]

In architecture, popular influence is even more widely visible, particularly in decoration. Many churches of the central Andes, from Quito southward to Arequipa and Potosí, have flat ornamentation resembling embroidery or woodcarving, cut deeply into the stone of their façades. Whether this decoration has its roots in native or European patterning has been debated; but the masons were Indian or mestizo, and to the viewer the work has a strong native American feeling. This "highland planiform decoration"[93] began to appear about 1650, and was used until the end of the next century. Its essence is distilled in the door surround of the small church of San Lorenzo in Potosí (1728–44). From a high niche, a squat St Michael oversees the entrance. Stylized foliage, in stone, covers much of the portal. In the upper corners, sun, moon and stars appear, and two mermaids playing guitars. The effect would be of coralline rococo encrustation, were it not for the weight of two large spiral columns, topped with heavily skirted stone caryatids, that flank the door itself. In New Spain a similar feeling of Indian-ness clings to various

churches of the southern, or Puebla, style, despite arguments that its inspiration is, again, European. This style, too, dates from the mid-1600s. One of its
many peaks is the parish church of Santa María at Tonantzintla (c.1700),
close to Puebla, whose interior is so convoluted and complete a mass of
polychrome stucco relief – leaves, fruits, cherubs' heads, scrolls, twisting
columns – that all but the most general shape of the building is lost. It is a
glory of gaudiness that may have sources in southern Spain; but even Andalusia falls short of this merry exuberance.

CREOLE NATIVISM

In the mid-colonial era, then, a creativity abounds in the popular arts, or the
popular side of the formal arts, that is weak in the paintings, buildings, and
music that come straight from European models. Creole high culture, it could
be said, was not markedly innovative. One exception to this must, however, be
made. And that is that some creoles of the middle period, especially in
Mexico, wrote histories that began to link the native, pre-conquest, past
with the colonial present in such a way as to suggest that there existed at
least a proto-national identity between the two. This was partly a revival of the
enthusiasm for Indian culture expressed in some early post-conquest writings,
most clearly those of Las Casas. One of the first of these historians, the
Franciscan Juan de Torquemada (not strictly a creole, but raised in New
Spain from early childhood), drew on Las Casas, and also on Sahagún. The
view given by his *Monarquía Indiana* (1615) of the Aztecs was certainly less
than wholly positive. He thought that the Devil had first entered Mexico in the
guise of Huitzilopochtli, their tribal god. But broadly Torquemada saw the
Aztecs as equals in civilization and morality with Greeks and Romans.[94] As
the century advanced, a few others, some in South America, found admirable
qualities in pre-conquest, and even present, Indians. But the creole most
notable in this line of thought was Sor Juana's intellectual companion, Don
Carlos de Sigüenza y Góngora. It was love for his fatherland (*patria*), he
declared, that moved him to delve into Mexico's native past. Following
European hermetic speculations of the day, particularly as developed by the
Jesuit Athanasius Kircher, Sigüenza argued for the descent of Mexican
Indians from the founding rulers of Egypt, whence all wisdom had ultimately
come. Egyptians had colonized Atlantis. It was only a short onward leap to
Mexico. Similarities of pyramids, glyphic writing, clothing and so on supported the Egyptian connection. Sigüenza gave physical form to his high
esteem for ancient Mexicans in a triumphal arch he designed for the entry
into Mexico City of a new viceroy, the Marquis of La Laguna, in 1680. On it
were displayed statues of the dozen native rulers of Tenochtitlan from its early
fourteenth-century foundation to the conquest, each of them representing
some particular political virtue. Sigüenza hoped that this would contribute
to a revival of the deserved fame of those native rulers, now unjustly ignored.[95]

It was, naturally, easier to find admirable qualities in distant Aztec kings
than in the downwardly leveled native commoners of late seventeenth-century

New Spain. These inspired in Sigüenza a deep distaste. Nonetheless, his arch signals an early stirring of movement toward a conscious converging, from the creole side, of the native with the imposed culture. It is a movement that has continued to this day, not only in Mexico but in other Spanish American regions that have a strong native cultural base. The convergence has gone furthest, however, in Mexico, in part because it first began there.

VARIETIES OF MESTIZAJE

Even without any such conscious effort, the seventeenth century advanced the mingling of American and European in the Spanish colonies. Though the proportion of people termed mestizos by themselves or by officialdom was still small, cultural *mestizaje* was now in full swing, as developments in religion, conceptions of the past, language, and the arts show. And the Euro-American blend was enriched and complicated by many African additions, across the board from religion to food. Cultural mixing was undoubtedly pushed forward by the demographic changes of this middle colonial time, particularly by the growing tendency of Indians, under various pressures, to leave their traditional communities for creole-dominated towns, haciendas, and mines. There, to the degree that they adopted alien ways, they became less Indian. And Spanish America as a whole was becoming less Indian; for, although native populations generally tended toward stabilization in the seventeenth century after the grim losses of the 1500s, and indeed rose in New Spain, native people became an ever smaller fraction of the whole as other segments of the population grew around them.[96]

After 1600, then, the blending of people and cultures for which the foundation had been laid in the previous century, and which is among the salient qualities – perhaps the most salient quality – of modern Spanish America, moved beyond any point of possible reversal. That is the chief accomplishment, for the long term, of the seventeenth century in Spanish American history. At the same time, ethnic and cultural mixing could only increase the divergence taking place between Spain and its American colonies – a splitting that was then more obviously visible in a range of practical changes in the operation of the empire: the growing role of creoles in their own administration, the fall in Madrid's receipt of American revenues, contraction in the official trade across the Atlantic, rising commercial contacts with foreigners, and growth of an autonomous American structure of production and exchange. These were problems, from the metropolis's point of view, that even the disorganized and unstable governments of the enfeebled Spain of Charles II (1665–1700) could not but notice. Nothing much could be done about them in that anarchic time of oligarchical adventurism in the peninsula. But the new Bourbon monarchy that after much effort finally brought order, if never greatness, back to Spain during the eighteenth century had no choice but to engage with them.

[12] EIGHTEENTH-CENTURY SPANISH AMERICA: REFORMED OR DEFORMED?

Spain at the opening of the seventeenth century suffered twinges of self-doubt. Spain at the opening of the eighteenth suffered sword thrusts of invasion and civil war. The death in 1700 without heir of Charles II, the last Habsburg ruler of Spain, was quickly followed by the outbreak of the War of the Spanish Succession. The great European powers wrestled mightily for the Spanish crown; or more precisely for the access to American wealth that possession of the throne should bring. Laughably trivial, indeed, if anyone remembered them, must have seemed the soul-searchings of the early 1600s, when in 1706 all the major cities of Spain, Madrid included, were occupied by forces of the Anglo-Austrian-Dutch Grand Alliance that was one of the contenders for control of the Spanish world. The most recent alien occupiers of Spain before then had been the Moors. The Alliance found internal backers in the peoples of the Iberian periphery: Aragonese, Catalans, Valencians, and Portuguese seizing the chance to avenge themselves of earlier slights and impositions from Castile and, in the case of the Spanish regions, to seek greater separation in the future. Opposing the Alliance was the Bourbon France of Louis XIV, whose grandson, Philip of Anjou, had been chosen by the moribund Charles II in his final days as his successor. Castilians accepted their former king's choice, and with it, necessarily, an alliance with France that from the start was a subordination.

The war, begun in 1701, dragged on, inside the peninsula and far beyond its bounds, until 1714. The allies were not able to hold for long what they occupied in 1706; but neither could France and Castile undo the Alliance. In 1712–13, in the multiple treaties of the Peace of Utrecht, compromises were negotiated that reflected the stalemate of the war. Philip was to keep the throne, being confirmed as Philip V of Spain but only on condition that he abandon rights of succession in France. Spain was to keep its American territories, but was stripped of its European lands. Minorca and Gibraltar went to Britain, Sicily to Savoy, and Flanders, Naples, Milan, and Sardinia to Austria. The British in addition gained a long-desired legal access to Spanish American markets through the concession of the *asiento de negros*, or monopoly right to sell African slaves to the Spanish colonies, for thirty years. With this went what was to prove the lucrative right to send with each Spanish trading fleet a ship of five hundred tonnes (no mean vessel by prevailing standards) laden with goods for sale at the trade fairs of New Spain and the Isthmus of Panama. With silver from the sale of slaves and merchandise in Spanish America the British aimed to quicken the growth of their trade with the Far East; again that endless oriental appetite for silver working its effect on the Western world.[1]

For Spain, the War of Succession and Utrecht were end and beginning. The end – the formal, unequivocal end after a century of decline – was of Spain's standing as an autonomous world power. The beginning was of a period – a long period that has lasted until very recently – of subordination to others' influence and will. It was now clear that Spain had gone from player to played upon. In the eighteenth century the main external directive force was France, to which Spain was tied by the Bourbon family link (though, true to Utrecht, the crowns were never united). Over and again in that century, and particularly in its second half, Spain was drawn in France's wake into costly conflicts. The enemy was usually Britain, with which France engaged in a century-long series of wars for world pre-eminence. Whatever weight Spain retained in European affairs came largely from its possession of the American empire. The Spanish state became a paradox: a second-rate European power holding the world's largest overseas colonies.

That Spain did continue to hold those colonies resulted from several causes. First was the sheer size of Spanish America. Even its subunits, such as the *audiencia* provinces and frontier governorships, were too large for any external power to bite off (without, at least, local collaboration, which was not offered). Again, America proved capable in the 1700s of providing funds and men for its own defense. Third, the sharing of wealth and administrative power with the monarchy that the colonies (or more precisely, the *criollos*) had achieved over the seventeenth century was conductive to preserving the status quo. At first sight, the absence of any colonial bid for separation during the War of Succession, when Madrid was powerless to thwart it, may seem striking. But in reality, whatever gains such an attempt might have brought were far outweighed by the risks of the unknown; much better to remain settled in the comfortable accommodation with the monarchy that long but largely gentle friction between rulers and ruled had produced over the previous century. It is in any case unlikely in the extreme that any colonial possessing political influence contemplated, even fleetingly, separation from Spain in the early 1700s. Only the experience of the Enlightenment and of reform would make time ripe for such notions.

After the War of Succession, Spanish affairs could hardly do other than improve; and so they did, slowly. Under the admittedly erratic leadership of Philip V (1701–46) and his successors Ferdinand VI (1746–59) and Charles III (1759–88), and under the French absolutist influence that the Bourbon line brought into Spain, the authority of the central government grew, that of the nobility fell, and limited economic recovery took place.[2] These changes were also in part the outcome of an intellectual renovation fanned by winds of change that entered the land, even if much attenuated in their crossing of the Pyrenees from their source in the French Enlightenment.

The American empire, too, propelled Spanish recovery with its growing contributions to the treasury. America was, in fact, notably more vibrant in all material respects than the home country throughout the eighteenth century, as almost all regions put behind them whatever contraction or stagnation they had known during the 1600s.

PEOPLE, PRODUCTION, AND COMMERCE

TRENDS IN POPULATION

Underlying this advance, first, was population growth. This is clearest for New Spain, where the total population grew from about 1.5 million in 1650, to 2.5–3.0 million in the early 1740s, to some 4.5–5.0 million in the 1790s, to above 6 million in 1810. These numbers suggest a rate of growth increasing with time. The same quickening increase can be seen in northern and central Chile (1 percent annually in the first half of the century, 2 percent thereafter), taking the population from c.95,000 in 1710 to c.583,000 in 1815. In New Granada a similar pattern seems likely, although the number of inhabitants early in the eighteenth century is unclear. During the 1770s the combined population of the *audiencias* of Santa Fe de Bogotá and Quito rose at the remarkable yearly rate of some 2.3 percent, and at perhaps 1.7 percent annually in the next decade. For Peru and Charcas demographic data are, unfortunately, still sparse for the eighteenth century. All indications are, however, that the population grew between 1700 and 1800. Crucial to that increase, whatever its pace, and to the clear acceleration of demographic growth in New Spain, was recovery of the Indian populations, founded above all on native peoples' improving resistance to the diseases that had for so long been so devastating. Native numbers rose particularly strongly after 1700 in Mexico, since that curve had touched its low point as early as the 1620s and was rebounding strongly by the end of the century. Standard opinion has long had the native population of the central Andes on a downward course until the 1720s, with a fierce epidemic of 1719–20 dealing a blow that reduced numbers to their minimum in colonial times. Recent, if very local, evidence, however, suggests that the low point may have come before 1660s, and that the epidemic of sixty years later, while undoubtedly severe, did no more than interrupt what was by then sturdy Indian growth. In the 1700s mixed-blooded people multiplied fast almost everywhere. It is said, for example, that New Granada then became "a fundamentally mestizo society." In Chile, too, mestizos flourished, but there it was the white portion of the population (including a mixed element generally regarded as white) that truly prevailed, laying the basis for the present nature of the country's population.[3]

By the close of the eighteenth century, the total population of Spanish America stood at some 12.6 million. By region, it has been reckoned as follows.[4] (Figures are rounded to the nearest 0.01 million).

region	millions	percentage of total
Mexico	5.84	46.4
Central America	1.16	9.2
Caribbean islands	0.55	4.4
New Granada	1.1	8.7
Venezuela	0.78	6.2
Quito	0.5	4.0
Peru	1.1	8.7
Charcas	0.56	4.5
Chile	0.55	4.4
Buenos Aires and Tucumán	0.31	2.5
Paraguay	0.1	0.8
Uruguay	0.03	0.2
Totals	12.58	100.0

Three points call for notice here. First is the preponderance of Mexico, with almost half the total population of Spanish America by 1800. This is an accurate indicator of its general, and especially economic, prominence in the empire in the eighteenth century. Second is the growth of the total population in that century. Although for very few regions are there reliable figures for its early years, almost every sign is of increase. And, given the great weight in the total of Mexico, for which estimates are available at least for the mid-seventeenth and mid-eighteenth centuries, it is likely that the whole Spanish American population grew between two and three times between 1700 and 1800. But, despite that, it should lastly be recalled that, before Cortés's arrival in 1519, the population of central and southern Mexico alone may well have surpassed the twelve million or so shown here for Spanish America as a whole. The gross demographic balance of the colonial period was categorically negative.

PRODUCTION

As in earlier times, it is in mining that growth is most incontrovertibly seen in the eighteenth century, thanks to the existence of continuous records of royalty taxes paid to the treasury. All major silver and gold regions managed an almost unbroken increase of production over the century. In silver output, the central Andes, after a steep decline throughout the 1600s, achieved an average growth of production of 1.2 percent annually in the eighteenth century. New Spain's rate of increase was the same or slightly higher from 1725 to 1810; and this was a continuation, after a brief dip in the early 1720s, of steady growth from about 1670 onward. In the closing years of the seventeenth century Mexican silver production exceeded Peru's for the first time. Mexico stayed ahead, by such a margin that c.1800 Mexican mines yielded some 25 million pesos yearly, against the central Andean total of 8–9 million. The combined amount was more than double the highest previous American yield of silver, achieved in Potosí's heyday c.1600. In fact, that earlier maximum was first passed between 1710 and 1720, and was exceeded in every year between 1750 and 1810.[5]

The reasons for such a general swelling of the silver stream flowing from Spanish American mines were, naturally, diverse. Some were particular to certain places, such as the continuation at Potosí of the state-run supply of cheap native labor through the *mita*. The recovery of Potosí's and Oruro's taxed production also fits with a cut in the royalty rate charged in the central Andes from a fifth to a tenth of output. Miners in Potosí had for a century or more pleaded for this reduction, which would make their tax load equal to the royalty charged in New Spain. Their petitions were finally answered in 1736. Mexican miners seem likely to have benefited from stable, or possibly even falling, labor costs that resulted from population growth in eighteenth-century New Spain. Generally stimulative of silver mining everywhere early in the century was the high valuation of precious metals in Europe at the time. Other broadly vitalizing influences were the spreading adoption of subterranean blasting, from about 1670 in the Andes and after 1700 in Mexico, and the greater availability of mercury resulting from new finds of ore at Almadén in Spain early in the eighteenth century. Blasting seems likely to have lowered the cost of both seeking silver ore underground and removing it once found. Increased mercury output at Almadén eased the tightness of mercury supply that had often hampered silver refining in the 1600s, and offset falling production at Huancavelica in Peru, the only substantial source of mercury in Spanish America.[6]

The general buoyancy of silver production in the eighteenth century brought rising revenues to the crown in royalties, sales of mercury, and taxes on general sales and trade. It stimulated the colonies' commerce, both internal and external, legal and contraband. Worth particular notice is the growth of output in the first half of the century that research has shown in recent years. The Mexican silver boom of the late 1700s, along with the relatively modest recovery of Potosí at the same time, were always obvious to historians, who tended to see them as the outcome of a planned revival of mining through policies applied mainly under Charles III. These included cuts in royalty rates and the mercury price, state-sponsored technical education, state-organized credit banks, the creation of privileged mining guilds, and social reward to successful miners in the form of noble titles. These measures certainly had positive effects. But now it is clear that late eighteenth-century growth of silver was also a continuation of a vigorously rising trend that had begun around 1670 in New Spain and perhaps fifty years later in the central Andes. This trend owed little to policy (except for the royalty reduction granted to central Andean miners in 1736), and much to the economic circumstances in which the industry operated, such as the technological advance of blasting, stability or possibly even decline (in Mexico) in the cost of labor, and a rise in the value of precious metals.[7]

Propelled by that same rising valuation, gold production in Spanish America also tended strongly upward after 1700. Much gold was found intermingled with silver ores in New Spain. It became there an important by-product of silver refining in the eighteenth century, especially at San Luis Potosí. With some interruptions, the largest in the 1780s, taxed gold output in Mexico grew by an order of magnitude between 1701–10 (c.1,980,000 grams in the decade) and 1801–10 (c.21,690,000 grams). Chile also produced much gold in the eighteenth century. Spanish America's best gold source remained, however, New Granada, where, according to records of both royalties collected and gold coins struck, the mines' output multiplied four or even six times between the early and late decades of the century. The royalty record, for instance, indicates an annual output for 1715–19 of gold worth c.440,000 silver pesos, against c.1,890,000 yearly in the 1790s. Apart from the rising worth of the metal, increased availability of labor seems to have underlain this mining growth in New Granada. Black slaves did much of the mining work, and imports of these were raised above earlier levels first by the French Guinea Company during the War of the Spanish Succession, and afterwards by the British South Sea Company operating the slave *asiento* under the terms set up at Utrecht. Population growth in general may also have provided new prospectors and workers, particularly for the important mining region of Antioquia in the center-north, where wage labor rather than slavery prevailed in gold extraction.[8]

Gold's value being so much more compact than silver's (the ratio of value of the two metals, weight for weight, in mid-eighteenth century Europe was about 15:1), gold was the easier of the two, and the more tempting, to smuggle. Hence production estimates drawn from royalty receipts are more likely to understate gold's production than silver's. Even so, the margin between the output of the two metals in the late Spanish colonies is worth noting. By official record New Granada, the main auriferous region, yielded gold worth a little less than two million pesos a year in the 1790s. New Spain, the main source of silver in the final colonial century, gave in the same decade some twenty-five million pesos annually. Silver remained to the last, as always, the prime metallic product, and the main export, of the American empire.

With the scale of its production, relative complexity of technique, and large formation of fixed capital in refineries, shafts and adits, Spanish American silver mining can properly be called an industry. The size, bustle, noise, smells, and dirt of such places as Potosí from the late sixteenth century, and Guanajuato from the mid-eighteenth, would incline a modern viewer to see them as industrial centers. But in that, mining was unique. The only other type of production that even approached industrial status was textile manufacture; and that only in New Spain.

Cloth, mainly rough woolen stuffs, and cottons where the fibre could be grown, continued to be made anywhere local demand existed. Native villagers spun and wove wool (from llamas, alpacas and sheep in the Andes, and sheep alone elsewhere) for domestic needs, as many still do today. Rural estates often had a weaving shop making cloth for residents' use. Regions particularly suited for raising wool-bearing animals tended to develop concentrations of *obrajes* for weaving. Conditions for production and sale might be favorable enough to induce local merchants and landowners to invest in these weaving sheds and the looms they contained. In South America the main such area after 1700 continued to be Quito. But the densest grouping of *obrajes* (and smaller establishments known as *trapiches*) in the eighteenth century was at Querétaro in the Bajío region of New Spain. While cloth output dropped in other Mexican textile zones, notably the Valley of Mexico and the Puebla area, it rose at Querétaro for most of the century, encouraged by population growth that provided abundance of both demand and labor. In the 1740s Querétaro had forty *obrajes*; and though the number fell thereafter, production was maintained by a multiplication of the smaller shops. The number of working looms rose until the independence wars began in 1810. There were 290 in that year.[9]

That concentration of weaving capacity undoubtedly made Querétaro the textile capital of Spanish America. But it was hardly an industrial town. *Obrajes*, and much less *trapiches*, were not factories. A large *obraje* was one with twenty looms. No power was used besides that of human operators. No technological advance is visible in eighteenth-century cloth making in Spanish America. As generally with Spanish American production in late colonial times, increased output was achieved by increasing inputs (in this case, of labor and wool), and not by improving productivity through technical change. Even at the best-case of Querétaro, then, textiles were a matter of a proto-industry comprising proto-factories. The result was that Spanish American textile production was increasingly undercut as the century advanced by ever cheaper cloths dispatched by the ever more efficient powered mills of Europe. So great were the price differences that finally developed that in the century's closing decades no regulation was capable of blocking contraband imports of those cloths, particularly printed cottons from England. And so began a long period, still continuing in some degree, in which Latin America found its possibilities for economic growth and change cramped by its degree of tech-nological backwardness compared with European (and, later, North American) producers.

Another activity on the border between craft and industry that continued strong in the eighteenth century was the building and repair of ships. Notable yards were at Guayaquil and Havana; and also, for vessels carrying the growing river traffic of the Río de la Plata system, a few miles downstream from Asunción on the Paraguay River. Suitable wood was at hand at all three sites.[10]

The processing of tobacco also came, in New Spain at least, to be a business impressive in scale, if again its techniques did not go beyond standard craft practices. Beginning in 1717, the Bourbon regime moved gradually to capit-alize on the healthy American appetite for cigars, cigarettes, and snuff by creating state monopolies on tobacco. In most regions the state controlled simply the sale of the leaf. But in the Philippines and New Spain it became not just the single buyer (at regulated prices) of leaf, but the maker of the end products. The Mexican monopoly, indeed, dating from the mid-1760s, over-saw manufactories in Guadalajara, Puebla, Oaxaca, Orizaba, and Querétaro – as well as a central plant in Mexico City, which in the mid-1790s employed over seven thousand workers, 60 percent of them women. Four out of five of them rolled cigarettes by hand.[11] Without mechanization this massing of labor, however impressive in numbers, brought few economies of scale. Like the *obrajes*, the tobacco-processing plants were still proto-factories.

Crafts practiced in the traditional small shops in every town continued to provide most of what most people wanted or needed by way of clothing, tools and utensils, household decorations, riding gear, and so on. The import trade, licit and contraband, brought in the luxurious and the novel; but now increasingly it also supplied what was more commonplace but simply cheaper, as in the case of factory-made cloth.

Spanish America's slowness in moving toward larger-scale manufacture was arguably above all the outcome of a resistance to innovation and change, and a parallel unreceptiveness to science and technology, that may be traced to Spain's cleaving to the Counter-Reformation, and deviation from many lines of European development, in the sixteenth century. As a result, the economic soil had not been prepared in the seventeenth century for the changes in productive methods that the eighteenth brought to the countries of north-west Europe. Bourbon attempts at innovation in production in the peninsula were, with rare exceptions, no more successful than America's. The Indies' lag was, though, also in part an outcome of policy. Since the late sixteenth century a thread of opposition to American manufacturing had run through the imperial administrative fabric. The fear was that what the colonies made they would not buy from Spain, and, besides, that any degree of economic autonomy could only promote political unruliness.[12] The thread was never prominent in Habsburg times, however, because of the impracticality of policing American production, and the unreasonableness of expecting colonials to import basic goods that they could make easily and cheaply themselves. But in the Bourbon urge to reform it was picked up again, as a central element in a new formulation of the entire imperial economic structure. One strong advocate of reform, Philip V's secretary of finance, war, the navy, and the Indies in the early 1740s, José del Campillo y Cossío, argued in his *New System of Economic Government of America* (1743) that the colonies must be seen as markets for Spanish goods; and that therefore factories and industries were "the only matter that must absolutely be forbidden in America."[13] Other influential planners were less insistent on this point. Nonetheless, orders were certainly given later in the century for the closing of *obrajes* and smaller textiles shops operating without viceregal permits. Although it is not yet clear how widely these commands were enforced, it is certain that a prospective colonial entrepreneur wanting to invest in some productive activity outside mining or agriculture was unlikely to find enthusiastic official backing for his efforts.

Along with mining, farming and stockraising were clearly the most dynamic elements of the eighteenth-century colonial economy. Total food production necessarily rose with the general trend of population growth, under all types of land use and holding, from the communal subsistence holdings of native villages to the large, privately owned estates. It may well be, however, that, at least in the more densely peopled regions, it did not altogether keep up with the increasing numbers. For just as it is likely that, in the seventeenth century, drastic shrinking of populations and their demand for food generally meant that farming was concentrated on the most productive soil, so conversely in the 1700s rising population and demand for food forced the use of progressively poorer lands, with a consequent drop in the general productivity of both land and farm labor. Similarly, where land came into high demand to meet a large local call for food, smaller and weaker owners or tenants might find themselves forced out by the owners of larger tracts. On these two counts, demographic recovery therefore brought falling living standards to at least some in the lower reaches of society. But farming for consumption in the colonies broadly and inevitably expanded over the century. It did so using the same techniques as before; and the same range of land units, from native communal plots, through various types of small holdings held by Indians, *castas* and Whites, to *haciendas* modest to vast.

Greater, however, was the growth of commercial, export-directed agriculture. This, indeed, was where true innovation in land use came in the eighteenth century; for although agriculture had yielded exports almost from the start (sugar, dyes, and cacao, for instance), these flows now grew so much that quantitative change became qualitative. Further, regions which before had been minor producers now began to export heavily.

Chile was one such place. Its production of livestock and arable crops (mainly wheat) grew almost without interruption by a factor of seven or more between 1700 and the early 1800s, partly as a response to rising demand for Chilean wheat on the coast of Peru. Annual exports of wheat through Chile's main port, Valparaíso, rose, for example, from some 66,000 to 120,000 *fanegas* between 1705 and 1735 (a *fanega* is about 1.5 bushels, or just over 0.05 cubic meters).[14]

Another rising exporter was Paraguay. In the final third of the eighteenth century, the province's long-established export of *yerba mate* to the downstream regions toward Buenos Aires expanded ten-fold. Shipments of tobacco, wood, sugar and sweetmeats also rose substantially. All these goods were carried on ships built and crewed by Paraguayans, whose province for the first time became economically integrated into its broader Platine region.[15]

A leading reason for that linkage was the economic growth of Buenos Aires itself, founded on the export of leather from the cattle roaming the town's pampas hinterland. Here since the sixteenth century herds of wild cattle had thrived. Hides had been carried away by the small official, and larger unofficial, trade in and out of Buenos Aires, some of them by Portuguese merchants operating from Brazil. In the War of Spanish Succession, however, the major buyers were the French, to whom the nascent government of Philip V had granted the slave *asiento*. Making full use of this legal access, French ships reached Spanish American ports in large numbers for the first time. And with their arrival in Buenos Aires there began an expansion in the dispatch of leather that persisted through the century. From 1708 to 1712 some 175,000 hides may have been exported. After Utrecht, and the transfer of the slave-importing *asiento* to the British, the South Sea Company carried Africans to Buenos Aires, and hides (and silver) from it: in 1715, some 45,000 hides, in 1718, some 40,000, in 1724, some 60,000. By the 1760s Buenos Aires exported 150,000 hides each year; from 1779 to 1795, about 330,000. With this growth went expansion of Buenos Aires's control over the interior plains. The nomads native to them were driven inward, away from water and the better pastures. The *cabildo* of the city began to grant *estancias* (not privately owned large tracts, as the term later came to mean, but rights to use grazing and water in specified areas). As shipments of hides multiplied, so began Buenos Aires's progression from small, isolated townlet to metropolitan city.[16]

Another region that after 1700 began to realize a long-apparent agricultural potential was Venezuela. Today Venezuelan coffee is renowned; but in colonial times the province's famous caffeine-containing product was cacao, exported mainly to New Spain in the 1600s, and thereafter to Europe as well. Production was rising fast by the start of the eighteenth century, to judge by the number of trees growing in the province of Caracas: half a million in 1684, three million in 1720 (and over five million in 1744). Until about 1730 Caracas-based growers and shippers rapidly enriched themselves from the sale of the booming bean, prized in Europe for not only its flavor but its supposed medicinal merits. The home government, its attention caught by these profits, decided to tap them for the peninsula's benefit by chartering in 1728 a commercial organization, the Guipúzcoa (or Caracas) Company, equipped with monopoly trading rights with Venezuela. In fact the Company's monopoly was never watertight. Venezuelans fiercely resisted the imposed attempt to make it so by, among other means, selling cacao to European contraband buyers. And the British South Sea Company, supplying black slaves to the Venezuelan cacao growers under the *asiento* until the War of Jenkins' Ear broke out in 1739, discovered it was highly profitable to exchange slaves for cacao in Venezuela, and then sell that cacao at Veracruz, in New Spain, for silver.[17] Thus Venezuelan chocolate found its various ways into the cups of imbibers on both sides of the Atlantic.

North from Venezuela, Caribbean islands large and small had shown themselves by the eighteenth century to be unmatched in soil and climate for growing sugar cane. The Spanish had ignored this opportunity. Although they had been the first to plant cane in the islands, in their earliest years on Hispaniola, the lure of mainland riches had distracted them from the islands' potential. Hence it was the French, English, and Dutch who drew sweet profits from the Caribbean as they occupied, in the seventeenth century, islands undefended or readily abandoned by Spain. By the mid-1700s St Domingue (now Haiti) was by far the largest American sugar producer, followed by Brazil, then Jamaica. The leading Spanish source was Cuba, ranking eleventh in America, below Dutch Guiana, Guadaloupe, and Barbados. English and French colonies provided over 80 percent of European sugar imports.[18]

From the mid-1760s, however, Cuba grew more sugar, as the Bourbon monarchy sought to develop the island's possibilities. The aim, apart from a general effort to increase royal income from America, was to create wealth locally to pay for improved defense of the island. The need for this had been made quite clear by the British capture of Havana in the closing stages of the Seven Years War in 1762. Over the next three decades Cuba's sugar output increased two and a half times (from some 6,000,000 kilograms in 1760 to

15,000,000 in 1792). Puerto Rico also became a substantial grower. By 1792 Cuba was the third-largest American source, after Jamaica and Brazil. St Domingue had vanished from the ranking. The French Revolution inspired a slave rising there in 1791, whose effects reduced sugar exports from 74 million kilograms in 1791 to 24 million in 1804, and a mere 900 kilograms in 1825.[19]

The rise of agricultural exports from eastern regions of Spanish America was the most striking change to appear in the colonial economy in the eighteenth century. Many causes underlay it, perhaps least among them the Bourbon developmental intent and policies visible over the century. More telling were: improvement in the performance and capacity of ships, so that freight of bulky goods became effectively cheaper; the inevitable rise, both legal and illicit (in the Spanish view), of foreign commercial contact with the colonies, as Spain's power waned and that of European rivals, and latterly of the United States also, waxed; and, overriding all else, the growth of population and wealth in Western Europe, especially as industrialization and, with it, urbanization took hold in the closing decades of the century. There then emerged the massive First World appetite for the foodstuffs and raw materials produced on tropical and subtropical plantations that has been one of the motors of the world economy for two centuries past. Thus in Spanish America, though precious metals were still the major export in the aggregate, for the first time large regions lacking silver or gold found their prosperity and populations rising. And along with that material growth went first a growing sense of local identity and then of future political potential.

TRADE

The fact that much of the rising demand for the products of Spanish America's land came from outside Spain complicated one of the central aims of Bourbon reform for America, which was to recover control of the transatlantic trade for Spain. The problem was twofold. First was the matter of goods arriving in America in foreign holds, whether smuggled or under some legal dispensation. Second was the predominance, even in the official transatlantic commerce by fleets, of foreign goods (a predominance clear in the late seventeenth-century revival of the value, if not the volume, of the fleet trade). Neither difficulty had an easy answer. But the first was the less challenging of the two. Foreign ships could be excluded by law backed by force. Providing that force in the form of naval defense might be costly; but it was far less costly, and less demanding of profound economic innovation, than replacing alien goods with Spanish products. For that would require a wholesale modernization of Spanish manufacture, to match economies already well on the road to mechanized industry.

The foreign presence in the Indies trade, in the form of ships actually docking in American ports, was huge at the start of the Bourbon era. France's holding of the *asiento* from 1701 to 1713 vastly stimulated a French interest in the Spanish American trade already quite clear before 1700. Improvement in ships and navigation now permitted safe and regular passage of Cape Horn for the first time. French merchants took such quick and sure advantage of this that no less than 68 percent of Peru's foreign trade is thought to have been carried in French vessels between 1700 and 1725 (twelve years after the British acquisition of the *asiento* at Utrecht). French traders were equally active in New Spain from 1700 to 1710.[20]

Then, after Utrecht, the British also shouldered their way into the Indies' markets on a scale they had previously only dreamed of. Not only could the South Sea Company smuggle in goods on its slave ships, but additions to the Utrecht treaty permitted the dispatch of five hundred tonnes of goods in a ship accompanying any annual Spanish trading fleet bound for America. It was a concession that the British pressed hard, especially after discovering that Spain was unable to dispatch fleets on the official yearly schedule. From premises (*factorías*) that it was allowed to build at eight major colonial cities, including Buenos Aires, Havana, Portobelo, and Veracruz, the Company distributed not only slaves but British goods. Spanish officials estimated that by 1728 it was the conduit for a third of the contraband entering America. In the late 1750s, long after the *asiento*, if not the Company, had disappeared, the British were still smuggling goods vigorously into the Indies, to the tune, by Spanish calculation, of six million pesos a year.[21]

By that time, changes were in train in the working of the official American trade that were intended to make it more resistant to interlopers and more rewarding to Spain. These changes, to be sure, were peculiarly slow in coming. The sluggishness resulted, it seems, mainly from the strong conservative influence over the government held still by the merchant houses handling the Indies trade in southern Spain. Their value as a credit source for the crown, and their control over a commerce seen as vital to national interests, preserved their weight in Madrid.

Hostilities during the War of Succession reduced the fleet trade almost to nothing, completing the decline in official transatlantic shipping that marked the late seventeenth century. Reinvigoration of the fleets was the government's main hope for recuperation of the trade for several decades after the war. This approach, given the costly and clumsy rigidity of the structure, surely all too obvious from the successes of interlopers using single ships, seems a self-defeating policy. But pursued it was with energy. One sensible change, by contrast, was the removal of the *Casa de Contratación* in 1717 from Seville to Cadiz; though even this relocation of the official base of the trade was simply recognition of a real shift that had been taking place for decades, as the Guadalquivir silted up between Seville and the sea.

A new master design for the fleets, the "Plan for the Galleons and Fleets of Peru and New Spain" of 1720, laid down that a fleet for each destination should sail yearly, at specified dates. This, in the event, proved no more practicable in the eighteenth century than it had in the sixteenth, with the result that for two further decades the fleet system did no more than sputter along. Suggesting, however, that something had been learned from the contrabandists, the 1720 Plan also proposed the use of specially licensed single vessels to supplement the fleets, and especially to relieve any shortages of goods that might arise in particular places. To these "register ships," colonial ports on the Atlantic side of America were declared open.[22]

The combining of sporadic fleets with occasional register ships brought a slight increase in the tonnage of the *Carrera*, from some 9,000 of total shipping annually in the 1720s to 11,000 in the thirties and early forties. Over those same years, also, Spain built up a defensive presence in the Caribbean. This considerably annoyed the British, who came to view their habit of sailing where they pleased in that sea as a proprietary right. It was, reputedly, the Spanish interception of a ship commanded by one Captain Jenkins, and the cutting off of his ear in the subsequent skirmish, that sparked off the War of Jenkins' Ear in 1739. The conflict was in reality more generally about access to Spanish America's trade as Spain's naval forces in the Caribbean began to display some teeth. It merged into the War of Austrian Succession (1740–8). During the decade of fighting Spain gave further signs of recovered strength in the Caribbean, succumbing in some instances to massive British naval attacks, but beating off others, notably Admiral Vernon's assault on Cartagena in 1741.[23]

It was, too, with the end of the war in 1748 that a vigorous expansion of the legal trade began that lasted for forty years. By the early 1770s the annual transatlantic tonnage had risen to some 28,000. This largely consisted of register ships. During the war no fleets had sailed; and after it they were unable to meet the challenge of the increasingly well-established single ship trade. Indeed, no *galeones* went to the Isthmus after 1748; and in 1776 the last *flota* sailed to New Spain, only the fifth since 1748.[24]

Rather as in silver mining, where the bulk of Bourbon reform was applied after many decades of expansion, so in the Atlantic trade the administration finally in the 1760s and 1770s gave legal form to what had long been increasingly successful practice. A series of concessions, beginning in 1764, gradually opened up Spain's major ports to single ship trade with, first, destinations in the Caribbean, and then others on the periphery, and lastly in core areas, of the mainland. The reforms were finally condensed into what is, after the New Laws of 1542, the most famous legal code applied to America by Spain in colonial times: the "Regulations and Royal Tariffs for Free Trade between Spain and the Indies" of 1778.

The aim of the code was precisely to liberalize trade between Spain and America, while excluding foreigners. The "freedom" of trade proclaimed in the title was only an intra-Hispanic freedom. And as the inclusion of "tariffs" in the title suggests, even exchange between metropolis and colonies was not to be untaxed. Because another intent of the code was to bring about what Campillo y Cossío and others had long since advocated – that Spain should be the manufacturing center of the empire, and America the source of the raw materials to be processed – tariffs were now revised to favor the movement of American primary exports to Spain, and of Spanish manufactures to America. True, an accretion of petty taxes on the Indies trade was eliminated, leaving only customs duties and the sales tax in place. One broad purpose of the "Regulations," that of removing red tape hindering Spanish transatlantic exchange, was certainly achieved.

The 1778 law brought some gains for Spain, although rather briefly. It really did not take hold until 1782, toward the end of Spain's engagement, in alliance with France, against England in the War of American Independence. And its effect ended in 1797 when England, at war with a French–Spanish alliance, blockaded Cadiz and effectively cut Spanish contact with America. In the fifteen-year interim, however, Spain's exports to America rose, on an annual average, to four times their level in 1778. And the Spanish share of this expanded export grew: Spanish goods made up, on average, 52 percent of the value embarked, against 38 percent in 1778. More striking still was the rise of colonial exports to Spain. Their yearly average value rose more than ten times for the period, compared with 1778. The abundance of primary products now pouring from the land in Spanish America (tobacco, cacao, hides, sugar, cochineal, indigo, cascarilla, and others) were worth 44 percent of the total export, more than ever before; the rest was gold and silver.[25]

The greater increase in Spain's imports from America than in its exports to the colonies also suggests (Spanish re-exports being ignored) a rising metropolitan gain from the transatlantic trade. But, if the 1778 "Regulations" were apparently effective in raising the value, and Spain's share, of the trade, they fell short of other aims. Most of the rise in Spanish exports consisted of agricultural products of the sort traditionally shipped to America: wine, brandy, flour, olive oil, preserved fruits, nuts, and the like. Even the improved selling possibilites in America under the new trading regimen, therefore, failed to stimulate Spanish manufacture. The sole and clear exception was Catalonia. There, direct trading between Barcelona and American ports, legal now for the first time, quickened the growth of the already established mechanized production of textiles. Barcelona was the second ranking dispatcher of exports to Spanish America in the 1782–96 period. Its share, however, was only 10 percent of the total value. Cadiz still dominated the trade, with 76 percent of America-bound exports. There was, therefore, little redistribution of the export business among Spanish ports. Andalusia controlled still, as from the start.[26] And in Cadiz, foreign merchants still prospered, handling the transshipment of manufactures of varied European provenance to America.

The trading link with the colonies was an early, and then constant, target of Bourbon reformers for obvious enough reasons. The century had begun with commercial disaster for Spain in America as, during the War of Succession, foreigners enlarged their already majority share of the business. But at least, after the war, the commercial problems it had made particularly manifest could be partly tackled close at hand, in Spain itself, through an attempted renovation of the shipping system. Hence naval and trade reform was pursued energetically in the 1720s. A broader reason for the close attention given to colonial commerce was that increasing Spain's control and share of it seemed, in itself alone, an obvious and direct means of economic, indeed national, recuperation. Spain could thereby secure a larger share of America's economic product, even before policies to mold and expand the colonial economies were devised and applied. All in all, the final outcome was positive. For while it is likely that more could have been done, and more quickly, if the past (as represented, for example, in the fleet system) had been cast off sooner, nonetheless the Bourbons' reforms did finally expand Spain's share of exchange with America. And if set in prevailing economic circumstances, especially Spain's growing backwardness in technology and financial organization compared with the leading European economies, then those commercial measures may perhaps be seen as surprisingly successful, an example of what policy can achieve against the odds of reality.

BOURBON REVISIONS OF RULES AND PRINCIPLES

GOVERNMENT

Bourbon reformers also sought, naturally enough, to renovate government, both at home and overseas; they were fully aware that the imperial system would not yield the fiscal fruits so essential to general Spanish recuperation unless the gaps and slackness in colonial government obvious by the late 1600s were remedied. For several decades, however, Spain itself absorbed most of the energy and attention of ministers. With one large exception, revision of colonial administration was limited to what could be done at home; and the major body with American tasks there was the Council of the Indies. As part of a general streamlining of government pursued immediately after the War of Succession, most of the old Habsburg councils of state saw their powers and functions passed to individual secretaries. Government by committee, safe but inherently slow, was now replaced in effect by ministerial decision. Louis XIV's administration was the model followed here. Among the councils losing executive force, in matters financial, military, commercial and governmental, was that of the Indies. A Secretary of the Indies and Marine now exercised those powers, overseeing both the colonies and the transatlantic link with them. Of its former functions, the Council kept little more than those of giving advice and acting as a final court of appeal from American *audiencias*.

The one large reform in government made in America before the mid-century was the addition of a third viceroyalty, New Granada, to the two (New Spain and Peru) founded soon after the military conquest. This was first attempted in 1718–19, partly to remedy disorder and inefficiency in the *audiencia*, at Santa Fe de Bogotá, that had previously run the region; and partly to strengthen Spain's capacity to collect taxes in a colony where gold production was rising, and to hinder foreigners from smuggling that gold out across New Granada's Caribbean shores. That first attempt failed. The man chosen to be viceroy, Don Jorge de Villalonga, displayed a mixture of personal extravagance and incapacity to control contraband that in 1722–3 resulted not only his own removal but also the dropping of the entire viceregal scheme. Perhaps it was still simply too soon for the post-war administration in Spain to take on such a major innovation in America. Sixteen years later the viceroyalty was successfully recreated, for the same purposes, though now made more urgent by the threat of the war that would break out in 1739.[27]

No such delay interrupted the formation of the fourth, and final, viceroyalty of Spanish America, that of the Río de la Plata, in 1776–7. The motives for this creation were similar to those behind New Granada's: the rising economic and commercial weight of Buenos Aires and its hinterland, and leakage of trading profits to foreigners, in this case the Portuguese in Brazil. An important Portuguese trading base on the north shore of the La Plata estuary, Colônia do Sacramento, long a thorn in the Spanish side, was seized for once and for all in 1777 by the man sent out to be first viceroy, Pedro de Cevallos. Cevallos then took charge of a viceroyalty embodying major jurisdictional revisions in southern South America. Not only Paraguay came under his command, but also the *Audiencia* of Charcas, known in the eighteenth century as Upper Peru.[28] Charcas had hitherto been firmly under Lima's thumb. Its transfer into the new viceroyalty had, particularly, the telling economic effect of diverting from Lima to Buenos Aires the silver flowing overseas from Potosí, Oruro, and other mines. The merchants of Lima complained bitterly. But at last, after 230 years, economic rationality was achieved, as Charcas's silver was legally permitted to follow its most direct channel, southward over the plains of the Río de la Plata, into the Atlantic trading system.

By the time this new southern viceroyalty was formed, administrative change in America had been gathering momentum for some fifteen years. While stirrings of activity can be found before 1760, it was really the dire consequences of Spain's late participation in the Seven Years War (1756–63) that made reform in America seem an urgent necessity. In 1761–2, Charles III, a king too ready to try war as a means of foreign policy – in this case to weaken British presence in North America – allied Spain with France against Britain in that contest. He grossly underrated British strength, and the outcome was the reverse of his hopes, a fortifying rather than a sapping of the British presence in America. The Peace of Paris of 1763 passed Florida (previously Spanish) to Britain, western Louisiana (previously French) to Spain, and all other French territory in North America to Britain. Thus France, Spain's natural ally through the Bourbon tie, was ejected from the North American mainland; and Spain was left alone there to face a British presence more massively menacing than before. By comparison, Britain's easy capture of Havana and Manila in 1762 (both returned to Spain by the Treaty) was a minor blow, though certainly a clear display of how strong Britain was growing at sea.

So there now arose in Madrid a resolve to gird up loins, and, with respect to America, to cultivate and draw upon the colonies' wealth to an extent and with a degree of intentionality and design without precedent in either the Bourbon or the Habsburg eras. The increased yield of America would support both its own defense and Spain's military sallies in Europe. The trading reforms already in train and later drawn together in the "Regulations" of 1778 were one facet of this comprehensive intent; the stimuli applied to mining late in the century, another; the creation of the new southern viceroyalty, a third. But there was scarcely a place, person, or activity, however marginal, in Spanish American lands that remained untouched by at least some ripple of reform over the final third of the century.

The first step to making America more profitable was to gather current information about it. To this end, reliable officials were sent from Spain to carry out thorough inspections, or *visitas generales*, of the major areas; the bureaucracy in place was seen as inherently unreliable and hence incapable of full and trustworthy reporting. The first region so examined was New Spain, thoroughly scrutinized over six years (1765–71) by a man, José de Gálvez, who was to come to epitomize the reforming effort in America, especially on account of his term (1776–87) as Minister of the Indies in the final decade of his life. As Minister, Gálvez sent visitors in the late seventies to Peru (Juan Antonio de Areche) and New Granada (Juan Francisco Gutiérrez de Piñeres) to imitate his own data gathering and disciplining of government earlier in Mexico.

Gálvez was typical of many of Charles III's high administrators: a lawyer, though not one trained in the leading colleges of the ancient Spanish universities that had traditionally supplied such officials, but a provincial from a family without social distinction. Reliance on men made zealous by their lack of conventionally privileged background and training was one aspect of the centralization of power pursued by Charles, whose reign represents the Spanish monarchy's closest approach to absolutism. Gálvez himself came to show the opinionated impatience of the self-made man; some around him found him "personally aggressive, ill-tempered, and intolerant, a bigot in the age of Enlightenment."[29] One prejudice that served well his own and the crown's political aims was the scorn he developed in Mexico for the colonial white population. They, the creoles, he judged to be "of a quick humour and understanding, but superficial and unreliable in judgement, even though remarkably presumptuous . . . They are of little spirit, being timid and submissive."[30] This disdain of the colonies' social and economic elite was fully shared, and reinforced, by his appointees to senior posts in America.

The reformers' contempt for creoles fitted well with what was, from the Spanish standpoint, a change quite essential in American administration if it was to serve Spain's purposes well: the weakening of its American-born component. Chiefly through the purchase of judgeships permitted from 1687, creole *oidores* were by the 1760s a majority in several *audiencias*, notably those of Mexico City, Lima, and Santiago de Chile. Creole numbers were large also, of course, in other branches of American government. Sales had already ceased in the 1750s, but the heavy American presence was by then installed for decades. Among Gálvez's first acts as Minister of the Indies in 1776–7 was to enlarge the *audiencias* by adding thirty-four judgeships to them. Only two of those appointed were creoles. In the entire period 1751–1810, 266 appointments were made to the American high courts; 203 of them went to peninsular Spaniards, only 63 to creoles.[31]

The retaking of the *audiencias* from the creoles was the most dramatic piece of renovation in American administration performed by Gálvez, his subordinates, and his successors. Perhaps more important, though, was the broader policy of replacing the patchwork structure of American government, bequeathed to the first Bourbons by the Habsburgs, with an efficient and professional bureaucracy. This Gálvez and others achieved by establishing promotion patterns and paying adequate salaries. There were limits to their success, of course. The features of the old system could not be completely erased. Creoles remaining in it could, and did, through ageless means of bureaucratic obstructionism, counter threats to themselves. And indeed the bureaucracy as a whole, even in its renovated state, could resist changes that seemed too radical or menacing to its interests. This is among the prime reasons for the limited success of the largest innovation attempted in colonial government by the Bourbon reformers, the installation of a system of intendants.

Intendants were a new variety of regional governors, holding broad executive and judicial powers, and charged especially with developing local economic activities and extracting income from them for the crown. Their model was in officials of the same name and function in Louis XIV's France. They were used in Spain to good effect, in the crown's view, from the mid-eighteenth century. The first American intendant was placed experimentally in Cuba in 1764. Gálvez saw in this species of official the answer to the ossified disorder of American administration, and was the most powerful, even fanatical, advocate of its installation in America. During his tenure as Minister he placed intendants in La Plata, Peru, and New Spain. Only New Granada and Quito finally remained without them.

The purpose was to centralize authority through an executive structure parallel to, and indeed short-circuiting, the old one of viceroys, *audiencia* presidents, *gobernadores*, and lesser local officials. The intendants, resident in provincial towns (eight in Peru, twelve in Mexico, for example), were to report to the Minister through superintendants placed in the viceregal capitals. But the new structure failed, essentially because the traditional bureaucracy, notably the viceroys, resented and resisted such a blatant subtraction from its authority. Removal of the superintendants followed quickly on Gálvez's death in 1787; and with them went the new system's crucial link with Madrid. The intendants remained in place until the end of colonial times, gathering information useful to government, overseeing economic activities and tax collection, and in many cases modernizing their cities with lighting, new tree-lined avenues, and improved water supply and drains – fine practical stuff of the Enlightenment, of which many intendants were by education and inclination good agents. But a clean sweep of colonial administration they never were.

This undermining of Gálvez's design notwithstanding, the general tautening of administration that he and others before and after him accomplished, along with tax increases, the efficient use of royal monopolies, and the placing of new treasury offices in economically growing areas (notably in New Spain), produced the desired result. Royal income in the colonies rose. While the fiscal yield of almost all regions had grown from early in the eighteenth century, reflecting mainly a broad economic expansion, the rate of growth accelerated dramatically in the period 1760–80[32] as the new efforts to raise revenues took hold. New Spain was the star of the fiscal stage, as its notable demographic and productive growth (especially in mining) would give reason to suspect. Exactly how much the royal income did expand there, particularly from the 1780s, is still uncertain because the accounts are hard to interpret. But a cautious estimate is that the crown's receipts rose from some three million pesos annually in the century's early years to twenty million near its close. Other considered calculations suggest that the average yearly growth in royal income in Mexico for the whole century was 2.6 percent; with, however, an acceleration to 5–6 percent from the mid-1780s to 1800; and, remarkably, a further doubling of the yearly rate from then to 1810. Part of the rise in these late decades, which far surpassed economic and demographic growth, was the result of heavy borrowing by the treasury from individuals and institutions. This constituted a deeper tapping by the state of late colonial Mexican wealth than even the revised and expanded structure of taxes and monopolies could achieve. On the other hand, inflation increasingly undercut the value of fiscal income as the century wore on. By one estimate there was no real growth at all in royal receipts in New Spain between 1793 and 1810, even though the number of pesos gathered doubled.[33]

New Spain is reckoned to have yielded two-thirds of the crown's income in America in the 1700s.[34] Much of this cash, however, never entered the coffers in Madrid, for the rise of the cost of American defense that began in the seventeenth century only quickened in the eighteenth. Raising funds for local defense was, of course, precisely one of the aims of reform, particularly from the 1760s onward. The fiscal yield of New Granada, for instance, grew strongly after the 1750s through the success of the royal monopolies on tobacco and *aguardiente* (brandy), and with the direct collection, rather than farming, of the sales tax. But with rising defense costs on the Caribbean coast and other administrative charges, it was only in the 1790s that New Granada had royal funds, and modest sums at that, to send to Spain. In Lima, from 1750 to 1800, 40 percent of treasury income went to defense; very little remained for remittance to Spain. Having a much larger income, the Mexico City treasury could dispatch more, and more consistently, to the peninsula. But Mexico carried the defense costs not only of its own coasts and its vast northern frontier, but also of the Philippines and parts of the Spanish Caribbean. Given the size of what needed to be defended and administered, it is testimony to the efficacy of the reforms that the American colonies, led by New Spain, were able to supply, in direct remittances, 15–25 percent of the crown's income in Spain in the closing decades of the eighteenth century.[35] And to this contribution should be added a variable, but often large, amount collected at Cadiz in taxes on the transatlantic trade and in fees, fines, and loans deriving from America.[36]

For one Councillor of the Indies in 1804, the colonies had become "those lands from which we seek to extract the juice."[37] The crudity of the comment perhaps reflects Spain's desperate fiscal state by that date, enmeshed as the country was in the Napoleonic conflicts; but the phrase was no more than a plain statement of the prime aim of Bourbon policy toward America, formulated before the mid-eighteenth century and applied mostly after then. The Habsburgs too, of course, had wanted to draw wealth from America, and had done so successfully, particularly in the time of Philip II and Philip III. But, partly through difference of imperial concept, and partly through force of circumstance, Habsburg exactions had seemed less severe. The prevailing notion before 1700 that the peninsular and American "realms" were united only in their subservience to the monarchy obscured the contrast of status between metropolis and colony. In principle, colonials served and supported the personal monarch rather than the abstract transatlantic state. And in practice, they viewed themselves to some extent in that light. Besides that, the rise of creole wealth and presence in American government made the final century of Habsburg rule a matter of politicized negotiation with colonials rather than of command. Further yet, Spain's preoccupation with internal problems in the seventeenth century caused her governing of America to become more a process of reaction than of proposal.

All this the Bourbon regimes sought to reverse. For planners instructed in the orderly ways of the Enlightenment, the American realms were to be treated more as a unit than as discrete and idiosyncratic territories. Their part, as that unit in the empire, was above all to support the imperial state. To the extent that reality allowed, they were all to be subject to the same broad schemes of development, taxation, and control: creoles excluded from administration, intendants inserted into it, new taxes and tariffs uniformly imposed. The rules and ethos of empire thus changed radically between the late seventeenth and the late eighteenth centuries.[38]

CHURCH AND STATE

Clearly displaying the new Bourbon manner was the monarchy's attitude to the church after the mid-century. For Charles III and his ministers the church was to be the servant of the state; serving, moreover, strictly within its own spiritual and pastoral sphere. To this extent, the older, indeed ancient, notion, preserved under the Habsburgs, of church as the partner with monarchy in governance (though in the Spanish case, a well controlled partner) was now eroded. The monarchy still certainly saw the church as its ally; but as an ally with its own set of separate tasks, fighting on a different, spiritual, front.

In this desire to restrain the church lay little anti-religious feeling. The portions of the Enlightenment that Spain imported barely included free-thinking. Rather, the motive for change was the regalism typical of the absolutist monarchies of the day. In the Spanish case, that desire to assert the monarch's supremacy in ecclesiastical affairs was combined with the highly practical notion that while the church's wealth in land and other property on the one hand tended to deflect ecclesiastics from their proper spiritual duties, on the other that wealth could serve the crown's fiscal needs very nicely.

With one exception, however, appropriation of ecclesiastical property did not begin until the century's end. Before then, the crown worked to control the clergy and reform it in the direction of zeal and spirituality. For both, an essential tool was a Concordat negotiated with Rome in 1753, granting to Spanish rulers essentially the same powers of nomination of clerical candidates in Spain as had been conceded for Granada and Spanish America around 1500. Some fifty thousand benefices in Spain, including bishoprics, now came under royal control; Rome's political influence in Spain and its ability to siphon money from the Spanish church were reduced. Gaining on both these counts, the monarchy saw the added authority won in Spain through the Concordat as an almost revolutionary advance.[39] Over the following decades, control over appointments brought into authority in Spain many bishops supportive of the crown's desire for a leaner, purer, politically detached church.

In America change on this scale was not possible, as the crown had already long controlled appointments through the Royal Patronage. There the main tool chosen for renovation was the convoking of provincial councils, the first, indeed, since the late sixteenth century. These gathered in the sees of archbishops (Mexico City, Lima, La Plata, and Santa Fe) in the early- to mid-seventies. Perhaps because the American church had undergone no organizational upheaval comparable to what Spanish clerics had experienced, these assemblies of bishops and parish priests showed small inclination to reform themselves. The councils achieved little. Through direct royal decree, however, the American clergy suffered curtailment of their legal privileges (right to trial by church courts, for example) and of other longstanding powers (for instance, the offering of asylum). Broadly speaking, the colonial clergy became more amenable to royal command.[40]

A loud warning shot across the colonial church's bows, fired by the crown early in the reform effort, doubtless contributed to this deference. In 1767 the Society of Jesus was expelled from the Spanish empire, as it was from Spain itself. In decreeing the expulsion, Charles III was in some degree following the example of rulers in Portugal and France, who in 1759 and 1764 had done the same in their realms. The Jesuits were suffering, broadly speaking, the effects of energetic regalism in Europe, where monarchs determined to take centralized control of their states were suspicious of what seemed an autonomous, secretive, international society. The distrust resembled in some degree the feelings sometimes inspired in smaller nations today by the presence of multinational corporations. To those organizations, in fact, the Society had some remarkable likenesses. The Jesuits' special allegiance to the papacy simply reinforced the distaste they inspired in rulers.

In America, the Society's efforts and achievements laid it open, in a time of political centralization, to suspicion and even charges of subversion. Its control of large mission areas (particularly eastern Paraguay, viewed by authorities as almost a state within a state), its possession of many prosperous *haciendas*, and its operation of most of the best schools and universities in the colonies, combined to make it the target of both the crown's distrust and envy. It supervised the education of many creoles; thousands of Indians lived under its tutelage; it was rich. "That pest," Charles III called it. In Spain its autonomy was not so obvious, but it was still seen as sapping the monarchy's power. There, with minimal justification, the Jesuits were accused in 1766 of fomenting popular riots in Madrid, troubles produced in part by the high price of bread, and probably whipped up by conservative nobles opposed to current reformism.[41] The expulsion followed a few months later. From Spain itself some 2,800 Jesuits were banished; and from America, 2,200, among them many creoles. The loss in dedicated missionaries, hard-working estate managers, and educated teachers was far more damaging than the numbers would suggest.

In the year after the expulsion, the crown called the rest of the regular clergy to order. It remained more elusive of the king's influence than secular clerics, as it had been in the sixteenth century. And indeed in what seems a replaying of Philip II's campaign to control the regulars precisely two centuries earlier, the crown in 1768 called on friars in America to restore their communal monastic life, fulfill their vows of poverty, abandon commerce, and study assiduously. They were, furthermore, bidden to "inspire in those most faithful vassals, as a fundamental maxim of Christianity, respect and love for the Sovereign, and obedience of the Ministers who in His Majesty's royal name rule and govern those provinces."[42]

The estates and other possessions of the Jesuits in Spain and America passed to the crown after the expulsion. Most were sold at auction over the next forty years. This was the first large seizure of church property by the Bourbon reformers. The next did not come until 1798, during times of fiscal crisis caused by war with Great Britain. Charles IV then ordered the disentailment and auction of various sorts of church-related property in Spain. The former owners were to receive 3 percent interest on the amounts raised, which sums went into a fund intended to repay, or consolidate, earlier loans the crown had received for war costs. Against those loans had been issued bonds, called *vales reales*. By 1808 about a sixth of church property in Spain had been disentailed.[43]

Fiscal conditions worsening, from 1804 part of the American church's property, its *obras pías*, was seized for the same purpose of consolidating the *vales reales*. These "pious works" were in fact large cash funds containing centuries' worth of donations by the faithful for the creation of chantries, chaplaincies, and the like. The funds had soon come to function as sources of loans, credit banks in effect, for colonials. Thus this category of church wealth now consisted largely of outstanding loans rather than land, buildings, or even cash. When, therefore, in 1804 the crown ordered the expropriation of *obras pías* in America, economic damage extended far beyond the church into civil society. For many of those who had taken loans from the *obras* funds were forced to sell real property to repay them; and widespread simultaneous selling depressed prices. The Consolidation decree of 1804 thus caused widespread bitterness in America, especially in New Spain, where it was more thoroughly applied than elsewhere. By late 1808 New Spain had yielded some 10.2 million pesos on this account; Peru, by contrast, produced only 1.2 million. In that year, the decree was canceled.[44]

Bourbon regalism thus drew on the physical resources of the church in America after having tried to renew the clergy's spiritual energy as well for better service of the state's ends. That attempt to create a church militant in the royal service had limited success, especially once the leaders in spiritual militancy, the Jesuits, considered too active to be safe, had been cast out. But the crown did at least achieve a "church compliant."

MILITARIZATION

The reformers were, on the other hand, more successful in raising the level of conventional militancy in the colonies; though the process of creating a useful and reliable armed presence in vast regions that had lacked one for two centuries was inevitably slow and difficult. From the start, the Bourbon regime had a more military cast than the Habsburg. Except for Navarre, those Spanish provinces that had been governed by viceroys came, with Philip V, under the control of captains-general. These officials also presided over regional *audiencias*, so that jurisdiction at the highest level was under strong military influence.[45] Then came from the 1720s the effective restoration of Spanish naval presence in the Atlantic, and in the mid-century an expansion of land forces also. Rising military presence in the Indies followed from the lessons learned in the Seven Years War. By 1771 some 43,000 troops were supposedly in place in Spanish America (doubtless many were there only on paper), mostly in garrisons in and around the Caribbean. Fear of internal disorder as well as a repetition of the foreign assaults inflicted during the war was, though, an impetus to expand the ranks. In New Spain, for example, substantial protests in 1766 in Guanajuato against new excise taxes, and then in 1767 about the expulsion of the Jesuits (into whose splendid church the city's wealthy had recently put much money, and the poor much work), were met by Gálvez, then visitor general, with hangings and multiple imprisonments. Then, to control "the perpetual disturbances and scandalous unruliness which the populace have maintained for so many years," he formed a new militia regiment with men from Guanajuato and nearby towns as well as a quasi-military police force for street patrols.[46]

Militias of Americans, rather than regular army units of Spaniards, inevitably became the majority of the growing soldiery henceforth. Only a few and, it was hoped, exemplary troops could be spared for America from Spain, given the home country's many European engagements in the late eighteenth century. And those men went preferentially to the exposed Caribbean garrisons rather than to the mainland. Nor could the colonial treasuries, even that of Mexico, fund the import of troops. Hence, local militias must do the job. But raising them was fraught with problems. As popular risings had suggested, and continued to suggest, it was potentially dangerous to arm the colonial poor. Governors hesitated particularly to give weapons to Indians and those with any degree of black origin, the latter always feared as possible trouble makers. On the other hand, the *castas* resisted being drafted and disciplined; desertion was rife. Hence creating substantial and reliable militia units was a slow affair. Numbers given in reports exaggerated effective forces.[47]

If, though, the mixed-blooded rank and file were hard to hold, there was no lack of creoles anxious for commissions. In the century's closing years, especially in the Andes, the motive in some was a conservative desire to help suppress further social disturbance. But improved status seems to have been the most general aim. One visitor to Venezuela at the turn of the century remarked of the rich creoles: "At present they seek an epaulette with as much avidity as they did formerly the tonsure." Of Peru, the most renowned traveler of Spanish America in its final colonial years, Alexander von Humboldt, noted: "It is not the military spirit of the nation but the vanity of a small number of families...that has nourished the militia in the Spanish colonies...It is amazing to see, even in the small provincial towns, all the businessmen transformed into colonels, captains, and *sargentos mayores*." Commissions could be bought. Rich white colonials spent heavily on them, thereby helping to support military growth in the colonies. By the decade 1800–9, creoles were 60 percent of the officer corps (including cadets and sergeants) in Spanish America, up from about 34 percent in the period 1740–69. Almost all other officers were peninsular Spaniards.[48]

Creoles, then, could assuage their frustration over exclusion from the higher bureaucracy by gaining a commission, a uniform, a title of rank. Allowing, even encouraging, this martial self-expression of creoles was, however, a dangerous policy for the crown. Selling army positions was just as foolish a short-term expedient as the sale of administrative office had been a century before. For though this apparently frivolous embrace of the military life by creoles betokens no particular rise of American praetorianism before 1800, nevertheless the outcome was that from 1810 many creoles found themselves suddenly transformed from salon soldiers into real men at arms. Most, initially, fought for the monarchy against revolutionary insurgents; a very few chose the independence cause from the start. But with time, growing numbers changed side, until royal armies in America found themselves at war with forces of independence led, in many instances, by creoles whom Bourbon reform had first drawn into the military life, and whose true martial abilities had been revealed, then honed, by combat on Spain's side. Reformers who had worried over arming the poor might reasonably have been expected to be equally cautious about creating the basis of a creole officer corps.

SOCIETY: CHANGE AND PROTEST

CREOLES, MESTIZOS AND OTHERS

If Spanish administrators saw creoles as acceptable soldiers but unacceptable bureaucrats, that was simply one instance of the mutability of white colonials' existence in the eighteenth century. Their numbers certainly rose. Despite the rarity of censuses until the late 1700s, there is little doubt that creole populations maintained a growth, strong in most regions, that had begun long before. Between 1646 and 1774, for example, the number of *vecinos*, or white householders, in eleven provincial Mexico cities (excluding Mexico City itself) grew eightfold, from 2,690 to 28,288. Assuming six people on average in each family, these urban Whites, most of them creoles, increased from some 16,000 to about 170,000. A more complete comparison can be made between the mid-1740s, when creoles were about 9 percent of the total Mexican population, and *c*.1803, when they were 18–20 percent of it. (Both percentages included some mestizos counted as white.) In the first decade of the nineteenth century, New Spain held some 5–6 million people altogether; hence in the final colonial years creoles numbered a million or more. New Spain's prosperity in the eighteenth century had favored their increase. Elsewhere, though multiplying, creoles were fewer. In the central Andes, for

FIGURE 12.1   The Metropolitan Cathedral of Mexico City. (© Tony Morrison, South American Pictures.)

FIGURE 12.2   The Capilla de los Reyes (Chapel of the Kings), in the Metropolitan Cathedral of Mexico City. (© Tony Morrison, South American Pictures.)

FIGURE 12.3   The Cathedral of San Luis Potosí, in north-eastern Mexico.

FIGURE 12.4   The façade of the Cathedral of Zacatecas, in mid-northern Mexico.

FIGURE 12.5   A country church near Bolaños, in western Mexico.

FIGURE 12.6   The tiled façade of the church of San Francisco, at Acatepec, near Puebla, in central Mexico.

FIGURE 12.7 Detail of the façade of San Francisco, Acatepec.

FIGURE 12.8 The high altar of the church of Santa María, at Tonantzintla, near Puebla, in central Mexico.

FIGURE 12.9   The Santuario de la Virgen (Sanctuary of the Virgin), at Ocotlán, near Tlaxcala, in central Mexico.

FIGURE 12.10   The central portal of the church of San Lorenzo, Potosí, Bolivia.

FIGURE 12.11 The façade of La Compañía, or Jesuit church, in Quito, Ecuador.

FIGURE 12.12 The gilded altar of La Compañía, Quito, Ecuador.

FIGURE 12.13 (*facing page, top*) The wooden parish church of Yaguarón, near Asunción, Paraguay.

FIGURE 12.14 (*facing page, bottom*) Yaguarón, interior view. Note the painted imitation of spiralling on the square columns.

FIGURE 12.15   Chapel of the Third Order of Saint Francis at São João del Rei, Brazil, by O Aleijadinho.

instance, eight major cities (including Lima) experienced a rise of only 1.4 percent in their number of *vecinos* between 1628 and 1764. A census of Peru in 1792 found a total population of 1,076,122. Of these, 13 percent, about 140,000, were "Spaniards" (that is, either creoles or peninsular Spaniards, these being in a small minority). The rising export zones of eastern South America, by contrast, though having smaller populations by far than New Spain, equaled or passed it in demographic growth. The city of Buenos Aires, for example, quadrupled in size between 1740 and 1776 (from some 5,000 to 20,000 inhabitants). Since in 1778 three-quarters of the population of the Río de la Plata basin was white, mostly American-born, creole numbers were clearly rising fast there.[49]

With these increases, the American-born part of the colonial white population further enlarged its long-standing majority. Migration from Spain to America was smaller in the eighteenth century than in the previous two, at about 53,000. Most of these people crossed the Atlantic in the later decades, attracted by economic growth. For that reason a disproportionate number went to New Spain. But even there the peninsular population *c.*1800 was no more than 15,000, outnumbered sixty-fold or more by creoles. In Peru, with fewer Spanish immigrants, creoles were probably similarly dominant, though censuses did not count them separately from the peninsular-born.[50]

Creoles, then, increasingly outnumbered Spaniards in America, while, from the 1760s, becoming ever more the object of at least official Spanish scorn. They found themselves assailed also from below, by the lower, and largest, segments of colonial society. This, first, was the outcome of the full ripening of the processes of ethnic mixing in the eighteenth century. Summarily stated, the number of mixed-blooded people was now rising exponentially, most of them the offspring not of two individuals of a particular ethnic identity, but rather of parents who were already of mixed origins. Hence in early nineteenth-century New Spain, by one estimate, mixed people were 22 percent of the total, against 18 and 60 percent respectively for Whites and Indians. (The mixed category here includes Blacks, but they were a small part of it.) The Peruvian census of 1792 showed 27 percent mixed (again including Blacks), against 13 and 56 percent White and Indian. In the two old central zones, therefore, Whites (very largely creoles) were now simply outnumbered not only by American natives but also by the mixed-blooded.

With mixing rampant, ever more of its products could not be securely or easily placed in any definite socio-ethnic category. A sign of the difficulty is seen in various series of paintings of *castas* done in eighteenth-century Mexico. The pictures typically show families of three, with each parent of a particular basic identity or mixture, and their offspring of yet another mixture. Indian and Black engender a *zambo*, for example; White and mestiza produce a *castizo* ("well bred," but not quite white). In their striving after subtle categorization, these paintings may seem relics of a medieval mentality; or perhaps the painters sought to entertain as they spun out the possible mixtures to baroque excess.[51] But in the everyday world such distinctions were not, and could not, be used. Genetics working as it does, a mestizo father, say, and a *mulata* mother might produce children varying in appearance anywhere within the bounds of a Black–Indian–White triangle. Appearance was thus a poor guide to parentage, and so the attempt to make fine ethnic distinctions from looks alone could only fail.

For purposes of social ranking, color and physiognomy still mattered, of course, as they do to this day in Latin America. But, increasingly, they could be overridden by other, acquired, traits. An Indian who spoke Spanish, and adopted the dress and short haircut typical of a mestizo, might well be generally reckoned mestizo. If he worked in a town at some task typical of mestizos, such as petty trade or a craft, rather than as a rural peasant farmer, he would almost certainly be so considered. Conversely, someone who was known to be of definitely mestizo parentage, but who married an Indian and lived among Indians, might for those reasons be considered, and even legally defined, as Indian.[52] Thus arose, and continued to strengthen, a partially cultural definition of ethnicity.

There were, it is true, limits to this "passing" from one attributed identity to another. An ethnic Indian who dressed as finely as a viceroy and who lived in a large house around the corner from the viceregal palace would not thereby be whitened, or generally be thought to belong to the gentility (unless he descended from the ancient native nobility, and the higher the better). Nor would a White ever be thought Indian or Black, no matter how like them he or she might behave. But a poor White, living by manual labor as an artisan, a small farmer, or a servant, might well be taken for a mestizo. And in the eighteenth century the number of such poor Whites rose.[53]

The lower border of white colonial society became increasingly frayed in the eighteenth century, as the mestizo population grew (and grew faster even than the white element). The fraying was exacerbated by the persistent influence of wealth on status; or rather the generalization of that influence now from Whites to other sorts of people. With the growing difficulty of locating individuals socially by their looks, the part played by what they could buy – housing, clothing, food – in indicating their status also expanded. Beyond this some general shift from honor to wealth as the prime source of status, perhaps in distant accord with the pragmatic spirit of the age of Enlightenment, may have been under way. Such, at least, has been proposed for eighteenth-century New Spain.[54] In any case, the easier accessibility of social standing now made available by money to *castas* as well as Whites inspired in leading creole families a strong desire to maintain their social superiority. (The fact that very few such families were completely free of mixture in their past can only have sharpened that desire.) One means of doing so was to acquire titles of nobility, for which they showed a keen appetite. The Bourbons greatly expanded the issue of American titles; and Charles III was the most generous of the Bourbons with them, granting twenty-three to New Spain alone during his three decades on the throne. The marquisates and countships were not sold, but awarded for notable service, mostly either military or economic. Hence rich mining entrepreneurs were rewarded for their success (and particularly, no doubt, for the cascade of silver into the treasury that resulted from it). Titles went both to creoles and to Spaniards living in America. But as many of the Spaniards founded families, or married into creole families, most of the titles remained there. In 1790 forty-nine titled nobles graced Lima alone. New Spain, between 1810 and 1820, had fifty-four titled families.[55]

CHALLENGE AND REBELLION

It was not merely a sense of creeping invasion of their social space from below that worried the white, very largely creole, population of the late colonies. Their unease had more palpable causes in the rising unrest visible at the lower end of society in the eighteenth century. To be sure, the previous century had not been wholly free of such troubles. The mountains of north-west Mexico, for example, were always a center of native resistance to missionary intrusion and economic burdens (specifically the demand for mining labor), and liable to ignite in revolt, as the Tarahumara Indians demonstrated several times in the late seventeenth century. Further north still, in 1680 the Pueblo Indians finally reacted to almost a century of unregulated pressures from settlers and evangelizing Franciscans by ousting them all from New Mexico for a dozen years. Such risings were, however, comfortably far from the heartland of New Spain. Right on high creole society's doorstep, by contrast, was the very noisy *tumulto* of June 8, 1692 in Mexico City. A mob of Indians and assorted *castas* invaded the main square and set fire to the viceregal palace, the town hall, and nearby shops. The central cause of this was a shortage and consequent high price of wheat and maize, resulting from excessive rains in the summer of 1691, followed by blight in the crops later in the year. The viceregal administration actually tried hard to remedy the scarcity with grain imports from other Mexican regions; but the efforts fell short, giving rise to resentment against a government popularly thought to have failed in its duty to the public good and to have refused to heed justified complaints. The riot was, then, an expression of suffering, with loud overtones of anti-governmental sentiment. The administration heard these, and, alarmed, reacted with harsh punishments, including several executions.[56]

Mexico City suffered no repeat of this eruption, however, in the eighteenth century, despite several episodes of crop failure, rising maize prices, and subsequent outbreak of disease.[57] In fact, central and most of southern Mexico were free of large risings, either urban or rural, in the 1700s. On the other hand, protest in native villages rumbled in the background throughout the century. In areas partly embraced by the present states of Oaxaca, Puebla, Hidalgo, and México, at least 142 minor revolts flared up between 1680 and 1811. What is surprising about these risings is that they remained local. They were, it seems, simply the product of specific grievances in individual native communities: a new *corregidor* who raised taxes, a priest who raised his fees for baptism, marriage, and burial, authorities who pushed up labor demands, or, particularly, violated what the village thought its rights of self-government. The fact that these sparks, generally fleeting, failed to ignite any larger fire suggests that there was not much tinder of broad resentment across the central and southern Mexican countryside in the eighteenth century. Native villagers apparently tolerated the colonial order as they found it, objecting violently only to what seemed unreasonable and unusual demands newly thrust on them. The colonial authorities, for their part, worked to preserve this *modus vivendi*, negotiating, and punishing only leaders rather than the whole community; and them, leniently. Only in the time of Gálvez's inspection of New Spain in the late 1760s did punishment grow fiercer (as, for example, in the suppression of scattered protests at the expulsion of the Jesuits); and that is hardly surprising, given Gálvez's authoritarian bent.[58]

Limited in physical range as these village risings were, however, they were common enough to provide, in the fear and mistrust of Indians they inspired among Whites, a rural parallel to the anxiety aroused in town dwellers by the growing crowds of *castas*. And if such worries became widespread in New Spain in the eighteenth century, creoles and peninsulars living in South America had far graver cause for concern.

The central Andes were the scene of as many risings in the eighteenth century as in southern and central Mexico; with the difference, however, that a few of the Andean movements became regional affairs that made the upper reaches of society more than merely nervous. These wider spread Andean revolts were often the work of mestizos as much as of Indians. That, indeed, is a strong reason for their extension: they were not limited to the insular concerns of single native communities. An early, if minor, example was the mestizo-led rising in Cochabamba, spreading to the neighboring province of Oruro, that took place late in 1730. This seems to have been a reaction to a new population count, made by order of the Peruvian viceroy of the late 1720s, the Marqués de Castelfuerte, for the purpose of upwardly revising assessments of tribute and forced labor levies. To that end, since mestizos were exempt from tribute and forced labor, some attempt to reclassify them as Indians was made. This naturally raised hackles, and an armed rising that led to the death of a government official was the outcome. Again, in Oruro itself in 1739, objections at all social levels to tax increases led to a planned rising including not merely mestizos and Indians, but creoles as well. In fact, the leader was a creole – and this shows how malleable ethnicity had become by the eighteenth century – who asserted his descent from the Incas and planned to be crowned as Andean ruler at Cuzco, the ancient Inca capital. The plan was indeed for a joint creole, mestizo and Indian fighting effort against the Spanish.

The Oruro plan has been described as "the first genuine rebel programme of the eighteenth century" in the Andes, and one that may have served as model for later movements, including the mighty shaking of the colonial order that Túpac Amaru II aroused in southern Peru four decades later.[59] What is new in it is, first, a sense of a multiethnic Andean unity reacting to attempts to impose change by outside forces, specifically the imperial government represented by the viceroy on the Peruvian coast. The blending of creole, Indian, mestizo, and other *castas* in at least some of these Andean movements distinguishes them from contemporaneous rebellions in New Spain. Second, the Oruro plan of 1739 brings out the messianic streak common in the Andean plots and risings, the theme of a restoration of Incaic rule that will rescue all those suffering under colonial oppression. There is little hint in eighteenth-century Mexican risings of any comparable vision of salvation through renewal of, say, Aztec power. The greater physical isolation of native peoples in the Andes, favoring maintenance of memories, may account for some of the contrast.[60]

Andean messianism soon became vividly clear in a more fully Indian, but still multiethnic, movement that arose on the forested inland slopes, or *montaña*, of the central Peruvian Andes in 1742. Its leader was a man named Juan Santos Atahualpa, who claimed descent from the Atahualpa captured and killed by Francisco Pizarro in 1532–3. Juan Santos titled himself *Apu-Inca*, or "Inca Lord." He was a mestizo, Jesuit-educated, who viewed the world as properly divided into three kingdoms – Spaniards in Spain, Africans in Africa, and God's "children the Indians and mestizos" in America.[61] His own contribution to realizing this schema was to begin in the eastern Andean forests, spread to the highlands, and end in his crowning as a new Inca ruler in Lima. The blending here of Incaic restoration with the reality of colonial rule (acknowledgment, in a concept completely alien to the Incas, that power in Peru emanated from a coastal city) is most striking.

In the event Santos Atahualpa had limited success. To the Spaniards' great frustration, he was able to repel four military expeditions sent in the 1740s to defeat him in the *montaña*; and he indeed achieved a long-lasting reversal of Spanish mission penetration of that zone of forested foothills. But in the highlands themselves he managed to gain only a brief and tenuous foothold on their eastern rim in 1752. On the other hand, the simple persistence of his movement away in the east may well have encouraged several other highland plots and risings in the mid-century. Notable among these was one in 1750 at Huarochirí, a region directly inland from the capital. This was, in fact, the continuation of a scheme devised by Indians living in Lima to destroy Spanish authority in the city by killing all officials, and, indeed, all Spaniards except priests. News of the plot got out, and it was suppressed. But its extension to Huarochirí over several weeks brought the death of most of the Spaniards in that province.[62]

Thus the Andes of what is now Peru and northern Bolivia became in the eighteenth century a seedbed for local revolt and broad sedition. The mountains, like those of north-western Mexico, but on a far larger scale, were ideal ground for this, their ruggedness as always blocking events from Spanish view, hindering attempts at control, and providing refuge for schemers. A crucial distinction from Mexico was that here the mountains stood close to the main centers of Spanish power and white population on the coast. The political menace they embraced was thus near to home. From the mid-century the rate of insurrection (mostly, it is true, minor) quickened: 1750–9, thirteen events; 1760–9, sixteen; 1770–9, thirty-one; 1780 alone, twenty-two; 1781, fourteen (including the start of Túpac Amaru's revolt in November). The pace increased in New Spain, also, but less than in the Andes.[63]

The rising rebelliousness of both regions reflected the ever heavier fiscal pressure that the Bourbon monarchy applied to the colonies after the mid-century. The greater unruliness of the Andes was probably the expression of lesser capacity to meet the crown's demands. Economic expansion there was slighter and later in starting than in New Spain, in part because the post-conquest recovery of the native Andean population had lagged behind that of Mexico. Growing tax loads therefore weighed more heavily on the Andean population; and did so to the extent, indeed, that not only Indians, but also mestizos, and even some creoles, were driven to protest. Native people, however, were certainly those who suffered most. They were the poorest; they alone paid tribute to the crown; and they alone were subject to a form of forced subsidizing of the administrative and commercial system known as the *reparto de comercio*.

Reparto simply meant the forced sale of goods to Indians by local governors. During the seventeenth century *corregidores* and *alcaldes mayores* had slipped into the habit of supplementing their salaries by using their authority to force the Indians under their control to buy various sorts of goods. Indeed, they often became monopoly suppliers by keeping other sellers out of their jurisdictions, and so controlled the selling price. The goods in question might be American products, such as mules or everyday cloths, or imported items for which few Indians had any desire or need. In time supply networks developed between merchants in the colonial capitals and the local governors, so that the merchants' livelihood came also to depend in part on the *reparto* system. The practice became more abusive of Indians in the 1720s, when the crown, still striving for economies after the War of Succession, stopped paying salaries to most *corregidores* and *alcaldes mayores* in America. The *reparto* then became these local officials' prime source of income. It even received the crown's legal license in the 1750s, though by then its abuses were well known, having been famously condemned in a report on affairs in the province of Quito written in the 1730s by two visiting officers of the Spanish navy. They, Jorge Juan and Antonio de Ulloa, found it a "system ... so cruelly wicked that it appears as if it were imposed on those people as a punishment," and declared that "A more tyrannical abuse could not be imagined."[64] The *reparto* inspired the same objection in Gálvez during his long inspection of New Spain thirty years later. His hostility to it was one source of his almost fanatical advocacy of the intendant system of local government during his decade as Minister of the Indies. Intendants and subdelegates (district officers within the intendancies) were to replace the previous local governors, and to receive salaries that would obviate the need for exactions like forced sales. In reality, late eighteenth-century attempts to uproot the *reparto* revealed it as less than wholly pernicious in its nature and effects; by then, though inherently exploitative of Indians, it brought supplies of some goods to remote places that other trading links could or would not reach. For this and other reasons it was never eradicated.

Still, for most native people most of the time, *reparto* was no small part of the multiple burden of support of the colonial state that they carried: headtax, formal forced labor, *reparto*, and the illicit labor demanded by both local officials and parish priests. The legalization of *reparto* in the mid-eighteenth century seems to have made that particular piece of the load more irksome, especially for the relatively poor Andean natives; and for that reason legalization may have contributed to the surge of local rebellion after the 1750s.[65]

The great Peruvian storm of the early eighties, however, while drawing energy from this native discontent, became large and regional because it embodied the anger of mestizos and creoles as well as Indians. Resentment rose rapidly in the seventies as the full flood of Charles III's reformism struck Peru, and especially after José Antonio de Areche, a man of the same rigid cast as his master, Gálvez, arrived as general inspector in 1777. Among the changes were these: increases in the general sales tax (*alcabala*) rate from 2 to 4 percent in 1772, and to 6 percent in 1776; fuller collection of the *alcabala*, by the treasury rather than by tax farmers; the imposition of a 12.5 percent tax on brandy (*aguardiente*) in 1777; application of the 6 percent *alcabala* to coca in 1779; establishment of customs houses in several major towns, to collect duties on internal trade; and in 1780 a royal command, intended to simplify tax gathering, that all artisans must belong to a guild.[66] These measures struck hard at many small and middling economic interests – mestizo and creole craftsmen, traders, muleteers, and small farmers. The customs houses were a particular target of ire; local revolts often followed their creation. The tax on brandy affected the same groups; that on coca, mostly Indians, who were the main chewers of the leaf.

In November 1780 began the most conspicuous reaction to this tightening of the fiscal screws, indeed what is now the most renowned revolt in the Spanish empire's entire history. Its leader was a mestizo named José Gabriel Condorcanqui, a *curaca* and landowner from the Cuzco district who claimed direct descent from the Incas. During the 1770s he sought formal recognition of this claim by the Spanish, and also pursued a Spanish title of marquis. Late in the decade he joined in the rising resistance to Spanish demands, finally taking the Inca name Túpac Amaru ("Royal Serpent" in Quechua) in intentional evocation of the last Inca noble, of the same name, to hold out against the Spanish in the sixteenth century. After his capture in 1572, that first Royal Serpent was executed at Cuzco by order of Viceroy Toledo. He remains to this day a powerful symbol of native resistance to European invasion.

The rising led by the second Túpac Amaru began at the native town of Tinta, in the south of Cuzco province, on November 4, 1780, with the seizure and execution of the local *corregidor*. This man, one Antonio Arriaga, was a notorious abuser of the *reparto* system, and was therefore an exemplary victim. In early December the rising turned south, to the area around Lake Titicaca; and then, late in the month, north again toward Cuzco, which Túpac Amaru briefly and unsuccessfully besieged in early January 1781. Another southward thrust followed, with an attempt, again fruitless, to drive the Spanish from the important trade center of Puno on the western shore of Titicaca. By then, however, the government in Lima had been able to send a large military force to the rebel area. Túpac Amaru was captured and, in May 1781, executed along with close relatives who had also been leaders of the rising. He then was drawn and quartered.

The revolt was remarkably violent, with much loss of life. It produced also much sacking of property, such as *haciendas* and *obrajes*, that belonged not to Indians but to creoles and mestizos. This destructiveness quickly deprived Túpac Amaru of most of his non-native support; most of the initial leadership had been mestizo, and there were creoles at first willing to back the rising in the hope of reducing the state's impositions on them. They were perhaps reassured by Túpac Amaru's early proclamations that he was acting in the king's interests, indeed at the king's orders, in ridding Peru of bad governors. There is here, as in many colonial risings, an element of the often-cited cry "Viva el rey y muera el mal gobierno" – "Long live the king and death to bad government" – implying a separation between the monarch and his agents, and a sincere belief that a just king could intend no harm to his subjects.

But the movement was sapped also by complex political and ethnic currents among the native population of southern Peru and northern Charcas.[67] Túpac Amaru, as a rural *curaca*, failed to gain the support of the old Indian nobility, sure also of its Inca origins, of Cuzco itself. Indeed, some of those noble *cuzqueño* families helped the Spaniards to suppress the rising. His self-proclamation as a restored Inca (late in 1780 he had himself and his wife portrayed in a painting as Inca king and queen), while fully in the now strong tradition of millenarian recreation of Inca rule, alienated those greater lineages. And adding to the weakening effect of disharmony among the Quechua-speakers of central and southern Peru was the ancient antagonism between them as a whole and the Aymará-speaking groups around Lake Titicaca and south of it. These, in the mid-fifteenth century, had been brought into the Inca state by force; the Spanish conquest had freed them from that domination. And though now, three centuries later, they had common grievances with the Inca descendants against the Spanish, a full and easy alliance was not possible. An Aymará rising had indeed begun in Chayanta, in present northern Bolivia, in 1777, led by one Tomás Katari, whose followers also saw in him a messiah. After Katari's capture and execution in January 1781, leadership of his movement passed to another Aymará speaker, who styled himself, like Túpac Amaru, "Royal Serpent" ("Túpac Katari" in that language). There was a strained alliance between Quechuas and Aymarás in a siege of La Paz, from March to October, 1781, that was Túpac Katari's most severe challenge to Spanish control. That investment was finally no more successful than the earlier attacks on Cuzco and Puno, although it briefly shook Spanish, and creole, confidence to the roots.

The Aymará movement ended shortly after the relief of La Paz by crown forces in October 1781. The Spanish captured Túpac Katari, perhaps with Quechua help. Túpac Amaru's followers continued to be active well after their leader's death, as the siege of La Paz shows. They finally made peace with the colonial government in January 1782, although aftershocks of the rising continued to ripple through the center and south for months after that.

The troubles of 1780–2 in southern Peru and northern Bolivia have been called a civil war. Certainly their violence and their cost in lives (possibly 100,000) justify placing them in that particularly bloody class of conflict;[68] as does the significance of their outcome. In the short term, the reaction of the colonial regime, led by Gálvez, to the conflict, once the leaders were punished, was to meet various of the rebels' demands. An *audiencia* was created in Cuzco in 1787–8, to provide the highland people with faster access to justice. Local government by *corregidores* was abolished and thereby, it was hoped, the *reparto* system also eliminated. (The hope was vain. The subdelegates within the intendant system, which was applied to Peru in 1784, perpetuated *reparto* for their profit.)[69] But it was the longer-term outcomes that were most telling for the course of central Andean, and particularly Peruvian, history. The war laid bare contrasts in mentality and material interest between natives and most of the rest of highland (and lowland) society. While many mestizos and even some creoles living in the mountains had been drawn into the Inca restoration current so clearly in evidence by the mid-eighteenth century, in its fully developed form that movement grew disquietingly extreme. It became messianic not only in the broad sense of Inca revival, but also in a narrower Christian frame, as, for example, Indian followers of Túpac Amaru began to view him literally as a redeemer who could raise the dead.[70] Although this fusing of Indian and Christian spiritual elements is wholly typical of native religion throughout colonial Spanish America, it was also, for conventional Catholics, heretical. But still more alienating of creoles, mestizos and other non-Indians was the destruction of lives and property that the war brought. Once the genie of native militancy had been unbottled, it was not, evidently, easily to be restrained or recaptured. The resulting fearful distrust of native Andeans broke up the multiethnic highland unity that was emerging by the mid-century; made most Peruvians chary of political movement and change for the rest of colonial times; and deepened an existing hiatus in Peru between coast and mountains that still impedes the country's progress today.

If never on the Peruvian scale, most of Spain's other South American colonies experienced growing internal disturbance after the 1750s. The city of Quito, for instance, was shaken through much of 1765 by violent opposition from mestizos and Indians, backed by much of the white upper crust of the city, including some clergy, to a broad sharpening of Spanish fiscal tools begun c.1760. This has been identified as the first large rising in America provoked by Charles III's reformism, though it did not spread outside the city of Quito.[71]

A later movement, similar in its temporary conjoining of all social ranks, but far wider in geographical range, was that of the *comuneros* of New Granada in 1781. From March to June of that year a large region of the eastern range of the Andes north of Santa Fe de Bogotá effervesced with hostility to tightening of the fiscal screws. Higher and better-collected *alcabala*, and the installation of royal monopolies on tobacco and *aguardiente*, which meant loss of profit to local growers and higher prices for local consumers, were the sorest points. In what was becoming a pattern, serious trouble started when a reforming visitor general, in this case Gutiérrez de Piñeres, enforced the new *alcabala* measures in March 1781. The focus of resistance was Socorro, a small town some 200 kilometers north of Santa Fe. Peasants there found the town's creole leaders, prosperous land owners in the main, quite willing to support the protest, disaffected as they were not only by fiscal demands but also more gravely by a sense that the crown's reformers were invading a political and social domain that they had long considered theirs alone. Inserting the state into places where it had rarely been a more than distant reality was, certainly, an aim of Bourbon reformism. That, precisely, was one of the purposes of the intendant system. In early May 1781, a large *comunero* force overwhelmed soldiers sent out from Santa Fe to suppress the protests. Later in the month 15,000–20,000 *comuneros* assembled to threaten Santa Fe; whereupon the authorities in the capital, notably the archbishop and the *audiencia*, decided that negotiation was the better part of valor. With the rebellion spreading into neighboring lowlands, the officials gave in on June 7 to most of the protesters' demands. Among these were the departure of the visitor general; a promise that no such officer should be sent again to New Granada; preferential appointment of creoles to administrative posts at all levels; reduction of tribute and *alcabala* rates; and abolition of the royal monopolies on tobacco and playing cards. All this, and more, the archbishop and judges conceded. The viceroy, who had been absent throughout on the Caribbean coast attending to its defense, later confirmed the agreement, and granted a general pardon.[72]

Like the Quito episode and the Túpac Amaru rebellion before it, and many other smaller movements, the *comunero* eruption in New Granada was above all a call for reversal of intrusive and exploitative change, rather than an attempt to destroy the system that had imposed that change. Although some historians in the countries concerned have liked to find early bids for national independence in these movements, they were not that. In that respect, the large South American insurrections and the local Mexican village risings of the eighteenth century have similarities. They aimed first to recover a status quo that familiarity had made tolerable. (Onto that basic purpose, certainly, radicals in Peru and Charcas grafted a desire to restore ancient, native government in the highlands. But that was far from a call to establish an independent Peruvian or Bolivian state.)

What is intriguing, indeed, about the New Granadan rising is its implicit appeal to an earlier political condition that was specifically colonial. In their public pronouncements, the *comuneros'* leaders referred repeatedly to the good of the *común*, the social community; hence the movement's name. And although upper class sympathy with Indians and *castas* must seem opportunistic (and indeed usually evaporated at the first outburst of destructive violence), nonetheless those references to the *común* were more than mere rhetoric. For they suggest a memory of the corporate, organic and hierarchical model of society implicit in the earlier Habsburg organization of the empire; and of the underlying notion that, although differences of wealth and status were in the nature of a hierarchical society, the common good was the final concern of the ruler. It was to what they saw as neglect of, or assault on, that common good that the *comunero* leaders objected in 1781. They had a sense, not perhaps conscious, of the degree to which Bourbon reformism after 1760 was attacking the deepest social and political assumptions that had underlain the empire for its first two hundred and fifty years.[73]

CREOLE SELF-AWARENESS: REJECTION AND RECEPTION OF EUROPE

Even though creole *comuneros* were, then, essentially conservative, in the sense of looking back fondly on an earlier mode of colonial existence, at the same time their dismay over the assault on that way of being in the late eighteenth century clearly implied danger for the Bourbon state. For the moment, they, like many other creoles elsewhere in America, might join with activists lower in society in blaming supposedly perverse agents of the monarchy, rather than the crown itself, for injuries received and the ills of the society around them. They would look on approvingly as rioters still shouted "Viva el rey" while sacking a customs house. But each new departure from the old model inevitably brought them closer to a political stance from which some of them would blame the Bourbon monarchy, and not merely its officials, for the losses and problems they perceived.

Such a political shift among creoles was encouraged also by their growing self-awareness. Spanish officialdom's disdain of them was one cause of this. A second source lay in the opinions of America and its inhabitants published by several European writers engaged in gathering knowledge of the natural world, and categorizing it in accord with the Enlightenment's desire for orderly patterns. America fared badly in these efforts. Prominent *philosophes* tended to abandon scientific rigor, indeed common sense, when attempting to rank it among the world's regions. Thus the Dutch writer Cornelius de Pauw, drawing on a climatic determinism advanced by others, found that the American tropics had produced, in the native population, a "degenerate species of humanity," and, in creoles, people given to indolence and vice. Georges-Louis Leclerc Buffon, eminent naturalist as he was, held that America was both geologically young and excessively wet and swampy; with the result, he sagely opined, that America's fauna were fewer and smaller than those of the Old World (save its snakes, lizards and insects). With few exceptions, American native people were also the feeble product of the same pernicious environment. In arriving at these conclusions, de Pauw, Buffon, and several similarly minded confrères twisted or simply threw out abundant contravening evidence.[74]

Creoles' reaction was twofold. They first sought refutations in America's Nature and in the reality of its pre-conquest and colonial history. Among the most forceful of writers in this line were creole Jesuits in European exile after the Society's departure from the empire in 1767. These were men personally familiar with the regions they described. They were also, ironically enough, well equipped mentally with the new rationalism to argue their case; for the Jesuits had been the chief importers and teachers in Spanish America of the science and mathematics of the seventeenth and eighteenth centuries. It was simple for them to show the falsity of European assertions about American natives, flora and fauna. The most complete of these refutations came from a Mexican exile in Italy, Francisco Javier de Clavijero, who produced in 1780–1 an *Ancient History of Mexico*, exalting a high culture that in his view began with the Toltecs in the sixth century after Christ and ended with the Aztecs. Clavijero also described the positive qualities, physical and mental, of present Mexican native people (while not denying their faults); and demonstrated, through an account of the geographical variety of New Spain, the absurdity of Europeans' gross generalizations about America's climate and landforms. But most striking was his praise of the politics, culture, rationality, and morals of the pre-contact cultures, which were comparable with Greece and Rome.[75] Clavijero here picked up threads first spun by the likes of Las Casas and, later, Sigüenza y Góngora. His work was a notable advance along the path, leading to the present, of incorporation of the pre-conquest cultures into Mexican national identity and consciousness. A further step in this process came in the 1790s, when Antonio de León y Gama, an official in the Mexico City *Audiencia* as well as mathematician, astronomer, and antiquary, published a study of two large Aztec carvings just found under the city's main plaza. These were two pieces that have come to stand as no others for the grandeur and complexity of the pre-conquest high cultures: the earth goddess Coatlicue, represented as a composite in stone of skulls, detached hands, and interwoven rattlesnakes; and the "Calendar Stone", a symbolic depiction of the five "suns," or ages, of the pre-conquest history of central Mexico.[76]

The creoles' second response to criticisms of America and its inhabitants was to collect and publish new knowledge of their continent's physical and human reality. Here the true spirit of the Enlightenment was a help, its concern with methodical accuracy a useful impetus for enquiry. Creoles had learned the new science from the Jesuits. They had also read widely among Enlightenment authors, most of whose work reached Spanish America with minimal censorship, either civil or ecclesiastical, until almost the end of the century. In New Spain, then, creoles published information on the geography, climate, plants and animals, economic resources and productive capacity of the territory in journals founded from the 1780s on. In Lima, the journal entitled *El Mercurio Peruano* carried the same range of data, among them the first year-by-year record of Potosí's silver production from the mid-1500s. In New Granada, Quito, Chile, and Buenos Aires the same spirit of practical inquiry arose. The outcome of this close attention to local conditions went beyond mere contradiction of European distortions of America, to produce among creoles a strengthening sense of regional identity and loyalty. Thus in the late eighteenth century there emerged a definite "creole patriotism" in Spain's colonies. The Mexican *Gaceta de Literatura* printed the phrase "our Hispanic American nation" as early as 1788.[77] Over the next two decades growing numbers of creoles came to share the sentiment contained in those words.

As their reactions to the Enlightenment suggest, creoles' intellectual awareness expanded in the eighteenth century. Whereas Spain had long been the natural point of reference, now, with the arrival first of the new science and then of a wider range of innovative thinking and writing, much of the rest of western Europe began to loom larger on creoles' mental horizons. Much contributed to this shift: Spain's political subsidence in the western world, set against the rise on every front of human activity of France and Britain; the intrinsic allure of the new thinking, in its rationalism and even its inherent secularism; late in the century, practical demonstration of the Enlightenment's political possibilities in North American independence and the French Revolution. Creole receptivity was not always and wholly welcoming, of course. Given the deep roots of Catholicism in Spanish America, secularism dismayed far more white colonials than it attracted. And the French Revolution, particularly after its American manifestation in a notably destructive slave revolt in Haiti in 1791, had the effect of purging all but the most radically inclined creoles of admiration for wholesale political innovation. Nonetheless, the creoles – native-born leaders of their several colonial societies – by the early nineteenth century had come to look on Britain, Germany, and particularly France as the prime sources of intellectual innovation and cultural creativity in the widest sense. This esteem of the European has continued in Spanish America, with the hesitations caused by the resentment that admiration can engender, down to the present. Added to the list of models, from the late nineteenth century, has been the United States.

The arrival of non-Hispanic European currents in the empire is clearly shown also in the music and art of the eighteenth century. In 1701 came the first known performance of an opera in Spanish America, *La púrpura de la rosa* (*The Purple of the Rose*), put on to celebrate the eighteenth birthday of the new king, Philip V. The libretto was by Pedro Calderón de la Barca, some would say the most profound dramatist of Spain's cultural Golden Age in the seventeenth century; and the score by Tomás de Torrejón y Velasco, a Spaniard who was chapelmaster at Lima cathedral from 1676 to 1728. But opera as a musical form was an Italian invention of the late sixteenth and seventeenth centuries, and its arrival in the colonies therefore marks a rising internationalization of taste in Spanish America. The first operatic performance in Mexico City (and indeed in North America) came ten years later, with *La Partenope*, written by the noted Italian librettist Silvio Stampiglia and scored by Manuel de Zumaya, a Mexican-born composer who later became chapelmaster of the cathedrals of Mexico City and Oaxaca.[78] The Italian influence in Spanish American music remained strong for the rest of the eighteenth century, partly in reflection of the esteem which Italian composers and players commanded at court in Spain. Local composers, both American-and Spanish-born, tended to follow Italian forms and styles. In Peru, the Milanese Roque Ceruti was a dominant force in music from his arrival in Lima in 1708 until his death in 1760. A comparable figure in New Spain was Ignacio Jerusalem y Stella, from Lecce in Italy, who was chapelmaster in Mexico City from 1749 to his death twenty years later. Even the remotest provinces felt the Italian musical touch. Domenico Zipoli (1688–1726), first a Jesuit church organist in Rome, spent the final decade of his life at the Society's house in Córdoba, in present Argentina. There he wrote liturgical music in a fully baroque style that Jesuits in the field carried to missions in Paraguay and Chiquitos (an area roughly corresponding with the Chaco of present north-western Paraguay). Not only did the Chiquitos Indians readily take to this music, but, having carefully recopied it over the years, still perform it today for the annual feast of Saint Ignatius of Loyola.[79]

In painting, sculpture, and architecture, the baroque prevailed for most of the eighteenth century, with continued development of the regional variations that had arisen earlier. Touches of rococo lightness appear here and there within the baroque. The two noted mestizo sculptors of eighteenth-century Quito, for example, Bernardo de Legarda (*d.* 1773) and Manuel Chilí (known as Caspicara), achieved this delicacy of touch: Legarda in his swaying "dancing Virgin" figurines of the Madonna, and Caspicara in a variety of gently done religious images from very late in the century.[80] In New Spain, the rococo is exemplified in architecture in the delicate façade of the Sanctuary of the Virgin at Ocotlán (1745), near Puebla, where slender bases veneered with red-orange tiles support "two lacy sculptured belfries, shining in the whitest whitewash."[81] Elsewhere, however, the urge to decorate surfaces so typical of the Spanish American baroque could yield a grandiosity that is far from rococo. The altar and reredos (1718–43) of the Chapel of the Kings in the Mexico City cathedral, for instance, form a massive gilded assemblage of architectural elements and vegetation-like decoration almost concealing a minor multitude of polychromed figures. In this "ultra-baroque" agglomeration the contours of the structure dissolve; the intent is apparently to submerge the viewer in a many-dimensioned opulence.[82] Rather more organized, and more powerful yet, is the stone façade (1752) of the parish church, and later cathedral, of Zacatecas in northern Mexico. Here it seems that the architect decided to offer to all and sundry passing by in the street the spectacle of a reredos taken to the baroque extreme. Into a display, over twenty meters high from pavement to pediment, of three orders of solomonic columns sharply carved with twisting grape vines, shells, and caryatides are inserted Christ and the Apostles, the four Fathers of the Church, and, presiding, God the Father set amidst angels with musical instruments.[83]

From the 1770s, and especially in the major cities, some reaction to baroque floridity appeared. Those creoles who were now busily absorbing European tastes turned from what they found provincial and popular. At the same time, the imperial administration sought to modernize and impose uniformity on public places in America. The aim was to impress on colonials the state's physical presence among them. Austere sobriety was the dominant note in the change. An early example was the new mint (Casa de Moneda) at Potosí, which, when finished in the 1770s, was among the largest secular structures in Spanish South America.[84] The façade has the bare simplicity of Spanish sixteenth-century building. Aversion to the baroque, however, typically took the form of neo-classicism, a then ascendant style in Europe that was carried across the Atlantic mainly by migrant Spanish artists and architects. Another Casa de Moneda of the late eighteenth century, that of Santiago in Chile, is a clear instance of the new stylistic preference. Its success in symbolizing authority is suggested by the fact that in republican Chile it has served as the country's presidential palace. Santiago also received a new neo-classical cathedral, as did Santa Fe de Bogotá. In New Spain the cathedral at Puebla was adorned with an imposing neo-classical baldachuin. Its designer, Manuel Tolsá, a sculptor and architect from Valencia in Spain, was the first director of sculpture at the new school of fine arts, the Academia de San Carlos, that Charles III founded in Mexico City in 1785 to stimulate artistic revival in Spain's richest colony. Tolsá left several lasting marks on Mexico City: the royally instituted School of Mines (built 1797–1813), the final portions of the towers and dome of the cathedral, and an equestrian statue of Charles III's son and successor, Charles IV (1788–1808), modeled on that of Marcus Aurelius on the Capitoline in Rome. The statue was the centerpiece of a renovation (the same reworking as uncovered the Aztec "Calendar Stone" and sculpture of Coatlicue) of the Plaza Mayor that another Spanish-born member of the Academia de San Carlos, Antonio Velázquez, oversaw in the early 1790s. The main architectural feature of the renewed plaza was a large elliptical balustrade, broken by four imposing iron gates, enclosing and isolating the king's statue. The effect was one of formal solemnity.[85]

THE EIGHTEENTH-CENTURY BALANCE

Tolsá's statue of Charles IV is long gone now from the main plaza, demoted to a more modest square nearby. With perhaps affectionate irony, present Mexicans call it "El Caballito," the "Little Horse," passing over the fustian presence of the tunic-clad, laurel-crowned monarch astride the animal's back. Well may they do so. For in hindsight there is truly a touch of absurdity in the representation of Spain's late colonial authority by the figure of Charles IV – a notably incompetent and inattentive king in whose reign Spain subsided into a mire of debilitating warfare that helped to precipitate the American empire's demise; and whose rule ended in ignominious abdication when France, under Napoleon, invaded Spain early in 1808.

It was in Charles IV's time, the last decade of the eighteenth century and the first of the nineteenth, that Spain reaped the richest gains from the reforms applied to America by his grandfather, Philip V, his uncle, Ferdinand VI, and particularly his father, Charles III. In the limited sense of producing more revenue for use in Europe and America, the wide innovations in taxation, officialdom, and territorial and administrative organization executed under the Bourbon kings were successful reform. For colonials of all social ranks, however, and above all for the growing creole population that was becoming the political nation of Spanish America, the aim of the changes seemed to be as much deformation as reformation.

Broadly speaking, by the early 1700s, Spanish America seemed set on a self-directed course, if not toward anything that could yet be called progress or development, at least toward creating an autonomous identity of its own. Abetting this process was the constitutionally equal standing of the individual colonies with the Iberian kingdoms (the Habsburg monarchy comprising discrete realms, such as Castile, Aragon, New Spain, Peru, Quito, and so on). This equivalence, admittedly legalistic but no mere fiction, was in practice increasingly undermined by the Bourbons as the eighteenth century advanced. Concrete aspects of Spanish American selfhood plainly visible by the early eighteenth century included: the rapidly growing mestizo population; a multiplying creole population which, through what was in essence long and informal negotiation with Habsburg administrators, had achieved a marked degree of political and administrative self-determination; wide freedom of access to foreign products both within the formal working of the *Carrera de Indias* and outside it through contraband; and development of internal trade among and within colonies.

With various aspects of this selfhood the Bourbons proceeded to meddle, more or less effectively, at different times and places after 1700. There was the attempt made in the late twenties in Peru, for purposes of raising tribute yields, to push at least some mestizos into the category of Indian. This was clearly an overambitious enterprise, flying in the face not merely of individuals' economic interests but also of biology; and it was not repeated or extended. But forty years or so later the assault on creoles' high influence in their own governing was a different story; and the assault expanded into an attack on their intellectual and moral capacity. At the same time, a large degree of *de facto* freedom of trade was being replaced by a so-called free trade operating strictly within the empire that was intended to subordinate the colonies more fully than ever to Spain's economic gain. And the economic interests of many, high and low in colonial societies, suffered as taxes grew in rate and application, as internal customs houses proliferated, and as royal monopolies expanded, all stifling the local and interprovincial trading that supported innumerable creoles and *castas* by the late eighteenth century. To this list of Bourbon distortions of the emerging Spanish American identity might be added measures to secularize the church (particularly as exemplified in the expulsion of the Jesuits, among whom were many creoles), and the reinsertion of a military strain into societies whose martial element had notably withered once the conquests were over in the sixteenth century.

Not all changes were unwelcome, of course. Most town dwellers benefited from the practical improvements in streets, lighting and water supply that many intendants brought to their provincial capitals. Those same intendants were a conduit by which new knowledge and ideas reached colonials, mostly creoles, living deep in the American interior. Almost all creoles were finally thankful for the presence of military forces that suppressed ructions in the lower reaches of society. But these were small compensations for the Bourbons' impositions on, and exactions from, America. Soon enough the costs of that imbalance would become clear.

PART V

PORTUGAL IN AMERICA

CHRONOLOGY OF PART V

1494   Treaty of Tordesillas

1497–9   First Portuguese voyage to India around south of Africa, led by Vasco da Gama

1500   Pedro Alvares Cabral, commanding second Portuguese fleet bound for India, touches on coast of Brazil

1501–2   Portuguese exploration of Brazilian coast

1504   First French ship on Brazilian coast

1516   Fortified Portuguese trading post founded at Pernambuco; first indication of sugar cultivation in Brazil

1532   Settlement at São Vicente by Martim Afonso de Sousa; settlement also inland, at Piratininga

Mid–1530s   Brazil divided into captaincies

1538   Probable date of first shipment of African slaves to Brazil

1548–9   Tomé de Sousa appointed and installed as governor general of Brazil; foundation of town of Salvador (Bahia) as capital; arrival of Jesuits; appointment of first *ouvidor geral*

1555–67   French colony of "Antarctic France" at Rio de Janeiro

1557–72   Governorship of Mem de Sá

1560s   First serious epidemics of Old World diseases in Brazil

1570   Indians declared free by Sebastião, king of Portugal

1578   Death of King Sebastião at Alcácer Quibir

1580–1640   Portugal and its empire under Spanish rule

c.1600   Beginning of slave-raiding *bandeiras* from São Paulo

1606   Founding of first Brazilian *relação*, at Salvador

c.1610   Three-roller sugar mill introduced into Brazil

1615   French finally driven away from Brazil

1621   Maranhão declared a separate "state" of Portuguese America. Dutch West India Company founded

1630   Dutch capture of Recife: beginning of Dutch occupation of north east Brazil

1637–9   Expedition of Pedro Teixeira from northern Brazil to Quito and back: Brazil's boundary extended far westward

1637–44   Brazilian administration of Johan Maurits van Nassau-Siegen

1640   Portuguese revolt against Spanish rule

c.1640   Beginning of large-scale sugar planting in non-Spanish Caribbean islands

1649   General Brazil Trading Company founded

1650–1700   Large inland movement of cattle

1654   Dutch leave Brazil

1661   Revolt of citizens of São Luís against Jesuits

1669   Fortress built at São José de Rio Negro, at confluence of Negro and Solimões rivers

Mid–1690s   Gold found in Minas Gerais

1703   Methuen Treaty

1720   Captaincy of Minas Gerais created. Abolition of General Brazil Trading Company. Chief executive in Brazil henceforth termed viceroy

1720s   Diamonds found in Minas Gerais

1724   Founding of the Academy of the Forgotten (*Academia Brasílica dos Esquecidos*) at Salvador, first of several Brazilian intellectual academies of the the eighteenth century

1744   Captaincy of Goiás created

1748   Captaincy of Mato Grosso created

1752   *Relação* of Rio de Janeiro created

1755   Lisbon earthquake. Beginning of the reform program of the Marquis of Pombal: creation of Board of Trade, and of Pará and Maranhão Company

1756–63 Seven Years War

1759   Creation of Pernambuco and Paraíba Company. Jesuits expelled from Portuguese territories

1763   Capital of Brazil shifted from Salvador to Rio de Janeiro

1775–83 War of American Independence

1777   Fall of Pombal

1778   Treaty of San Ildefonso, fixing southern boundaries of Brazil

1791   Slave revolt in Saint Domingue

FURTHER READING FOR PART V

Bradford E. Burns, *A History of Brazil*, has much on the colonial period. For a native account, if brief, José Honório Rodrigues, *Brasil: período colonial*. The multiple works of C. R. Boxer remain eminently readable: *The Portuguese Seaborne Empire, 1415–1825*; *Salvador de Sá and the Struggle for Brazil and Angola, 1602–86*; *The Dutch in Brazil, 1624–1654*, *The Golden Age of Brazil, 1695–1750*; *Race Relations in the Portuguese Colonial Empire, 1415–1825* (Clarendon Press, Oxford, 1963). To these should be added the works of Stuart B. Schwartz, notably *Sovereignty and Society in Colonial Brazil. The High Court of Bahia and its Judges, 1609–1751*, and *Sugar Plantations in the Formation of Brazilian Society. Bahia, 1550–1835*; those of A. J. R. Russell-Wood: *Fidalgos and Philanthropists. The Santa Casa da Misericórdia of Bahia, 1550–1755* (Macmillan, London, 1968), and (as editor), *From Colony to Nation. Essays on the Independence of Brazil*; and Kenneth R. Maxwell, *Conflicts and Conspiracies. Brazil and Portugal, 1750–1808* (Cambridge University Press, Cambridge, 1973). For the eighteenth century, especially, see Caio Prado, Junior, *The Colonial Background of Modern Brazil*.

[13] COLONIAL BRAZIL: SLAVES, SUGAR, AND GOLD

EXPLORERS, INTERLOPERS, AND SETTLERS

Brazil is today by far the largest Latin American country. At 8.5 million square kilometers, it is not much smaller than Canada and the continental USA (respectively 9.9 and 9.4 million square kilometers). But its beginning was quite modest. And indeed the very existence of this large nation, the greatest concentration of Portuguese speakers in the world, has in its origins a certain air of chance. For in 1494, the year in which Spain and Portugal concluded the Treaty of Tordesillas, dividing the western hemisphere between them into separate zones of exploration, influence, and commerce, the geography of the western Atlantic shores was all but unknown. There was therefore no suspicion in that year that the placement of the line of demarcation 370 leagues west of the Cape Verde Islands would give Portugal territory in America. That realization did not come until exploration of the South American coast revealed how far eastward the land extended. Then it became clear that the Tordesillas line sliced off for Portugal all of South America to the east of the mouth of the Amazon.

Even when the first Portuguese touched on the coast of Brazil, in 1500, they did not realize that they had reached a part of the American mainland. In that year, the second Portuguese fleet bound for India (the first had been Vasco da Gama's of 1497–9) swung far westward in the Atlantic en route to the Cape of Good Hope, propelled, so it seems, more by winds and currents than by any exploratory intent. The ships came upon the Brazilian coast at about 16 degrees south, and there rested for a week. The fleet's commander, Pedro Alvares Cabral, took the discovery for another island, to be added to the Azores, Madeira, and the Cape Verdes in Portugal's collection of Atlantic island colonies. He named the discovery "Island of the True Cross."

The island notion was soon dispelled. An exploratory flotilla sent from Lisbon in 1501 reconnoitered most of the eastern coast of Brazil. One outcome of this voyage was the permanent, if highly debatable, naming of the emerging continent; for in the Portuguese caravels sailed a Florentine explorer, merchant, and chronicler named Amerigo Vespucci, who in 1499 had already surveyed much of the north coast of Brazil. Vespucci's reporting, or rather the publication in Florence of inflated accounts based on it, led within a few years to the attachment of "America" to what in justice should bear Columbus's name.[1]

The exploration of 1501–2 revealed the enormous length of the new coast, but found little else to engage the Portuguese attention, with the striking exception of abundant wood yielding a red dye. Doubtless some remembered that the first salable product of Madeira had been a red dyewood. So vivid a colour did the American wood (*Caesalpinia echinata*) give that it suggested to the Portuguese glowing coals – *brasas*. And after these the land soon came to be named (or so the most appealing etymology of "Brasil" would have it). For the next four decades, Brazil wood was the main economic attraction for the Portuguese in this portion of South America that the fortune of Tordesillas had bestowed on them. The crown immediately set up a royal dyewood monopoly, and then secured an income from it by licensing private traders to obtain logs from Indians and sell them in Europe.

It was not only the Portuguese who came to load logs. From 1504, when a French ship happened on the Brazilian coast, merchants from several northern French ports made every effort to profit from the strong European demand for good red dyes. Competition between Portuguese and French for dyewood quickly grew into general hostility at sea, with each seizing the other's ships where possible. The presence of French shipping on the Brazilian coast was also a threat, in Portuguese eyes, to the safety of the fleets returning from India around the south of Africa. Hence some form of defense of the Brazilian coast was needed. In 1516 came the first royally directed attempt at this, with the dispatch to Brazil of coastguard ships, and the founding at Pernambuco, at the top of the eastern coastline, of a fortified factory, or trading post.

This was not enough to deter the French. In the 1520s French corsairs plagued Portuguese shipping not merely along the Brazilian coast but during the Atlantic crossing as well, taking perhaps twenty Portuguese vessels a year on average throughout the decade.[2] Behind the French persistence was not just the pursuit of profit, but also practical expression of resentment at their legal exclusion from America. The exclusion was in part the outcome of the Spanish and Portuguese agreement at Tordesillas to divide the non-European world between them. But underlying that agreement was the papal approval of such a division, which rested in turn on the late-medieval doctrine that popes possessed temporal powers over the entire globe. There were, by the early sixteenth century, theologians who regarded that doctrine with suspicion; in Spain itself Francisco de Vitoria publicly challenged it in the 1530s. And France, clearly for practical as well as theoretical reasons, joined the critics. Brazil offered an irresistible opening for a real test of the doctrine. It was easier to reach than the Spanish American territories, ensconced as they were in the Caribbean, or lying beyond it. And Portugal, poorer in money and men than Spain, was a less dangerous adversary than its large Iberian neighbor.

COASTAL SETTLEMENT

The Portuguese, then, for the rest of the century, and indeed early into the next, found themselves continually obliged to swat at Frenchmen buzzing around this or that site on Brazil's vast coastline. The English became a smaller nuisance of the same sort late in the century, and on the north coast for some decades thereafter. There was, in truth, only one means of securing the coast, and Portugal's claim to Brazil, from such meddling, and that was to root settlements there. Portugal set about this in earnest in the 1530s.

Up to that time, with the exception of the factory at Pernambuco, which proved short-lived, and a few other royal factories, about which almost nothing is known, built as collection points for dyewood, settlement of Brazil was unplanned and minimal. Most of the Portuguese in Brazil in the first three decades were deserters, castaways, survivors of shipwrecks, and convicts (known as *degredados*) exiled from Portugal. These were all men. Some of them, from choice or necessity, took to living among Indians, sometimes becoming leaders of the natives' small communities. One such was Diogo Alvares who, under the name Caramurú, became prominent among the natives of Bahia. These early nativized settlers set in motion the miscegenation that has ever since marked Brazilian social history. They also learned native languages and customs, so that they were valuable middlemen once formal colonization began.

The dawdling pace of Portuguese settlement in Brazil had several causes. One was certainly lack of economic allurement, apart from dyewood, the extraction of which barely required settling since the coastal Indians would happily cut it in return for trinkets and metal knives and axes. The Indians themselves were not such as to attract settlers. Brazil lacked the native states, large towns, elaborate works of art, and accumulated metallic wealth that drew the Spanish on across Middle America and Western South America once they had encountered the Aztecs. Most telling of all, however, was that, by the time that Brazil made its appearance as a part of Portugal's Atlantic domains, that country's attention was already firmly fixed on West Africa, a rich source of gold and slaves, and even more on southern Asia. With Vasco da Gama's voyage in the late 1490s the Portuguese had achieved, after a century of dogged preparatory exploration, what Europeans had long dreamed of: linkage by sea, with all the potential for huge cargoes which that implied, with the fabled sources of pepper, cinnamon, cloves, and other spices, not to mention silks, ivory, and precious stones, of the Orient. With the vast profits of that trade in prospect, why bother with the Island of the True Cross, whose main claim to attention seemed to be a native people in whom was disconcertingly combined naked innocence with a propensity to roast and eat their captives?

If, indeed, it had not been for the interloping French, Portugal might have left Brazil to a few *degredados* and their companions for some time to come. But though Portugal had little urge to settle it, that anyone else should frequent it was intolerable. And so in 1530 John III's administration decided to create a permanent colony. Martim Afonso de Sousa, a well-tried naval commander, was sent off with five ships in that year to patrol the coast, explore the mouths of the Amazon and Río de la Plata to locate them relative to the Tordesillas line, and set up a royal colony. His ships carried 400 settlers for that purpose. After extensive surveying, Sousa in 1532 chose São Vicente, close to present Santos in the south, as the settlement's site. His brother reported the allocation of land for farms, and the establishment of order and justice "to the great satisfaction of the men, for they saw towns being founded, ... the celebration of matrimony, and living in civilized communion, with each man as lord of his own property... and all the other benefits of a secure and sociable life."[3] Sousa may have chosen so southerly a site because it offered the potential of easier access to the interior; and by this time rumors had filtered even to Brazil of the existence of a "white king" (the Inca) rich in precious metals who lived far inland.[4] Given that report, it is notable that town founding was not limited to the coastal plain. A small place, Piratininga, was also settled some 50 kilometers from the sea, facing inland from the top of the coastal escarpment. In 1562 Piratininga was united with a nearby Jesuit mission named São Paulo. It was therefore one parent of the town which centuries later would become Brazil's, South America's, and indeed the Southern Hemisphere's largest city, with a population, c.1990, of 16.7 million. In the much nearer future, particularly in the seventeenth century, São Paulo would also be the base for expeditions that explored much of Brazil's interior, and, in doing so, effectively pushed the colony's boundary far westward of the Tordesillas limit. Martim Afonso de Sousa, when he returned to Portugal in 1533, can have had little inkling of what he had set in motion in planting those urban roots inland from São Vicente.

Nevertheless, the São Vicente colony was only one small area of settlement on 5,000 kilometers of coastline. Occupying any large fraction of the rest with crown colonies was far beyond the monarchy's means. Hence in the mid-1530s John III had resort to an essentially private form of colonization. He divided Brazil into fourteen territories extending westward from the coast to the Tordesillas line, and granted these to twelve "donatary captains," whose heirs might succeed to them in perpetuity. The captains were minor nobles and respectable commoners. Most of them were military men and bureaucrats, in either case with good connections to the court. They received, as had comparable grantees of land in medieval Portugal, and in the Atlantic islands in the 1400s, vast powers.[5] Particularly notable was the king's permanent ceding of civil and criminal jurisdiction. The captains might name judges at all levels, execute criminals who were commoners, and exile those of higher social standing. They might found towns, and allocate lands to colonists. They themselves became owners of specified tracts of land, and received a small portion of the taxes due to the king on fish caught and dyewood cut in their territories. Fiscal control, including the royal dyewood monopoly and taxes, was, indeed, the sole major authority that the king retained. Notable is the lack of reference to Indians, except for a permit to send a certain number of them annually as slaves to Portugal, duty free. Christianization of the natives receives no mention.[6]

Despite the immense opportunities for autonomous seigneurial rule which that captaincy plan offered to the donees, the project did not, in general, promote settlement as the king had hoped. Colonizing was an expensive proposition, and only one of the captains was truly rich. Three of the appointees never made any attempt to settle their grants. Native resistance and the indiscipline of the people sent out (and of those already there) made the settlement of most of the others tenuous. Two captaincies, Bahia and São Tomé, that did well initially were abandoned in the mid-1540s as a result of native hostility. The Indians resented loss of land to settlers and, even more, the enslavement to which they were increasingly subject as farming began to expand. The sole true successes were in the far north and in the south, at Pernambuco and São Vicente. The first had the advantage of short sea passages to Europe, and also of able leadership from its captain, Duarte Coelho, who set about defending the coast and promoting agriculture with great energy. São Vicente benefited from being the site of Sousa's settlement a few years earlier. Although by the mid-thirties Sousa was captain-general of Portuguese India, São Vicente was donated to him; and the capable lieutenants whom he appointed ran it well.[7]

The two exceptions were not enough to offset the broad failure of the captaincies to raise the level of Portuguese presence in Brazil. By the late 1540s some fifteen towns and hamlets along the coast held a bare 2,000 settlers. Further direct royal intervention seemed indispensable. Hence in 1548 John III dispatched Tomé de Sousa, a cousin of Martim Afonso well tried in the royal service in Africa and India, to be governor general of Brazil. The captaincy of Bahia, between Pernambuco and São Vicente, was bought back from its original grantee, to be established as a royal captaincy by this second Sousa. In 1549 he chose a site overlooking the entrance to the great Bahia de Todos os Santos – All Saints' Bay – for the capital of the new crown colony. The town that arose there, Salvador (often known itself as Bahia), became the capital of Brazil and so remained until 1763.

Thus it was that, almost fifty years after Cabral's landing, royal government finally came to Brazil. The governor general had supreme executive authority in Bahia, and broad, if ill-defined, oversight of the private captaincies. Some of these survived into the eighteenth century, with varying degrees of autonomy. Generally speaking, the crown and its colonial officials interfered least in those that were best run by their donatary captains. Naturally enough, also, those that were simply furthest from the base of royal authority in Bahia tended to be left alone. Disputes between royal and private administration were common enough; but they were usually settled *ad hoc* by the crown itself without any damaging jolting of Portugal's hold on Brazil.

Defense, against both native and outside threats, figured largely in Tomé de Sousa's orders. Salvador itself should be built, of masonry, around a strong central fortress. Sousa was to see to fortification of the little towns already existing in various captaincies, and to the arming of their inhabitants. He was also to gather ships to drive away the French.

Military men were among the thousand people who went with Sousa to Brazil in 1549, his party instantly adding 50 percent to the existing colonizing population. Among the new arrivals were some 400 *degredados*, Brazil having by now replaced the west African island of São Tomé as the main zone of exile for miscreants. Sousa also brought peasants and craftsmen; and, to staff his new government, lawyers and treasury officials. More serious attention was now given than before to the application and collection of taxes throughout Brazil.

INDIANS AND JESUITS

Most notable, however, among Sousa's founding force for the new crown colony of Bahia were six Jesuits. These were not only the first priests from the fifteen-year-old Society to reach America, but a clear sign that the Portuguese crown finally intended to activate its long proclaimed policy of protecting and evangelizing the Brazilian natives. From the earliest years of the century Portugal had held that its title to Brazil was justified in large part by christianization. But missionary attempts had in reality been rare, the work of a small number of friars, some Franciscans among them. John III now decided that the new Society's blend of spirituality and worldliness fitted it to attack the long delayed task. The number engaged in it was not large; by 1598, 128 Jesuits had reached Brazil.[8]

Their work was twofold: to protect the native people from the settlers' depredations, and to make Christians of them. By 1549, the depredations had become severe, as the native reaction to them in the form of attacks launched on colonial settlements in the mid-decade would suggest. By then dyewood was no longer the sole profitable product exported from Brazil. Its rising rival, an introduced plant, was sugar cane. For cane to grow, land must be cleared, then kept free of weeds. The cane must be cut, and hauled quickly to a mill for extraction of its juice. All this demanded heavy physical effort, far more tiring, disciplined, and continuous than what was needed to fell the Brazilwood trees and drag their trunks to the shore. The Portuguese were too few (and far too unwilling) to provide the necessary labor. Hence Indians must perform it. But in the dominant native culture of the coast, that of the Tupí speakers, agriculture was the women's work. And, moreover, it was relatively light and intermittent work, since the staple food, manioc, grew abundantly with minimal attention. Money was no work incentive for Indians, since they exchanged only by barter; and they had accumulated enough of the tools and trinkets that the Portuguese and others had bartered for dyewood. Further, lacking any political structure larger than the village, the native people also lacked any centrally directed system of labor that the Portuguese might have adapted to their own use. The outcome of all this, from the late 1530s on, was the Indians' enslavement.[9]

Thirty years passed before the crown finally came to grips with the question of Indian slavery. In the meantime, it entrusted the native people to the care of the Jesuits, who took on the challenge with all the enthusiasm to be expected of so young a body. Like the first Portuguese to see the Brazilian natives fifty years before, the Jesuits were initially struck by their apparent simplicity and receptivity. The Indians, it seemed, were sponges ready to soak up Christianity. The Jesuits' leader, Manoel de Nóbrega, wrote of them, "They are not certain about any god, and believe anyone who tells them he is a god ... A few letters will suffice here, for it is all a blank page. All we need to do is to inscribe on it at will the necessary virtues, be zealous, and ensure that the Creator is known to these creatures of His." Indians seemed superior to Christians in their practice of morality and natural law.[10]

Brief experience changed the tune. Although many native people came to the Jesuits eager for teaching, and many thousands were baptized, it soon became clear that they were impelled as much by a hope that the priests would protect them from the settlers as they were by any thirst for the true faith. Further, and worse, the christianity that they absorbed did not displace their own religious beliefs, of whose presence and complexity the Jesuits soon became all too aware. They "return to the vomit of their ancient customs" after being baptized, reported one. By the mid-1550s Nóbrega was disillusioned enough to call them "pigs in their vices and way of life."[11]

From the start of their evangelizing efforts, the Jesuits saw their best chance of success in removing Indians from their communities and regrouping them in new villages (aldeias). One such aldeia was set up in Bahia in 1552. But the Indians' natural urge to flee once relocated, added to settlers' objections to Indians' being taken from the potential slaving pool, made the Jesuits uncertain about the village scheme for a few years. Then, though, realization that they were failing to convert Indians in their own settlements revived the aldeia project in the late fifties. From then on the villages were a standard feature of colonial Brazil; so was argument about them between Jesuits and colonists. As in the Jesuit reducciones in Paraguay, in Brazil too the aim was both to pluck native people from a familiar environment that would tend to preserve traditional habits, and to deposit them in alien, essentially European surroundings in which it would be easier to teach them new behaviors. So, for example, in the aldeias they should not live in multi-family long houses. In the small huts preferred by the priests, nuclear families would thrive, and the promiscuity supposedly encouraged by communal living would find no home.

Support for the creation of aldeias came from Mem de Sá, governor general from 1557 to 1572, in both principle and action. On his arrival in Bahia Sá quickly decided that the constant warfare among neighboring Tupí in the captaincy's interior must stop. He set out to achieve this through a mixture of force and enticement: peaceful Indians would be free and protected; those who insisted on fighting would be punished. The outcome for Indians who ignored Portuguese authority was quick and sharp. Sá attacked with great violence, his men's arquebuses mowing down native archers. By one report, 30 native villages were burned in Bahia; by another, from a Jesuit, 160. One outcome was that displaced and defeated Indians flocked to the aldeias. At the start of Sá's term these numbered two or three; by 1561, there were eleven, with a population in early 1562 of 34,000.[12] After his campaign in Bahia, Sá extended his disciplinary action to the north. There, between Bahia and Pernambuco, a particularly bellicose native sub-group named the Caeté fought not only other Indians but the Portuguese north and south of them.

They had, moreover, in 1556 captured, after a shipwreck, the first bishop of Brazil, who was returning to Portugal from his see at Bahia; and, having taken him, they cooked and ate him. In 1562 Sá declared a general war of punishment on the Caeté. Anyone might attack them; any Indians captured could be enslaved. The outcome was near annihilation of the Caeté. Even those who had taken refuge in Jesuit *aldeias* were seized. Any who avoided capture fled into the interior.[13]

The 1560s were dismal years for the natives of the Brazilian coast. After Sá's assaults, which were really the colonizing state's first large attempt to control the Indians, they next suffered what seems to have been the first major onslaught in Brazil of imported disease. It would be puzzling if Old World bacteria and viruses had not attacked the immunologically defenseless Brazilian natives earlier; and indeed the Jesuits reported high local mortality in the early fifties.[14] But pandemic diseases, penetrating the interior far beyond European settlement, did not appear until *c.*1560. The first seems to have been a hemorrhagic dysentery, perhaps combined with an influenza that had afflicted Europe in 1557.[15] In 1562 both plague and smallpox, the prime killer of American natives in the sixteenth century, arrived. The Jesuits did what they could for both those in their *aldeias* and others who came for treatment. "I peeled part of their legs and almost all their feet, cutting off the corrupt skin with scissors and exposing the live flesh ... and washing that corruption with warm water. With which, by the goodness of the Lord, they were healed."[16] Concentrating Indians in *aldeias*, alas, encouraged the spread of the pathogens. With the many deaths inevitably came lack of food, since there were too few free of infection to grow even the undemanding manioc. Most *aldeias* near Bahia and Olinda, the chief town of Pernambuco, disappeared. Even in those where the dead were replaced by natives brought from the interior, the numbers dropped from thousands to hundreds.

Reports to Lisbon on Indian matters by the Jesuits and the governor general, and a rising awareness that the Indians' decline meant lack of labor in Brazil at a time when sugar cultivation was rapidly expanding, now led to more serious thinking about the Indian question, particularly slavery, than ever before. At orders from Portugal, Mem de Sá called a junta in Bahia for that purpose in 1566. Its members were leading Jesuits, the bishop of Brazil, and royal judges. They found in favor of the *aldeia* system: Indians under Jesuit supervision would be protected from the settlers' demands. At the same time, though, the junta did not condemn enslavement, but merely urged that Indians not legally enslaved should be freed. These conclusions were sent to the king, Sebastião (1568–78), a young man predisposed to favor Indians, since, it has been said, if not king "he would probably have been a zealous missionary."[17] And in 1570 Sebastião issued the first statement to come from Portugal affirming the liberty of Brazilian native people. Indians might "on no account and in no way be enslaved." But, in recognition of the colonists' need for labor, the law immediately backed away from that ringing declaration, making exceptions of those found to be cannibals, those taken in just war (that is, war made by settlers in self-defense or retaliation), and those who repeatedly assaulted colonists or other natives. Such sinners and trouble makers might still be enslaved. And in practice, even the crown's qualified ban on Indian slavery was quickly diluted still further in Brazil itself. The rising demand for labor, together with a loss of moderate voices with the death of Nóbrega in 1570 and Sá in 1572, led to revocation of the 1570 law, and its replacement in Brazil from 1574 on by much laxer rules. The colonial authorities now decided that Indians taken by other natives in tribal conflicts, and in danger of their lives, might be bought out of captivity by colonists. This was a procedure known as *resgate* (a combination of ransom and rescue) that had long served the Portuguese as a means of acquiring slaves, but which had latterly drawn increasing official disapproval. At the same time the notion of just war was allowed to become so loose that almost any pretext sufficed for slave raiding.[18]

SUGAR

CANE AND MILLS

Many of the wounds that the Indians of the Brazilian coast were now suffering were inflicted, at a distance, by Europe's increasingly prominent sweet tooth. The Portuguese naturally experimented from their early years in Brazil with the profitable sugar cultivation that they, and Italians working from Lisbon, had begun in the 1450s in Madeira. As the first tentative colonization of Brazilian was beginning after 1500, sugar growing was starting to thrive also on the island of São Tomé, in the Gulf of Guinea of central West Africa, which Portugal had occupied in the 1480s.[19] In Brazil itself the first sign of sugar making appears in 1516, when the colonial administration in Lisbon, the Casa da India, ordered the dispatch to Brazil of an expert capable of building a sugar mill. Brazilian sugar may have been sold at Antwerp as early as 1519.

It was, though, in the 1530s, those years when Portugal finally focused its attention on the territorial, administrative, and defensive ordering of Brazil, that sugar truly began to find its place in the colony. Among Martim Afonso de Sousa's people in 1532 were Portuguese, Italians, and Flemings who knew Madeira's sugar business. It was natural, as the idea of settlement prevailed over the earlier view of Brazil as a place mainly valuable for its bartered dyewood, that thoughts should turn to cultivable crops. And it was soon obvious that much of the east coast was ideally suited by temperature, rainfall, and soil to the raising of sugar cane. The two thriving captaincies among the dozen created in the mid-thirties owed their success largely to sugar: São Vicente in the south, and Pernambuco in the north. Sugar mills (*engenhos*) quickly appeared in both (and a few in other captaincies also). Pernambuco, for reasons of both climate and proximity to Portugal, developed into the prime sugar province of Brazil in the sixteenth century. By 1550 it had five *engenhos* running; in 1585, sixty-six. Duarte Coelho, the founding captain of the territory, imported craftsmen from Portugal and from the Canaries, where in the sixteenth century the Spanish, also, grew sugar. He organized the sale of sugar in Lisbon, where a considerable degree of north European interest, mainly Dutch but also German, in the production, freight, and marketing of sugar arose as the century proceeded.[20] In Brazil the north-east became still more clearly the prime sugar region, when Bahia, after its recreation as a crown colony in 1548, imitated Pernambuco in building *engenhos*. Tomé de Sousa, the first governor general, came with orders to set up mills and plantations. The land around the Bay of All Saints proved excellent for cane. Mem de Sá's subjugation of the Indians of the interior of Bahia in the late 1550s made planting that land safe. Sá himself built a large refinery. In 1570 the captaincy had eighteen mills, and by 1590, perhaps fifty. By then, Pernambuco and Bahia together yielded possibly three-quarters of Brazil's sugar. By the end of the century Brazil was producing some 600,000 *arrobas*, or *c.*8.8 million kilograms, annually, the great part of which was exported to Europe, drawn by the constantly rising prices that accompanied the incipient transformation of sugar "from a luxury of kings into the kingly luxury of commoners."[21]

With the sixteenth-century ascent of sugar, Brazil took on the part of tropical agricultural exporter that it has played, with until recently only minor qualification, down to the present. Within the colony, the sugar *engenho* had become by 1600 the dominant economic and social unit, and was long to remain so. Its central position in the colony's being put a rural stamp on Brazil as a whole. The colony was not one in which towns prevailed, controlling hinterlands. Rather, the defining trait was the rural plantation, with urban settlement secondary to it.

The sugar estate consisted of cane fields, typically under 1,000 hectares in total area, surrounding a nucleus of buildings. Of these the most important were the sheds sheltering the machinery for crushing the cane, and others, adjoining, that held the cauldrons and kettles in which the juice squeezed from the cane was boiled down to make crystalline sugar. The other major buildings were the workers' living quarters, the owner's house (often simply called the "big house," or *casa grande*), and a chapel.

Heavy physical labor went into every stage of sugar making. Virgin ground being readied for planting was cleared with hand tools, and for almost all the colonial era further tilling and weeding was also done by hand, with little use of ploughs until the late eighteenth century.[22] The production process started with the planting of small pieces of cane. These took fourteen to eighteen months to grow to harvestable size. From the stump left after cutting, another cane would develop, although after three or four cuttings from the same root, the amount of juice yielded began to drop, and a new planting was needed. Once cut, the cane was quickly hauled to the mill on carts. If it was not crushed within forty-eight hours, the quality and quantity of the juice began to fall. The urgency of milling newly cut cane clearly placed limits on the practicable size of plantations.

The first type of crushing device used in Brazil was a simple millstone that rolled on its rim over chopped up pieces of cane. An improvement on this was a machine consisting of two horizontal wooden rollers, geared together, and made to rotate either by the power of animals (oxen, horses, or mules), or by a water wheel where there was enough water at hand. Only around 1610 did the more efficient design present in New Spain in the sixteenth century reach Brazil. This had three vertical rollers, the middle one being turned by a shaft descending from above, while the two on each side, linked by gearing with the driveshaft, rotated in the opposite direction to it. This device was lighter, cheaper to build, and more effective in crushing cane than the earlier, two-roller, apparatus. It was quickly adopted in *engenhos* after its appearance, and seems to have been the sole major technological advance made in sugar processing in colonial times.

The juice from the cane flowed through a pipe or channel to the boiling house. There it was heated several times, to different temperatures, in copper vats of various sizes set over furnaces. The aim of the heating was to bring impurities and lighter sugars to the surface, where they could be skimmed off. From some of the skimmings alcoholic and non-alcoholic drinks could be made, though not rum (*aguardente*), which was distilled from the molasses separated from the sugar later in the refining process. After a final boiling in small kettles, the now thick syrup was poured into bell shaped molds made of clay, and there left to cool. The molds were then set, narrow end down, in suitably pierced racks in the *engenho*'s purging house. There, over several weeks, the liquid would crystallize into a brown sugar. Further refining in the molds could convert part of their contents into white sugar. For this, a thin covering of wet clay was applied to the hardening sugar at the upper, open end of the mold. Water from the clay filtered down through the sugar, removing coloration and the last impurities from the upper layers. What flowed out of the hole at the base was molasses, which could be used as such, for distillation, or for recrystallization into a lower grade sugar. After up to six clayings, the sugar in the top two-thirds or even three-quarters of the mold was white. Below it was a fine brown sugar called *mascavado* (muscovado in English). The solid loaf of sugar was tipped out of the mold, the white cut from the brown, and both pounded by hand with a mallet to a fine texture. Brazilian growers exported mainly muscovado and white to Europe, where the latter was particularly esteemed.

Sugar making was, then, a complicated and delicate process, whose many components had to intermesh closely if the optimal end product was to be obtained from the potential in the cane. Once the cane was cut, delay or interruption in processing would cause loss in quality or quantity up to the point where the molds filled with syrup were placed in the purging house. Optimizing the product required the use of skill and judgment by overseers in the boiling and purging houses. Cutting, hauling, and feeding the cane between the mill's rollers was hard and constant work; and even dangerous, since inevitably hands and arms were occasionally caught in the machinery. Most striking of all was the continuous intensity of labor in sugar making. Climatic conditions on the northern Brazilian coast allowed the cane harvest (the *safra*) to proceed for at least nine months out of the twelve. Since cane could not be stored, the mill had to be in operation for that time as constantly as possible. That meant, in practice, all but continuous work, day and night, in the boiling house, and milling stints of eighteen to twenty hours. The other hours went to cleaning and repairing machinery and caldrons. For months at a time, then, apart from admittedly frequent religious holidays, workers had minimal opportunity for rest, and for gathering and preparing food.[23]

The *engenhos'* complement of buildings, machinery, caldrons, furnaces, hand tools, and draft animals also made these plantations the most capital intensive of productive units in colonial Brazil. One *engenho* in late seventeenth-century Bahia had copper cauldrons with a total weight of over 5,000 kilograms. All copper was imported from Europe.[24] Where water power was used, aqueducts were needed. Some growers built large storage tanks to provide a reserve of energy.

SUGAR WORKERS: SLAVES, INDIAN AND AFRICAN

A grower's largest investment, however, was in labor; for most of the work in sugar production was done by slaves. In the sixteenth century, most of these were Indians, obtained by slave raiding in the interior or through *resgate*. As both Sebastião's 1570 declaration of natives' freedom and its subsequent dilution in Brazil suggest, the colonists' demands on the Indian population became constantly heavier in the middle decades of the century. The severe losses of people to disease in the 1560s resulted only in greater pressure on the survivors. The number of slaves taken did not fall; quite the reverse. Thus in the 1580s many thousands of enslaved natives were at work producing sugar. The 66 *engenhos* operating in Pernambuco in 1585 used some 4,000 of them. In 1589 the fifty or so *engenhos* in Bahia had, by one estimate, some 9,000 Indian slaves.[25] By that time, it is true, not all natives working on plantations were slaves. Some, a minority, were free people paid in goods, such as metal tools, for their labor. They came either from nearby native communities, or, more commonly, from Jesuit *aldeias*. In the early seventeenth century, by which time contact with colonists had made at least some natives familiar with European monetary practice, a few instances of actual wage labor appeared.[26] But this never became a standard type of employment in sugar.

While the numbers of Indians on plantations rose in the closing decades of the sixteenth century, sugar growers were also looking outside Brazil for workers. The soaring demand for sugar, the persisting toll of disease among the natives, the underlying opposition in Lisbon to Indian enslavement, and the rising cost of expeditions deeper into the interior to seize or ransom workers, all united to persuade planters to turn increasingly to Africa for their workforce. Powerful precedent for the use of Blacks of course existed in the Atlantic islands on which Portuguese settlers had raised sugar, particularly Madeira from the mid-fifteenth century and São Tomé in the sixteenth. Both had quickly become successful exporters of sugar. Slaves to grow it had been easily available from west African sources to which the Portuguese, as a result of their explorations and factory building in the 1400s, had almost monopoly access. As experience with native slaves accumulated in Brazil, settlers there came to realize the attractions of Africans in comparison with Indians: greater technical skills, in farming, animal tending, and even metal working; greater physical strength and endurance; and greater resistance to disease.

Africans are reported as present in Brazil in 1535, working on early sugar plantations in São Vicente, though whether as slaves or free laborers is unclear. The date of the first shipment of slaves from Africa is probably 1538.[27] Until the mid-century, however, the African presence in Brazil was very small. After then it began to grow, as imports of slaves quickened. The import curve steepened notably after 1570, in response to the burgeoning of sugar. There began in that decade a slow substitution of African for Indian coerced labor on the plantations that would take fifty years to complete. For a time, the great pace of sugar's expansion led to continued growth of the native labor force. But then the Indian component shrank, and Indians were finally, by the 1620s, all but wholly replaced by Blacks in the cane fields and mills. The Africans transported to Brazil came mainly from the part of west Africa whose shore runs east–west from Cameroon to Senegal. Late in the century the Portuguese began to draw also on more southerly sources of slaves in the Congo and Angola. The numbers of slaves arriving in Brazil are uncertain, except in their upward trend. By the close of the century perhaps 10,000–15,000 may have been landed yearly. The total number of Africans present by then is not at all clear. Some idea of their rising prominence is given by the fact that, in the late 1580s, 25–30 percent of slaves in Pernambuco and Bahia were black. Pernambuco's *engenhos* employed some 2,000 black slaves in the mid-1580s; in 1589, Bahia had 3,000–4,000 of them.[28]

PEOPLE AND GOVERNMENT

POPULATION TRENDS

Numbers are barely any more certain for other components of the population in the sixteenth century; or for most of the rest of colonial times, for that matter, since no official counting took place until after 1750. Portugal imposed no head tax on the Brazilian natives, so even that basic fiscal motive for keeping track of Indian numbers was lacking. Of the white population, the same in one respect can be said as of the African: that its growth accelerated notably after the mid-century. By 1570 the Whites (very largely Portuguese) had reached some 20,700, concentrated, as would be expected, in the captaincies of Bahia and Pernambuco (each with some 6,000), and São Vicente (3,000). By the mid-eighties the white total had risen to 29,400. By then Bahia and Pernambuco, prospering from sugar, had both increased their share, to some 12,000 each; while São Vicente had fallen back to 1,800. It is likely, then, that by 1600 Brazil held some 40,000–50,000 Whites, most of them in the north-east.[29]

Notwithstanding the lack of censuses, every indication is that over the sixteenth century the fall of the native population was more dramatic by far than the rise of immigrant numbers. No one now doubts that the Indians exceeded a million in 1500. A series of "educated guesses" suggests, indeed, that in the entire area of modern Brazil they may have then numbered some 2.4 million; and a reasoned proposal exists that Brazilian Amazonia alone may have held five million before the Europeans' arrival.[30] It is probable, as with Blacks and Whites, that only after 1550 did important changes begin. The first severe set of alien epidemics struck in the sixties, their effects sharpened by the famine that followed them. Local outbreaks of disease followed in the seventies and eighties. And in 1597 came another broad onslaught of microbes on the coast, especially in the north-east. To be added to disease, of course, are the destructive effects of enslavement, and particularly of the raiding carried out to procure slaves. Though no reliable global figure for Indians is available for the late sixteenth century, the trend is clear in this contrast: in 1562 the Jesuit *aldeias* in the single captaincy of Bahia had 34,000 natives, whereas in 1585 the total of Indians in *aldeias* in Brazil as a whole was only 18,000. Flight to the interior may explain some of that fall; but disease and slaving were by all accounts the prime culprits.[31]

COLONIAL ADMINISTRATION

The growing complexity of Brazil and Brazilian issues in the late sixteenth century – among them, the rising urgency of the Indian question, the growth of African and European populations, the multiplication of settlements, and above all the expansion of sugar raising and export – made the existing governmental forms seem wanting. The Portuguese monarchy had throughout the century pursued centralization of power at home. To secure a hold on its Asian possessions it had installed in them some of the institutions tested in Portugal. Now, with Brazil proving to be far richer and therefore more attractive to settlers than had seemed possible for its first fifty years under Portugal, it was time to tighten the transatlantic reins as well.

Portugal shared with Castile the Iberian conviction that the supreme task of monarchs was to provide justice in their realms. Courts, judges and lawyers, therefore, played just as prominent a part in the Portuguese world as they did in the Spanish. Judges, being the embodiment of royal law, also came to be seen, in the places to which they were appointed, as natural founts and appliers of new regulation. There was in Brazil, then, as in Spanish America, a blending of the executive, legislative, and judicial tasks of government. In Brazil, the first legal figure with such powers was the *ouvidor geral* ("general judge," or high royal magistrate) sent out in 1549 with Tomé de Sousa, the first governor general.[32] A sign of the weight given to the office of *ouvidor* was that in 1554 it was combined with the post of *provedor mór da fazenda*, or chief treasury officer, in the colony. Judges were the men to entrust with gathering the king's Brazilian income.

Up to 1549, the law had been represented in Brazil by municipal magistrates, and more powerful figures, also termed *ouvidores*, appointed, one per captaincy, by the donees. The new *ouvidor geral* heard appeals from these lower judges, and was also charged with visiting the various captaincies to monitor the application of the law. Naturally enough, those inspected resented this intrusion by royal officers. This was one aspect of a broad resistance from town councils, the religious, and assorted colonials, to the imposition of royal authority in the second half of the century. The chief royal magistrates thus found themselves caught up in many sorts of business besides the strictly legal. On occasion they became interim governors general. A small number found themselves leading military forays against refractory Indians.[33]

By the 1580s it was clear that a single superior magistrate could not adequately oversee the exercise of law in such a vast territory as Brazil's, and among a population quickly rising in number and wealth. This realization coincided with a radical change in Portuguese political affairs. For in 1580 began a period of sixty years in which the crowns of Spain and Portugal were united, and in which Madrid, at least nominally, became the master of Portugal's empire.

The union of crowns followed from the death, without heir, of the young king Sebastião during an assault on the Moors of Morocco in 1578. Sebastião, never in his young life an exemplar of stability and good sense, had been made foolhardy by a blend of religious zeal and imperial ambition. His somewhat rag-tag expeditionary army was routed at the battle of Alcácer Quibir by a much larger Moorish force, with great loss of men and at a total cost of six months' royal revenues. Several contenders for the Portuguese throne then presented themselves. The one who prevailed was Philip II of Spain. He was not only the son of a Portuguese princess, but the ruler of the first European military and political power of the day; and that power, of course, loomed over Portugal's land frontiers.

In the event, Spain left the administration of Portugal and its empire largely to the Portuguese themselves, under general supervision from Madrid channeled through a viceroy in Lisbon. But it is not surprising that the Spanish, in that Philippine age of newly achieved "government by paper," found defects in Portuguese administration both at home and abroad. One perceived deficiency was in justice. The remedy finally went as far as the promulgation of a new code of Portuguese law, the *Ordenações filipinas* (Philippine Decrees), in 1603.[34]

The practical need to improve the exercise of law in Brazil, then, coincided in the 1580s with reformist pressure coming from Spain. The upshot was a decision to install in Bahia a high court of appeal, known in Portuguese lands as a *relação*. By the mid-1580s such courts existed in Lisbon, Oporto (in the north of Portugal), and Goa (where one had been created in 1544 to enhance the legal and political presence of the monarchy in the Indian Ocean). Philip II had apparently concluded by 1586 that Brazil needed a *relação*. And three years later ten magistrates were chosen to staff it. The ship carrying most of them, however, was unable to make Brazil because of adverse winds. The judges were scattered and no court took form. The setback gave opponents of the change, some of them high in Portuguese administration, the chance to marshall their arguments. Some feared that a larger judiciary in Brazil would only stimulate litigiousness there. Others saw a simpler solution in simply increasing the number of magistrates. The outcome was that the High Court of Brazil was not founded until 1606. Thereafter, but for a gap from 1626 to 1652, it was a permanent part of the colonial governing apparatus.

The *relação* of Bahia was founded with, at least nominally, ten judges. Most of these had the title of *desembargador* (literally, and rather optimistically, a remover of hindrance). Some *desembargadores* dealt with civil suits. Appeals from their verdicts, in cases worth substantial sums, went to the *Casa da Suplicação* in Lisbon, the senior *relação* in the Portuguese legal system. Other *desembargadores* were available for general assistance in trials where needed. Appeals in criminal suits were heard by the *ouvidor geral*, the prior senior magistrate in Brazil, whose office was now integrated into the high court. Cases involving royal interests, including of course treasury matters, went before a special judge, the *juiz dos feitos da coroa e fazenda*. These were the principal magistrates of the court. It was equipped also with a secretarial staff, a doctor, a chaplain, a bailiff, and a custodian. And at its head was a *chanceler*, or chancellor, who was finally responsible for the consonance of the court's rulings with existing law. His functions extended also, however, into executive business. He might examine regulations issued by the governor general to ensure their legality. He received and ruled on accusations made against the governor general. In the governor's absence, it was now he, rather than the *ouvidor geral*, who assumed executive command of Brazil.[35] The *relação* at Bahia was a Portuguese parallel with the Spanish American *audiencias* that sat in viceregal capitals (at this date, Mexico City and Peru). They had a similar role of collaboration, but also inherent confrontation, with the colony's chief executive, in the Spanish case the viceroy. And like viceroys in Peru and Mexico, the Brazilian governor general was the *ex officio* president of the high court, with voice though no vote in its decisions. What Brazil lacked, however, was the series of regional high courts far from the colonial capitals that in Spanish America were so potent reminders of the monarchy's existence and authority. The absence of any such state agencies outside Bahia was a reflection of Brazil's smaller size and population, and particularly of the persistence of private colonization in most of the captaincies. Although Lisbon gradually pressed in on the donees' powers, the notion of private control and jurisdiction died hard in Brazil, whereas in Spanish America the crown had smothered it almost at birth.

As Portuguese Brazil neared its first centenary, then, it was at last acquiring a organizational form and a distinct identity that during the first half of the century seemed hardly to be developing. Sugar was now clearly the foundation of the colony's being, as its prime source of income and the *raison d'être* of its defining social institution, the rural plantation. Sugar had caused colonists already in place to put down roots, and drew newcomers from Portugal. Its labor demands had shaped the treatment of the native people by colonists and colonial government alike, and ultimately driven rising numbers of Indians to flee from the coast to the relative, if only temporary, safety of the interior. Those same demands had energized the trade in African slaves, who, by 1600, were well on the way to supplanting native slaves on the sugar *engenhos*. By then, indeed, Brazil was firmly set on its road to becoming predominantly a society of Whites, Blacks, and, with time, Mulattoes.

Brazil had lagged behind Spain's American colonies in acquiring a clear sense of self. Portugal's Asian orientation, perfectly reasonable given the wealth that it promised to yield, accounts in part for the difference in timing. A larger cause was the absence among the Portuguese of the almost crusading determination of sixteenth-century Castilians to bring American natives into the faith and culture of Europe. That, though – nor any difference in governance or even ethnic and social development – was not the deepest contrast between the two Iberian colonial presences in America. The most striking difference is, rather, Brazil's relative openness to the exterior. Its geographical position on the east side of South America, and the fact that its sixteenth-century settlement all took place within a few miles of the coast, made it a part of the Atlantic world in a way that no substantial piece of Spanish America would be until the eighteenth-century emergence of the Río de la Plata and Venezuela. Spain's first major American territory, Mexico, lay shielded by the Caribbean and its barrier of islands. The second, Peru, was still further from other Europeans' reach, hidden away beyond Panama, beyond the South American rainforest and the inner Andean ranges. For purposes of religious purity and economic security Spain found this geographical arrangement most advantageous. And in the sixteenth century it was able, to a remarkable degree, to maintain a hermetic American empire, one linked to Europe by the narrow and sealed channel of the *Carrera de Indias*. By the end of the century, to be sure, the seals were clearly starting to leak; and from then on they did little but fail. But still, for that first century, in both aim and reality, comparatively speaking, Spain made a closed empire in America and Portugal an open colony.

OUTSIDERS: THE DUTCH, AND OTHERS, IN BRAZIL

The Portuguese did not, of course, indiscriminately welcome outsiders to Brazil. The French annoyance was a leading reason for the installation of royal government and defense from the 1530s. And after French Protestants founded, in the 1550s, a settlement that they named "Antarctic France" in the bay of Rio de Janeiro, Mem de Sá reacted forcefully, so that the colony lasted only twelve years (1555–67). But a less aggressive foreign presence was easily tolerated. From the start Italian, Flemish, and German capital flowed into the sugar business.[36] Dutch ships carried much of the sugar trade later in the sixteenth century. And even in the second decade of the new century, after a long period of hostility between Portugal and the Netherlands had begun, Dutch merchants reckoned that their ships carried, with Portuguese approval, 50–75 percent of the trade between Brazil and Europe.[37] Another transatlantic trade was, alas, well developed by then, run by colonials themselves, as Brazil sent its tobacco to the west coasts of Africa to be exchanged for slaves.

A little later in the seventeenth century, beginning in the 1620s, Brazil found there was a price attached to its easy Atlantic accessibility, as it suffered the only major foreign invasion in its history to the present day. The attackers were the Dutch, who proceeded to ensconce themselves in the north-east of the territory for twenty-five years.

The origin of this change in the Portuguese–Dutch relationship, which until a few years before the attack was mutually beneficial, though certainly with its ups and downs, lay in the union of the Spanish and Portuguese crowns in 1580. For although in everyday affairs the union's effects had been minimal, since Spain's policy was to leave Portuguese officials and practices in place, at a higher political level the story was quite different. Portugal and its possessions had become part of the Spanish state. Enemies of Spain were now Portugal's too. Spain, from the late 1560s until the mid-seventeenth century, had no foe more relentless than the Dutch. And the Dutch, correctly perceiving Portugal as the weaker and poorer part of the union, brought their firepower to bear on Portugal's overseas holdings. As themselves Europe's dominant new trading power, abundantly equipped with ships and deep-sea mariners, they would undoubtedly have been tempted to try their own fortune in business long controlled by the Portuguese. But the knowledge that a blow struck against Lisbon was also a blow against Madrid quickened their efforts.

The Dutch aimed first at Portuguese interests in west Africa. On the Mina coast, the western end of the present Ghanaian coast, the number of Dutch trading vessels multiplied in the 1590s, so that by 1600 Hollanders had largely displaced the English and French as rivals of the Portuguese in the exchange of gold for European cloths and metal goods.[38] Further concentration on this area's trade culminated in 1606 in a Dutch attack on the venerable fortified trading station of São Jorge da Mina. The Portuguese, with the help of African allies, repulsed the attack. But the Dutch persisted with their exploitation of the trade and with their attacks on Portuguese positions, even during the truce between Spain and the Netherlands from 1609 to 1621. After the truce ended, neither the military nor the commercial situation improved for Portugal. And indeed in 1637 the Dutch finally captured São Jorge; and in 1641 Luanda and Benguela also fell. These Portugal recovered in a final peace with Holland in 1663. But the Dutch had taken and now kept control of the Mina coast. Portugal was now gone from west Africa, and could trade there only with Dutch license.

In Asia, Portugal lost far more still to Holland. The main Spice Islands went in 1605, though part of the loss was recouped in 1606 by a Spanish force from the Philippines. In 1622, Hormuz, on the Persian Gulf, fell; as did Malacca in 1641, and various Portuguese coastal places in Ceylon between 1638 and 1658. Slightly to the west, Cochin and other places on the Malabar coast of western India succumbed to the Dutch in 1663. Macassar in the Celebes, to which the Portuguese driven from the Spice Islands had retreated to maintain their trade in spices and sandalwood, was finally taken in the late 1660s.[39] Having stripped Portugal of so many ports in southern and eastern Asia, the Dutch then took over the large share of the ship-borne carrying trade in the Arabian Sea, the Bay of Bengal, and the China Seas that had so profited Portugal in the sixteenth century. Finally the Portuguese were left with just Diu, Damão, Bassein, and Bombay, in north-west India; Goa, half way down the western coast; Macao, on the south China coast; and part of Timor in eastern Indonesia, where their sandalwood trade survived.

Dutch successes against Portugal in Africa and Asia had profound effects. One was to make the Netherlands an enduring colonial power in the east. Another was to leave Brazil as Portugal's pre-eminent overseas possession, a position for which the success of sugar had now well equipped it. The Dutch, naturally, did not neglect Brazil. Their West India Company, created in 1621 at the end of the twelve-year truce, was a device designed to harass and profit from all and any Iberian lands in America. As a result of Dutch familiarity with it, its accessibility, and its perceived weakness in defenses, Brazil was the Company's preferred target. The first assault, on Salvador, came in May 1624, directed by Piet Heyn. The townspeople fled in great panic. The Dutch held the town, though hardly any more, until April 1625, when a powerful fleet of Portuguese and Spanish ships ousted them. Salvador resisted two more attacks in 1627. But then in 1630 the Company shifted its aim further north, to Recife, the chief town of Pernambuco. Now, with silver seized by Heyn from the Spanish at Matanzas in 1628, the Company had funds to throw a force more than twice as large as that of 1624 (67 ships and 7,000 men, as against 23 and 3,300) against Brazil. Portuguese resistance was stiff. But the attackers prevailed; and so began a Dutch presence in the Brazilian north-east that lasted until 1654.[40]

At its maximum extent the Dutch occupation stretched 1,800 kilometers around the shoulder of Brazil, from a little south of the São Francisco River on the east coast to a little west of the Paranaíba on the northern. It went no further inland than the Portuguese had gone. Nor did it need to, for the West India Company had its eyes on sugar above all else, and sugar was a coastal crop. By occupying Pernambuco, the Dutch took charge of Brazil's leading sugar region. The Company, in its best years for sugar, 1637–44, apparently controlled at least a quarter of total sugar exports from Netherlands Brazil, and took taxes on the rest.[41] Most *engenhos* during the occupation stayed in Brazilian hands. Although a plan existed for emigrant European farmers to take up sugar cultivation, in the event time was too short even to reveal if this was practicable. Other exports were tobacco, hides, and, as ever, dyewood, on which the Company set up a trading monopoly.

The broad impression remaining of the Dutch occupation of the north-east is one of rather open-minded civility on their part (despite Portuguese horror at heavy Dutch imbibing). Not all, naturally enough, was harmony and light. Having resisted the Dutch invasion and expansion, the Portuguese colonists who chose to stay in the occupied area did so resentfully. On the edges of the Dutch zone there was continual skirmishing, with both sides working to attract Indian auxiliaries for their efforts in the field. Certainly, too, an undercurrent of religious hostility was present. The West India Company had been the creation of strict Calvinists, for whom abhorrence of the Catholicism of Iberoamerica was as much a spur to action as the political and economic damage the Company might inflict on Spain. Nevertheless, despite the presence of zealous Calvinist preachers, the Dutch administration in Brazil was in practice tolerant of the exercise of Catholicism, even of the continued existence of monasteries and nunneries, supported by their traditional revenues.

The strong sense of enlightenment left by the Dutch regime owes much to Johan Maurits van Nassau-Siegen, from 1637 to 1644 governor general of Dutch Brazil, and a scion of the family that had produced William the Silent two generations before. Though a Calvinist and a soldier tempered by experience in the Thirty Years War, he officiated in Brazil more in the spirit of the humanistic education he had received. He developed much affection for Brazil; Dutchmen nicknamed him, indeed, "Maurits the Brazilian."[42] To indignant Calvinist preachers he promised repression of Catholicism; but did little or nothing to effect it. He tried to diversify agriculture in Brazil away from sugar; but also cut taxes and made credit available to sugar planters for repair of *engenhos* damaged in the invasion. He set up town and rural councils, on which both colonials and Dutchmen should sit, in an effort to create representative government. In 1640 he went so far as to call a brief assembly of Portuguese settlers from the occupied zone, in an effort to give them a say in their government, and to hear and remedy their complaints about the behavior of the Dutch soldiery and local officials. The gathering has been described as "the first ... legislative assembly in South America."[43]

In the long term, though, Johan Maurits is best remembered for his efforts to gather and record accurate information about the people, fauna, and flora of Brazil. There he supported six artists, among them Albert Eckhout, who was particularly adept at painting humans and animals, and Frans Post, a specialist in rural views and scenes. He took with him to Brazil also one Georg Marcgraf, a German naturalist, who dispatched to Europe collections of specimens of plants and animals. Marcgraf died young in Angola in 1644. But a compilation of his Brazilian notes was published in the Netherlands in 1648 as *Historiae Naturalis Brasiliae*, a work which provides the first systematic accounts of Brazil's flora and fauna, of native groups, and of the geography and climate of Pernambuco (with records of rainfall and winds).[44] The information emanating from Johan Maurits's entourage was much better than anything previously collected, and remained central to the study of Brazil until the nineteenth century.

Late in 1640 Portugal rose against Spanish rule. The times had grown desperate for Spain. Military defeats on land were followed, in October 1639, by the destruction by the Dutch admiral Tromp of a large Spanish fleet in the Downs, off the Kent coast of England. In January 1640 another naval force, Spanish and Portuguese, sent to Brazil to oust the Dutch, was scattered by a smaller Dutch fleet near Itamaracá island, off the coast of Pernambuco. In May 1640 began the revolt of Catalonia against the centralized rule and fiscal impositions of Madrid. The loyalty of other Spanish provinces seemed doubtful. In December the Portuguese proclaimed the Duke of Braganza as John IV.

Portugal and the Netherlands were now therefore united in hostility to Spain. And indeed they agreed upon a ten-year truce in June 1641. But it was a truce limited in practice to Europe. The Dutch continued to gnaw at Portugal's holdings in Asia and Africa; and they made no move to leave Brazil. And Portugal, caught up in a war of liberation with Spain that continued fitfully into the mid-1660s, could do little to oppose Dutch hostility overseas.

In Brazil, however, the events of 1640–1 had their effect. With the Dutch–Portuguese truce signed, the West India Company decided to cut costs in Brazil by reducing its garrison there. It also recalled Johan Maurits, whose enthusiasm for Brazil had, so the Company's directors thought, led to excessive spending on activities besides the martial. After protesting about both his removal and the risky economizing, he left Brazil in May 1644. And with him went a powerful force for mediation between invaders and colonials, for there were many in all parts of the population – Dutch, colonials, Blacks, and Indians – who had come to regard him as a just and trustworthy governor.[45]

In the mid-forties, therefore, with the Dutch apparently hesitant, the guerrilla warfare that had always flickered on the edge of the occupied zone began to burn more steadily. Though it was the Portuguese governor general at Salvador, Antônio Telles da Silva, who first directed the anti-Dutch effort, its final success was very much the work of residents of Brazil, acting independently of Portugal, which remained focused on its own contest with Spain. The retreat of the Dutch to Recife and its close vicinity by 1648, and their final withdrawal in 1654, have been seen moreover as the doing not only of white colonials, but of mixed bloods, Blacks, and even Indians fighting alongside the others more or less willingly. For some more recent Brazilians, indeed, the process of ejecting the Dutch both encouraged and revealed the start of a sense of multiracial national identity in the colony. And while it is rather easy to find signs of such sentiment where none may really exist, there is no denying that it was the colony and not the homeland that began and sustained the practical effort against the Dutch.[46]

In other respects, the Dutch presence was too brief to leave much permanent imprint on Brazil. One lasting change was that the great rise of population and commercial energy that the town of Recife experienced during the occupation persisted after the Dutch left. The external outcomes, however, range from the simply interesting to the historically fundamental. An example of the first sort might be the departure from Recife with the Dutch, who had been notably tolerant of them, of a number of Jews who chose not to return to the Netherlands but to try their luck in Dutch territories in North America. Those arrivals in New Netherland in the mid-1650s became "The Pilgrim Fathers of American Jewry."[47] A far more telling movement was the extension in the Dutch period of sugar growing from Brazil to the Caribbean. In Barbados, for example, where English settlers had first raised tobacco in the late 1620s, sugar planting began in earnest c.1640. A rise in the European price of sugar after 1633, caused by disruption of Pernambuco's production after the Dutch invasion, was the first stimulus for the change of crop. The Barbadian English overcame their early problems in sugar making by sending men to Pernambuco to learn the methods developed in Brazil.[48] Other islands, both English and French, took to sugar at the same time. And when the Dutch were driven from Brazil in the fifties, they too began planting cane in their Caribbean colonies. Doubtless the new European colonists of the Antilles would in any case have developed the islands' potential for sugar sooner or later. But the easier access to Brazilian techniques provided by the Dutch occupation of Pernambuco quickened the process. The outcomes included Brazil's loss of a near-monopoly on the supply of sugar to Europe, and, conversely, vast and enduring gains in income for the northern European powers now building up their colonial presence in the Caribbean.

MOVEMENT INLAND: SLAVERS, PROSPECTORS, AND STOCKMEN

EXPLORERS AND *BANDEIRANTES*

While the north-eastern and northern coasts of Brazil were held by the Dutch in the 1630s and 1640s, the interior was finally, if slowly, starting to yield to a variety of probings by other residents of the territory. With these tentative inward movements began a process at least as important to the formation of modern Brazil as any multiethnic effort to expel the Dutch. For it was above all in the century between, roughly speaking, 1650 and 1750 that Brazil grew from its early coastal form to approximately its present size.

In the north a key event in this expansionary process was the final driving away of the French in 1615. Immediately after this a Portuguese expeditionary force was sent to found a settlement on the Amazon. On the Pará River, actually the southern arm of the Amazon estuary, this was done. A fortress was built, the nucleus of what soon became the town of Belém. Five years later, in 1621, the entire northern coastal region, generally termed Maranhão, was declared a separate *estado*, or "state," of Portuguese America, separate from the "State of Brazil," and with its own capital at São Luís, halfway along the north coast.[49]

From this new northern base area, exploration of the Amazon now proceeded, driven in large part by slaving of Indians along the river's banks. Native communities around the shores of the enormous estuary were all but destroyed. English ambitions for settlement along the Amazon were another spur, in the 1620s and 1630s, to surveying of the river.[50] Portuguese movement upstream was eased, too, by the union of crowns, because while Brazil was formally in the Spanish domain, Madrid seemed little concerned by what would otherwise have been violation of the Tordesillas treaty. In fact, Philip IV encouraged exploration by the Portuguese and Brazilian colonials, and in 1637 went so far as to grant to a Portuguese a hereditary captaincy extending some 400 kilometers up the north bank of the Amazon from the sea. It was in 1637, also, that a canoe bearing two Spanish Franciscans appeared at the mouth of the river. The two had left a failing mission attempt on the Napo river (in present Peru), and, fearless friars that they were, decided to see the Amazon rather than reclimb the Andes to the Spanish-settled regions. This feat moved the Portuguese governor at São Luís to send a strong expedition of seventy Portuguese and 1,100 Indians upstream to forestall any Spanish claim to Amazonia. Under Pedro Teixeira remnants of this force finally in 1638 reached the city of Quito. Then, in 1639, Teixeira went back down the river; and, following orders, founded a settlement at Tabatinga on the Napo as the new marker between Spanish and Portuguese territories in the interior of northern South America. With this one astounding stroke the demarcation line was pushed almost 2,500 kilometers west of the old Tordesillas limit, where it has remained, at that latitude, until now. Tabatinga is at the modern convergence of the boundaries of Brazil, Colombia, and Peru. The Spanish, blocked by the Andean foothills from sending any large body from Peru, and now generally beset by far more urgent problems in the Iberian peninsula and elsewhere in Europe, did nothing to drive the Portuguese back. In Teixeira's wake others began to use the Amazon and its tributaries for access to the salable products of the rainforest, such as wild cacao, hides, wood, spices, and medicinal herbs.[51] A clear mark of growing colonial activity in Amazonia was the building in 1669 of a fortress, São José de Rio Negro, at the confluence of the Negro and Solimões rivers, near the present site of Manaus. Men from Pará explored the upper waters of Amazon tributaries in present Ecuador and Peru in the 1680s. Another variety of European presence along the rivers was the mission *aldeia*. Franciscans, and particularly Jesuits, tried as always to defend the forest peoples from the rising labor demands and the slave raiding of the colonists. Carmelites seem to have been the most active evangelizers in western Amazonia, broadly speaking beyond the fort at São José.[52]

Some would see in Pedro Teixeira the very embodiment of the spirit of that classic and mythologized Brazilian type, the *bandeirante*. *Bandeirantes* were members of *bandeiras* – roving bands of armed men who traversed the interior of Brazil in the seventeenth century, hunting for sources of wealth (which they found mainly in the form of Indians taken for slaves), and in doing so exploring and extending westward the colony's territory. The word *bandeira* means, first, "flag;" but it was used in medieval Portugal as a term for a small armed unit, a raiding party detached from a larger company. In Brazil the word was current by 1635 to mean a group of backlands militiamen.[53] But the cultural implications that it has accumulated in more recent times are what has given it so much weight in Brazilian self-consciousness. *Bandeirantes* set out on their journeys from several areas on the coastal periphery of Brazil. But the prototypical *bandeirante* was a *paulista*, a native of São Paulo in the south-east. And a distinctive trait of *paulistas* by the end of the sixteenth century was the degree to which they were the product of racial mixing – mixing not, however, of European and African, as was by then growing common elsewhere in Brazil, but of European and Indian. The term used for this combination, the Brazilian equivalent of the Spanish American mestizo, was *mameluco*. And what has made the *bandeirante* from São Paulo so important a part of Brazil's view of its past is that he was part Indian. It is perhaps through the phenomenon of the *bandeira* that the Indian has been most fully drawn into the Brazilian sense of self.

The *bandeirantes*, men of the seventeenth century, were the prime discoverers of Brazil, in the sense that what their journeys revealed in the interior was larger by far, and more varied, than what European explorers had found earlier on the coastal plains. With only minor exaggeration, in fact, the *bandeirantes* might be called the makers of Brazil, because it was their roaming of the interior that established Portugal's claim to vast tracts west of the Tordesillas line.

The *mameluco* nature of São Paulo's people went back to the start of European settlement in the area where the town developed. The first Portuguese there, well before Martim Afonso de Sousa's arrival, was João Ramalho, one of those deserters or castaways who were the main Portuguese vanguard in Brazil. He became a famous warrior and local leader of Indians, took a chief's daughter as wife, and before his death had innumerable children, grandchildren, and great grandchildren.[54] Piratininga, and São Paulo after it, did not draw large numbers of new arrivals from Portugal in the sixteenth century. Isolated as they were at 700 meters, just over the crest of the coastal escarpment, indeed the only colonial places so positioned until much later, they were less attractive to immigrants than the developing sugar areas further north. Early São Paulo had both the advantages and the drawbacks of its relative isolation: freedom from governmental meddling, but poverty in its apartness from the rising prosperity of the sugar-rich coast. Its own economy before, and after, 1600 was largely a matter of subsistence farming and the raising of pigs, cattle, and horses on rural estates.[55] There were typically patriarchal Iberian figures among the landowners and the leaders of town government (often the same men); but at the same time the simple and rough conditions of the plateau frontier made a man's standing dependent to an unusual degree, for the time, on his own efforts and ability.[56] By 1600 the town of São Paulo had some 120 houses and 2,000 inhabitants. Most of them were white, *mameluco*, and Indian, although by then some Blacks were also present. It is a clear sign, though, of the region's ethnic and cultural nature that, even a hundred years later, the commonest language used by all those in and around São Paulo was not Portuguese, but Tupí.

The *bandeiras* of São Paulo are above all a seventeenth-century phenomenon. But the many defensive sallies launched by the *paulistas* in the late 1500s against hostile native people in the region around the town were clearly, in effect, rehearsals for them.[57] With the turn of the century came a distinctly offensive *bandeirismo*, aimed mainly at slaving; although two wide-ranging expeditions from São Paulo were organized in 1601 and 1602 by the then governor general of Brazil, Dom Francisco de Sousa, specifically to look for gems and precious metals in the interior. This was part of a continuing search for mineral wealth in Brazil that might match that of Spanish America. Later in the century *bandeirantes*, some at the colonial government's behest, were to make that their first object; and in the end their efforts yielded rich fruit.

For the next fifty years, however, the *bandeiras* from São Paulo were first and foremost slaving expeditions. Some of them were veritable small armies, in which a few dozen white *paulistas* commanded hundreds of *mamelucos* and even more numerous Indian auxiliaries. Slave taking, indeed, often enough meant fighting. These forces went off into the interior for months or years at a time. As a practical guide to the territory they used its many rivers, following their valleys inland, down the slope of the plateau toward the major streams of Amazonia or the Paraguay-Paraná-Uruguay system. In this they perhaps imitated the travel patterns of native people of pre-contact times.[58] But it was not until the eighteenth century that explorers of the interior used boats on the rivers to move themselves and their goods. The seventeenth-century *bandeirantes* went on foot.

The slaves whom they captured were put to work locally on the plateau in and around São Paulo, or were sold on the coast for labor in sugar making and other tasks. Although the proportion of African slaves in the *engenhos* was by this time rising fast, the vibrant growth of the sugar business still produced a demand for Indian slaves; and especially so because the early 1600s were a time of growing Dutch interference at the sources of the slave trade in west Africa. Coinciding with this difficulty was the appearance of a tempting source of Indian slaves in the form of the mission reductions that the Jesuits were now starting to create east of Paraguay. The first of these, set up in 1610, were within 600 kilometers of São Paulo, almost due east of it on the southern bank of the Paranapanema river. Over the following decades the Jesuits gathered Indians into other reductions further west and south, in what are now parts of eastern Uruguay, north-eastern Argentina, and southern Brazil (but, even there, areas that lay west of the Tordesillas line). There ensued a protracted battle between the Jesuits in these areas and the *paulistas*. The raiders on occasion found themselves abetted, if not aided, by the Spanish governors of Paraguay and even by the secular church authorities there, since both groups saw the Jesuits as intruders in their own jurisdictions. The missionaries resisted with unexpected, if thoroughly Jesuit, vigor and practicality, arming their neophytes and fielding them as surprisingly effective defense forces of their communities – and, for that matter, of this particular eastern limit of Spanish America, though the Spanish administration was not grateful. Finally, however, by *c*.1640, *paulista* pressure drove the Jesuits back behind the Uruguay and Paraná rivers. From then, also, Portugal's revolt against Spain inclined the local Spanish governors to take stronger action themselves against the *bandeiras*. In those forty years after 1600, nonetheless, the *paulista* raiders had in reality greatly extended Brazil's reach to the west, and southward into what is now Uruguay.

After the mid-century, the *bandeirantes* broadly turned from a hunt for slaves to one for precious metals and stones. The reasons were several: the greater remoteness and defensive strength of the Jesuits' reductions by then; the improvement of the African slave supply as Portugal took back gathering areas from the Dutch in Angola, though not in western Africa; and Portugal's need for a source of wealth and income to make up for losses in the sugar business to the new plantations on the Caribbean islands. And so, though slaving of Indians in the interior still continued to a degree, the *bandeirantes* now functioned mainly as prospectors. They were employed and organized as such, indeed, by the crown.

By 1650, the pursuit of minerals had already led to some spectacular incursions into the interior (journeys sometimes called *entradas*) from various coastal towns. From Bahia expeditions had gone west to the São Francisco river valley, and ranged southward along it, covering many thousands of kilometers. One *entrada*, from Sergipe, just north of Bahia, had stayed in the interior for eight years around 1600. But it was after 1650 that these prospecting ventures ranged furthest, pushing the limits of Brazil (particularly of its central section between 10 and 20 degrees south) far westward, in the sense of both the political boundary and geographical knowledge. Now *paulistas* trekked over areas that were to become known as Minas Gerais, Goiás, and Mato Grosso, 1,500 kilometers and more to the north and north-west of São

Paulo. One of the most remarkable of them, Antônio Rapôso Tavares, spent the years 1648–52 on a formidable journey up the Paraguay river to some point in the eastern Andes, and thence back via Amazonia.

GOLD

These explorations revealed enough gold to keep the prospecting effort at high pitch. But it was not until the mid-1690s that the great rewards came. And they appeared, ironically enough, really quite close to home, not deep in the western interior but near the Velhas river, 500–600 kilometers north-east of São Paulo. Among several discoverers was Antônio Rodrigues de Arzão, who set out from Taubaté, near São Paulo, in 1693. A rash of strikes elsewhere followed in the next few years, some as far north as Bahia. But no other region proved to have gold in the amounts quickly found in the Velhas area. As a result, in 1709 the crown set up a new administrative unit, São Paulo and Minas do Ouro (Gold Mines); and in 1720 this gold zone was made a quite separate captaincy, Minas Gerais (General Mines), a name that persists to the present.[59] With the gold strikes began a new phase of colonial Brazilian history, a "golden age" lasting half a century or more (c.1700–60) in which Brazil imitated the central Andes and Mexico in exporting large quantities of bullion, and in which gold gave a superficial gloss of wealth to Portugal as well. During that period, as might be expected, prospecting continued with still greater energy, resulting in further major gold finds now far into the interior in Goiás and Mato Grosso. Large deposits of diamonds also came to light in the late 1720s in Minas Gerais; and others, though smaller, later in Bahia and Goiás.

With the gold discoveries, the pioneering work of the *bandeirantes* was done. Gold prospecting soon gathered a momentum of its own in the interior; and mining brought more or less fixed settlement with it, so that for the first time towns appeared far inland. Fortune seekers, and supplies, were carried after 1710 or so to the mines and new towns by the *bandeiras'* successors, expeditions known as *monções*, or "monsoons" (so named, apparently, from the meaning of "season for travel" given to the word by the Portuguese).[60] These were freighting ventures, using long, dug-out canoes to take people, domestic animals, food, and other goods into the interior. Now the rivers flowing inland over the plateau proved their worth as means of transport, though their abundance of rapids and waterfalls made the freighting business slow and arduous.

In the early 1970s, Embraer, Brazil's principal aircraft building company, produced its first successfully exported aeroplane. It was named the "Bandeirante." The pathfinders of the seventeenth century occupy a place in the Brazilian memory comparable to that of cowboys in the USA or gauchos in Argentina, as the expression of an independent and hardy national spirit, and as the men who unlocked the nations' interiors. In truth, the *bandeirantes* fill this image far more completely than the other two types. They were active for better than a century; they ranged astonishingly deep and wide; their journeys were arduous without parallel. They were, of course, far from unsullied heroes. For fifty years they were out-and-out slavers, responsible for the uprooting, and probably the early death, of hundreds of thousands of natives of the interior.

THE CATTLE FRONTIER

Understandably less well remembered than the frontier-expanding *bandeirantes* of the 1600s are the cattle that moved into many of the opening spaces of the interior behind them. But the animals deserve recalling, because they were the most obvious alien presence in much of the *sertão*, or backlands, for a long time; and ranching drew colonists (land owners and herders, or *vaqueiros*) inland, admittedly in small numbers, long before the great inward flood of gold seekers took place in the early eighteenth century. Cattle were an important instrument of the European occupation of the land in Brazil, as they were also in the pampas further to the south, or in northern Mexico.

Martim Afonso de Sousa brought the first cattle to Brazil in the early 1530s. They multiplied on the coastal plain in step with the growth of the sugar industry, since the *engenhos* needed meat for food, and, more crucially, oxen to pull carts and turn crushing mills where water could not be used.[61] Hides served any number of purposes, and candles made from tallow were a basic source of light. As sugar output and the colonial population grew, cattle raising spread inland from the coast, making good use of land that was too dry and infertile for cane. The easiest access to the interior was up the valleys of the rivers that cut through the coastal ranges, such as the Paraguaçu in Bahia, and above all the great São Francisco, which entered the sea halfway between Salvador and Recife, giving entry to an enormous area of the interior extending down almost to São Paulo. Throughout the seventeenth century, but mostly after 1650, stockmen and cattle pressed inland up the valleys. By the 1680s they had gone north from the São Francisco valley into the inner marches of the northern captaincies of Paraíba and Ceará. The land there is the epitome of what the word *sertão* brings to mind: arid, infertile, thinly covered with brush.[62] Only extensive ranching was possible on such land; and enormous estates came into being covering hundreds of square kilometers. On such areas the numbers of animals could, however, be very large. In the somewhat less forbidding interiors of Bahia and Pernambuco, 500,000 and 800,000 head of cattle were reported in 1711. And despite the existence of such numbers close to the large population centers of the north-east coast, great drives of animals from distant areas took place. In 1709, for instance, cattle were herded overland some 800 kilometers from Maranhão, which by then had become an active stockraising area, to Bahia. Some, indeed, were driven a further 1,000 kilometers southward, to feed the teeming gold-seeking population of Minas Gerais.[63] A northward flow of cattle also developed after 1700, drawn by demand in the mining areas. Stock estates appeared in the lowest reaches of Brazil, the Rio Grande do Sul of today, and sent their animals 1,500 kilometers or so north to the gold regions.

As in northern Mexico, native people in Brazil reacted fiercely to the bovine incursions. Cattle, large and easily hunted beasts, were a splendid new source of food. But this immediate gain was more than offset by the damage they did to farming land, and the human presence and the taking of open territory for estates that came in their train. Resolute Indian resistance to the spread of ranching punctuated the second half of the seventeenth century, especially in the interior of Bahia and in the extreme north-east. Colonial governors of the region, driven to distraction by these risings, called in seasoned *bandeirantes* from São Paulo to suppress them. With much violence the job was done.[64]

SEVENTEENTH-CENTURY SOCIETY

As the appearance of the *bandeirantes* shows, by the late 1500s Brazil was developing its own social types. The colonial society, indeed, was beginning to acquire its own identity, as, for example, *engenhos* multiplied and the imports of African slaves to work them rose. This growth of distinctiveness in the society and divergence from its Old World sources accelerated in the seventeenth century, and has continued since then.

It would be easier to follow these changes if the size of the several components of the population were better known. But, in comparison with colonial Brazil, even the Spanish colonies seem rich in demographic data. It is clear enough, however, that the non-Indian population was growing in the seventeenth century, as a result of both natural increase and of immigration. The 40,000–50,000 Whites present *c.*1600 had increased to perhaps 100,000 a century later. Scattered figures are available for particular places. The white population of Salvador early in the seventeenth century was perhaps 4,000; in 1709 the town had some 21,600 communicants, most of whom were probably white. The total population of the town *c.*1700 was over 40,000, and is thought to have tripled between 1647 and 1717. Recife rose from a total of some 2,000 in 1639 to become the second town of the colony by the early 1700s, with 10,000 or so citizens in 1709. In 1646 São Paulo had 600 Whites and *mamelucos* capable of bearing arms; in 1700, 3,000 of the same.

The ethnic make-up of the population is even less clear than its total size. In 1700, Whites, at 100,000, were about a third of an estimated total, in the colonized areas, of 300,000. By 1680 the slave population (very largely black) may have reached 150,000, so that by 1700 it would have been rather more than half the total. The balance at that date of perhaps 40,000 presumably consisted of free Blacks, Indians, and ethnic mixtures. The basic types of mixture were *mamelucos* and *pardos* (all those with some degree of African blood).[65]

As in Spanish America, social divisions and rankings went, with time and the rising diversity of the population, from the simple to complex. At the start there were just Portuguese (and Portuguese mostly of low social or economic standing) and Indians (Indians, moreover, largely lacking the contrasts of rank, wealth, and power found in the high-culture areas of Spanish America). To these were added in the sixteenth century an African component. For an understanding of the social structure that arose from these basic elements, it is useful in the Brazilian case, as for the Spanish colonies, to suppose a transfer of the notion of estates from the home country. In America, all Portuguese and Spanish settlers, whether commoners or of higher rank, became the colonies' *de facto* nobility. In Brazil, Indians, then Africans also, took the role of the commoners, specifically of a commoner peasantry. These categories seemed at first distinct and fixed. But with miscegenation, acculturation, economic diversification, and the appearance of legal distinctions such as those between slaves and free people (whether black or native), the initial pattern lost its simple clarity. The free black artisan ranked higher, in both ascribed and real status, than the black slave domestic in the town house of a wealthy family. This domestic, however, was a social cut above the slave servant in the estate house of an *engenho*; who in turn saw himself, and was seen by all others, as superior to the field hand. Similarly, Indians in the seventeenth century who lived in villages near *engenhos* or towns, and who worked for wages in some craft or other task useful to the Portuguese, were in a quite different social category from those in mission *aldeias*. Generally speaking, ethnically mixed people, while subject to the same sort of suspicion about morality and trust-worthiness as was common in Spanish America, had an advantage in practical opportunity over pure Blacks and Indians. An appreciable whiteness in appearance tended to make for access to the white segment of society and its economic offerings.[66] The *mamelucos* of São Paulo were a case in point.

Working and living conditions for the mass of commoners, the Blacks, varied widely with their occupation and status. The free urban smith or carpenter had a material life not much different from his white or mixed counterpart. On the sugar estates, field and mill slaves were worked hard and long, with some risk of injury from knives, crushing machinery, and furnaces. The combined tolls of heavy labor and disease undoubtedly led to a short life for most rural slaves, although life expectancy cannot be accurately calculated for the seventeenth century, nor is it clear how much shorter the slave's life was on average than that of other poor people. What is clear is that there was no natural increase in the rural slave population. If left to itself, indeed, it would have fallen. The rise in the number of African slaves in seventeenth-century Brazil was, then, the result of large imports. The reasons for the tendency toward natural decline were several. A central one was the high cost to the owner of raising a slave child compared to the price of a newly arrived captive from Africa. Owners were little concerned that their slaves should reproduce. They were therefore unwilling to buy many women. Consequently, fewer women than men were shipped to Brazil. Among such children as were born, early mortality seems to have been high, in part because mothers suffered the effects of hard physical labor and inadequate diet. The outcome was (in Bahia, at least) that from 1600 to the early 1800s, some 70 percent of slaves present at any time had been born in Africa. The steady influx made for a constant reinforcing of African culture in Brazil, in religion and social custom, and possibly a parallel slowing of the "Brazilianization" of the Black. From the eighteenth century, for example, comes evidence that, in such church-consecrated marriages as did take place, ethnic and regional origin in Africa was still influential, like seeking like as partner.[67]

Blacks naturally produced a variety of reactions to their forced removal to Brazil and to the different hardships they suffered there as slaves. For most, religion gave comfort and a sense of community. African religions lived on in Brazil, and in fact continue to do so in vibrant, if transmuted, forms. Many slaves added to the beliefs they brought from Africa some elements of Catholic faith and practice, such as marriage by the church. Some undoubtedly found solidarity in sharing Christian beliefs, and besides that the church could actually offer some practical framework for community, such as religious fraternities that provided not only a sense of belonging but also funds for dowries, burials, and some insurance against hard times in life. More violent resistance to slavery and to specific ill treatment was also common enough, though no slave rebellion took place before the nineteenth century. At the individual level, cases of abortion, infanticide, and suicide can be found. Much more common, though, was running away, which began to happen in the late 1500s. The coastal forests and mountains, and the *sertão* inland from them, offered plenty of hiding places. *Mocambo* was the name used in the seventeenth century for a community of escaped slaves; *quilombo* became the usual term after 1700. Such groups often survived by combining subsistence farming with assaults on estates, towns, and travelers. Their existence naturally gave rise to considerable nervousness and irritation among officials, estate owners, and other colonials. Governors organized attacks on the communities, often using friendly Indians as troops; a special rural police was set up to hunt escaped slaves. But the outlaws were resistant. The most famous community of escapees in Brazilian colonial times, Palmares in the interior of Pernambuco, existed for almost the entire seventeenth century. It grew to a size of many thousands. Its fortifications and well-organized militia held out against all attacks until in 1694 a tough force of *paulista bandeirantes* was sent against it, and finally prevailed, overthrowing its King Zumba. The depiction of Palmares and its fall in *Quilombo*, a film of 1984, reinforced its place in the Brazilian memory.[68]

A less drastic and more frequent reaction to slavery was to seek to escape from it by becoming free. A custom existed among owners of granting liberty in their wills to favorite slaves. Most of these were women. Black mistresses of *engenho* owners quite commonly were manumitted in this way, along with their children. Loyal male slaves also benefited from the custom; although for people past the prime working age the gain was dubious. In letting such slaves go, owners may have benefited more in saved maintenance costs than they lost in production. Slaves often also bought themselves out of servitude. Owners of sugar estates sometimes gave their more skilled slaves chances to earn small sums for extra work, apparently as a stimulus to productivity. Determined slaves might eventually save up enough to buy their liberty. Towns offered better earning opportunities, so that self-purchase was more easily managed there. Most freed slaves indeed lived in towns, for the same reason of more abundant work. Since mulattoes and Brazilian-born Blacks (*crioulos*) were generally closer to the dominant European culture than the African-born, they were more able to find paying work. And so it was mulattoes and *crioulos* who predominated among the free. In the long term, since children born of the manumitted were also free, the cumulative effect of liberation was large, and notably offset the continued import of enslaved Africans. In the early 1820s, of Bahia's total population of half a million, some 170,000 were slaves, while 250,000 were freed men and women, or descendants of freed people.[69]

THE INDIANS AND FATHER VIEIRA

If seventeenth-century Blacks had some chance of escaping from slavery, for the native people of Brazil the century offered only minimal chances of relief. For some along the settled coast, there were opportunities for a meager independence as occasional wage workers or suppliers of food to colonists and the slave population. But for the great majority of Indians, living in the interior, the century brought only harassment by slave raiders, or at best well-intentioned disruption by missionaries. Philip III, king of Spain and Portugal in the first two decades of the century, in 1609 asserted that the Brazilian Indians were by nature free, though strictly as legal minors whose care he entrusted to the Jesuits. Of their own villages and lands, however, Indians were to have control; such land was inalienable. These rulings provoked a rising by the Bahian colonists, and reinforced an already well established hostility between settlers and Jesuits, with the settlers accusing the priests of monopolizing Indian labor for their own gain in the *aldeias*. The protest was forceful enough to bring cancellation of Philip's rulings in 1611.

Slaving then proceeded without legal hindrance in the interior. The Jesuits found it particularly damaging in lower Amazonia, where the native population was exploited unmercifully by the newly arrived settlers of the Maranhão coast. That northern region was short in resources and economically isolated; throughout the century it was the poorest part of Brazil. Settlers there could not afford black slaves. So they seized Indians to work the small tobacco and cotton farms that provided the area's sole salable products. From the 1620s the Jesuits saw this exploitation of the natives as a challenge needing their attention. But for lack of numbers they could do little until the 1650s. Then they began in Maranhão and Pará a brief but furious pro-Indian campaign under the leadership of the most distinguished Jesuit to appear in colonial Brazil, António Vieira (1608–97).

For his pro-Indian efforts, Vieira seems to the modern eye to have been the closest Portuguese equivalent to Bartolomé de las Casas. But his fame at the time had other more intellectual sources. He was born in Lisbon, but educated in Bahia by the Jesuits. There his brilliance emerged early, showing itself in his splendid oratory. His writing, and the record of his speaking, have sustained to the present his ranking as one of the greatest literary masters in Portuguese. His linguistic abilities extended to other languages; he learned Tupí (and also Kimbundu, a language of the Angolan Blacks in Brazil). During the 1630s in Bahia he became the town's most renowned preacher. In 1641 he was one of a party chosen to go to Lisbon to congratulate the king, John IV, on Portugal's casting off of Spanish rule. The king was drawn by his talents, and sent him around Europe on secret diplomatic missions. John also heeded Vieira's accounts of the sufferings of Brazil's native people.[70] The king reiterated the principle of Indians' liberty, and tried to regulate their wages and maximum periods of work, though to little effect.

By 1650 Vieira was a preacher celebrated in various European lands, an influential diplomat, and a powerful courtier in Lisbon. The missionary vocation that he had felt as a young man still tugged at him, however, and he decided that northern Brazil was the place to exercise it. He reached Maranhão in 1653, and there proceeded to chastise the thousand or so white settlers of the north with sermons that seem to echo Antonio de Montesinos's excoriation of the citizens of Santo Domingo in 1511. On the first Sunday in Lent, 1653, he berated them thus:

> Christians, nobles, and people of Maranhão, do you know what God wants of you during this Lent? That you break the chains of injustice and let free those whom you have captive and oppressed. These are the sins of Maranhão; these are what God commanded me to denounce to you ... All of you are in mortal sin; all of you live in a state of condemnation; and all of you are going directly to Hell. Indeed, many are there now and you will soon join them if you do not change your life.[71]

But he did not persuade them of their imminent perdition; nor that they should give up the labor of slaves and do the necessary physical work themselves. "It is better to live from your own sweat than from the blood of others."[72] But they thought not, and protested to the king about prevailing pro-Indian rulings. John IV thereupon gave new approval to slaving. Vieira saw no choice but to return to Portugal to lodge his protests in turn. The result was a temporizing decree in 1655 that gave the Jesuits charge over all native villages, and discretion to permit *entradas* to obtain slaves by *resgate*. Vieira in reality conceded that the combination of the north's poverty of resources with the ambitions of the settlers, largely Portuguese peasants, meant that some degree of native enslavement was inevitable. He granted that genuine *resgate* – the ransoming of Indians who were truly in danger of being killed by their native captors – was an admissible source of slaves; but strove to stop *resgate* from being used, as it long had been, as a blanket pretext for seizing all or any Indians.

His concessions did not, however, remove the tension between Jesuits and colonists, who still saw the mission presence as a threat to their access to labor. The intensity of the Jesuits' evangelizing efforts in the late fifties only reinforced this feeling. Fifty-four *aldeias* were set up around the mouths of the Amazon, and filled with Indians persuaded to abandon their own communities along the shores of the rivers that flowed into the lower Amazon. But this exposed them to imported diseases, from which many died.

Finally, in 1661, the settlers' resentment exploded. The spark was perhaps provided by a severe epidemic of smallpox in Maranhão in 1660 that killed many natives, so shrinking still further the accessible labor supply. Settlers complained to the crown in January 1661 of such penury that the daughters of "nobles" among them (those with most land, rather than title holders) had no suitable clothes to wear to Mass at Christmas.[73] In May of that year the citizens of São Luís revolted against the Jesuits. The settlers had the sympathy of other religious orders in the region, put in shadow by the Jesuits, and even of the governor, previously a backer of Vieira and his men. Vieira was confined, and with his fellows shipped back to Portugal. There his fortunes rose and fell erratically with political shifts in the court. But he never regained the authority he had held in the early 1650s. He later spent six years in Rome, confirming there in the pulpit his earlier European repute as a great preacher. In 1681 he returned to Brazil, where he persisted in the Indian cause until his death at a great age in 1697. He was never again, however, so influential a pro-native voice as before. The crown, inspired in part by his arguments, did once more forbid Indian slavery in 1680 and restore control of the northern *aldeias* to the Jesuits. But another rising by the settlers followed. The Society was again ousted. Vieira's strivings lived on mainly in the rules for running *aldeias* that he had created; and in the long term in his lasting fame as the chief champion of native interests active in colonial Brazil.

GOVERNMENT AND ECONOMY IN THE SEVENTEENTH CENTURY

COLONIALS PURSUE THEIR INTERESTS

While Indians generally continued to suffer at the base of seventeenth-century Brazilian society, the white segment of the population diversified in wealth and standing, as it did in Spanish America. The growth of towns provided an expanding range of opportunities for Brazilian-born and immigrant Whites in crafts and in services such as small trading. In towns the possibility of social ascent through economic gain was probably greater than in the plantation-dominated countryside.

Particularly striking in the seventeenth-century history of Brazil's white population is the rise in political power of its upper end. As in the Spanish colonies, this clearly happened because of the increase, by 1600, of the number of locally born Whites who had known nothing but Brazil; and also because of Portugal's difficulty, given such challenges as the union with Spain and the Dutch assaults in Asia, Africa, and Brazil, in administering Brazil as tightly as it might have desired.

As towns grew in size, the *câmara*, or municipal council, became a useful vehicle for the expression of colonials' wishes, likes, and dislikes. It was such councils in the north that sent protests to Lisbon about the Jesuits' activities. Aldermen and town magistrates were elected by local property holders, with the result, predictable enough, that members of *câmaras* everywhere in the colony tended to be men prominent in local economic affairs. In Bahia, for example, the councils were dominated by sugar planters and merchants. Since the crown depended for its colonial income on the prosperity of these leading groups, it had a political interest in heeding the wishes of town councils. This, together with the absence in Brazilian provinces of any powerful agencies of royal will to compare with the Spanish American *audiencias*, perhaps explains why these Brazilian councils seem to have had more political weight than their counterparts in the Spanish empire, the *cabildos*.

In the 1600s Brazilian colonials influenced government also by joining the bureaucracy in growing numbers, and at ever higher levels. By the mid-century, they held many of the middle level posts that had previously been filled by European-born men, becoming "treasury officials, customs collectors, market inspectors, probate judges, scribes, and watchmen."[74] Such offices could be bought or inherited. Then in 1653 the barrier to the highest level of the judiciary was breached, with the appointment of the first Brazilian-born *desembargador*, Simão Alvares da Penha Deusdará. Alvares was the son of one Manoel Alvares da Penha, a leading citizen of Pernambuco during the time of the Dutch occupation, and a man who had given supplies to anti-Dutch forces there. This activity had brought him the nickname, subsequently added to the family name, of "Deusdará" ("God will give"); and a grateful king had granted him a title of nobility as well. The son's appointment to a judgeship in the high court at Salvador also probably followed from the father's patriotic services. The fact that he was the husband of a sister of Father Vieira, then at the height of his influence at court in Lisbon, can only have brought him further favor. This was the first of ten namings of colonial-born men as *desembargadores* before the mid-1700s.[75]

Even without Brazilians on the bench, however, leading colonials had, from early in the seventeenth century, close connections with the judges of the high court that gave them influence at the top of the colony's government. Despite rules to the contrary, the judges in the *relação*, like the *oidores* in Spanish American *audiencias*, were keen participants in the colonial economy. Some lent or borrowed money; some traded; some bought land. These and many other dealings inevitably created close ties with colonials, who used them to sway judgments in their favor. More personal links also developed from the start. Again ignoring regulations to the contrary, some *desembargadores* married into local families. Their high status and power made them desirable candidates for the hands of daughters of even the most prominent of colonial families; while the wealth of such families, and the potential that their local contacts offered for making money, made such alliances attractive to the judges, who were generally not rich. Almost a fifth (32 of 168) of the *desembargadores* appointed to the court at Salvador before 1759 married Brazilian women.[76] The children of such unions were well placed, in turn, for office and influence. Another strong family linkage was *compadrio*, or ritual coparenthood, into which a person from outside the family might be drawn by acting as a marriage witness or a godparent. The connection was thought almost as close as a blood tie. High court judges were much sought after as *compadres*. And since a person might connect himself thus to any number of families, the potential for locals' influence on government was even greater here than through matrimony.[77]

From the early 1600s, but especially after the mid-century, marriage ties developed between judges of the *relação* and some of the powerful and extended families, almost clans, that had become by then a salient feature of Brazilian society. Some of these families had branches in several regions of the colony, which they used for wide-reaching business and political purposes.

The seventeenth-century extended family in Brazil has indeed been described as a corporation, in which the creation of wealth (and typically clannish feuding with other families) was seen as a collective rather than an individual enterprise.[78] One powerful northern family that linked itself early to the *relação* was that of the Cavalcanti de Albuquerques, who traced their descent in part from the sixteenth-century proprietary donees of Pernambuco, the Albuquerque Coelhos. A Cavalcanti daughter from Pernambuco married Manoel Pinto da Rocha, whose term as *desembargador* in Salvador began in 1609. Later in the century, three other judges in the high court married into the Cavalcantis, who in turn had marriage ties with other major families. Ownership of sugar estates was common in these groups. Judges also married the daughters, and sometimes the widows, of those other families. And so the supreme judicial body in the colony was extensively linked with the producers of Brazil's main export crop. This, broadly speaking, suited the interests of both crown and colonial leadership. The sugar barons, as they may perhaps be called, could count on the support of the high court in legal disputes. And the crown could thereby hope to promote the output of the product that was the prime source of fiscal income from Brazil. By modern standards, the judges' patterns of behavior – in marrying into local wealth and power, in using their positions to advantage for private business and gain – were clearly corrupt. At the time they were acceptable if not pressed to excess. By the early eighteenth century, the point of excess seems to have been reached, at least in the crown's perception. In the 1720s various judges were investigated for illicit business activities, and two actually removed from office. But the attempted reform was not harsh enough, or the temptations were too strong. Later *desembargadores* continued to trade.[79]

The *relação* of Salvador was suspended between 1626 and 1652. Several reasons led to the removal of the court. The main one was the need to find funds to divert to defense after the initial wave of Dutch attacks in the early twenties (which had, of course, resulted in the attackers' year-long occupation of Salvador in 1624–5). After ordering the elimination of the court early in 1626, Philip IV of Spain reassigned the salaries paid to its staff to the town's garrison.[80] But local opinion also had a large part in the matter. In the *Dialogues of the Great Things of Brazil* (c. 1618) attributed to Ambrosio Fernandes Brandão, a well-to-do sugar planter and trader of Pernambuco and Paraíba, the author's spokesman, Brandônio, criticizes the *relação* on several grounds: its expense, its inaccessibility from distant parts of the settled coast (and the resulting expense of litigation for many parties), its slowness in dealing with business, and lastly its simple superfluousness, since most disputes are resolved privately before reaching the high court level. These were quite specific and practical complaints, doubtless justified in some instances. More generally it is clear that leading colonials, often speaking through the *câmaras*, objected to what they saw as encroaching royal centralism in the presence of the high court. The Albuquerque Coelhos of Pernambuco, for instance, the wealthy descendants of the first donee of that captaincy, still tried to run it as their own domain, and resented the availability of the high court to those who wished to raise objections to their administration. There was here, also, an element of simple regional contention between Brazil's most prosperous area, Pernambuco, and the center of its royal government, Salvador. From influential colonials in Brazil, then, there sounded no voice defending the *relação* when the king decided to remove it in 1626; indeed, persuasive evidence exists that their complaints about the court contributed to Philip IV's decision.[81]

With the *relação* gone, the *ouvidor geral* again became the highest source of justice in Brazil. A separate position of *ouvidor* had already been created for the southern captaincies, and this judge remained in place. The removal of the high court, however, while an economy for the crown, did nothing to make colonials' access to justice simpler or cheaper; quite the opposite, in fact, since the final court of appeal was now in Lisbon, and crossing the Atlantic was dangerous and slow while the war between Spain and the Dutch lasted. And so, reversing its opinion completely, the *câmara* of Salvador began in the early forties to argue that the court should be reinstated. In 1652 Lisbon finally heeded the town council's repeated requests. In March 1653 new judges took their places in Salvador.

And so, once again, weighty colonials had shown the influence they could exert in the government of Brazil. And now, indeed, after the expulsion of the Dutch from Brazil mostly through home grown effort, colonials found the restored Portuguese crown willing to give them a larger say than before in their own affairs. Among the new judges in 1653 was Simão Alvares da Penha, from Pernambuco. The next year, a second Brazilian, Cristóvão de Burgos, a prosperous and well-connected Bahian, was raised to the bench.[82] These high appointments were a natural culmination of the movement of colonial-born men into the governing bureaucracy's lower strata that had been advancing throughout the century. And while that movement has several possible explanations, its central impetus was simply the growing number of American-born men of influence in Brazil. Especially with the growth of the great extended families, the reality of white Brazilians' local political weight could not be ignored. The colonials' success in driving out the Dutch served simply to sharpen the point. And so, from exercising influence on officials through ties of kinship and business, the colonial elite now advanced to direct action at the highest levels of government. As with the Spanish American creoles after 1600, there was no stopping Brazilian Whites from gaining a large say in their own government.

PRODUCTION: SUGAR ABOVE ALL

Underlying the political advance of the colonials in the seventeenth century, in some measure, was certainly the more central economic role in the Portuguese empire that Brazil acquired as a result of the Dutch attacks in Africa and the Orient. Its economic weight continued to lie in sugar. The trend of sugar exports (which differs little from the production trend) seems clearly to have been upward from the beginning of the century until the late seventies. Annual exports from 1600 to 1620 averaged in the 800,000 *arroba* range (11.75 million kilograms). After then, every available estimate is higher than that average, though the estimates are regrettably few:

1627 or 1628	900,000 *arrobas*	(13.2 million kilograms)
1643	1,200,000	(17.6)
1650	2,100,000	(30.9)
1670	2,000,000	(29.4)

Supporting these large exports were steady or rising prices of sugar in European markets until almost 1660. Naturally the upward trend of exports had its interruptions; weather and wars took their toll. Within Brazil an important geographical shift in production occurred. The Dutch occupation of Pernambuco cost that captaincy its lead in output. Some 60 percent of Brazilian sugar was Pernambuco-grown *c.*1600; but only 10 percent fifty years later. Many Pernambucan planters fled with their slaves and money to Bahia during the 1630s, with the result that Bahia then became, and from then remained, Brazil's prime sugar region. By 1660 European prices of sugar were starting to soften, under the influence of the rapidly expanding sugar production of the Caribbean islands. Up to then the possibility of holding back exports had given Brazilian growers some control over the European price.[83] Now other suppliers would step in to fill any gap. And so Brazil, after a century as, in essence, the monopoly supplier of sugar to Europe, found itself in the uncomfortable position of being at the mercy of the external market in which its major product was sold. It is a position that many other producers of primary products have had to endure since then. But Brazil, having had the distinction of being the first large region in the world to produce plentifully on tropical plantations, now also became notable as the first major primary producer to become dependent on external economic conditions on which it had minimal influence. Still, European demand for sugar continued strong; and the Caribbean producers were subject to the same sorts of natural and humanly caused difficulties as affected Brazil. And so, always with fluctuations, Brazilian sugar sales to Europe remained high in the eighteenth century.

Brazil sold other products of the land in the seventeenth century, though none approached sugar in value. The multiplication of cattle in the interior meant that the colony became self-sufficient in leather and meat about 1640. Having previously imported hides and salt meat, it gradually began to export at least leather. In the first decade of the eighteenth century, Brazil sent some 110,000 hides yearly to Lisbon (50,000 from Bahia, 40,000 from Pernambuco, and 20,000 from Rio de Janeiro and other southern places); much leather, though worth barely 2 percent of the yearly sugar export of the period.[84] Spices, also, were to be found in the interior forests, especially once Maranhão was settled and became a base for up-river exploration. Types of pepper, clove, and cinnamon grew wild. The main exportable spice, however, was ginger, which was smuggled from Brazil into northern Europe in the early 1600s. Its cultivation in Brazil was encouraged by royal decree in the 1640s. For another forest product, dyewood, European demand continued, and so exports also. The largest export from the land, however, was tobacco. The plant was native to Brazil. The leaf entered Portugal from the colony before 1550, and was considered a medicine, good for toothache, asthma, and indigestion. Its pleasurable qualities were soon also appreciated. In the seventeenth century Brazil became the largest producer, and the first large producer, of tobacco in the world. The growing areas were Bahia and Pernambuco, and then Maranhão, of which it was the sole exportable product of high value. In an effort to take full advantage of this, the Maranhão settlers petitioned in 1637 that foreign tobacco should be excluded from Portugal. Tobacco's profitability was such that in 1639 the town council of Salvador forbade its planting for fear that insufficient land would be available to grow food for the local population. In the second half of the century, tobacco was often the means of payment for slaves in Africa.[85]

SHIPS AND TRADE

Aside from standard craft goods, Brazil produced little in the way of manufactures. The sole important exception was ships. Bahia was the main center for this, with a yard set up in the final years of the sixteenth century. The local supply of wood for hulls and masts was abundant; there were local resins and cotton for caulking; black slave labor was at hand; skilled iron workers could be found on the sugar *engenhos* (though the iron itself was imported from Europe). In 1650 the crown ordered the building of one 700–800 tonne galleon a year at Bahia. A vessel of a thousand tonnes was laid down in 1659. These were very large ships for their day.[86] Shipyards came to exist also in Pernambuco, and, after 1650, at Rio de Janeiro and on the Paraíba coast in the extreme north-east.

Brazilian-built ships were used in the transatlantic trade. They also carried goods along the South American coast, where for much of the seventeenth century a frequent destination was Buenos Aires. During the union of crowns, Spain gave the Portuguese the advantage of lowered barriers to the markets of the American empire; and Brazilian ports then became lively entrepôts for the transmission of sugar, European goods, and African slaves into southern Spanish America. Silver from the Andean mines paid for these imports. After Portugal departed from the union in 1640, that trade continued as contraband (in which Europeans, notably the Dutch, participated as well as Brazilian merchants). Late in the century Buenos Aires ceased to be the target of Brazilian merchants. The colony's southward expansion had by then advanced so far that in 1682 a Portuguese town could be founded on the north shore of the Río de la Plata, 60 kilometers north-east across the estuary from Buenos Aires. This was Colônia do Sacramento, which as a point of infiltration of alien goods into Spanish America was to be a thorn in the Spanish side for almost a century. Only in 1778, by the Treaty of San Ildefonso that fixed the southern boundaries of Brazil close to their present position, did Portugal finally yield Colônia to Spain.[87]

Like Brazil, Buenos Aires had the advantage (or in the official Spanish view, the drawback) of being on the Atlantic, and therefore easily accessible to ships and nations trading in that ocean. With few exceptions, such as concessions to the Portuguese after 1580, the Spanish colonial administration, aiming to reserve Spanish America commercially for the home country alone, tried to counteract that natural advantage with exclusionary rules that banned foreign entry into Buenos Aires. (Smugglers, local settlers, and often enough even officials took little notice, it is true.) By contrast, Portuguese policy makers generally accepted that geography was destiny, and in general produced a trading policy far less rigid than the Spaniards'. This is most clearly shown in the absence, in the Portuguese case, of a fleet system designed as the sole carrier of goods to and from Brazil. Despite some attempts at organizing convoys in the sixteenth century for protection of shipping, Portuguese merchants, then and after 1600, preferred to entrust their goods and fortune to large numbers of caravels sailing independently. The loss of one such small ship was not overwhelming. Only in the late 1640s, after drastic losses of ships to the Dutch during the contest for north-eastern Brazil, did the Portuguese crown, partly at the urging of Father Vieira, finally go about providing naval defense by chartering a trading company. This, the General Brazil Trading Company (*Companhia Geral do Comércio do Brasil*), founded in 1649, was to be the sole supplier to Brazil of four foodstuffs basic to the Portuguese diet: wine, oil, flour and salt cod. On exports from Brazil, it could charge duties. To secure the Company's monopoly, in the future only a few ports would be open for transatlantic trade: Lisbon and Oporto in Portugal, and Recife, Salvador and Rio de Janeiro in the colony. The price to the Company of its privileges was the provision, within two years, of thirty-six warships, each with twenty to thirty cannon and a full complement of sailors and soldiers. These ships were to escort trading convoys across the Atlantic. The Company was funded with private investments, mostly from merchants in Lisbon who were "New Christians" (that is, Jews who had converted to Christianity); but, in another example of Portuguese openness, shares were offered in Amsterdam, Paris, and Venice.

The Company had mixed success for rather a short time. Its first defended fleet left Lisbon in December 1649. Its warships helped to weaken the Dutch hold in Brazil in the early fifties. But there were difficulties in raising the intended capital, despite pressure on the New Christian subscribers. Never did all thirty-six ships appear. Complaints came, as was to be expected, from merchants and ship owners in ports excluded from the Brazil trade. And so, as early as 1654, ships were again allowed to sail without convoy, provided they did not leave from Lisbon or carry goods covered by the monopoly. The Company soon proved, however, a poor supplier of those monopoly items. Hence, in 1658, the crown abolished its monopoly, and at the same time reduced to ten the number of warships to be provided. In 1664 the governing nine-man council was disbanded; the running of the enterprise passed to the crown. In 1694 the government appropriated the Company's funds, compensating shareholders with bonds in the royal tobacco monopoly. In 1720 the Brazil Company was abolished.[88]

The institution of the Company did make the escorted trading fleet a permanent feature of Portuguese transatlantic commerce. But, as the exception granted in 1654 shows, independent sailings still continued. Such ships were probably more numerous than those in the fleets. And smuggling, though impossible to quantify, also persisted, doubtless energized, in fact, by the attempts to regulate the trade more tightly. Many in Brazil, including lower officialdom, stood to gain through contraband. Portuguese smugglers, then, and Englishmen and others arrived with little hindrance in Brazil to sell and buy.[89]

The scant success of the Brazil Company in the long term is a further demonstration of Brazil's easy accessibility to all maritime nations with Atlantic shores. That accessibility may help to account for various distinctive features of Brazilian economic life in the seventeenth century. One is the lack, relative to the Spanish colonies, of economic diversification. The directness of Brazil's contact with Europe, and hence its low cost, made the supplying of European manufactures cheap, and therefore weakened incentives to produce them in Brazil itself. Similarly, the sparsity, in comparison with Spanish America, of internal trade and the resulting absence of inland trade networks (apart from cattle drives from around 1700 onward), reflects the ease with which ships could reach the regions where demand existed. (The nature of Brazilian colonization before the eighteenth century was of course perhaps an even larger influence here. The economic geography of sugar growing meant that population was densest near the coast.) Third, accessibility may have promoted the robustness that the Brazilian economy seems to show in the seventeenth century. Trade to and from Brazil was largely free of the inefficiencies of the fleet system of the *Carrera de Indias*, and associated costs (the high taxes, for example, levied to pay for escort vessels) that burdened Spanish American commerce. That advantage can only have helped to stimulate production in Brazil.

One of the most remarkable qualities of seventeenth-century Brazil is precisely its freedom from almost any hint of economic depression; and this in a period when much of Europe suffered at a minimum decades of difficulties, and for which the economic vitality of large parts of Spanish America is at least debatable. Only after about 1670 did Brazil, apparently, feel any economic pinch, after losing its place as sole major supplier of sugar to Europe. Clearly its well-being up to then owed much to the sustained demand for sugar that even a war-torn and plague-ridden Europe could offer. And Brazil escaped in good part the problem of rising shortage and cost of labor that the disastrous post-conquest collapse of native population presented to Spanish America. Native Brazilians, of course, also died from the imported diseases, and the numbers of them available for work also fell as they fled inland. But Brazilian natives were never so valuable as workers as the Indians of the main areas of Spanish settlement, lacking as they did most of the skills and also the familiarity with labor organization possessed by the natives of the central Andes and central Mexico. Hence, in crude economic terms, the loss of native labor was less severe a blow for the Portuguese than it was for the Spaniards. More telling still, though, was that the Portuguese were so easily able to make up the loss with African slaves. Again Brazil's geographical position was an immense help. It was closer to the African sources of slaves than any part of Spanish America. Further, the Portuguese already had long experience as slave buyers in Africa, and had established bases there precisely for that purpose. So powerful were these circumstances that Brazil would most probably have become a land largely of Whites and Africans even had its native people not so severely declined.

THE AGE OF GOLD

SHIFTS OF PEOPLE AND POWER

With the discovery of plentiful gold at the end of the century, Brazil regained whatever economic momentum it had lost. Indeed, the outcomes of the gold strikes were more than merely economic. Most aspects of the colony's life felt gold's influence. The demographic effects appeared almost immediately. As news spread of the finds made in what was to become Minas Gerais, hopeful prospectors began to arrive. The first came from the Brazilian coast. Then the lure of gold began to draw men from the Azores, Madeira, and Portugal. Once again little record exists of numbers; but in the 1740s some 1,500 a year may have left Portugal for Brazil.[90] The exodus was large enough to cause worries that a decline in Portugal's population and economy might follow. More acute still was the concern in Brazil itself about the movement of slave labor from coastal plantations into the mining zones. By 1715 or so, Minas Gerais had 30,000 black slaves, nearly all of them new arrivals from the coast. The coastal plantations suffered double damage: loss of hands, and a rise in price of newly imported slaves caused by the miners' avid demand for workers. Whether black or white, almost all the newcomers to the mining interior were male. Very few miners, and even fewer slaves, were married. Such unions as existed were informal. Since white colonials consorted eagerly in such arrangements with black and *mulata* women, the mining towns were places of unusually rapid ethnic mixing.

Inland towns were the most durable result of the gold boom. In areas where previously barely a hut could be found, substantial towns quickly developed. Minas Gerais had eight before 1718. One of the first was Vila Rica do Ouro Prêto. Today Ouro Prêto (Black Gold) is still very much in place, and has come to stand as the representative symbol of the gold era. In Goiás and Mato Grosso, where mining developed a little later than in Minas and was never so productive, fewer towns were founded.[91] But at least two, Vila Boa de Goiás in Goiás and Cuiabá in Mato Grosso, still stand. In Brazil, as in Spanish America, even infant mining centers were often far more than mere encampments. In both colonial systems these new places were generally set down in remote and previously deserted areas. They necessarily and immediately became centers of government and justice; and as such quickly took on urban traits.

The building of towns and the influx of thousands of newcomers inevitably impinged on the native peoples of the interior. Most Indians had already disappeared from the initial gold area of Minas Gerais around the headwaters of the Velhas river. But prospectors pushing further west ran into native resistance, some of it distinctly fierce. Those travelling from São Paulo to

Mato Grosso in the canoes of the eighteenth-century monsoons were likely to be attacked along the rivers by swift and able warriors from various tribes. The Guaicurú of the Chaco, for example, had mastered the wild horses of their region; intruders could do little against them. Such resistance clearly slowed access to the goldfields deepest in the interior. But it did not block it. On the other hand, attempts to put Indians to mining work were rarely successful for long, although destructive while they lasted.[92]

In the strict sense of underground work, there was little mining in Brazil. Only in Jacobina, in inland Bahia, was tunneling into veins the usual form of extraction. In Minas Gerais vein working was rare. There and further west, washing of gold-bearing sands and gravels on the surface was what "mining" meant. The dangers of darkness, airlessness, and collapsing roofs and ladders typical of Spanish American silver mining were largely unknown in Brazil. But the work was still hard and bad for the health. Slaves, and the occasional Whites to be found physically laboring, shovelled and bent for long hours, sweating in the sun but with legs and feet chilled by the water in which they generally stood. One physician of the time observed that the contrast laid the workers open to "very severe pleurisies, apoplectic and paralytic fits, convulsions, pneumonia, and many other diseases."[93] Washing did not consist simply of digging up stream beds and panning material in wooden bowls. Where possible, dams and channels were used to divert water from streams and rivers so that it flowed over promising strata, washing gold particles (or diamonds) free. This hydraulic work was arduous; and dams were known to break. Slaves were expected to last as useful workers for only seven to twelve years.

The swelling mine populations of the interior took a good deal of feeding, and of supplying in general. Their demand for foods and other goods had a broadly invigorating effect on many types of Brazilian production. The cattle raisers of Maranhão, the north-east, and then the south, responded readily to the challenge, sending off great numbers of cattle on the hoof, and quantities of salt beef. Live cattle also carried their hides with them; and leather had multiple uses in gold extraction and in everyday life in the mining towns. Coastal sugar growers were presented with a new internal market for their product. And both artisans and importing traders in the coastal towns found new selling opportunities. Quickly enough, of course, the mining areas began to produce for their own needs. Around the mining centers, and along the routes to them, estates and farms appeared, raising cattle, smaller domestic animals, and foods such as the ubiquitous manioc. But local production never filled local needs. One result for the coast, at least in the early mining years, was inflation, of the price not merely of slaves, but of many goods, foods included. Producers gained, but consumers suffered. The crown's early response was to try banning trade and communication between Bahia and Minas Gerais, and even forbidding the making of roads linking the two regions. But trade was not to be stopped. The motive of profit was reinforced, as in similar Spanish American situations, by the fact that what the miners offered in trade – gold – was itself money. Sellers got gold in hand; they needed to make no further exchanges or sales to realize their gains.[94] And so the mining region, particularly Minas Gerais itself, became a powerful force for the economic articulation of a vast area of Brazil, just as the silver mines of the Potosí district had become a century or more before, 2,300 kilometers away to the west.

Just how much gold Brazil produced is hard to say for sure. The crown assessed a royalty of a fifth on production; but collecting that tax in the frontier-like conditions of inland Brazil was no simple matter, so that taxes are a poor guide to output. A substance so compact in value was easily hidden and carried away, no matter what efforts the government might make to seal off the mining zones and control trade. Cattle drovers and other traders who knew the terrain well could spirit gold to the coast with little difficulty. There, in a variety of ships – naval and commercial, Portuguese and foreign – amateur and professional merchants stood ready to bear it away, openly or hidden, for profitable exchange in Europe or west Africa. The scale of smuggling is suggested by the contrast between two recent sets of figures, one for production and the other for arrivals of Brazilian gold in Europe. The first gives total output from 1711 to 1769 as 129,830 kilograms. (Of that amount, Minas Gerais yielded 96,250 kilograms, or 74 percent.) By the second, 619,000–639,000 kilograms reached Europe between 1711 and 1770.[95] Perhaps the labors of historians will some day reveal clearly how Brazil managed to send to Europe almost five times more gold than it produced. For the moment it seems safe to say that the production figures given here certainly understate reality; and that arrivals may have been exaggerated. A large margin of contraband gold remains. A lesser contrast between the two sets of figures is in timing. Arrivals in Europe were highest in the decade 1726–35; while production is shown as peaking from 1735 to 1744. It seems safe to conclude that Brazilian gold production was at its height c.1720–45.

If much gold slipped through the tax collecting net, it was not for lack of effort by the government. Numerous new officials were appointed to the mining zones, charged, among other things, with applying a new mining code of 1700–3. At least three foundries were set up in major mining towns after 1720, to which miners were to bring their gold to pay the royalty and have the rest cast into ingots bearing the royal arms. These fiscal innovations were only one side of the administrative response to the growth of mining. New judicial districts and local courts appeared. Militia companies were often raised to enforce law in the backlands, patrol for smugglers, and deal with the occasional disorders that arose in towns as, for example, miners protested against taxes. On a larger scale, first the captaincy of Minas Gerais was created in 1720, to be followed by those of Goiás and Mato Grosso (areas previously inland sections of the São Paulo captaincy) in 1744 and 1748. In 1752 came the very large innovation of the creation of a second Brazilian *relação*. It was sited at Rio de Janeiro to give people in the mining region, and others in the center and south, relatively quick and economical access to a court of appeal. And finally, eleven years later, arrived the most telling change of all with the raising of Rio, in place of Salvador, to the position of administrative capital of the colony. The official view now was that the success of gold mining, and the expansion of other production connected to mining, had shifted Brazil's economic and demographic weight from the north-east to the center south. That was now also where the weight of government must be. Henceforth the colony's chief executive (the post had been upgraded in 1720 from governor-ship general to viceroyalty) officiated from Rio. And Rio remained the capital of Brazil after independence until 1960, when the new city of Brasília, pur-pose-built for that role, assumed it.

Rio's rise to pre-eminence actually took place when the decline of gold mining had begun. The city's elevation did not, however, prove harmful or inappropriate, since the economy of the center and south, after a brief hiatus, again flourished with a resurgence of coastal agriculture. Gold output fell in the mid-century at bottom because the most accessible placer deposits were by then depleted. To tackle others would have required larger hydraulic efforts (longer diversions of water courses, for instance) than had hitherto been attempted. And for that neither the necessary capital nor entrepreneurial will, or probably skill, seem to have been present.[96]

ECONOMIC RESILIENCE AFTER THE GOLD BOOM

The end of the mining boom in the mid-century left both Brazil and Portugal in the economic doldrums for a time. For Portugal, indeed, that is an under-statement. Over the half-century of Brazilian mining, Portugal had grown to depend on the constant inflow of gold, and of diamonds, to balance its foreign trade. Especially in need of balance was the trade with Portugal's main commercial partner, Great Britain. Existing trading patterns between the two countries had been reinforced in 1703 by the Methuen Treaty, which gave preferential tariff treatment to imports of British wheat, cloth, and other manufactures into Portugal, and to imports of Portuguese wine and olive oil into Britain. The negative effects of this agreement for Portugal, in discour-aging industrial development there and in making the country dependent on Britain for manufactured goods, have become a commonplace. Part of the responsibility, however, must lie with the products of the Brazilian mines; since, with gold and diamonds to offer in payment, it was simpler to import than to produce. Whatever the allocation of blame, if such it be, it is plain that from 1700 to 1750 Portuguese purchases from Britain were enormously larger than sales to Britain: by one estimate, 8,737,000 pounds' worth of imports against 3,209,000 pounds of exports. Brazilian gold and diamonds made up most of the difference. With these in dwindling supply after the mid-century, overseas trade necessarily had to adjust severely; and not only trade, in fact, since a good part of the crown's income came directly or indirectly from gold and diamonds. The solution to these problems was a combination of what in modern terms would be called "import substitution industrialization," ap-plied from the 1760s onward, with reinvigoration of Portugal's system of foreign trade. Partly through governmental effort (in, for example, granting of loans) and partly through private initiative, Portugal built factories, most of them small, to produce the mainly luxury goods that had previously come in from abroad. Exports of wine and oil continued; to them were added re-exports of Brazilian plantation products, in rapidly growing quantities. And thus the deficit with Britain shrank in the 1770s and 1780s. In the 1790s Portugal actually achieved a surplus in its British trade.[97]

Brazil filled the gap left by the shrinkage of mineral exports by turning back to the land; or more exactly, to the plantation agriculture along the coast that had created such wealth in the century from 1550 to 1650. Sugar remained the most valuable crop and export. But the difference from that earlier period was that plantation owners now found large profits in other tropical crops. This diversification only reinforced Brazil's primary identity as a tropical plantation colony.

The effects of persistent warfare of the late eighteenth century did much to revitalize Brazilian sugar, making it once more the economic backbone of the colony. The Seven Years War (1756–63) brought conflict to the Caribbean. The resulting interruption of sugar supplies from the islands drove up European prices, much to the benefit of Brazilian planters. Prices sank again after 1763, however; and it was not until the War of American Independence (1775–83) that a new rise began. What finally guaranteed a lasting buoyancy in the price was the slave revolt in St Domingue in 1791. That French colony had long been the prime producer of sugar in the Caribbean. With the near-disappearance of that source, supply fell sharply below European demand, bringing gain to the remaining producers, the Brazilian planters among them. A rush of *engenho* building followed. Bahian production entered on an expansion that continued until the 1840s. Pernambuco, the other old sugar center, thrived too. And in the middle south Rio de Janeiro and São Paulo became major growers and exporters.[98]

Tobacco was another lively export in the late 1700s. It grew widely in the north and north-east, but above all in Bahia, which provided over 90 percent of the commerical crop. Exports possibly doubled from the fifties to the eighties, again in response to rising European prices. Italy, Germany, Spain, and France received the better quality tobacco produced in Brazil, mostly via Portugal. The poorer leaf stayed in Brazil, or was sent, as for long past, to Africa to be exchanged for slaves.

Four other plantation crops prospered in the economic conditions of the late eighteenth century. Cotton was first exported in the sixties. Maranhão was the main growing area until 1800, though the crop spread to other parts of the north coast, and also to the north-east. After 1800 the north-east, especially Pernambuco, took the lead in cotton. Simplicity of cultivation, good quality, and strength of price resulting from the growing mechanization of textile making in Britain and France underlay cotton's success. Like tobacco, and sugar as well, cotton reached its final European markets mostly as a re-export from Portugal. By 1792 Brazil was the source of 30 percent of the cotton fiber that British mills spun and wove.

Three foodstuffs complete the list of agricultural exports. Rice first left Maranhão for Portugal in the sixties. By 1781 enough was being shipped to replace the home country's previous imports (mainly from South Carolina). Cacao, almost all from Pará on the north coast, prospered particularly in the decade after 1800, finding profitable markets in Portugal, and via Portugal in various European countries. Lastly, there began the rising trend of coffee exports that, in the nineteenth century, was to reach such heights that the crop became almost synonymous with Brazil. Portugal began importing coffee in the 1730s, from Belém in the north. But it was only with the spread of cultivation further southward – to Pernambuco, Bahia, Rio, Minas Gerais, and São Paulo – between 1760 and 1800 that the plant found its true homes in Brazil. In 1807 the export of coffee reached some 1.5 million kilograms, seven times more than a decade before. By then Brazilian coffee could be drunk throughout western Europe, and from Moscow to north-west Africa.[99]

If rice, cacao, sugar, and coffee lacked the glamor of gold, they were in the long run much more valuable to Brazil. Gold was still being exported early in the nineteenth century. But in 1796 it made up only 17 percent of total exports (to Portugal), and in 1806, a mere 6.6 percent; while at those two dates the four foodstuffs amounted to 51 and 46 percent of all exports. Cotton was the next most valuable product sent to Portugal. Secondary effects of the great shifts in productive lines that Brazil experienced after the 1750s were quick to appear. Naturally enough, as mining subsided, so did the flow of people inland. In fact the flow stopped and may have reversed. The town of Ouro Prêto, for example, had some 20,000 citizens in the 1740s, but only about 7,000 in 1804. Fewer people ate less, so that the farming and stock-raising base that had developed around mining now contracted. At the same time, new labor demand and economic opportunities arose on the coast with the resurgence and diversification of agriculture. Coastal towns grew, as these examples show:

Belém	1749,	6,574	1801,	12,500
Recife	1750,	7,000	1810,	25,000
Salvador	1757,	35,922	1807,	51,000
Rio de Janeiro	1760,	30,000	1803,	46,944
São Paulo	1765,	20,873	1803,	24,311

Demographically, Brazil reverted considerably to its pre-mining contours in the late 1700s. The headcounts of the population that reforming adminis-trations, seeking higher tax income, now finally began to make show that c.1800 about 73 percent lived near the coast, most of them in and around the long-standing major ports of Paraíba, Pernambuco, Bahia and Rio de Janeiro. The most heavily peopled coastal captaincy was Pernambuco, at 19 percent of the total population. It seems at first contradictory, given the near demise of gold, that Minas Gerais, at that date, led all captaincies in numbers of people, with 19.7 percent of the total. That figure, however, reflects the success of Minas's conversion by the end of the century to plantation agricul-ture, particularly in sugar and coffee. The total population of Brazil as the nineteenth century began was between two and three million. It had grown between 2.5 and 4 times since a hundred years before.[100]

The fundamental reason for Brazil's success as an agricultural exporter in the late 1700s was rising demand for its crops in European countries that were experiencing population growth and early industrialization. But policy also had a part in the colony's agricultural boom. Authorities in Lisbon drafted and applied stimulatory measures. These, it is true, were conceived largely with the benefit of Portugal itself in mind. But thanks to the developing economic reality of which Portugal and Brazil were a part, some of those plans had expansionary effects that spread beyond the mother country.

POMBAL AND REFORM

Serious efforts at economic reform began during the period when Portugal was governed by Sebastião José de Carvalho e Melo, better known as the Marquis of Pombal (a title bestowed in 1769). For almost the entire reign of Joseph I of Portugal (1750–77), Pombal was secretary of state and of foreign affairs. In effect, the contrast between his own concentrated energy and the indolence of the king left him as an almost autonomous first minister of the realm and the empire, an aristocratic exponent of a despotism that in most of its applications did not stray far from Enlightenment.

Pombal had great and comprehensive schemes for the economic restoration of Portugal, an undertaking that became ever more necessary as the inflow of gold from Brazil dwindled. The devastation of Lisbon by a great earthquake in 1755 added urgency to this need. A third of the city fell on November 1 of that year, including its administrative and business center; and 15,000 or more died in the collapse of buildings, or the subsequent flood and fire.[101] It was as master of the city's rebuilding that Pombal first gained almost limitless power. The outcome was the elegant, open, geometrically regular city that still exists, a monument to enlightened orderliness.

A French visitor to Lisbon shortly before the earthquake noted in his journal: "[Portugal] is more of a province than a kingdom. One might say that the King of Portugal is a potentate of the Indies that lodges in a European land."[102] In hindsight the comment seems arrestingly prescient, though it is unlikely that its author lived long enough to know of the move to Rio de Janeiro that the Portuguese court was to make in 1807–8. It was also, especially in the economic sense, an accurate assessment of Portugal's position in the empire. Pombal set out to change that position, or at least to modify it to Portugal's advantage.

Broadly seen, Pombal's design for the empire resembled what reform-minded political economists had by then already proposed in Spain: that the colonies' central task was to serve the interests of the metropolis by producing raw materials needed by manufactories in the home country, and then by providing a market for what was made. To expand manufacture in Portugal Pombal created in 1755 a *Junta do Comércio*, or Board of Trade, to set up workshops and factories, import foreign craftsmen, provide loans, and broadly oversee production. He was keen that both large factories and smaller workshops supplying them with partly finished items should prosper. And indeed they did, producing a wide range of cloth and leather goods, clocks and watches, glassware and hardware, and sundry luxury items, from the 1760s until after 1800. Private effort responded well to governmental encouragement, and thus home-made goods displaced much that had previously been imported into both Portugal itself and the colonies (above all Brazil) from foreign sources (notably Great Britain).[103]

For the profitable and efficient working of the trading link between Portugal and Brazil, the main source of useful raw materials, Pombal also produced a set of reforms. In his view, only large and well-capitalized merchant houses could compete with the British traders who dominated the Anglo-Portuguese commerce, and also sent large contraband cargoes to Brazil. He actively suppressed small traders, whom he saw as weak, inefficient, and not least as collaborators with the British in smuggling. The government-created Board of Trade of 1755, indeed, replaced an old corporation of Lisbon merchants, which was abolished. In that same year Pombal's government chartered a company designed to trade with, and develop, Pará and Maranhão in the north of Brazil. Anticipating later Spanish reformers of American silver mining, who gave social reward, such as titles, to successful entrepreneurs, Pombal encouraged investment in this and other companies by offering membership of military orders and chances of ennoblement to prospective shareholders.[104] His aim was to dispel the social disrepute that still hung around commerce. A second Brazilian company was formed in 1759, created to trade with Pernambuco and Paraíba. Like the Maranhão company, one of its tasks was to supply adequate labor, in the form of African slaves, to its appointed region. The companies were broadly speaking corporations for development, charged with experimenting with new crops and farming methods, advancing shipbuilding and navigation, and regulating production so as to stabilize the selling price of tropical crops. They were buyers of the products of their regions, and monopoly sellers of imports from Portugal, for which they were to open up markets. Generally speaking, the companies seem to have fulfilled their developmental aims, by, for instance, promoting in their areas trials of new crops which then were exported profitably from Brazil. They operated, of course, in times when demand for such crops was rising; so that the degree to which their efforts truly propelled development is hard to say. The fact that they did not long survive Pombal, being abolished in 1778–9, may suggest that they were not as useful as he had hoped; or perhaps simply that they had done their job by then. In any case, the post-Pombaline government bent to the wishes of merchants in Portugal, and merchants and planters in Brazil, all of whom objected to the companies' control of prices, especially those of slaves.[105] Under the free trade between Portugal and Brazil that then resumed, plantation exports continued their vigorous growth.

Pombal did not stop at economic reform, in either Portugal or the empire; although all his innovating aimed to bring material benefit to Portugal. Like Gálvez and others in Spain, he sought to achieve this through tighter control by colonial government, a gathering up of the reins of power. The number of officials in Brazil was already rising when he came into office, and he added more. In 1767 an improved treasury structure was put in place, after similar reforms in Portugal itself in 1761. In the sixties, also, the colonial militia was upgraded, in part by the importation of English and German officers to train it.[106] Naturally, not all changes were fully effective; but the net result was to narrow colonials' margin of self-determination, and to make the state a more palpably intrusive presence in Brazil.

Some of Pombal's reforms managed to combine enlightened modernity with practical gain. His abolition of slavery in Portugal in 1761 seemed a humanitarian measure; but it left more slaves available for Brazil. In the middle and late fifties he asserted once again the freedom of Brazilian Indians. He went further than merely ending native slavery, however; he favored removing all distinctions between Indians and Whites. The goal seems admirable, if impossibly idealistic; but Pombal had a very practical outcome in mind. He hoped that a decreed social equalizing of American natives and Europeans would promote marriages between them (which he saw as entirely honorable) and hence quicken population growth in Brazil. For it seemed to him that the colony was underpeopled, that Portugal could not control or defend it if it were not more completely settled. Pombal came close, indeed, to the idea famously aphorized by the nineteenth-century Argentine political thinker, Juan Bautista Alberdi, as "to govern is to populate" ("gobernar es poblar").[107] But these were the fantasies of a remote theorizer. If he had ever seen in person the size of Brazil, and the social and cultural contrasts between Indians and Whites, he would perhaps have concluded that governmental promotion of mixed marriage was unlikely to add much to the population density.

Pombal's Indian policies had, however, a most tangible effect in his administration's relationship with the leading advocates of native Brazilians, the Jesuits. For them, separation of natives from colonials had always been fundamental to the Indians' well-being and survival. Pombal's wish to blend native people into the general population was therefore anathema. Without doubt, less noble issues were also at stake. For the Jesuits, control of Indians was a political as well as a humanitarian matter. Politics, and economics also, were very much in Pombal's mind: the Jesuits, with their many mission villages, seemed to be running large areas of Brazil amounting to a veritable "state within a state"; and their possession of large, profitable estates was a temptation to him, as it was also to Spanish reformers in the 1760s.

Pombal, however, was possessed of, or rather possessed by, a special animus toward the Jesuits that made his hostility to them more virulent by far than anything that Spanish officials could muster. The sources of this detestation are unclear; but it grew as his power rose in the fifties. The fact that the Society, a markedly international body, had sent foreign priests to Brazil clearly fed his suspicions. He informed the papal nuncio in Lisbon that some, at least, of the Jesuits in Amazonia were in reality disguised European engineers using the slave labor of countless Indians to build fortifications (presumably to exclude Portugal from the region). With perhaps more reason, he believed that Jesuits in the south were collaborating with the British in illegal trade. Quite clearly in the realm of reality was the Society's dominance of education in Brazil, which gave it a unique influence among the white population. To his accusations, imagined or otherwise, about Jesuits' doings in Brazil, Pombal added allegations that they had been involved in political unrest in Portugal itself, including an attempt on the king's life in 1758. The upshot was the government's decree, in September 1759, expelling the Jesuits from Portuguese territories. The number ejected from Brazil was about 670.[108] And so began the assault on the Society that was to continue in the French and Spanish expulsions in 1764 and 1767, and culminate in its suppression by Rome from 1773 to 1814. The royal treasury gained from the sale of some of the Jesuits' lands in Brazil; other estates remained under crown supervision, and indeed passed into the national government's control after Independence. Nor were Jesuit estates the only church property to be taken. The seizure of Mercedarian lands in lower Amazonia in the mid-sixties, and the recall of the friars to Portugal, suggest that Pombal was inspired not simply by his private hatred of the Jesuits, but also by the prevailing regalism of the day, reinforced by the secularism of the Enlightenment.

In a limited way he was also a man of the Enlightenment in his attitudes to education. There was, apparently, little notion in him of the intrinsic worth, or pleasure, of gaining knowledge; but he did esteem new knowledge and ways of thought for their utility in material development and administration. For that reason he created a system of secondary schooling in Portugal, and oversaw a modernization of the University of Coimbra in 1772, adding to it faculties of mathematics and philosophy (which embraced the natural sciences).[109] Coimbra remained as the sole Portuguese university; the only other, at Evora, was a Jesuit institution, and was closed. From Coimbra in the late eighteenth century duly emerged modern-minded men, some rising to the peaks of government, who worked for the material advance of the empire, Brazil included.

In Brazil itself, however, education did not progress under Pombal; the reverse, in fact. The Jesuits had maintained seventeen secondary colleges and seminaries in the colony, and with them had provided almost all the available education. With the expulsion, these schools were without teachers. Colonial Brazil had no university. The contrast with the Spanish colonies, where universities were founded in the sixteenth century, is striking. The Portuguese crown, perhaps because its colonial apparatus was generally smaller and looser than the Spaniards', saw political advantages in making colonials dependent on Coimbra for their higher education. For similar reasons, and again in stark contrast to Spanish America, Brazil had no printing press until 1808. Two attempts to set up presses in the eighteenth century were blocked by the government. Pombal, wishing to center the empire on Portugal, logically upheld the prior line. For him, publishing and higher learning had no place in Brazil.

Brazil, then, felt Pombal's imperious touch in a number of instances, and with it a sense of new subordination to Portugal's interests: more taxes, more officials, new monopoly companies, control of import and export prices, hostility to local manufacture, foreign military instructors, attempts at radical social engineering, and much else. That said, very few in the colony seem finally to have found this increased Portuguese pressure intolerable.[110] Perhaps the reason was in part that the pressure eased after Pombal fell from power in 1777, and Portuguese administration lost the sharp edge that he had put on it. Perhaps also his reforms seemed, on balance, more developmental than extractive. Certainly neither they, nor any measures applied later, had quite the extortionate quality that is evident in Spain's fiscal treatment of the American colonies in the 1790s and later. Again, prosperity may have blunted protest. The same wars that in the nineties made Spain desperate for American income brought great trading profits to Brazil as well as Portugal. To rising industrialism's demand for raw materials was added that caused by preparations for war in northern Europe. Finally, that unblockable accessibility of Brazil should not be forgotten. Despite any efforts that Portugal could make to stop it, contraband trade persisted on the Brazilian coast. The British, above all others, were constantly there, by-passing Lisbon to exchange their growing abundance of manufactures for Brazil's growing cornucopia of tropical plantation produce. The resulting gains to the upper segment of colonial society can only have served to allay distress about Portuguese reformism among those best placed to take action against it.

PRODUCTS OF MIND AND SENSIBILITY

If Brazil lacked universities and presses, it was not, in the eighteenth century at least, without a life of the mind. Such activity is most easily seen in various academies that appeared from the 1720s onward in the larger towns. Salvador and Rio de Janeiro were the main places where these groups arose. The names chosen suggest, with the exception of the first, a certain self-confidence or perhaps enlightened optimism. The earliest was the Brazilian Academy of the Forgotten (*Academia Brasílica dos Esquecidos*, Salvador, 1724–5). Then followed the Academy of the Fortunate (*Academia dos Felizes*, Rio, 1736–40); the Academy of the Select (*Academia dos Selectos*, Rio, 1751–2); the Brazilian Academy of the Reborn (*Academia Brasílica dos Renascidos*, Salvador, 1759–60); the *Academia Scientífica* (Rio, 1772–9); and finally the *Sociedade Literária* (Rio, 1786–90, 1794). The transience of these groups possibly indicates that they were the products of the coincidental presence of men of like interests; there was not perhaps the "critical mass" of the intellectually inclined needed to make them permanent. Nonetheless, they left a mark. From the start with the "Forgotten," for instance, they called attention to Brazil itself – its wealth, beauty, and economic centrality in the empire. One of that group, Caetano de Brito e Figueiredo, proclaimed in his *Dissertação Terceira* ("Third Dissertation") that "Golden Brazil is the depository of the most priceless metal, fertile producer of the sweetest sugar canes, and generous cultivator of the most useful plants ... Brazil is the most precious jewel of the Lusitanian sceptre, the most valuable stone in the Portuguese crown, which of itself possesses much majesty and beauty."[111] Sebastião da Rocha Pita, another member of the group, produced in 1730 his *História da América portuguesa*, a renowned history of Brazil that expresses his pride of identity with the colony. Later in the century members of the academies, like parallel figures in Spanish America at the time, made studies of Brazil's animals, plants, agricultural and mineral resources, and geography. Hard fact thus came to reinforce sentiment as a foundation for proto-national feeling, even if that feeling was limited to a very few at the upper end of society.

Many of those who gathered information about Brazil had been educated at Coimbra, and were products of that university's modern reorientation after its reform by Pombal. Their own fascination with the physical reality of Brazil derived from a physiocratic concern with land and agriculture that they absorbed in Portugal. Later they brought Adam Smith to Brazil. The *Wealth of Nations* was among the first works to appear from the newly installed presses after 1808. Two different translations, in fact, appeared from presses in Rio and Salvador, in 1811 and 1812 respectively. Free traders and economic liberals in general then had the classic theoretical statement of their positions close at hand.

The mining town of Ouro Prêto was a third intellectual center of eighteenth-century Brazil. Particularly notable was a group of poets who wrote there late in the century. Generally speaking, however, colonial Brazil's literary production was small in comparison with what emerged from Spanish America. Chronicles, histories, and descriptions from the sixteenth century onward certainly exist, but not on the scale produced by either of colonial Spanish America's central regions. The same may be said of formal music in colonial Brazil. Such music as is known dates from the second half of the eighteenth century. The first piece with a Portuguese text is a cantata that was sung in Salvador at an early meeting of the *Academia dos Renascidos* in July 1759. In Rio de Janeiro and various towns of Minas Gerais a number of mulatto church organists and choirmasters were also active as composers. No trace of Africa appears in their work, however; their inspiration was in European composers of the time, who were the admired models. One of them, José Maurício Nunes Garcia (1767–1830), a leading musical figure in Rio, conducted there in 1819 the first American performance of Mozart's *Requiem*.[112]

Buildings, above all churches, are the richest artistic relic of colonial Brazil. And among them, the most distinctive are those of the second half of the eighteenth century. Sixteenth-century churches were simple, largely wooden, structures. Greater size and complexity came in the 1600s with the arrival of the baroque. The churches, though often now splendid, were, however, similar in plan to those of Spanish America: an essentially flat, tripartite façade (a central section flanked by towers), fronting a rectangular structure containing three aisles. The interiors were at first, also, of a similar simplicity and restraint. But from the 1660s a notion of the "church wholly of gold" ("igreja toda de ouro") influenced Portugal and Brazil. Interiors decorated with gold leaf laid over carved wood began to appear. An early Brazilian example is the "Gilded Chapel" (1695–1702) of the Franciscan Third Order at Recife.[113]

By that time gold was becoming abundantly available for such purposes; and the previously plain interiors of various large churches in the coastal cities were fitted with dense, even overpowering, gilded and polychromed ornamentation that comprised spiraling columns, masses of carved foliage, gamboling cherubs, and sacred figures peering from niches. In Minas Gerais itself, however, which was the source of the gold used both to gild and pay for these creations, a greater simplicity, at least in decoration, prevailed. Here substantial building in masonry began *c.*1730. It was after 1750, however, that most of the distinctive churches of the region appeared, churches that now seem to epitomize the architectural style of colonial Brazil. In them, the imposing mass of the baroque gave way to the daintiness of the rococo. The churches were smaller and lower. In the clearest cases, straight lines were replaced by curves. Façades were convex curves; towers were cylindrical; ground plans were rounded, oval, or even double-oval in form. Interior decoration was sparer, with delicate and fanciful traceries set rhythmically in open spaces of wall and ceiling. A light, shell-like frame was placed around windows. These churches seem to draw on the rococo style of Bavaria and Austria in the mid-eighteenth century. And in reality they may well do so. The suggested linkage is through the marriages of Peter II of Portugal (1667–1706) to a Bavarian princess, of his successor, John V (1707–50) to an Austrian princess, and of Pombal, no less, to another Austrian princess.[114] The Austrian rococo is present in eighteenth-century Portugal; and Portugal is its supposed stepping stone to Brazil.

Among the designers of the churches of Minas Gerais was a mulatto born in the captaincy's major town, Ouro Prêto, who has been described as "the greatest architect and sculptor Brazil has produced."[115] This was António Francisco Lisboa (c.1738–1814), better known as O Aleijadinho, the little cripple. He is so called because from the age of about forty a disease, possibly leprosy or syphilis, attacked his hands and feet, and deprived him of movement. Latterly he worked with pen, chisel, or mallet strapped to the remains of his hands. The local soapstone that served for both building and sculpture is, fortunately, soft when newly quarried; it hardens with weathering. Aleijadinho is the architect of the church of São Francisco in Ouro Prêto, among others. He did much decorative stonework, such as portals, altars, and pulpits, for yet other churches. But his most admired creation is one of carved human figures: the ensembles of sixty-six statues in wood, and twelve in stone, at the pilgrim church of Bom Jesus de Matosinhos, overlooking the town of Congonhas do Campo in Minas Gerais. The wooden, polychromed figures are set in six small chapels along the rising approach to the church. They depict scenes from Christ's Passion. The stone statues, representing Biblical prophets, stand on plinths built into the walls of a double stairway leading up to the church.

> Placed in strategic positions, the huge figures seem to dance a tremendous ballet as the visitor winds his way back and forth walking up the steps. He is made to see the statues from all sides and angles. From a distance all twelve prophets, in diverse attitudes, greet him. As one comes nearer, they act in ever-changing groups of different sets of eight, six, four, even two... Their features are harsh and sharp, their costumes fantastic, with Oriental overtones, their expressions prophetic.[116]

In their scale and severity, these statues seem far from the rococo. Their emotional force and their exoticism perhaps hint at some early infiltration of romanticism into this remote interior of Brazil; or perhaps they are *sui generis*, simply the late product of Aleijadinho's singular sensibility. Still, it is the rococo that dominates Brazilian architecture in the late eighteenth century, and which can be taken as the closing style of the colonial era. Neo-classicism, in contrast to its prevalence in the late Spanish colonies, barely makes an appearance in Brazil before 1800. The Brazilian reaction to the heavy excesses of baroque ornament was not the grave austerity of classical imitation, but the lighter, more graceful decorativeness of the rococo. The Spanish crown, whether with inherent political message or not, tried to impose the new solemnity of neo-classicism on its American territories in the late 1700s. The Portuguese did not. The contrast perhaps signals how much lighter the reforming touch of the Portuguese rulers generally was than that of their Spanish counterparts. And that difference was to have a large effect on the manner in which the two colonial structures were soon to gain independence; and, indeed, a bearing on the development of their respective histories through much of the nineteenth century.

PART VI

SELF-DISCOVERY: THE NINETEENTH CENTURY AND BEYOND

CHRONOLOGY OF PART VI

1778   Birth of José de San Martín

1778–9   The *Inconfidência Mineira* in Brazil (*Tiradentes'* plot)

1783   Birth of Simón Bolívar

1790–1873   Life of José Antonio Páez, *caudillo* in Venezuela

1791   Slave revolt in Saint Domingue (Haiti)

1793–1877   Life of Juan Manuel de Rosas, *caudillo* in Río de la Plata

1794–1876   Life of Antonio López de Santa Anna, *caudillo* in Mexico

1795   Peace of Basle between France and Spain

1797   Spain forced to allow colonies to trade with neutral countries

1798   "Tailors' Plot" in Salvador

1803   Louisiana sold by Napoleon Bonaparte to the United States

1805   French–Spanish naval defeat at Trafalgar by Britain

1806   Miranda tries, and fails, to start rebellion in Venezuela

1807   Franco-Spanish invasion of Portugal

1808   Abdication of Charles IV of Spain. Accession and abdication of Ferdinand VII. French occupation of Spain. Joseph I placed on Spanish throne by Napoleon. British expeditionary force sent to Spain. Emergence of Spanish national junta. Viceroy deposed in New Spain by *Audiencia* of Mexico. Arrival of Portuguese royal family in Rio de Janeiro

1809   Risings in Buenos Aires and Quito

1809–10   Independence declared in La Paz (Bolivia), but quickly suppressed by Spanish forces

1810   Declarations of self-government in Caracas, Santiago de Chile, and Buenos Aires (effective permanent independence of Río de la Plata). Viceroy deposed in New Granada. Return of Miranda to Venezuela. In Mexico, the "Grito de Dolores," and multiple risings in the north. Treaty of Navigation and Commerce between Great Britain and government in Brazil

1810–14   Deliberations of Cortes (Parliament) of Cadiz

1811   Defeat, and execution, of Hidalgo in Mexico. Effective achievement of independence by Paraguay. French expelled from Portugal

1812   Constitution of Cadiz

1813   French expelled from Spain. Morelos captures Acapulco

1814   Ferdinand restored to Spanish throne. First Mexican constitution issued, at Apatzingán

1815   Final defeat of Napoleon Bonaparte. Execution of Morelos. Brazil raised to status of kingdom, constitutionally equal with Portugal

1816   Death of Miranda

1817   Battle of Chacabuco. Republic of Pernambuco briefly declared in Brazil

1818   Battle of Maipú. Independence of Chile

1819   Battle of Boyacá. Independence of Colombia

1820   San Martín lands on Peruvian coast, at Pisco. Military revolt in Spain, and restoration there of liberal constitution of 1812. In Portugal, military revolt, adoption of Spanish constitution of 1812, and declaration of constitutional monarchy

1821   Battle of Carabobo. Independence of Venezuela. San Martín named Protector of Peru. Plan of Iguala in Mexico, and subsequent independence. Return of John VI from Brazil to Portugal

1822   Battle of Pichincha. Independence of Ecuador. Confidential meeting of Bolívar and San Martín at Guayaquil, and San Martín's withdrawal from the independence movement. In Brazil, proclamation of Peter I as emperor, and independence

1824   Battles of Junín and Ayacucho. Independence of Peru. Federalist constitution in Mexico, and beginning of first federalist republic (ended 1836)

1825   Independence of Bolivia

1828   Effective independence of Uruguay

1830   Death of Bolívar

1832–3   First modern factory built in Latin America (a powered cotton mill near Puebla in Mexico)

1836–9   Confederation of Bolivia and Peru, under Santa Cruz

1844   Independence of Hispaniola (Dominican Republic), from Haiti

1845–51   First presidency of Ramón Castilla in Peru (second, 1855–62)

1850   Death of San Martín

1852   Rosas driven from power in Buenos Aires

1853   Argentine federalist constitution

1855   Final exit of Santa Anna from politics in Mexico

1857   Reform (liberal) constitution of Mexico

1860s   Beginning of boom in Latin American primary exports (lasting until c.1930), and of age of oligarchies in government

1864–7   Reign of the Archduke Maximilian as emperor of Mexico

1870s   Beginning of large (especially southern) European emigration to Latin America (continuing until c.1930). Revival of foreign lending to, and investment in, Latin America. Start of major railway building, and of industrialization in form of small factories. Beginnings of organized labor. Rising influence of positivism

1871   "Free-womb" law in Brazil

1877   Beginning of Porfiriato (the age of Porfirio Díaz) in Mexico

1879–84   War of the Pacific

1886   Abolition of slavery in Cuba

1887   Statue of Cuauhtemoc erected in Mexico City

1888   Abolition of slavery in Brazil

1889   Abdication of Peter II in Brazil, under military pressure. Brazil proclaimed a republic

1891   Federal constitution in Brazil

1898   Spanish–American War. Independence of Cuba and Puerto Rico

1903   Separation of Panama from Colombia

1904–14   Panama Canal built

1910   "Plan of San Luis Potosí" issued in Mexico by Francisco Madero

1911   End of Porfiriato in Mexico. Madero assumes presidency

1913   Madero removed from Mexican presidency by military coup, and killed. Beginning of great violence of Mexican revolution (lasting until 1915)

1917   Mexican constitution, statist and nationalist, replaces that of 1857. Election of Venustiano Carranza as president of Mexico

1920   Flight, and death, of Carranza in Mexico. Election of Alvaro Obregón to Mexican presidency

1920s   Rising political influence of working class in much of Latin America. United States now the dominant financial and economic influence in Latin America

1929   Crash of stock market in New York. Beginning of economic depression. In Mexico, foundation of the National Revolutionary Party (precursor of the PRI, or Institutional Revolutionary Party), and beginning of the *Maximato* of Plutarco Elías Calles (to 1934)

1930s (to 1950s)   Period of populism in politics, and internally directed industrialization in economic policy

1930–45   First presidency of Getúlio Vargas in Brazil (second, 1951–4)

1934–40   Presidency of Lázaro Cárdenas in Mexico

1937   "Estado Nôvo" ("New State") declared by Vargas in Brazil

1938   Foreign oil companies expropriated in Mexico

1945–late 1970s   Period of exceptionally high economic growth across Latin America

1946–55   Presidency of Juan Domingo Perón in Argentina (second presidency 1973–4)

c.1950   Policies of Import Substitution Industrialization (ISI) implemented in much of Latin America, under the influence of the Prebisch thesis

1952   Revolution in Bolivia

1959   Revolution in Cuba

1960s–1980s   (dates vary in different countries) Period of military government ("bureaucratic authoritarianism") in much of Latin America

1968   Coup by reformist military in Peru

1973   Overthrow in Chile of socialist government of Salvador Allende, by military (under General Augusto Pinochet)

1979   Sandinistas oust Somoza regime and dynasty in Nicaragua

1982   Debt crisis (economic difficulties for rest of the decade in most of Latin America). Britain retains Falkland (Malvinas) Islands in war with Argentina

1988   Military rule (Pinochet regime) ended in Chile by referendum

1990   Sandinistas voted out of office in Nicaragua

1992   Abimael Guzmán, and other leaders of the Sendero Luminoso, captured in Lima: effective end of Sendero's guerrilla activities

2000   Election of first president in Mexico since 1929 not from the dominant party: Vicente Fox (of PAN, or National Action Party)

FURTHER READING FOR PART VI

The standard account in English of the movements of independence is John Lynch, *The Spanish American Revolutions, 1808–1826*. A succinct work is Richard Graham, *Independence in Latin America. A Comparative Approach* (2nd edn, McGraw-Hill, New York, 1994). William S. Robertson, *Rise of the Spanish-American Republics as told in the Lives of their Liberators,* is a traditional but still engaging approach to the subject. For Brazil, see Roderick J. Barman, *Brazil. The Forging of a Nation, 1798–1852.* Volume 3 of *The Cambridge History of Latin America* contains essays on the independence of individual regions.

For the nineteenth century a good survey is David Bushnell and Neill Macaulay, *The Emergence of Latin America in the Nineteenth Century*; and for the nineteenth and twentieth, see the standard studies by Tulio Halpern Donghi, *The Contemporary History of Latin America*, and Thomas E. Skidmore and Peter H. Smith, *Modern Latin America*. For the second half of the twentieth century, John Ward, *Latin America. Development and Conflict since 1945*, is a succinct survey, with illuminating comparisons with other parts of the world. For economic matters, Victor Bulmer-Thomas provides a broad synthesis in *The Economic History of Latin America since Independence*; for twentieth-century economic affairs, see also Rosemary Thorp, *Progress, Poverty and Exclusion*. In addition to the chapters treating particular countries in volumes 3, 4 and 5 of *The Cambridge History*, consult the country studies in the Latin American Histories Series published by Oxford University Press (various dates, some studies in second editions): Charles C. Cumberland, *Mexico. The Struggle for Modernity*; Herbert S. Klein, *Bolivia. The Evolution of a Multi-Ethnic Society*; Franklin W. Knight, *The Caribbean. The Genesis of a Fragmented Nationalism*; John V. Lombardi, *Venezuela. The Search for Order, the Dream of Progress*; Brian Loveman, *Chile. The Legacy of Hispanic Capitalism*; Louis A. Pérez, Jr., *Cuba. Between Reform and Revolution*; James R. Scobie, *Argentina. A City and a Nation*; Thomas E. Skidmore, *Brazil. Five Centuries of Change*; Ralph L. Woodward, *Central America. A Nation Divided*. Also see: for Mexico, Alan Knight, *The Mexican Revolution*; for Argentina, David Rock, *Argentina, 1516–1987. From Spanish Colonization to Alfonsín*; and for Peru, Fredrick B. Pike, *The Modern History of Peru*. The Duke University Press (Durham, North Carolina) is publishing an attractive set of *Readers* on Latin America, country by country, each book containing a selection of translated documents, commentary by historians, and illustrations. An example is Robert M. Levine and John J. Crocitti (eds), *The Brazil Reader. History, Culture, Politics* (Durham, 1999). Informative discussions of broad topics in Latin American affairs after 1930 (politics, society, economy, church, and so on) are to be found in *The Cambridge History*, Volume 6, parts 1 and 2. Two well illustrated and comprehensive works on Latin American art are Dawn Ades, *Art in Latin America. The Modern Era, 1829–1980*, and Jacqueline Barnitz, *Twentieth-Century Art of Latin America* (University of Texas Press, Austin, 2001).

[14] *INDEPENDENCE*

Between 1810 and 1825 all the Spanish territories on the American mainland gained their independence from Spain. In the Caribbean, by contrast, Cuba and Puerto Rico remained under Spanish rule until 1898; and Hispaniola was occupied and controlled by Haiti from 1822 to 1844, at which point it broke free. Two other large islands once held by Spain had yielded to English attack, Jamaica in 1655 and Trinidad in 1797, and remained British colonies until 1962.

For obvious enough reasons of national sentiment and historical drama, the fight for independence, and the origins of that fight, have long drawn historians' scrutiny. Their only rival for attention in Latin America's past has been the European conquest itself. The fascination with independence is justified. The story of its achievement is a stirring one; and a tracing of its sources shows them to have been deep and numerous.

Latin American independence came in the midst of an era of sweeping change in the Western world. It was indeed part of that change. The Enlightenment, in advertising the potency of human reason, had accustomed those whom it touched to the notion that change was a normal state of being; for what was dangerous, damaging or demeaning in the human condition could be remedied by the proper application of the mind's power. Progress was easily within the human grasp. This message had penetrated Spanish America by the late eighteenth century. Educated creoles (though, it is true, few others) had read and debated the writings of the European Enlightenment. Literary societies of the late eighteenth century, some of them set up by intendants, had often provided a forum for such discussion. Some creoles had also conversed with visiting European savants sent by the Spanish crown to modernize mining or make scientific surveys of the land and its resources. Others, though fewer, had visited Europe, and continued to do so at the opening of the new century. They brought news back with them of all manner of European innovation. But news came from abroad under its own impetus. Colonials were well aware, for instance, of the United States' independence, of the drafting of the new nation's constitution, and of the development of federal government. They were the target of political tracts brought by North American traders, who also on occasion gave out copies of the US Declaration of Independence and of the constitution. They were equally informed of the course of events in France after 1789. Those happenings struck some colonials as inspiring and admirable; but, especially as the French Revolution took an extreme turn in the nineties, far more found them unnatural and frightening (a view that was reinforced by the eruption of the revolution's American offshoot in the form of the Haitian slave revolt of 1791).

Thus change was in the political air of Spanish America as the eighteenth century ended. Or, better, the possibility of change was in the air. That possibility, rather than any particular set of beliefs, was the political legacy of the Enlightenment to the Spanish colonies. Creoles did not necessarily take up notions of inherent human freedom and equality, nor accept that government should follow the popular will; though some did. But most, perhaps almost all, inevitably absorbed the pervasive questioning of traditional order and stability that the Englightenment radiated. Only those living in extraordinary isolation escaped it.

In the preliminaries to the independence conflict, and to a considerable degree in its conduct as well, creoles were the prime political actors on the American side. They were the potential political nation in the various colonies. To their number may be added a scattering of mestizos, men such as Túpac Amaru who, for particular reasons of birth or personal qualities, were able to make a political mark. But in general creoles were those in the colonies with the educated awareness needed for the conception of political schemes at a regional or national level. Hence their increase in the eighteenth century, which made them by far the largest part of the white population in the colonies, had great political meaning. Rising creole consciousness of the several colonies' geographical, economic, and human realities; creole reaction to European, and especially Spanish, disdain of America and its inhabitants; creole resentment at exclusion from office; creole acceptance of the pervasive notion that the traditional order was not immutable: all these gained a political charge proportional to the rise in creole numbers. If reasons for changing the old order became potent enough, there were now, as the nineteenth century began, many capable of acting on them.

In the opening years of the century, the causes for creole discontent accumulated. Some were specific to particular colonies, sometimes indeed to particular areas within colonies. Others were more or less generalized. There was certainly a current of "pure" desire for escape from Spanish rule. This was strongest among urban creoles on the east side of South America. They were inhabitants of places that lacked, by the standards of, say, Mexico City, Quito, or Lima, a sense of deep colonial tradition, having grown fast in the eighteenth century from the export of agricultural products to Europe. Some, at least, of their creole citizens tended to radicalism for its own sake. The preeminent example is Francisco de Miranda (1750–1816), a merchant's son from Caracas who well before 1800 began to seek foreign support for the ejection of Spain from America. His first inspiration was the United States, which he came to know through residence and travel in 1784. His second was France. He spent much of the nineties there, actually commanding French revolutionary troops in the field as a general in 1792, and then being considered by the French as the leader of a projected revolutionizing attack on Spanish America.

This came to nothing, as did Miranda's efforts at various times to persuade the United States and British governments to back his schemes of liberation with men and materials. In 1806 he raised a volunteer force of 150 men in the United States in the hope of igniting a rebellion in Venezuela, but failed to do so in two attempts. It was only in 1810 that he finally returned to Venezuela, after a declaration against Spain had already been made in Caracas. Briefly in 1812 he was given supreme powers by the rebels. But soon afterward the Spanish prevailed. Miranda was captured, and died in prison four years later.[1] He has gone down as the greatest of the "precursors" of Spanish American independence. He was not alone. Other expatriate creoles in European capitals imitated him on a smaller scale. One was Antonio Nariño, from New Granada, who sought British help; another, Pedro Fermín de Vargas, also from New Granada, in Paris.

A more concrete issue in the exporting regions on the Atlantic coast of South America was free trade. For Buenos Aires, Spain's basic policy of blocking free exchange with lands outside the empire was particularly irksome. The pampas hinterland of the city was an apparently limitless source of the leather for which excellent markets existed in the industrializing countries. Mariano Moreno (1778–1811), a creole lawyer who was one of the chief agitators for change in Buenos Aires, wrote forcefully in 1809 in favor of free trade.[2] Moreno greatly admired Rousseau, and indeed was the editor of a translation of the *Social Contract* published in Buenos Aires. In 1810 he was one of the leading spirits in Buenos Aires's declaration of self-government. For the progressive authors of that action, there was no more burning issue than freedom of trade.

For merchants on the west coast of South America, and in Mexico, by contrast, the question was less urgent. Neither region sensed such potential gain from open participation in the Atlantic trading system as did Caracas with its cacao, and Buenos Aires with its hides. Traders in those older sections of the empire had learned to work, though not without frequent complaint, within the restrictive limits of Spanish trade policy. But other discontents with Spanish government were widespread enough by 1800, even in those more traditional, and in most respects more conservative, regions. There was a sense of the invasiveness of the enlarged bureaucracy that had resulted from the reforms of Charles III's time, an increased awareness of Spanish control (or at least intention to control). Tax rates had risen, and taxes were now more efficiently gathered than before. Indeed, the state's demands seemed to be progressing from taxation to outright seizure, as in the forced liquidation of the *obras pías*. And particularly vexing was the knowledge that these exactions were being made by an enfeebled European state, one that had become in all but name the lackey of France.

Spain's junior position in the association with France founded on the Bourbon link had been clear enough from the beginning of the eighteenth century. It became painfully obvious in the 1790s, when Charles IV had to decide how to treat revolutionary France, a challenge that led to Spain's bouncing between France and England in a seemingly helpless fashion. Faced in 1792 with growing radicalism in the revolution, confirmed by the execution of Louis XVI in January 1793, Spain first formed an alliance with Britain against France.[3] This led to a Spanish invasion of southern France in 1793, a larger retaliatory French movement into northern Spain the next year, and in consequence the Peace of Basle between France and Spain in mid-1795. A year later the two countries allied against Britain. Now disasters rained on Spain thick and fast. Britain was more powerful at sea than France and Spain combined. In February 1797 Admiral Jervis defeated a Spanish fleet off Cape St Vincent at the southern tip of Portugal; and in America the British took Trinidad. A British blockade of Cadiz and broad assault on Spanish shipping all but severed Spain's links with America, halting the commercial gains that had resulted from the trade reform of 1778, and cutting the flow of silver from America at a time of general mining boom. Few were the occasions in the empire's history when American silver was more desperately needed. Then, to meet the colonies' needs for imported foods, manufactures, and raw materials, and to allow them to sell their exports, Spain was forced to let them trade with neutral countries. Permission for this was given in late 1797, and was withdrawn in April 1799; but trade with neutrals did not thereby cease. And in reality it was all but free trade, since the origins of cargoes could not easily be checked, and ships might enter colonial ports under false papers.[4] Colonials grew used to this open commerce. And the United States, a major neutral trader, sent ships to ports throughout Spanish America, and with them spread word of its political successes among increasingly receptive creoles.

Hostilities ceased, though only briefly, with the Peace of Amiens in 1802. But even the treaty cost Spain dearly. For Napoleon, first consul of France since 1799 and soon to be emperor, yielded to Britain Spain's title to Trinidad. Then, when hostilities between France and Britain resumed in May 1803, he sold Louisiana to the United States to raise money, in spite of an obligation by treaty with Spain never to dispose of that territory. In late 1804 Spain was again pulled into France's combat with the British. An early outcome was Nelson's crushing of the combined allied fleets at Trafalgar in October of 1805 – a defeat that signaled the end of an epic of doughty Spanish seagoing that had begun with the voyages of exploration in the late fifteenth century. For France, the blow was less telling. Although Trafalgar brought Napoleon's naval schemes to a halt, he proved irresistible on land over the following two years, dominating much of Europe through brilliant victories. In October 1807, by the Treaty of Fontainebleau, he concerted with Spain an invasion of Portugal, Britain's continental ally. The Franco-Spanish invasion took place in November 1807, with French troops crossing Spanish territory to participate. Shortly before Lisbon was occupied, British vessels spirited away the Portuguese royal family and court to Rio de Janeiro. France had negotiated the 1807 treaty with Manuel Godoy, Charles IV's first minister, who by its terms was to become prince of the southern tier of Portugal, the Algarve. But in March 1808, Prince Ferdinand, Charles IV's son, led a rising against Godoy, not concerned by the possibility (or perhaps welcoming it) that the king might fall along with his minister. That in effect was the outcome. Charles abdicated in favor of his son, who then became king, as Ferdinand

VII. Napoleon, observing the chaos into which Spanish government had descended, and the fall of Godoy, the minister with whom he had dealt in Spain, then resolved to cut through the Spanish tangle with a military occupation of the country and the installation of his brother Joseph as monarch. Napoleon had, indeed, for some years past contemplated placing Spain under his direct control; the confusion of early 1808 provided an easy opening for doing so. On March 23 French troops entered Madrid. Ferdinand believed that they had come in his support. But Napoleon ordered both him and his father to Bayonne, in south-western France. In May he was forced to abdicate in favor of Joseph, who became José I of Spain. And in France Ferdinand was detained until Napoleon's own abdication in 1814.[5]

1808–1809

A hundred years had passed since Spain had last been filled with foreign troops, in the War of Succession that had confirmed the Bourbons on the throne. The subordinate linkage to France that had begun with that war and its settlement at Utrecht had now drawn Spain down into the mortification of both occupation and an imposed, alien monarch. But from this humiliation arose a powerful popular reaction, "the first great people's war of modern history."[6] Spaniards, again drawing perhaps on a genius for military improvisation that they had shown in the American conquests, began a dogged guerrilla war against the French. Spanish resistance was soon backed by the arrival of British troops, sent by a government which saw the Iberian peninsula as the only European land arena on which Napoleonic France could now be fought. A British force landed in Portugal in August 1808. Its commander was Arthur Wellesley, whose actions over the next five years in what became known in Spanish history as the War of Independence brought him the title of Duke of Wellington. The expulsion of the French from Spain in 1813, coupled with the loss of the Grand Army in its retreat from Moscow in the winter of 1812–13, marked the collapse of Napoleon's imperial design.

The French invasion produced a political as well as a military reaction in Spain. In response to the disappearance of the monarchy, local and regional governing councils, or juntas, sprung up across the country. It was a remarkable practical demonstration of the rooting in Spain of eighteenth-century notions of popular sovereignty; and also, some have argued, of the emergence from long suppression of medieval Spanish notions of participatory government. In September 1808 a national junta formed, asserting itself as the legitimate source of Spanish and imperial government in defiance of the French regime. This Junta Central met first at Aranjuez, just south of Madrid. French military advance gradually pushed it southward in 1809. Early in 1810, the Junta yielded to the demands from local councils for a more representative form of national government, and made arrangements for the gathering of a parliament, or cortes, with delegates from those parts of Spain still able to send them, and also from the colonies. By mid-1810 almost the only city in Spain secure from French attack was the port of Cadiz, in the far south. The town stands at the end of a long and narrow promontory, which made for easy defense on land. Spanish and English ships provided protection from seaborne assault, and also brought in supplies. It was here that Spain's first national parliament met in September 1810, and deliberated over the following three and a half years. This Cortes of Cadiz was a remarkably liberal body, in part because local people were named as substitutes for delegates from areas of Spain under French occupation, and also for American representatives who were slow to arrive because of distance. Cadiz itself, an outward-looking, middle-class trading community, was markedly liberal in its attitudes. The effect of the substitutions, then, was to emphasize liberalism in the assembly. And this body, in 1812, produced not only Spain's first written constitution, but one that has been called "the banner of liberalism throughout southern Europe and Latin America for decades."[7] On the movement toward independence, the immediate political issue in Spanish America, the effects of the document were certainly telling.

In the colonies the political outcome of the French invasion was as immediate as it was in Spain, and still more profound. Wrenching disputes over how government should proceed produced splits within single administrations. The key issues were those of sovereignty and legitimacy. Clearly the imposed French monarchy possessed neither. The exiled Spanish monarchy had both, but was inaccessible. What was to be made, then, of the Junta Central, once it appeared? Could it be accepted as the current source of Spanish political will and power? To many senior administrators in America, the Junta, and even more the Cortes after it, seemed not only suspect in claiming to be Spain's supreme governing entities, but also dangerously radical in the manner of their formation. If popular representation were to be admitted as the basis for legitimacy in Spain, might not creoles, on the same principle, insist on participating in American government? Some creoles, indeed, did precisely that. In Mexico, by the late summer of 1808, the viceroy seemed to be entertaining demands from the *cabildo* of Mexico City, which was dominated by creoles, that authority be shared between it and the *audiencia*. The proposal was, in effect, that sovereignty shift from Spain to America. The *audiencia*, whose judges were Spaniards, took conservative alarm at this, and found backing for its opposition among rich, immigrant Spanish merchants and land owners. This alliance was powerful enough to depose the viceroy, in September 1808, and send him back to Spain. A period of authoritarian, indeed repressive, rule by the *audiencia* then ensued, in which private Spanish interests were favored at the expense of the creoles, and wealthy peninsulars set up a semi-private militia, the Volunteers of Ferdinand VII.[8]

Far away to the south a similar fissure in Spanish authority developed a little later in the *Audiencia* of Charcas, seated at La Plata in the central Andes. There the president of the court, supported by the archbishop, inclined to accept the authority of the Junta Central in Spain. But the judges of the court saw threatening populism in the Junta's claims to authority, and took the position that the *audiencia* itself must be the supreme governing body in its jurisdiction, which it should rule, according to existing law, in the name of the exiled king. Ambitious creole lawyers in the University of La Plata saw in this division a chance for political power of their own. Feigning alliance with the *audiencia*, and its proposal for self-government for Charcas during the king's forced absence, they plotted to bring about declarations of local self-rule, nominally on behalf of Ferdinand, in various towns in the territory. Only in La Paz did they have success. There, in July 1809, a group of adventurous creoles arrested the Spanish governor and the bishop. A governing *junta tuitiva* (protective council) formed, under the leadership of a mestizo named Pedro Domingo Murillo, and briefly took control of La Paz. Dropping any pretence of governing in the king's name, it issued a proclamation stating that "It is now time to overthrow the [Spanish] yoke...It is now time to organize a new government based on the interests of our fatherland...It is now time to declare the principle of liberty in these miserable colonies acquired without any title and kept by tyranny and injustice."[9] This was clearly a declaration of outright independence. It was indeed the first such in Spanish America; Bolivians are still proud of that fact, as they are of Murillo himself. Spanish military force was, however, close at hand in Peru; and the insurgency was undone by the end of January 1810.

Other risings took place in 1809: one in Buenos Aires in January, of royalists opposing a viceroy whom they suspected of liberalism; one in Quito in August, of rebellious upper class creoles who overthrew the *audiencia* and set up a governing junta, ostensibly in Ferdinand's name. This movement collapsed in late October, on the approach of Spanish troops from Guayaquil and the south.[10] Everywhere, in fact, the ground seemed to tremble under Spanish administrators' feet as a result of the French invasion of Spain. No definitive movement toward independence, however, took place in that year.

1810

The following year was a different matter. As French troops pushed southward in Spain it seemed, by early 1810, as if there would soon be no haven left in the country for any native governing body. No one could predict that Cadiz would hold out as it did. As news of the French advance in Andalusia reached America, therefore, it sparked explosions of political action among activist creoles whose radicalism had fed on the instability of the two previous years.

The first outbreak came in Caracas on April 19, 1810. On that day the city council called a *cabildo abierto*. This was a limited sort of town meeting, an "open council" to which, however, only notables had right of attendance. It was a congregation usually convened by the local governor for mainly cere-monial purposes. But on this occasion, the captain-general of Venezuela, who was the supreme local authority, was prevented from entering by apparently organized mob action. And the creole-dominated town council, with a few added members, transformed itself into a "Junta for the preservation of the rights of Ferdinand VII" that rejected any claim to authority in Venezuela by bodies in Spain. And so in April 1810, Venezuela (or rather Caracas, since the town council could speak only for the capital and its immediate surroundings) declared itself to be self-governing. Its manner of doing this prudently preserved at least the pretence of loyalty to the Spanish monarchy.[11]

A month later Buenos Aires followed suit. Arrival of the news that Seville had fallen to the French provoked implementation of a scheme that creoles in the city council had planned from late 1808. This was, precisely as in Caracas, to summon a *cabildo abierto* and set up a junta to displace the chief local Spanish authority. In Buenos Aires, this was the viceroy of the Río de la Plata; and it was he who was persuaded to call the meeting, apparently expecting to become the leader of the junta. The "open council" convened on May 22, 1810. As in Caracas, organized mobs played a part, excluding men who seemed likely to object to the plan. In this the radicals' control of the local militia also helped. From the meeting emerged a junta that assumed local government in the name of the king. Its leaders were creole, among them the most ardent advocates of free trade. On May 25 this body arrested the viceroy, and in so doing ended Spanish rule in what was to become Argentina.[12] For unlike Caracas, Buenos Aires and its hinterland never reverted to Spanish control after that date. Hence, although the *cabildo abierto* had not declared independence, the Río de la Plata can rightly claim to be the first region of Spanish America in which colonial rule ended.

The same movement of ejection of royal governors by juntas of local notables quickly spread to New Granada. It started in Cartagena on June 14, and extended to Cali, Pamplona, Socorro, and finally, on July 20, to Santa Fe de Bogotá itself, where the viceroy was deposed. On September 18 Chile made its move – again the *cabildo abierto* (in Santiago), again the junta of notables taking up the reins of government in the name of Ferdinand VII.[13]

By late September 1810, therefore, most of Spanish South America outside the central Andean heartland of present Peru and Bolivia had passed into creole control. As it turned out, only in the Río de la Plata was that control permanent; elsewhere Spain struck back before self-government was finally established. But the political shift was already immense. In the space of five months vast and economically vibrant areas of the empire had become autonomous. In general they had proclaimed autonomy within the monarchy. But the monarchy was a conveniently vaporous entity at the time. It was unclear, and still remains so, what the implied assertions of loyalty were worth.

Two days before Santiago de Chile convened its *cabildo abierto*, however, a very different sort of movement had begun in Mexico, with the famous *grito de Dolores*, or "cry of Dolores," issued by Father Miguel Hidalgo y Costilla, parish priest of the town of that name, before dawn on September 16, 1810. So began a short-lived but spectacular rising, initiated by creoles but soon taken over by unruly popular force. The conservative crack-down precisely two years earlier had driven creole activism underground in Mexico. No possibility of town meetings existed there once the *audiencia* took control in the autumn of 1808. The constitutional route to creole autonomy was blocked. Resistance festered, however, in secret, especially in provincial towns. One of those was Querétaro, 200 kilometers north-west of Mexico City, in the south of the rich arable zone known as the Bajío. There a small group of prosperous creoles, some of them military officers, plotted to ignite a rising against the central *audiencia* and its rigid peninsular backers in October 1810. Hidalgo joined this group in the summer of that year, Dolores being only some 80 kilometers from Querétaro. He was himself a creole, now in his early sixties. Though a priest, he was a man of no great spirituality; most of his career had been spent in teaching rather than in pastoral work, and he seems to have had a greater interest in the writings of the *philosophes* than in those of the Church Fathers. He certainly had absorbed the Enlightenment's message that improvement of the human condition was possible through practical means. And as parish priest of Dolores he spent more time seeking to better the material lives of his flock than praying for them. To that end he put his own money into small local industries, such as silk raising, pottery manufacture, tanning, carpentry, and bee keeping. This solicitude for his parishioners' well-being brought him their affection and loyalty; and perhaps especially so in 1810, since the previous two years had been a time of drought, shortage of food, and consequent high prices in central Mexico.

The Querétaro plot was discovered by the authorities, and its leaders in the town seized on September 13. Hidalgo received word of this setback. In one of the iconic scenes of Mexican history, he summoned his parishioners, mostly Indian and mestizo, with the sound of the church bell and exhorted them to support him in a rising against Spanish rule. Without planning, therefore, and with no semblance of a trained military force, Hidalgo's rebellion began. He led his people south and west across the Bajío toward Guanajuato, a natural target given the fame of its mines. On the way, they took from the parish church of Atotonilco an image of the Virgin of Guadalupe, which became the movement's symbol. On September 23 Hidalgo led into Guanajuato a much expanded force, a horde indeed, of 23,000 men. Sacking of the city and killing of the intendant and many other Whites followed.

The destruction of Guanajuato revealed the insurrection for what it was quickly becoming: an onslaught on white people, no matter whether Spanish or creole, and on their property, by massed peasants and elements of the urban poor. Sparks from the conflagration quickly flew far and wide, igniting risings as far away as Zacatecas and San Luis Potosí in the north, and in Guadalajara in the west. By early October Hidalgo's own force numbered 60,000. In mid-October he occupied Valladolid (now Morelia) in Michoácan. From there he advanced with 80,000 on Mexico City, and seemed poised to attack it. But in the capital the government had many thousands of trained militiamen, under the command of a most capable Spanish officer, Félix María Calleja; and at Hidalgo's approach almost all creoles in the city forgot their grievances against the Spanish administration, and closed ranks with it. Hidalgo prevailed, by force of numbers, in a small contest on October 30. But that was the high point of his campaign. Tens of thousands of his followers deserted after this battle. And from there the rebels' road led downward, to Calleja's definitive victory over them near Guadalajara on January 17, 1811. Hidalgo and his creole lieutenants fled northward, hoping to reach the United States. But they were captured, and executed in the summer of 1811.

There is irony in Father Hidalgo's ranking as the greatest hero of Mexican independence, for his rising almost certainly did more to delay the break from Spain than to advance it. The rising was from the start an ethnic-cum-class war rather than a war of liberation. Given the circumstances of its beginning, it perhaps could hardly have been otherwise. The effect was to alienate from it all but the most extreme of creoles. And, as the story of the movement clearly demonstrated, as long as unity existed between Spaniards and a majority of creoles, independence could not come. It is not even completely clear that independence was, as the movement progressed, Hidalgo's prime aim. He had declared initially that he acted in the king's name; later he called for independence. But, responding to the demands of his followers and to the nature of the movement, he became as much a social as a political reformer. His pronouncements, at least, indicate as much: abolition of the Indian tribute, abolition of the distinctions of *castas*, abolition of slavery, restoration of lands taken from native communities.[14]

Few years in Spanish America's history have been more dramatic than 1810. Between May and September Spain's colonial apparatus suffered a series of hammer blows that seemed to the creoles who inflicted them heavy enough to alter its structure, if not to damage it beyond repair. Precisely how many of the radical creole groups who seized local power in 1810 were at that stage pursuing outright independence is hard to judge. But all were seeking at the very least home rule within a far less demanding colonial system than had emerged from Bourbon reform in the eighteenth century. In the event, only the Río de la Plata achieved that self-governing aim permanently in 1810. Elsewhere, although that year certainly marks a historic break with the past, self-determination still lay some ten to fifteen years in the future. The road to it was to prove long and arduous in most regions.

SPANISH SOUTH AMERICA, 1811–1825

The chronology of independence in the mainland countries of Spanish America is as follows. (The dates are not those of declarations of independence, but of the effective and permanent break from Spanish rule. In some cases, single battles, named here, brought about that separation.)[15]

Río de la Plata (later Argentina)	May 1810
Paraguay	May 1811
Chile (battle of Maipú)	February 1818
Colombia (colonial New Granada, battle of Boyacá)	August 1819
Venezuela (battle of Carabobo)	June 1821
Mexico (colonial New Spain)	August 1821
Central America	August 1821
Ecuador (colonial Quito, battle of Pichincha)	May 1822
Peru (battle of Ayacucho)	December 1824
Bolivia	January 1825
(Uruguay	October 1828)

Clarification is needed in two instances. First, Central America, *c.*1800, consisted of an area now comprising Chiapas and Soconusco (in present southern Mexico), Guatemala, Honduras, Nicaragua, El Salvador, and Costa Rica. Together these regions formed the Captaincy-General of Guatemala, which was a unit of the Viceroyalty of New Spain. When New Spain gained independence, then, in 1821, Central America did so also, almost without violence. Then, in 1824, the several provinces broke away from Mexico, as the United Provinces of Central America. Late in the 1830s, this attempt at federalism collapsed, and the five present national states emerged as separate units. Panama, which today is the southernmost Central American nation, was at the time a province of Colombia, and so remained until 1903. Second, the territory of present Uruguay was contested in the independence period between Buenos Aires and Brazil. After a period of much uncertainty in the 1820s, during which the region was administered at different times by both, an agreement made between Brazil and the Argentine Federation, at British urging, created the sovereign nation of Uruguay.

The first colony to achieve self-rule, after the Río de la Plata, was Paraguay. The process here was simplicity itself, and consisted of two military defeats, not of Spaniards but of a force from Buenos Aires. After their coup in May 1810, the creole leaders in Buenos Aires were keen to extend their authority northward. They had at least three reasons. First, the viceroyalty of the Río de la Plata, created in 1776, had included both Paraguay and Upper Peru (soon to be Bolivia), and Buenos Aires hoped to keep that unit intact and under its control. Second, Upper Peru was still the great silver producing zone of South America, and for that reason Buenos Aires was particularly anxious to keep hold of it. Third, control of northern territories would provide a deep buffer against possible attacks from the Spanish base of administrative and military power in South America, Peru. To begin the northward push, since a Spanish intendant still governed Paraguay, Buenos Aires despatched an army to Asunción in late 1810. But Paraguayans, long conscious of their cultural and political separateness from Buenos Aires, resisted the threat rather than yielding to it and beat the invading force in January and March 1811. In May of that year, a junta led by José Gaspar Rodríguez de Francia and others deposed the intendant and declared independence. In 1814 Francia received from a national congress what amounted to dictatorial powers. He remained head of state, authoritarian and isolationist, until his death in 1840.[16]

Buenos Aires had no more success in its efforts to control Upper Peru. Between 1810 and 1817 it sent no fewer than four expeditionary forces up into the mountains of the future Bolivia. But they generally met with indifference or hostility from the local people, who were no more attracted by the prospect of a new source of external control than the Paraguayans had been. The Spanish authorities in Peru proper also sent armies southward into the highlands to combat the incursions from Buenos Aires. As a result, Upper Peru was much fought over, with loss of life and damage to property, after 1810. Adding to disorder and destruction from then until about 1816 were the guerrilla activities of several local leaders, mostly mestizos, who emerged in this period, seeking regional power in the mountains and in the east. These men, while being little concerned by the large issue of national independence, probably helped Buenos Aires unwittingly by tying down Spanish forces. With the increase, however, of Spanish strength in South America after the fall of Napoleon and the restoration of Ferdinand VII in 1814, guerrilla activity in the Upper Peruvian highlands was gradually suppressed. And the leaders of the now-emerging Argentina decided that an attack on the Spanish base in Peru via Chile would serve their security needs better than further attempts across the central Andean highland.

That story should not be told, however, before events in northern South America from 1810 onward are related. If Buenos Aires, capital of the Río de la Plata, was one focus of resistance to Spanish rule in South America, Caracas, capital of Venezuela, was the other. And no other single figure was so influential in the struggle for the independence of Venezuela, of northern South America, and indeed of South America as a whole, as that son of Caracas, Simón Bolívar. Although it is obvious that in the insurgents' final success against Spain a multitude of people and circumstances played essential parts, it is also true that Bolívar was a central figure in so much of the independence process that his career illustrates it comprehensively.

Simón Bolívar (1783–1830) was the son of a landed family of Caracas, one that dated from the sixteenth century but had become rich and prominent in the cacao boom of the eighteenth. He was educated privately, and evidently to little academic effect, since when he visited relatives in Madrid in 1799, they were struck by his ignorance.[17] The previous year he had been commissioned as a sub-lieutenant in a militia battalion in Venezuela; but that, and it was very little, was the sum of his military instruction. His great military feats later in life were clearly the fruit of innate ability. His first visit to Europe, mainly to Spain, was from 1799 to 1802. He married in Madrid in May 1802 the daughter of an ennobled Caracas family, and with her returned to Venezuela. The marriage was terribly brief; his bride died in January 1803. By the end of that year Bolívar was back in Europe, now spending much time in Paris, where, by his own account, he read widely, especially in the writings of the Enlightenment. He met Alexander von Humboldt, recently back from his long visits to South and Middle America. He briefly flirted with freemasonry, then a fertile breeding ground for radical political thought. In this second stay in Europe, Bolívar became a convinced republican. And he absorbed from Machiavelli and other humanists of the Italian Renaissance the notion that active citizenship in the republic was the source of true virtue.[18] Political activism was indeed soon to become his life's central business. It was in Italy, on one of the hills of Rome, that in 1805 Bolívar (as was many years later reported) made a vow that conveys the fire of a young man newly captivated by a political cause. "I swear before the God of my fathers, by my fathers themselves, by my honour and by my country, that my arm shall not rest nor my mind be at peace until I have broken the chains that bind me by the will and power of Spain."[19]

After his return to Venezuela in 1807 he attended to his family estates in a manner of which Voltaire, whose free-thinking he already admired, would have approved. But he also associated with other young creoles resentful of

Spain's grasp on Venezuela. In 1810 he was one of the activists in Caracas who deposed the Captain General. He then made a brief diplomatic visit to London to solicit British governmental aid for the Venezuelan insurrection. He was unsuccessful, and returned to Caracas in December 1810. Whatever sympathy the British may have had for the rebels in Spanish America, and whatever hopes for free commercial access once the colonies were independent, they could hardly help while allied to Spain against France.

The salient events of Bolívar's career after 1810 provide a rough geographical and chronological map of the independence movement in northern South America.[20]

1811

July–August. He helps to suppress a counterrevolutionary movement in Valencia, 100 kilometers west of Caracas.

1812

August 12. He leaves Venezuela for New Granada after Spanish forces regain control of Venezuela.

December 15. In New Granada, he issues his "Cartagena Manifesto" explaining the failure of the first republic in Venezuela and asking for New Granada's help in a new attempt to free Venezuela.

1813

May 7. The president of the New Granadan federation gives Bolívar permission to invade Venezuela.

August 6. Bolívar re-enters Caracas. For the next thirteen months, the period of the second republic, he rules Venezuela as military dictator.

1814

June 15. Bolívar suffers heavy defeat at La Puerta by José Tomás Boves, a Spanish general. Venezuelan patriots abandon Caracas in July.

August–December. The patriots retreat from Venezuela, with much dispute in their ranks. Bolívar again moves to New Granada, where he is given command of troops of the United Provinces of New Granada to force the state of Cundinamarca, in which Bogotá lies, into the New Granadan federation. Cundinamarca is not royalist, but has rejected ties with other now-independent regions of New Granada. It surrenders on December 12.

1815

May 9. Bolívar leaves New Granada, which will soon be retaken by Spanish forces, for Jamaica.

September 6. He issues his "Jamaica Letter," which summarizes the current state of affairs in Spanish America and urges new attempts at independence.

1816

Year spent partly in Haiti, gaining support from its independent government. Bolívar's attempts during the summer to regain a hold in Venezuela fail. But on December 28 he enters the colony east of Caracas, beginning his third and ultimately successful effort to liberate northern South America.

1817

He creates a base of operations in the distant east of Venezuela, in the plains of the Orinoco, at the town of Angostura.

1818

January. He begins westward movement up the Orinoco, and gains the crucial support of José Antonio Páez, leader of the *llaneros* (cattle herders of the plains), who had hitherto fought well, though as an independent agent, against Spain.

Fighting in Venezuela between insurgents and Spanish forces under General Pablo Morillo, who is strong in the Andean west of Venezuela. This continues into the spring of 1819.

1819

February 15. Installation of the Congress of Angostura, gathered to provide a legal basis for an insurgent government in Venezuela.

In May, Bolívar begins a campaign to liberate New Granada. After crossing the Andes, on August 7 he defeats the royalists at Boyacá, 110 kilometers north-east of Bogotá.

December 17. Republic of Colombia (New Granada and Venezuela) formed, at Bolívar's urging.

1820

September–October. Bolívar begins to engage Spanish forces in western Venezuela.

1821

June 24. Bolívar defeats Spanish forces definitively at Carabobo, south-west of Valencia in Venezuela. He enters Caracas in triumph on 29 June.

September 7. He is made first President of Colombia by the constituent Congress of Cúcuta, which since May 1821 has been drafting a constitution for the new nation. The constitution is highly centralist, though it includes liberal measures such as the abolition of Indian tribute and a law freeing slaves' children at birth.

December. Bolívar goes south from Bogotá to pursue the war of liberation in southern New Granada, a region conservative in both politics and religion.

1822

May 24. Insurgents' victory at Pichincha in Quito (Ecuador), under the command of Antonio José de Sucre, by now Bolívar's most able lieutenant. This victory ends Spanish rule in the territory of Quito, since Guayaquil, the other major town, has cast off Spanish government, in a rising of October 1820.

July 13. Bolívar incorporates Quito into Colombia.

July 27. He meets, at Guayaquil, with José de San Martín, the liberator of Chile, and now Protector of Peru. Apparently as a result of this meeting, which was held in secret, San Martín retires from the campaign for independence in South America, leaving Peru still largely in Spanish hands.

1823

March–April. Bolívar sends two large forces south to Peru. He arrives there himself in September, and begins a political struggle with leading creoles in Lima.

1824

February 10. A Peruvian congress makes Bolívar dictator, to cut through political infighting.

August 6.   Bolívar defeats the Spaniards at Junín in the central Peruvian Andes.

December 9.   Sucre inflicts a final defeat on Spanish forces in Peru (and in South America) at Ayacucho, in the Andes 240 kilometers west of Cuzco. He pursues the remnants of the Spanish army southward into Upper Peru, where they scatter without further combat.

1825

August 6.   The Upper Peruvian assembly creates the nation of Bolivia, named in honor of the Liberator, who enters La Paz in triumph on August 18.

1826

April 30.   Bolívar is re-elected President of Colombia.

May 25.   He completes his constitution for Bolivia (a most centralist document providing for a life-long president with powers to name his successor), which he hopes Colombia will also adopt. It does not.

Having been the most influential single contributor to the liberation of Venezuela, Colombia, Ecuador, and Peru, and having brought these four new nations together in the federation generally known to historians as Gran Colombia ("Greater Colombia" in English), Bolívar spent the rest of his days trying to maintain that union. But this was to go against three colonial centuries' worth of separate regional development, three hundred years' worth of largely separate local government, in the four components of his new state. His problems were compounded by the extreme regionalism of Colombia itself. In this grand scheme, then, Bolívar failed. He died, of consumption, on December 17, 1830, a grimly disappointed man; and a man abandoned by most, and reviled by many, of those who had once been his friends and allies in the great struggle for independence.

How quickly his role in that struggle grew after 1810 is clear enough in the bare facts of his career just presented. He took part in the unsuccessful fight of the Venezuelan insurgents in 1811–12 against Spanish troops and their loyalist allies in the colony. He, with many other Venezuelan rebels, took refuge in New Granada, many areas of which had already, if temporarily, freed themselves from Spain. There, with the Cartagena manifesto, he clearly emerged as the leading political voice among the insurgents in northern South America. The rising esteem in which he was held as a military leader is shown by New Granadan support in 1813 for his proposed re-entry into Venezuela. His success in this made him the natural political leader there. As that leader he demonstrated in 1813–14 the penchant for centralizing executive power that was to become an ever more prominent part of his political personality. He by now saw concentrated power as the sole practical counter-poise to the fissile tendencies so obvious to him in the politics of Spanish America.

The restoration of Ferdinand VII to the throne early in 1814, after the Spanish War of Independence had been won, allowed Spain to focus attention and manpower on suppressing rebellion in America. This is visible in Bolívar's defeat by Boves in June 1814, and the subsequent demise of the second republic. New Granada also succumbed in due course to the Spanish counter-attack, and Bolívar took refuge first in Jamaica and then in Haiti. Only at the end of 1816 did he return to Venezuela to begin his third and, as it proved, finally successful effort at liberation. Now he had a new strategy. He spent 1817 creating a remote base in the Orinoco plains in the extreme east of the territory. From here, early in 1818, he began a slow advance westward; but not on Caracas, the Spanish stronghold, but further south, aiming for New Granada. In August 1819 he defeated the Spaniards decisively at Boyacá, ending colonial rule in New Granada. Late in 1820 Bolívar carried the fight back eastward into his homeland, and there inflicted the final defeat on the Spaniards at Carabobo in June 1821. Now his military and political eminence was so great that in September he was the obvious choice as first president of Colombia. Almost immediately, however, he decided he must direct the campaign southward toward Peru, the bastion of Spanish power in South America. In the years 1822–4 he and his most capable military lieutenant, Antonio José de Sucre, inflicted a series of defeats on Spain in Ecuador and Peru, culminating in Sucre's victory at Ayacucho at the end of 1824. With that, Spain was effectively dismissed from South America. As Ecuador and Peru were liberated, Bolívar, whose political authority was now irresistible, incorporated them into Colombia to form, if only briefly, what was in area the largest Spanish-speaking nation ever to exist in South America.

Below the surface of this bare relation, lies, of course, a multitude of events and stories – complex, tragic, heroic. There were stirring crossings of the Andes in both directions to take the Spaniards by surprise; intricate political maneuverings to bring and hold together feuding insurgent factions, especially in New Granada; constant political planning, with congresses assembling and constitutions a'drafting, to give legal substance to what had been gained by force; ceaseless exercise of persuasive charm to bend others to the Liberator's will and purpose. No writer of that morning of the Romantic age could have invented as protean a hero as Simón Bolívar.

Yet Bolívar died, only five years after reaching the pinnacle of his accomplishments, a despairing and rejected man. In 1826 he had been re-elected President of Colombia. But the centralization of authority that he thought essential to hold that confederation together grated on many political figures in its four constituent states. In 1828 his rule became no less than dictatorial, and in September of that year men who called him "tyrant" tried to kill him in Bogotá. Late in 1829 Venezuela seceded from the federation, and in May 1830 Ecuador did the same. Bolívar had by then resigned from the presidency, and was on his way to retirement in Venezuela. But he did not see Caracas again. He died in December near Santa Marta on the coast of New Granada. On November 19, 1830, six weeks before his death, Bolívar wrote to Juan José Flores, a Venezuelan who had been one of his generals in the independence wars, and was now president of the recently seceded Ecuador, a letter that contains his most remembered phrase:

> You know that I have been in command for twenty years; and from them I have derived only a few sure conclusions: first, America is ungovernable for us; second, he who serves a revolution ploughs the sea; third, the only thing that can be done in America is to emigrate; fourth, this country will fall without fail into the hands of an

unbridled multitude, to pass later to petty, almost imperceptible, tyrants of all colors and races; fifth, devoured as we are by all crimes and destroyed by ferocity, the Europeans will not deign to conquer us; sixth, if it were possible for a part of the world to return to the primeval chaos, the latter would be the final stage of America.[21]

But he had not "ploughed the sea." For all the political storms that he had suffered, and for all the greater tempests that he rightly predicted would follow, he had been the chief pilot of Spanish South America's departure from the empire. In the broad regions whose affairs he had in varying degree directed, the political present in 1830 was unalterably different from what it had been in 1810. They were now, for better or for worse, politically sovereign nations.

Bolívar's thirteen-year campaign, from the events of April 1810 in Caracas to his arrival in Lima in September 1823, was one arm of a pincer movement that closed on Peru from north and south. The southern arm was built and guided by the other great independence leader in South America, José de San Martín. His story is both shorter and simpler than Bolívar's, but nonetheless one full of inventiveness and exceptional capacity in command.

San Martín (1778–1850) was a creole from Corrientes, in the north of present Argentina, but from early youth lived and was educated in Spain. At the age of only eleven he became a cadet in the Spanish army, and in the next two decades fought for Spain in a variety of campaigns, rising to the rank of lieutenant-colonel. But late in 1810, the news of the risings in Caracas and Buenos Aires crystallized in him his previously unformed sympathies for the insurgent cause. He left Spanish service, and returned via London to the Río de la Plata.[22] There he soon received command of a cavalry regiment, began to take part in politics, and made a good marriage. In January 1814 he was given command of the army of the north, with the task of directing Buenos Aires's third attempt to take Upper Peru, and from there move on to attack Spain in Peru itself. But, reflecting on this strategy and its two past failures, he conceived the idea of attacking Peru through Chile rather than through the central Andes. He therefore resigned, on grounds of ill health, his command in the north, and obtained the post of governor of Cuyo, west of Buenos Aires under the mountains. There, in the provincial capital, Mendoza, from early 1814 to late 1816 he made preparations for an attack on the Spanish regime in Chile, which forces sent from Peru had restored late in 1814.

In January 1817, San Martín's Army of the Andes crossed the mountains into Chile, using several passes. The army numbered altogether some five thousand, among whom were a substantial minority of Chileans. Chile provided some of the commanders, notably Bernardo O'Higgins, who had been one of the leading lights of the colony's attempted break from Spain between 1810 and 1814. Once the crossing, extremely arduous even in midsummer, had been made, detachments from the main force occupied large areas north of Santiago. But San Martín led the bulk of the army to victory over the Spaniards at Chacabuco, near Santiago, on February 12. Two days later he and O'Higgins entered Santiago in triumph. Unlike Bolívar, San Martín had little interest in political leadership; nor did he have any grand scheme for Spanish America that he felt impelled to promote through political activism of his own. For these reasons, and perhaps even more because for him Chile was primarily a stepping stone for the liberation of Peru, he refused the offer, made by the city's *cabildo*, of supreme political power in Chile. That role fell to O'Higgins, whose distinctly dictatorial government lasted until he was driven from the country in January 1823.

San Martín had not yet, in fact, completed his military business in Chile. Spanish forces managed to regroup south of Santiago, and in March 1818 inflicted a defeat on him that brought a new threat to Santiago. But he struck back, and on April 5 at Maipú, near the capital, won the victory that freed the colony from Spanish control for once and for all. In accomplishing that, Maipú also secured Chile as a base for San Martín's assault on Peru. And it was to that greater purpose that he now turned.[23]

There was no question of a land attack on Peru. The utter dryness of the Atacama desert stood in the way. Therefore ships had to be gathered. The cost of these, and indeed of the whole expedition, fell on Chile and Argentina; and, in the event, rather more heavily on Chile, which became awkwardly indebted to foreign lenders as a result. To command the naval force, Chile engaged Thomas Cochrane, a British naval officer who had risen to eminence in the Napoleonic wars. Now he joined the many British, North American, and other soldiers of fortune in the force destined for Peru; the numbers of these mercenaries had risen in all insurgent forces in South America with the passage of time, and some played distinguished senior roles in the wars. Cochrane was one who did so. Though wayward and impulsive, and for those reasons often at loggerheads with San Martín, who was planned caution itself, Cochrane served the attack on Peru well, holding Spanish naval forces on the west coast fully in check. The invading force left Chile in August 1820. It consisted of twenty-three ships manned by 1,600 sailors, and carrying some 4,500 troops, largely Chilean and Argentine. Cochrane argued for a frontal attack on Lima; but San Martín chose to land at Pisco, 220 kilometers further south, in the hope that his presence there would stir more radical elements in Peru into action against the Spaniards.

It was at this point that San Martín's grand scheme began to lose momentum. The situation was different from the one he had faced in Chile as he laid plans for that campaign. He had known that in Chile he could count on a large group of influential opponents to Spanish rule; some were indeed already in his army. But in Peru very few such people were to be found. While he had come to Chile, therefore, as an ally, he arrived in Peru as an intervener, almost perhaps an interloper. He seems to have been only too conscious of that. "How could the cause of independence be advanced by my holding Lima, or even the whole country, in military possession?" he asked an interviewer in 1821. "I wish to have all men thinking with me, and do not choose to advance a step beyond the gradual march of public opinion."[24] Bolívar would not have been, and two years later was not, troubled by such scruples.

The loyalty to Spain of the Peruvian creoles was without equal in Spanish America. Those in Lima were the most faithful of all, and Lima was the unchallenged center of political power in Peru. It was probably the most patrician city of the empire, its leading families proud of their origins in conquerors and early settlers, its lesser creole lights conscious of the city's centuries-long role as viceregal and ecclesiastical capital of Spanish South America. It was more removed from modernizing European influences than even Mexico City. The issue of free trade loomed far less large than in the newly expanded cities of the Atlantic coast of the empire. And it may well be that as rebellion spread in the periphery of Spanish South America from 1810 onward, creoles in Lima found for themselves a rewarding new role as pre-servers of colonial rule, in an effort that restored luster to Lima and to themselves. The creation of new viceroyalties in the eighteenth century had reduced the city's political standing, robbing it in 1739 of authority over New Granada and Quito; and in 1776 over Charcas (Upper Peru), Paraguay, and the Río de la Plata. After 1810, however, Lima became the hub of Spanish efforts to reverse the current of insurgency; and with that it partly regained its place as the imperial center of South America. The viceroy in those years, José Fernando de Abascal, seems to have had the political wit to capitalize on this revival of the city's status by placing creoles in responsible posts (the presidency of the *Audiencia* of Cuzco, for example, and the intendancy of La Paz).[25] For reasons, then, of present politics as well as tradition, many notables in Lima held to the Spanish side while mutiny sprouted to the north and south. And finally, those who might still feel the attractive tug of change were likely to be brought up short by the memory of the great rebellion in the Andes of 1780–1. That store of Indian hostility was still there in the interior, ready perhaps to erupt again if the old order were changed. The Haitian rebellion in the early 1790s, and Hidalgo's rising in New Spain much more recently, served only to keep alive fears of the consequences for Spaniards and creoles if imperial control were to lapse.

San Martín therefore faced great inertia in Peru's creole political nation, inertia that he was never able to overcome. Eventually he abandoned his waiting game and advanced on Lima; whereupon the Spanish authorities left the city, and he entered it on July 10, 1821. Faced with this reality, the *cabildo* of creole notables issued a declaration of independence on July 28. On August 12 San Martín accepted the title of Protector of Peru, appointing to advise him a cabinet drawn from his own followers and from local creoles of apparently liberal inclinations. He, in good liberal fashion, declared free the children of slaves born after July 28, 1821; he abolished Indian tribute and all types of forced native labor; he ordered that Indians should in the future be called simply "Peruvians." But all this applied only to the area that he controlled, which was merely Lima and its immediate surroundings. In the mountains the only threat to Spanish dominance was from bands of creole and mestizo guerrillas, who were as much bandits seeking to gain from looting as they were freedom fighters. He waited once more for creole support to accrete around him. But rather the reverse happened, as the creoles of Lima grew resentful of the presence of his army and the cost of supporting it, which now fell on them.[26]

And so, when San Martín sailed north to meet Bolívar at Guayaquil in July 1822, he went in relative weakness. Bolívar's southward sweep from New

Granada, through Quito toward Peru, was in full flood; San Martín's masterly plan to free Peru, and by doing so to secure the permanence of rebel gains everywhere in South America, had stalled in creole conservatism, fears, and apathy. Only speculation exists about what was said in those interviews. San Martín's inclination to believe that monarchy would be the best guarantee of order in Spanish America may well have clashed with Bolívar's adamantine republicanism; for however authoritarian a government Bolívar came to believe Spanish America needed, he always drew the line at kings. Any debate they may have had about how to proceed in Peru (and that must surely have been the crux of their discussions) would almost certainly have ended in disagreement. The outcome was that two months later in Lima, San Martín resigned as Protector of Peru. He returned via Chile to Mendoza, and in 1823 left Argentina for France, England, Brussels, and ultimately Brunoy, on the outskirts of Paris. He never again set foot in Argentina, Chile, or Peru. He died in 1850 in Boulogne, to which he had moved to escape the dangers of the February Revolution of 1848 in Paris.[27] Twenty-six years before his death, in the manner already related, Sucre and Bolívar, unencumbered by San Martín's political or ethical reservations, had done in Peru what they saw must be done, ending 292 years of Spanish imperial rule in South America.

NEW SPAIN, 1811–21

About a month after San Martín's final entry into Lima inspired the town council there to declare independence from Spain, New Spain, in August 1821, departed from the empire. That was a coincidence, not a connection – except in the broadest sense that movement toward independence took place in all the mainland colonies during the same years and for the same range of reasons. Quite remarkable, in fact, is the almost complete detachment of the independence process in New Spain and Central America from the parallel unfolding of events in South America. There was next to no contact between the insurgents in the two regions, much less any mutual support with, say, men or money. That, perhaps, is a mark of the great degree to which Middle America and South America had become separate political and cultural entities even before the empire disappeared.

In Mexico, the defeat of Hidalgo in January 1811 had not brought insurgency to an end. The torch was taken up by perhaps a greater figure, the mestizo priest José María Morelos y Pavón (1765–1815). He was by far a humbler figure than Hidalgo, a carpenter's son, and a man who in his youth worked as a mule driver on the road between Mexico City and Acapulco. In so doing he gained a knowledge of that south-western region of Mexico that later stood him in good stead as an insurgent leader. He trained for the priesthood at the college where Hidalgo taught, though no record exists of any particular attachment between the two at the time. After taking orders in 1799 he tended parishes in the western lowlands of Michoacán, an isolated, hot area. He approached Hidalgo after the *grito de Dolores* in 1810, and was told to organize a military force on the southern Pacific coast, the area familiar to him, with the aim of taking Acapulco. Morelos persisted in this task after Hidalgo was defeated and executed. By late 1811 he had gathered a force that differed from Hidalgo's in being relatively small, at 9,000, and well-equipped, with weapons captured from the Spanish. But it was most notably different in being well disciplined.

With this potent army, Morelos gave the Spanish administration of Mexico grave cause for concern for two years. By late 1812, indeed, he controlled much of the south, including the cities of Oaxaca and Orizaba; and in April 1813 he took Acapulco after a long, and probably wasteful, siege. He menaced communication between Mexico City and Veracruz, and the capital certainly lived under the threat of his attack for some time. In the large region under his control he enforced order strictly (in great contrast to Hidalgo, executing soldiers convicted of theft), collecting taxes, and appointing local officials. Finally, however, Morelos fell, like Hidalgo, to the military ability of Calleja, the Spanish commander (who also became viceroy in March 1813). When in December of that year Morelos moved north to attack Valladolid, in Michoacán, Calleja sent a force to intercept him. Morelos was defeated. One of the key royalist officers in the battle was a creole colonel named Agustín de Iturbide, who seven years later, having changed sides, was to play the central role in Mexico's break from Spain. Morelos was not captured in this engagement, but after it spent almost two years in southern Mexico in slow retreat before an increasingly powerful Spanish opposition. In September 1813 a congress of representatives from areas then free of Spanish control had gathered at the small town of Chilpancingo, some 80 kilometers north of Acapulco. Members of this body stayed with Morelos in 1814, and in October of that year issued, at the town of Apatzingán, Mexico's first constitution. It was a liberal document that declared an independent republic. It did not have, however, the desired effect of attracting to Morelos the wide creole support that any successful bid for independence needed. Finally, in November 1815 Morelos was captured. Being found guilty of both heresy and treason, he was defrocked, and then shot on December 22, 1815.[28]

For five years after Morelos's capture late in 1815, guerrilla activities were almost the sole sign in Mexico of hostility to Spanish rule. Even Calleja, viceroy as well as military chief from March 1813 to September 1816, was unable to eradicate this elusive, fragmented resistance. And when his harsh regime was replaced by a more conciliatory administration, the guerrilleros had greater freedom of action. It has been long known that small bands operated from remote mountainous areas; but only recent research has shown that raiding took place close to cities. The Mexico City to Veracruz road, for instance, which was Mexico's busiest trade route, was under constant threat, and was sometimes cut. The outskirts of Mexico City itself suffered raids in 1816. *Haciendas* around Querétaro were assaulted in 1818. These constant pinpricks, while unlikely in themselves to cause the Spanish to leave, certainly lowered morale among officials, troops, and creole loyalists. The administration's inability to deal with the irritation tended to add to the discontent of those already impatient of Spanish rule; and that impatience certainly grew with the imposition of taxes to pay the costs of keeping men in the field to chase guerrilleros.[29]

Just as an event in Spain, Napoleon's occupation in 1808, had set in motion the movements toward independence in America, so again in 1820 another occurrence in the peninsula was instrumental in driving those movements toward their conclusion, and especially so in Mexico. The event was the quite unexpected rising of an army, on the point of sailing from Cadiz to attempt a retaking of the Río de la Plata, against Ferdinand VII.[30] Other army units across Spain quickly joined the revolt, the inspiration of which lay partly in resentment of the large cuts made in the military after 1814, and partly in the hostility of all shades of liberals to the rigid absolutism that Ferdinand had displayed.

The immediate political result of the risings was the restoration of the Cadiz constitution of 1812. Under its terms, Ferdinand found himself suddenly a king subject to the control of a parliament. He did not have to bear the liberal yoke for long; in 1823 Louis XVIII of France sent an army to free him of it. But by then the damage in America had been done.

Mexican independence in 1821 has long been viewed as a reaction to the liberalism of the revived Spanish Cortes, a rejection by influential conservative Mexican creoles of, for example, anti-clerical legislation coming from that parliament, and deriving in turn from the constitution. In that there is a degree of truth. But the move toward independence in 1820–1 was, not surprisingly, the work of a much wider segment of political opinion among the creoles. Broadly speaking, most creoles had few objections to the constitution. The 1812 constitution was in fact preserved in the scheme of Mexican independence that was soon to be proposed. But the conduct and the attitudes of the Cortes toward the colonies did cause a fatal resentment in Mexico. The parliament now, just as in Cadiz eight or so years before, seemed to contradict its own liberalism by showing itself resolved to keep America subservient to Spain. Many creoles' ideal political arrangement was self-government within a loose imperial framework, a commonwealth indeed. There had never been any likelihood, of course, that the monarchy under Ferdinand VII would contemplate any such change. But the maintenance of a strictly imperialist line by the otherwise reforming Cortes of 1820–3 was intolerably galling. When, therefore, under the terms of the 1812 constitution, elections to town councils and provincial assemblies once again took place in Mexico in mid-1820, and when the viceroy of the day restored the freedom of the press that had been canceled late in 1812, loud protest at restrictive Spanish policy was heard. Urgency was added to the search for a solution by reports of internal conflict among liberals in Spain. Mexicans feared that such disagreements might open the way to restoration of absolutism; in which case reformers in Mexico could expect renewed repression. So it was that when in February 1821 a proposal appeared for Mexican self-government, it received wide support.

The main author of this proposal, the Plan of Iguala, was Agustín de Iturbide (1783–1824), the creole who as a royalist officer in 1813 had taken part in the definitive defeat of Morelos. Smarting perhaps under his removal from command in 1816 for supposed misconduct, and possibly also sensing the new wind's gathering force, in late 1820 he changed sides. The following February he and Vicente Guerrero, one of the prominent guerrilla leaders of the years before 1820, published the Plan. It was a clever proposal, calculated to appeal to and unite most shades of opinion. By it, Mexico was to become a Catholic monarchy, separate from Spain but ruled by Ferdinand VII as emperor, or by one of his brothers if he declined the throne. Mexico would have a Cortes. This new government would guarantee independence, the existence of Catholicism as the sole state religion, and the equality of Spaniards and Americans. These guarantees – of religion, independence, and union – were to be protected by the "Army of the Three Guarantees," consisting of ex-insurgents and former royalist troops who, like Iturbide, had shifted their allegiance. Property also was guaranteed. And all those who held positions in the church, the military, and the government would remain in them if they accepted the Plan. Even the viceroy and the judges of *audiencias* might have a role in the new regime, in a Sovereign Junta that would govern while permanent arrangements were developing. Offices in government, though, were to become available to all inhabitants, and caste distinctions were to be abolished.

The Plan of Iguala, replete as it was with carrots for Spaniards, all manner of creoles, monarchists, seekers of autonomy, churchmen, and even the lower orders of society, was, for long enough, welcomed by all except those on the political extremes. Throughout the first half of 1821 great numbers joined Iturbide. Many royalist troops, most of whom were, like him, Mexican born, deserted to him. With such forces he easily overran the colony. Cracks developed, predictably enough, in the Spanish side. Dissatisfied with the viceroy's inability to control Iturbide's revolt, Spanish troops mutinied in Mexico City early in July 1821 and deposed him. In late August Iturbide met the incoming captain-general of Mexico, Juan O'Donojú, at Córdoba, near Veracruz. The two negotiated a treaty there in which O'Donojú, the senior Spanish official in Mexico in the absence of a viceroy, recognized the existence of the independent Mexican empire. He and Iturbide then moved to Mexico City with the Army of the Three Guarantees. There the remaining Spanish forces, acknowledging O'Donojú's authority, surrendered. Iturbide entered the capital on September 27 as head of the new government. And so Mexico entered its independent existence, with, in that final act of the drama, very little bloodshed, and more in exasperation than in anger.

In contrast to Peru at about the same time, independence did not have to be forced on New Spain, even though its coming was above all a response to external events. The politics that brought self-rule were an internal invention. Mexico's greater willingness to break away, in comparison with Peru, reflects at least its greater absorption over the previous half-century or more of recent European ideology. It had, by 1820, plenty of moderate liberals. Mexico was also more confident of its wealth and resources than Peru; it had been the rich jewel in the empire's crown throughout the eighteenth century, and still possessed the resources to prosper as an independent economic entity. And although Hidalgo's insurrection had been cause for much alarm among creoles as well as Spaniards, Mexico did not suffer from any internal division comparable to that great cultural hiatus between coast and highlands, European and native, that had long afflicted Peru, and would continue to do so until the present. Indian, mestizo, and White had long lived in Mexico in greater familiarity than in Peru, if not in perfect harmony. The coastal Peruvian creole's fear of the alien, in the form of highland Indians, had therefore no full counterpart in Mexico. Hence nervousness about Spain's departure was less of a check on movement toward independence there than in Peru. Finally, Mexico left the empire because no good reason remained to stay. Under Charles IV and Ferdinand VII, the monarchy had lost whatever numinous quality it had previously possessed. Parliamentary government by Spain, even with representatives from America sitting in the Cortes, seemed unlikely to offer any improvement in colonial status. The cost of defending Spain's hold on the colony against challenges from guerrillas fell on the colony itself. Spanish power was incomparably diminished from what it had been a century, even half a century, before. The stem had withered; the branch, Mexico, fell off. That same image of the independence process applies to the other mainland colonies in some measure; but in Mexico's case it is peculiarly fitting.

Cuba, however, did not break from the stem. For this there were two main causes, one external and one internal. The external reason was the Haitian slave rebellion of 1791. If alarming tremors from this earthquake reached distant regions of Spanish America, in Cuba, close to the epicenter, the revolt caused far greater consternation. The flight of some thirty thousand Frenchmen from Haiti to Cuba between 1709 and 1808, with news of destruction and death, kept this fear alive.[31] To be sure, Cuba benefited economically from the revolt, since it replaced Haiti as the main source of sugar in the Caribbean. But the expansion of its production required larger imports of African slaves after 1790. The rising proportion of black slaves in the island's population naturally made Spaniards and creoles more fearful still. It is no surprise that the ending of Spain's colonial presence, administrative and military, was too dangerous a prospect for most to contemplate.

Within Cuba, even before the Haitian eruption, creoles had had less cause for discontent with Spanish rule than their counterparts almost anywhere else in the empire. From the end of the Seven Years War, in 1763, Cuba had enjoyed a peculiarly favored position in the Indies. The ease with which Havana had been captured by the British in 1762, and the political and strategic outcome of the war – Spain's being left almost alone to face the consolidated and potentially aggressive British presence in North America – made Madrid acutely aware of the need to build up its military presence in Cuba. The island was, after all, in a key strategic position for the defense of New Spain and other Spanish holdings around the Caribbean. But improvement of Cuba's defenses must be paid for in larger measure than before by the island itself. Spain, therefore, set about modernizing and developing Cuba with remarkable vigor. In 1764 the first intendant appointed to America took office in Havana. The following year free trade was permitted between the Caribbean islands and seven major ports in Spain (the beginning of the expansion of free exchange between Spanish territories that culminated in the trade law of 1778). Restrictions on the import of slaves were eased in practise, if not in law. British and North American slave traders began to sell slaves in Cuba, and in the nineties foreign merchants were allowed to settle and buy property in the island. From 1790, in fact, Cuba enjoyed greater freedom of commerce, and generally a greater openness to the exterior, than any other part of the empire. In that year it was given permission to trade with allies and neutral countries. Much Cuban sugar went to the USA. All this came about with much consultation between creole planters and merchants and local Spanish government, with the administrators often bending the regulations in the colonials' favor. The Cuban elite, a combination of creole sugar planters and Spanish merchants, in fact achieved by 1800 a considerable amount of say in its own government. It was not the autonomy that more demanding creoles elsewhere would have liked. But in combination with the need to keep Spain on the scene as a guarantee of security, it was more than enough to deflect creoles away from hankerings for independence.[32] For similar reasons, although its economic improvement did not come until after 1810, Puerto Rico also stayed in the fold after the mainland empire fell.

BRAZIL

In its approach and entry to independence Brazil was, as in its entire history down to the present, more tranquil than Spanish America. The same resentments of the home country's demands and restrictions, the same tensions between colonials and peninsular emigrants to America, and the same sense of a developing separateness were to be found as in Spanish America. But all this was more muted, less urgent. In part the difference lay in a relaxation of pressure for reform in Portugal after the fall of Pombal in 1777. Again, Portugal did not impose on Brazil the weight of fiscal demands that Spain laid on the Indies after 1790. Brazil, rather, in the nineties enjoyed the gains that accrued to it, as they did to Cuba, from the fading of Haiti as a sugar producer. And in general Brazil's final colonial decades were a time of prosperity, as its enlarged range of plantation products found ready markets in Europe. Members of upper colonial society, therefore, had few complaints on material grounds against Portugal. They might have found more cause for discontent in political or intellectual matters. The *câmaras*, or town councils, did lose some of the local authority they had possessed earlier in colonial times. The crown refused to the end to allow the establishment of a university or printing presses in Brazil, so that colonials had to go to Europe (usually to Coimbra) for higher education, and could, in principle, read only such books as the administration allowed to cross the Atlantic. Portugal's efforts to keep Brazil free of alien and disturbing ideas was quite overt. Brazilians who received education in France in the revolutionary years were not allowed to return home.[33] But such open restrictions brought very little reaction in Brazil. One reason for the compliance of potentially active and influential colonials was their general social conservatism. For most of them the French

Revolution had the same message as it had for Spanish American creoles: radical political change was fraught with social hazard. The Haitian revolt simply added to their caution. Again, late colonial Brazil was still highly regionalized. Pure distance made concerted action by leading colonials in, say, Rio, Salvador, and Recife unlikely. And such feelings as existed of a distinct American identity were generally focused on a person's region of origin, rather than Brazil as a whole. *Pátria* meant one's own captaincy, or some even smaller area.[34]

Only two instances of Brazilian opposition to Portuguese rule stand out in the late colony. The first came just before the French revolution, in 1788–9, and took place in Minas Gerais; hence its usual name, the *Inconfidência Mineira*, or "Minas disloyalty." Its cause was a heavy-handed attempt to raise local taxes and collect debts owed to the crown. Merchants and other socially prominent people of the region stood to lose severely, and some (but fewer than twenty all told) began to conspire to make Minas Gerais into an independent republic. Perhaps, they thought, other captaincies would imitate it. Among the plotters were notable intellectuals of the captaincy, some of them the products of Coimbra. Their inspiration was in the unthreatening precedent of the United States' independence.[35] But the plot was soon uncovered, and its authors were arrested. One of the most active was Joaquim José da Silva Xavier, a junior army officer who also on occasion performed as a dentist, and so gained the nickname *Tiradentes* ("Toothpuller"). The *Inconfidência* is often referred to as his movement, in part because he was the only conspirator punished by execution.

Ten years later came a very different intrigue, the "Tailors' Plot" in Salvador of 1798. Here the plotters were mainly Blacks and mulattoes, half of them slaves or freedmen. Most were city-born, and most were manual workers. Ten of the thirty-two men finally arrested were indeed tailors. Some of the group, at least, had read or heard read French revolutionary writings. The notices that they posted in Salvador in August 1798 called for social and racial equality as well as republican independence (first of the city, and then of the captaincy of Bahia). One of the conspirators declared that it was "necessary for all to become Frenchmen," whereupon "everything being levelled in a popular revolution, all would be rich, released from the misery in which they were living, discrimination between white, black, and mulatto being abolished; because all occupations and jobs would be open and available without distinction to each and every one." Any proposal less likely than this to attract the support of the mass of influential colonials is hard to imagine. Of the conspirators, four of the poorest, doubtless picked as an exemplary warning, were hanged, drawn, and quartered.[36]

It is difficult to see in either the *Inconfidência Mineira* or the "Tailors' Plot" any serious threat to the political or social status quo of Brazil at the end of the eighteenth century. They were straws stirring in the gentlest of breezes. When, therefore, the Portuguese royal family along with several thousand courtiers and officials arrived in Rio de Janeiro on January 22, 1808, they came to a colony that bore them few grudges. With the arrival of Prince John (regent of Portugal in place of his disturbed mother from 1792 to 1816, and then king as John VI until 1826), an age of monarchy began in Brazil that lasted until 1889.

So much larger was Brazil than Portugal, and Portugal so much dependent on Brazil for its economic well-being, that it could easily be argued that the colony had really become the empire's center of gravity, at least in the material sense. Suggestions that the monarch might move across the Atlantic had indeed been made before, though perhaps not seriously. The Prince Regent, however, took to Brazil, or at least to Rio, with gusto, and finally left in 1821 only under fierce political pressure from Portugal.

During his thirteen years of residence, Brazil gained in political self-esteem. The particular part of it that gained most in that respect was, of course, the capital, Rio de Janeiro, and the area surrounding it. Rio became a far more imposing center of government than it had ever been as a mere viceregal capital. John had brought with him many state papers and much of the Lisbon bureaucracy, since it would clearly be necessary to duplicate in Rio many of the governmental bodies existing in Portugal. Printing presses, initially for government purposes, were set up for the first time, in Rio and then in Salvador. Other innovations, in 1808, were schools of surgery, again in Rio and Salvador, created not so much for the public good as to improve medical services to the military. In the same year, the crown created a Bank of Brazil capable of issuing notes and making loans to the government. Two years later, a Royal Military Academy appeared in Rio, to train officers for the Brazilian section of the Portuguese army (soldiers in the homeland being committed at the time to the fight against the French in the peninsula).[37] These were only some of the accoutrements befitting a metropolitan capital that Rio acquired during John's stay. Inevitably, also, its population grew concurrently, rising from c.50,000 in 1808 to c.100,000 in 1821. Among the citizens were many outsiders. The largest group of these was naturally Portuguese, who came to number (including some who had been there before 1808) around 24,000. But other European nationalities were well represented: 1,500 Spaniards and Spanish Americans; 1,000 Frenchmen; 600 Englishmen; 100 Germans; and others, to a total of over 4,200, from assorted European countries and the United States. These numbers refer to men alone, most of whom were professionals and craftsmen.[38] Rio thus became cosmopolitan as well as politically powerful.

Neither the final ejection of the French from Portugal in 1811 nor Napoleon's abdication three years later provided persuasion enough for Prince John to return to Lisbon. He was contentedly settled in Rio, comfortably distant from the importunities of the Portuguese nobility, most of which had not followed him to Brazil.[39] Late in 1815, partly in response to appeals from Portuguese authorities for his return, he officially made Brazil a kingdom, and created the "United Kingdom of Portugal, Brazil, and Algarves." Brazil was now the constitutional equal of Portugal, and therefore no longer a colony. The crown was as properly resident there as it was in the traditional homeland.

Although messages of gratitude allegedly poured in on the Prince Regent from around the newly elevated territory, not all in Brazil were happy with the prospect of his remaining indefinitely. The influx of foreigners, especially artisans, to Brazil that had followed the monarchy's arrival had led to some radicalization of political ideas. Republicanism, along North American lines, and denunciation of absolutism, in the French style, gained currency in the port towns, especially among the growing numbers of freemasons now to be found in Brazil. This radicalism joined, in the north, with resentment of the promotion of Rio de Janeiro that had taken place after 1808. The regional rivalry was already old, dating back to the pre-gold age when the north-east was the heart of Brazil. It was in Pernambuco, once the richest of the sugar captaincies of the north-east, that serious trouble broke out in March 1817. The spark was the attempted arrest, by the governor of the captaincy, of an army officer who belonged to a masonic lodge. The officer, forewarned, instead raised his men in revolt against the local government. Within a day a republic of Pernambuco was proclaimed and a new government set up. The rebellion spread quickly into the next captaincies northward, Paraíba and Rio Grande. But almost as quickly it subsided, as loyal troops came into action, and local opposition developed. For many, especially among the more prosperous, the movement was still too extreme in its republicanism, and in its implicit hostility to slavery. Pernambucan autonomy was not worth the possible sacrifice of that age-old economic prop.[40]

However brief the northern rebellion may have been, nevertheless, and however cheering Rio's support of the now King John VI in that crisis, the monarchy suffered in both image and confidence as a result of it. Late in 1817 more troops were brought over from Portugal; in March of the following year, secret societies, including freemasonry, were banned. The crown no longer rested easily in Brazil. At the same time, impatience with royal government was rising in Portugal, where economic conditions remained difficult after the long war against the French. In 1819 discontent in Portugal spread to the army when pay fell several months behind. In August 1820 the garrison of Oporto, in the north of the country, revolted; in September the garrison at Lisbon overthrew the king's regents there and installed a new provisional government. And in November 1820 the military, imitating the radical model of the Spanish army in the same year, pressured that government into adopting, for interim purposes, the Spanish constitution of 1812.[41] Portugal now became a constitutional monarchy (though with an absent king), directed by liberals.

The course of Brazilian independence, from this point, has certain resemblances to the independence process taking place in Mexico at the same time. Briefly stated, it runs as follows. A parliament was quickly elected in Portugal, and met for the first time in late January 1821. Brazil was allocated 70–75 of the 200 total seats in this assembly; but no Brazilian representatives arrived before August 1821, and from some regions none ever arrived; hence crucial decisions were taken without Brazilian participation. One of these was that the king should return to Lisbon. John briefly hesitated before acceding to this demand on March 7, 1821; not to return would possibly mean his loss of Portugal. On April 26 he and some four thousand Portuguese, along with the funds held in the treasury and the Bank of Brazil, departed for Lisbon. As 1821 proceeded, the Portuguese parliament showed ever more clearly its intent to treat Brazil once again as a colony. In September it ordered that all governmental bodies set up in Rio in 1808 should be abolished; in October it named military governors, under direct orders from Lisbon, to all regions of Brazil. Brazilian deputies arriving to take their parliamentary seats were treated with scornful hostility, as inhabitants of a "land of monkeys, of little black men caught on the coast of Africa, and of bananas," in the words of a leading Portuguese liberal.[42] An energetic debate ensued in Brazil about the best course of action to take. No one was prepared to accept anything less than political autonomy. The options ranged from the radicals' preference for independence as a republic to the moderate-liberal and conservative solution of a dual monarchy, with John VI on the throne in Portugal and his son, Peter, on that of Brazil. Peter had not returned to Portugal with his father, who may possibly have advised him to collaborate, if necessary, with Brazilians seeking autonomy. By so doing he would preserve at least the possibility of future reunification of the monarchy. In January 1822 Peter formally announced that he would stay in Brazil. He became the focal point of the attentions of competing political factions. As the story of the final break with Portugal goes, on September 7, 1822 Peter received renewed demands from Lisbon that he return to Portugal and restore Brazil to Portuguese rule; his own orders in Brazil were overridden. He was at that moment on the bank of the River Ipiranga, between Santos and São Paulo. Grinding the papers under his heel, he reportedly announced, "From today on our relations with them are finished. I want nothing more from the Portuguese government, and I proclaim Brazil for ever more separated from Portugal. Long live independence, liberty, and the separation of Brazil." A month later Peter was proclaimed Emperor, and in December crowned as Peter (Pedro) I of Brazil in Rio de Janeiro.[43]

That was not quite the end of the story. In the north and the north-east considerable Portuguese army and naval forces remained in place. To dislodge them Peter engaged Thomas Cochrane, who, after winding up his services to the independence movements on the west coast in 1822, was now living on an estate he had acquired in Chile. Early in 1823 he put together an improvised Brazilian squadron at Rio, commanded and crewed partly by other British seamen. Although this force was inferior to the considerable Portuguese flotilla that was lying at Salvador, Cochrane's reputation made up the difference in strength; so that when he arrived off Salvador in July 1823, the Portuguese troops embarked and sailed away under the escort of the warships. Cochrane gave chase as far as the Canaries (and one of his captains, as far as Lisbon), taking or destroying most of the Portuguese vessels. A similar show of naval force along the north coast in late July and August was enough to end the Portuguese presence there. In November 1823 Cochrane was created Marquês de Maranhão in recognition of his part in bringing Brazilian independence to a successful conclusion.[44]

[15] *Adrift in Storms:*
Caudillos and Penury

"The number of madmen in Bolivia is not large." So wrote José María Dalence, head of the recently created national Statistical Council of Bolivia, in his most useful *Statistical Sketch of Bolivia*, published in 1851.[1] He was referring to people in institutional care. And by that definition he was right. He had found only 116 such men, and 106 women, among a population of 1.38 million in 1846. But almost any outsider, contemplating the political history of Bolivia over the decade before 1850, and willing to stretch the definition of *locos* a little wider, might well have wondered if many, or most, of the population must not be mad in a country so fraught with governmental chaos, coups and counter coups, and wild political rantings. And worse, indeed, was still to come.

Bolivia was not alone in suffering such disorder. Almost all the new Spanish American nations went through periods of great political instability for several decades after gaining independence. Some were emerging from it by the 1850s; but others, like Bolivia, remained in greater or lesser turmoil until the 1870s. From that post-independence period, in fact, dates the beginning of the faintly comic-opera image that still clings to Latin America in the popular view. It was the period in which Antonio López de Santa Anna, nine (or more) times president of Mexico between 1833 and 1855, having lost a leg in a battle against French invaders of the country in 1838, had it disinterred from its first resting place in 1842 to be ceremonially reburied, with funeral discourse, in Mexico City.[2] It was the period in which Mariano Melgarejo, the wayward mestizo dictator of Bolivia in the 1860s, allegedly amused himself by ordering his troops to march out of second floor windows, and forced his officers to dance with each other at balls that no society ladies of La Paz would attend. These, and many others like them, are the ancestors of the heavily goldleafed and sunglassed Latin American military heads of state of a thousand twentieth-century cartoons.

Although it would be foolish, and wrong, to dismiss the post-independence decades as simply a period of indescribable chaos, political calm was notably absent from a time when it was much needed. A simple index of the degree and persistence of disorder lies in the number of constitutions proclaimed in the various countries before a sustainable legal frame was finally devised. The Andean countries fared worst. Among them, Ecuador is perhaps the extreme case. None of its eight constitutions in the nineteenth century proved lasting, and since 1900 it has had eleven more. Bolivia had nine before arriving at a document in 1878 that remained in effect for sixty years. Peru had eight, the last of which, in 1867, endured until 1920. Colombia's total was seven; but the last of them (1886) was in force until 1991. Mexico did considerably better, with three constitutions before the notable charter of 1857, which was superseded only in 1917. The countries in southern South America were the most stable on the constitutional score:

- Argentina 1819, 1826, 1853 (in force until the present, except for 1949–55);
- Paraguay 1813, 1844, 1870 (in force until 1940);
- Chile 1822, 1833 (in force until 1925);
- Uruguay 1830 (in force until 1918, but replaced four times since then).[3]

These numbers certainly provide only a crude measure and comparison of political stability in the various new nations. But they are a rather striking index of how much uncertainty existed among the politically active groups about the forms of governance that they should pursue. That uncertainty was natural enough. Having thrown their captains and officers overboard, the creoles now found themselves adrift aboard their various ships of state, with, they suddenly realized, at best a theoretical knowledge of navigation. They had not been prepared for this task; and, given the nature of Bourbon colonialism, they could hardly have prepared themselves, in a practical sense, for it. In the circumstances, it is no surprise that political creeds were dogmatically advanced and argued, that local interests often had remarkably free play, and that it was usually might, rather than principle, that finally prevailed.

POWER AFTER INDEPENDENCE

The mightiest figures in the political landscape after independence would certainly seem to have been the triumphant heroes of the struggle for liberation: the Bolívars, the San Martíns, the Sucres, and others in their several places. These were the men with the greatest moral authority to lead, and with the charisma, both inherent and reinforced by their exploits, to unite divergent political elements in their train. But in the event even these remarkable men found themselves quite powerless when confronting a combination of deep rooted geopolitical inertia in Spanish America and newly imported political principles. San Martín, having had a taste of local politics in Lima during his time as Protector of Peru, and perhaps with an inkling of how much more of the same, or worse, would follow, decided to withdraw from the scene even before the Spanish were ousted from the Andes. Sucre did two years as president of Bolivia (1826–8). He strove for enlightened and modernizing government, but found himself falling from a position of adulation as heroic liberator of the nation to one of resented outsider. (He, like Bolívar, was a Venezuelan.) Bolívar himself played for the highest stakes – the creation of a multi-nation federation in north-west South America – and, losing, suffered the hardest fall. As an outsider, he was fatally handicapped in New Granada, Ecuador, and Peru; and his efforts to glue together what for centuries had been discrete political and even cultural entities in the end brought him only rejection in all of them. In Mexico, Iturbide's exit came even more quickly than Sucre's or Bolívar's. He was, in any case, a man of far smaller moral and military stature than either of them; at best, a most ingenious trimmer. In May 1822 he had himself crowned as Agustín I, Emperor of Mexico. But his high-handedness as instant royalty lost him the support of both the army and civilians, so that in March 1823 he had to abdicate and move to exile in Italy. When in 1824 he returned to Mexico with hopes of re-establishing his political position, he was captured and executed.

Men who had led in the wars of independence, but at less than the highest level, often had longer political careers in the new states. Among many examples, one striking case is that of Andrés de Santa Cruz (1792–1865), a mestizo who succeeded Sucre as president of Bolivia, so becoming the country's first native-born leader. Santa Cruz at first fought for Spain against the insurgents in the central Andes, and changed sides late, after being captured in 1820. He then served under San Martín in Peru, showing himself to be a poor field commander, but a good organizer. As such he later drew the attention of Bolívar, who made him his chief of staff, and in 1826 left him as *de facto* ruler of Peru during his own absence. Two years later Sucre named Santa Cruz as his successor in Bolivia. He presided over the country from 1829 to 1839, and in general proved an able, thrifty, honest, and progressive head of state. Under his guidance Bolivia gained a firm financial footing, and seemed well set for recovery from damage suffered in the independence period. All was lost, however, when Santa Cruz – overreaching from his prior accomplishments, and perhaps hoping for success of a sort that had eluded Bolívar – tried to combine Peru and Bolivia into a single state. The attempt seemed possible because by the mid-1830s Peru had subsided into extreme regional conflict, whereas Bolivia was under centralized control. Santa Cruz proclaimed the confederation in October 1836. External interference, however, naturally had the effect of increasing political unity in Peru to oppose it; and the cost of the enterprise made it unpopular in Bolivia. But the definitive resistance to the plan came from neighboring countries, which saw in it a threat to the balance of power in western South America. Chile declared war on the confederation in December 1836, and Argentina five months later. Argentina invaded; but the major effort came from Chile, which defeated the confederacy in January 1839 and thereby brought it, and Santa Cruz's presidency, to an end. Santa Cruz went into European exile. Eventually he regained some favor in Bolivia and was named ambassador to Belgium and then the Vatican. He died, though, in France in 1865.

Santa Cruz initially succeeded in Bolivia because of his personal qualities, the prestige he brought from his activities as an independence leader in the 1820s, and because he was a native of the country. It was in his foreign hankerings that he lost his way (and in doing so helped send Bolivia down a path of political disorder that was fifty years long). In Venezuela in those same years a man resembling Santa Cruz in some respects, but perhaps crucially different in lacking external ambitions, managed to keep a far longer hold on power. This was José Antonio Páez (1790–1873), the leader during the independence wars of the *llaneros*, the cattle herders of the Orinoco basin.

Páez was born of humble, though probably white, parents in the western interior plains of Venezuela. His father was a minor official in the royal tobacco monopoly.[4] At an early age he became a cowhand himself, and like many other *llaneros* lived an existence that alternated between cattle raising and banditry. He had natural qualities of leadership, and by the opening of the independence period had gathered a small following of men whom he put into the field against the Spanish. So adept did he prove as a guerrillero in the plains that in 1816 he became the leader of insurgent efforts there. In 1818 he recognized Bolívar, somewhat grudgingly, as the supreme authority in the struggle for independence in Venezuela, and joined forces with him. At Carabobo, in 1821, his *llaneros* (whom Bolívar later termed "our cossacks") played a central part in the rebel victory; and he was with Bolívar in his final and triumphal entry into Caracas after the battle, on June 29, 1821.

Páez, then, emerged from the independence conflict in Venezuela as a hero of a particularly authentic sort, a man of the people whose courage and innate abilities to lead in war had raised him from near nothingness to national eminence. Such men might seem, to the populace at large, more admirable than even the heroes who chose a larger stage, such as Bolívar himself, or Sucre, since these had started from positions of social superiority and advantage. The esteem that Páez had achieved by the early 1820s (sustained, it is true, by later military and political actions) underlay a long and on the whole distinguished career. He was the dominant political figure in Venezuela for the next twenty-five years. He was the man who led the country out of the Colombian federation at the end of 1829. He was president from 1831 to 1835, and again from 1839 to 1843. After 1847 he spent most of the rest of his life in exile, in the United States. But he still commanded enough respect to be called back to Venezuela by conservatives in 1859 to do battle with federalism; and from 1861 to 1863 he was again president.

CAUDILLOS

A better example than Páez can scarcely be found of that ubiquitous political figure of Spanish America in the early decades of independence, the *caudillo*. The word is the diminutive form of *cabo*, which in turn descends from the Latin *caput*, "head." The *caudillo*, then, is the "little head" or "little chief." The diminutive says much about the source of authority of this political type. He was the familiar local leader, the common man risen to power but still close to his, and the populace's, roots; or so, at least, he would have the people think. The word carries also a strong military connotation; the means of gaining prominence is martial prowess. A man did not become a *caudillo* as a strategist but as a successful fighter, in person, in the field. Santa Cruz, therefore, who was not a notable warrior, barely qualifies as a *caudillo*. Páez, who could fight hand to hand, ride, swim rivers, and live off the land as well as the toughest *llanero* – and was to boot a most capable commander – was almost a living definition of the type.

The *caudillo* was one of the independence wars' chief legacies to the working of Spanish American politics. Before the wars, there were no *caudillos*; after them, scarcely a country was without them. Their dramatic appearance, in the course of those ten or fifteen years of conflict, is a crucial event in the development of the militarism that has characterized (some would say dogged) Spanish American political life ever since.

The *caudillo* was typically the product of rural, often isolated, areas, far from the colonial capitals in which politically informed creoles made bids for autonomy in 1810 and later years. If there was any part of the Spanish empire in which force had endured in colonial times as an instrument of order, it was in those isolated regions. To the extent that such areas felt the Spanish hand, it was applied by quasi-military figures, the occupants of the office of governor and captain general that was usually the highest Spanish authority on the periphery. But in many such areas power was shared in practice between officials and the owners of great estates. These men were in effect march lords, exercising jurisdiction in their domains and sometimes keeping what amounted to a private militia. Thus, by both public and private example, in remote rural areas the potential *caudillo* had models to follow. And when Spanish rule faltered after 1808, and the colonial centers became engrossed in their own affairs, there were ambitious or needy men, like Páez, who saw and seized the opportunity to better themselves through some blend of banditry and guerrilla warfare. Local warlords, some of them white, others mestizo, but almost all of humble origins, multiplied in the rebelling colonies. They fought for their own gain; and possibly, when it seemed beneficial to them, for the freedom of the colony in which they lived. Their activities became, as it were, a constant background noise behind the strategic efforts of the prominent liberators. And, at the end of the day, a very few of them, like Páez, emerged from the background as national leaders. More remained armed and ambitious in the provinces, out of the limelight but a potential threat to the stability of the newborn nations.

The appearance of *caudillos* was part and parcel of another legacy of the wars of independence to the new states. And that was regionalism. Just as the Spanish military conquest, three hundred years earlier, had, by destroying the large native states, allowed a resurgence of localism in Mexico and the Andes, so the process of independence, in removing Spanish controls, left the way open for regions to break loose from the new national capitals. The term *republiquetas*, "little republics," has been applied to the fiefdoms that ambitious local leaders tried to create in Bolivia during the wars. For several decades after independence, that same tendency plagued most Latin American countries. It was the outcome of natural geographical divisions – a river basin, perhaps, or a series of valleys isolated by mountains – added to the political ambition of local figures.

More prominent even than Páez in Spanish American history as *caudillos* on the supra-regional scale are Juan Manuel de Rosas (1793–1877) and Antonio

López de Santa Anna (1794–1876), in, respectively, Argentina and Mexico. Rosas was not the product of quite the classic *caudillo* mold. He was born in Buenos Aires, the son of a long-established creole family of office holders. The family also, however, had land, and it was on their *estancia* that Rosas gained his important, practical education. He had minimal military experience. There was no fighting of the Spaniards in the Río de la Plata after 1810; Rosas did, though, take a brief part in a civil conflict in 1820. By that time he had he acquired land of his own; the focus of his life, indeed, both personal and political, was on the land, and on the people who raised cattle on it.

Among those people were the gauchos, the local equivalent of the Venezuelan *llaneros*. And just as Páez had risen to prominence as a leader of *llaneros*, so Rosas advanced with the support and loyalty of his herdsmen and other workers, whom in the twenties he made into a disciplined force for labor, and, potentially, for military action as well.[5] Rosas was politically ambitious, and became, as the twenties advanced, increasingly prominent among the *estancieros* (estate owners and cattle breeders) around Buenos Aires. His chance came amidst growing political conflict at the end of the decade. Using as a fighting force his own men, together with other landowners' workers, he imposed himself in 1829 as the governor of the province of Buenos Aires. He remained governor until 1832, and then returned to the office from 1835 to 1852.

In formal political terms, Rosas was a contradiction. He had allied himself politically to those who promoted federalism in the early Argentina, in opposition to advocates of centralized government. But this was pure convenience; for there was in fact no more convinced a centralist than Rosas. And though he was never more, in name, than the governor of the single province of Buenos Aires, in reality he rapidly came to dominate the entire Argentine territory. He was able to do so because he had the backing of the cattle breeders, who were the prime economic force and the source of the major exports, salt beef and hides. If he had need of military force, or the threat of it, he could count on them to send him their own gauchos. He was careful to keep up the image of strong, practical man of action, which gave him the loyalty of rural workers. He drew the approval of urban artisans, also, by protecting them with tariffs from the threat of cheap manufactured imports. His control of Buenos Aires itself, essentially the country's sole port, made this protection effective. By force, the threat of force, and political maneuver, he controlled the provincial *caudillos* who dominated the interior. And, in case force were not enough, he used political terrorism, the instrument of which was a para-military political club named the *Sociedad Popular Restauradora*, or People's Society for Restoration. He gave an armed section of this, named the *mazorca*, a free hand to cull the political opposition. (The word means "ear of maize," the tight packing of the kernels reputedly symbolizing the closeness of the organization's ranks. But in Spanish American pronunciation *mazorca* has the same sound as *más horca*, "more gallows;" the name was, then, a grim pun.) Estimates vary widely of the number of political killings; it reached perhaps two thousand for his entire period of rule.[6] This mode of keeping order seems to prefigure Argentine practices in decades only recently passed. But neither terror nor networks woven of loyalty or intimidation remained effective when the underlying structure of Argentina began to change. By the mid-century, sheep were displacing cattle on the pampas, and wool was rising in importance as an export. The owners of the sheep pastures were new men, many of them foreigners, who were not part of Rosas's system. Far more serious than this, however, was the growing challenge presented to him by the so-called Littoral, the north-eastern provinces through which the three great rivers, the Paraguay, Paraná, and Uruguay, flowed. This region was beginning to rival Buenos Aires in the production of cattle and sheep; and as it grew economically, so it did also in resentment of Buenos Aires's centralization of political power and taxation. In one of the Littoral provinces, Entre Ríos, there had appeared by 1850 a *caudillo* named Justo José de Urquiza, who dared to challenge Rosas. He did so in part because he had the backing of Brazil, a country entering in the mid-century on a period of economic prosperity, and hostile to what it saw as the dangerous northward expansion of Buenos Aires's influence. Uruguay, also, was still a bone of contention between Brazil and Buenos Aires, despite its legal status as a sovereign state lying between the two. Brazilians as well as Uruguayans were alarmed by Rosas's suspected designs on it. The outcome of these tensions and fears was that in 1851 a Triple Alliance of Brazil, Entre Ríos and Uruguay sent an army, under Urquiza, southward toward Buenos Aires. It approached the capital early in 1852. Rosas's forces had perhaps gradually grown hollow behind their intimidating façade, and in February 1852 he was defeated. Rosas retreated to the house of the British minister in Buenos Aires, and then sailed off on a British naval vessel to exile in England. There he died, twenty-five years later, near Southampton.[7]

The Rosas years in Buenos Aires coincided almost exactly with Santa Anna's period of political prominence in Mexico. Other similarities between the two exist, notably the fact that they were both indisputably *caudillos*. On the other hand, the contrasts are also clear. Santa Anna was the son of Spanish immigrants to New Spain, his father being a subdelegate (a district administrator serving under an intendant) in the Veracruz region of the Gulf coast. In the independence wars in Mexico, Santa Anna fought for the crown until 1821, when, along with many others, he changed sides and joined Iturbide's movement. That late, and slight, participation in the independence movement was the point of departure of his political career. Physically speaking, his base always lay in rural Veracruz, where he became an estate owner and could count on popular support.

To follow the story of Santa Anna's political career is a challenging task at anything below the most general level. It is even hard to say for sure how many times he was president (at least nine, perhaps eleven), and for how long he held that office (about twelve years, all in all). He first became president in 1833, and left office for the last time in 1855. During that period he was certainly the country's most prominent military leader; and it was largely as a result of that sort of prominence that he was chosen as president. But that in itself is puzzling; for Santa Anna's military failures far outweighed his successes. He was the field commander responsible for Mexico's loss of Texas (first to independent status in 1836, and then to the United States in 1845).

A decade later he was president and commander in chief during the war of 1846–8 with the USA that cost Mexico its remaining territories in what is now the western United States (roughly speaking, present-day California, Arizona, and New Mexico). It may be that no one could have done better. Certainly the westward advance of the United States was an almost irresistible force. After these catastrophes and lesser setbacks, Santa Anna usually retreated to his estate in rural Veracruz and awaited the next call to action. The memory of both the politically active class and the people seemed short; and the crises were frequent. The new call, therefore, generally came quickly; and once more Santa Anna would don a splendid uniform and ride up to a tumultuous acclamation in Mexico City. It was a pattern whose crudity seems to be in contradiction with the sophistication and intelligence visible in many Mexican political figures during those decades.

Perhaps, however, it was precisely the presence in Mexico of intense and often acrimonious civilian politics that created both need and openings for a figure like Santa Anna. More telling still may have been Mexico's lack of a persistently dominant economic and social group comparable with the *estancieros* of the Río de la Plata. It was above all their support that kept Rosas, who was one of their kind, in place for so long. Santa Anna was a landowner; but in the Mexico of his time landowners, though among the rich and powerful, did not monopolize politics and wealth. The absence in him of commitment to any political creed confirms this explanation of his seesawing career. By Santa Anna's standards, Iturbide had been a mere dabbler in trimming. Santa Anna accepted happily enough the politics of whoever most recently had called upon him. It is true, however, that over the course of his presidential career he moved broadly rightward. At the start, in 1833, he had very briefly acquiesced in the distinctly radical liberalism of the day. His final presidency, of 1853–5, was one of extreme centralization; and in December 1853 he accepted the title of *alteza serenísima* ("most serene highness"). In this last period of rule Santa Anna indeed behaved in a dictatorial fashion that was worthy of Rosas, setting up a secret police and decreeing the death penalty for political opponents. The harsh arrogance of his government served, though, only to precipitate the onset of a powerful liberal reaction that for several years past had been brewing. Santa Anna was unable to resist this storm, which quickly developed into the great Mexican Reform movement of the mid-century. He abandoned the presidency and left the country on August 17, 1855 in a steamship named, ironically enough, *Iturbide*. Like Iturbide, he evidently hoped to return to Mexico at some future date and regain power. For that reason, perhaps, in contrast to many ejected *caudillos*, he did not choose Europe for exile, but went instead first to Colombia and then to the Danish West Indian island of St Thomas. Early in 1864 he did in fact attempt a return, seeing an opportunity for himself in the newly established and monarchical French administration of the country. But the French would have no truck with him. He was finally readmitted in 1874, when he was old and worn. He died two years later in Mexico City.[8]

Most Spanish American countries had periods of *caudillo* rule during the half-century after independence, though few had men of the power and endurance shown by Páez, Rosas, and Santa Anna. The *caudillo*, as type, was not without variations. Some of these leaders seem to have relied particularly on their direct attractiveness to the mass of people for legitimacy and authority. Examples of this more "folk" or "populist" variety of *caudillo* are Rafael Carrera, who dominated Guatemala from 1839 to 1865, and Manuel Isidoro Belzu, president of Bolivia from 1848 to 1855. A case can be made for classifying as folk *caudillos* the first three rulers of independent Paraguay: José Gaspar Rodríguez de Francia (in power from 1814 to 1840), Antonio Carlos López (1840–63), and his son Francisco Solano López (1863–70).[9] But appeal to the masses alone could rarely sustain power for long. The successful *caudillo* drew also on the support of the upper end of society, gaining it by catering to their interest. Favorable tax and tariff regulations, opening of access to public or Indian land, patronage in the form of employment or pensions – these and much else drew social and economic notables to the *caudillo*. But above all the upper (and middle) classes clustered around these men because they offered the promise of order at times when order was the exception rather than the rule. The provincial and often lower class origins of the *caudillos* might be expected to have made them unattractive to the relative sophisticates of the capitals. But it was precisely their inferior and regional origins that gave them their allure: those who were from the people and the provinces should know best how to control the people and the provinces. In the phenomenon of *caudillismo* there was much irony and seeming contradiction. Uncouth warlords, bred by the wars of independence and in all appearance destabilizing elements in the newly independent Spanish American states, were often and soon enough welcomed as restorers of stability. There is more than a hint of their being seen by all levels of society as surrogates for the departed figure of king or viceroy. Santa Anna was surrounded in government by upper class, conservative Mexicans at the time he became his "most serene highness"; Páez's troops are reported to have gone into combat in 1848 crying "Long live the King José Antonio Páez."[10]

CONSERVATIVES AND LIBERALS

Monarchism, in fact, was a notion with many adherents during the struggles for independence and their agitated aftermath. It had a natural fascination for conservatives, for those, almost all of them creoles, who yearned for the orderly certainties of the colonial regime. San Martín was far from being the only leading light of the independence movement who thought that a king or prince would be the best solution to the obvious problem of legitimacy in postwar administrations. Advocates of constitutional monarchy under European princes appeared in both Chile and Argentina before 1820. Iturbide, in 1821, proposed that Mexico become such a kingdom, under Ferdinand VII or another Spanish prince. Ferdinand, however, was far too rigid a personality ever to have seen in this a means of preserving Spain's hold on Mexico. And in the event Iturbide himself became king, indeed emperor – only to fall in short order because by definition no creole could satisfy the requirement of legitimacy that was supposed to inhere in royalty. But the notion of monarchy died hard in Mexico. In 1830, Lucas Alamán, a leading conservative figure and yet more distinguished chronicler of his times, reported that many believed the answer to political disorder to lie in the import of a European prince.[11] And it was in Mexico, in the 1860s, that the experiment was finally tried. Mexico owed, by then, large debts to France. The French ruler of the time, the Emperor Napoleon III, had long contemplated setting up a French protectorate over Mexico. He concerted with Mexican conservative refugees, desperate foes of the liberal reformers then in power, to back them with a sizable French army. Mexico, in return, would pay its debts. The army was also to support the establishment of a monarchy, to be occupied by Maximilian (1832–67), the younger brother of the Austrian emperor. These ostensibly improbable schemes were actually put into effect. Maximilian, with his Belgian wife Charlotte (Carlota in Spanish), arrived in mid-1864 to assume the throne as emperor. He proved a disappointment, however, to his conservative backers. Maximilian was a well-intentioned young man, broadly inspired by a faith in democracy and equality. He had in fact much more in common with Mexican liberals than with their opponents. He approved, for example, of laws the liberals had passed in the late fifties that stripped the church of its lands and other real property. He drafted progressive labor legislation. He chose moderate liberals as well as conservatives for his cabinet. But for more radical liberals he remained the creature of conservatism, as well as the symbol of foreign intrusion into Mexico's sovereignty. His presence, then, was a goad to the committed opponents of conservatism. And in the civil war that ensued, he was finally captured and, in June 1867, executed by firing squad at Querétaro. Carlota lived on another sixty years in Europe, though in a state of apparently paranoid disturbance. So ended Mexico's second and last attempt at formal monarchy.[12]

After independence, it was generally more extreme conservatives who were drawn to monarchy. The moderate conservatives' preference was for a firmly centralized republican government; and this they could achieve by backing able national *caudillos*, who in return would supply a variety of political and financial favors. "Conservatism," in the post-independence context, meant the preservation, as far as possible, of the social and political conditions of late colonial times ("political" in the sense that power should remain the exclusive possession of the traditional upper reaches of society). Conservatism was not so much a political creed as a form of political inertia, a quite expectable and natural clustering together of many of the rich and eminent who suddenly found themselves deprived of the props that the Spanish presence had provided. Externally, their new countries stood exposed, largely defenseless, to the forces of international politics and economics. Inside the countries, the rich and notable now lacked the assuring reinforcement of social hierarchy that the presence of orderly Spanish administrative and legal structures had implied. If conservatives had any ideology, it was in a shared belief in the central role of the Catholic Church in their societies. For the church was, for them, not just the source of spiritual certainty and help, but also the bearer of a long social and cultural tradition; and, beyond that, a force that could and

FIGURE 15.1 Santiago Matamoros (Saint James the Great) as killer of Moors. Saint James was patron saint of Spain, and allegedly the helper of Spaniards in battles against American natives, as well as in earlier conflicts with the Moors. (Cuzco School, Peru, eighteenth century. New Orleans Museum of Art.)

FIGURE 15.2 *Cortés and Victory*: José Clemente Orozco's vision of the *conquistador* as machine. (Mural, 1936–9. Hospicio Cabañas, Guadalajara, Mexico. © Tony Morrison, South American Pictures.)

FIGURE 15.3 Don Antonio de Mendoza, first viceroy of New Spain (1535–49).

FIGURE 15.4 Don Francisco de Toledo, fifth viceroy of Peru (1569–81). (From Felipe Guaman Poma de Ayala, *Nueva Coronica y Buen Gobierno* 1936.)

FIGURE 15.5 Saint Rose of Lima, canonized in 1671, the first American-born saint. She appears here as a Dominican nun, bearing the infant Christ on a bed of roses. (Unknown artist, Cuzco School, late seventeenth century. New Orleans Museum of Art.)

FIGURE 15.6 Sor Juana Inés de la Cruz, scholar and greatest of colonial Mexican poets. (Miguel Cabrera, 1751. Museo Nacional de Historia, Chapultepec Castle, Mexico City.)

FIGURE 15.7 Equestrian statue of Charles IV, in bronze, originally placed in the center of the Plaza Mayor of Mexico City. (Manuel Tolsá, 1796. © Tony Morrison, South American Pictures.)

FIGURE 15.8 Antonio José de Sucre (bronze statue, Plaza Mayor, Sucre, Bolivia).

FIGURE 15.9 Simón Bolívar. (Mary Evans Picture Library.)

FIGURE 15.10 José de San Martín, with his staff. (Unknown artist, nineteenth century. © Corbis-Bettman.)

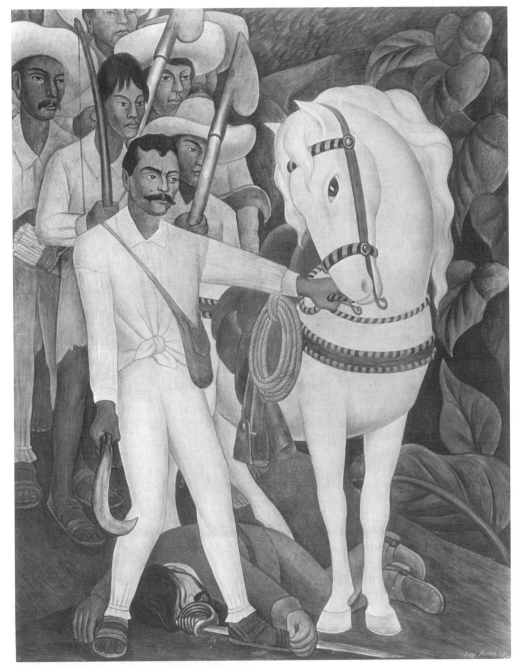

FIGURE 15.14 *Agrarian Leader Zapata.* (Diego Rivera, 1931, fresco, The Museum of Modern Art, New York. Abby Aldrich Rockefeller Fund. Photograph © 1997 The Museum of Modern Art, New York.)

FIGURE 15.11 (*facing page, top left*) Juan Manuel de Rosas, reproduced with permission of the General Secretariat of the Organization of American States.

FIGURE 15.12 (*facing page, top right*) The young Porfirio Díaz.

FIGURE 15.13 (*facing page, bottom*) Porfirio Díaz as elderly president, with civilian and military supporters, entertained by dancing girls. (David Alfaro Siqueiros, mural, 1957, in the Museo Nacional de Historia, Chapultepec Castle, Mexico City. © Roger Scruton.)

FIGURE 15.15   Pedro I of Brazil. (Timepix / Rex Features.)

FIGURE 15.16   Pedro II of Brazil. (Timepix / Rex Features.)

should bind society together. Any attack on the church, whether on its spirituality or on its material possessions, was likely to inspire conservatives to furious response.

And attacked the church certainly was. Its assailants were the numerous adherents of liberalism to be found in the newly independent Spanish America. Unlike conservatism, liberalism was clearly an ideology; and, moreover, one alien to the Spanish world. Its origins were in north-western Europe in the eighteenth century, and particularly in the rationality of human beings emphasized by the Enlightenment. The eighteenth century's confidence in the power of human reason to solve problems made liberalism inherently a doctrine of change. Its confidence that reason resided in every human being made liberalism naturally a doctrine of individualism, and, by derivation, one of individual liberty and equality also. All this – the emphasis on interlinked individuality, liberty, and equality – was contradictory to the body of social and political beliefs that passed to independent Spanish America from the colonial period. Those beliefs were, in essence, an extension of the medieval view that society properly consisted, not of separate individuals, but of estates and corporations, in which people occupied fixed and largely unchangeable positions, forming a firm and strong hierarchy. In colonial times this model of society had, as suggested earlier, lost some of its rigidity in Spanish America. But it was still the underlying pattern, and one to which conservatives reverted, especially in times of uncertainty or disorder.

Liberalism came to Spanish America by two main routes. One was creoles' reading of political and philosophical writings from Europe and North America, together with the direct experience that a rather small number of them had, as travelers, of political life in those two regions in the late eighteenth and early nineteenth centuries. The other, and more important, means of transmission was the Cortes of Cadiz, and above all the constitution produced by that parliament in 1812. The fact that the constitution was the product of a modernizing Spanish body, in which creoles had had at least some participation, made it especially appealing to reform-minded men in the colonies around the time of independence.

Generally speaking, those in post-independence Spanish America who were drawn to liberalism were likely to be dwellers in provincial cities, and more of the middle range than of the upper crust of white society.[13] Although great landowners and great merchants might disagree on economic issues, specifically on tariff questions, broadly viewed wealth was a good predictor of conservatism. Just as in Europe the rise of liberalism was linked with the expansion of a bourgeoisie in the eighteenth century, so in Spanish America the existence and growth of a population of professionals and middle-level traders in regional cities provided fertile soil for liberalism there. Liberals might be inspired not only by abstract principle, but also by envy (or, more delicately put, by a desire for equality with the rich and influential of the largest cities). For the same reason of geographical distribution, liberalism generally went hand in hand with federalism in the early decades. Liberals were likely to press for greater autonomy of provincial government, while for conservatives power naturally resided in the center. The lines, however, were not always clear cut. "There is nothing quite so much like a Conservative as a Liberal in office," remarked a nineteenth-century Brazilian nobleman. The same could have been said of Spanish America.[14] Given the political disorder of the time, liberals were often enough ready to strike bargains with *caudillos* in order to gain access to power; arguing, perhaps, that strong central government was needed precisely for the protection of the individual freedoms that they held so dear. And in times of severe stress, many a moderate liberal might find himself slipping into the conservative camp, leaving only his radical brethren to continue the true fight.

The liberal–conservative conflict naturally played out with different intensity and with different speed and rhythms in different places. Almost everywhere it was, at one level, a disruptive tension, bringing political and sometimes military battles, and creating conditions in which *caudillismo* could flourish. The persistence of the *caudillo* after independence, in fact, was in some part the outcome of political instability caused by this particular antagonism. At another level, however, the duel between conservatives and liberals, between traditionalists (more or less inert) and innovators (more or less doctrinaire), between the native and the alien, can be seen as a phase of Spanish American political and cultural development that was bound to arrive sooner or later. It was part of the process of self-definition and of establishment of identity *vis-à-vis* the outside world that had to be undertaken.

Among the many examples that could be taken of liberal–conservative contention, the story of the first federalist republic of Mexico (1824–36) is an illustrative case. It is especially so because it culminated in a fierce dispute about the church; and it was the issue of religion that generally provoked the most ardent feelings on each side.

In summary (for to go into detail would quickly produce confusion), the first federalist republic proceeded as follows. In 1824 a Mexican constituent congress produced the country's first post-independence constitution. Broadly speaking it was a reaction to the authoritarian centralism that Iturbide had shown during his brief reign as emperor. The congress was dominated by federalists (liberals by nature, if not yet by name), and the constitution was itself a federalist, and republican, document, very much along the lines of the United States' constitution. It divided Mexico into nineteen states, most of them with the borders of the present states. Each of these was to have its own congress, making state law, and its own constitution. The national government, of an elected president and a congress, received powers to tax nationally and to make wars and treaties.

The first three years of the new republic were tranquil enough. The president was Miguel Fernández y Félix, a man who had been one of the most active insurgents against Spain after Morelos's demise in 1815, and who had later been imprisoned for his opposition to Iturbide's regime. He is better known by the pseudonym "Guadalupe Victoria" he had chosen for himself as an insurgent: Guadalupe to invoke Mexico's own version of the Madonna, and Victoria simply for victory. He was, then, a far more authentic hero of the independence struggle than Iturbide had ever been, and by that measure a natural occupant of the presidency. He inherited financial difficulties from

Iturbide's time; but loans and investments from Great Britain deferred the urgency of resolving them. Elections in 1826 brought still more federalists into the national congress. But a conservative reaction was quick to develop; and this, added to the reappearance of fiscal problems once the loans were used up, resulted in the election as president in 1828 of a centrist general. The defeated candidate, another famous ex-guerrillero of independence, Vicente Guerrero, challenged the election, and with the support of Santa Anna, then the military commander of Veracruz, forced another early in 1829, in which he was successful.

Already, therefore, three challenges to constitutional process were visible in Mexico. One was the conflict, as old as politics itself, between "ins" and "outs." Conservative centrists simply became impatient with the hold that federalists possessed on congress after 1826. Another was the intrusion of the military, and of force, into politics. The opposition candidate in 1828 was a general; Guerrero prevailed against him with at least the threat of force provided by Santa Anna. The third was the destabilizing effect of economic and fiscal problems.

Worse was very soon to come. Guerrero appointed as his finance minister one Lorenzo de Zavala. He was a man who, after first supporting Iturbide, had become a radical federalist. In 1827 he was elected governor of the state of México in the center of the country, where he legislated for disentailment of church properties and removal of communal lands from villages in order to promote private ownership. In national office he pursued the same line, seeking to resolve what was by now a severe lack of public funds by forcing the sale of church property, and setting up a progressive income tax.[15] The result was a lurch to the right, in the form of a coup in December 1829 by the vice-president, Anastasio Bustamante, a military man who not only reversed Zavala's fiscal policies but also had Guerrero shot. His conservative regime lasted until 1832. But late in that year, a reactive coup took place that brought on to the scene one of Mexico's prominent liberals of the nineteenth century, Valentín Gómez Farías. Gómez was almost a model of the Spanish American liberal of the time. He was a middle-class provincial – a native of Guadalajara who had practiced medicine in another provincial capital, Aguascalientes, before becoming a national congressman for Zacatecas, a state that showed a fierce attachment to regional autonomy in Bustamante's regime. The force necessary for the coup was provided, once more, by Santa Anna, who, although without any commitment to federalism or liberalism, saw a chance for personal advancement in a change of government. Santa Anna quickly emerged as the new national president (his first occupancy of the office), but, retiring to his *hacienda* in Veracruz to see what might eventuate to his still greater advantage, left Gómez Farías in charge as his vice-president.

Gómez immediately picked up threads that Zavala had been forced to drop in 1829 and added some of his own. He revived discussion of the disentailment of church property. He seized the property of missions in Upper and Lower California. He decreed an end to obligatory payment of tithes to the church. He declared monks and nuns free to retract their vows. In a revival of the colonial *patronato real*, he asserted the government's power to name bishops and archbishops. He removed the University of Mexico, seen as a bastion of conservatism, from church control; and created a Directorate of Public Education to control schooling, previously dominated by the church, throughout the country. Priests were forbidden to bring politics into their preaching. And then, extending his attack to another perceived reactionary force besides the church, he canceled the *fueros*, or special privileges, of the military. These consisted essentially of the right to trial by special courts.[16]

Vast indignation resulted among the clergy, the army and many of their allies among the wealthy of Mexico. *Religión y fueros* ("religion and privileges") was the conservative cry. And so loudly did it sound that in April 1834 Santa Anna dismissed Gómez Farías and the congress, repealed the anticlerical and other measures, and crushed by force a protest by liberals from Zacatecas. Before dissolving congress he pushed through it a decree declaring that in him "resided, by the will of the nation, all the extraordinary powers necessary to make as many changes in the constitution of 1824 as he should think suitable for the good of the nation, without the hindrances and delays which that instrument prescribed."[17] He seized, then, dictatorial powers, and ruled with them, and military backing, until late 1835, when he went north to combat, unsuccessfully, the newly declared independence of Texas. Enough respect for constitutional forms remained in him, however, for him to order the election of a new congress in 1834. This body, dominated by clerics, military men, and their supporters, first met in September of that year. As instructed, it drafted a new constitution. This, sometimes known as the "Seven Laws," appeared finally in 1836. It was, as would be expected, a centralist document, providing for abolition of state legislatures, conversion of states into "departments," presidential appointment of departmental governors, a large role for an outgoing president in the choice of his successor, an eight-year presidential term, and the creation of a cabinet of thirteen presidential advisers, two of whom should be military men, and two priests.

Thus Mexico formally moved from federalism to centralism in the space of a dozen years, in fits and starts along a zig-zag path of conservative and liberal, militarist and civilian, religious and secularist excursions. All over Spanish America during those years the same play was being acted out, with of course local variations; nor did large alterations in the script begin to appear for another quarter of a century.

In most regions, a central theme in the action was the mutual hostility of liberals and the Catholic Church. This issue was most contentious in Mexico and New Granada, where liberalism took its firmest hold and where church leaders, perhaps in reaction, were notably intransigent. Liberal hostility to the church had a number of sources. One underlying tension was the rationalist's scorn of the irrational, as religious faith might be seen to be. This, though, was generally not in Spanish America a powerful cause of antagonism, since many liberals were practicing Catholics. Even those who were, however, thought, like the Bourbon reformers of the late eighteenth century, that the church had no part to play in politics, that it should be limited to its proper spiritual sphere. This was going against a long colonial tradition. And, of course, the fact that the upper clergy usually lent their political weight to conservatism, of which the church was a large and natural part, irked liberals all the more. Again, the privileged position that clerics held in society, as a result of long tradition and their special rights (above all, having their own courts) offended liberalism's basic notions of equality. Privilege granted to any group in society was a loss of freedom to the rest. Above all, however, it was the church's wealth that liberals could not abide. Its continued holding of legally inalienable land and buildings at a time when countries and governments were in dire economic straits was indefensible. The objection was theoretical as well as practical. Liberals generally accepted Smithian notions of the economic efficiency of competition. Through the operation of markets the greatest material gain would accrue to the greatest number of people, provided that all competed on an equal footing. And the protected status of church property meant that it competed at an advantage. Church property, therefore, must be freed from the dead hand of entail and offered for purchase. Then it would be put into efficient production, and society as a whole would benefit.

Such radical change took time to accomplish; early attempts were beaten back, as Gómez Farías's experience in Mexico illustrates. Generally it was not until the mid-century, when a new generation of liberals had matured and lent new vigor to the cause, that attacks on the church wrought lasting damage. In New Granada in the early 1850s came various anti-clerical measures, including abolition of church *fueros* and of obligatory collecting of tithes; definitive creation of religious toleration; and legal separation of church and state. In 1861 the further steps were taken of suppression of monasteries and convents, and then seizure and sale of church property.[18] In Mexico during those same years similar measures were placed on the books. Together these laws constitute a good part of the Mexican Reform movement, one of the crucial periods in the political history of the country after independence. The first was the Juárez Law of 1855 which, in the name of equality, restricted the *fueros* of church and army by limiting the jurisdiction of these institutions' own courts to matters of internal discipline.[19] The second was the Lerdo Law of 1856 which, broadly, aimed to disentail lands belonging to all corporations, both ecclesiastical and civil. And then, a year later, came the Iglesias Law, designed to restrict the fees that parish priests could charge their people for such services as burial, marriage, and the like. Excessive charges levied on poor peasants had been among the most severe criticisms of the church made by this activist group of liberals. The authors of these laws, Benito Juárez, Miguel Lerdo de Tejada, and José María Iglesias, all members of the liberal government that replaced Santa Anna's final dictatorial regime in 1855, were among the leading lights of the Reform movement. Late in the following decade, after Maximilian's brief empire, Juárez became president; but it is for the entirety of his actions from the mid-fifties onward that he has become perhaps the country's most revered political figure. (One reason for that, among many, is that he is the only Indian to have been president.) In the short term, the three laws brought a tempest down on their originators and on those around them in government. The measures were incorporated into the 1857 constitution, which proved in the end to be a solid foundation for the country's political existence, and remained in force until 1917. But before it was finally set in place, its framers passed through the fire of civil war. First came their conflict of 1858–60 with the conservatives opposing the Reform; and then followed war against the conservative-backed French intervention and Maximilian's monarchy, ending in 1867.

Although liberals' most serious quarrel, in property matters, was with the church, they objected to the legal isolation from market forces of any property, ecclesiastical or not. This is clear in the Lerdo Law of 1856, which was aimed at the holdings of civil as well as religious corporations. The civil property in question was mainly the common land of towns, from the largest down to the level of Indian villages. There was no suggestion, naturally, that land occupied by public buildings, squares and streets should be offered for sale. But common lands around communities used for farming, grazing and gathering wood were another matter. Spanish colonial law had guaranteed Indian villages' possession of lands ranging in area from a dozen or so to hundreds of square kilometers. This guarantee had been largely effective. Now the economics of free competition, espoused enthusiastically by nineteenth-century liberals, posed a threat to these holdings. To protect native villages from loss of land, Lerdo de Tejada specifically excluded Indians' commons from disentailment in his 1856 measure. But that exclusion was omitted from the version of the law placed in the 1857 constitution. As a result, native communities began to lose land. The same happened in New Granada, for the same reasons, from the 1850s onward; and also in Bolivia, from the mid-sixties, and more seriously from the late seventies onward.[20] Indian communities were weakened as a result, and some disappeared.

Nineteenth-century Latin American liberals were not necessarily friends of the humble. They did not try to redistribute wealth from the rich to the poor as their twentieth- century descendants have typically sought to do. Their aim was to create as many independent economic actors as possible, each competing on terms as equal as possible, so that markets should work with maximum efficiency. The hope, then, in the case of Indians, was that they would buy pieces of disentailed communal land and work them as small-holders. But in reality the buyers were typically the owners of surrounding estates, who stood to gain doubly: they added to their own holdings, and could often employ as wage laborers villagers who now had little or no common land to work themselves. Disentailment under liberal economic principles thus contributed much to the phenomenon of the landless and dependent peasant, a Spanish American figure becoming far too typical by the late nineteenth century.

Post-independence Economies

Ironically, then, liberals' hard-headed dedication to economic egalitarianism (in the sense that everyone should be free to compete on equal terms in markets) tended to increase rather than reduce inequalities of wealth. Liberal policies did not take into account, and were certainly not radical enough to overcome, the prevailing differences of wealth and power in societies. And the existence of those differences made it hard for the poor to succeed as independent economic actors of the Smithian sort. Conservatives, on the other hand, to the degree they held to the seigneurial and patriarchal models of colonial times, may have done less harm to the poor. Broadly speaking, however, most of the politically active class, in the different nations, whether liberal or conservative, adopted the precepts of free market economics. That was the theory of the times. And one of its major propositions – that free international trade among regions possessing natural advantages for producing this or that range of items would benefit all participants in it – held immense attractions for the economically and politically powerful in Spanish America. From time to time tariffs might have to be imposed to protect local production, or (more probably) to raise money for governments; but for most large producers and merchants, a high degree of freedom of trade, in normal circumstances, promised the most profitable outcomes.

The goods exported after independence until the mid-century were very much the same as before 1810, although some changes in the regions of production took place. For lack of records, especially for the early post-independence years, it is hard to compare volumes of production and export in, say, 1805 and 1830. Everything points, however, to a decline. The bases of most productive activity suffered from the effects of the independence wars.

One such effect was to slow dramatically the rapid growth of population visible almost everywhere in Spanish America by the end of the eighteenth century. Between 1810 and 1823 the total number of people in Spanish America rose perhaps by half a million, at a growth rate of 0.3–0.4 percent annually. The following list gives populations in millions of large regions for which reasonable figures are available for both 1810 and 1823.[21] Populations *c.*1850 are added to give a longer view.

	1810	*1823*	*c.1850*
Mexico	6.0	6.8	7.66
Peru, Ecuador, and Bolivia	1.45	1.4	4.19
New Granada	2.0	2.0	2.2
Venezuela	0.95	0.79	1.49

These figures suggest that in areas that saw prolonged and heavy fighting, populations stagnated or fell a little from 1810 to the mid-twenties. The post-war economic outcome was probably that labor was in less abundant supply than before 1810, and, other things being equal, at least no cheaper than before. Other things, however, were not entirely equal. For the wars, by all accounts, did as much harm to the physical means of production as to people, so that the demand for labor may have fallen. Mining machinery was smashed (the example of Guanajuato assaulted by Hidalgo's men in 1810 comes to mind), buildings were damaged, and animals were seized for war purposes, leaving farmers without means of ploughing and hauling, and freighters short of mules and llamas (in the Andes) to carry goods. Simple neglect and lack of upkeep were probably as harmful, though, as outright damage. That was certainly so in mining, where constant maintenance was needed to keep mills and pumps built from wood in action. Liquid capital naturally became scarce during the wars. Production of gold and silver fell, so that cash reserves could not be replenished. Money was exported to buy arms. Those who had cash tended to guard it rather than invest during such troubled times. Spaniards departed for Spain or some other safe haven, taking their money with them. And so, even when the fighting was over, the funds needed for reconstruction were scarce and expensive.

It was not until about 1850 that in Peru and Mexico silver production again reached its late pre-independence levels, at, respectively, about 110,000 and 560,000 kilograms annually. (It is worth noting in passing that despite the post-independence depression of mining, Mexico still was the source of 50–60 percent of the world's new silver down to 1860.) Spanish American silver production received an unexpected boost in the 1830s with a new ore discovery at Chañarcillo, near Copiapó in the arid mid-north of Chile. Even more spectacular in Chile, however, was the rise of copper mining from the 1830s onward. By 1850 mines in the north, at various sites in the Coquimbo and Atacama provinces, were yielding over 12 million kilograms yearly; by 1860 Chile was the world's leading copper exporter.

Far more regions, however, had products of the land to sell abroad than had minerals. The Río de la Plata, still blessed with vast areas of cheap grazing land, continued to export hides to Europe and salted beef to Brazil and Cuba, where it was a basic item in the slave diet. By 1820 salt meat exports from the Río de la Plata had again reached their pre-independence levels; large salting plants, some of them employing hundreds of workers, came into existence in the Río de la Plata, and also in Chile, which was another South American exporter of salted beef. The Río de la Plata sold increasing amounts of tallow, another cattle product, to Europe after 1830. Among export crops, cacao continued to be important for Venezuela; and also for Ecuador. Venezuela also rapidly developed into a large exporter of coffee. By the mid-century, coffee provided 40 percent of Venezuelan exports, and the proportion rose after then. Cuba, still under Spanish administration, was the largest and most efficient producer and exporter of sugar in Spanish America in the nineteenth century. Its success was in large part the result of the use of growing numbers of slaves, imports of whom continued until the 1860s. Technological advances also had a substantial part to play in rising Cuban output of sugar. The island had a railway before any other Latin American country (or indeed Spain), built in the mid-1830s to lower the price of moving sugar from plantations to ships. Steam driven machines for crushing cane also brought economies in the refining of sugar. With the arrival of steam power for transport and milling, estates grew larger and economies of scale in production accrued. In consequence, Cuba has been described as "the greatest economic success story of the first half of the nineteenth century in Latin America."[22] The capital needed for modernizing the sugar industry came from three sources: from Spain; from Spaniards who had left other American colonies, bringing their money with them; and from Cuba itself. Not having suffered wars, the island, and notably its merchant community, had funds to invest.

The only large new export from Spanish America between 1825 and 1850 was guano. On the Chincha islands, off the Peruvian coast about 200 kilometers south-east of Lima, bird droppings had accumulated over many thousands of years to depths of up to 30 meters. The substance was an indirect product of the teeming fish population of Peru's cold and food-rich offshore waters. It was rich in nitrogen, and had been long used by native people as a fertilizer. "Guano" is in fact simply the hispanized spelling of the Quechua *huano* (manure). Peruvian guano was first analyzed chemically in Germany in 1840, and its potential as a fertilizer confirmed. Exports began in 1841 to the industrializing countries of Europe, notably Great Britain. They continued into the 1870s. By the mid-1850s some 500,000 tonnes were being shipped annually, and guano was one of the most valuable of Latin American exports. With the trade the income of the Peruvian government rose dramatically, as did its ability to raise loans on the international market. Both gains contributed to the easing of political chaos that had plagued Peru during its first two decades of independence.[23]

Guano was a mineral export, but one needing no processing. Nor did its extraction require technique or investment. It was, in fact, largely dug by hand and taken to waiting boats in wheelbarrows. Peru imported many thousands of indentured Chinese workers to do this hot and unpleasant work. For a country as disorganized and poor as Peru in the 1830s, guano was a godsend, a commodity that commanded a good price at almost no cost.

Other Spanish American states, in exporting above all the products of the land and of mines, in effect exported goods that were as close to this ideal as possible. They had nothing new to match guano. But in concentrating on what could be produced by existing methods, they made the best of difficult internal economic conditions. Volume of production was generally raised simply by the use of more land and labor, both of which were at hand. The Spanish American population, for example, grew between the 1820s and 1850s at about 1 percent annually, a slow rate but faster than that of the war years. With additions of land and labor available at low cost, technological innovation was not indispensable, and was indeed rare. This sort of growth in a traditional mode depended, of course, on continuation of the demand from Europe and North America for primary goods that had developed in the late eighteenth century. But this demand did continue to rise as industrialization advanced in those regions. The prices of Latin American primary exports stayed relatively strong. Some (the price of hides, for instance) did fall nominally; but they fell less than the price of the manufactured imports into Spanish America for which they were being exchanged. In other words, Spanish America's terms of trade (indeed, Latin America's, since the same was true of Brazil) improved over the thirty or forty years after independence, as industrialization spread in Europe and North America, costs of production there dropped, and a growing number of manufacturers competed in world markets. By the mid-century, for example, the price of British manufactured exports (still largely textiles) stood at about half what it had been in the decade 1810–20. Thus Latin America benefited, without itself industrializing in any significant degree, from the industrialization of the emerging economic First World.

The benefit came, nonetheless, with a cost. And that was dependence on foreigners for the supply of manufactured goods. For the long term, such dependence held risks: the obvious one of interruption of supply for some uncontrollable reason, and the more serious one of having to pay whatever manufacturers might charge for their goods. A yet more danger-fraught dependence was that of being at the mercy of foreign markets for the sale and selling price of Latin America's primary products. The positive balance enjoyed by Latin America between the price of primary exports and that of manufactured imports in the three or four decades after independence was the product of passing economic conditions. Prime among these was the growing scale and efficiency of manufacture, which reduced the price at which factory-made goods could be profitably sold. But there was no reason why such conditions should prevail permanently, and in fact they did not. Since the mid-nineteenth century, indeed, Latin America, along with other primary producing areas around the world, has more often than not found itself in the opposite position, with the price of its exports falling in relation to that of manufactured imports. Dependence on external markets is something that every economy that engages in overseas trade has to face in some measure. But primary producers are in a particularly exposed position.

But what else, in the circumstances, could be done? If Spanish America wished to be able to import foreign manufactured goods, it had no choice but to exchange for them whatever it could sell. And what it could sell was hides, salt beef, tallow, coffee, cacao, copper, guano, and the like. Spanish American countries could have chosen to do without manufactured imports. But that, at a time when mass production in factories was making many items of common use, particularly textiles, cheaper than ever before, would have meant a loss of living standard for most people. An obvious third course would then seem to have been to build factories in Spanish American countries themselves, to add manufacturing, with its attendant efficiency, to the existing farming and mining. But this was then, and has continued to be, a remarkably difficult process. Factories were expensive; and after the wars capital was scare and dear in the new countries. National markets were small, limiting the potential gains of economies of scale. It would still, therefore, have been difficult to match the low prices offered by European makers. Spanish America had not passed through the slow, broad, and progressive advance in science and technology toward mechanized production that Great Britain, France, Germany, and the United States had known and were still experiencing. There was not, then, a base of knowledge, education, practice, and labor to sustain new, technically advanced, industry. These obstacles to industrialization have persisted from then until now; only with difficulty and patience have they been, to a greater or lesser degree, surmounted.

The sole success in industrialization soon after independence was achieved in Mexico, in the form of mills for spinning and weaving cotton built near Puebla and in the state of Veracruz in the 1830s and 1840s. The first mill, proudly named "Mexican Perseverance" (*Constancia Mexicana*), appeared at Puebla in 1832–3. It was a water powered spinning mill. By the mid-forties fifty other such mills existed, and a number of weaving establishments also. This new industry produced 45,000 bolts of cloth in 1837 and no fewer than 656,500 in 1845, meeting a good part of the country's mass demand for cheap cotton fabric.[24] The keys to this successful, if limited, industrialization in Mexico were the relatively large size of the buying population, the presence of a large number of skilled artisans in Puebla as an initial workforce, and the availability of start-up capital from the government. A investment bank, or *Banco de Avío*, had been set up in the early 1830s precisely to provide funds for textile manufacture. It was the creation of Lucas Alamán, who at this point in his varied life was Minister of Internal and Foreign Affairs in the conservative government of the day. Alamán also provided tariff protection for the new mills, with income from the import duties going to fund the bank. The success of this official investment scheme was limited, it seems, to textiles. Alamán was soon out of office, the regime to which he belonged replaced in 1833 by liberals who objected to governmental provision of credit as a distortion of the free market. As the thirties advanced, political disorder grew. By 1840 the *Banco de Avío* was without funds, and in 1842 it ceased operation.

The obvious place to turn for credit to set up manufacturing, in the absence of local sources, would seem to have been abroad. But, first, foreign lenders had little interest in helping to create factories whose products would compete with those they wanted to export to Spanish America. They did show an initial interest in investment in primary production, specifically mining, so that Spanish America would have goods to exchange for manufactured imports. Independence was followed by an immediate rush of British funds into mining from Mexico to Chile. But restoration of the mines and refineries to their pre-war state proved far more demanding than eager investors, still dazzled by the silver exports of the late empire, expected. Almost all those mining investments failed; and creditors retreated, with burned fingers, from Spanish America as a whole.

Foreign reluctance to invest in Spanish America only increased when in the late 1820s various countries defaulted on public loans they had received, very largely from Great Britain. In the first half of the decade the new governments of Mexico, Colombia, Peru, Chile, and Buenos Aires had borrowed from British banks to buy, above all else, arms and ships for the final stages of the wars. The total was some seventeen million sterling, with more than six million going to both Colombia and Mexico.[25] But the depressed economic state into which the countries descended before 1830 made repayment impossible, as it was generally to remain until 1850 or later. As a result new foreign loans became virtually unobtainable until the second half of the century. The only exception in Latin America was Brazil, which, having largely escaped war and its attendant costs and destruction in breaking from Portugal, was able to service its borrowings.

The evident drawbacks of direct investment in enterprises within Spanish America and of lending money to governments left commerce as the main means open to outsiders of extracting wealth from the new states. Again the British were the leading players for some time, as they finally gained the easy and legal access to Spanish American commerce that they had pursued since the mid-seventeenth century. The first great opportunity came with the move of the Portuguese government to Rio de Janeiro in 1808. The Prince Regent immediately opened Brazilian ports to free trade; and then in 1810 succumbed to pressure from the British for privileged trading rights by signing a Treaty of Navigation and Commerce that gave them preferential tariff rates.[26] These lasted, in the event, until 1844. As a result, British sellers not only did well in Brazil, but also were able to use Rio as an entrepôt for trade with the Río de la Plata and, a little later, the west coast of South America. The commercial opening of Brazil came at a moment when Britain was avidly seeking outlets for its exports, since France had blocked access to European markets. Just how important the Latin American market was at that juncture is shown by the fact that in 1809 and 1811 no less than 35 percent of all British exports were sold there. The proportion then dropped. But until the end of the Spanish American wars of independence in the mid-twenties Britain held a near-monopoly on Latin American foreign trade. Over the next quarter-century that stranglehold relaxed somewhat, as primarily the United States, but also France, Germany, and other European countries, moved into Latin American markets.[27]

Lack of data makes for difficulties in assessing economic conditions and change in Spanish America in the decades after independence. This is particularly so for production for internal sale and supply, which was still by far the largest portion of national output. The presumption on that score is that change was generally small and slow until the mid-century. Although, for instance, economic liberalism decried any sort of corporate privilege in land-holding, and hence from the 1820s policies were suggested or enacted to deprive Indians of common lands, in fact hardly any such land was lost until the 1860s or 1870s. It was not until then that demand from internal and external markets for farm products rose to the point of making acquisition of Indian commons attractive to neighboring landowners or other business-like investors in agriculture. Hence almost all Indians continued, for at least forty or fifty years after independence, to farm in their established ways for subsistence or small-scale selling in local markets. Similarly, craftsmen in towns and cities continued to work, and in some cases to thrive. Manufactured imports were certainly a threat to some of them; again, textiles are the prime example. But freight to the remoter places was still difficult and expensive, so that craftsmen in inland towns were less exposed to competition from imports than their fellows in coastal cities. Again, it is possible that those same artisans may have benefited from the growth of export agriculture after independence, finding good selling opportunities in the rising populations of the inland agricultural "frontiers." In the importing cities themselves, retail trade may have expanded as the flow of foreign goods rose. It is possible that the urban lower classes were generally better off after independence than before it.[28] All such generalizations, of course, are open to many specific contradictions.

Spanish America's exporting performance is a little clearer. Clearly the wars of independence caused a severe decline in overseas sales, from which recovery was slow. The impression is of a gradual quickening of exports from a low point in the 1820s. By 1850 or so the export curve was perhaps beginning to steepen, marking the start of the export boom that dominated the latter part of the century. Growth before 1850 was certainly not dramatic. Indications are, for instance, that the value per head of Latin America exports in the years

1829–31 was some US$5.10, and that this figure rose to only $5.20 in 1850. Since the population seems to have grown in that period at about 1 percent annually, per capita export growth was therefore also about 1 percent a year. At that pace exports, per person, would have taken a little over seventy years to double. The mainland leaders in per capita exports in the mid-nineteenth century were the sellers of cattle products. Uruguay, with a population of only 132,000, was in first place by an extraordinary margin at $54.90 per person. Argentina, with 1,100,000 people, managed $10.30. Cuba's advanced sugar production gave it an export figure of $22.20. Costa Rica was already showing signs of future prosperity, with $11.40 per head; coffee was its leading export item.[29]

In recent decades, historians, sociologists and other students of development have debated strenuously whether political independence brought Latin America a parallel economic independence. A powerful current of thought has had it that the new states simply passed from being economic colonies of Spain (and Portugal) to being those of the financial and industrial powerhouses of the day (notably, in the first instance, Great Britain). There is some truth in that proposition, especially if attention is focused on exports. For as exporters, Latin American countries were by definition dependent for their foreign income on markets over which they had no control. And as Britain was their largest market, it had a dominant influence over the price paid for hides, coffee, cacao, and the like. Nonetheless, as industrialization expanded in other First World countries, the range of potential markets for Latin American exports widened, bringing at least some greater possibility of the sellers shopping for the best price for their goods. With time, the range of suppliers of manufactures widened similarly, with increased chances, again, of shopping for the lowest price for imports. Very few, if any, producers, buyers, or sellers in Latin America would have willingly returned, after independence, to the trading restrictions imposed on the colonies by Bourbon Spain in the late eighteenth century. And above all, the independent nations were free of perhaps the greatest burden of formal colonial status, which was to have been part of a structure designed by Spain to extract wealth in the form of taxes (and forced loans) as well as exports from the American territories. The whole intent of Bourbon fiscal and commercial policy had been to make the colonies send more to Spain than they received from it. The necessity, rigidly imposed after independence by economics, that trade should be balanced in anything beyond the short term, prevented such wholesale suction of wealth. Exports may possibly have been undervalued by Britain or other overseas buyers; but increasing competition over the nineteenth century among those who bought from Spanish America provided some remedy for that. And the fact that terms of trade between Spanish (and Latin) America and its suppliers of manufactures improved to the mid-century at least casts doubt on the degree of undervaluation.

Economic and political woes were inextricably linked in the decades after independence. Politics, on the grand scale of national government, was an art in which Spanish Americans had had almost no practical experience. The aftermath of economically destructive wars was a poor time for political learning and experimentation. Conversely, political disruption deterred potential investors, both native and foreign, and thereby hindered economic recovery. Within the simple circular connection between economics and politics was a lesser but crucial sub-linkage, that of governmental income. State formation promised to be problematical in any case; on a shoestring it was a daunting challenge. Damaged economies did not easily yield the funds needed to operate government at even a low level. The difficulty was exacerbated in some countries by the liberal-inspired abolition of Indian tribute soon after independence. That was certainly a progressive measure, but one that took from those governments a major remaining source of income. That being so, tribute was generally reimposed within a few years, to be abolished finally only when receipts from other sources began to rise in the mid-century.

Governments, then, were perpetually short of funds. Nevertheless, they had money, and because of that were a tempting target for those who were, or thought themselves, needy. Access to the national treasury was, then, a powerful stimulus for political ambition, struggle, and disorder. The constant changes in regime so typical of Spanish American government in the 1820s, 1830s, and 1840s were in some part the result of different interest groups simply taking turns in office for mercenary ends. This pursuit of profit in government had good colonial precedent, though in that time offices had been sought for their safe salaries or because they gave power to make local exactions. In some countries one group that was in a uniquely strong position to lay claim to public funds, and thereby aggravate existing fiscal (and political) difficulties, was the military. To secure its own financial support, it could either seize power, or merely threaten to do so. Perhaps the clearest, and worst, example is that of Mexico, where military spending averaged about 60 percent of the central government's outgoings in the 1820s, and generally between 20 and 30 percent from 1830 to the mid-fifties (with the astonishing exception of eight months in Santa Anna's final regime in 1854–5, when it reached 93.9 percent of the total).[30]

[16] CALMER WATERS AND A NEW COURSE: OLIGARCHS AND EXPORTS

With time came economic reconstruction and political experience. As resources became more abundant, and competition for them slackened a little, and as a sense of what was politically practicable grew, the first signs of rising order appeared in various countries' affairs. It was a rocky and fragile order, to be sure, often enough a matter of two steps forward and one back. The fact that in 1857 Mexico could produce a constitution that proved to be good for sixty years would at first impression suggest that calm had descended on the country by then. But in reality the decade after its promulgation was among the most violent and unpredictable in the country's national history, containing as it did both civil war between the liberal framers of the constitution and their conservative opponents, and foreign intervention and monarchy in the mid-sixties. Only after all that did a long period of stability begin. Argentina, too, produced a durable constitution in the 1850s. The 1853 document, providing for federalism along United States lines, has indeed remained in force ever since, apart from a brief interruption from 1949 to 1955 during the regime of Juan Perón. But much friction, including actual fighting between Buenos Aires and the interior provinces, had to be overcome before national unity finally arrived in the late 1870s.[1]

Peru was among the first countries to begin moving toward greater calm, despite the extreme disorder of the 1830s in the country. The presence of guano income from the early 1840s onward proved a considerable emollient of political strains. This can be seen in the two presidencies (1845–51 and 1855–62) of Ramón Castilla, the man who has been called the founder of the Peruvian nation.[2] Castilla (1797–1867), a mestizo who began what was to be a long military career as a royalist officer in the independence wars, can be classified as a *caudillo*. But he had, or developed, a sense of the need for orderliness in national affairs that signals a shift away from the intense personalism of post-independence politics in Peru. He was also keen on modernization in the material sense. As finance minister in the early 1840s he both set up the first contracts for guano export, and successfully negotiated with William Wheelwright, a British shipbuilder, to start a steamship business along the Peruvian coast. In 1851, at the end of his first presidency, a railway opened

between Lima and its port, Callao. More important in Castilla's first administration, though, were two financial measures: the drawing up of a first national
budget, and a law, in 1850, providing for amortization and repayment of the
national debt. Rising guano income, much of it going to the national government, did much to make these fiscal advances possible. Political conduct, it is
true, did not improve commensurately for some time. Castilla, with liberal
support, had to fight for his second presidency against the general he had
named as his successor in 1851. During the brief civil war, in 1854, he ended
both slavery and Indian tribute in Peru. Undoubtedly both measures were
taken for reasons of convenience as well as principle: they reinforced his
support among liberals, and provided grateful recruits, in the form of freedmen, for his forces. But both proved permanent. And, again, both were in
good part the fruit of guano, since the funds entering the treasury from those
exports replaced income from the Indian head tax, and also allowed for
compensation of slave owners for lost labor. During his second term, Castilla
moved away from his liberal support, and was the force behind the centralist
constitution of 1860. Yet it is notable that he did not execute liberals who
plotted against this document, but sent them into exile. In 1845, in his
inaugural address, he had proclaimed that "Power in my hands will be the
power of the law." And, all considered, the description sometimes applied to
him of "Soldier of the Law" seems merited.[3]

BOOMING EXPORTS

Peru's deep and growing reliance on guano exports in the middle decades of
the century may stand as a prototype for the condition of almost all Latin
American states for a half century or more after 1860. There is hardly an
aspect of Latin American affairs between the 1860s and the depression of the
1930s that does not carry the impress of the great export boom that developed
in those decades.

Between c.1850 and c.1912, Latin America's exports, measured in US
dollars, grew a little more than ten times, from some 155 million to about
1,580 million a year. This equates to an average annual increase of some 3.77
percent, an unusually high rate of growth for any large economic measure over
a long period.[4] The increase was a response to quickening industrialization
and population growth in the technically and economically advanced countries of the time (France, Germany, Great Britain, and the United States);
and, late in the century, to rising industrialization in other states in northern,
eastern and southern Europe, and in Russia and Japan. With the industrial
development of these places came large demand for a wider range of raw
materials than before, and hence an expansion of Latin American exports in
both volume and variety. To precious metals, for instance, though they were
still major exports from Mexico and Colombia, were added base metals. The
spread of electrification created a need for huge amounts of copper. Hence, by
the start of the First World War, copper was the leading item sold abroad by
Peru, and the second by Mexico and Chile. Similarly, there was now a call for

unprecedented amounts of tin, to plate the recently invented steel can so as to prevent rusting, and spoilage of the preserved food. Bolivia's major export, as a result, shifted from silver in the 1890s to tin in the early 1900s. By 1913 or so, 72.3 percent of the country's overseas sales were of tin, and only 4.3 percent of silver. Another mineral substance for which there seemed to be endless demand was the nitrates of the northern Atacama. On the eve of the War, these, sent abroad for use as fertilizer and chemical feed stock, made up 71.3 percent of the value of Chile's exports. Finally, soon after 1900 came the opening scene of a long Latin American economic story with the discovery of large oil reserves on the Gulf coast of Mexico. Foreign sales soon followed.

To these new mineral exports were added overseas sales of new products of the land. Of these perhaps the most remarkable, on various counts, was rubber. Demand for it rose fast in the late 1800s for use in both electrical insulation and inflatable tires for cars and bicycles. That need was first met by the tapping of wild rubber trees in the Amazonian regions of Brazil, Peru, and Bolivia. A remarkable rush of attention and people to previously ignored parts of the rainforest ensued, leading most notably to the explosive growth of the town of Manaus, on the Rio Negro in Brazil near its junction with the Amazon. During its two boom decades Manaus was equipped, among other things, with its always-mentioned opera house, and with electric lighting (the first town in Brazil to have it). The Amazonian rubber boom suddenly collapsed, however, in 1911–12. Seeds of the wild rubber tree (*Hevea braziliensis*) had been illegally exported from Brazil in 1876, and via Kew Gardens in London became the source of rubber plantations in south-east Asia, particularly Malaysia. Once those plantations began to yield, the price of raw rubber dropped so sharply that gathering it from forest trees became immediately unprofitable.[5] Considerably longer lived was the growing of henequen, or sisal, in Yucatan. Henequen cultivation was much stimulated by the invention of mechanical reaping of grain crops in the USA in the 1870s, and the resulting call for great quantities of twine to bind bales. Henequen was raised only in the relatively dry north-western corner of Yucatan. As it was rising in importance there, however, another new plantation export was coming into being in the far more extensive wet lowlands all around the Caribbean (and also on the coast of Ecuador): bananas. In fast steamships this extremely high-yielding but delicate fruit could now be sent to market in temperate countries. United States companies dominated the business from the start; and in 1899 two of the leading enterprises joined to form the United Fruit Company, of long and controversial fame.

Demand rose for traditional as well as new agricultural exports, although some shifts took place in areas and emphasis of production. Argentina and Uruguay, for instance, continued to export hides and meat. Indeed, beef and mutton exports grew as refrigerated ships became available in the 1880s, and as the quality of meat was improved through the import of breeding animals and their segregation from existing stock by barbed wire fencing.[6] But on the eve of the First World War, the leading Uruguayan export was not meat (24 percent of the total), but wool (42 percent); and Argentina by then sent abroad chiefly grains: maize (22.5 percent of all exports) and wheat (20.7 percent). For several countries, the raw materials for caffeine-containing drinks became the primary exports. Paraguay, for centuries the main source of *yerba mate*, exported it within South America; by *c.*1913 *mate* made up 32.1 percent of the country's foreign sales. In Ecuador and the Dominican Republic, cacao was the leading export by that date (64.1 and 39.2 percent of all exports, respectively). But most prominent by far in this line of agricultural goods was coffee, which was the leading export, *c.*1913, of no fewer than seven countries: Brazil (62.3 percent of its total exports), Venezuela (52 percent), Colombia (37.2 percent), El Salvador (79.6 percent), Guatemala (84.8 percent), Haiti (64 percent), and Nicaragua (64.9 percent). The small Central American countries, but Brazil also (the largest producer), relied to an extraordinary and risky degree on the industrial countries' demand for coffee.[7] That demand had accelerated from the 1870s.

Over the second half of the nineteenth century the world market for Latin American goods expanded and diversified. Most notably, Britain lost its overwhelming role in Latin American trade, although it retained a major one. In 1850 it had been the main export market for most countries. By 1913 it was the leading buyer from only four of them: Argentina, Bolivia, Chile, and Peru. France was the main market for Ecuador, Haiti, and Venezuela; and Germany for Guatemala, Paraguay, and Uruguay. From both France and Germany, some fraction of what arrived from these countries may have been exported to other European destinations. It was, however, the United States that by 1913 had become the leading market for the largest number of Latin American nations: Brazil, Colombia, Costa Rica, Cuba, the Dominican Republic, El Salvador, Honduras, Mexico, Nicaragua, Panama, and Puerto Rico. With the exception of Brazil, these countries are in or around the Caribbean. The emergence of the USA as the major buyer of their goods is one aspect of a developing United States influence over its immediate and near neighbors to the south. A crude count of numbers of countries does not, however, reflect trade patterns quite accurately. The United States, by 1913, was certainly the major buyer of Latin American exports, with 29.7 percent of the total. But Britain still took 20.7 percent, largely because it still received a quarter of Argentina's exports; and Argentina was the source of almost a third of all Latin America's exports (510 million dollars' worth of a total of 1,588 million). Germany and France bought, respectively, 12.4 and 8.0 percent of all exports. Thus almost 30 percent of Latin American sales, in 1913, went to markets other than the "big four."[8] A substantial diversification of the selling pattern had taken place.

The same was true of imports into Latin America. Whereas in the mid-nineteenth century Great Britain had been the major seller of goods, by 1913 the United States had overtaken it by a small margin (with 25.5 percent of imports against Britain's 24.8). Germany (16.5 percent) and France (8.3 percent) were the two other major suppliers; hence about a quarter of Latin America's imports now came from sources other than these four. British exports still consisted, as they long had, of textiles and clothing. In these Britain kept its pre-eminence. But in other lines of factory-made goods other suppliers advanced more quickly, raising their market share in Latin America.

The United States sold, for example, much mining and farming machinery. One of the prime destinations for such items was Mexico, almost 54 percent of whose imports came from the USA. Britain was the leading supplier still to southern South America, with 31 percent of Argentina's market and barely less of those of Chile, Uruguay, and Paraguay. British sales were still strong also in Brazil, at 24.5 percent of the total, compared to the United States' 15.7 percent.[9]

Latin America, then, as a whole advanced economically from the mid-nineteenth century in enlarging its export volume most impressively, and in expanding both the range of its exports and the variety of its trading partners. The high growth rate of exports brought unprecedented wealth into all Latin American countries, which revealed itself in everything from vast new individual and family fortunes to growth and splendid renovation of towns and cities.

If, though, the rapid rise of exports is set against the increase of population that was taking place at the same time, the performance is rather less remarkable. Between c.1850 and c.1912, the total Latin American population grew about two and a half times, from 30,381,000 to 77,456,000. The average growth rate for the period was 1.52 percent yearly. The pattern was, though, of acceleration, such that an increase of perhaps 1.25 percent annually in the 1850s had risen to 1.85 percent after 1900. This was the prelude to the Latin American population explosion of the twentieth century. Great variations of course can be found from country to country. The largest increase was probably in Uruguay, whose population rose at an average annual rate of 3.55 percent from 132,000 in the early 1850s to 1,144,000 around 1912. At the other end of the scale was Bolivia, rising at only 0.5 percent yearly from 1,374,000 to 1,866,000. Of the large countries, the fastest growing was Argentina (1,100,000 to 7,333,000, at 3.1 percent annually), and the slowest Mexico (7,662,000 to 14,262,000, at 1.0 percent). Between these two, with a growth rate of 2.0 percent, was Brazil; although its population of 24,386,000 c.1912 (up from 7,230,000 about 1850) was by far the largest in Latin America by then (Mexico being second).[10] The reason for the rising populations and rising rates of growth was more a decline in death rates than rising numbers of births. And the decline in deaths was above all the outcome of public health improvements, in the form of safe water supplies, underground sewerage systems, inoculations against smallpox and bubonic plague, and eradication of mosquitoes to combat yellow fever. The richer countries were better able to make these improvements, so that it was in them that numbers increased most quickly.

Certainly the combination, in the sixty years after 1850, of a tenfold rise in exports with a two and a half times rise in population suggests an improvement in general wealth and living standards in that period. And that was probably so, even though gains from exports were unequally spread in the populations, and exports were still the smaller part of Latin American economies' total output. Nonetheless, a recent calculation of the export boom's contribution to national wealth suggests that it was not large enough to bring dramatic improvements in living standards. In that same period of c.1850–1910, the United States achieved an increase in gross domestic product

(GDP), per capita, of 1.5 percent a year. (At that rate, living standard doubles in about fifty years.) The only two Latin American countries to match that rate of improvement were Argentina and Chile. And even if the desired rate of annual GDP increase per person is reduced to 1 percent, only two more Latin American countries, Cuba and Uruguay, qualify.[11]

The export boom, then, although enormously influential on the course of Latin American history in the late nineteenth century, seems not to have been as complete an answer to the region's needs as its promoters would have liked. Export-led growth had its limitations. But if more could have been sold abroad, it would have been more successful.

The restraints on exports seem to have been both external and internal. The industrial economies' demand for Latin American products was at least high enough to prevent a long-term decline in their price between 1850 and World War I, although within that period numerous fluctuations naturally took place. And, in general, and in the long term, Latin America's terms of trade did not decline in those years, as has sometimes been thought. They may, indeed, have improved, though certainly not as dramatically as in the thirty years after independence. Again, various products and various countries had differing experiences in this respect; and upward and downward movements occurred within the longer period. The growth of the purchasing power of Latin American exports, for instance, was higher in the decades 1870–90 than in the twenty years before or after then, which suggests that trading terms may have moved in Latin America's favor particularly in that period.[12]

If demand existed, then, for what Latin America had to sell, what prevented more of it from being produced? Land, it seems, was not generally in short supply, although its increasing concentration in large estates in the second half of the century may have made for less than fully efficient use. Offsetting this was the increasing accessibility of land brought about in many regions by the wide extension of railways from the 1870s onward. Trains could move crops economically to ports, where distance had previously made that uneconomic.

Labor, on the other hand, was scarce in most countries, despite population growth; or so, at least, employers' complaints suggest. The outcome was, first, internal migration of workers in a number of countries, some of them drawn by higher wages. On the whole, however, few employers were willing to use higher pay to attract labor, fearing that it would reduce or remove their competitiveness and profit. In labor-intensive agriculture, this was an understandable enough anxiety. Other incentives might be used, such as providing workers with plots on which they could grow food for subsistence or possibly for sale. Force and intimidation could be, and were, used to hold labor where attractions failed. Retention by debt (created by paying wages in advance or by overcharging workers for goods bought from the employer or company) was clearly another well used device in the late nineteenth century. It was common, for example, in several states in southern Mexico where great numbers of new estates were formed to grow coffee, tobacco, and sugar for export. The local population was growing, but was still too sparse to supply all the hands needed. And so indebtedness became a common means of preventing workers from moving, especially once local and national governments made the police and military available to pursue any who tried to leave. Estate owners took to buying and selling workers' debts among themselves. In doing so they moved the laborers' obligations from one place to another, and treated the men in effect very much as possessions.[13] Outright slavery, of Blacks, did persist strongly until late in the nineteenth century in two Latin America countries, partly as a survival from the colonial centuries and partly as an outcome of labor shortage in a time of high production for export. It was the dominant labor form in export agriculture in Cuba (still formally a colony until 1898) and Brazil. In them slavery was not abolished until 1886 and 1888 respectively.

African slavery was one aspect of the large immigration that took place into Latin America in the nineteenth century, drawn in part by the need for labor. The slave trade continued until the mid-century, when it finally succumbed to the British opposition to it that had been growing almost from the start of the century. Still, great numbers of slaves arrived after 1800. A million and a half were landed in Brazil before the trade ended in the early 1850s. Spanish America took nearly three-quarters of a million, most of them going to the Caribbean. Arrivals in Puerto Rico ceased *c.*1845, and in Cuba in 1867.[14] Other immigration with some element of coercion in it, though not at the level of slavery, included the import of Chinese. They went not only to Peru, but also to Cuba for work in sugar, to Costa Rica for building railways, and to Mexico for henequen cultivation. Koreans also labored on the Mexican henequen plantations. For banana growing around the Caribbean, for rail work, and for excavation of the Panama Canal after 1903, workers (mainly black) were drawn from the British West Indies. Puerto Ricans went to work on sugar plantations in Cuba; and Haitians on those of the Dominican Republic.[15]

Apart from African slavery, however, these movements did not match in numbers the influx of Europeans into a few countries late in the nineteenth century and early in the twentieth. The outstanding case is Argentina. Between 1871 and 1915, 2.5 million Europeans took up permanent residence in the country, four-fifths of them from Italy and Spain. One effect of this was that in 1914 a third of the Argentine population was foreign-born; and since many of the new arrivals took root in Buenos Aires (making it, incidentally, the first Latin American city with more than a million people), the population of the capital became predominantly foreign. Indeed, for more than sixty years two-thirds of its adult citizens were people born outside Argentina. A genuine basis exists for Buenos Aires's frequent assertion that it is a European city. Large, but lesser, migrant currents flowed into Brazil and Uruguay. The net number entering Brazil ("net" because, as in Argentina, many of those who came subsequently departed) was between 1.7 and 2.0 million. Again, most of these were Italians; second in numbers were Portuguese; and third Spaniards. There were also Germans and Russians, and then people from other parts of Europe, and the eastern Mediterranean. Substantial numbers of Japanese arrived after 1907. They, like many of the earlier immigrants, went mainly to the state of São Paulo. Italians were the commonest newcomers also to Uruguay, most of them settling in Montevideo itself. In 1908 immigrants made up 17 percent of the national population.[16]

In these three countries and some others (Mexico, for instance) it was national policy in the late nineteenth century to encourage Europeans to emigrate. Financial aid was sometimes offered to help them to move. The aim was not just to enlarge the labor force, but also to raise the level of national culture, since Europe was still generally perceived, as it had been since independence, as the home of true civilization. Many regimes of the day were influenced by positivism, a theory of social development which both advocated what could be called "social engineering" by governments and implicitly held Europeans to be further along the road of human progress than most others in the world. To such governments, massive European immigration seemed an obvious shortcut to faster modernization and development. The strategy seems to have been successful where large numbers of newcomers arrived. Thus Argentina, with the comparatively high literacy and skills of its immigrants, gained an unusually able labor force by the beginning of the First World War. There, also, immigrant settlement of underpopulated rural areas resulted in the rise of prosperous small farming. In Brazil, immigrants proved an effective replacement for slaves on coffee plantations; in fact, they were seen there precisely as a replacement for slave labor.

In some, but few, countries, then, mass immigration served to resolve or relieve the labor shortage that limited exports. Probably only in Argentina did it do so completely; and that, coupled with the existence there of a functioning market in labor (so that wages moved up and down according to demand for workers in this or that activity), contributed much to the country's economic pre-eminence in Latin America early in the twentieth century. A few of the countries that did not receive large numbers of immigrants, but whose exports came mainly from mines, also escaped labor shortage in their export efforts, since mining was more in need of substantial capital than of labor for its success. These were Bolivia, Chile, and Mexico. But elsewhere shortage of workers, at the wage levels that employers thought themselves able to offer, generally prevented the full export potential from being developed.[17]

Capital seems to have been less of a restraint. One notable economic change after the mid-century was the greater and better-ordered availability of investment funds. Before then, as before independence, the church and merchants had been the major sources of loans. But in difficult post-independence times, merchants were less able to lend than before; while church wealth was under constant liberal attack. Foreigners were unwilling to make loans after the mid-1820s because of Latin America's poor record of repaying credits received before then. The 1860s, however, brought a revival of outside financial interest in Latin America. This showed itself first in the form of banking. In that decade, foreign banks appeared on the streets of a few large cities alongside the home-grown banks that had begun to be founded in a few countries in the 1850s. In 1863, for instance, the Bank of London and the River Plate began business in Buenos Aires, with a million pounds of capital. Its operations in trade and exchange enabled it to double that sum by 1870.[18] With the prospect of such quick gains, it is no surprise that by 1870 three British banking companies had numerous Latin American branches. Italian, French, and German banks quickly appeared in their train. This form of foreign re-entry into Latin American finance carried relatively low risks, since the funds made available for lending were largely the accumulation of local deposits.[19] The banks' European origins made them seem particularly respectable and safe, and hence attractive to depositors.

The development of banking, then, whether locally or foreign owned, began to provide a formal and orderly access to credit in the middle decades of the century. To that source of funds was added, in growing amounts, whatever sums immigrants brought with them. But substantial investment, from the 1870s onward, was mainly the outcome of renewed foreign willingness to risk money in Latin America. And that, in turn, was a response to improved political and economic conditions in at least some of the countries.

The revived foreign investment took two forms. One was purchase of bonds issued by Latin American governments. The larger and already economically more robust countries had the greatest success in selling government securities. They – Argentina, Brazil, Chile, Mexico, and Uruguay – particularly attracted the British, who, by 1914 or so, had sent to those five countries 90 percent of the investment they had made in Latin America in the form of government bonds. At that date, in fact, 67.8 percent of the public external debt of Latin America was in British hands (against the USA's share of only 13.8 percent). It is particularly striking that Britain held 92.1 percent of Mexico's public foreign debt, against the United States' 7.9 percent, at a time when the USA was otherwise so dominant in Mexican economic affairs (receiving, for example, 75.2 percent of the country's exports, and providing 53.9 percent of its imports, against respective figures for Great Britain of 13.5 and 11.8 percent). In finance, therefore, Britain remained the dominant foreign presence in Latin America even though it had yielded much in trade there to other industrial powers. It had, c.1914, US$1,511 million invested in Latin America's external public debt – a little above two-thirds of the total foreign holding ($2,229 million) of that sort.

In absolute terms British participation, at that same time, in the second form of foreign investment was still larger. This was direct investment in different lines of production and service. The British share of the $7,569 million of foreign capital of this sort was $3,588 million, or 47.4 percent of the whole. In this category the United States' share was higher than in bond holdings, though not greatly so, at 18.4 percent. Direct investment from the USA had gone mostly into mining, petroleum, and agriculture (Caribbean banana growing, for example, and Cuban sugar). The British, by contrast, held 71.2 percent of all foreign investment in Latin American railways, and 59.7 percent of that in public utilities.[20] France and Germany were also substantial direct investors.

What proportion of all investment in Latin America was of foreign origin is hard to know. In Argentina by 1914, according to one estimate, public and private investments from abroad together made up about half the country's total capital stock, and were worth two and a half times the annual GDP.[21] Since Argentina was the target of choice for many foreign investors, the proportion was probably smaller elsewhere. But the implication is that investment had given foreigners a very large, though not majority, stake in the Latin

American economies by the opening of the twentieth century. On the other hand, the sums quoted for external investment should not be taken wholly at face value. For it is clear that some large proportion of the money invested by foreign companies active in Latin America was in fact of local origin: deposits by local people in foreign-owned banks, for example, or local investments in foreign-owned enterprises, or reinvestment of locally generated profits. Foreign companies, then, had become important not only as channels for the import of capital, but also as stimulants to the accumulation of local capital.[22]

That stimulating or facilitating role suggests how thoroughly foreign economic actors penetrated Latin American economies from the late nineteenth century on. It also points to what is indeed true: that influential Latin Americans, both public and private, generally welcomed the influx of foreign funds. There was little concern at the time about possible surrender of economic sovereignty or even, apparently, about the export of profits. Foreign money was generally more warmly received than even foreign immigrants. Outside investors found willing allies in the middle and upper classes for their projects. Such collaborators have sometimes been damned in more recent times as *vendepatrias*, "sellers of the fatherland." Undoubtedly many of them looked to profit from their foreign connections, and many did indeed do so. But the prevailing view, founded in economic liberalism and its support of free trade, was that to facilitate the import and investment of external funds was also to advance economic progress and modernization.

And it is hard to dispute the proposition that foreign investment did contribute mightily to change of that sort, particularly in the sense of enabling Latin America to enlarge its participation in the booming world market (or, more precisely, the North Atlantic market) of those decades.[23] Without railways, for instance, to provide cheap and rapid freight of ores, grains, hides, wool, and so on, to ports (or, in Mexico, to the frontier with the USA), export volumes could barely have increased. Railways, furthermore, served to open up areas previously isolated by distance from participation in markets. They did not necessarily do so, because the foreigners who largely financed the building of railways were mainly concerned to funnel exports to points of exit. And areas distant from the rail routes might find themselves in relatively greater isolation than before. But that was not the dominant economic effect of the enormous growth of rail transport in late nineteenth-century Latin America. That growth was no less impressive than the rise in exports. In 1870 South America had a total of 2,850 kilometers of track; in 1900, 42,000 kilometers. Mexico in 1876 had 650 kilometers; in 1910, 25,000 kilometers.

Rail transport was the new technology tied to foreign investment that was most in the public view. But much other technical innovation accompanied the capital inflows. It was important in, for instance, mining, agricultural processing, and the rather limited range of manufacture for domestic markets that developed in the larger countries before the First World War (mostly cloth, clothing, processing of food and drink, and building materials, such as cement).[24] Immigrants from European countries that were already industrialized brought familiarity with factory production with them; some also brought investable funds. The small factories that sprang up in growing numbers from the 1870s onward, mostly in Brazil, Argentina, Mexico, Chile, and Colombia, were often the creations of these newcomers.

With rising foreign investment also came modernization in what might be called the culture of business and production. There was a new injection of entrepreneurship (reinforcing immigrants' efforts in that line), the opportunity to observe and acquire new methods of business and management, and to learn the importance of advertising. Foreign concerns provided business apprenticeships for many local people. These matters had been studied abroad by those Latin Americans able to afford such excursions; but as the foreign business presence expanded, local opportunities multiplied to edge into the mainstream of modern business practice.[25]

POLITICS DURING THE EXPORT BOOM

The export boom began in part because improving political conditions were favorable to it. But as it gained momentum, it became the force that conditioned politics. The general political color of Latin America during the sixty years of the boom is caught by such descriptions as "authoritarian liberalism," or "progressive authoritarianism."

The essence of politics in the period was that it was dominated by the groups who produced goods for export and who received a large share of the profit from the sale of those goods. Plutarchy was the political order of the times; rich men and families in most countries came together in oligarchies that ran regions and nations. The members of the oligarchies were the owners of estates and mines, and to a lesser extent those who took leading parts in the business of export; but in that, foreigners had a much larger share than in production for export.

If questioned about their political tenets, most of these people would have defined themselves as liberals, and their period is sometimes thought of as one of liberal ascendancy in Latin America. It was so, but in a limited sense. What triumphed, under the persuasive influence of profitable exporting, was liberalism in its economic aspects: an emphasis on open competition, on the unacceptability of economic privilege, on the freedom of all to seek a share of the fruits of open markets. If political freedom seemed likely to act adversely on this economic liberty, then it should, at least for the time being, be curtailed. Economic liberalism would, in the end, bring wealth enough for all; and then political freedom could be realized. The liberalism of the late nineteenth and early twentieth centuries was, then, a highly pragmatic affair. It had lost much of the dogmatism of liberalism in the half century after independence. The church, for example, was no longer the prime target of reform that it had long been. That, it is true, was in part because reforms applied to it in the mid-century, such as the removal of its property, had been largely accomplished; and broadly speaking by 1900 church and state had been separated, so that the church's political role was no longer such a large bone of contention. Again, late nineteenth-century liberals had little concern about due political process. Elections took place, but few worried if they were blatantly manipulated. Priority had to be given to maintaining order, because order was conducive to material advance, and material advance was the essence of progress. For the preservation of order, liberals now favored activist government. And where government action seemed likely or necessary to promote progress, they even approved of economic intervention by the state, in the form, say, of protective tariffs or public spending on infrastructure, which was a contradiction of even economic liberalism.

POSITIVISM

Many liberals were in fact, knowingly or otherwise, under the influence of the positivism of the day from the 1870s onward. It was positivism that provided the welcome theoretical framework that linked order with progress, and hence justified strong and interventionist government. Positivism, indeed, has been seen as a healing balm of previous frictions between liberals and conservatives, because it offered compromises in which both sides could acquiesce, at least in the benign context of the wealth-generating export boom.[26]

The positivism that many wealthy Latin Americans eagerly consumed was the work of Auguste Comte (1798–1857), a French social philosopher who had sought an orderly explanation of the development of human societies. He hoped to formulate hypotheses and laws about social development along the lines of the laws of the "positive" sciences (mathematics, physics, chemistry, and biology). As a starting point, Comte proposed a three-stage development of human understanding of the natural and social world. The first step was "theological," where understanding was cast in terms of religion and irrational speculation. The second was "metaphysical;" now humans approached nature and society with logic and analysis. And the third and final stage was "positivist," in which the basis of reasoning and comprehension was empirically verifiable, "scientific" knowledge. The advanced countries of the nineteenth century were entering their positivist stage.

Though Comte saw this progression as applicable to all human society, and hence movement from one stage to the next as being universally possible, if not inevitable, it seemed to leading Latin Americans that their countries could be actively lifted onto the third step by the conscious promotion of science, and general import of what was modern. An early exponent of the system in Latin America was a Mexican doctor, a liberal named Gabino Barreda, who had studied under Comte in Paris. In 1867 Barreda expounded Mexican history in positivist terms. The colonial period had been the country's theological stage. Post-independence liberalism had raised it to the metaphysical level. Now that liberalism had triumphed (with the defeat of conservatism, Maximilian, and obscurantism generally in 1867), Mexico was ready for its next upward step. This advance should be achieved through education. Here Barreda added a contribution of his own to the positivist scheme, possibly in reaction to the chaos of the previous ten years in Mexico. He proposed that this education should not be merely general or even scientific, but one that strengthened the impulse to follow moral law (which he clearly perceived as a universal constant). Who or what should provide this teaching? His answer was the state. Thus, for Barreda the state was to become not only the source of the knowledge that would lift Mexico to the third and final level in the positivist series, but also the tutor and guardian of the nation's morality.

Benito Juárez, the radical liberal reformer of the late 1850s, but now president of a country recently rent by civil war, found Barreda's views attractive. He took him as adviser on educational reform, and appointed him director of the National Preparatory School (*Escuela Nacional Preparatoria*) that was founded in that same year of 1867 to train teachers for the country. The school's syllabus, not surprisingly, was strongly Comtean. Over the next decade the *Prepa*, as it eventually became known, educated a number of young men who became influential political voices in the country in the closing years of the century. Before they did so, some of them published a journal called *La Libertad (Liberty)*. This might seem a promising title, a survival of liberal principle. But the journal's motto was "Order and Progress," and the pub-lishers argued that order must come before all else. They objected to a stress on individual autonomy that they found in the 1857 constitution; it could lead only to anarchy as long as Mexico lacked inherent order and greater material progress. And the achievement of order, one of the editors of *Liberty* paradox-ically argued, might require dictatorship, an "honorable tyranny" that would offer "fewer rights and fewer liberties in exchange for greater order and peace."[27]

Positivism could thus be drawn out in menacing directions. When a social application of Darwinism was added to it, it became even more pernicious. The moneyed were happy to assume that a process of natural selection had lifted them to their superior position in society. They found it equally com-forting to think of the poor as naturally being so as a result of innate incapaci-ties. And yet more convenient was the notion that governments would be going against principles of Nature if they tried to raise the poor and servile from their inferior state. Traces of this reasoning appear in Barreda's opinions. Order, he argued, would allow the material development of the "most apt individuals among Mexicans." That is, those who had the knowledge and skills to prosper could and would do so in orderly social and political condi-tions. The more "apt" people there were, the more orderly conditions would become, and then the number of the *aptos* would multiply further. The state should therefore not interfere in the growth of prosperity among certain people. (Here economic liberalism makes a reappearance.) But it should use education as a means of directing the prosperous to work for the general good of society. This did not in the least mean, however, that wealth should be taken from them for social improvement. The positive potential in great wealth would indeed be jeopardized if it were broken up. The state, then, should encourage the wealthy to become richer still – while persuading them to put their wealth to socially useful purposes.

Positivism and Darwinism thus instructed the wealthy and the aspirants to wealth in Latin America that possession of riches was part of the natural order of things, an outcome of their inherent superiority, and that conscious attempts to improve the conditions of the poor were doomed to failure because they contradicted natural laws. Conservatives were drawn to the doctrines by their blessing of wealth and their confirmation of the social order. Liberals could find in them affirmations of individual liberty within the "natural" order of society, and the expectation that, in some undefined future, prosperity would filter down to the base of society.

While positivism was widely influential in Latin America, above all in the last thirty years of the century, it found its keenest following in Mexico, Chile, and Brazil. In Brazil it was taught particularly in the national Military School. Its modernizing tenor was opposed to the traditionalism inherent in monarchy. It therefore played a part in turning the Brazilian army against the empire and was one inspiration for the military's large part in the removal of the Emperor Peter II in 1889. It was in Brazil, also, that the only positivist church in Latin America was founded. In a curious twist of his admiration for science, Comte late in life created an elaborate church-like organization to spread positivism's effects in society. A Brazilian, Miguel Lemos, who had absorbed Comte's message in Paris in the late seventies, created a branch of this church on his return to Brazil in 1881. It still functions today in a small way. Another enduring reminder of Comte's influence in Brazil is on the national flag. It was originally designed by a positivist, and to this day bears the motto *Ordem e Progresso*.

FAMILIES

Prominent in the late nineteenth century oligarchies were large families, or linked groups of families, whose origins long antedated the rise of exports. Typically, in Spanish America, they were the descendants of successful immigrants of the late 1700s; of Spaniards, that is, who had been drawn to the colonies in the time of Bourbon reforms, particularly to seek profits in the stimulus that the monarchy had then applied to imperial trade. Many of those newcomers had married into propertied creole families, adding energy to wealth. The period after independence was one in which family organization flourished. The first half-century of the countries' national existence has parallels with the half century after the military conquests in the 1500s. Both were times of internal conflict, weak government, and social fluidity in which family seemed a rare solid bedrock, the source of people who could be relied on in business or in politics when most others, mainly concerned with their own interests, were suspect. And while it seems overstated to suggest that the notable families that appeared shortly before 1800 "may be the pivot around which Latin American history moved from the late colonial period through the early twentieth century," no doubt exists about the breadth of influence and power of large kin groups.[28] In their second generation (that is, in the years after independence) these families tended to intermarry their prolific offspring, often to "round out" influence and economic activity. Thus a family with land might link with one rich in urban property. Other combinations were of military and political influence, or of commerce with agriculture. This model of extended and complementary economic interests and wide professional range can still be seen in large and prominent Latin American families. Besides land or business interests, they may include, among cousins, nephews, in-laws, and other relatives, a doctor, a lawyer, a priest, an academic, a military man, a local or national politician, and so on. There is still perceived safety in having access to reliable and loyal representation and advice in many fields of social activity. And, of course, the wider the geographical range of the family, the better; influential members in the local or national capital are keys to a family's fortunes.

CHILE: WAR, OLIGARCHY, AND PARLIAMENTARY RULE

Oligarchies, then, were to some extent alliances of notable families, or, in the larger countries, assemblages of various such alliances. Chile provides an exemplary case of the rise of an oligarchy, and its activities in the late nineteenth-to early twentieth-century decades. The social elite of the country as it entered independence had consisted almost entirely of the families formed by recent immigrants from Spain, many of them Basques who then made money in commerce. (The modern Spanish philosopher Miguel de Unamuno, himself a Basque, once proposed that Chile and the Society of Jesus were the two greatest Basque creations.)[29] This Basque and Castilian aristocracy remained in place throughout the nineteenth century. In 1908, eighty-eight (more than a fifth) of the largest estates in the country were still owned by twelve surnames from that group. To that colonial-based nucleus of notable families, however, had by then been added others who had been lifted to prominence by export profits over the previous forty years.

Export of nitrates had been the most powerful vehicle of their advance. These minerals, in great demand abroad as fertilizer, mostly lay in what was initially a Bolivian section of the Atacama desert. There, in the 1870s, and by agreement with Bolivia, Chileans began mining nitrates for export. In 1878 the Bolivian government raised the tax it charged to the Chileans on the mineral removed, contravening a term of the agreement between the two countries. The dispute escalated into a war, the War of the Pacific (1879–84), into which Peru was drawn also, as a result of a secret treaty of mutual defense that it had made with Bolivia. Chile prevailed in this struggle. In doing so it enlarged its area by a third, and gained effective control of all the nitrate bearing territory in the Atacama, whether previously Bolivian or Peruvian. Those nitrates then became the basis of Chilean wealth and progress for several decades.

From the start foreigners had a large share in the Chilean nitrate business, and may always have maintained a majority interest. Governments did not contest this foreign presence, preferring to secure income by taxing exports rather than by establishing national control of the deposits. The ensuing income was certainly very large. It allowed the reduction of other taxes, to the benefit of large landowners, and provided the government with funds in the eighties for greatly expanded public works, including southward extension of the railway system. Competition, however, for these new and enormous sums soon brought political trouble. In 1890 the national congress, already resentful of the power gained by the presidency as a result of nitrate income, was unable to produce a new budget of its own, and refused to approve the proposal by the then president, José Manuel Balmaceda, that the previous year's spending allocations should be extended. The contest, aggravated by other issues, degenerated into a civil war in 1891, from which the congressional side, supported by the British and other foreign interests, and by the navy, emerged victorious. And so began a parliamentary dominance of Chilean politics that lasted until 1924.[30]

The congress was a body in which the single largest group was landowners. Half the senators and deputies had owned large estates in 1875; in 1902, 57 percent of all congressmen did so; and fifteen years later, 46 percent held land among their assets. Most of them, it is true, had other possessions besides land. Foreign companies owned much of Chilean mining, but native landowners bought shares in mining, and in other businesses, such as banking. Under the stimulus of the nitrate boom, Chile developed a surprisingly large industrial base by the early twentieth century. At least 6,000 factories employed some 75,000 workers by 1911. Members of the oligarchy had shares or directorships in these, also. Their children often found lucrative homes in bureaucracy and the professions, both of which swelled under the effects of nitrate income. But despite all such diversification, landowning remained the cultural ideal, a powerful colonial survival. Those who first made money in other enterprises often invested it in rural estates. As in colonial times throughout Spanish America, also, the landed gentry preferred life in the city, the locus of true civilization, to the delights of the country. So it was observed, even after the end of the parliamentary period, that the whole country was controlled by families who inhabited four square blocks in central Santiago.[31] Higher civilization still, of course, was to be found in European cities, of which Paris was the cultural pinnacle. Plenty of Chileans, and other Latin Americans, were to be found there by the end of the nineteenth century. The story goes that in 1891 a large Parisian ballroom did not give space enough for the number of Chileans who had gathered to celebrate Balmaceda's defeat, most of them members of old landowning families. To live in Europe was the highest fulfilment of cultural ambition. Those who stayed at home did their best to replicate European life in Santiago. The oligarchy's extravagant tastes during the period of parliamentary supremacy led to its being tagged as the *clase derrochadora*, the "spendthrift class."

THE LOWER ORDERS

THE MIDDLE CLASS

Although liberalism and positivism, the underlying ideologies of Latin America in the late 1800s, provided excellent reasons for the concentration of wealth and power, gains from the export boom could not be monopolized by the oligarchies. Notables took the best of the bureaucratic and business jobs that appeared as governments grew and companies proliferated; but there were far more at lower levels, and these went to people of lesser wealth and standing. The jobs appeared above all in towns and cities, and it was there that toward the end of the century a substantial middle rank of society developed. "Middle sectors" is the term many historians of Latin America have chosen to apply to these people, since they are hard to define and even the loose "middle class" seems too precise. But that term is good enough for present purposes. Just how large this class was in a particular country, or how fast it grew, is also hard to say. In Mexico, in the mid-nineties, it may have made up 8 percent of the population (against an upper class of 1 percent, and a "lower class" containing everyone else). Almost every country, however, offers good anecdotal evidence of having noticeable and influential numbers of these lawyers, doctors, engineers, teachers, middling traders, lower administrators, and clerks by the start of the new century. In 1911 the British vice-consul in Guadalajara, Mexico's chief western city, remarked that a decade earlier "the palm hat and cotton trousers were predominant on every main street while European costume was confined to a few... [but] within these ten years we have seen the peon on the main street become a rarity, while the European garb is everywhere... In fact, a middle class, hitherto lacking, has sprung into being."[32] Although it is impossible to tell from this whether it was those same wearers of palm hats and cotton trousers (or at least some of them) who had now taken to European costume, it is certainly true to say that some who came into the middle class were mestizos and other mixtures; though very rarely Indians. As throughout Latin American history, wealth still had the power to raise people in ethnic and social standing. And it is probable that the arrival of the export boom quickened the pace of that economically based upward movement, after a lapse during the slow recovery of production and trade after independence. Another distinguishing middle class mark was literacy. To the degree that reading ability may be reflected by newspaper circulation, Mexico by that measure had one of the smaller middle classes in Latin America. Its newspaper circulation, c.1910–14, was twelve copies per thousand people. Three countries which, on other evidence, seem to have had particularly strong middle classes headed the newspaper-reading table: Argentina (87 copies per thousand people), Uruguay (80), and Chile (44).[33]

The middle classes had no single political orientation or effect. For some years, at least, they posed no challenge to the oligarchies of their countries and in fact mostly sided with them in seeking material progress through exports, industrialization, and strong central government. They tended to nationalism, especially in the face of the rising financial, political, and even military presence of the United States, particularly in and around the Caribbean, from the 1890s onward. At the same time they admired North America's wealth and economic modernity, seeing there an enviable model of middle class prosperity. They did not fully share, then, the cultural orientation of their social superiors toward Europe. Another and more telling contrast was in the middle class's pursuit of education. Schooling gave access to better jobs, and hence to greater income and status. But all this was a matter of reform rather than revolutionary change. And in the cases where middle classes did finally help to weaken oligarchic rule, as, for example, in Argentina after 1912, and in Chile in the mid-twenties, they did so largely through elections in which their growing numbers gave them political weight.[34]

URBAN LABOR

A much greater potential hostility to oligarchic interests lay among the working population that the export boom had brought into existence, in the production of export goods, in their processing and handling, or in the industrialization that export revenues had stimulated. Even in the most advanced countries, that industrialization was not yet large. Many so-called factories were not much more than overgrown artisan shops. Hence the numbers of factory workers were still small percentages of total populations: 75,000 in Chile in a national total of some 3.4 million *c.*1911; 59,000 in Mexico in about 14 million at the same time; 242,000 in Argentina in 1914, among 8 million; 275,000 in Brazil, of a total of 30 million in 1920.[35] Still, these were people concentrated in cities and large towns. If and when they acted in concert, they could frighten and perhaps coerce.

Latin America absorbed radical politics slowly. Liberalism was the most extreme set of ideas to take firm root there for almost the entire nineteenth century. The European utopian socialism of the early decades made no inroads. Labor activism was therefore slow to develop. Almost everywhere, mutual aid societies among artisans, deriving from colonial brotherhoods, were the fullest extent of workers' organization until the 1870s. In return for a regular subscription these societies provided some benefits for accidents, illness, and death; often enough the members included the masters of craft shops as well as their workers, so that the brotherhoods served to ally employers and employees, rather than to set them apart. In Mexico, where the societies were particularly common, they joined together in the early seventies in the *Gran Circulo de Obreros* ("Great Circle of Workers"), the first example of some wider labor organization. At its start this body came under the influence of a brief burst of anarchism that is the first sign of the arrival in Mexico of European revolutionary ideas. But that influence quickly lapsed, and the "Great Circle" itself faded in the 1880s as the government of the day first tried to accommodate labor and then forcibly suppressed what would not yield. Mexico, however, had seen some twenty strikes during the 1870s, organized by the mutual aid groups.

Elsewhere the 1870s were also a time of incipient labor activism that then subsided as the export boom grew and the tolerance of oligarchical governments declined. Local sections of the First International (1864) appeared briefly in Argentina and Uruguay, though with only a few hundred members. Anarchism was the idea with the widest penetration, although its practical effect was reduced by its extremist advocacy of revolution and dismissal of unionism as merely "reformist." Anarcho-syndicalism, in the 1890s, proved more realistic, and hence more influential, with its support for union action in the form of strikes, boycotts, and sabotage as means of undermining the state.[36]

The revolutionary general strike was one means of changing the political and social order that anarcho-syndicalists proposed. And while no national strike ever developed in the export-boom period, general strikes of city workers took place in Rio de Janeiro, São Paulo, Buenos Aires, and other towns in the opening years of the twentieth century. Argentina had the strongest labor movement, in part because its enormous immigrant population inevitably brought with it a measure of European radicalism. Generally speaking, though, immigrants were not agitators; and governments took care to identify and oust those who were. Argentine labor organization and activism, then, were probably just as much the outcome of the country's economic prosperity as they were of the arrival of political extremists. By 1896, twenty-six or more unions existed in Buenos Aires; in 1907, 231 strikes took place in the city, with some 75,000 workers engaging in them altogether. Labor protests continued despite the promulgation of repressive laws and physical attacks on strikers by police and military.

As would be expected, few types of opposition were more provocative to progressive authoritarians than strikes, and not just in Argentina. The Chilean government used force to repress strikes and demonstrations in the port of Valparaíso in 1903, in Santiago (1905), and the northern coastal city of Antofagasta (1906), killing hundreds. Worse still was the slaying in 1907 of over a thousand men, women and children in the nitrate center of Iquique, during a protest over wages and working conditions. Workers died in similar circumstances in Mexico in two major strikes in 1906 and 1907. The first was against the US-owned company operating a copper mine at Cananea, in the far north; the government's acquiescence in the company's use of men brought in from Arizona to attack the Mexican strikers was especially resented. In the second, the government used force against workers at the Río Blanco textile mill in Orizaba, between Mexico City and the Gulf coast, killing probably over a hundred.[37]

RURAL LABOR

Unionization and strikes became the standard forms of protest used by workers in factories, mines, and railways because these men were largely town-dwellers with quite distinct places of work. They could organize themselves and choose the targets of their action. The lot of most rural workers, on the other hand, was quite different. Being spread out over the countryside, and having perhaps ancient ties to their communities and long-standing attitudes of deference to their employers, they could far less easily arrange concerted protest against worsening conditions of life, whether material or cultural. When discontent became extreme, local or regional revolt against a class of employers was a possibility; and such cases certainly occurred in the late nineteenth century. But generally the peasant was less able to defend himself and his kind against exploitation than the urban worker. Only in the case of plantations producing coffee, sugar, cacao, bananas, and other tropical export crops did the conditions of labor and the workplace resemble those in a factory. Here work was largely for money; hours of labor were fixed; conditions of work were closely defined; the plantation, or the company that owned it, was a discrete economic unit. Strikes could be an effective defense against exploitation and abuse in such a setting, and they happened (though not as often or as soon as in urban industry).

Other rural workers did not have that option. Laborers on estates often faced a landowner whom long tradition had made a culturally dominant figure, a force hard to oppose. In more remote areas, the owners might still be *de facto* local judges. In such a situation aggrieved workers had few choices. They might leave; some did, and that accounts for part of the rapid urban growth of the late nineteenth century. Or they might make themselves less available to landed employers. Some certainly seem to have taken that course, which may explain to a degree the puzzling but quite general complaints from estate owners that they could not find enough hands. The complaints are odd because the period was one of population growth, so that, other things being equal, workers should have been more abundant than before. It may be that the alleged shortage was less an absolute dearth than a lack of men who would work with the reliability and intensity that the owners wanted.[38]

Population growth should certainly have made for downward pressure on pay; and for that effect persuasive evidence exists, although remuneration is hard to measure absolutely because most of it was not given in cash but in payments in kind, provision of land for cultivation, and food and drink. As, however, estates became more commercially oriented from the mid-nineteenth century onward, producing either for export or for sale in growing national markets, owners tended to seek greater efficiency than before. The less useful, perhaps underemployed, residents that many *haciendas* had long tended to accumulate were dismissed. Owners tended to replace resident workers, who represented a constant cost, by temporary workers hired when the occasion demanded it. Although enormous variations existed from place to place and from time to time, the wide impression is, then, that from the mid-1800s rural workers received less for their efforts than they had before.

In some areas, the option of resisting poorer pay or declining conditions on estates by avoiding work became ever less available, as other sources of sustenance for country dwellers dwindled. Cottage industry in villages, which had long produced rough cloth, clothes and footwear, shrank as rail freight brought imports cheaply into the interiors, as national production rose in factories, and as free trading liberals reduced import tariffs.[39] More damaging than this in regions with large peasant populations, though, was the liberal inspired attack, already mentioned here several times, on communal lands. Given the clearly serious losses of land to peasant villages caused by that sort of policy, it is odd that historians have not yet documented it more closely. But it is plain that especially in areas with large numbers of Indian (and by this time also mestizo) communities, such as the Andes from Colombia south to Bolivia, liberal efforts to turn villagers into independent small farmers by abolishing communal lands largely failed. It was too easy for surrounding landowners to persuade poor and gullible people to sell whatever title to their individual plots they had received. Central Mexico is the region for which the process and its result are most precisely known. Francisco Bulnes, a Mexican politician and journalist, wrote in 1916 that only 15 percent of all Mexican communal villages had kept their lands. In the small state of Morelos, immediately south of Mexico City, almost all villages had lost their land to estates, and some villages had indeed totally disappeared. The result was that rural people had no choice but to leave, or to work on whatever terms the neighboring estate owners offered. A rural proletariat had appeared, which was doubtless part of the landowners' aim in absorbing community lands.[40] For excellent reason, then, Morelos was the most ardent source of opposition to the national government in central Mexico when the country's revolution began in 1910. It was, to be sure, an extreme case. More typically, in Mexico and elsewhere, villagers would be left with some land, too poor to be of use to local estates, on which to eke out a living. To the degree that they could do so, they escaped working for hire; but their margin of independence and security had become thin.

MEXICO: DÍAZ AND THE REVOLUTION

It was in Mexico that the discontents of urban and rural workers reached such a pitch as to lead them to rise violently against the national controllers of politics and economic resources. Their efforts were reinforced, and indeed catalyzed, by support at crucial moments from parts of the middle class. For the years around 1900, in fact, Mexico provides a unique example of willingness in the middle ranks of society to take strong action against an oligarchical regime. The alliance between middle and lower classes was unstable and fragile, and sometimes gave way to hostility. But in the end it prevailed, with both groups making gains in the struggle at the expense of the previously rich and powerful. And so the vicious and destructive civil war that afflicted Mexico for much of the second decade of the twentieth century is generally, and properly, called a revolution.

Discontent in early twentieth-century Mexico gained force from having a most concrete and identifiable target: the regime of Porfirio Díaz, the apparently perpetual head of state. The Colombian novelist Gabriel García Márquez perhaps had Díaz in mind when he conjured up in *The Autumn of the Patriarch* – his surreal vision of Latin American dictatorship – the "historic night . . . the immense date on which we were celebrating the first centenary of his rise to power, so that visitors had come from all over the world captivated by the announcement of an event which it was possible to witness only once in the passage of the longest of lives."[41] Díaz in fact first came to the Mexican presidency in 1877; and, in living mockery of his declared principle of "No Re-election," remained ensconced in the national palace (apart from the years 1880–4) until 1911. Except for Fidel Castro in Cuba, no other Latin American leader has stayed in office so long; very few have remained close to the center of power, in and out of office, for like periods.

Díaz came to power partly by force; and he owed the eminence that made him a contender for the presidency to his successes as a military commander on the liberal side in the 1860s. He took office, therefore, as a figure in the authoritarian mold, and remained so throughout his long regime. He was a dictator, although not a classic military dictator. He used the army, certainly, to deal with regional revolt or the threat of it. He took full advantage of the spread of telegraph lines and railways through Mexico that occurred in his time, with his encouragement, to listen for dissidence, and dispatch force to subdue it. But military power was not central to his political longevity. Nor, to any large degree, was political terrorism (although, as one comment has it, "it began to be said that presidential ambition was a disease that usually ended fatally").[42] Rather, he owed his long tenure to a symbiotic relationship with the order-and-progress minded oligarchy that was in its first flowering in the 1870s. He, like the liberal Juárez before him in his last years, invested in that positivist program and spent the rest of his life enabling its application to Mexico. So, then, he favored the privatization of Indian communal lands; he promoted the development of ever larger estates by selling public lands and granting large areas of them to those who contributed to a national land survey in the eighties; he welcomed foreign capital; he attracted foreign mining investment by annulling in Mexico the ancient Spanish legal principle that subsoil rights always remained the property of the state. He worked to enable Mexico to profit from the export boom in whose early years he came to power. In that he was successful, and the producers of export crops and of minerals, and their allies the foreign investors, saw to it that he remained in place.

The export growth and the profits, however, came at a cost to the mass of the population. The Yaqui Indians of Sonora, in the north-west, who rebelled in the 1880s to stop the conversion of their lands into cotton and rice plantations, found themselves first put down by force by the state government, and then sold as laborers to the henequen plantations of Yucatan. Mostly, however, the people suffered by omission rather than commission; such, precisely, is what a combination of positivism and socially directed Darwinism was likely to produce. The living conditions of the masses were not the proper concern of government. The outcome of such a belief was sometimes great suffering. Infant mortality, for instance, could reach some astounding levels. In the mid-northern state of Aguascalientes 800 of every 1,000 children born alive in 1893 died before their first birthday; the national figure was 493; and the figure for Mexico City was 323 (against 120 in Boston and 114 in London at the same time). That was perhaps an exceptionally bad year; but the national rate from 1896 to 1898 was still 324 per thousand. Average life expectancy at birth in 1910 was thirty years (against fifty in the United States by then).[43] It is possible, in fact, that for the mass of the people living standards fell during the *Porfiriato*, as Díaz's period is known. A combination of rising population with reallocation of land to export crops seems to have worked in that direction. Maize production may have fallen absolutely (and it has been proposed indeed that per capita production of maize was higher in 1810 than in 1910). Beans and chili, too, were less abundant, per person, at the end of the period than at the start. Food prices rose, especially in Díaz's final decade, so that real wages for the many declined.[44]

Such pressures, added to dismal working conditions in the growing number of factories, brought rising labor activism after 1900. It also spurred, in the same years, the development of political opposition to Díaz, particularly among the professional middle class that had flourished on the borders of the export boom. By now the president, his ministers, and his generals were mostly elderly and increasingly remote figures. A generational urge for renewal was added to a feeling of exclusion from national affairs, and to whatever awareness of social injustice potential reformers may have had.

The first notable body of political opposition was the *Partido Liberal Mexicano* (PLM; Mexican Liberal Party). Revived liberalism appeared on the scene in San Luis Potosí, a silver town in the mid-north, in 1900. Its animator was Camilo Arriaga, the son of a prominent local mining and landed family, though himself a professional (a mining engineer), educated partly abroad, and a reader of European socialist and anarchist literature. His stimulus to action was that old liberal bugbear, religion. Díaz had allowed the church to re-emerge in Mexico, and to gather some property again; though he took care never to repeal the anti-clerical laws of the fifties, or to move toward a reunion of church and state. But in San Luis Potosí, under the leadership of a bishop who declared the reform laws to be dead wood, the priesthood was again a very obvious urban presence. Arriaga therefore publicly called for the formation of liberal clubs across Mexico, and the gathering of a national convention in San Luis.[45] Some fifty such clubs arose, mainly in the north, and their first general meeting duly took place in February 1901. Debate began with anticlericalism, but quickly moved to a wider range of more political issues under the radicalizing influence of Ricardo Flores Magón, a lawyer from Oaxaca. The convention then criticized Díaz's methods of political control, urged restoration of justice and freedom of speech and the press, and called for democracy in politics.

In 1904 Flores Magón formally founded the PLM. By then the liberal movement had swung considerably leftward, in part in response to repression by the regime in the form of closing down publications, and exiling or jailing prominent figures, some of whom had begun to make loud attacks on the government. Leaders of the movement extended its concerns to the problems of the poor; it began to propose social reforms. By late 1903 the leaders were in voluntary or imposed exile in the USA. A split among them left the lower middle class element dominant. Support came from United States socialist and anarchist groups; and the US government sent spies and finally imprisoned some of the leading lights, including Flores Magón. Finally, however, in 1906 in St Louis (Missouri) the PLM published a program. It was a radical document, anticipating some of the provisions of the Mexican constitution of 1917, the charter that emerged from the revolutionary struggle. In 1906 the PLM called for universal free education in Mexico, a minimum wage, the end of child labor, guaranteed job security, land redistribution, and much else. The manifesto ended with various ringing declarations, including an assurance that "No longer will there be present the Dictatorship, always at hand to advise the capitalists who rob the workers or to use the armed forces as protection for foreigners who reply to peaceful petitions of Mexican workers with showers of bullets."[46] While the drafters of the constitution, ten or so years later, may not have had this document in hand as they worked, its production clearly shows that there were Mexicans, in the years before the great storm began, who had in mind the radical and nationalist reformism that the constitution displayed.

By 1906, in fact, the PLM had become too radical for most other critics of the regime. Its extremism eroded the middle class base with which it had started. It was active in the Cananea and Río Blanco strikes of 1906 and 1907, and in another rail strike in 1908. It began organizing direct revolutionary risings, although only two actually took place, in 1906 and 1908. The first was in Veracruz and the second in the northern states of Coahuila and Chihuahua. Neither was large, and both were put down easily by government forces (with helpful information about the party's activities north of the border supplied by US authorities).

Middle class reformists now gathered around the *Partido Democrático* (Democratic Party), an organization created early in 1909 to promote improving social programs; or, more precisely, they gathered around Bernardo Reyes (1850–1913), an army general and former minister of war who seemed a likely candidate for the vice-presidency in the elections of 1910. Reyes was the Democratic Party's choice for that position. Over the course of 1909 a great tide of support for him arose across the country, especially in his home state of Jalisco, in the west, and in the north-east, where he was well known as the governor of the state of Nuevo León. The government was severely alarmed. No such open political activity had taken place in Mexico for decades past, nor had so much discontent been so openly voiced. Reyes, moreover, had many loyal supporters among his subordinates in the army. Díaz reacted with propaganda and by removing prominent backers of Reyes from their military and civilian positions. In the event, however, the reaction proved unnecessary, and the danger exaggerated. Reyes himself, a man who had risen to eminence in the porfirian world, could not ultimately bring himself even to seem to oppose it. The threat of *reyismo* to the regime quickly evaporated because its figurehead proved no more than that.[47]

The support, middle class and other, that had so eagerly clustered around Reyes's supposed candidacy was, though, soon inherited by a true challenger to Díaz. This was Francisco Madero (1873–1913). Madero is certainly among the most intriguing figures in Mexican political history. He was the son of one of the richest families in the country. Its base was in Coahuila in the north, but it had economic interests throughout the national territory in banking, commercial agriculture, textiles, wine making, copper mining, and iron and steel manufacture. The family, like others of its sort, had long and close ties with the Díaz regime; Madero's grandfather had been governor of Coahuila in the early eighties, and he himself corresponded with the president on friendly terms.

Madero was educated, as were many similarly placed young Spanish Americans of the time, in France. He also studied agriculture at the University of California at Berkeley. With the knowledge gained he ran, from the mid-nineties, part of his family's estates in Coahuila. He was, then, an "agribusinessman," a young man fully immersed in the technocratic, modernizing current that coursed through Mexico in those times.

He was also, however, an idealist, a student of Hinduism who believed that in any profession a man could reach the highest level of virtue if his acts were beneficial to human welfare and progress. Perhaps this conviction gave him a persuasive altruism that made him attractive to a very wide social range in Mexico. For broad support was what he received, at least for long enough to enable him to upset the dictator.

Madero admired French republicanism, and came to believe that Mexico could rise to its full potential stature only under democracy. He was one of those who had felt the attraction of revived liberalism at the turn of the century, but who then turned away from its rising extremism. He dabbled in electoral politics in Coahuila in 1905, backing an opposition candidate for the governorship. His man lost, and he was briefly harassed by the *porfirista* state authorities. (Díaz himself, it seems, told them to stop.) After this clearly uncomfortable experience, he decided to desist from politics until the approach of the next presidential elections, due in 1910. In 1909, encouraged by the degree of political uncertainty that had developed, and being deflected from working with the Democratic Party by its close association with Reyes, he created his own Anti-Reelectionist Center of Mexico, with the slogan, partly borrowed from the Díaz of long before, of "Effective suffrage, no re-election." Branches of this sprung up around the country. Díaz, perhaps to maintain a show of democracy, tolerated Madero's activities almost until the time of the presidential election, in late June 1910. Shortly before then he had Madero arrested, for making allegedly inflammatory statements. In the election Díaz received his customary huge number of votes, and Madero 196. After being released on bail, Madero declared that only violence could bring change to Mexico. In November he issued a "Plan of San Luis Potosí," and retreated to the United States to organize revolutionary action. The Plan was a call to arms for a revolt against Díaz. It simply declared the June elections void and Madero to be provisional president of Mexico. With this manifesto the Mexican revolution began.

The first few months were unpromising. Díaz's government captured plans for risings in central Mexico, and only in the far north did active resistance develop. When, however, Madero returned to the country in February 1911, insurgents rose in many regions. Díaz then yielded with surprising speed. On May 21, 1911 a peace treaty was signed with Madero, and four days later, Díaz gave up the presidency. Soon he was in exile in Paris, where he died in 1915.

Madero entered Mexico City to triumphal acclaim in early June 1911. All must have seemed accomplished; and with, indeed, remarkable ease. But this was not even the end of the beginning; it was hardly the beginning of the beginning. With the common enemy gone, those who had gathered around Madero's standard – they included former political associates of Díaz in Mexico City, guerrilla leaders in the far north, and Emiliano Zapata, the emerging great peasant leader of the center south – tended to fly off in their different directions. In October 1911, true to his democratic principles, Madero submitted himself to a presidential election, and was duly chosen by an overwhelming majority. But by the time he took constitutional office in early November, much of his popular support had gone. The subsequent fourteen months of his presidency were filled with regional revolts, as once again, in a time of a weakened center, provincial political ambitions flourished. Madero could not act quickly enough to dispel social tensions in the country and thus maintain the popular support he needed. Some promising beginnings were made. A Department of Labor was set up in December 1911 to mediate in labor disputes and act as an employment agency. Other labor measures were decreed, including a minimum wage, and a maximum work day of ten hours. These were certainly innovatory concerns in a Mexican administration; but they were too little to ensure labor's wholesale support for Madero. Similarly, his division of remaining public lands into lots for small farmers was a step in the right direction, but many more were needed. He proposed no plan to break up estates.

With his government much weakened by revolts and the cost of putting them down, and by the loss of mass support, Madero fell, finally, to a military coup in February 1913. Resentful conservative army commanders released from jail two leaders of earlier risings. One was Bernardo Reyes, the reluctant candidate of 1909, and the other, Félix Díaz, nephew of the departed dictator. These two launched an attack on the national palace. Madero called on his army chief, Victoriano Huerta, to resist the assault. After several days of artillery exchange in the center of Mexico City, Huerta decided to change sides. Madero and his cabinet were arrested on February 18. Four days later he, his vice-president, and two loyal generals were shot while being removed from the palace on the supposed first stage of a journey into exile. Huerta or Félix Díaz are the prime suspects in the ordering of this assassination. Active behind the scenes in the final days of Madero's government was the United States ambassador, Henry Lane Wilson. From the start he had regarded Madero's rise to power, and the ending of the porfirian order, as a threat to US interests and capital in Mexico; and he clearly supported Huerta against Madero's continuation in power. His part in Madero's fall was substantial.

If Wilson, however, had hoped that Huerta would bring back the *pax porfiriana*, he was sorely disappointed. For now began the most violent phase of the revolution, and its full degeneration into civil war. This conflict had two main phases. The first (February 1913 to July 1914) was the contest that Huerta and his old guard backers fought with the "constitutionalists" (those who broadly speaking approved of Madero's actions and who claimed to be acting to sustain the 1857 constitution, which Huerta had clearly violated in overthrowing Madero). The second (mid-1914 to late 1915) was a terrible internal fight among the constitutionalists. It was during these two and a half years of unrelenting warfare that most of the estimated million deaths in the revolution took place.

The main opposition to Huerta came from the far north. Three states bordering the USA (Coahuila, Chihuahua, and Sonora) refused to recognize his regime. This was a continuation of opposition to the center that had already shown itself in northern support for Madero. More broadly it was an expression of the already fully apparent prosperity of the north, founded on agricultural and mineral exports to the United States, and a connected rising sense there of progressive modernity that contrasted with the traditionalism of the center and south. The man who emerged as leader of the northern

FIGURE 16.1 Indigenous and alien still at odds: Bolivian Indians versus donkey (an animal introduced from Spain in the sixteenth century).

FIGURE 16.2 Still the all-purpose beast of the Andes (freight, wool, meat, sacrificial victim): young llamas in Bolivia.

FIGURE 16.3 A modern example of the three-roller mill for crushing sugar cane, in Santa Cruz, eastern Bolivia.

FIGURE 16.4 Preparing *chicha* for the Feast of the Three Kings (January 6), in highland Bolivia.

FIGURE 16.5 La Glorieta, near Sucre, Bolivia. The oligarchy triumphant: the neo-Moorish cum Italianate palace of Francisco Argandoña, a Bolivian banker, in the 1890s. (In Unknown, *Sucre, capital de Bolivia, 1897*.)

FIGURE 16.6 The oligarchy at play: music and boating at La Glorieta, 1890s. (In Unknown, *Sucre, capital de Bolivia, 1897*.)

FIGURE 16.7 Urban improvement in the late nineteenth century: the new municipal theater rising in Sucre, Bolivia, in the 1890s. (In Unknown, *Sucre, capital de Bolivia, 1897.*)

FIGURE 16.8 Sucre in the 1890s, with the Prado, or formal public park, in the foreground. The park was later adorned with a miniature Eiffel Tower. (In Unknown, *Sucre, capital de Bolivia, 1897.*)

constitutionalist opposition was Venustiano Carranza (1859–1920), the governor of Coahuila. In March 1913 Carranza issued his "Plan of Guadalupe." This declaration was something of a repetition of Madero's San Luis manifesto in that it called for a restoration of constitutional government, announcing Carranza to be the First Chief of the constitutionalist army, and provisional president.

The United States now lent great weight to the reformist side. Another, and greater, Wilson, President Woodrow Wilson, who found Huerta's usurpation offensive to his ambitions for responsible self-government in Latin America, first tried to persuade Huerta to declare an armistice with the constitutionalists and hold elections. That bringing no satisfactory result, Wilson in late 1913 began efforts to oust Huerta. His most direct actions were (in February 1914) to allow the supply of arms from the United States to Carranza (previously banned, to promote a peaceful solution in Mexico); and (in April 1914) to send US troops to Veracruz on the pretext of preventing the unloading of a cargo of arms destined for Huerta. The occupation of Veracruz was, though, more broadly a warning to Huerta; and also a heavy financial blow to him, since a quarter of the government's revenues still came from duties charged at the Veracruz customs house, and these were now cut off. At the same time, constitutionalist forces were advancing down the north-west coast from Coahuila, under the man who was to be the key military leader for the rest of the revolutionary period, Alvaro Obregón. He drove Huerta's forces back with several defeats, taking Guadalajara and other western towns during the summer. Huerta resigned and left the country. The subordinates he left behind surrendered Mexico City to the constitutionalists on August 20, 1914.

Then the real social conflict began. With Huerta out of the way, the reformists again splintered, as they had on the departure of Díaz. The main groups can be identified by their leaders. Carranza, the First Chief, a man now in his mid-fifties, was the son of an estate owner in Coahuila and a former governor of the state in the final Díaz years. He had been among the first national figures to join Madero in 1910. But he had less radicalism in him even than Madero. He was aloof, honest, and most aware of that honesty. Though he was far from being, as one unkind comment has it, "bourgeois mediocrity incarnate,"[48] he lacked the attractiveness that had drawn wide support to Madero. That defect, however, was considerably offset by the greater personal appeal of his right hand man, Alvaro Obregón (1880–1928). Obregón was from Sinaloa, from the impoverished side of a wealthy family. He had worked with his hands, then as a schoolteacher, and then as a successful small farmer. He had a common touch that Carranza lacked. His innate capacity for strategy and military command, which had been made clear by mid-1914, also gave him a heroic quality absent in Carranza.

Also from the north was a very different figure, perhaps the best known of the revolution: Francisco ("Pancho") Villa (1878–1923). Villa was the son of a northern estate worker, and had himself worked as such, in addition to being at one time or another a muleteer, miner, trader, cattle rustler, and bandit. He represented the underside of northern prosperity, the workers who made it possible and who had suffered from difficult, possibly declining, laboring conditions before 1910. His followers were a mixture of miners, railwaymen, migrant farm workers, and the unemployed. If, as some argue, the north was, and is, mestizo Mexico *par excellence*, Villa was the prototypical mestizo: restless, rootless, and, in upper class judgment, dangerous and shifty. In 1910 Villa had been drawn to Madero, and took part in the fighting in Chihuahua against Díaz during the winter of 1910–11 that had initiated combat against the old regime. In the first half of 1914, while Obregón was advancing against Huerta on the west coast, Villa was taking towns in the north for the constitutionalists.

Emiliano Zapata (1879–1919) was, in representing the interests of the poor, Villa's counterpart in the middle south. But by most measures the two were contrasts. Zapata was from a peasant family and village. His primary aim was land reform, the restoration to traditional villages of lands lost to estates. His personal ambition for power was far weaker than Villa's. And he never operated far from his base and homeland in Morelos.

In outline, the constitutionalist infighting of late 1914 and 1915 went as follows. A contest for control of the movement immediately developed between Carranza and Villa. After fruitless negotiation between them, conducted for Carranza by Obregón, Carranza abandoned Mexico City in November 1914 for Veracruz, leaving the way open for Villa to occupy the capital in December. Zapata joined him there from Morelos. Once at the center, however, Villa seemed uncertain of how he should proceed to consolidate national authority. As a result, public attention once again turned to Carranza, down on the Gulf coast. Open fighting broke out, and in January 1915 Obregón began inflicting defeats on Villa's troops. Carranza and Obregón now also shifted their political stance somewhat leftward, to attract lower class allies to their side. One decisive success of this tactic was their gain of the support, in the form of both political backing and men willing to fight, of urban workers in Mexico City. And again the United States came to Carranza's aid, with arms, and in October 1915 diplomatic recognition.

In January 1915, under pressure from the *carrancista* side, Villa retreated northward from Mexico City. Obregón pursued him, leaving the capital still occupied by Zapata, as it was to be, on and off, for several months more. In April 1915 Obregón defeated Villa decisively at Celaya, 220 kilometers northwest of Mexico City in the Bajío. Villa's past successes in battle had come from his use of wild charges of thousands of horsemen. Obregón used trenches and barbed wire to counter these. First at Celaya, and then on fields further and further north, Villa lost. By the end of 1915 he had been driven back to Chihuahua and reduced to guerrilla activity in the mountains: a nuisance but no longer a threat to the main course of the revolution. Zapata, meanwhile, was faring no better. In August 1915 his men were finally dislodged from Mexico City. He retreated to Morelos, which Carranza's troops entered early the next year. Under pressure, splits developed in the movement, weakening it. Finally, in 1919 Zapata was lured into an ambush set up by the central government, and was shot.

By the start of 1916, then, Carranza, and his increasingly prominent lieutenant Obregón, had prevailed. They had done so by military force and skill;

and also by making their version of constitutionalism more widely attractive. Besides holding out the prospect of political influence to urban labor, Carranza published in January 1915 an outline of radical agrarian reform, to include the dissolution of large estates and the return to villages of lands unjustly taken from them. He probably did not like such measures, but saw their political potential in the circumstances of 1915. Late in that year he set off on a six-month tour of the country to familiarize himself with it, and it with him. In many areas local political bosses ruled; but there was no one capable of challenging him at the center. In October 1916 national elections were held (with, for the first time, universal adult male suffrage) to choose delegates to a convention that should write a new constitution. This body met in Querétaro (a site selected in commemoration of the liberals' defeat of Maximilian there in 1867) in December. Hardly anyone had been elected to represent the views of Zapata, Villa, or, on the opposite extreme, survivors of Díaz's regime. A good many moderates were present. But supporters of Obregón's positions, usually to the left of Carranza's, were the largest influence at the convention, in part because they were mostly military men, and therefore spoke with the threat of force behind their words.[49] As after the independence wars, therefore, the military was politically influential; but now what it stood for (aside from its own preservation) was change rather than continuity.

The new national charter was the work of only two months, December 1916 and January 1917. In some respects it rehearsed the constitution of 1857; but in more it broke new ground, broadly reversing the precedence of individual interests over those of the state (a precept dear to nineteenth-century liberals) to put the state first. In doing this it revealed the enduring influence of positivism in Mexico; but the most obvious stamp was now that of socialism.

The clearest legacy from 1857 was in the constitution's anti-clerical provisions. Freedom of religion was guaranteed. But no church or sect might conduct its rites except in places of public worship, which were to be supervised by the state. Much was forbidden: no religious processions; no property owning by a church, and no operation or supervision of charities; no holding of public office by priests; no clerical criticism of the government; no exceeding of government-approved numbers of priests in any locality; no foreign priests, no matter which the sect; no church schools (education was to be wholly secular). People might go through a religious marriage ceremony if they wished; but since marriage was now defined as a civil contract, no union was valid without a civil ceremony as well. The target in 1857 had particularly been Catholicism. Now all religion was restricted. These controls had a nationalist aspect, since Protestant sects had become active in Mexico, and many Protestant priests were from the United States.

A second major focus of the new constitution was labor. Here various concerns already addressed at least tentatively by Madero and Carranza received definitive treatment and emerged as regulations: an eight-hour day; no work by women and children after 10 p.m.; no work by children under six, and no more than six hours for those under sixteen; a rest day every week; guarantees of minimum wage; equal pay for equal work; wage payment in cash; limits on overtime. Labor unions were authorized, and the right to strike was guaranteed in most circumstances. More advanced were requirements that industrial companies with more than a hundred workers should set up schools for the employees' children; and the inclusion in the constitution of the principle of profit sharing between employees and workers.

The most radical section of the document, however, was its treatment of land and subsoil rights. Article 27 reversed changes made in the 1880s and 1890s under Díaz that allowed full ownership of these by foreigners. Now the subsoil remained national property, no matter who owned the surface. Petroleum deposits were included in this principle. Further, no foreigner might own land or water within 100 kilometers of national frontiers or nearer than 50 kilometers to the coast. The prohibition was made retroactive, in a clear attempt to restore national sovereignty. More startling still, though, was the declaration by article 27 that "all contracts and concessions made by former governments which shall have resulted in the monopoly of lands, waters, and natural resources of the nation by a single individual or corporation are declared subject to revision, and the executive is authorized to declare those null and void which seriously prejudice the public interest." This gave near-arbitrary power to the presidency to take lands from corporations and individual owners, and opened the way to the revocation of grants and sales that had occurred from the time of the disentailment laws of 1856.[50] Peasant communities which could show that their losses of land to surrounding estates had harmed the public interest now stood well placed to recover them. The tenor of the constitution's provisions on land was to make all ownership provisional – provisional, that is, on governmental consent, which in turn depended on use.[51]

Still as First Chief, rather than president, Carranza accepted the constitution. The Querétaro convention had called for presidential and congressional elections. These were held in March 1917, again with full adult male suffrage, which had been written into the constitution. Carranza was elected president and remained so until his untimely death in May 1920. It was a difficult period for him and for Mexico. The constitution was more innovative than he would have liked. It gave him, however, great executive power, and with that he was able to avoid applying many of its radical measures. Many of them, indeed, such as those regulating labor, have never been applied to the full extent of the law. Land reform did not reach its full force until the 1930s. More immediate and urgent problems of government pressed on Carranza. The fighting of 1914–15 had inevitably done much economic damage, especially to agriculture. By 1918 production of almost all common foods was lower than in the last years of the Porfiriato. Food prices rose; the inflationary trend was worsened by the government's resort, confronted by low revenues, to printing paper money. Carranza used force to put down strikes resulting from falling living standards. As he did so, he sacrificed the remaining popular support that he had.

The military, too, remained a large problem, and on two counts. First was the persistent survival of many small and essentially private militias in the regions, now shoring up the local political pretensions of their leaders. Only slowly, therefore, could central government extend its hold into much of the country. Second, the regular army remained large, over-officered, and greedy. In 1914, under Huerta, the military had taken 31 percent of the national budget; in 1917 the fraction was 72 percent, and in 1919, still 66 percent.[52] Only in the 1920s, through a mixture of bribery and political maneuver skillfully applied by Obregón, was the military residue of the revolution worn down – and to such good effect, in fact, that since then the armed forces have taken, by Latin American standards, an unusually small part in Mexican political life.

Perhaps Carranza's most persistent source of worry was Obregón himself. For he was the revolution's military chief and its great hero. In 1916 he had become minister of war; but he resigned the office when Carranza was elected president in 1917, and retired to Sonora to recuperate and plan his bid for the presidency in the 1920 elections. The long-impending split between the essentially conservative, though pragmatic, Carranza and the more radical, though always careful, Obregón finally opened up as that election came near. Carranza decided that Obregón's military past made him an unsuitable candidate for the leadership of a country striving to escape militarism. He therefore put forward his own civilian contender, a diplomat little known in Mexico. Fearing that Carranza intended to control the election, Obregón's supporters in Sonora called for his removal; and in a repetition of the events of 1914, a Sonoran "Liberal Constitutionalist Army" began, early in 1920, to move down the west coast toward central Mexico. Regular army leaders thereupon abandoned Carranza, who tried to escape eastward. But he was captured, and died in May 1920 either by assassination or by suicide. With him finally died nineteenth-century liberalism in Mexico. And with Obregón, elected president later in the year and in office until 1924, began, if haltingly, the age of the interventionist state from which the country may only now be slowly emerging.

THE 1920s: POLITICS AND EXPORTS

In its combination of geographical scope, duration, broad involvement of urban and rural laborers, sharp changes in social and economic policy, reform of political leadership, and not least in its toll of perhaps a million dead, the Mexican revolution was an event without parallel in Latin America in the early twentieth century. Indeed in the entire history of Latin America from independence to the present the only process comparable in its political, social, and economic effects in one country is the Cuban revolution that began in 1959. But even that did not include a civil war on anything approaching the Mexican scale of combat and casualties.

Although estates, landless peasants, low wages, inequality of wealth, foreign ownership, and other concerns of the revolutionaries did not disappear from Mexico after 1917, or 1920, or any other later date, nonetheless the days of unquestioned oligarchy were now over. The old order, an outgrowth above all of the export boom, was gone. New forces ran the country. In the decade or two after the revolution, the old order changed substantially elsewhere in Latin America as well. It did so partly in response to conditions resembling those in Mexico before 1910, though less acutely or powerfully present. No other country had had a Porfirio Díaz for three decades and more. In few others was inequality of wealth so blatant and as widespread. But in almost all countries forty or fifty years of flourishing exports had created economic and social tensions that would demand political release.

In some cases, the release came largely through democratic means. Argentina is the best example of this process. Immigration, industrialization, and the rise of small farming had produced a large and relatively prosperous urban and rural working population, and a substantial urban middle class, even while exports continued to swell the fortunes of the rich. From the 1890s these people found a political home in the *Unión Cívica Radical*, the Radical Civil Union, a movement that in its beginnings, at least, stood mainly for observance of the 1853 constitution and honesty in elections. In 1912 the then president, Roque Sáenz Peña, the son of a wealthy family but a longstanding opponent of political corruption and personalism, introduced a law requiring all males over eighteen to vote, and to vote, moreover, by secret ballot. In the next presidential election, in 1916, the outcome was that the leader of the UCR, Hipólito Yrigoyen, became president. The UCR then remained in power until 1930. Although there were instances of violence between conservatives and labor, the party's mild reformism, combined with Yrigoyen's immense personal popularity, kept organized labor and rural workers generally content while slowly undermining conservative interests.[53]

In Chile labor had a rather briefer impact on national politics. Its vote was instrumental in the election as president in 1920 of Arturo Alessandri, a reformist who planned wide economic and social change in the country. Labor's political force rose during his first years in office; but circumstances forced him into alliance with a portion of the army, so that from the middle of the decade his influence was increasingly pushed aside by a centralist, though materially progressive, military regime.

Something of the same pattern can be seen in Peru, where in 1912 Guillermo Billinghurst, the grandson of a British naval officer who had fought for Buenos Aires in the independence wars, was elected president. He was a businessman, rich from the nitrate trade, who had been a popular mayor of Lima in 1909–10. He is sometimes accounted one of the first "populist" politicians of twentieth-century Latin America, but was probably above all a man who believed that the wealthy, for their own future safety, should make overtures to the growing working populations. He reduced the military budget and put the money so saved into a public health service. He introduced obligatory collective bargaining between workers and employers, and began an assessment of the living conditions of Indians in the Andes of southern Peru. When the congress objected to his progressive projects, he encouraged workers in Lima to demonstrate against it. In 1914 he was removed by an army coup after having tried to shut down the congress.

Some of Billinghurst's concern for the life of the masses carried over into the administration of Augusto Leguía from 1919 to 1930. Like Billinghurst, Leguía was a successful businessman. Unlike him, he was an open dictator, who entitled his regime the *Patria Nueva*, or "New Fatherland," a title with perhaps a distant whiff of fascism. He courted the support of Lima workers to undermine the influence of the remaining oligarchy, and paid some attention – how sincere is arguable – to Indians' complaints about loss of land. Like the military regime to the south, in Chile, however, Leguía was mainly concerned with Peru's material development. During his years in office investment in Peru from the United States ran high, as it did in much of Latin America in the 1920s, and Leguía took advantage of the resulting tax revenues. Very large loans, likewise mainly from the USA, also paid for his projects. Public works, such as roads in the mountains giving Indians access to the more developed regions of Peru, were high on his agenda. Irrigation, modernization of agriculture, public health, primary education, beautification of Lima; on all these too his government spent heavily.[54]

Examples could be multiplied. Across Latin America in the 1920s governments and informal holders of power and influence were forced to come to terms with large and increasing working populations. The desires and the demands of those populations grew more urgent. The Mexican revolution provided them with some inspiration. But since it had a less defined overarching ideology than the Russian revolution, it was that distant eruption that had the greater effect. Disruptive shock waves from it traveled to Latin America, amplifying workers' own protests and arguments. University students were among the first to feel those tremors, and began to develop into the powerful political force for change that they have continued to be in Latin America.

It was, however, once again external economic change that brought the age defined by exports and oligarchies to a close, and tipped Latin America into a new political era. That change was the depression that began in 1929 with the stock market crash in New York.

Up until then, Latin American countries on the whole continued to export successfully. The outbreak of war in 1914 had at first dragged exports down. But as the demand for strategic materials grew, those countries that possessed them benefited. At least for those items terms of trade improved in the short term. Mexico sold rising amounts of oil from the fields on the north Gulf coast, an area mostly free of revolutionary fighting. Venezuela began to export oil for the first time. Peru's sales of copper, Bolivia's of tin, and Chile's of nitrates, all boomed. Countries whose main exports were non-strategic, on the other hand, suffered from the fall in demand and the disruption caused by the war. Brazil, for example, saw its income from foreign coffee sales drop sharply.

Exports in the 1920s continued on the whole to do well, though no longer growing at pre-World War I rates. For that, changes in international trade wrought by the war had some responsibility. Britain, which had already ceased to be Latin America's main trading partner before 1914, was now burdened with the costs of war and hence stopped being its main source of capital. That role passed to the United States. In the 1920s the USA also continued to increase its commercial dominance of Latin America as both importer and exporter. Germany had all but disappeared as a trading partner for Latin America during the war, and remained out of the picture in the twenties. The slowness of the postwar restoration of the gold standard made for uncertainties about currency exchanges and about investment flows that hindered commerce and economic change in the twenties.[55]

Other negative pressures on Latin American exports in that decade included technical developments that, for example, substituted factory-made dyes for natural products, and synthetic fibers for raw cotton. A yet more general brake on trade was the slowing rate of population growth in the industrial countries, felt economically elsewhere as less buoyant demand for primary products. Latin America's terms of trade worsened during the twenties – as they had indeed since the start of the war (strategic materials excepted).[56] Nonetheless, partly through more efficient production and improvements in transport resulting from foreign (largely North American) investment in the twenties, individual Latin American states had some success in increasing their shares in world markets for several commodities. These included meat and some grains (Argentina), bananas (Colombia and various Central American countries), sugar (Cuba, the Dominican Republic, Puerto Rico, and Peru), copper (Chile and Peru), oil (Venezuela), silver (Bolivia, Mexico, and Peru), and tin (Bolivia).[57] As a result, and despite the fact that foreign markets were less predictable than before, almost all countries maintained a rising value of exports until 1929.[58]

The depression put an end to that. Export sales fell in 1930, and continued to decline sharply until 1932–3. The political outcomes were rapid and striking. With varying degrees of direct and indirect causality, the subsidence of exports resulted in the following: military coups in Peru (against Leguía) and Argentina (against Yrigoyen) in 1930; the weakening of the coffee oligarchy as a political force in Brazil, and the ascent to power, partly by military intervention, of Getúlio Vargas, who was to dominate Brazilian politics until 1945; the fall of the military government of Chile, as a result of loss of control of public order, and the beginning of a political recasting of the country into new forces that would persist for forty years; a brief military regime in Bolivia, and the setting of the scene for the outbreak of the Chaco War (with Paraguay) in 1932 – a conflict that changed the course of Bolivian history from the mid-thirties; the ending of several decades of conservative domination in Colombia, with the election of a liberal president; and the fall of the Ecuadorean government in 1931 and the start of a long period of political turbulence. In other countries, the depression's effects were present, but less easy to define. The country possibly least touched by them was Venezuela, where the dictator Juan Vicente Gómez was well ensconced and where exports (very largely of oil) quickly recovered from a minor dip in 1931–2.

BRAZIL: EMPIRE AND COFFEE

Much of what has been said in the preceding pages, the primary focus of which has been Spanish America, applies equally to Brazil. In fact, various Brazilian examples, particularly of social and economic processes, have been cited, since, broadly viewed, Portuguese and Spanish America followed the same paths in the nineteenth century (and have continued to do so since). One outstanding political contrast remains, however; and that is the persistence of monarchical government in Brazil until 1889.

Brazil had only two royal rulers: Peter I (1822–31) and his son, Peter II (1840–89). The two reigns were separated by a regency, since Peter II was only five when his father abdicated (and, indeed, only fourteen when he himself came the throne in 1840). Just as the presence of the Portuguese prince regent in Rio after 1808 helped Brazil to move into independence with a minimum of conflict and bloodshed, so the continued presence of the monarchy after John VI was summoned back to Portugal in 1821 contributed to Brazil's avoidance of the political chaos suffered by much of Spanish America down to the mid-century. Everything interconnects, of course. The lack of a war of independence meant that Brazil did not suffer the economic disruption that afflicted Spanish America. That, in turn, meant less political scrapping after independence for economic crumbs, because the cake was much as it had been in late colonial times. Funds had not been borrowed to support the war against the colonial power; and what was borrowed after independence did not have to go to replacing what had been destroyed, but could be used for new investment. Production and export of coffee continued to leap ahead. By c.1850 Brazil was by far the largest exporter in Latin America, with overseas sales of almost 36,000,000 dollars (coffee bringing in half that sum); its nearest rival was Cuba (26,000,000 dollars of exports, largely in sugar).[59] And because Brazil suffered no economic hiatus, it was able to service its foreign debts and so continue to borrow while the Spanish American states could not. A deeper common causality may be found under all this: the generally less oppressive nature of the Portuguese colonial regime, relative to Spain's, especially in the final quarter of the eighteenth century, after the fall of Pombal. That led to the royal family's being received tolerantly, even gladly by some, when it moved to Brazil. And that, in turn, favored the preservation of monarchy after the colony's break from Portugal, a continuity helpful to political calm and economic advance.

The political framework within which the two emperors ruled until 1889 was provided by the 1824 constitution. It was a document in whose drafting Peter I had much influence. First he called an assembly in Rio in 1823 to prepare a constitution. The dominant tone of the congress was liberal, generally in line with Peter's own inclinations. But he grew impatient with its wranglings and appointed a committee of ten, drawn mostly from the congress, to work with him on the document. It was quickly written, and sent to town councils around the country for ratification. The procedure is typical of the style of rulership that father and son used in Brazil. They were latter-day enlightened despots, willing to bend so far towards representative and participatory government, but with limited patience. If anything, Peter II was more conservative than his father; but he was longer in power, and time may have brought greater rigidity with it.

The 1824 constitution gave the monarch large powers, making him a chief executive aided by a cabinet whose members he chose. A "moderating" power contained in the charter enabled him to adjudicate among other branches of government, and also to dissolve the legislature at any time and call for new elections. Both emperors used this prerogative. The subordination of the legislature was increased by the monarch's part in selecting senators for its upper house: he was to choose one candidate of three put forward by local electors. The constitution gave no rights or claim to citizenship to the two million or so black slaves in the country (in a total population of slightly under four million).[60] Peter himself seems to have been completely opposed in principle to slavery, but could hardly have risked touching that issue, given Brazil's almost total reliance at the time on slave labor to produce its major exports, sugar and coffee.

Brazil had its share of the regionalism that did much to keep Spanish American countries in political turmoil before the middle of the century; and to this Peter's concentration of power at the center, in Rio, was a response. In the north-east resentment over the shift of political power southwards in the mid-eighteenth century still festered. In 1824 parts of the north, led from Pernambuco, tried to break from Brazil as a separate "Confederation of the Equator." The attempt was put down within a few months, largely because Rio had the naval force necessary to dominate the sea. Regional restlessness continued, however, into the forties. Brazil was never in real danger of breaking up, but the centrifugal movements were a political demonstration of the fact that the country still consisted of somewhat isolated economic regions which traded more with the exterior than among themselves. It was not until the 1840s that the Rio government, under the young Peter II, was able to enforce its will consistently in the north-east and elsewhere. Only in that decade, it has been said, did Brazil become consolidated as a nation-state.[61]

Peter I abdicated suddenly, and to general surprise, in April of 1832. There was perhaps in him a touch of impetuosity or impatience, visible in his reaction to orders from Portugal on the Ipiranga in 1822 and his dismissal of the efforts of the constituent congress in 1823. He had in fact, though, been losing support for several years. An element of nativism existed in Brazil that objected to foreign influence or incursion, of which he could be accounted an example. Further, he had argued for European immigration, partly to strengthen Brazil's armed forces. Hundreds of Irish and German immigrants did in fact enter the army. Riots broke out in Rio in 1828 between these troops and local people. A later influx of Portuguese, largely liberals fleeing from the rightist government by then in power in Lisbon, gave rise to more objections in 1831. There were Brazilians who saw these arrivals as a threat to independence. Two more general complaints undermined Pedro. The first was his failure to attach Uruguay to Brazil. Argentina had designs on it also. British intervention arranged that neither should get it (though both persisted in trying for several decades more), and resulted in the emergence of Uruguay as a separate state in 1830. Second, and possibly most distressing of all to powerful economic interests, was Peter's negotiation in 1826–7 with Great Britain of a treaty stopping the slave trade between Africa and Brazil. The ban was to start in 1830. In fact, it did not, and the slave trade continued, against British objections, until 1851. But the challenge to slavery put Peter in bad odor with important Brazilians. The final straw came early in 1831 with street fighting in Rio over the recent influx of Portuguese. Peter reacted to the disorder by dismissing his cabinet and replacing it with another staffed by his closest allies. He refused demands that he restore the first cabinet, saying that he "would do everything for the people, but nothing by the people." The next day he renounced the throne, naming his very young son as successor. He retreated to Portugal, where he died of consumption in 1834.

Brazil was in name governed by a regency during the thirties, but in reality the congress had a large say in administration. The interruption of the monarchy gave a space in which political adjustments took place that would reinforce the basic stability of the state. Conservatives and liberals began to organize themselves into recognizable parties. The Additional Act of 1834 amended the constitution to allow for provincial legislatures.

Monarchy was still seen, however, by those in high political places as the keystone of the state structure. Hence Peter II was installed as emperor in 1840 at the age of fourteen, four years short of the constitutional age of accession. He was clearly a precocious youth, dismissing senior men from his cabinet in his early days. During the rest of the decade he enlarged his knowledge of Brazil, in part by travel, and developed his considerable innate ability to govern. He was lucky in presiding over a country growing ever more prosperous, at least at its upper social levels and in its foreign trade. He was a model of energy and practical intelligence. He was free of pretension and anxious for honest government.[62] He promoted modernization: the first iron mill was built near Rio in 1846; steamboats started sailing the Amazon in 1852; the first railway began operation in 1854, from Rio a little way into its hinterland; in 1867 a longer and economically more significant line opened between São Paulo and the port of Santos, making coffee growing practicable on the terrain westward of São Paulo.

The middle decades of the century, 1850–70, were the golden age of the empire. Not surprisingly Brazil began to flex its political muscles in this period, as the expression partly of its prosperity, partly of its political consolidation. Its contribution to the liberals' ousting of Rosas from Buenos Aires in 1852, in working to unite his Argentine opponents, seemed a diplomatic coup.[63] Rosas had long been an irritant and a threat, blocking the movement of ships down river from Paraguay and Brazil, and constantly stirring up the question of Uruguay. He, in fact, regarded both Uruguay and Paraguay as insolent provinces of Argentina.

In the 1860s Brazil's new confidence in South American affairs, and a resurgence of the Uruguayan question, led the country into a major external conflict – the Paraguayan War, or War of the Triple Alliance. The immediate genesis of this was convoluted and is still a matter of debate. Generally speaking, though, the territorial ambitions of both Brazil and Argentina had much to do with it, as did the foolhardiness and resentment towards Argentina of the then ruler of Paraguay, the dictator Francisco Solano López. The war began with a Brazilian invasion of Uruguay, in September 1864, and Uruguay's calling on Paraguay for support. Solano López then sent troops northwards into Brazil, and also across northern Argentina, in defiance of an Argentine warning. Brazil and Argentina in early 1865 joined forces against Paraguay. And a political change within Uruguay brought that country into the alliance. The Paraguayans fought heroically and at enormous cost, both economic and human, for five years, until Solano López was finally killed in battle in March 1870. It was long thought that Paraguay lost half of its population in the war; but this estimate has been much lowered, to between some 9 and 19 percent. Most of the casualties were among adult men. Almost 40 percent of the country's pre-war territory became Brazilian or Argentine. To Brazil went a broad segment of the north between the Paraguay and Paraná Rivers. Argentina took a similar area in two pieces, one west of the Paraguay and between the Pilcomayo and the Bermejo Rivers, and the other further east, bounded by the Paraná, the Uruguay, and the Iguassú.[64] The war also ended a long post-independence period of isolated economic development in Paraguay, which had yielded some success in sustaining the living standard of the mass of the people. The country had been politically stable, though at the cost of harsh dictatorial rule. That now ended as well, and a long period of political disorder ensued.

The allied victory, though it could never really have been in doubt, added to Brazil's rising self-confidence as well as to its territory. But the effects of the conflict went deeper and wider, so that the war takes on a transforming role in Brazilian national history.

First, success added to Peter II's confidence and increased the inclination towards autocracy that he was already showing. This was one reason for the appearance in 1870 of an offshoot of Brazilian liberalism, the Republican party, which was the first openly anti-monarchical political organization in the country. The Republicans favored a federal system of the North American sort. They were not a powerful political influence until the eighties, but drew the support of the rising number of educated young people in the country.

Second, the war pushed the issue of slavery into the foreground. The good fighting performance of slaves in the army had led to increased questioning of the existence of slavery in Brazil. Two earlier events had already given the matter prominence. One was the final ending of slave imports into Brazil, under intense British pressure, in 1850–1, and the other, formal emancipation of slaves in the United States in 1863, during the Civil War. Both influenced opinion in Brazil. With no more slaves arriving, coffee growers in the south began to be concerned about their future work force. They proposed immigration from Europe as a solution (which, indeed, it did become); but some Europeans objected to moving to a slave-owning country. And so, even among those who in the past had completely depended on slavery, a sentiment for abolition began to appear. Sensing this multiple current, in 1871 the emperor allowed passage of a "free-womb" law, by which the children born of slave mothers would from that date be free (although the mothers' owners could put the children to work until they reached twenty-one). So the matter rested legally until 1885, when slaves aged sixty or more were declared free. The multiplying advocates of full abolition (among them now army officers who in 1887 said they would no longer pursue fugitive slaves) continued to press. And in 1888, with almost unanimous political support, slavery came to its end in Brazil.

A third major effect of the Paraguayan War was the entry of the Brazilian military onto the political stage. Before the war neither army nor militarism in general had played a noticeable part in politics. That was another positive outcome of a largely peaceful independence process. The war, however, enlarged the army in both numbers and in its sense of importance. In the following decades positivism gave it a sense of modernizing purpose. At the same time its neglect by the government after the war, resulting in officers' advancing neither in rank nor in pay, created a resentment towards the imperial regime. It was in fact the army, a substantial presence in a country now with a large progressive element in its mentality, that dismissed the aging and ailing emperor in 1889. In November of that year Peter's slowness in reacting to political demands that he disband his chosen conservative government provoked an army coup. Told one day that he must leave the country, he did so the next (15 November), and retreated, like many banished Latin American leaders before him, to Paris. There he died two years later. The Brazilian Republic was proclaimed on 16 November 1889.

Brazil then passed through a rapid recapitulation, in politics at least, of Spanish America's experience after independence. It might be said, in fact, that politically speaking Brazil did not become fully independent (in the sense of breaking free of the colonial past) until Peter II's reign was over, and that therefore some reiteration of what the former Spanish colonies had gone through would be expected.

The Republicans held power after the abdication. In 1891 they adopted a new constitution much influenced by that of the USA, and emphatically federal in content. States, for instance, could maintain their own armies; they could raise their own foreign loans and collect their own customs duties. With physical and fiscal force at their disposal, the states gathered strength at the expense of the center. In the mid-nineties national political parties that had formed after 1889 decayed. National politics became a matter of competition for the presidency among states, with the richest ones dominant. Local political bosses, known as *coronéis* ("colonels"), in the manner of regional *caudillos* in Spanish America, arose and joined forces with local oligarchies consisting of alliances of rich families. São Paulo and Minas Gerais were the most prosperous states, both as large exporters of coffee (of which Brazil provided more than half the world's supply by 1890). These two states controlled the presidency until 1930; of the fifteen presidents holding office between 1889 and 1930, six came from São Paulo, and four from Minas.[65] In the 1920s, after a generation's span of this order, a renovatory spirit appeared in the form, first, of a group of middle class nativists, who wanted to replace republicanism, which they saw as a product of European liberalism, by something more genuinely Brazilian and "tropical;" and second, of junior army officers, known as the *tenentes* ("lieutenants"), who, like the military of the 1880s, resented their neglect by the national government, but also called for honest elections and greater attention to social needs by the state. This movement ran parallel to the growing political weight of labor in various Spanish American countries in the same decade. The *tenentes* even started local revolts in the early and mid-twenties. But they were not enough to upset the prevailing political order, founded as it was on the wealth of coffee. Only an assault on that wealth could produce such major change; and that assault was provided, after 1929, by the depression.

DEFINING THEMSELVES

In economic matters, there was no breaking loose from the rest of the world. Latin America still finds that true today, despite efforts to create a measure of autonomy during and after the thirties by, for example, investment in manufacture to produce items that had previously been imported. This in turn, it was hoped, would reduce the need for exporting primary goods to pay for imports, and so reduce exposure to the whims of international markets. The strategy had some success, but most countries still rely heavily on income coming from foreign sales of oil, minerals, tropical foods, and the like.

For much of the nineteenth century, breaking loose, economically or otherwise, was not a leading concern. Or rather, separation from the outside world was not the aim. What many members of the various political nations wished to break from was the colonial past, and to do that they actively sought patterns to follow in the exterior, above all in Europe. And some or many of them seized eagerly on alien political models and ideas – liberalism, positivism, federalism in the North American style – and chopped and changed between them, with varying degrees of success, to fit Latin American reality. Even conservatives, who found value in colonial culture and comfort in its continuation, welcomed certain of those imported ideas: the economic aspects of liberalism, for instance, or Darwinism (as a justification for the existence and maintenance of the social and economic hierarchy).

The "modern" countries of Europe seemed to offer the greatest range of contrasts with Spain and Portugal, and among those, as a number of earlier references here have suggested, France was the most admired, the cultural ideal, the acme of civilization. Almost anyone who could do so gravitated to Paris, from superfluous heroes of independence, to discarded dictators, to painters and poets wishing to advance to the leading edge of their arts. A sonnet ("In Winter") written by the Nicaraguan poet Rubén Darío (1867–1916) catches this admiration nicely:

> In these long, slow winter hours my Carolina
> Sits by the fire that glimmers in the salon
> Curled up or half curled up in the softest chair
> Enveloped in her enormous sable coat.
>
> The white angora stretches out beside her,
> Rubbing his nose against the lace of her skirt;
> Behind them, the porcelain jardinieres from China
> Loom up against the Japanese silk screen.
>
> Carolina is drugged with the sly philters of sleep.
> I enter without a word, take off my gray coat,
> And kiss her face, which is as rosy and bright
>
> As a red rose that once was a fleur-de-lis.
> She opens her eyes and looks at me with a smile.
> Outside, the snow is still falling over Paris.[66]

The poem appeared in a collection named *Azul* (*Blue*) that Darío published in 1888 while he was in Chile. It was there, in the company of other young literati, that he first delved deeply into French poetry, responding particularly to the work published by the Parnassians in the sixties and seventies. That movement's preference for cool, precise statement and exotic and classical subject matter captivated him. It became the point of departure for *modernismo* (modernism), the dominant mode of poetry in Spanish in the late nineteenth and early twentieth centuries. Darío was a leader among modernists, and, in the opinion of many, the best poet in the Spanish-speaking world of his time.

What is particularly touching, and revealing, about "In Winter" is that it was written before Darío had visited France, before, in fact, he had been outside Spanish America. It was the product of idealization, of distant admiration, and of yearning.

In some measure it was possible to bring Paris, and other European places, to Latin America. The import had begun in some places, in fact, in the late eighteenth century with the shift in art and architectural style away from the baroque to the neo-classical. The transfers continued and accelerated in the nineteenth century. The first large example is the arrival in Rio de Janeiro in 1816 of a French commission on fine art led by Joachim Lebreton. This was a group of planners, artists, and architects invited by John VI to advise on the remodeling of Rio in the neo-classical style into a truly imperial capital.[67] French town planning remained the ideal for Latin Americans throughout the century. "The Chilean Haussmann" was the nickname given to the politician, historian, and savant Benjamín Vicuña Mackenna after he redesigned the center of Santiago de Chile in the 1870s. Haussmann's spacious renovation of central Paris, with its wide, open boulevards, squares, and parks, was much imitated across Latin America in the late nineteenth century, as export-derived funds became available for the removal of congested central areas and reconstruction. Large, grandiloquent buildings – palaces, ministries, theaters – in a loosely neo-classical or beaux-arts style were strategically placed along and around these new thoroughfares. The newly rich housed themselves in imitation French mansions, of two or three stories and with slated, mansard roofs.[68]

The drawback of borrowing from Europe was that, although it made a modernizing break with the colonial period, it did little to give Latin American nations a sense of their own identity. They might be modern in taste, but on that road they could hardly become more than simulacra of the originals. One European domination was being swapped for another. Awareness of this danger rose during the second half of the century. The paintings of that period demonstrate its appearance especially well.

By the middle of the century various influences on Latin American painting were starting to converge, and from the meeting more distinct local schools were developing. One influence was the tradition of scientific illustration that had begun with the scientific and geographical expeditions of the late 1700s. The same sort of expeditions had continued after independence, generally led by curious Europeans. Sometimes they engaged local artists to record their discoveries of flora and fauna, and some of those painters and draftsmen added landscapes to their production. A second influence was the arrival of a goodly number of European painters, drawn by the newly accessible exoticism of the independent nations, and intending to record it to meet the demand for the picturesque that was so strong in Europe at the time. These artists painted and drew dramatic landscapes, genre scenes of Latin American popular life, and images of the ruins of native antiquity (the latter particularly in southern Mexico and northern Central America). They may have done little direct teaching of painters in the countries where they worked, by they provided examples of subject matter and technique that locals might imitate. Third was the survival and expansion of national academies of art. Only in Mexico had one, the Academia de San Carlos, been founded in colonial times. Two more appeared early in the nineteenth century: the Brazilian Imperial Academy of Fine Arts, in Rio de Janeiro, in 1826; and the Academy of Painting and Sculpture, at Caracas in Venezuela, in the mid-1830s. Other states had to wait for the late nineteenth or early twentieth centuries for their national academies.[69] The three academies that did exist for most of the 1800s, however, played a large role in keeping neo-classicism and academic treatment of art present in Latin America. Many of their directors and instructors were formally trained Europeans who carried to Mexico, Brazil, and Venezuela rather jejune visions of their own countries' traditions in painting and sculpture.

A common part of those traditions, however, was history painting – the depiction of historical scenes with generally a morally uplifting or nationalistic intent. This concern joined with the interests in landscape and genre sustained by illustrators and visiting Europeans to stimulate production of paintings on national themes in many Latin American countries. The linkage between subject matter and the politics of the moment could on occasion be remarkably close. For example, during Maximilian's brief empire in Mexico in the mid-1860s, Santiago Rebull (a Mexican, but trained partly in Rome) directed the production of a series of portraits of independence heroes. The aim was to attach the new regime to the Mexican past. But as soon as the empire was over, and republican government by the liberals restored, academic painters turned to celebratory portrayal of the native past, with, for instance, José María Obregón's *The Discovery of Pulque* (1869), or Rodrigo Gutiérrez's *The Senate of Tlaxcala* (1875). In these scenes in the "academic nationalist" style,[70] and others like them, ancient Mexicans are painted, with high technical and compositional skill, to resemble unspecified figures of the classical European past. They look little like modern Indians, nor do the settings in which they are shown much resemble Mexican pre-Columbian building, even as it would have been known *c*.1870. What can be seen here is a continuation of efforts made a century before to recast native Mexican antiquity in the European classical mold. Indians of the day counted for very little. But their remote ancestors were once more being summoned up as proof that the country had a deep and noble past. There may perhaps be a connection between the fact that the president of the restored republic, Benito Juárez, was himself a full-blooded Indian and this celebrating of pre-Columbian natives around the end of his life. But the appearance of this theme in Mexican art at the time is certainly also a tentative expression of rising consciousness of the nation as a combination of European and native elements. The Indian element here is "sanitized" by its presentation as a parallel of European classicism. A decade or more later, under Porfirio Díaz (a mestizo rather than an Indian), a reminder of a less remote native past appeared prominently in Mexico City. In 1887 a monument to Cuauhtemoc, the Aztec leader whose capture signaled the fall of Tenochtitlan to Cortés in 1521, was unveiled.[71] The figure stands to this day atop a tall column on the Paseo de la Reforma, the grandest (and most Haussmannian) avenue of Mexico City.

A particularly elegant demonstration of a rising awareness of Mexico's native past (or, perhaps, of the need to add a native component to the self-image of the country) can be found in two landscapes by José María Velasco (1840–1912). He was a painter who delighted in great sweeping views of the central Valley of Mexico. He had learned his landscapist's trade from Eugenio Landesio, an Italian brought to Mexico to teach at the Academy in 1855. In 1875 Velasco produced a view entitled *The Valley of Mexico*. It is done from the north. It shows the lakes that still existed then on parts of the Valley floor. Mexico City lies in the distance. Further away still, to the south, rise the snow peaks of Popocatépetl and Ixtaccíhuatl. In the foreground, very much in the classical European style of landscape, are small figures: a woman, a child, and two dogs. Two years later Velasco painted another view of the Valley (*View of the Valley of Mexico from the Hill of Santa Isabel*) from almost the same vantage point, and showing the same physical features. In this second painting, however, the figures are gone. They are replaced by nopal cactuses, and, small but distinct against shadow in the center, a flying eagle. The reference to the foundation myth of Tenochtitlan is clear: the city was to be built where the wandering Mexica tribe found an eagle perched on a cactus with a snake in its claws. Velasco subtly reminds his viewers that this is the valley in which the Aztec capital stood.[72]

Throughout Latin America in the later decades of the nineteenth century painters abounded who, though less formal and ambitious than Velasco, depicted their nations in a variety of styles. Landscapists and genre painters (known as *costumbristas*) seem to have been active everywhere. A country particularly rich in that sort of work was Ecuador. Merely as an example, Joaquín Pinto (1842–1906) may be briefly mentioned. He was taught by other Ecuadorians, including one, Juan Manosalvas, who had trained in Rome. Pinto was briefly director of an Academy of Painting in the provincial town of Cuenca after 1900, and then was a founding member of the new National School of Fine Arts in Quito from 1904. He painted portraits and religious scenes, but also landscapes, and above all genre representations of common people, including lively, unsentimentalized urchins. In his work, then, the popular puts in a strong appearance. His street people are, moreover, clearly mestizos or *castas* of one type or another.[73]

By the start of the twentieth century, lower class people and their everyday lives were receiving growing attention from painters and other artists across Latin America. Pedro Figari, for instance, a Uruguayan lawyer and politician who was for a long time merely an amateur painter, produced somewhat primitivist scenes of street life and people's gatherings in their houses, including dancing by the remaining black population of the country. José Guadalupe Posada, a Mexican printmaker who would probably not have considered himself an "artist" but simply an illustrator, produced many thousands of images for sale to the common people of Mexico City. In many he was a satirist commenting on behavior at all social levels. Best known now of his work are his engravings of skeleton figures taking part in the annual Day of the Dead celebrations.[74]

It was in Mexico during, and more definitively after, the revolution that painting most fully reflected a changed national self-definition. In the early twenties, Obregón's minister of education, José Vasconcelos (1882–1959), imitating Soviet post-revolutionary models, organized a program of mass education through the arts. A central part of this effort, and the one that is certainly most celebrated, was the employment of various artists to paint murals on the walls of numerous public buildings, particularly in Mexico City. Among these muralists was the great trio of Diego Rivera (1886–1957), José Clemente Orozco (1883–1949), and David Alfaro Siqueiros (1898–1974). These men were by no means in agreement on either artistic or political questions. Vasconcelos, moreover, gave them great freedom of subject matter. But broadly speaking the message that emerged from their often vast paintings was an "indigenist" one, celebrating the perceived native identity of the country, whether pre-conquest or present. It was, then, also a nationalist message. As such it was consonant with the tenor of article 27 of the 1917 constitution, which attempted to exclude foreigners from ownership and exploitation of Mexican resources, and, more broadly, made all private property rights subordinate to those of the nation.

Vasconcelos himself had a nationalist side; after the revolution there were few eminent Mexicans who did not. But his view of the essence of Mexico was different from the muralists'. He rightly saw the culture as fundamentally no longer Indian, but mestizo. Furthermore he upended the centuries-old view of mestizos as being intrinsically inferior to the stocks of which they were a mixture. For him, rather, mestizos were a step on the way to the *raza cósmica*, a "cosmic," or fifth, race that he predicted would develop in Latin America, combining but transcending the qualities of the four existing races (white, red, black, and yellow) to form a new and superior sort of human being.[75] While, therefore, the muralists tended to depict the Spanish conquerors negatively, as, for example, monster man-machines, Vasconcelos later produced a small laudatory biography of Cortés describing him as "creator of our nationality."[76] He declared that it was foolish to begin Spanish-American patriotism with Hidalgo's "cry of Dolores" or with Bolívar's exploits. It must be rooted in Cuauhtemoc and Atahualpa and also in its Spanish source.[77] The overriding point, nonetheless, is that both the muralists' definition of Mexican identity, and Vasconcelos's, were far from what had prevailed barely more than a decade before. There was no longer any notion that the country should strive to resemble Europe (or the United States). Whether Indian or mestizo, its cultural reference point was, and must be, internal. With the necessary local variations, other Latin American countries followed Mexico to that conclusion in due course. Since then, expectably enough, rejection of "first world" or "metropolitan" models and behaviors has waned and waxed. But Latin American countries today survey the outside world from a far more secure cultural base, and with a far firmer sense of self, than they had sixty, seventy, or eighty years ago.

IMPERIALISM REVIVED?

The nationalism that appeared in Mexico with the revolution, and which became common elsewhere in Latin America in the 1930s, was a product of the growing prominence of the mass of the people in political life. It was a useful tool for leaders wishing to marshal political backing for themselves and their programs. It was an effective social glue where the rising political weight of the majority put the old hierarchical ranking of society under strain.

Nationalism, though, was also a reaction to foreign pressures and intervention. Its appearance coincides with a rise in those pressures from around the beginning of the twentieth century, and particularly with the growing intrusiveness of the United States into Latin American affairs.

With certain signal exceptions, such as the Mexican–American War of the 1840s, the United States did not exert its weight in Latin America for most of the nineteenth century. In 1823, with the Monroe Doctrine, it had in a sense unilaterally drawn Latin America into a political enclosure of which Washington was unmistakably the dominant occupant. With the aim of forestalling Spanish attempts to recover the colonies, possibly with the help of other European powers, the doctrine pronounced that the western hemisphere was now closed to European colonization or other forms of political control; in return, the United States would not interfere in European affairs. But in fact the doctrine remained a somnolent, if not quite dead, letter for the rest of the century. The United States raised little objection, for example, to the French imposition of Maximilian on Mexico in the 1860s. Part of the reason was undoubtedly the distraction of the US Civil War at the time. But the lack of reaction in this case was not exceptional. The United States had not objected strongly to the British presence and influence in Belize and adjacent parts of eastern Nicaragua.

But with the rise of US economic and military strength after the Civil War, the inclination to direct intervention grew. One obvious target was Cuba, which was both still a colony and still, until abolition in 1886, a slave territory. By the 1880s, furthermore, Cuba (along with Puerto Rico and Santo Domingo also) was selling almost all its sugar to the United States, which, as an essentially monopoly buyer, was able to control price, and hence production levels, closely.[78] Cuba was becoming, indeed, an economic dependency of its large northern neighbor. And after the colony became engaged in 1895 in its second war of independence against Spain (the first having been fought from 1868 to 1878, with limited success in the form of increased autonomy), President McKinley's administration decided that the United States was obliged to intervene. The purpose was not so much to take control as to ensure that an independent Cuba would be able to govern itself and resist other possible interventions from Europe. Rich and prominent Cubans also called for action by the United States in the interests of restoring order. In February 1898 the battleship *Maine*, sent to protect US citizens, exploded in Havana harbor. Since the explosion had no apparent cause in the ship, blame fell on Spain. And when Spain refused to pay compensation, the United States declared war. The conflict lasted seven months or so, from late April to early December of 1898. In that time, a Spanish fleet was destroyed in the Philippines, another off Cuba, combined US and Cuban insurgent forces defeated the Spaniards on the island, and US troops occupied Puerto Rico. As a result of the war, Spain finally lost the remnants of its American empire, and most of its surviving colonies elsewhere. By the Treaty of Paris of late 1898, Puerto Rico passed to the United States, and has remained in colonial or quasi-colonial status since. The Philippines also became a US possession, until finally achieving independence in 1935 after tortuous negotiation. Cuba was placed under US military government until 1902. After then democratic self-rule began, but very much in the North American shadow. The notorious Platt Amendment of 1903 laid down the United States' authority to intervene in Cuban internal affairs, and was in force until 1934. Direct investment in sugar from the United States rose sharply, and spread to mining, tobacco, and the railway. By the 1920s the North American financial grip on Cuba was strong, and even the depression did little to weaken it.

For a blend of economic, strategic, and idealistic reasons (since the interventions were generally quite honestly seen as necessary to instill order and good government among its southern neighbors), the United States quickly expanded its reach in and around the Caribbean in the twentieth century. The United Fruit Company bought large areas of land in Guatemala, Honduras, Nicaragua, Costa Rica, Panama, Colombia, and Venezuela to grow bananas. The fruit became the leading export of several of the Central American states, and the primary buyer was the USA.[79] In 1903 the USA was instrumental in bringing about the separation of the province of Panama from Colombia, so that a canal could be built linking the Atlantic and the Pacific (as it was, between 1904 and 1914). A canal between the oceans had seemed essential, for both trading and military purposes, once US settlement of the north American west coast began in the mid-1800s.

To this assemblage of territorial and financial interests that the United States created in the islands and along the margins of the Caribbean, the term "neo-colonial," or even "neo-imperial," seems fittingly applied. British authority in Latin America in the nineteenth century has sometimes been described in the same terms. But the British influence was founded almost entirely in commerce and finance. And although the British preponderance in those for much of the century brought with it great political persuasiveness, it was a force qualitatively different from the power gained by a nation willing to send troops when diplomacy, manipulation of tariffs, blockades, and other arm twisting failed. Over the course of the twentieth century the United States sent troops into various nations of Middle America and the Caribbean. It is unlikely that the most recent of these incursions, the intervention of 1989 in Panama for the removal of the country's drug-rich military boss, Manuel Noriega, will be the last.

To Theodore Roosevelt, the president who oversaw a good part of the United States' assertion of authority over its Caribbean neighbors, Rubén Darío addressed a poem in his collection *Songs of Life and Hope (Cantos de Vida y Esperanza)* of 1905.[80] The poem reads, in part,

> You are the United States,
> Future invader of our naive America
> With its Indian blood, an America
> That still prays to Christ and still speaks Spanish...
>
> The United States is grand and powerful.
> Whenever it trembles, a profound shudder
> Runs down the enormous backbone of the Andes.
> If it shouts, the sound is like the roar of a lion.
> And Hugo said to Grant: "The stars are yours."
> (The dawning sun of Argentina barely shines;
> The star of Chile is rising...) A wealthy country,
> Joining the cult of Mammon to the cult of Hercules;
> While Liberty, lighting the path
> To easy conquest, raises her torch in New York...
>
> But our own America...
> O men with Saxon eyes and barbarous souls,
> Our America lives. And dreams. And loves.
> And it is the daughter of the Sun. Be careful.
> Long live Spanish America!
> A thousand cubs of the Spanish lion are roaming free.
> Roosevelt, you must become, by God's own will,
> The deadly Rifleman and the dreadful Hunter
> Before you can clutch us in your iron claws.
>
> And though you have everything, you are lacking one thing:
> God!

The terms of the relationship, and the Latin American view of the United States, have not changed greatly since Darío wrote these lines. For Latin America, the USA has been the "Colossus of the North," or, in the phrase used in the title of one of the many studies of inter-American relations, a "Hovering Giant" always threatening to descend with mighty political, economic, and sometimes even military force to assert its will. [81] Besides that, US popular culture, transmitted through music, film, writing, and even such apparent trivialities as fast food (epitomized by the ubiquitous McDonald's hamburger), has seemed irresistibly invasive. But the McDonald's restaurants proliferate because people choose to eat in them. Similarly, many Latin Americans find much in the politics, way of life, and culture of the USA to envy, admire, and emulate. Inconsistencies exist also in the giant's attitudes towards Latin America. Since the enunciation of the Monroe Doctrine, at the time when Latin American countries were taking their first independent steps, the USA has broadly regarded Latin America as its own sphere of interest.

Latin America has been a part of the world to be protected from external interference and harm, and guided along roads to greater well-being. That there has been a benign undercurrent in US intentions toward Latin America cannot be denied. Greater prosperity under greater democracy has been a constant goal of the USA for Latin America. Equally undeniable, however, is the clearly proprietary cast of US attitude and policy. And that has led to much highhanded action, whether diplomatic, economic, or even military. As examples given in the next chapter show, the USA has often enough acted thus, indeed over-reacted, especially when its own interests have seemed challenged. Threats to its investments in Latin America, for example, have long been likely to bring fierce retaliation in the form of political pressure and economic sanctions. It was, though, the onset of the Cold War in the mid-twentieth century, with Washington's resulting fear that Marxism would spread in Latin American countries, that gave rise to the starkest contradictions in US policies and actions in Latin America. Cruelly authoritarian and anti-democratic regimes received backing from the United States if they opposed and suppressed Communism. Like the Catholic missionaries in sixteenth-century Spanish America who were willing to use most un-Christian violence to extirpate idolatry and enforce conversion, the democratic United States, in the twentieth century, was capable of resorting to most undemocratic means of eradicating a political doctrine that it abhorred, hoping that nonetheless democracy would finally prevail.

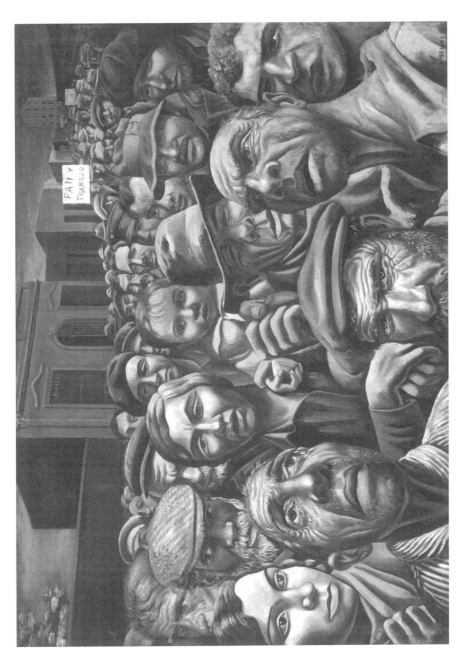

FIGURE 17.1 *Manifestación (Demonstration)*, 1934 (oil on hessian, 180 x 249.5 cm), by Antonio Berni (Argentina, 1905–81. Malba–Colección Constantini, Museo de Arte Latinoamericano de Buenos Aires).

FIGURE 17.2 Mario Vargas Llosa (Peru). One of Spanish America's two best-known novelists of the twentieth century (the other being the Colombian, Gabriel García Márquez). Photo © Geraint Lewis / REX

FIGURE 17.3 Latin American industrialization at its most successful: the Brazilian-made Embraer RJ (regional jet) 145 – one of several models of small-to-medium sized passenger aircraft sold in large numbers by Embraer from the 1970s onward in the USA, Europe, and elsewhere. Embraer is now (2002) the fourth-largest producer of passenger aircraft in the world.

[17] *People, Politics, and Economies Since 1930*

Rising Numbers

In the twentieth century, the population of Latin America underwent its most dramatic change since the sixteenth, growing from 59.6 million in 1900 to 473.4 million in 1996. This almost eight-fold increase is on the same scale of magnitude as the perhaps ten-fold decline that took place among, for instance, the native people of central Mexico and of Peru in the century or so after the arrival of the Spaniards. Latin America's population grew more between 1930 and 1990 than did that of any other large region of the world, except Africa. Until late in the twentieth century, the increase took place at an increasing rate. So, for example, the population in 1930 (102.8 million) was 1.73 times greater than that of 1900, while the total in 1963 (222.4 million) was 2.16 times larger than it had been in 1930, and that of 1996, 2.13 times bigger than the number in 1963. The four countries with most people in 1900 still headed the list in 1996:

Country	Population (in millions)	
	1900	1996
Argentina	4.61	35.22
Brazil	17.98	157.87
Colombia	3.89	35.63
Mexico	13.61	96.58
Total	40.09	325.30

The fraction of the total population of Latin America living in these four countries also stayed much the same from the beginning to the end of the century: 67.3 percent in 1900, and 68.7 percent in 1996.[1]

Natural increase (an excess of births over deaths) was the main reason for what can truly be called a population explosion. The increase was boosted until about 1930 by a continuation of the massive immigration into some countries that had started in the 1870s. The immigrants were mostly from southern Europe: Italians, Spaniards, and Portuguese. The numbers of people who arrived and stayed were as follows:

To	1881–1900	1901–20	1921–30
Brazil	993,400	823,400	486,100
Argentina + Uruguay + Chile	1,292,000	2,079,400	1,206,000
Totals	2,285,400	2,902,800	1,692,100

The four countries shown in the table were the main destinations for immigrants. A large number also went to Cuba: a net total of 596,100 people between 1902 and 1930, 58 percent of them from Spain and most of the rest from Haiti and Jamaica.[2] Other Latin American countries received far fewer newcomers than these five.

It was, though, mostly the fact that more people were being born than were dying, and that those who were born lived on average increasingly long lives, that accounts for the population boom of twentieth-century Latin America. The crude birth rate – the number of live births per thousand of population – remained high in most countries until the 1970s, at between 40 and 50; only after then did a decline begin that led to rates of between 20 and 30 per thousand by the mid 1990s. (For comparison, the birth rate in the USA in the mid-nineties was about 15.)[3]

While birth rates (fertility) stayed high, however, rates of death (mortality) began to fall. Children born in Latin America around 1930 could expect to live for an average of some thirty-five years. By the early 1980s, life expectancy had generally increased to sixty-five or more. The numbers naturally varied from place to place. In the richer countries (Argentina and Chile, for example) mortality was far below the Latin American average in 1930, and the typical life therefore longer. Those differences have persisted, but are now much less marked. That has come about because the conditions that led to falling mortality in those richer countries became more widespread across Latin America, particularly after the mid-century. The conditions in question were largely those of public health, including the wider availability of clean water supplies, extension of sanitation systems, campaigns against disease-carrying insects, and inoculation of growing numbers of people against diseases such as smallpox, diphtheria, and typhoid.[4]

As mortality dropped, fertility remained high, and the broadening gap between the two rates produced, until the 1970s, the fastest population growth in Latin America's history. By the early eighties, though, fertility had also clearly fallen. By 1980–5, a Latin American woman of child-bearing age (15–49 years) could be expected to give birth, on average, to 3.9 children. Only twenty years earlier (1960–5) that average had been 6.0.[5] The number of children being born in Latin America, per potential mother, had dropped in twenty years by a third.

How to account for this dramatic change? One broad shift underlying it may have been a "demographic transition" comparable to what happened in nineteenth-century Europe once mortality was reduced there. Two to three decades after death rates fell, birth rates followed suit, as parents realized that children were increasingly less likely to fall prey to previously common diseases; hence fewer children "needed" to be born. Reinforcing the parents' choice of fewer children may well also have been the realization that a larger family would threaten the rise in living standard that ever more people were enjoying as the prosperity brought by industrialization spread through society.[6] Both conditions (reduction in disease and material gains from industrialization) were present in much of Latin America by the 1970s, favoring a demographic transition. That change had taken place earlier in the twentieth century in a few, richer countries (notably Argentina, Chile, Uruguay, and Cuba), and their birth rates dropped accordingly well before the 1970s.

More specific explanations can, though, be found for the striking fall of fertility in the 1970s. One was increased use of reliable contraceptive methods, such as the birth-control pill and sterilization. (These added to the effects of abortion, which, though generally illegal in Latin America, was nevertheless remarkably common, being estimated to have ended 300 of every 1,000 pregnancies in 1974.)[7] Awareness and use of contraception grew in the seventies as more governments, including those of Mexico and Brazil, created policies and programs for population control. These had been slow in arriving because of a variety of objections to birth control: the traditional Catholic opposition, and frequently a sense that limiting population was an affront to national status. Quite possibly, however, the most powerful influence tending to reduce fertility was that ever more women were being educated, and to an increasingly higher level. It may well be, world-wide, that the strongest predictor of falling fertility is women's education. The educated woman is more likely to be aware of contraception, and confident in using it. She is also more likely to work gainfully outside the home, and may well be unwilling to give up such opportunities in order to have a large number of children. Education and work may well lead her to delay marrying, and hence have fewer fertile years in her marriage. In recent decades, rising numbers of women across Latin America have received schooling, and to higher levels. Between the mid-seventies and the mid-nineties, for instance, the percentage of females enrolled at the secondary level grew in many countries by 20 to 30 percent.[8] The consequence of the resulting downward pressure on fertility, and other such pressures, has been that the population of Latin America, while still growing, was at the century's end strikingly smaller than earlier calculations had projected it would be. One serious estimate, made by CELADE (the Latin American Center for Demography) as late as 1972, put the probable total in 1995 at 558.7 million, and in 2000 at 637.2 million.[9] The actual population in 1996, as already stated, was 473.4 million.

The racial or ethnic composition of this population is now hard to specify because national censuses have largely stopped showing such distinctions among individuals. That those differences are no longer recorded shows how far genetic and ethnic mixing has proceeded in most of Latin America. If in the eighteenth century it was already impossible to describe individuals' genetic heritage accurately from their appearance, so that census takers and parish scribes resorted to broad descriptions such as mestizo or mulatto, by the mid-twentieth even those wide categories had disappeared in most places. Further and constant mixing had produced greater homogenization of color and features; in some countries mixing had come to be seen as desirable rather than degrading, so that there was ideological reason to stop recording it. Now, in any case, in those regions that once held developed native cultures, or to which large numbers of African slaves were imported, most people are the product of the mingling of one, or both, of those genetic streams with the one coming from Europe, consisting both of settlers in colonial times and immigrants later on. (The migration from Asia, smaller but influential in particular regions, should not be overlooked: Chinese to Peru and Cuba in the nineteenth century; Japanese also to Peru, but mainly to Brazil, in the twentieth.) Traces persist – sometimes strongly – of old distinctions. Lighter skin color and fairer hair are almost everywhere considered desirable, and are socially advantageous. But the broad reality of racial and ethnic mixture as distinctively Latin American is accepted by most, and welcomed by many.

That said, the survival of large numbers of indigenous people in a few areas has to be noted. (The standard identifying mark of such people is that their primary language is one of the native tongues.) The areas where they are found correspond closely to the heartlands of the most advanced pre-Columbian cultures: central and southern Mexico, northern Central America, and the Andes in Ecuador, Peru, and Bolivia. According to 1980s' national censuses, Bolivia had some 2.8 million native people, making up 54 percent of the total population; Guatemala, 2.3 million (42%); Mexico, 5.2 million (9%); and Peru, 3.6 million (25%). A non-census estimate for Ecuador put the number there in 1980 at 3.1 million (30% of the total). Far smaller numbers were also present in Argentina, Brazil, Chile, Colombia, Costa Rica, El Salvador, Honduras, Nicaragua, Panama, Paraguay, and Venezuela.[10] That Indians are still so widely present, and in fact slowly growing in numbers, is more the outcome of the resilience of their cultures than of policies favorable to them over the almost two centuries that have passed since independence.

The almost eight-fold demographic growth that Latin America experienced over the twentieth century as a whole was an imposing change. While growth on this scale is not as shocking as the immense drop in the native populations in the sixteenth century, and will not have long-term outcomes of similar consequence, such vast and rapid increase could not but alter many aspects of Latin American life. It meant, for example, that for much of the century countries had very large proportions of children in their populations, who contributed little or nothing to national economic products while being a source of constant pressure on educational systems and other social services. Growing populations constantly strained economic resources, particularly those of land and the agriculture that took place on it. Indeed, people born in rural areas where there was little or no cultivable land left for them to work had little choice but to move away. Migration from the land was certainly among the most notable of social phenomena in twentieth-century Latin America. People typically moved to towns and cities. But many of them could not afford to live inside existing city limits, and so formed shanty settlements around the edges. In this informal and often illegal way, mid-

and late-twentieth-century Latin America gained some of the world's most populous cities (Mexico City, São Paulo, and Buenos Aires, for example) while becoming ever more urban. In 1930 only some 17 percent of the population lived in towns of 20,000 or more; by 1980 that fraction had grown to 65 percent, and still rises.[11] Migrants also, of course, might move beyond national borders, when conditions abroad seemed attractive enough. Examples include Bolivians going to Argentina, Central Americans to Mexico, and, of course, Mexicans to the USA.

ECONOMIC CHANGES

Less obvious than migration, but important, has been the broad economic outcome of high population growth in helping to perpetuate inequalities of income and wealth in Latin America. The constantly abundant supply of labor has tended to depress the wages of the great majority. In doing so, it has made upward social mobility more difficult, and hence preserved the existing social stratification. The persistence of economic inequality is one of Latin America's most obvious failures in the twentieth century. It is especially so because, contrary to widespread views, the economic performance of nearly all Latin American countries over the century was in fact good. Except in times of economic crisis, such as the early 1930s and the 1980s (and excessive attention to these difficult periods may well have given an unduly negative impression of the general performance), Latin America did well, judging by the standard broad measures of economic achievement. There was no period of more than a few years in the twentieth century in which the gross domestic product of Latin America, taken as a unit, failed to grow. The same can be said of individual countries.[12] Over the entire century, the combined GDP of Latin American countries rose at more than four percent a year on average, a rate of sustained economic growth that would be considered remarkably high in current developed and industrialized countries. For three decades or more after the end of the World War II – a period of high economic growth almost everywhere in the world – the Latin American economies expanded particularly fast. Between 1950 and 1973, for example, their aggregate growth rate was 5.2 percent annually, quicker than that of the developed industrial countries, at 4.8 percent, and that of most of Asia. Only the newly industrialized countries of Asia, such as Singapore, South Korea, and Taiwan did better than Latin America, though not remarkably better, with a world-leading growth rate of 5.7 percent annually in that 1950–73 period.[13]

Furthermore, Latin American economic growth in the twentieth century outpaced even the high rate of population growth, so that on average the economic condition of individuals improved. From about 1928 until 1980 the average improvement in per capita income was 2.1 percent a year – a distinctly respectable figure – with high rates (among the big countries) being found in Venezuela, Brazil and Mexico (3.6, 2.9, and 2.6 percent respectively) and low rates in Chile and Argentina (1.3 and 1.2 percent). (The latter two entered this period, however, with far higher per capita income levels than the first three.) In the 1980s per capita income actually fell, at an average rate of 1.1 percent annually across Latin America, undoubtedly the longest period of such decline in the century; per capita growth then resumed, though slowly, in the early 1990s.[14]

For a clearer and closer view, economic affairs in Latin America since the Depression can be usefully divided into three periods: from the early thirties to the mid-century, from then until the late seventies, and from the early eighties to the end of the century. There are, naturally, continuities running through all three periods, but each has its own distinctive traits.

The first period (the 1930s and 1940s) was one of transition, in which many Latin American countries, having experienced the dislocating shock of the Depression, sought to reduce their dependence on exports. They particularly tried to change the engine of economic growth from export (of very largely primary products) to manufacture (of goods for consumption at home). This was a fundamental shift from traditional practice that was hard to accomplish, and therefore slow.

Recovery from the effects of the Depression arrived, in fact, remarkably quickly in Latin America. Beginning at different points in 1931 or 1932 in different countries, gross domestic product again started to rise, and continued to do so throughout the decade. By 1939 it had grown in eight countries by more than half, and in three others by over a fifth. The rest did less well.[15]

How to account for this economic resilience? It seems, in fact, that the jolt of the Depression served to accelerate positive changes that were already taking place. As world prices of Latin America's exports fell, from 1929, income from those exports necessarily followed suit. Foreign exchange was then clearly lacking to buy manufactured imports on the previous scale. This difficulty acted as a stimulus for growth of manufacturing within Latin America – a faster expansion of the industrialization already in place in the twenties and earlier. Manufacturing, it is true, was still largely limited to consumer goods, such as textiles and prepared foods; complex and heavy capital items still had to be bought abroad. And no country could be described as having an industrialized economy by the end of the thirties. Argentina was the only one in which manufacturing output in 1939 exceeded 20 percent of GDP (at 22.7%). It was followed on that measure by Chile (18%), Mexico (16%), Uruguay (15.9%), Brazil (14.5%), Peru (10%), and Colombia (9.1%).[16] Everywhere else, manufacturing provided a smaller fraction of the domestic product.

Governmental action helped this energizing of industry; the 1930s, indeed, saw Latin American governments becoming more active in economic matters, often to useful effect. Industry benefited from the tariffs placed on imports, and from devaluation of currencies. Both measures increased the price of imported goods, and so encouraged consumers to buy more locally-made products. With the advance of industry, and the growth of urban working populations that went with it, there came in the thirties a distinct advance towards a desirable economic situation in which internal demand would be large enough to drive growth, replacing the pattern in which growth was achieved by expanding the volume and value of exports.

Except in Argentina, however, internally-driven growth was not achieved in the 1930s. Exporting, indeed, continued to be a major component of Latin America's economy, and remained the major source of growth, especially in the smaller countries. Almost all Latin American governments continued to support sales of the traditional exports – primary products from the land and from mines. Intentional devaluation of currencies benefited exporters, and where there was not actual devaluation, governments offered exporters advantageous exchange rates. Again, demand in the world's industrialized countries for primary products from Latin America picked up in 1932–4, and generally speaking, terms of trade were more favorable to Latin America in the mid- and late thirties than they had been in the twenties. Prices of the non-consumer manufactured goods that Latin America still imported tended to have fallen from the twenties more than the prices of primary exports. The metals that various countries produced for export (gold, silver, copper, and tin) were priced relatively high by world markets as the thirties progressed. Brazil, which had the highest increase in export volume (10.2 percent annually, 1932–9) overcame weak coffee prices by moving quickly and strongly to the production and export of cotton. The United States, despite the Depression, remained the main buyer of Latin American exports, though with a slightly falling share. In the late thirties Latin American exports to Germany grew.

The economic trends of the thirties in Latin America persisted through the next decade. Broad economic growth continued, as did per capita growth (with a tendency to be stronger in the larger countries). The share of industry in the total output of the economies grew still further. Whereas in 1939 Argentina had been the only country in which industry yielded more than 20 percent of output, by 1950 that level had been reached or passed also by Brazil (21%), Chile (23%), Cuba (26%), and Uruguay (20%); and Mexico was close, at 19%.[17] Exporting continued to be strong, however, in part because World War II created higher demand for various primary items, such as metals. Although the war made for difficulties in exporting to Europe, increased sales from Latin America to the United States more than compensated. The United States, indeed, became more deeply involved in Latin American economic affairs than ever before during the war. It became now practically the sole source of external finance. It sent advisory missions to various countries, some of them with the aim of pressing for the development of heavier, more basic, industry than had existed before. At the same time, because fewer imports of any sort could be had during the war years from the industrialized countries, Latin American manufacture of consumer products necessarily expanded, providing substitutes for what had previously been imported; and trade in manufactures among Latin American states became a significant part of their external commercial relations for the first time.[18]

All this continued essentially unchanged in the years immediately after the war. Primary exports thrived, with demand for them rising as the combatant countries recovered, and then, in the early fifties, as the new conflict in Korea began. Terms of trade became notably more positive for Latin America, with particularly buoyant world prices of oil and minerals after 1945 benefiting Venezuela and Mexico, and strong demand for coffee and other foods working to the advantage of Brazil and others.[19] And manufacture remained on its rising track. Whereas, though, manufacturing had expanded up to this time more as a result of economic circumstances (primarily the difficulty of paying for imports after the Depression, and later the simple difficulty of obtaining them during the war) than of policy, now, in the mid-century, it became the object of planned stimulation. This active governmental promotion of industry in Latin America is closely associated with the ideas of Raúl Prebisch, an Argentine economist, and with the appearance of the Economic Commission for Latin America (ECLA), an agency of the United Nations founded in 1948 in which Prebisch was the leading theorist. He, in the late 1940s, began to think of Latin America's position in the global economy as the outcome of the relationship between the Center (the rich industrialized countries) and the Periphery (the poorer countries, whose existence depended heavily on their exports of primary products to the Center). The duality of Center and Periphery (often Center *versus* Periphery) has since then been a constant in much thinking about the economic working of the world. Among Prebisch's influential ideas were the following. In the economies of the Center, technological advances (which were constantly being made) resulted less in lower prices of the goods produced than in higher wages for the workers who made them. Hence the benefits of technology were retained in the Center; the price paid by the Periphery for goods bought from the Center did not fall. By contrast, workers' wages in the Periphery generally tended to fall, because a surplus of labor often existed there. This was particularly so when agriculture in the Periphery was made more efficient by modernization; then it needed fewer workers than before, and the average rural wage dropped. Further, within the Center economic hegemony (i.e. power) had shifted, between the mid-nineteenth century and the mid-twentieth, from Europe (especially Great Britain) to the United States. And the United States had a lower propensity to import primary products than Europe had had, because the United States was able to grow a larger proportion of its own food than Europe could (while also possessing large reserves of minerals, including oil, within its borders). Hence the Periphery had difficulty in achieving balanced trade with the USA; what it could offer in exchange for industrial imports were goods that the USA might not particularly need. That imbalance boded ill for Latin America's terms of trade with the Center.[20]

Prebisch's proposed solution was that Latin America should now itself industrialize as a matter of economic strategy, with far more planning and support of manufacture by governments than before. The growth of industry that had already been under way for several decades thus received a boost from economic theory, and accelerated. It also acquired a formal name: import substitute industrialization (ISI); though in reality providing locally-made substitutes for previously imported items was what industry had always done in Latin America. A better term for the broad economic aim now pursued, above all in the larger countries, is perhaps "inward-directed industrialization" or even "inward-directed development" (in contrast to the export-led growth of earlier times).

For more than twenty years this inward focus of economic policy proved a positive strategy for Latin America. The period from 1950 to the early seventies was one of economic vigor for almost all countries around the world, and Latin America certainly gained from that general expansion. But its economies performed exceptionally well as a whole, reaching GDP growth rates of 5.1 percent annually (1950–60) and 5.9 percent (1960–73), while for the whole period 1950–73, the growth rate in the world's industrialized economies was lower, at 4.8 percent annually. In Latin America's growth, expansion of manufacturing had a leading part. Industrial output rose, across Latin America, at 6.6 percent per year in the 1950s, and 7.3 percent yearly in the 1960s. Those increases led to a rising share of manufacture in total production: 18.4% in 1950, 21.3% in 1960, 24.0% in 1970 (and 25.4% in 1980). To be more specific, by 1970 almost a third of Brazil's GDP came from industry, about a quarter of Argentina's and Chile's, and more than a fifth of Colombia's, Mexico's, and Peru's.[21] Meanwhile, even though terms of trade became less favorable for Latin America, as Prebisch had foreseen, the general world economic boom meant that Latin American exports continued to rise. In the fifties, almost all exports were still of primary goods; but in the early sixties manufactures became a noticeable, and growing, component of overseas sales.

As manufacturing grew in the fifties and sixties, the goods produced expanded not only in quantity but in range. In most countries, the emphasis up to then had been, as for many decades past, on processing foods and making non-durable consumer items such as textiles and clothing. Now came a move to durable consumer goods, such as machinery for household use, and cars, and then beyond that to intermediate and capital goods – the materials, tools, machinery, and equipment needed to enable further manufacture to take place. By 1970 items such as the following were being produced in many Latin American countries: thread, cloth, cigarettes, cement, fertilizers, industrial chemicals (such as caustic soda), paper pulp (and paper), pig iron, steel (crude, rolled, bars, rods, and wire), televisions, tires, and cars, buses and trucks. Naturally the heavier and more complex items were mainly produced in the larger economies. About 87 percent of the cars and 86 percent of the commercial vehicles made in 1970, for instance, were made in Brazil, Argentina, and Mexico. The smaller and poorer countries produced none.[22]

The industrialization that took place from the 1950s onwards did not happen, and could not, without the support of governmental policy. The problems that had dogged Latin American manufacture since its nineteenth-century origins were still very much present. Even in the large countries, the market for goods remained small, when compared with the home markets of the mature industrialized countries of the world; hence economies of scale in manufacture were rarely available. And economy in manufacture was also generally reduced by the lower level of technology existing in Latin America (in comparison with those same industrialized countries). If industry was to grow, therefore, it must be favored and protected. Governments in the fifties and sixties provided help in various ways: by placing high tariffs on imported manufactured items that would compete with what was now produced at home, so that the imports became expensive; by setting import quotas for imports, so that they were scarce (and therefore dear); by ruling that foreign companies manufacturing in Latin America must use a certain percentage of locally made parts in their final products; and by artificially adjusting currency exchange rates to raise the effective price of imports (and also to lower the price of exports to make them more competitive). Governments sometimes also provided direct subsidies for new industry, or went still further, creating state-owned companies to accelerate industrialization, particularly in the case of basic inputs essential to manufacture, such as electricity, oil products, and steel.

The money that governments put into such companies indeed made up a good part of the very large investment required for industrialization. In the 1960s, for example, public investment – money spent by governments – constituted between a half and a third of all capital formation in Latin America. A high rate of investment was indeed one of the outstanding features of that dynamic decade for Latin American economies. Investment grew at 9 percent annually, so that total investment in 1973 was more than three times higher than in 1960. For the longer period 1950–81, the average annual growth of investment was 7.4 percent. As would be expected, countries with the highest rates of investment growth, notably Brazil and Mexico, also achieved the highest increases of GDP. What was particularly notable about investment in these decades (in contrast to much of the earlier history of capital formation in Latin America) was that most of the funds invested were not from abroad, but raised domestically. That was particularly so in the 1950s, when Latin America had little access to international money markets. In the sixties, it is true, inflows from abroad rose, partly in the form of multinational corporations building plants in Latin America or buying existing companies, and partly as long-term official loans and credits coming from the USA, Japan, and Europe. The sixties were the decade of the Alliance for Progress, a set of policies put into effect by the United States in 1961 to advance democracy and political stability in Latin America. Political change of that sort would be more likely to happen if wealth increased (and were more equally distributed). Hence, under the Alliance, the United States provided funding for economic diversification and growth of infrastructure in Latin America. This was also the time when the Inter-American Development Bank was established: it began its appointed task of furthering economic and social development in the Americas in 1960. But despite the growing availability of funds from these and other overseas sources, investment from domestic sources continued to dominate, still making up three-quarters, or more, of the total in 1981.[23]

Greater economic internationalization of Latin America did, however, occur in these decades in a new and particular fashion. This was the creation of regional economic groupings of countries designed to resolve the problem of inefficiently small markets. Forming groups of countries, with reduction or elimination of tariffs within the group, would provide larger domestic markets for industry, while also improving efficiency in production, as industries in the various countries within each group became obliged to compete directly with each other. Four major organizations were created: the Central American Common Market, in 1960; the Latin American Free Trade Association (comprising Mexico, Brazil, and all of Spanish-speaking South America), also in 1960; the Andean Common Market (Bolivia, Colombia, Chile, Ecuador, and Peru), in 1969; and the Caribbean Free Trade Association, in 1968. Success with these innovative economic units was mixed. Trade within Latin America certainly did increase as a result of their existence – particularly trade of manufactures. And the new arrangements stimulated industrial production, as hoped. But the larger economies benefited more than the middling and small ones, some producers protested against the creation of large economic regions, continuing to prefer the comfort of monopoly within their own domestic markets and foreign economic interests objected to the formation of large, tariff-protected blocs. For these and other reasons, integration was less complete than originally intended, and the benefits somewhat smaller.[24] Still, the creation of regional markets was clearly something new in Latin American economic history, and also something rather striking in Latin American history generally, given the almost complete separateness of the countries of Middle and South America after the failure of Bolívar's attempt to create a greater Colombia in the 1820s.

(In 1991 a further regional market group came into being, with the creation of the *Mercado Común del Sur* – the "Common Market of the South" – generally known by its abbreviation *Mercosur*. This brought together Argentina, Brazil, Paraguay, and Uruguay in a union of lowered tariffs and coordinated economic policy. Chile joined the group in 1996. *Mercosur* immediately became the largest trading block in Latin America: 190 million people, 55% of Latin America's GDP, and 55% of its industrial trade. In the years after the foundation of the group, the aim of increasing trade among the members was achieved.[25])

If regional integration has received mixed judgments, so also has the inward-directed development of which it was a part. There can be very little doubt that the inward economic focus, with the attendant accent on industrialization, that prevailed from about 1950 brought about an acceleration of economic growth, and thus raised the average per capita income in Latin America. As is true of any set of policies, the inward focus could certainly have been better applied and managed. Protection of industry has, for example, been criticized as excessive, with the result that manufacturers in Latin America (whether native or branches of foreign companies) became fat and lazy. Tariffs, subsidies, and import quotas guaranteed them high profits and little competition. Hence there were few incentives for efficiency, or for research to improve products. The result was that consumers in Latin America paid ever higher prices for goods that were often of poor quality and out of date in design and construction. For the same reasons, the full export potential for Latin American manufactures was not reached. The growth of government-run enterprises exacerbated the already strong Latin American tendency to bureaucratization. Borrowing in the 1960s by governments to fund new state industries resulted in expansion of the money supply in various countries, and hence in inflation. Generally speaking, investment in industry was excessively stressed and investment in agriculture consequently neglected, so that the production of food and other agricultural goods for both home consumption and exports suffered. With the potential for exports less than fully realized, foreign income was lacking to import new technology and necessary capital goods (this adding to the technological lag already resulting from inadequate research).[26] It could also be said that while the post-1950 inward focus certainly reduced Latin America's economic dependency on the industrialized countries – since many manufactured imports were now replaced by local products, and, even more impressively, most of the investment needed to create new industries was locally raised – nonetheless technological dependency still remained. But that criticism is perhaps excessive: the scientific and technological gap between Latin America and the industrial countries was too wide, and too deep in its origins, to be eliminated in a few decades.

The accumulating drawbacks of inward-directed development grew more apparent as the 1970s progressed. In that decade the share of industry in GDP rose less than it had in the fifties and sixties, and GDP itself grew more slowly. Then, in the early eighties, economic events moved quickly to force the majority of Latin American countries that for thirty years had pursued inward-directed economic advance to abandon that focus, and to turn once again to expanding their exports to the rest of the world.

This quick, indeed dramatic, shift back to an older economic pattern and purpose had its origin in external events in the 1970s. In 1973 the Organization of Petroleum Exporting Countries (OPEC), which then controlled most of world oil production, raised the price of crude oil fourfold. Further increases followed later in the decade, notably in 1979. The immediate outcome in Latin America of these upward price jumps was gain for the countries that exported oil (notably Venezuela, Mexico, and Ecuador), and loss for those that imported it (almost all the rest). Brazil – the largest country, with a by-now rather highly industrialized economy – suffered severely from the high cost of imported oil. In 1983, 54 percent of its payments for imports went to buying oil.

A second effect of higher oil prices, ultimately more damaging for Latin America, was the borrowing of money on international markets that many of the countries indulged in during the second half of the seventies. Much money was available for lending. The income of the OPEC countries had multiplied faster than they could use it internally, and they therefore deposited vast sums in private banks in various of the industrialized countries of the world. The banks actively sought to lend these deposits. Their efforts were successful: by 1980, they held 80 percent of Latin America's foreign debt.[27] They had been helped in placing so many large loans by the internationalization of banking that had come about by the mid-1970s. Capital could now flow around the world more quickly, and with fewer restrictions, than ever before. Almost all Latin American countries chose to take advantage of this easy availability of capital, both to pay for the increasingly expensive oil and to maintain industrialization and economic expansion ("debt-led growth" is a name sometimes given to this choice of policy). Such was the abundance of funds around the world that borrowing was extremely cheap. Borrowing even had the apparently paradoxical effect of driving interest rates still lower, since as countries received loans, their reserves of foreign currency rose, with the effect of strengthening their own currencies. Thus real interest rates actually became negative for several years after 1973: a country could profit simply by taking loans, since the true cost of repayment was less than the value of the sum originally borrowed. It was, many naturally thought, foolish not to borrow in such circumstances. The sums that flowed into Latin America were enormous. In 1971–3, the total inflow of capital was US$ 9.1 billion; in 1974–7 (immediately after the rise in oil prices), US$ 25 billion; and in 1978–81, US$ 38 billion.[28]

By 1980–1 almost all Latin America was awash in borrowed money. The abundance was often unwisely used. Governments and companies over-invested in large, expensive projects. Military regimes seized the chance for unnecessary updating of national arsenals. As the inflow of loans drove up the value of national currencies, export of money, particularly to the United States, for investment or simply safer deposit, became common. Some of this exported money was simple domestic savings. Overvaluation of currencies depressed exports. Imports of all sorts swelled in volume and value. Governments, well supplied with loans, had little incentive to address the key question of tax reform. Latin American countries remained generally undertaxed, to the advantage of the rich and the disadvantage of government. Both governments and private companies neglected to economize in their operations and keep them efficient.

Few, however, it seems – whether Latin American governments, foreign creditor banks, or expert international bodies like the World Bank – saw the developing danger of the borrowing countries' constantly falling capacity to repay their debts. When that realization did ultimately come, in the summer of 1982, the result was a crisis, more devastating and longer-lasting in its effects for Latin America than even the crash of 1929. The blow fell first on Mexico, which was by then the largest producer of oil in Latin America, and which had therefore suffered from the decline in the price of oil that had finally begun, after so many years of increase, in 1981. Finding its foreign reserves dwindling fast, Mexico in August 1982 announced that for ninety days it would make no payments on the principal of its external public debt. The suspension of payment was soon extended into 1983.[29] Suddenly, to the eager lenders of the past several years, all Latin America looked a bad risk; they began to demand quick repayment. The borrowers' difficulties were aggravated by the quick jump in interest rates that took place in the USA in the early eighties. Loans that had been free or even intrinsically profitable in the late seventies now became expensive. Lenders wanted their principal back, in the near future, and with substantial interest.

To make those repayments, most Latin American countries were in essence forced, for the rest of the decade, to transfer to their foreign creditors money that would otherwise have been spent within their own boundaries. A large net transfer of wealth occurred to the lenders' countries, principally the USA, but also Britain and others. The result was that most of Latin America became poorer (for briefer or longer periods, according to the country). Nearly all its countries went through two or more years in the 1980s in which their GDPs fell. The average yearly growth rate of GDP across Latin America in that decade was a mere 1 percent, in severe contrast with the 5–6 percent annual growth of the preceding decades. And since populations were still increasing at more than 1 percent annually, income per person necessarily fell. Even in the mid-1990s it was still lower than its 1980 figure. In 1983, for example, GDP per capita was at only 91.3 percent of the 1980 level, in 1985, 92.7 percent, and in 1994–5, 95.8 percent. The debt crisis therefore produced the longest period of shrinking individual wealth suffered by Latin Americans in the twentieth century. Real wages (earnings measured by their actual purchasing power) fell on average, by 17 percent from 1982 to 1984, and inequality of income increased almost everywhere. Governments had to cut spending on social services, such as education and health; it dropped by some 10 percent from 1982 to 1986. Unemployment rose, as did the numbers of the poor. The fraction of poor households among all households increased from 35 percent in 1980 to 41 percent in 1990; in 1995 the percentage was still 39.[30]

The most obvious means available to governments of finding money with which to service the suddenly overwhelming debts was to cut imports. Funds that had previously bought goods from abroad now went to pay principal and interest. Imports were reduced by direct controls and also by devaluation of currencies, which made them less affordable to local buyers. Devaluation should also have produced a surge in exports, by making them cheaper abroad, but this desirable effect was reduced by weakness of overseas demand in the eighties for Latin America's primary products. Devaluation, by increasing the price of imports, also tended to increase inflation. People on fixed incomes, or, even worse, newly out of work, particularly suffered from this. A further cause of inflation was the fall in governments' tax income that resulted from the contraction of economies. To meet that difficulty some governments resorted to printing more money – a measure almost bound to be inflationary. A striking case of this was Bolivia, where in mid-1985 prices were rising at an annual rate of 20,000 percent;[31] to send an ordinary airmail letter from Bolivia to the United States at that time required half a million pesos' worth of stamps.

Clearly, "debt-led growth" had proved to be a disastrous failure. The policy yielded growth, in fact, only for a few years in the late seventies and early eighties; after that it resulted in lasting economic stagnation, accompanied by the impoverishment of most Latin Americans. It also left most of Latin America with a millstone of long-term financial obligation around its neck, since, although countries renegotiated their debts from the late eighties onward, lightening the terms of repayment in various ways, they were left owing enormous sums – sums that indeed still grew, thanks to interest charges and new loans taken to service the old ones. In 1996, for instance, the total amount owed by Latin America to foreign creditors was an estimated US$ 612 billion, up from $419 billion in 1990 and 382 billion in 1985. By then, renewed economic growth meant that, for most countries, foreign debt was falling as a proportion of national product. But the cost of paying interest and installments on the debts was still rising in several cases (including the biggest economies) as a percentage of exports. In 1996, for example, the cost of Argentina's debt service was 44% of the value of its exports (up from 37% in 1990); for Brazil, 41% (up from 22%); and for Mexico, 35% (up from 21%).[32] A large part of what these countries earned by exporting, therefore, was going to service loans instead of buying foreign goods that directly or indirectly would have benefited the populations.

The debt crisis brought about deep changes in economic policy in Latin America – changes that persisted into the new century. Many governments, often under the influence of foreign economic theorists (particularly in the United States) and pressure from foreign lenders (above all, powerful bodies such as the International Monetary Fund), now took measures to open their economies, to a greater or lesser degree, to the free play of market forces. This was a retreat from the governmental intervention in economic life that had so greatly expanded in the wake of the Depression in the 1930s, and a readoption of the economics of liberalism that had prevailed in Latin America in the nineteenth century. "Neo-liberalism," indeed, was the term often applied to this new ordering of things economic. The broad intention and hope, central to this sort of policy since its origins in Adam Smith, was that the more freely markets (both domestic and international) were allowed to work, the more efficient economies would become; and high efficiency, in turn, would maximize gains to those economies and the people within them. Restoring liberal economics seemed, then, to be the quickest means of escaping from the burden of debt and of once more raising the rate of economic growth. In practice, neo-liberalism meant such changes as reducing or eliminating tariffs on foreign trade; "privatization" – the selling off of government-owned enterprises (such as utility companies, telephone systems, and airlines) to private buyers, either national or foreign; and emphasizing commerce with the rest of the world more than with trading groups within Latin America (which now tended to be seen as limiting the full potential of free market economics). In the 1990s financial reform was added to liberalization, in an attempt to improve the working of banks and capital markets in various countries.[33]

By the first half of the 1990s, Latin America was once more growing economically; GDP rose at an annual rate of 3.3 percent between 1990 and 1996. By 1990 exports were also rising strongly. Neo-liberal policies doubtless had some part to play in these improvements, though it is difficult to apportion credit between them and other influences, such as positive economic conditions in the rest of the world. Neo-liberalism did certainly, however, open Latin America more fully once again to external economic influences, reversing the half-century trend to inwardly-directed development, and, indeed, reviving pre-1930 economic traits. Much of export growth, for instance, consisted of primary products, such as copper from Chile, and coal from Colombia (which by this time was also benefiting from enormous illegal exports of drugs, notably cocaine). Even the apparently large manufactured exports of countries such as Brazil and Mexico consisted in part of goods that were assembled from imported components.[34] Thus Latin America continued in its dependency on unpredictable world commodity prices, and on foreign technology. Occasional signs of escape from this situation were, nonetheless, visible. One such was the great success of the Brazilian company Embraer in selling sophisticated regional jet airliners in the USA, Europe, and elsewhere.

Latin America's economic difficulties and backslidings in the last two decades of the twentieth century should not, though, be allowed to obscure its notably positive achievements before 1980: almost constant growth in most countries (except for the brief hiatus of the Depression in the early 1930s) from the start of the century; growth, moreover, for three decades or more after World War II, at a rate close to the world-record pace of the "Asian Tigers;" and growth vigorous enough until the 1980s to raise per capita average income, despite the vast increase that took place in its population.

A catch lies, however, in that "average." For while nearly all Latin Americans are better off now than their social counterparts were a century ago, the degree of gain has not been equal across social levels. Inequality of income has generally increased, leaving Latin America with some of the highest disparities of earnings in the world. The following table gives figures for some the largest Latin American economies (showing the share of total household income received by the 20% of households that earn least, and the 20% that earn most):

Country	Year	Lowest 20%	Highest 20%
Argentina	1989	4.1	52.6
Brazil	1989	2.1	67.5
Chile	1994	3.5	61.0
Mexico	1992	4.1	55.3
Peru	1994	4.9	50.4

Source: Wilkie, *Statistical Abstract*, vol. 35, table 1417; (Argentina only) Mamalakis, "Income Distribution," p. 252.

(For contrast, in the United States, in 1985, the lowest-earning fifth of households received 4.7% of total income, and the highest-earning fifth, 41.9%. Poor households did little better than those in Latin America; but the richest had a significantly lower share of the total.)

Several causes, both practical and intangible, have led to this unequal sharing of income. One that has acted powerfully to perpetuate and possibly increase it has been high population growth (especially once the growth rate accelerated in the middle decades of the mid-twentieth century). The constantly rising supply of new workers has exceeded the demand for labor, with a depressive effect on wages. This problem has been particularly clear in cities, to which enormous numbers of rural people have migrated. Out in the countryside poverty has persisted because land is still concentrated among rather few owners. In some countries (Mexico, for example, in the 1930s, Bolivia in the 1950s, and Peru for a few years after 1968), large land holdings were broken up and redistributed among peasants. But the scale of those reallocations was not big enough to have more than a passing effect on rural poverty. In Mexico, for instance, in 1960, 66 percent of landholdings were of 5 hectares or less, and occupied only 0.8 percent of all agricultural land by area, whereas a mere 1.7 percent of holdings exceeded 1,000 hectares, but made up 78 percent of the country's total farmed area.[35] Thus in the Latin American state most noted for land reform in the twentieth century, barely two decades after the largest redistributions had taken place, farm land was still heavily concentrated in large units owned by a few people. It might be wondered, of course, whether land redistribution, however desirable for reasons of social justice, could possibly have been carried out on a large enough scale to remove poverty from rural areas, given, once more, the population surge of the twentieth century.

Concentration of land in few hands has, of course, a long history in Latin America, and is generally seen as an inheritance from colonial times. While it is certainly true that the great estate, the *hacienda de campo*, was a colonial creation, particularly of the eighteenth century, it was heavily reinforced as an institution in the nineteenth. Liberal laws made the land of corporations, notably the church and Indian communities, available to existing or aspiring estate owners. And the export boom decades showed that rural *haciendas* could be profitable as never before. Unequal distribution of land, therefore, and the inequalities of income that follow from it, are as much a product of decisions taken after Independence as of conditions carrying over from colonial times. It is similarly arguable that the social attitudes embodied in positivism and social Darwinism (both of them sets of ideas adopted in Latin America in the export boom era) worked in the twentieth century to sustain notions that societies contained naturally superior and naturally inferior groups. Those persisting notions, in turn, may well have worked in various ways to promote income differentials – to make the rich believe that they were rightly and deservedly rich, and the poor justly poor. Hence governments may have invested less than they might have in social services for the mass of the population, such as education and health. Such underinvestment, it has been argued, resulted in people unprepared and unfit for anything but the simplest work, and that, in turn, led to continued low wages at the bottom of society.[36]

Nonetheless, it still has to be said that inequalities of income (and therefore of wealth) were to some degree offset by social spending in the twentieth century, as the increasing length of Latin Americans' lives, already mentioned, would suggest. (By 1995 average life expectancy for a new-born in Latin America was 69, only seven years less than in the USA.) Governments spent on education, health, retirement payments, and other social benefits, though programs were often inefficiently run and unequally applied. Except in their funding of education, which was generally directed at entire populations, governments tended to apply social spending piecemeal, granting benefits (for, say, medical treatment or pensions) first to groups that had some political or economic influence, such as employees of state bureaucracies, or union members. Only gradually did social spending extend, therefore, to those in the lowest layers of society – those who needed it most. And the rural poor were generally left to last, usually having even less leverage with governments than the self-employed and unemployed dwellers of cities and shanty-towns. Nonetheless, numbers of medical personnel and hospital beds increased faster than the size of populations, making medical attention broadly more available with time, and increasing standard of living and longevity across the breadth of societies. Education for all, at least at the primary level, was generally made compulsory, and free, by the 1940s. The result was some acceleration of the already rising rates of literacy across Latin America. In 1920 some 59% of Latin Americans were considered illiterate; in 1950, 42%; in 1970, 28%; and in 1995, 13.6%. It is striking that rates of school enrollment, literacy, infant mortality, and life expectancy continued to improve, though at a slower pace, during and after the debt crisis of the 1980s, despite severe cuts in social spending. The reasons may well be continued momentum from earlier decades (when, for instance, large numbers of medical staff were trained), the arrival of cheaper and better medical techniques, and more efficient use of the reduced funding.[37]

The following basic measurements give some indication of Latin America's economic and social standing in the world at the end of the twentieth century. The figures are largely self-explanatory, but the low levels of illiteracy in Latin America and the Caribbean are notable. Latin American efforts in the education of women are apparent in the closeness of the male and female illiteracy rates.

1999	Population % growth rate	Life expectancy at birth	Per capita income (US$)	% adult (i.e. 15+) illiteracy
Latin America & the Caribbean	1.5	69.8	3,640	male 11.0 female 12.8
East Asia & the Pacific	1.1	69.0	1,010	male 8.4 female 21.5
Sub-Saharan Africa	2.5	46.8	490	male 31.1 female 47.4
High income OECD countries	0.6	77.9	27,020	not available
World	1.4	66.5	4,990	male 17.5 female 31.1

Source: The World Bank Group, http://devdata.worldbank.org/external/CPProfile. Country groupings: East Asia and the Pacific – 23 countries, including China and South Korea, but excluding Japan; Sub-Saharan Africa – 48 countries, including South Africa; OECD (Organization for Economic Cooperation and Development) – 52 countries, mostly western European, with Greece, Israel, Qatar, United Arab Emirates, Iceland, Canada, USA, Japan, Australia, New Zealand, and other smaller high-income economies.

POLITICS AFTER 1930

POPULISTS

Given the rather rapid recovery of Latin American production and trade from the Depression, it seems fair to say that that great shock had more persistent and transforming effects on Latin America's politics than on its economies. Many changes of regime followed quickly from the sudden blow of 1929, and political instability remained a trait of many countries throughout the 1930s, and in some beyond that decade. Shifting patterns of governmental forms swirled across Latin America in the 1930s and 1940s, in which dictatorship, military or civilian, and democracy, electoral or controlled, combined in differing proportions.

Very broadly speaking, the Depression marked the end of oligarchies' domination of political life – the domination that had had its roots in the wealth of the export boom of the late nineteenth and early twentieth centuries. Challenges to national oligarchies were, of course, clearly present before 1930, in the form of growing middle classes and increasing organization of labor, to name only two examples. The ground was already trembling under oligarchies' feet. The Depression, with its abrupt shrinking of exports, had a far more unsettling effect. After it, the presumption no longer stood that small, rich groups existed at the top of society that possessed natural rights to dominate political life. Oligarchies did not, of course, disappear. They adapted themselves to new conditions, took in new members as new sources of wealth arose (from manufacturing, for instance), and constantly sought to exert political influence. But now they had to contend, far more seriously than before, with other groups who thought they had at least as good a claim, if not a stronger one, to a loud political say.

One such group was the swelling number of poor people born in the population explosion that was so prominent a feature of Latin America's twentieth-century history. More specifically, the enormous expansion of urban populations, particularly from the 1930s onward, produced a new political force. Those unprecedented and concentrated masses of largely poor people living in and around big cities were seen by politicians as both a challenge and an opportunity. The increase in numbers of urban dwellers merits brief emphasis with figures for some representative cities, all of them Spanish American capitals. (Where there are two figures in an entry, the first gives the population in millions, and the second shows the percentage of the national population then living in the city in question.)

	1930	1950	1970	1990
Buenos Aires	2.18	5.13 29.9%	8.31 34.7%	11.58 34.8%
Lima	0.27	1.01 13.2%	2.84 21.5%	6.50 29.1%
Mexico City	1.05	2.88 10.3%	8.74 16.6%	19.37 21.9%
Santiago (Chile)	0.70	1.33 21.9%	2.84 29.9%	4.70 35.7%

Brazilian cities saw similar changes. The population of Rio de Janeiro, for instance, went from 1.7 to 5.61 million between 1930 and 1995, and that of São Paulo from 2.58 to 18.42 million between 1950 and 1990 (growing as a fraction of the national total from 4.9% to 12.2%).[38] What is striking about these figures is that they show large cities (principally the capital cities) not only growing fast in the twentieth century, but also becoming home to an increasing share of the national populations. The reason for this was in-migration from rural areas, resulting from declining opportunities for work in the country and expanding urban employment in industry and services. Thus politicians, as the twentieth century progressed, found themselves ever more obliged to address the needs – and seek the support – of ballooning urban populations.

At the time of the Depression, the urbanization of Latin America was still in its early stages; c. 1930 only a sixth of the population lived in towns of more than twenty thousand. The urban poor were therefore only one constituency that politicians seeking to remove countries from the control of the old elites had to address. A good case in point is the appearance of the APRA party in Peru, led by a man who, judged by the length of his influence, must rank as the most prominent political figure in the country's twentieth-century history: Víctor Raúl Haya de la Torre (1895–1979). Haya was from Trujillo, the largest town on the northern coast of Peru, the son of a journalist and printer who had married rather above himself into a local landholding family. He showed an early interest in politics as a law student at the university in Trujillo, but seems to have begun acquiring his social and political radicalism only when, in 1917–18, he spent several months in the Andes as secretary to the prefect of Cuzco. There he developed a great affection for the highland Indians, and a deep sympathy for their poverty. After returning to the coast, Haya plunged into student politics at the University of San Marcos in Lima, at first taking up issues of university reform, and then, as he became aware of the industrial working population of Lima, pressing for night schools for those workers. By 1921 these "popular universities" were in action in Lima. Haya then came to national prominence in 1923 as the leader of a demonstration against the plan of the then president, Augusto B. Leguía, to dedicate Peru to the Sacred Heart of Jesus. For that effort he was exiled – moving to Mexico at the invitation of José Vasconcelos, the renowned post-Revolutionary minister of education.

It was in Mexico that Haya, in 1924, founded the American Popular Revolutionary Alliance (APRA), intended to be a pan-Latin American vehicle by which "oppressed peoples and classes" could oppose imperialism. Only in Peru, however, did APRA become a political force. There it burst onto the scene in 1931. In that year Haya lost a presidential election to Lieutenant Colonel Luis Sánchez Cerro, the man who in 1930 had led the military coup that brought Leguía's presidency to an end. APRA, nonetheless, won numerous seats in the Peruvian parliament, and became nationally prominent as an opposition to what was by now traditional in Peruvian politics: dominance of national life by a small oligarchy closely allied with foreign capital. Often, though not always, the oligarchy had been backed by the military – another traditional source of power in Peru whose permanent hostility APRA now quickly earned. First APRA resisted Sánchez Cerro's attempts to suppress the party by staging a revolt in 1932, centered on Trujillo, in which army officers were killed; then, the next year, a member of APRA assassinated Sánchez Cerro.

The Trujillo rising attracted to APRA many workers from the sugar estates of the north coast – a rural proletariat that had appeared once traditional sugar raising in the north became an agribusiness in the late nineteenth century. The estates, well supplied with national and foreign capital, expanded to occupy small farms, leaving country people little choice but to work in sugar, on the owners' terms. APRA sought, with considerable success over the following decades, to draw such people under its umbrella, along with Indians in the Andes, and the rising numbers of industrial poor in the coastal towns. In the early 1930s Manuel Seoane, a Lima journalist who was one of APRA's central figures, announced that "Basically we aspire to the liberation of our human capital, the worker... from the economic slavery that weighs on him." Seoane went on, "Our true capital is not only the Peruvian citizen but also the riches of our soil, which is also enslaved. The principal Peruvian products, our copper, petroleum, cotton and sugar, are monopolized by imperialistic enterprises or by creole minorities who exploit and tax the country without giving it any benefit, but rather leaving a sorry trail of arbitrariness, theft, and abuse."[39]

APRA had, then, taken up a nationalist stance, which complemented its patronage of workers, whether rural or urban. It sought, indeed, to become still more inclusive socially, welcoming the middle class since some of that group, for instance small businessmen, also suffered under the dominance of the old elite and its foreign backers. Much of this sounds imported. Nationalism was rampant in the Europe of the 1930s, while anti-imperialism and exaltation of workers (though not of the bourgeoisie) ring clearly of Marxism. But Haya explicitly separated *aprismo* from Marxism – which he considered an ideology drawn from European circumstances, and not necessarily applicable to America.[40] He had indeed publicly broken in the late 1920s from Peruvian Marxists and their distinguished theoretician, José Carlos Mariátegui. The set of beliefs and policies that APRA presented, then, was for him Peruvian and Latin American in its inspiration and its pertinence.

Haya de la Torre never became president of Peru. His closest approach to the office came in the final year of his life when he was appointed president of the constituent assembly of 1978–9 charged with drafting a new national constitution. But throughout the century the party remained a powerful leftist force for change in Peru, in opposition to moneyed interests and their allies in the military and in the Church. An APRA candidate, Alán García Pérez, was finally elected to the presidency for the period 1985–90. Times were hard in the aftermath of the debt crisis, and the clumsily nationalist economic policies pursued by the APRA government only made matters worse – disastrously so, in fact.[41] At the start of the twenty-first century, nevertheless, APRA is still an active contender in Peruvian politics.

As Haya de la Torre was emerging on to the political scene in Peru in the 1920s, in Brazil another prominent politician of twentieth-century Latin

America was doing the same. This was Getúlio Vargas (1883–1954), a man whose career offers clear parallels with, but contrasts to, that of Haya. The most obvious difference is that Vargas became president of his country, and indeed held the office longer than anyone else in the century, first from 1930 to 1945, and again from 1951 to 1954. Only Pedro II, in fact, outdoes him in years as chief executive of Brazil. Vargas and Haya differ also in that the first was above all a practical and highly pragmatic politician, not an originator of political thought, and indeed a man without any clear ideological position or attachment; whereas Haya is remembered above all for the ideas incorporated in APRA. But the two were alike in the appeals they made to the mass of their countries' populations, and in the support they received from workers, both rural and urban.

Both also were provincials – Haya from the north of Peru, and Vargas from a small town in the southernmost state of Brazil, Rio Grande do Sul, where his father, a general, prospered in raising cattle. After a brief spell in the army, he trained as a lawyer, practiced briefly, and then entered politics as a member of the state legislature. The dominant political organization in the state, whose line Vargas soon learned to toe, was the Republican party. Its thought was strongly influenced still by Positivism, giving to state administration an emphasis on order, hierarchy, and centralization of authority that Vargas himself was later to adopt as national president. He moved toward politics at the national level in 1922, when he became a state representative in the Congress (which sat in Rio de Janeiro). In 1926 he was appointed finance minister of Brazil, and in 1928 returned to Rio Grande do Sul as state governor.

Vargas came to the presidency of Brazil in 1930 as a result of a brief rising, against a national political system long dominated by rural-based oligarchies, by a broad "Liberal Alliance" acting with the support of reformist elements in the army. Late in that year the army high command, in a coup, removed the government of President Washington Luís Pereira de Sousa, and installed Vargas, the leading figure of the opposition, as provisional president. As such, he remained in office until 1934, when he was elected president by the Congress. Before his four-year term was over, however, he staged his own military-backed coup in 1937, creating the *Estado Novo* ("New State") and establishing himself as dictatorial ruler of Brazil until 1945. His final term as president (and the only one to which he was nationally elected) ran from 1951 to 1954.

The dominant political theme of Vargas's first, long, fifteen-year spell in the presidency was centralization of power (closely associated with a determination to exercise that power himself). One of his earliest steps was to suspend the federalist constitution (of 1891). He replaced state governors with officials reporting directly to himself. He disbanded state legislatures and the national Congress. These measures, and others like them, provoked in 1932 a short but sharp constitutionalist revolt in the state of São Paulo, set in motion mainly by the established rural elite of that traditionally rich and powerful coffee-growing state. The Paulista oligarchy, however, found itself isolated. Backing for it came from neither rural nor urban workers in São Paulo, nor the corresponding upper class in surrounding states, such as Minas Gerais.

Consequently the revolt subsided after a three-month siege of the city of São Paulo. Its failure reflects not only Vargas's quick acquisition of authority, but also the weakening of the coffee growers by the collapse of the world coffee price after 1929.

Vargas did not further punish the *paulistas*, but now moved to regularize his position and forestall similar opposition in the future by arranging the drafting of a new constitution. A constituent assembly gathered in November 1933, elected under a new code issued by Vargas that lowered the voting age to eighteen and gave the vote for the first time to working women. The new constitution, of July 1934, maintained federalism in Brazil, but gave more power than before to the presidency. That same movement toward concentration of power at the center is also visible in the constitution's allowing nationalization of some parts of the economy, including newspapers, advertising, insurance, and mining. The state was now able to increase its control of information and have a bigger say in directing economic development. Other parts of the document increased the state's attention to labor and family matters.

From the start, in fact, Vargas had shown much concern for labor, and particularly urban labor. In 1930 he set up a ministry of labor, and, in clear contrast to earlier regimes, moved quickly to provide workers with benefits, while organizing them under government control. In 1931, for example, the ministry began creating new unions in a process that led to a doubling of the number of organized workers by 1944 (to over half a million, in contrast to about a quarter of a million in 1930). The fascist regime of Mussolini in Italy provided the pattern for this incorporation of workers into the state through government-run unions. Eight hundred or so unions existed by 1944. Strikes were forbidden, but the state gave protection to workers through courts and labor laws. They also received more concrete help in Vargas's time in such forms as pension plans, paid vacations, maternity benefits and child care, minimum wage guarantees, training and education programs, safety regulations, and security of employment. Vargas thus sought to match the benefits of Brazilian urban workers with those received by labor in the industrialized countries of the world; in Latin America comparable benefits existed only in Mexico, Chile, and Uruguay.[42]

The attention that Vargas gave to labor clearly had several motives. Among them was very probably a desire to increase social justice and, in doing so, to modernize Brazil. At the same time the tight control that the state now imposed on labor, in exchange for aid granted to workers, was likely to contribute to the national economic development that Vargas pursued. Besides that, he, as the first national leader of Brazil to give protection and favor to labor, naturally gained enormous political support from these policies. And although he did little for rural workers (for example, he avoided land reform), nonetheless, by the end of his second term and of his life in 1954, he was widely regarded as the "father of the poor" across the country. It has been said of him, also, that "he was the first politician to extend dignity to the Brazilian people."[43] He can, indeed, be properly called a populist politician – one who appealed directly to the mass of the people, and who received their direct support in return. From the start he took great care to make himself known, traveling to all parts of the country in his first years, and then making good use of the new medium of radio to speak directly to the people. He gave the impression, in fact, of talking with them person to person.

The broad backing he gathered enabled him in 1937 to expand the executive power he held under the 1934 constitution by carrying out, in November of that year, a coup against his own government, and declaring the creation of a "New State" in Brazil. Extremist movements had by that time appeared in the country's politics. On the far right there was a strong "Integralist" party, highly nationalist and openly imitating European fascism (even down to the salute with the raised right arm). On the left, Communism had done well in Brazil after the tottering of capitalism in the Depression, attracting followers also with a nationalist message, though one that had a xenophobic, anti-imperialist base.[44] Seeing in these, and other, political organizations a threat to order and progress in Brazil, and with the immediate pretext of a supposed Communist plot for terrorism in the country, on November 10,1937 Vargas, backed by the military, seized all political power for himself, disbanding the congress and canceling the presidential election of 1938. As a dictator, though not as repressive as others before and after him in Latin America, he then ruled Brazil until 1945. In that year the military forced him out of office; with the defeat of dictatorships in World War II, and the victory of the democratic Allies, it seemed inappropriate for authoritarian government to continue.

Before and during the war, Brazil prospered under Vargas. Initially there had been strong economic links with Germany, but after the United States entered the war at the end of 1941, Vargas aligned the country with the Allies, declaring war on Germany and Italy in August 1942. Brazil profitably exported raw materials to the USA, which also encouraged (with advice and credits) the growth of heavy industry, such as steel, in the country. With the industrialization and economic expansion that Vargas pursued, a new wealthy elite developed and joined the remnants of the traditional rural oligarchy. Vargas worked with the new rich; he could hardly do otherwise if he was to achieve his economic aims. It is said that his long years in power left Brazilian society little changed in its basic elements. But it is plain enough that by extending suffrage and organizing labor, even if in the form of government-dominated unions, he brought the mass of the people further out on to the country's political stage than they had ever come before.

In the presidential elections of 1950 popular support for Vargas carried him easily back to office. In this final term, however, inflation and other problems made it difficult for him to produce what he had promised. In August 1954, beset by scandals over corruption and crime among his followers, and fearing imminent removal by the military, he resigned, and killed himself. His death was widely and intensely mourned throughout Brazil.[45]

A famous contemporary of Vargas, at the head of another of Latin America's largest countries, was Lázaro Cárdenas (1895–1970), president of Mexico from 1934 to 1940. He was from the state of Michoacán in western Mexico, a mestizo, the grandson of a Tarascan Indian, and the son of a small-town shopkeeper. From 1913 he fought in the Mexican Revolution on the rebel side, distinguishing himself in the field as an officer. He campaigned mostly under the command of Plutarco Elías Calles, one of the small group of prominent constitutionalist leaders from Sonora, in the north-west of the country. In 1924 Calles was elected president of Mexico, succeeding Alvaro Obregón, the preeminent Sonoran revolutionary. Cárdenas's links with Calles continued during the latter's four-year term. Cárdenas was now military commander of the Huasteca, a region of eastern and northeastern Mexico rich in oil, which was being extracted by foreign companies. In 1928 he entered civilian politics with his election as governor of his home state, Michoacán.

Calles's presidential term ended in that year. Through an amendment by Congress to the 1917 constitution, which had forbidden second presidential terms, Obregón was able to run again, and was indeed elected. But only seventeen days after his victory, he was, on July 18,1928, assassinated by a rightist Catholic. This jarring event proved both a significant end and a significant beginning for Mexico. First, Obregón was the last of the supreme leaders of the armed Revolution (Madero, Carranza, Zapata, Villa, and himself) to die. Second, his death was instrumental in the creation of the political structures that would dominate Mexico until the end of the century.

In that process of political refashioning, Calles played a central part. His presidential term did not expire until November 1928, and he was in any case clearly the senior figure on the political scene after Obregón's death. Taking charge in the post-assassination disorder, he set about creating a new party that would draw into itself existing sectoral parties and organizations (peasant, agrarian, and socialist groupings, for example), with a leadership consisting of existing prominent political figures, supreme among whom would be Calles himself. On December 1,1928, the day after he had handed over the presidency to an interim holder of the office chosen by the Congress, Calles announced the formation of this new party – the National Revolutionary Party (or PNR, *Partido Nacional Revolucionario*).[46] This entity, via its brief modulation (1938–46) as the Party of the Mexican Revolution (*Partido de la Revolución Mexicana*), was the origin of the famous and sometimes notorious PRI (*Partido Revolucionario Institucional*) – the Institutional Revolutionary Party that controlled most of Mexican politics until the 1990s, and made the country unique in Latin America as a state dominated by one party for more than half the twentieth century.

Through the PNR Calles and his close associates from earlier in the twenties ran Mexican politics at the center until 1934, exercising powerful influence over three short-term presidents in a period that has come to be known as the *Maximato* (Calles being the *jefe máximo*, or "supreme boss"). In these years Calles continued a rightward movement, already visible in his own presidency, away from realizing revolutionary ends, such as redistribution of land, and back toward more conventional policies such as development of economic infrastructure, and increasing investment (even foreign investment). Difficult economic conditions resulting from the Depression doubtless contributed to this retreat from radical change.

The PNR, however, embracing as it did assorted earlier political entities, also contained those for whom the Revolution still provided an inspiration and a program of desirable change. Splits therefore developed in the party as the years of the *Maximato* passed. One of those remaining on the left, though far from the extreme, was Lázaro Cárdenas. When the PNR came to choose its candidate for the presidential race in 1934, it settled on him: a man of military and, by now, political note, reliable, clearly capable, and, so it seemed, safe – even a touch dull.

But once Cárdenas began campaigning, any impression of workaday ordinariness soon evaporated. He traveled endlessly, trekking into the most remote of places; a story has him swimming ashore from a ship to reach a place otherwise inaccessible.[47] The result of these efforts was victory by a large margin in the election of July 1934. Calles and his entourage, hoping to prolong the *Maximato* and its control from behind the throne, were soon undeceived. Cárdenas acted quickly, building on the immense popular support that the election had shown him to have, to move Mexican politics back onto the track laid down in the Revolution.

The opportunity offered by mass politics was there, ready to be seized. In the early thirties, as Calles had shifted rightward and the Depression dragged on Mexico's economy, more radical labor movements than in the twenties had appeared, some of them with strong Communist influence. One outcome was rapid multiplication of industrial strikes: as Cárdenas came to the presidency at the end of 1934, Mexico City alone was threatened with sixty stoppages. Parallel pressures were mounting in the countryside. There had been some redistribution of land to peasants in the twenties, but by the early thirties it had all but stopped. Calles had declared in 1930 that agrarian reform was a failure, should be halted, and replaced with private, capitalist farming.[48] By the time of Cárdenas's election in 1934, strikes, seizures of land, and peasant discontents in general were multiplying in rural Mexico.

Calles was, then, increasingly out of tune with mass aspirations and needs as the years of the *Maximato* accumulated – and increasingly associated in popular opinion with owners of wealth, land and industry. What had become of the gains for the people implied in the Revolution and laid out in the 1917 Constitution? In the first eighteen months of his presidency Cárdenas made adept use of that question to separate himself from Calles (long his sponsor) and from the political trends of the *Maximato*. Using the authority of the vote that had elected him, he forced followers of Calles out from all levels of government, whether national, regional, or local. Much the same was done in the army, potentially a severe threat to Cárdenas, although his own military pedigree gained him credit there. He also moved away from the hostility that Calles had shown toward the Catholic church, manifest most clearly during his presidency in his fierce efforts to suppress the *Cristero* rising in western central Mexico – a peasant protest against government anticlericalism that became a guerrilla revolt. The outcome of Cárdenas's maneuvers was that by early 1936 he was firmly enough in control to send Calles into exile in the USA. The recent *jefe máximo* returned to Mexico only in 1941, after Cárdenas's term had ended, there to live out his four remaining years.

Over the next two years, 1936–8, Cárdenas implemented the radical changes from the conservative *callista* line for which he remains famous. First and foremost came agrarian reform, aimed above all at creating more *ejidos*: units of land communally owned and worked individually (or in a few cases collectively) by peasants. Cárdenas saw *ejidos* not just as a source of food, but as a means by which the peasantry could grow more confident, independent, educated, and ultimately more engaged in the political life of the country.[49] The amounts of land and the numbers of people affected by the *ejido* project are impressive. By 1940 around 800,000 rural dwellers had received 18 million hectares; *ejidos* then occupied 47 percent of Mexico's farmed land (in comparison to 15 percent in 1930). The number of people without land had dropped from 2.5 million to 1.9 million (and that in a decade of accelerating population growth). The government, moreover, provided not only land, but also credit to work it, along with investment in irrigation, roads, and electricity supply. It also encouraged peasants to organize politically, though under state auspices, a process culminating in 1938 in the formation of the CNC, or National Peasant Confederation. The peasantry thus became incorporated into the single national party (until 1938 the PNR, then the PRM, and finally in 1946 the PRI).

The creation of *ejidos* meant, of course, loss of land to private owners. In the fierce heat of Cárdenas's reform, protest had little chance of success. But when, after his time, national government again moved to the political right, private landowning reasserted itself, whether at the small peasant level or in medium or larger units. After the mid-century, indeed, the state encouraged private ownership of medium land holdings (in the 100–300 hectare range), since they proved to be efficient sources of food for both national consumption and export. Meanwhile, *ejidos* lost their economic vitality; nor did their peasant holders mature politically as Cárdenas had hoped. Nonetheless, the great transfer of wealth and resources brought about by land reform in the late thirties was in some measure permanent. It stands as one of the major outcomes of the Revolution.[50]

Though Cárdenas is remembered above all for his attention to country people and to the land, in basing his presidency on mass support, he obviously had to draw to himself industrial workers as well. These, by the 1930s, included not only urban people, but labor in mines, the electrical and oil industries, and on railroads. During the regime of the Sonorans – Obregón and Calles – in the twenties, large numbers of workers had been gathered together in the CROM (the Regional Confederation of Mexican Workers). This umbrella organization declined, however, early in the *Maximato*. Cárdenas, once president, sponsored a rival confederation, the CTM (the Confederation of Mexican Workers), which persists to the present. In charge of the CTM was Vicente Lombardo Toledano, a leading Mexican Marxist intellectual of the time, and a figure in the late thirties whose political power was exceeded only by Cárdenas's. Through the CTM workers were attached, like the peasantry, to the state and its dominant party, the PNR. They received, in return, important support from the state, particularly in the years immediately after the CTM's foundation in 1936. Cárdenas's government tended to support labor against employers in the many strikes of that time. In his final two years, though, Cárdenas moved from active encouragement of industrial action by workers to trying to ward off strikes, not for the benefit of employers but for that of the economy as a whole.[51]

It was a labor issue that led to an action by Cárdenas's government that remains as emblematic of his regime as redistribution of land: the expropriation and nationalization of the Mexican oil industry, dominated since its late-nineteenth-century origins by British and United States companies. As military chief in the Huasteca – Mexico's prime oil area – in the twenties, Cárdenas had not liked the high-handed and often corrupt behavior of those companies. He had himself resisted their attempts at bribery. Then, in 1935, with the foundation of a new national oil workers' union, began a long and fierce battle between the companies and labor over wages and benefits, length of the work week, and the filling of jobs by union members. The companies resisted union demands stubbornly. The government, keen to avoid loss of oil production, advocated arbitration. A federal commission was set up, and reported in mid-1937 in the workers' favor. It went beyond the issues of the dispute, however, to criticize the companies for political manipulation, fraudulent accounting, and other offenses. The companies reacted predictably, refusing to improve their earlier offers to workers. Thus a labor conflict grew into a battle of wills between powerful foreign interests in Mexico and the national government. As each tried to stare the other down, compromise became ever less possible. Finally, in March 1938, Cárdenas, in a national radio broadcast, announced the expropriation of the oil industry. The companies were to be compensated, and Mexicans, in a great surge of national self-affirmation, contributed sums large and small to the payment. The government turned the oil industry over to the union, which operated it capably. But hostility from the expelled companies, in such forms as refusal to buy Mexican oil and to supply equipment, brought difficulties and falling production. The government therefore quickly joined the union in the running of the industry, creating in June 1938 a national company, PEMEX (*Petróleos Mexicanos*). The company still operates, and, indeed, with the discovery in the 1970s of far larger oil reserves farther south on the Gulf Coast of Mexico became a weightier entity in the country's economy than ever before, while Mexico grew as a force in the world oil market.[52]

The oil expropriation raised Cárdenas to a level of national eminence – almost heroic standing – that his earlier and, in truth more complex, undertakings in land and labor reform had not brought him. It was seen as an act of national self-assertion in which almost all Mexicans might find satisfaction and pride, whereas redistribution of land and support of labor had inevitably angered many in the middle and upper classes. Thus March 1938 marks the political high point of Cárdenas's presidency. Economic difficulties, however, were already present that would make his final two years to some degree a time of retrenchment and of a shift toward the political center that would be continued rightward by his immediate successors in the presidency. Government spending was by then in growing deficit; inflation was rising, export income was falling. Even though Cárdenas never ceased in his commitment to workers over employers, labor over capital, nonetheless in the late thirties economic necessities forced his government to be less supportive of strikes than before, and, for example, to cut back on the expensive program of rural education that it had created to raise the political awareness and activism of the peasantry.

Still, Cárdenas's place in Mexican history is as the champion of peasants and the embodiment of national pride. Until the end of his life, in 1970, he remained for Mexican peasants, and especially for those of his native Michoacán, the all-capable *Tata* ("Father" – and it is worth recalling that for centuries Bishop Vasco de Quiroga, another memorable benefactor of the Indians of Michoacán, was remembered with the same title). For Mexicans more generally, he became in later life "an icon, a kind of moral *Jefe Máximo*, the only true living Mexican Revolutionary, the moral conscience of the Revolution."[53] And yet Cárdenas's legacy is not only a moral or symbolic one. He was a transitional figure of practical politics. He worked hard to gather great political authority to himself through his overtures to the mass of the people, and then, as the individual bearer of that power, used it to oust Calles, creator of the *Maximato*. He might well have set up a popularly-based *Maximato* of his own, but instead sought to establish, or encourage, mass organizations, such as the CTM and CNC, that would serve as the component parts of a corporate state. In that state the president, while endowed with great influence, was less the individualist *caudillo* of old than the representation of the will of the dominant party of Mexican politics. The original party had been Calles's PNR of 1929, created to pull together a variety of political and social interests. Nine years later Cárdenas recast Calles's creation as the PRM, with a clearer corporate structure. The two major components of the PRM, and therefore, in effect, also of the Mexican state, were to be the workers' CTM and the peasants' CNC; to them were added a popular sector (comprising organizations unconnected to labor or peasantry), and a military sector. The latter drew the armed forces into the party – but only briefly, since in 1946 Cárdenas's chosen successor as president, Manuel Avila Camacho, abolished the military sector, and renamed the resulting three-part structure the PRI. This Institutional Revolutionary Party dominated Mexican politics until the 1990s and still remains a most powerful political force in the country.

As, for many Mexicans, Cárdenas's presidency began to gather golden hues in memory, at the southern end of the South America another political career was taking flight that soon enough would acquire its own near-mystical qualities. On June 4, 1943 a military coup brought an abrupt end to a post-Depression period in Argentina in which conservatives – including the old oligarchical elite of big land owners – contrived to take back political power that they had earlier lost. Participating in the coup was one Juan Domingo Perón, a colonel in the army. Perón was to become the most prominent figure in Argentine public life in the twentieth century, and quite possibly in the country's entire independent existence.

The resurgence of the old elite in the country during the thirties was an oddity in Latin America. Part of the explanation lies in the fact that when the Depression struck, in 1930, it was not the oligarchy that was in power, but the middle-class-backed Radical Civil Union, led still by Hipólito Irigoyen. In any country the woes of the Depression tended naturally to be associated with the current regime, and so Irigoyen, despite his once-great popularity, was ousted by an army coup in September 1930. This was the first of many military coups in twentieth-century Argentina.

For thirteen years conservatives ruled Argentina. They did so by manipulating elections and relying on military backing; generals indeed occupied the presidency until 1938. They benefited also from Argentina's unusually rapid recovery from the Depression's effects, particularly in the form of rising exports (and prices) of grain from as early as 1933. Like others in Latin America at the same time, but more fully, the conservative governments pressed ahead with inward-directed industrialization in the thirties. Ever more of Argentina's consumer goods were domestically made during the decade.[54] Government income was, moreover, invested in a multitude of public works: roads, railroads, airports, and hospitals, for example.

Far from everything was negative, therefore, in what is sometimes called the "infamous decade" (década infame) of 1930s Argentina. But it was in truth a time of rearguard action for the conservative elite. Corruption of elections was one source of accumulating hostility toward them. A more serious cause for concern, however, was the growing weight of potential political opposition in the cities, and especially in Buenos Aires itself. The industrialization that conservatives promoted, and which developed first and most fully in the capital city, attracted great numbers of people from rural areas, beginning with the pampas. Migration into Buenos Aires from the interior averaged 70,000 yearly between 1937 and 1943, and 117,000 from 1943 to 1947. Higher urban wages attracted large inflows of people. The population of the city rose as a result from 3.4 million in 1935 to 4.7 million twelve years later. The number of industrial workers increased from 544,000 in 1935 to 830,000 in 1941, and then to more than a million by 1946.[55]

It was with the support of these urban workers that Colonel Perón rose to national prominence between 1943 and 1945, then to dominate Argentina as president from 1946 to 1955. The 1943 coup was the work of officers from the middle ranks, like him. The group had other qualities in common: they were not from the upper crust of society, as many senior officers of the time were, and they were strongly nationalistic, critical in particular of the powerful influence Great Britain had long had in the country. Since that influence had continued very strongly in the 1930s, benefiting the landed oligarchy and its high-ranking backers in the military, the younger officers had cause for complaint.

In this new military regime, Perón maneuvered his way to ever greater influence by making good use of the two rather junior posts he held: minister of labor and secretary of the army. The second position gave him the power of patronage in the army, and he quickly saw that the first could bring him vast civilian support if properly employed. He began to give governmental support to workers' demands that employers offer better wages and working conditions, and on a larger scale he took advantage of ideological splits in Argentina's largest labor organization, the CGT (Confederación General de Trabajo, or General Labor Confederation), to bring it under his own influence (the model of mutual support of state and labor was Mussolini's Italy, where Perón had spent 1938–40 as Argentine military attaché).[56] By 1945 many in Argentina were beginning to be alarmed by Perón's popularly-based authority: not only employers whose labor costs had risen, and upper- and middle-class people alarmed by his playing to the crowd, but also unionists on the left who resented his usurpation of organized labor. Some, even, in the military government increasingly found him an intolerable threat. Under pressure in October 1945, Perón resigned his offices. Arrest quickly followed.

Before entering jail, however, he made a radio broadcast in which he promised workers that he would soon return. The message had an effect that even he could hardly have expected. On October 17,1945 vast numbers of urban workers streamed from poor suburbs into central Buenos Aires, converging on the presidential palace in a demonstration that forced the regime's leaders to pluck Perón from jail and present him on the palace balcony late that night to the gathered throng. A week later came the formation of a Labor party, backing his candidacy in the presidential election of February 1946. In his campaign across the country, Perón had the company and help of his wife, the famous Evita (born Eva Duarte), an actress of lower-class origins. His appeal was above all to the poor throughout Argentina, the *descamisados* ("those without shirts"), but his nationalism also drew substantial backing from the middle class, especially when the US ambassador tried to influence voters against him.[57] He was elected president by a clear margin.

Perón came to power in propitious economic times for his political program. At the end of World War II the country was not only free of foreign debt but indeed held large credit balances abroad, particularly in Great Britain, for goods supplied during the war. Beyond that, demand stayed strong for Argentina's food exports, and prices accordingly high. Money was therefore plentiful to fund the changes that Perón thought the country needed.

His plan was first one of centralization of power. The military was clearly a potential ally in achieving that aim, but also a threat if discontented, as the events of late 1945 had shown. Perón kept the armed forces with him for many years by making their allocation in the national budget larger than in any other Latin American country at the time. Generals proliferated, and had at their disposal abundant new equipment. And although Perón had resigned from the army before running for president, he could always evoke his military background to maintain his link with the armed forces. A slight military flavor persisted, indeed, throughout his regime.

His nationalist aims were clearly expressed in economic matters. Industrialization was to continue, with the aim of reducing still further the country's dependence on foreign manufactures. The government provided credit for investment. Industrial production (though still largely of consumer goods) rose by some thirty percent in the years 1946–8.[58] Enterprises that were foreign-owned were to be nationalized. Thus the telephone and electricity-generating systems became state property, as also, most famously, did the British-owned railroads. Allies of the regime began in 1947 to buy the national broadcasting system; the state within a few years controlled not only radio but most other media.

Foreign trade was also taken under government control. The state bought agricultural exports from producers at an officially set price, and then sold them at the higher prices prevailing on the world market. The result was a loss to old landed interests that were the main source of exported grains and meat, and a profit to the government that enabled it to expand its hold on the economy and fund its social programs. This transfer of wealth from the old elite to industry, social services, and other destinations naturally increased hostility to Perón among the remnants of the oligarchy. Despite threats, however, actual expropriation of land did not happen.

All other economic changes notwithstanding, it is the shift of wealth to the poorer end of society that took place, at least in the early years of Perón's presidency, that is its best remembered feature. Expansion of industry and enlarged government spending led to an increase in real income of over forty percent in the 1946–9 period, with much of the gain going to workers as Perón continued to support strikes for better pay and conditions. With the regime's approval strikers multiplied in numbers, increasing in Buenos Aires alone from 50,000 in 1945 to 335,000 in 1946 and almost 550,000 in 1947. The number of unionized workers rose from 877,300 in 1946 to almost 1,533,000 in 1948.[59] And beyond the gains going to workers from industrial action, they also benefited from greatly increased social spending by the state: housing projects, schools, hospitals, clinics, stadiums sprung up around the country. For the poorest in the population help came above all from the charitable foundation set up by Eva Perón to provide health and social services, as well as useful items such as sewing machines and bicycles. Eva also pressed for women's suffrage. This was achieved, in 1947, and another enormous pro-Perón voting block in the population came into being.[60]

In all Perón's and Evita's support of workers, it is of course easy to see only a self-serving pursuit of political backing. But there was more to it than that. In the first place, as a militarily-trained politician enamored of order and organization, he saw improving the lot of the great majority as a means of preserving order, and of forestalling violent revolution that would cost the holders of wealth in Argentina far more than they lost to his political programs. Beyond that, it is difficult to deny in him, and in Eva (perhaps particularly in her, given her lowly origins), an intrinsic desire to relieve the sufferings of the poor. Social justice was an end in itself. The state had a responsibility to work for it. The qualities of which Peronism was ideally composed, by one description, were "justice, sovereignty, welfare, emancipation, harmony, [and] progress."[61] These were elements of *justicialismo* – a neologism used by Perón from 1948 onward to describe his political and social doctrine, a supposed third way between capitalism and communism.

Progress toward those goals slowed severely after 1950. Economic problems were partly to blame. The reserves stored up in World War II had been used up in the nationalization program. Then export prices fell, trade surpluses vanished, the government's deficits rose, and inflation along with them – with the effect that real wages dropped in the early fifties. In an effort to stop inflation, the government imposed a price and wage freeze from 1952 to 1954. With the treasury less well lined than before, from 1952 Perón yielded on the nationalist front and encouraged foreign investment in Argentina. Economic conditions actually improved somewhat after 1953, but the regime had lost the golden touch with which fortunate post-war conditions had temporarily blessed it.

Perón was easily re-elected in 1951 (having amended the constitution in 1949 to allow a second term). Eva helped him in that campaign; but she was already suffering from cancer, and died in July of 1952. Immense national mourning followed.[62] The mass of the people stayed with Perón, but opposition swelled up elsewhere – in the military, where the president's interference seemed ever more intrusive, and in the middle class, which wondered if there was to be any end to the gifts bestowed on workers. Expression of civilian opposition was by now difficult and even risky. But finally it found a home in an unexpected quarter – the Catholic Church. Relations between Perón and the Church had been generally comfortable. The Church was, for him, a conservative force in a good sense, promoting social order and naturally opposed to disturbing doctrines of the Left. But by the mid-fifties discord was growing. The Church disliked Perón's presentation of *justicialismo* as a doctrine, equipped with "believers" and occasionally even an "apostle" (himself). It reacted negatively to a proposed canonization of Eva. Above all, perhaps, it objected to the government's interference in education.[63] It began to act as a base for those with objections to Peron's regime. He, in turn, found fault in mid-1954 in senior churchmen's supposed backing of a new Christian Democratic Party. Rallies and counter-rallies of Peronists and Catholic activists began to take place, first in Córdoba, north-west of Buenos Aires, and then in the capital itself at the end of the year. As varied opponents of Perón gathered strength and confidence in 1955, conflicts became more overt and violent. In June, naval aircraft attempting to bomb the presidential palace instead mistakenly killed several hundred pro-government demonstrators gathered in a show of CGT strength in central Buenos Aires. The army hesitated a few months in following this naval lead. But finally on September 19,1955, after army revolts at Córdoba and Bahía Blanca, on the coast south of Buenos Aires, Perón resigned. Soon after, he departed into a seventeen-year exile. Though excluded from Argentina he still exercised considerable, and generally disruptive, influence in the country's politics. Finally in 1973, after the military government of the day allowed him to return, he was again elected president. He was now seventy-eight, and had less than a year of life left. His brief restoration only added to the political disorder from which Argentina was already suffering; rising political and economic disarray led to a period of harsh military rule from 1976 to 1982. Such was the impact, however, that Perón had made on Argentine consciousness – and particularly on that of the mass of the population – in the 1940s, that Peronism lives on in the country, as a powerful, though ever less definable, political and ideological force.

In the public careers of these four prominent men – Haya de la Torre, Vargas, Cárdenas, and Perón – can be found much of the political behavior and many of the political attitudes, preferences, and beliefs that characterized Latin America as a whole in the post-Depression decades. The period presented somewhat the same question as the years after Independence a century or so earlier: what to put in the place of a well-established mode of government that had suddenly ended? Colonial administration had departed in the 1820s, while, with the Crash of 1929 and the Depression that followed, the well-established dominance of oligarchies was to a large degree undone. A casting-around for new ideas, structures, and practices in politics then ensued, resulting in the regimes that have just been described in Peru, Brazil, Mexico, and Argentina, and others, not greatly different, elsewhere in Latin America.

What common features are worth noting in the post-Depression politics of the four countries briefly treated here? One obvious shared trait is increased military intervention in government. The oligarchical period had been a time of largely civilian rule, in great contrast to what came before it. Now, again, officers seized power in coups, or armed forces acted as underpinning of regimes that backed them with money and *matériel* and agreed with them ideologically. Only in Mexico, of the four cases described, was this not so. There Obregón and Calles, in the post-Revolutionary decade of the twenties, had astutely defused the military danger remaining after the years of fighting were over. Cárdenas inherited a military already well on the way to being integrated into a powerful national state (a process illustrated by his own inclusion of it as a sector of the PRM in 1938). Elsewhere no such state existed; the armed forces thus had greater freedom of action, and indeed were keen to act, generally as restorers and keepers of order, and sometimes also (as in Brazil and to some extent in Argentina) as promoters of nationalism and social justice.

Amidst militarism there sprang up, however, persistent sprigs of representative democracy – always an end to be pursued, in the view of at least some segments of Latin American populations, even if only as a distantly realizable ideal. But all four of the major figures here described were elected to office (though Haya never to the presidency, and Vargas as president only in his final, ineffective term). Perhaps the surest sign of advancing democracy in this period is the extension of voting to women. The arrival of women's suffrage in Brazil (1932) and Argentina (1947) is wholly representative of what took place elsewhere. Ecuador had been the first in Latin America to give women the vote, in 1929; Paraguay was the last, in 1961.[64]

Even though elections brought Cárdenas, Vargas, and Perón to presidential office, however, these men had little interest in thereafter governing democratically. Elections conferred legitimacy – but legitimacy was then used for concentrating power and acting with the greatest possible executive independence. Regional and local opponents tended to be replaced with loyalists. Messages from the political center were now more effectively sent to entire countries than ever before through the medium of radio (which governments sought to control). If the message was nationalist (as in Cárdenas's broadcast announcing the expropriation of foreign oil companies), its power of binding a country together, and the country to the national leader, was even greater. The political pursuit was above all one of order. To that end governments aimed to preserve ranking in society, though not necessarily the same ranking as before (the old upper crust was severely hurt by the policies of Cárdenas and Perón, for example). There might well be, as in the cases of Haya, Cárdenas, and

Perón, sympathy for the suffering and harsh lives of the poor. Such deprivation had to be remedied through the support of unions, distribution of land, and social services. But workers and peasants were to remain workers and peasants. They were to be incorporated into political and national life through organizations and unions that formed sectors of the state, and that were under state control. The parallel with medieval social estates may perhaps be drawn. And indeed it may be that, although Latin American countries in the thirties clearly imitated the fascist European nations of the time in trying to build corporate states, they were particularly inclined to do so because that model of the state lay embedded in them from their deep colonial past.

These four great national figures were then, for all their concern with the needs of the masses, not social revolutionaries. The way forward for their societies, as they saw it, was not through class struggle, but rather through the harmonious regulation, from the political center, of a social order in which all were to be made content in their stations. It seems likely that an underlying notion of this sort still strongly persists in Latin America. And that may go some way toward accounting for the striking fact that, although Latin American Marxists abounded in every country in the twentieth century, no Marxist regime (with the obvious but single exception of the Cuban case) survived long.

And finally, to come full circle to the point of departure of this discussion of post-Depression politics, as practical politicians Haya de la Torre, Vargas, Cárdenas, and Perón were above all populists – leaders who saw that the surging populations of their countries presented new political opportunities while demanding new political attention. Perón, in particular, coming on the scene later than the other three, and in a country that was in any case more fully industrialized and urbanized, saw the opportunity and challenge of the booming numbers of poor city workers. But the careers of all four represent a political response to one of the prime changes taking place in twentieth-century Latin America: unprecedented growth in the number of Latin Americans.

THE 1950S AND 1960S

The variety of political modes and practices seen in the 1930s and 1940s continued in the next two decades, although there appeared no new political giants to compare with Vargas, Cárdenas, and Perón. The nearest approach to these populist reincarnations of nineteenth-century *caudillos* was perhaps Fidel Castro, master of Cuba after the revolution he led there from 1959. Nor was there any clear trend in political forms in the mid century. In Venezuela a string of military dictatorships that had begun in 1908 finally came to an end in 1958, yielding to what was initially highly insecure civilian government. In Peru, also, the military continued to be strong, either in the presidency, or close to it. Their keen fear of, and hostility to, APRA kept them on the highest political alert. A particular example of this was the fiercely repressive rule of

General Manuel Odría, dictator from 1948 to 1956. In post-Perón Argentina, the military were likewise never far from the political front lines, ousting a civilian president in 1962, organizing a new presidential vote, but removing in 1966 the man who had been elected, and then occupying the presidency themselves until the brief return of Perón in 1973–4. The case of Colombia was unusual, with only four years of military rule (the dictatorship of General Rojas Pinilla, 1953–7) in the mid century, despite a resurgence between 1948 and 1966 of the rural violence that has so often marked the country's history. The length and ferocity of this particular period of rural conflict were such that it has become known as simply *La Violencia*. Such disorder might well have been expected to provoke military intervention in government. But, apart from Rojas Pinilla's four years, the traditional Conservative and Liberal parties continued to rule, going indeed so far as to agree, in 1956, that for the next sixteen years the presidency and other offices would alternate between them. This pact in fact meant power sharing between different segments of an oligarchy that had survived far more intact than almost anywhere else in Latin America, and that survival was much to blame for the rural violence of those decades, and indeed for the continuation of violence and guerrilla warfare in the country into the twenty-first century. In Chile, also, though to a lesser degree, traditional social and economic differences persisted. The political culture of honest elections and constitutional government accommodated them for many years. When, however, it finally brought to power in 1970 the socialist regime of Salvador Allende, and that regime moved still further leftward, conservatives were provoked to take violent measures. In 1973 a military coup killed Allende, and initiated eighteen years of harsh dictatorship by General Augusto Pinochet.

Changeability was, then, the dominant trait of Latin American political arrangements in the middle decades of the twentieth century. Given the exceptional prosperity of the three decades after World War II, that may seem surprising. In the nineteenth century, political stability had increased as the rising export boom improved economic conditions. But then, politics had been in the hands of the elite that profited, more than any other part of society, from the growth of trade. Now, almost a century later, the remains of that elite had to share the political field with a substantial middle class, and a vastly larger and better organized mass of workers, both rural and urban. Wider suffrage, large and powerful unions, professional organizations, big and entrenched bureaucracies, and of course large and professionalized militaries – these and other forces now added greatly to the complexity, and hence instability, of politics in the mid-twentieth century.

Only one major country managed to avoid this general unsteadiness: Mexico. There, the rule of the dominant party, the Institutional Revolutionary Party (PRI), rolled resolutely onward, with little change of line except perhaps a slight alternation between right and left after every other presidential term.[65] The title of the party seems odd, even self-contradictory, but in truth it reflected what had happened by the 1940s in Mexican politics: the Revolution had itself become not only the dominant, but the defining, event of the country's recent history. The Constitution of 1917, cast, as it were, in the heat of that devastating civil war, became enshrined as the country's guiding icon. In reality the Constitution often went unobserved, in letter and in spirit. Employers, for example, ignored the clauses that defined working conditions; corruption became endemic in the working of politics; economic inequality was not reduced in the long term. But so strong was the connection linking Revolution, Constitution, and Mexico itself that any radically new political activism could be presented by the political establishment in the Party as nothing less than an assault on the nation. Most Mexicans came to accept that notion, and although minor opposition parties existed, political aspirants had strong incentives to work within, not against, the PRI. This seems the best explanation for the exceptional absence in Mexico of military, or military-backed, bids for power.[66] Any attempted coup would have been perceived by many Mexicans as treasonous.

It is tempting, given Mexico's political calm after 1930 or so, to think that a dominant-party political system could have served other Latin American countries well. The inclusive, corporate state represented by such a party perhaps seems a useful bridging device between the political structure of colonial times and a fuller representative democracy. It is true, of course, that the Mexican arrangement did not free the country from political corruption or even, on occasion, from violent repression of political dissenters. But corruption and repression were, in the twentieth century, no less prevalent elsewhere, and in some parts of Latin America, a good deal more in evidence. On the other hand, the Mexican dominant-party state may have functioned only because of the particularities of the country's early twentieth-century history, as just suggested. And besides that the question remains of whether dominant-party politics benefited Mexico in anything but politics itself. Economic gains, for instance, are not so obvious: in 1996 the country's per capita domestic product, at $2,953, was less than half Argentina's ($6,191), and lower than Chile's ($3,440), Uruguay's ($3,258), Venezuela's ($3,143), and Brazil's ($3,007)[67] – all five of those countries that had gone through periods of severe political turbulence in the twentieth century.

The most dramatic political change undergone by any Latin American country in the mid-1900s was plainly the revolution that began in Cuba in 1959. The guerrilla campaign started by Fidel Castro in 1956 in the coastal Sierra Maestra in the east of the island had origins in Cuban history that were both deep and recent. First it was an expression of Cuban nationalism, a sentiment almost continuously threatened since independence in 1898 by the country's close ties – by its physical proximity, indeed – to the United States.[68] Even after the USA's legal capacity to intervene in Cuban internal affairs ended, in 1934, with the cancellation of the Platt Amendment, the country remained deeply in the economic and cultural shadow of its large neighbor. The United States provided the major market for Cuba's prime export, sugar, and invested heavily in sugar production, mining, public services, and banking in the island. Second, internal conditions in the fifties created growing discontent. The dictatorial rule of Fulgencio Batista, the dominant figure in Cuban politics from the mid-1930s and now president after a military coup in 1952, grew ever more corrupt. The international price of sugar became unsteady, creating unemployment in the countryside, where the lot of peasants was already grim as a result of high concentration of land ownership. The middle class, though rich by Latin American standards, felt poor by those of the ever-present North America. Per capita gross domestic product indeed did not grow from 1947 to 1958.[69] As Castro, therefore, emerged in the late fifties as the leader of resistance to Batista, he found little difficulty in attracting wide support. Indeed as his insurgent force advanced westward toward Havana in 1958, it grew constantly, and finally the army, sent by Batista to oppose the rising, itself largely gave up the effort and dissolved. On January 1,1959 Batista fled into exile (dying in Spain in 1973), and Castro entered Havana without difficulty.

The full political force of the revolution, and its wider impact on Latin America, did not become apparent immediately. It was only after the failure of a attempted counter-coup – the landing in April 1961 at the Bay of Pigs by 1,300 Cuban exiles, backed in a limited and tentative fashion by the USA – that Castro declared Cuba to be a Marxist-Leninist state, began organizing it internally as such, and proclaimed an intent to foment revolution elsewhere in Latin America. Tension between Cuba and the United States rose markedly as a result, and even more when in October 1962 US reconnaissance revealed that the Soviet Union was building a missile base in Cuba. That highly alarming "missile crisis" was defused by an exchange of undertakings between Moscow and Washington: the first would withdraw the missiles if the second promised to withhold support for future invasions of Cuba. But the hostility between the United States and Castro's regime was now profound and has continued, with only minor variations in its intensity, to the present. It was exacerbated by the USA's imposing a strict economic boycott on Cuba. This had severe consequences for the country's economy, especially after Soviet aid ended (with the collapse of the USSR) in the 1990s.

In the event, Cuba's attempts to stir up revolutionary movements across Latin America failed, and after the late sixties its efforts in that line largely ceased, or were redirected to Africa. But early in the decade it was not obvious that they would fail. Hence Latin America seemed a prime field of contest in the Cold War between the USA and the USSR, capitalism and Marxism. The United States' response included directing development programs toward Latin America (notably the Alliance for Progress) that would promote economic growth and diversity, and hence also political stability (in the form, it was hoped, of more fully representative democracy).

RESURGENT MILITARIES

These programs contributed to the vigorous economic growth that was already taking place in most of Latin America in the sixties, but they had little success in raising the level of democracy. Indeed, to judge by the broad political trend in Latin America in the sixties, continued and strengthened in the seventies, just the reverse was the outcome. What these two decades in fact brought was a resurgence of military government. It was, however, not so much the classic individual dictatorship that reasserted itself (though there were examples of that, most notoriously General Alfredo Stroessner in Paraguay, in power from 1954 to 1989), but government by groups or committees of generals and admirals. "Bureaucratic authoritarianism" is one name that has been given to this style of military rule. Of the large countries, only Colombia, Mexico, and Venezuela escaped government of this variety at some period in the sixties, seventies, and eighties; few of the smaller states avoided it.

Although specific explanations can be found in each country for the intrusion of the military into politics, the broad conditions that favored it call for most attention. First, the movement can be seen as a reaction against populism in politics – against politicians' favoring the mass of the people at the expense (or so it could be perceived) of holders of wealth. The wealthy, mostly conservatives, welcomed the intervention of military men who seemed likely to resist those transfers; or, at least, likely to work to maintain the old, ranked, social structure that would sustain inequalities of wealth and status. Second, conditions particular to the sixties worked to sharpen the sense of threat that conservatives felt. The most obvious danger was precisely Cuba's proclaimed intention, backed by the Soviet Union, to sow revolution in Latin America. Across the western world, moreover, the sixties (particularly the latter years of the decade) were a time of social unrest and challenge to entrenched politics. Students in the United States protested specifically against the Vietnam War and generally against established values. European students pressed for a leftward shift in their countries' politics and for a greater say in university government. They had Latin American counterparts, some of whom, however, went much further, founding or joining guerrilla groups that used violence in the service of political and social change. The *Montoneros* of Argentina were one such youth organization, a guerrilla offshoot of Peronism which in 1970 assassinated a former president, General Aramburu. Across the Río de la Plata in Uruguay a revolutionary urban guerrilla group calling itself the Tupamarus caused great disorder in the 1960s. More generally, in the same years, workers' strikes and demonstrations added to the sense of growing disorder felt by existing holders of power and influence, and their military allies. Ironically the Alliance for Progress itself added to the potential for military intervention in politics. Its promotion of democracy came to seem misguided to those who thought that the majority had already gained enough influence, and under the Alliance the USA provided generous military funding so that the means would exist to combat the insurgencies that Cuba threatened to stir up. With larger and more modern forces at their disposal, commanders gained confidence.

The dates of the notable conservative military regimes in the decades following the Cuban revolution are as follows: Argentina, 1976–82 (although the military had dominated Argentina's politics for most of the sixties and the early seventies); Bolivia, 1971–9 (although, again, military men had occupied the presidency since 1964); Brazil, 1964–85; Chile, 1973–88; and Uruguay, 1973–85. In addition to these the conservative dictatorship of General Stroessner continued in Paraguay until 1989.

The actions and attitudes shared to a greater or lesser degree by these regimes included limitation of mass political activities and organizations (with particularly harsh attacks on leftist political bodies of any sort); assertion of a traditional Catholic conservatism; political and economic collaboration with holders of land and wealth (and also to some extent with middle classes alarmed by the self-assertiveness of the masses, as particularly in Chile in the early 1970s); and suppression of cultural, artistic, and intellectual activities and expressions that could be construed as challenging the militarized state and its values. These governments are remembered particularly for the violence of their assaults on the political left. In 1973 the Uruguayan army simply destroyed the Tupamaru guerrilla organization in the country. In Chile, collaborators with the socialist regime of Salvador Allende between 1970 and 1973, and other suspected leftists, were hunted down by military and intelligence forces, tortured, and summarily executed. Many just disappeared. Disappearances, however, were even commoner in the early years of the 1976–82 military regime in Argentina. There the campaign against leftist dissidents, or those remotely suspected of such dissidence, is recalled as the "Dirty War" because of its viciousness. Weak control of investigators may have been some part of the reason for what can only be called the evil of this campaign. The government itself was split among the three branches of the Argentine military, and divided authority persisted downward through the state structure, so that police and other groups looking for dissidents could act very much as they pleased.[70] The use of torture, however, was clearly part of the policy of the military leadership. Among the most potent adversaries of the Argentine military regime were the mothers of those who had disappeared – the famous mothers who quietly but relentlessly paraded in protest in front of the presidential palace in Buenos Aires. They put the regime in a quandary. Their presence was an embarrassment, but they could hardly be forcibly removed because motherhood was central among the Christian virtues that the generals declared themselves to be defending.

The long-lived military regime in Brazil also had its moments of violent political oppression, but broadly speaking military rule there was less extreme than in Spanish American countries – another example of the generally more moderate tone of Brazilian affairs. Civilian elites were more of a restraining influence on the military in Brazil than in Argentina or Chile. Part of the reason for the relative moderation of Brazil also lay also in the exceptional economic performance of the country from 1969 to the late seventies – the "Brazilian miracle" whose benefits spread widely among the upper and middle classes (though hardly reaching the mass of the population).

The poor majorities were not ignored by quite every military regime in these decades. General René Barrientos, ruler of Bolivia from 1964 to 1969, chose to reinforce his authority with peasant support, which he drew to himself by continuing the programs of land distribution, rural welfare, and popular education that had begun in the country in the fifties. By contrast, however, he firmly suppressed labor organizations, notably that of the miners, which had become a potent force in Bolivian politics.[71] After his apparently accidental death in 1969, two other military governments followed, increasingly leftist and chaotic. The second of them was in turn ousted in 1971 by a coup led by Colonel Hugo Banzer. So began a typical right-wing military regime, allied with business interests, that ruled Bolivia until 1978.

The military government that came to power in Peru in 1968 had a still greater popular orientation than Barrientos's in Bolivia. Its mass-directed reforms indeed were designed not just to bring it political support, but as part of a strategy to promote national development, and hence increase security. One concern of the officers who led the coup against the civilian government of the day was the considerable unrest, some of it violent, that had broken out among the Andean Indian peasantry in recent years. The specter of the Cuban Revolution seemed to be on the prowl in the central Andes. The Peruvian officer corps of the time was educated to a degree unusual in Latin America, and saw the solution to this security problem less in the repression of peasant movements than in reform that would improve living standards. Much else went into their development-for-security program: nationalization of foreign-owned companies in mining, fishing and agriculture; replacement of these by workers' cooperatives or state companies; expansion of the state in the form of new ministries and regulating agencies; attempted improvement of public services; and broadly the creation, under military supervision, of a well-ordered corporate Peruvian state.[72] But the lasting bequest of this military regime – which in its combining of reform with social ordering and assertion of nation recalls the Cárdenas years in Mexico – was redistribution of land. Almost all large estates in Peru, both coastal and Andean, were broken up and distributed among some 360,000 farming families, most of them organized into farming cooperatives.[73] Though considerable areas of land, particularly in the mountains, were returned to earlier owners after the military years ended in 1980, nonetheless the Peruvian generals of the seventies differed from their peers elsewhere in Latin America in leaving at least some country people better off than they found them.

Almost all the bureaucratic–authoritarian military regimes came to an end in the first half of the 1980s. As with their appearance, the stories of their ending vary from country to country. The clearest case of a particular national circumstance leading to the exit of the military is that of Argentina. In April of 1982 the generals then in charge, facing mounting domestic pressures, sent an invasion force to recover the Malvinas (or Falkland) Islands, in the Atlantic off southern Argentina, from British control. To the surprise of the regime, Great Britain immediately despatched troops, ships, and aircraft to challenge the invasion. In mid-June the Argentine occupation ended in surrender. The quick reversal of fortunes – from the apparently easy recovery of what Argentines had long considered their own national territory to its being snatched away again – so discredited the military establishment that its regime collapsed. In 1983 a civilian government returned to Argentina.

But even in Argentina, broader causes underlay the end of military rule. The generals had undertaken the Malvinas venture to deflect rising criticism of their administration and to distract public attention from growing inflation (the result of deficit spending by the government) and from the looming problem of vast foreign debt.

For this was the time of the debt crisis, the severest challenge to Latin Americans' economic well-being in the twentieth century. It had been military governments that had borrowed so eagerly in the late seventies, the recent time of cheap loans. That borrowing had briefly extended Latin America's long post-World War II economic boom. But now, in 1982 and the years immediately following, the costs of the loans quickly became overwhelming, and the incompetence of the governments that had taken them a cause for criticism. High government spending at home had brought inflation, escalating interest rates in world money markets made the loans suddenly very costly, and lenders began to demand repayment of principal as well. The outcome for those in Latin America lucky enough to keep their jobs was reduced real income; many simply lost their jobs. For almost everyone, the debt crisis meant a notable and lengthy fall in living standard.

The crisis added powerful new force to what was already a rising current of discontent in most countries with military rule. The armed forces had originally intervened, in almost every case, to restore order in countries where labor unrest, guerrilla activities, and even simple fighting among political parties looked likely to produce disarray, or even disintegration, of society and politics. They had, by means foul and fair, restored order to a considerable degree. But that once done, even those in the upper and middle classes who had most gladly welcomed them began, sooner or later, to chafe under the limits imposed – bans on political expression and party activity, exclusion of businessmen from decision-making in state-run economies, suppression of cultural and intellectual diversity. Beyond that, abuses of human rights had become ever more widely known inside Latin America, while international pressure to end them (notably the reproofs of the Carter administration in the USA from 1976 to 1980) had risen.

Under this growing burden of external disapproval and domestic pressure, to which the debt crisis added a crushing final weight, the military regimes one by one withdrew to the barracks during the eighties. As they went they negotiated with those politicians from pre-military days who were still active and interested in affairs of state about the transition to civilian rule. In every case, but in some only after a tense period of confusion, elections took place and a new representative government entered office. Of the big countries, Chile was last to change. By a referendum in 1988 which gave Chileans the choice of continuing under military control for eight more years, Augusto Pinochet, the man who of all Latin American ruling generals of his time most clearly resembled a classic nineteenth-century *caudillo*, was removed from office. Chileans voted "No" to the possibility of continued military rule, led in all probability by Pinochet, by a margin of 55 to 43 per cent. A substantial minority, it would seem, still had positive memories of the armed forces' intervention in the midst of multiplying disorders fifteen years before.

RURAL TROUBLES

The post-military years were not calm everywhere. Conflicts continued, or began, in several countries between central governments and rural guerrillas.

They were the expression of persisting differences in living standard between urban and rural people, broad neglect of the peasantry, and particularly of unequal distribution of land in the countryside. They were also to some extent the expression of the continued existence of far-leftist politics in Latin America. The advocates of revolutionary change (many of them coming from the middle class) saw in rural discontents the best soil for cultivating violent movements with which they might reshape politics and societies.

A prime case is the movement known as the *Shining Path* (*Sendero Luminoso*) in the southern highlands of Peru; or, to give it its full name, the *Communist Party of Peru by the Shining Path of José Carlos Mariátegui*. The complete title asserts continuity with the aims of the leading Peruvian Marxist of the twentieth century, and a political thinker who had, moreover, particularly concerned himself with the problem of the Andean peasantry in Peruvian society and politics. The *Sendero Luminoso* was the creation of, above all, Abimael Guzmán, a teacher of philosophy at the University of Ayacucho in the southern Andes. He used his position of authority in the university to spread a Maoist brand of Marxism in the surrounding region. Mao having developed his theory of revolution with peasants especially in mind, this particular variety of Marxism matched Andean conditions most closely. In later years, indeed, Guzmán, under the assumed title of "Presidente Gonzalo," came to see himself as the successor to Mao, and indeed to Marx and Lenin as well, in world socialist thought.

The *Sendero* flourished between 1980 and 1992. It gained support among peasants in Ayacucho because the province, apart from being among the poorest in Peru, had also seen some reversal of the land redistributions made by the military government of the 1970s. Peasants had gained land, then lost it again. But the movement counted less on attracting peasants than on imposing itself on them, and its prime means of self-imposition was violence. The *Sendero* saw itself as a movement of cleansing fire; all evidence of existing structures of power in Peru was to be burned away, and a new and just society built on the resulting sterilized ground. Thus groups of guerrillas would descend on highland villages, enact summary trials of officials, and, if evidence gathered called for it, execute them. Killing was often by stoning. Judgment and punishment might also extend to moral offenders in the village population – people who had maltreated others – since the *Sendero*'s notion of revolution included ethical as well as political cleansing. Villagers, generally fearful by now, would be instructed to resist reimposition of government control and to support the revolutionary movement. The Peruvian government, however, sent police and troops into the highlands to combat the *Sendero*. Villages that had suffered the attack of one side would then be assaulted by the other. Thus the peasantry suffered from a double violence. Some 25,000 people are thought to have died in this struggle by 1992.

The *Sendero Luminoso* seemed to gain strength through the 1980s and on into the early 1990s. Its area of influence grew northwards in the mountains, reaching as far as the upper valley of the River Huallaga, on the eastern side of the Andes north and east of Lima, where large amounts of coca were grown for processing into cocaine in Colombia. From the growers the *Sendero* demanded payments, which became one of its main sources of income. Its strategy included surrounding the cities of Peru in preparation for taking them. It became ideologically well established in Lima at the public University of San Marcos. It went to work in the shanty towns around the capital, assassinating even community leaders who had emerged in them and who were no political friends of the central government, the justification being that any authority that was not the *Sendero*'s was corrupt and hostile. Not reform, but complete revolution, was the movement's aim. It reminded Lima of its presence by frequently blowing up electricity pylons, so causing black-outs in the city. All changed, however, suddenly and unexpectedly in September of 1992, when the security forces of President Alberto Fujimori's regime located and arrested Guzmán and other leading *senderistas* in Lima. The arrest also yielded much information about the movement. With this capture, the steam went out of the *Sendero Luminoso*. Its activities declined sharply after 1992; and though it still (in 2002) exists, there is little sign of its resurgence.[74]

The same cannot be said of the other Andean state afflicted with large guerrilla movements in recent times. In that country, Colombia, guerrilla action is all too present in the opening years of the twenty-first century, mainly in the form of the FARC (the Revolutionary Armed Forces of Colombia). It is true that other guerrilla movements existing in the country in the late twentieth century came to terms with the national government in the early 1990s, and that besides the smaller ELN (National Liberation Army) only the FARC remains active. But it is a salient presence in the country's life, dominating large rural areas and constantly reminding city dwellers of its existence through kidnappings. It is a Marxist organization dating to the 1950s and 1960s, a guerrilla offshoot of the Colombian Communist Party. As such its aim has been to overthrow the existing political, social, and economic order of Colombia and put a Marxist–Leninist state in its place.[75] It has always been a rural-based organization, attracting the support, or at least toleration, of peasants for at least two reasons. The first is unequal distribution of land in Colombia, which would presumably be remedied in the sort of state the FARC would create. The second is political neglect of the peasantry, and indeed lack of any beneficial attention to it, by the central government. It seems that Colombia owes much of its chronic political instability, including its long spells of civil war (among them guerrilla activities), to the traditionally exclusive nature of its national political system. Liberals and Conservatives, parties founded in the nineteenth century, have dominated the country's political life, while also strictly limiting effective political participation. The peasantry has had little direct political say, therefore. The country's geography, finally, only compounds its difficulties. Sprawling as it does, in its western half, across three major Andean ranges and their intervening valleys, it presents central government with severe problems of simple access – and opponents to government with many safe havens. In the 1980s and 1990s, control grew yet more difficult with the rise of the refining and export of cocaine. As drug cartels developed in regions of the country, sometimes in league with land owners who already possessed their own private militias to combat the alliance of guerrillas and peasants, local civil wars erupted. The national government thus lost still more control over its territory, and much still remains beyond its effective reach.

Damaging, and even locally devastating, as internal conflict was in parts of Peru and Colombia in recent times, its effects were yet more destructive on the national scale in three Central American countries, for the simple reason that they are small places and fighting spread over much of their areas. The three are Guatemala, El Salvador, and Nicaragua.

All of them suffered particularly severe conflict – civil wars in fact – during the 1980s. Several common causes exist for these simultaneous episodes of violence. The most general condition underlying conflict was that, in those three countries, the traditional social, political, and economic order had changed less in the twentieth century than almost anywhere else in Latin America. More specifically, political parties originating soon after independence in the nineteenth century continued to dominate politics, under the largely exclusive control of people with high economic and social standing. During much of their time of political sway, these parties had collaborated closely with the military, which had usually (though in fairness it must be said not always) been a conservative force. The typical outcome in the twentieth century had been dictatorships interspersed with periods of severe disorder. Severe economic inequities had persisted. Unequal distribution of land was an especially negative trait because, these countries being small in size and population, they had not provided markets large enough to enable much industrialization to take place; consequently a great many people still depended on farming for a livelihood.[76] Inequalities clearly worsened in the 1970s. The three countries' economies grew strongly for most of the decade, but the gains went mainly to the upper end of society, with the majority facing inflation and rising unemployment as the eighties approached. Finally, in the 1970s and 1980s the countries were also the object of much pressure from the USA, which saw leftist movements in them as a dangerous extension of Marxism onto the American mainland. It was not at all obvious at the time that the Cold War was in its final phases; the rise of Marxism in Central America therefore seemed a direct political threat to the United States, whose Republican administrations of the eighties did all they could to support conservative opposition to leftist movements in the area.

The United States tried to influence the course of events above all in Nicaragua, where in the late seventies spontaneous popular protests had coalesced behind the reformist FSLN. This body – the Sandinista National Liberation Front – was a political alliance named after Augusto César Sandino, a national hero who in the early 1930s had fought against both Conservatives and a military intervention by the USA. In 1979 the FSLN forced out Anastasio Somoza, a dictator whose father and brother, also dictators, had ruled Nicaragua from 1936 onwards. The Sandinistas then proceeded to govern the country until 1990, with some support from Cuba and the USSR. Their presence in government gave rise to great and disproportionate consternation in the United States, which proceeded to arm and finance a conservative guerrilla opposition, generally known as the *Contras*. In response the Sandinista government greatly expanded its own army, finally spending over sixty percent of its budget on defense. Constant fighting ensued, costing an estimated 40,000 lives between 1983 and 1987, and perhaps as much as four billion dollars in damage.[77] In the end the United States prevailed, though not militarily. Despite the considerable redistributions of land and other reforms benefiting the mass of the population that the Sandinistas carried out, war expenses created such stringency in the country that when national elections were held, in 1990, they were voted out. Administrative incompetence had mixed with corruption and political infighting among the Sandinistas to contribute to that election result.

In El Salvador and Guatemala, the United States had no revolutionary regime to face in the early 1980s, but it gave strong support to traditional governments facing guerrilla insurrections (providing, for example, more than five billion dollars for improvement and enlargement of the Salvadoran army in the eighties). In both countries popular unrest had grown in the 1970s, for reasons similar to those visible in Nicaragua, though neither possessed so obvious a target for resentment as the Somoza dynasty. But the long alliance of the military and the "haves" in both societies against the "have nots" was just as plain. A distinction in Guatemala, though, was that the "have nots" consisted largely of Indians – speakers of different Maya tongues living in the hilly terrain of the north-west of the country. The holders of wealth and power, on the other hand, were white and mestizo. Hence in Guatemala racial difference added to the socio-economic tension found in Nicaragua and El Salvador (in both of which Indians were fewer). Although the story of events in both countries is full of political twists and turns, in essence both passed through a decade in which revolutionary groups, consisting mainly of peasants, fought for greater political voice, land, and broadly a larger share of the national wealth. The human losses were high: fifty to seventy thousand, mostly Indians, killed in Guatemala between 1978 and 1985, and perhaps a million forced to migrate, either to other parts of the country or northward into Mexico; and in El Salvador, seventy-five thousand dead, and, again, a million displaced.[78]

What was gained at such high cost is still hard to say. If wealth and land have become less unequally shared among the populations of El Salvador, Guatemala, and Nicaragua, numbers have yet to prove that outcome (the probability, at least for land, being highest in Nicaragua, where some land reform did take place in the eighties). It does seem, however, that a result of the conflicts in these three countries was a greater openness of politics, and a greater sense among the mass of the people of their influence in matters of government, if and when they combine to exercise it. On the other hand, only in El Salvador did the armed forces seem to have withdrawn from politics.[79]

RECENT YEARS

In the closing years of the twentieth century, Latin American continued along courses established in most of its countries in the mid-eighties: governments at all levels chosen in popular elections, and economies run on neo-liberal lines. Economic growth resumed in the nineties, though with interruptions from time to time in various countries, and generally at a lower rate than before the late seventies. No obvious trends, nor any clear innovation, are visible in politics in recent years. One important external condition did change, however: with the ending of the Cold War, *c.*1990, Latin America ceased to be territory on which the United States and the Soviet Union fought proxy battles between capitalism and Marxism. Outside Cuba (after 1990 little more than an irritating insect buzzing at the window, at which Washington took occasional reflexive swipes), the USA had scant cause for ideological concern in Latin America as the century ended. That change lowered the likelihood of US intervention, with either arms or money, in Latin American affairs; it also diminished the United States' general interest in the countries to its south. The one outstanding exception to that generalization is the North American Free Trade Agreement (NAFTA) of 1992–3. That was, and is, an economic project, grounded in neo-liberalism, and designed to increase freedom of trade and investment among the United States, Canada, and Mexico for the benefit of all three.

It was Mexico that, in the final year of the twentieth century, sounded perhaps the most positive note in recent Latin American politics. In the presidential election held in July 2000 a candidate won, for the first time since 1929, who was not a member of the single, controlling party (PNR–PRM–PRI). The victor was Vicente Fox, the candidate from the PAN (National Action Party), a conservative, business-oriented, and Catholic organization whose influence had long been rising in the north of the country. At the same time, the single party failed to gain the two-thirds majority needed in the national congress to ensure passage of legislation. These election results were a large step forward in the political maturing of the second largest country in Latin America (by population and economic product).

EPILOGUE

In February 1996 the mayor of Santa Fe, the capital of the state of New Mexico in the southwestern USA, approved the appointment of a new chief of police for the town. The appointee, Carlos Jaramillo, was the brother-in-law of the mayor, Debbie Jaramillo. The appointment was actually made by the city manager, Isaac Pino, who was the mayor's brother. Mr Jaramillo had a somewhat checkered record. In the 1970s he had been the state liquor director, in charge, among other things, of assigning licenses for the sale of alcoholic drinks. He had been accused, though never found guilty, of taking bribes for the granting of licenses, which at the time were very costly in New Mexico because a fixed number had been issued for the entire state. When questioned, Mr Jaramillo had "taken the Fifth Amendment." That is, he had made use of the amendment to the US constitution that excuses an accused person from being a witness against himself.

New Mexico is a state that was once (before 1848) a part of Mexico. In it, especially in the north where Santa Fe lies, a large part in politics is taken by people who call themselves "Hispanics." They are the descendants of colonial settlers of the region; and mainly of people who arrived in the eighteenth century, after the suppression of the Pueblo Indian revolt of the 1680s and 1690s against the Spanish colonial presence. Nowadays Santa Fe also has a large non-Hispanic, or "Anglo," population, since for most of the twentieth century it was known as an artistic center, and in recent decades has become a fashionable place of residence for people, many of them well-off, escaping from the faster pace of life on the east or west coasts of the United States.

From Anglos and some Hispanics came cries of protest over the nepotism of Carlos Jaramillo's appointment. One local wit, a sign painter, replaced the sign outside the town hall with a new one reading "Jaramilloville Municipal Building." The mayor justified the choice and her approval of it by explaining "This community has always been a community that was related to one another. It's no different than anything that has gone on in this community for four hundred years." Later she added "You can pick your nose, you can pick your friends, but you can't pick your family." To explain that cryptic piece of down home wisdom, she went on "I'm trying to be humorous about the crap that they're trying to lay on members of my family – they can't help who they are."

On several counts she was right. Juan de Oñate, a member of a rich silver mining family from Zacatecas, began the Spanish settlement of New Mexico in 1598. Since then the number of Hispanic families in the state has always been small, and they have always intermarried, forming wide kin groups. What elsewhere would be called nepotism has long been, in New Mexico, almost inevitable; although this, to be sure, was a particularly provocative case, especially since Carlos Jaramillo had been the only man considered for the job. Another generally accepted truth seems to have been hidden in the mayor's outspoken elucidation of the business: that relatives who are qualified for jobs should get them, no matter how dubious the appearance (for, after all, "they can't help who they are").[1]

Hispanic politics lives on in New Mexico, helping to give the state the air of a foreign enclave in the United States, an ironic survival of departed empire within a nation that itself has been considered imperialist towards its closer Latin American neighbors. And it is not just in that charming remnant of the Spanish empire that politics is often regarded as a family business, or as providing opportunities for the family to do business. The same still holds across Middle and South America. Raúl Salinas, elder brother of Carlos Salinas de Gortari, president of Mexico from 1988 to 1994, somehow contrived to accumulate between eighty and two hundred million US dollars in a Swiss bank account between 1989 and 1994, while earning, or at least receiving, a bureaucrat's salary of US$ 190,000 annually. The administration of Carlos Menem, president of Argentina, wobbled in the early nineties under the impact of charges that his relatives were drug traders. A decade later, a good part of Argentina's new economic and fiscal crisis resulted from political patronage – the stuffing of government at all levels with the friends and relations of office holders. Many of them appeared at their workplace only to collect their salaries. The state paid out vast sums to such people (by one estimate US$ 2.2 billion in 2001) for very little work in return.[2]

In present Latin America, the primacy of family across the range of life's activities is a barely diminished survival from colonial times. In politics, the inheritance is harmful, since it destroys hope and confidence in reform, and so hinders true democratization. Why bother with the complicated proceedings and forms of representative government, if the elected leaders' relations (and friends) will continue to do as they have always done? In other aspects of life, the role of family is sustaining, both of personal well-being and public order. Fewer people are cast adrift in (or out of) society than in most countries of the industrial world. The willingness of the family, both nuclear and extended, to absorb and support people temporarily or permanently incapable of sustaining themselves certainly works for social and political stability.

There are, of course, in Latin America other impediments to representative government besides its subversion by family and personal interests. The authoritarian centralism of colonial times (although it was for much of them more ideal than reality) has proved durable. In part that may be because the idea also endures that it is the common, not the individual, welfare that really matters; and that therefore the voice of the individual is, in most cases, unimportant. A concern for the health of the whole would, ideally, be well served by enlightened despotism. Latin America has been rich in despots in the past 170 years, but few of their claims to enlightenment would stand close scrutiny. And the good of the whole is too easily transformed into the good of the part, on the grounds that once the part is well established, it will be able to work more effectively for the benefit of all. But the time when it does so has generally been slow in coming.

The combining of governmental powers in single figures and institutions that was standard practice in colonial times has also proved hard to discard, and has sustained authoritarianism. The post-independence *caudillo* was an unmatchable example of the conflation of executive, law-maker, and judge, with military force added to strengthen him in all three roles. In times of political disorder and economic difficulty, often mutually reinforcing, the model has remained seductively attractive. And it has been so not only to those in a position to take power themselves, but to people at all social levels who longed for calm. A notable example in the 1990s was provided by Alberto Fujimori, the son of Japanese immigrants who, to general surprise, was elected president of Peru in 1990. Still greater was the surprise, however, when in April 1992 Fujimori, confronted with rising economic and political dislocation of the country by the *Sendero Luminoso*, suspended the legislative and judicial branches of his government and took dictatorial powers. This *auto-golpe*, or coup against his own administration, had military backing. More significantly it also drew large popular support from a citizenry tired of internal warfare and collapsing living standards. In due course Fujimori convened a constituent congress which drafted a new constitution. That document concentrated power at the center, reduced the congress to one chamber, and allowed for re-election of the president. In 1995 Fujimori, still admired for his autocratic action in 1992, and also receiving credit for the remarkable economic recovery that Peru was by then undergoing, was indeed re-elected. He was the first president of the country to be voted into office for a second successive term. (That term came to an abrupt end, however, in 2000, when he fled the country amidst growing, and undeniable, charges of massive bribery and blackmail in his government.)

In Latin America, then, the strong man at the center may well have the support not just of those around him, or even just of a class that stands to benefit from his presence, but of most of the populace. Whether this predilection for authority is a matter of ingrained political culture, or of reaction to difficulties that it seems only the use of central power can resolve, is open to debate. Certainly the past, extending back to early colonial times, has many models to offer. But little, perhaps nothing, in human behavior is immutable. If and when circumstances of life in Latin America improve sufficiently, the penchant for the strong-armed man may decline. That, after all, is what has happened in European countries that now consider themselves orderly, prosperous, and democratic. They were not always so – some, indeed, were not so within living memory.

At the start of the twenty-first century all Latin American countries, except Cuba, possess elected governments. Those governments, moreover, have been put into office by universal adult suffrage, male and female. Elective democracy has never before seemed so well set in Latin America. What is especially striking is that this upsurge of democracy, after the period of military authoritarianism in the 1970s and 1980s, happened in years of economic downturn. There were fears at the time of violent, perhaps even revolutionary, popular reaction to the fall in living standards that most people experienced. But, except for the guerrilla activities in rural areas already mentioned (most of which had roots further in the past), no such thing happened. The great majority entrusted its future to democratic processes. Optimists may see in that choice a sign of some major reorientation of Latin American political preferences. Skeptics, on the other hand, may read Peru's long admiration of Alberto Fujimori, or the election in 1998 of the former colonel Hugo Chávez – the epitome of the populist *caudillo* – to the presidency of Venezuela, as signs of a still deeper persistence of continuity with the past.

However hard to predict politics may be, close to immutable is another characteristic of Latin America that had its origins in early colonial times, indeed in the first moments of the conquests. That is the ethnic and cultural fusion visible in the populations of almost all the present states, the product of five centuries of *mestizaje*. It is difficult to see how this mixing could be undone, or how its product could be genetically displaced. Only, perhaps, some immense and sustained immigration of people of one particular genetic stock could now overwhelm the mestizos' presence, and a migrant movement of such scale can hardly be imagined. Far more likely is that *mestizaje* will continue to do its work, so that in time an ever larger proportion of national populations will be products of the blending of the Indian and the European, or (as in Brazil and the Greater Antilles) of the African and the European, or, in a few areas, of all three.

All considered, Paraguay is the country in which blending has advanced furthest to date. By one count, for *c.*1990, 76 percent of the population was of mixed white and native origin. By this measure, Honduras and El Salvador were yet more mixed, with 92 and 89 percent of mestizos respectively. But Paraguay has arguably most fully integrated its native past into its present culture, as is shown by the adoption of Guaraní as an official language, and, more significant, its actual daily use by a great part of the population. (Another estimate, for the early 1960s, shows Paraguay as 94 percent mestizo. The contrast with the lower figure quoted for thirty years later does not indicate a whitening or indianizing of the population, but the difficulty of deciding whether many mestizos are more white or native than mixed).[3]

Of the large countries, Mexico had the largest proportion of mestizos *c.*1990, with 75%, followed by Chile and Venezuela, both with 70%, Colombia with 50%, Peru 42%, and Bolivia 32%. Lowest on the mestizo scale in Spanish America were Uruguay (7.5%), and Argentina (2%). Both these are largely white countries, in which large immigration from Europe a century ago overwhelmed other genetic elements in the populations. Brazil, *c.*1990, was estimated to be evenly divided between Whites and those with a greater or lesser degree of African blood; Indians survive in the interior, but in numbers that come to less than one percent of the total population.

In no other large region of the world in recent centuries has a such extensive ethnic mixing taken place. (The population of Latin America in 1990 was 448 million, almost a tenth of the global total.) Vasconcelos's contention that the future "cosmic race" of Latin America would be superior to any of its four predecessors is no more defensible than the colonial Spaniards' belief that mestizos compounded the worst of both Indians and Europeans, but the cultural blending produced by physical mixing has given rise to a particular human inventiveness that has already produced notable results and should give many more. There is the intermingling of religion that in the Andes and elsewhere has drawn Christian saints and ancient native deities together into single cults, or which has blended Catholicism and African beliefs to produce Umbanda in Brazil (a spiritist religion with both a working- and middle-class following), and Voodoo in Haiti and other Caribbean places. There is the blending of musical traditions that has yielded at the popular level the central Andean *cueca*, and, better known, various dance forms (often songs as well) with a strong African base: the Argentine tango, the Brazilian samba and bossa nova, the Caribbean son, cha-cha, *salsa*, *cumbia*, and others. In formal music, the combining of European and native influences can be heard in the work of Carlos Chávez, who drew inspiration from the rhythms of pre-Hispanic Mexico, and more clearly yet in the compositions of Heitor Villa-Lobos, the most widely known composer of "art" music in Brazil and indeed in all of Latin America. His greatest inspiration came from the folk music of the interior, in which he traveled for several years as a youth, gathering material. There is the art of the muralists and others in Mexico, and a variety of painters elsewhere in Latin America, which takes as part of its subject matter the mestizo, the mulatto, and the historical interaction of Europeans and American natives. There is the fiction of recent decades, the work of such world-class writers as Gabriel García-Márquez and Mario Vargas Llosa, which is shot through with the mestizo presence. Far from least there is food, almost everywhere a combining of Old and New World ingredients and preparation. It is in Mexico that mestizo cuisine rises to its greatest height, blending wheat, meat, and dairy products from Europe, with maize, beans, and chiles from Middle America to produce one of the world's great culinary forms.

Middle and South America are distinctive not only in their degree of ethnic mixing and its cultural outcomes, but in the post-colonial identity with which *mestizaje* left them. Brazil and the former Spanish territories occupy in this respect a middle position in the range of ex-colonies of recent times. To one side of them stand former possessions like the United States, Canada, Australia, and New Zealand, in which colonials, with or without violence, rejected colonial rule and themselves became the masters of their own affairs. The native people of these regions had little or no say in independent government, either at the time of independence or later. On the other side are many other states, mainly in Africa and Asia, from which, again with or without fighting, the colonial powers departed, leaving native people in charge of government. Spanish and Portuguese America occupy an intermediate position, of which Spanish America provides the clearer illustration. After the colonizing power was expelled, those who gained authority were neither simply ex-colonials nor native people. Political power passed after independence in part to creoles, and in part to mixed elements in the population. Creoles certainly shared the values and culture of the departed colonial rulers to a degree; some shared almost all of them, others very few. But nearly all creoles were in some measure also culturally mestizo, in that the American homelands with which they identified in a range of affective and material ways were partly defined culturally by their Indianness (with the exception of Argentina and Uruguay). Most creoles, perhaps, were in some measure genetically mestizo, though they would have denied it. And then, of course, there were undisputed mestizos who after independence exercised great political and military power, mostly as regional *caudillos*, but two, at least, as national presidents: Santa Cruz in Bolivia and Castilla in Peru. (To drive home the point, it is worth recalling that Benito Juárez, liberal president of Mexico, was genetically Indian, although education and profession made him culturally a mestizo). The point is, then, that political control in the national period of Spanish America did not remain in the hands of outsiders nor revert to those of natives, but rather became the possession of groups who to differing but significant degrees were the product, the new mestizo product, of what had once been the conquering and the conquered elements of the population and culture. (In Brazil, much the same has happened, although, as was the pattern in colonial history, somewhat later than in Spanish America. And in Brazil the mixture is not to any significant degree of White and Indian, but of White and Black.)

In Latin America, therefore, after independence, the clear-cut identity issue of natives *versus* ex-colonials did not exist. The Spanish American "we" was inescapably part of both, and has since then become ever more fully so. (In the Brazilian version of the process, the native is replaced by the African.) This fusing can quite properly be seen as the ultimate derivation of Spain's early wish to "incorporate" the American territories. That was, in the sixteenth century, seen as a political and legal matter. The American "realms" were to be equal parts of the Spanish body politic with the Iberian kingdoms, each of them directly attached to the head, the monarchy. But incorporation was a wider aim, an ethos of colonization rather than a simple matter of law or policy. The attachment of the American natives was also to be achieved through christianization and what the Spanish considered "civilization" – teaching them to behave in every way as much as possible like Spaniards. With limitations, some of which have been recounted in this book, that happened. But what the Spanish policy-makers and theorists of empire did not see in the sixteenth century was that America would in its own ways "incorporate" the colonists. Not only was the American Europeanized, but the European Americanized. And in the convergence lies the present and future identity of Latin America.

Further Reading

Mountainous quantities have been written on twentieth-century Latin America, by, in addition to historians, legions of anthropologists, economists, political scientists, and sociologists. Volumes 6 to 10 of *The Cambridge History of Latin America* are devoted to the period between 1930 and the present. A most attractive survey of recent times, however, can be found in Peter Winn, *Americas. The Changing Face of Latin America and the Caribbean* (Pantheon Books, New York/University of California Press, Berkeley and Los Angeles, 1992, 1999).

GLOSSARY

aguardiente "Burning water" – i.e. brandy, usually made from wine. In Brazil, *aguardente* was rum, prepared from sugar.

alcalde mayor See *corregidor*.

aldeia A mission village in colonial Brazil, into which Indians were "congregated" by evangelizing priests, mostly Jesuits.

altiplano "High plain." A word applied to the northern Mexican plateau (1,200–2,400 meters), and the plain between the western and eastern Andean chains in Bolivia (*c*.4,000 meters).

arroba A measure of dry weight, in Brazil about 14.75 kilograms, and in Spanish America about 11.5 kilograms.

asiento (de negros) A contract for the supply of African slaves to colonial Spanish America.

Audiencia A regional court of appeal, and administrative tribunal, in colonial Spanish America.

Bajío Fertile area of central Mexico, north of Mexico City, and merging northwards into the *altiplano*; excellent land for grain.

bandeirantes "Pathfinders" of the interior of Brazil, typically from São Paulo, pursuing Indian slaves and precious metals, and active mainly in the seventeenth century.

boucanier "Buccaneer." A informal French settler in the Caribbean, particularly in western Hispaniola, in the seventeenth century, generally of a piratical nature. So named from the use of the *boucan*, or grill, to smoke and so preserve meat.

bureaucratic authoritarianism Military government by the military as an institution, rather than by a single figure from the armed forces; best exemplified in Argentina, Brazil, Chile, and Uruguay in the 1960s, 1970s, and 1980s; often harsh and neglectful of law and human rights.

cabildo Town council, in Spanish America.

cabildo abierto "Open council." A town meeting in colonial Spanish America, supposedly open, but in fact usually attended only by local notables.

cacique An Indian leader. Colonial Spaniards took the term from the Caribbean and applied it to native leaders of all levels on the mainlands.

Carrera de Indias The "Indies run," or shipping of goods to and fro between Spain and America in the officially permitted *flotas* and *galeones* (q.v.).

castas A generic term for all people in colonial Spanish America who were not Whites or Indians.

caudillo A political boss, either regional or national, in Spanish America. The term applies mostly to nineteenth-century figures, but some twentieth-century leaders may be ranked as *caudillos*.

chácara   Land for planting, in the Quechua speaking parts of the Andes.

Charcas   The sixteenth- and seventeenth-century name for the area corresponding roughly to modern Bolivia; more commonly known in the eighteenth century as *Alto Perú*, ("Upper Peru").

chicha   A mildly alcoholic drink of the Andes, consumed from pre-Columbian times to the present, fermented from chewed maize.

coca   *Erythroxylon Coca*, or its dried leaves, which from time immemorial native Andeans have chewed to relieve hunger, thirst, and fatigue.

congregación   In colonial Spanish America, the gathering of more or less scattered Indians into a single community, existing or new. Also known as *reducción*.

Consejo de Indias   See Council of the Indies.

consulado   In Spain and its colonies, a tribunal overseeing a community of large merchants in a particular place, and trying cases in which they were involved.

corporate state (corporatism)   Variety of state in which the political community consists not of individuals but of a number of economic and functional groups (such as labor unions or peasant organizations) of which individuals are members. In principle a system allowing expression of the interests of group members, and giving them joint influence in the affairs of state; in practice often a means by which central authority controls large segments of a population.

corregidor   A "co-ruler." In Spain a royally-appointed governor of a town. In the colonies, the same, or more commonly, a district officer at the lowest level of the bureaucracy, governing one or more native communities. Difficult to distinguish in Spanish America from the *alcalde mayor*.

Council of the Indies   The supreme administrative council of state for colonial Spanish America.

creole   See *criollo*.

criollo   Literally a native of a particular region (from Spanish *criar*, "to raise"); a term applicable to any non-native American born in Spanish America, but normally applied to Whites born in the colonies.

crioulo   A slave born in Brazil, whether of African- or Brazilian-born parents.

curaca   The Quechua term for a local Indian leader in the Andes.

degredado   A criminal exiled from Portugal (often to Brazil, in the early sixteenth century).

desembargador   A judge in a Portuguese high court.

doctrina   A rural parish in colonial Spanish America.

ejido   In Spain and colonial Spanish America, public lands around a town or village for communal use (mostly grazing of animals); in post-Revolutionary Mexico, pieces of farm land collectively held, but usually divided into smaller units worked by families that are members of the holding community.

encomendero   A Spanish colonist to whom an *encomienda* was granted by the crown or its authorized agent.

encomienda   A grant to a Spanish colonist of the tribute (consisting of goods, sometimes cash, and, in the early post-conquest decades, labor) of a number of Indians. In return the colonist was to teach the Indians given in *encomienda* (trust) to him or to her both Christianity and "civilized" conduct.

engenho   A sugar mill and estate in colonial Brazil.

entrada   "Entry." In Brazil, an exploratory expedition into the interior, mainly in the seventeenth century. Also used in early Spanish America in the same sense.

estancia   In Spanish America, a private landholding, usually small, for farming, and particularly for raising livestock. Specifically, in the usage of the Río de la Plata in the eighteenth century, an area of usufruct of pasture and water.

factoría   A factory, or premises, in Spanish America for the reception and housing of slaves newly arrived from Africa.

factory   A trading post (in, e.g., the Portuguese empire), sometimes fortified.

flota   Literally, "fleet." Specifically the trading fleet intended to sail annually from Spain to New Spain (i.e. Mexico) and back for most of the colonial period.

forastero   Generally, "outsider." Specifically, in the central Andes, an Indian who had moved permanently from his or her native community to another.

Friars Minor   The Franciscans (the Order of Friars Minor).

galeones   Literally, "galleons." Specifically, for most of the colonial era, the trading fleet intended to sail annually from Spain to the Caribbean side of the Isthmus of Panama carrying goods for the west coast of South America, and returning goods thence to Spain.

garúa   A thick mist covering parts of the Peruvian coast during the winter.

hacendado   The owner of an *hacienda*.

hacienda   Rural estate in Spanish America, both colonial and national, often very large in remote and infertile regions, smaller in areas of good farm land close to population centers. A defining socio-economic unit of Spanish America.

hidalgo   Literally, "child of something." A person of nobility.

Liberation theology   A movement in Catholic thought and action, particularly associated with Latin America, and deriving from the Second Vatican Council (1962–5); principally the proposition that the Church should take practical action in the world to address the needs of the poor, if necessary through participation in politics, and even in violent action aimed at reform.

mestizaje   "Race" mixture.

mestizo   A person of mixed parentage; usually, in Spanish America, of mixed European and Indian blood.

México-Tenochtitlan   The name given to Mexico City for a few decades after the military conquest by the Spanish.

mulato   A Mulatto, or person of mixed African and European blood.

naboría   Originally, someone who was the personal dependent of a native leader in the Caribbean. The Spanish took the term to New Spain, where it came to mean an Indian who was the personal servant of a Spaniard; and, more loosely, an Indian who worked for wages.

Neo-liberalism   Resurgence in the late twentieth century of classical liberal economics, emphasizing the efficacy, for creating wealth, of unrestrained competition, open markets, and the unimpeded movement of capital.

New Galicia   The name given by the Spanish to a large region of northwestern Mexico in colonial times. The capital was at Guadalajara.

New Granada   The name used in colonial, and early national, times for the territory covered by present Colombia. ("Colombia" came into use in 1863.)

New Leon (Nuevo León)   A province of northeastern Mexico in colonial times, and a modern Mexican state in the same area.

New Mexico   The northernmost province of colonial Mexico, beyond the Rio Grande; now a state in the United States.

New Spain   The usual term for Mexico in the colonial period. Strictly speaking, as a viceroyalty "New Spain" embraced not only Mexico, but Central America (as far south as, but not including, Panama), Spanish possessions within the present limits of the United States, Spanish Caribbean islands, and the Philippines.

obraje   A spinning and weaving workshop, equipped with spinning wheels and mechanical looms.

oidor   A judge in an *Audiencia*.

ouvidor geral   A higher crown magistrate in a territorial section, or province, of colonial Brazil.

pardo   In Spanish America, a person with some degree of African blood. In colonial Brazil, a slave of mixed ancestry.

paulistas   The inhabitants of the town or city of São Paulo in Brazil; particularly famous as *bandeirantes* in the seventeenth century.

Peru   In colonial times, the name commonly used for the territory corresponding roughly with present Peru. As a viceroyalty, however, "Peru" embraced until 1739 the whole of Spanish South America, and Panama. At that date the viceroyalty of New Granada was created. In 1776 another viceroyalty, that of the Río de la Plata, was added. The Peruvian viceroyalty then consisted only of present Peru and Chile.

peso   A widely-used term for a coin or unit of currency. The basic meaning is simply "weight." A peso originally was a certain weighed amount of gold or silver. In colonial Spanish America, the largest commonly circulating coin, weighing one ounce, was the *peso de a ocho*, or "piece of eight" – eight referring to the number of *reales* composing the peso. A common unit of account, though not an actual coin, was the *peso ensayado* of 13.25 *reales*.

Quito   As a province of colonial Spanish America, the area roughly corresponding to present Ecuador.

Real Hacienda   In colonial times, the Spanish royal treasury.

real oficial   A treasury official in colonial times.

reducción   See *congregación*.

regular clergy/regulars   Members of religious orders (e.g., Franciscans, Dominicans, Jesuits, Augustinians).

relação   A high court in Portugal and its colonies, corresponding to the Spanish *audiencia*.

repartimiento   Broadly, "distribution." Used in several senses in colonial Spanish America: as a near synonym for *encomienda*; as the name for the state's assignment of Indians to colonists for labor; as the term for the forced sale of goods to Indians by local officials of colonial government. In the latter sense also found as *reparto* (*de comercio* or *de efectos*).

resgate   In colonial Brazil, the ransoming of Indians taken captive by other Indians, and supposedly in danger of their lives, for the purpose of enslaving them. Considered a licit means of obtaining slaves, but much abused.

residencia   In colonial Spanish America, the investigation of an official's conduct in office that his successor was legally required to perform.

safra   In Brazil, the harvesting of sugar cane.

Sapa Inca   The "sole" Inca; i.e. the supreme Inca leader, or emperor.

secular clergy   Clergy not belonging to any religious order, but living in the "world" as part of the central church hierarchy of archbishops, bishops, parish priests, etc.

sertão   A general term for the interior of Brazil; more specifically, the dry and infertile interior of the north-east of Brazil.

situado   In colonial Spanish America, a subsidy from one treasury office to another, generally to cover military expenses.

Spanish Main   See *Tierra Firme*.

Tierra Firme   The Spanish Main[land]. A general term for the first shores of the American mainland explored by the Spaniards, from Panama to the Guianas.

tlatoani   "He who speaks" (Nahuatl). The supreme leader of a polity in pre-conquest Mexico.

trapiche   Generally a small mill of some sort, for, e.g., silver refining, sugar processing, or cloth making.

Upper Peru "Alto Perú." The eighteenth-century term for Charcas (now, roughly speaking, Bolivia).

Valley of Mexico The large valley in which Mexico City, formerly the Aztec capital Tenochtitlan, lies.

vaqueiro Cowherd in colonial Brazil.

vecino Literally "neighbor" in Spanish. In colonial times a householder in a town, usually of some social standing, and therefore usually white.

viceroy The supreme executive authority in colonial Spanish America, where, before the eighteenth century, two viceroyalties existed: New Spain (1535–) and Peru (1544–). In 1739 New Granada became a viceroyalty; and in 1776, the Río de la Plata also.

visita In colonial Spanish America, a "visit" or official inspection of some administrator, administrative body, or region by a high-ranking bureaucrat. Generally speaking a *visitador* was sent to resolve some particular problem that had arisen.

yanacona/yana In the central Andes, an Indian who, like the *naboría* in the Caribbean, was before the conquest the personal dependent of some powerful figure. After the conquest, an Indian who was the personal servant of a Spaniard.

zambo A person of mixed African and American Indian parentage.

Notes

Chapter 1: Lands and Climates

1 Arregui, *Descripción*, pp. 164–5.
2 James, *Latin America*, p. 21.
3 Ibid., p. 77.
4 West and Augelli, *Middle America*, pp. 30–1.
5 Ibid., p. 33; Clapperton, "Tectonic history," pp. 12–14.
6 James, *Latin America*, pp. 21–2; Smith, "The Central Andes," p. 256.
7 Clapperton, "Tectonic history," p. 18.
8 *Hammond Comparative World Atlas*, 1989, p. 13.
9 James, *Latin America*, p. 24.
10 Ibid., p. 334.
11 Ibid., p. 24.
12 Henshall and Momsen, *A Geography*, pp. 189–96.
13 James, *Latin America*, p. 836.
14 Ibid., p. 837.
15 Henshall and Momsen, *A Geography*, p. 4; Galloway, "Brazil," in Blakemore and Smith, *Latin America*, p. 326.
16 Zepeda, *República mexicana*, p. 28.
17 *Hammond Comparative World Atlas*, p. 37; James, *Latin America*, pp. 242–3.
18 *Hammond Comparative World Atlas*, p. 36.
19 James, *Latin America*, p. 419.
20 Ibid., p. 441.
21 Lanning, *Peru before the Incas*, p. 10.
22 Ibid., p. 9.
23 James, *Latin America*, p. 553.
24 Ibid.
25 Ibid., p. 572.
26 Ibid., pp. 401–3.
27 Ibid., pp. 437–9.
28 Conrad and Demarest, *Religion and Empire*, pp. 161–2.
29 Ibid., p. 162.
30 Dobyns and Doughty, *Peru*, p. 15.
31 Blakemore and Smith, *Latin America*, pp. 256–7.
32 Larson, *Colonialism*, 1988, pp. 28–9.
33 Bennett and Bird, *Andean Culture History*, p. 60.
34 Ibid., pp. 60–2.

35 Blakemore and Smith, *Latin America*, p. 459.
36 James, *Latin America*, pp. 570, 577.
37 Ibid., pp. 25–6.
38 West and Augelli, *Middle America*, p. 47.
39 James, *Latin America*, pp. 596, 621–2.
40 Burns, *A History*, pp. 135–7.
41 Wilkie, *Statistical Abstract*, vol. 17, p. 50 (table 400).

Chapter 2: American Peoples

1   Cortés, *Letters*, p. 108.
2   *Cabildo* of Jauja to Charles V, cited in Hemming, *The Conquest*, p. 120.
3   Conrad and Demarest, *Religion*, p. 84.
4   Davies, *The Aztecs*, pp. 8ff; Clendinnen, *Aztecs*, pp. 22–3.
5   Conrad and Demarest, *Religion*, p. 22.
6   Ibid., p. 30.
7   Calnek, "Patterns," p. 55.
8   Davies, *The Aztecs*, p. 54.
9   Calnek, "Patterns," p. 48.
10 Davies, *The Aztecs*, pp. 41–3.
11 Broda et al., *The Great Temple*, pp. 65ff.
12 Conrad and Demarest, *Religion*, p. 38.
13 Clendinnen, *Aztecs*, p. 28.
14 Cook, "The Historical Demography", passim.
15 Rojas, *Mexico Tenochtitlan*, chapter 3.
16 Conrad and Demarest, *Religion*, pp. 173–8; Hassig, *Aztec Warfare*, pp. 263–6.
17 Conrad and Demarest, *Religion*, p. 38.
18 Clendinnen, *Aztecs*, p. 91.
19 Ibid., p. 97.
20 Ibid., pp. 216–18.
21 Brundage, *A Rain of Darts*, passim.
22 Clendinnen, *Aztecs*, pp. 79–80, 156.
23 Ibid., pp. 48–54.
24 Morris, "Progress and prospect," p. 236.
25 Conrad and Demarest, *Religion*, p. 97.
26 Stern, *Peru's Indian Peoples*, pp. 4–9.
27 Rostworowski de Diez Canseco, *Historia*, pp. 46, 59. For Huari, Isbell, "City and state," passim.
28 Conrad and Demarest, *Religion*, p. 111.
29 Rostworowski de Diez Canseco, *Historia*, pp. 59–60.
30 Hemming, *The Conquest*, p. 132; Mason, *The Ancient Civilizations*, pp. 208.
31 Conrad and Demarest, *Religion*, pp. 100–10; Rostworowski de Diez Canseco, *Historia*, p. 76.
32 Hyslop, *The Inka Road System*, passim.
33 Rostworowski de Diez Canseco, *Historia*, pp. 100–3, 132.
34 Ibid., pp. 122, 132–3.
35 Cf. Brundage, *Two Earths*, pp. 35–7.
36 Conrad and Demarest, *Religion*, pp. 124–5.
37 Ibid., pp. 112–21.

38 Mason, *Ancient Civilizations*, p. 174.
39 Patterson, *The Inca Empire*, p. 76.
40 Ibid., p. 81.
41 Rostworowski de Diez Canseco, *Historia*, pp. 122–5.
42 All above from Helms, "The Indians," pp. 37–45.
43 Juan de San Martín and Antonio de Lebrija to Charles V, in Parry and Keith, *New Iberian World*, vol. 4, p. 412.
44 Hidalgo, "The Indians," p. 106.
45 Ibid., p. 116.
46 Hemming, "The Indians of Brazil," p. 133. This description of Brazilian native people is largely based on Hemming's account.
47 Hulme, *Colonial Encounters*, pp. 61–4; and chapter 2 passim.
48 Discussion of the Arawak here closely follows Helms, "The Indians," pp. 49–54.
49 Wilson, *Hispaniola*, p. 2.
50 Ibid., pp. 6, 15, 32.
51 See, for example, Pendergast, "Up from the dust."
52 Schele and Freidel, *A Forest of Kings*, chapters 9, 10.
53 "Chichimecs," in Tenenbaum (ed.), *Encyclopedia of Latin American History and Culture*, vol. 2, p. 94.

Chapter 3: Iberia

1 Morison, *Admiral*, p. 221.
2 McAlister, *Spain and Portugal*, p. 42.
3 Oliveira Marques, *A History*, p. 145.
4 John Noble Wilford, "Norsemen in America flourished, then faded," *The New York Times*, "Science Times," July 7, 1992.
5 Parry, *The Age*, p. 117.
6 Oliveira Marques, *A History*, p. 133.
7 Ibid., p. 148.
8 O'Callaghan, *A History*, p. 397.
9 Oliveira Marques, *A History*, p. 137.
10 Ibid., p. 130.
11 Diffie and Winius, *Foundations*, p. 34.
12 Ibid., p. 77; Oliveira Marques, *A History*, p. 158.
13 Fernández-Armesto, *Ferdinand and Isabella*, p. 155.
14 Diffie and Winius, *Foundations*, p. 104.
15 Ibid., p. 306; Oliveira Marques, *A History*, p. 154.
16 Oliveira Marques, *A History*, p. 154.
17 Ibid., p. 153.
18 Ibid., pp. 240–1.
19 Fernández-Armesto, *Ferdinand and Isabella*, p. 144.
20 Diffie and Winius, *Foundations*, pp. 42–4.
21 Fernández-Armesto, *Ferdinand and Isabella*, pp. 144–5; Diffie and Winius, *Foundations*, p. 59.
22 Diffie and Winius, *Foundations*, p. 58.
23 Elliott, *Imperial Spain*, chapter 1.
24 Le Flem et al., *La frustración*, p. 145.
25 Elliott, *Imperial Spain*, p. 7.

26　Ibid., p. 86.
27　Lunenfeld, *The Council*, pp. 99–107.
28　Kamen, *Spain, 1469–1714*, p. 21.
29　Le Flem et al., *La frustración*, p. 152.
30　Joseph Pérez, in Le Flem, *La frustración*, p. 153.
31　Kamen, *Spain, 1469–1714*, p. 38, and *The Spanish Inquisition*, pp. 36–7; Le Flem et al., *La frustración*, pp. 156–7.
32　Kamen, *Spain, 1469–1714*, p. 39.
33　Ibid., p. 41.
34　Bénnassar, *Inquisición*, passim, and pp. 337–41.
35　Le Flem et al., *La frustración*, p. 160.
36　Fernández-Armesto, *Ferdinand and Isabella*, p. 92.
37　Kamen, *Spain, 1469–1714*, p. 34; Fernández-Armesto, *Ferdinand and Isabella*, p. 99.
38　Fernández-Armesto, *Ferdinand and Isabella*, p. 89.
39　Kamen, *Spain, 1469–1714*, pp. 35–6.
40　Garrido Aranda, *Moriscos*, p. 51.
41　Kamen, *Spain, 1469–1714*, p. 37.
42　Phelan, *The Millennial Kingdom*, p. 45; also Liss, *Mexico*, pp. 14–15.
43　Diffie and Winius, *Foundations*, p. 155.
44　Ibid., pp. 159–65.

Chapter 4: Columbus and Others

1　Diffie and Winius, *Foundations*, pp. 58, 88; Phillips and Phillips, *The Worlds*, p. 98.
2　Phillips and Phillips, *The Worlds*, p. 108; Fernández-Armesto, *Columbus*, p. 30.
3　Morison, *Admiral*, p. 68.
4　Phillips and Phillips, *The Worlds*, p. 130; Fernández-Armesto, *Columbus*, p. 52.
5　Fernández-Armesto, *Columbus*, p. 45–6.
6　Ibid., p. 70; Phillips and Phillips, *The Worlds*, pp. 133–4.
7　Fernández-Armesto, *Columbus*, p. 26.
8　Ibid., pp. 49–50; Todorov, *The Conquest*, p. 26.
9　"Oath sworn regarding Cuba," cited in Todorov, *The Conquest*, p. 32; also Morison, *Admiral*, p. 466.
10　Sauer, *The Early Spanish Main*, pp. 72–7.
11　Phillips and Phillips, *The Worlds*, pp. 206–11.
12　Vigneras, *The Discovery*, p. 19.
13　Morales Padrón, *Historia del descubrimiento*, chapter 4.
14　Parry, *The Discovery*, p. 222.
15　Ibid., p. 217.
16　Morales Padrón, *Historia del descubrimiento*, p. 140.
17　Ibid., p. 151.
18　Ibid., chapter 6.
19　Sauer, *Sixteenth Century North America*, pp. 154–6.
20　Parry and Keith, *New Iberian World*, vol. 3, p. 475.
21　Spate, *The Spanish Lake*, p. 104.
22　Oliveira Marques, *History of Portugal*, p. 229; Diffie and Winius, *Foundations*, second map following p. 192.

23 An English translation of the treaty in Parry and Keith, *New Iberian World*, vol. 1, pp. 275–80.

Chapter 5: Experiment in the Caribbean

1   Ferdinand Columbus, *The Life*, p. 85.
2   Sauer, *The Early Spanish Main*, p. 81.
3   Chaunu, *Conquête*, p. 121.
4   Ibid., p. 122; Sauer, *The Early Spanish Main*, pp. 105–6.
5   Rouse, *The Tainos*, p. 155.
6   Cook and Borah, *Essays*, vol. 1, p. 410.
7   Ibid., vol. I, chapter 6; Cook, "Disease," pp. 214–20.
8   Sauer, *The Early Spanish Main*, p. 181.
9   Gómara, *Cortés*, p. 5.
10 Quoted in Sauer, *The Early Spanish Main*, p. 183.
11 Chaunu, *Conquête*, p. 131.
12 Góngora, *Studies*, pp. 4–5.
13 Tyler, *Two Worlds*, pp. 137–8, citing Las Casas, *Historia de las Indias*, book 1, chapter 92.
14 Ibid., p. 213, citing Las Casas, *Historia de las Indias*, book 2, chapter 6.
15 Sauer, *The Early Spanish Main*, p. 156. For mining and agriculture under Ovando, see Lamb, *Frey Nicolás*, pp. 167–75.
16 Lamb, *Frey Nicolás*, p. 170.
17 Pagden, *The Fall*, p. 15.
18 Sauer, *The Early Spanish Main*, p. 151; Parry and Keith, *New Iberian World*, vol. 2, p. 256.
19 Sauer, *The Early Spanish Main*, p. 152.
20 Lamb, *Frey Nicolás*, pp. 191–2.
21 Sauer, *The Early Spanish Main*, pp. 199–200.
22 Lamb, *Frey Nicolás*, p. 182–3.
23 Sánchez Bella, *La organización*, p. 12.
24 Ibid., p. 14.
25 Lamb, *Frey Nicolás*, p. 186.
26 Ibid., p. 184.
27 Las Casas, *Historia de las Indias*, vol. 1, chapters 27–30, cited in Parry and Keith, *New Iberian World*, vol. 2, p. 270.
28 Sauer, *The Early Spanish Main*, p. 149; Tyler, *Two Worlds*, pp. 219–24, citing Las Casas, *Historia de las Indias*, book 2, chapter 9.
29 Las Casas, *Historia de las Indias*, book 2 chapter 8, quoted in Tyler, *Two Worlds*, p. 216.
30 Zavala, *La encomienda*, p. 13.
31 Ibid., p. 15.
32 McAlister, *Spain and Portugal*, p. 157.
33 Lamb, *Frey Nicolás*, p. 213.
34 Floyd, *The Columbus Dynasty*, pp. 144–5.
35 Haring, *The Spanish Empire*, p. 22.
36 Schäfer, *El Consejo Real*, vol. 2, p. 66.
37 Haring, *The Spanish Empire*, p. 84.
38 Lamb, *Frey Nicolás*, p. 212.
39 Haring, *The Spanish Empire*, p. 180.

40 Lamb, *Frey Nicolás*, p. 210; Floyd, *The Columbus Dynasty*, p. 149.

41 Floyd, *The Columbus Dynasty*, pp. 150–1.

42 Ibid., pp. 153–5.

43 Dussel, *Historia general*, vol. I/1, p. 304, quoting Las Casas, *Historia de las Indias*, book 3, chapter 4.

44 Dussel, *Historia general*, vol. I/1, p. 304.

45 Zavala, *La encomienda*, p. 22.

46 For a translated text of the Laws of Burgos, Parry and Keith, *New Iberian World*, vol. 1, pp. 336–47. See also Simpson, *The Encomienda*, pp. 33–4, and Zavala, *La encomienda*, pp. 22–4.

47 Zavala, *La encomienda*, p. 27.

48 Simpson, *The Encomienda*, p. 53, and chapter 4 passim.

49 Zavala, *La encomienda*, pp. 32–7.

50 Chaunu, *Conquête*, p. 132.

51 Sauer, *The Early Spanish Main*, pp. 159–60.

52 Cook and Borah, *Essays*, vol. 1, p. 401.

53 Ibid., vol. 1, pp 409–10; Cook, "Disease," pp. 236–9.

54 Sauer, *The Early Spanish Main*, p. 203.

55 Ibid., p. 203.

Chapter 6: Military Conquest

1 Díaz del Castillo, *The Conquest*, p. 16.

2 Ibid., p. 47.

3 Prescott, *The Conquest*, vol. 1, p. 164.

4 Cortés, *Letters*, p. 113.

5 Parry and Keith, *New Iberian World*, vol. IV, pp. 48–50.

6 Lope de Vega, *Arauco domado*, act 1 (p. 117).

7 Hemming, *The Conquest of the Incas*, pp. 154, 201; Espinosa Soriano, *La destrucción del Imperio*, passim.

8 Todorov, *The Conquest of America*, p. 74.

9 Kubler, "The behavior of Atahualpa," p. 421. Discussion of the Aztecs here draws from Clendinnen, " 'Fierce and unnatural cruelty'," and *Aztecs*, chapter 11; Díaz del Castillo, *The Conquest of New Spain*; Hassig, *Aztec Warfare*, chapter 16; Todorov, *The Conquest of America*, especially chapter 2; Vaillant, *The Aztecs of Mexico*, chapter 14.

10 Clendinnen, *Aztecs*, p. 269, quoting from Sahagún, *Florentine Codex*, book 12.

Chapter 7: Administration: the Power of Paper

1 See Cortés, *Letters*, passim.

2 Gómara, *Cortés*, p. 327.

3 Cortés fourth letter to Charles V, October 15, 1524, in *Letters*, p. 336.

4 Simpson, *The Encomienda*, p. 61.

5 Cortés, *Letters*, pp. 511–12. For the ordinances on Indian treatment, Parry and Keith, *New Iberian World*, vol. 3, pp. 350–2.

6 Gibson, *The Aztecs*, p. 60.

7 Himmerich, *The Encomenderos*, p. 58.

8 Gómara, *Cortés*, pp. 340–1.

9 *Historia verdadera*, vol. 3, p. 138.

10 Simpson, *The Encomienda*, pp. 164–7; also p. 391, note, of his translation of Gómara, *Cortés*.

11 Riley, *Fernando Cortés*, pp. 29–30.

12 Elliott, *Imperial Spain*, p. 163.

13 Gómara, *Cortés*, p. 408.

14 Schäfer, *El Consejo*, p 16.

15 *Leyes y ordenanzas nuevamente hechas por su Magestad para la gobernación de las Indias y buen tratamiento y conservación de los indios ...* (complete text, Escuela de Estudios Hispanoamericanos, Seville, 1961); partial translation in Parry and Keith, *New Iberian World*, vol. 1, pp. 348–56.

16 Vargas, *Historia del Ecuador*, pp. 78–9.

17 Lockhart, *Men of Cajamarca*, p. 179.

18 Bataillon, "Les colons ...," p. 492.

19 Garcilaso, *Royal Commentaries*, vol. 2, p. 1217.

20 Simmons, *Albuquerque*, pp. 100–2.

21 Mora Mérida, *Historia social*, p. 3.

22 Loveman, *Chile*, p. 70.

23 Parry, *Audiencia of New Galicia*, p. 19.

24 Schäfer, *El Consejo*, vol. 2, p. 68.

25 *Leyes y ordenanzas nuevamente hechas*, clauses 10 and 11.

26 Haring, *The Spanish Empire*, p. 131.

27 Elliott, *Imperial Spain*, pp. 71, 166.

28 For Mendoza, see Aiton, *Antonio de Mendoza*.

29 Parry, *Audiencia*, pp. 27–8.

30 Aiton, *Antonio de Mendoza*, p. 87.

31 Góngora, *Studies*, p. 76.

32 *Recopilación*, book 3, title 3, laws 3, 65.

33 Cf. Leonard, *Baroque Times*, chapter 1.

34 For Toledo, see Zimmerman, *Francisco de Toledo*; for amalgamation and mining labor, Bakewell, *Miners*, chapters 1, 3.

35 Lohmann Villena and Sarabia Viejo, *Francisco de Toledo. Disposiciones ...*

36 Elliott, *Imperial Spain*, p. 161.

37 Burkholder and Johnson, *Colonial Latin America*, p. 74.

38 Elliott, *Imperial Spain*, p. 160.

39 Himmerich, "The Encomenderos", pp. 58, 92.

40 Lohmann Villena, *El corregidor*; Ramírez, "El Dueño de Indios"; Bakewell, "La maduración". For *corregimientos* in New Spain, Ruiz Medrano, *Gobierno*, esp. pp. 69–79 and appendix 1; also Burkholder and Johnson, *Colonial Latin America*, pp. 78–9.

41 For local government, see, for example, Marzahl, *Town in the Empire*.

42 Sánchez-Bella, *La organización financiera*, pp. 97–100.

43 *Recopilación*, 3, 8, 38.

44 Phelan, *The Kingdom of Quito*, p. 145, and chapter 6 passim.

45 Borah, "Representative institutions," passim.

46 Dealy, *The Latin Americans*, p. 23.

Chapter 8: Church: Friars, Bishops, and the State

1 Morison, *Admiral*, p. 397.

2 Barnadas, "The Catholic Church," p. 512.

3   For patronage, see Barnadas, "The Catholic Church," pp. 512–13; and Dussel, *Historia general*, vol. I/1, pp. 241f. For *Inter caetera* in translation, Parry and Keith, *New Iberian World*, vol. I, pp. 271–4.

4   Schwaller, *The Church*, p. 68.

5   Schäfer, *El Consejo*, vol. 2, p. 192.

6   Barnadas, "The Catholic Church," pp. 517–8.

7   Parry and Keith, *New Iberian World*, vol. I, pp. 385–6.

8   Dussel, *Historia general*, vol. I/1, pp. 552–8.

9   Ricard, *Spiritual Conquest*, p. 80.

10 Dussel, *Historia general*, vol. I/1, p. 553.

11 See, in general, Phelan, *The Millennial Kingdom*.

12 Baudot, *Utopía*, p. 96.

13 Clendinnen, *Ambivalent Conquests*, p. 48.

14 Mendieta, *Historia*, book 3, chapter 29; translated and quoted by Clendinnen, *Ambivalent Conquests*, p. 49.

15 Ricard, *Spiritual Conquest*, p. 219. This account of the Tlatelolco college is drawn from ibid., chapter 14.

16 Dussel, *Historia General*, vol. I/1, p. 318.

17 Clendinnen, *Ambivalent Conquests*, pp. 74–5.

18 Padden, *The Hummingbird*, pp. 259ff.

19 Gibson, *The Aztecs*, p. 117.

20 Archivo General de Indias (Seville), Indiferente General 2859, vol. 2, f. 1–18, "El Rey. Despacho que se dio a Don Francisco de Toledo, virrey del Perú," para. 20.

21 Ibid., para. 15.

22 Gibson, *The Aztecs*, pp. 106, 110.

23 Schäfer, *El Consejo*, vol. II, p. 565ff.

24 Phelan, *Millennial Kingdom*, p. 106.

25 McAlister, *Spain and Portugal*, pp. 427–8; Greenleaf, *The Mexican Inquisition*, passim; for the Inquisition's political role in Spain, Bennassar, "Por el estado," passim.

26 Zavala, "La 'Utopía'," and "Sir Thomas More," passim.

27 Miranda, "El Pátzcuaro de Don Vasco," passim.

28 López Lara, "Los Hospitales," pp. 119–25.

29 Quoted by Zavala, "Sir Thomas More," p. 105.

30 Zavala, "La 'Utopía'," p. 15.

31 Pagden, *The Fall*, pp. 52–5.

32 Discussion here of natural slavery and Vitoria draws heavily on ibid., chapters 3 and 4.

33 Ibid., pp. 94–107.

34 Parry and Keith, *New Iberian World*, vol. I, p. 387.

35 For Vitoria's reasoning, ibid., pp. 300–6.

36 Góngora, *The Spanish Empire*, p. 56.

37 Baudot, *Utopía*, p. 102.

38 Ricard, *The Spiritual Conquest*, p. 47.

39 Baudot, *Utopía*, p. 175, and chapters 3 and 4, on Olmos generally. Also Wilkerson, "The ethnographic works".

40 Discussion of Sahagún here draws heavily on Brading, *The First America*, pp. 119–24. See also Edmonson, *Sixteenth-century Mexico*.

41 León Portilla, *The Broken Spears*, p. 93. This work is compiled from *Codex Florentino* and other early native accounts of the conquest.

42 Brading, *The First America*, pp. 121–2.

43 Baudot, *Utopia*, pp. 108–12.
44 Cf. Elliott, *Imperial Spain*, pp. 209–17.
45 Wagner, *The Life*, pp. 5–6.
46 Sanderlin, *Bartolomé de las Casas*, p. 87, from Las Casas, *Historia*, book 3, chapter 79.
47 Ibid., p. 16, quoting Antonio de Remesal, *Historia general de las Indias occidentales* (Madrid, 1619), vol. 2, p. 108.
48 Brading, *The First America*, p. 63.
49 Wagner, *The Life*, pp. 135ff.
50 Ibid., pp. 167–8.
51 Hanke, *The Spanish Struggle*, p. 121.
52 For the text, Parry and Keith, *New Iberian World*, I, pp. 366–71.
53 Wagner, *The Life*, p. 239.
54 Sanderlin, *Bartolomé de las Casas*, p. 115, citing *Apologética Historia*, introductory argument.
55 Ibid., p. 202, quoting *Apologética Historia*, chapter 48.
56 For this, more subtly put, Pagden, *The Fall*, chapter 6, particularly pp. 141–3.
57 Brading, *The First America*, pp. 104–10.
58 A close analysis in MacCormack, *Religion*.
59 Fraser, *The Architecture*, pp. 156–9; Kubler, *Mexican Architecture*.

Chapter 9: Society: Old Orders Changed

1 Newson, "Indian population," p. 41.
2 Cook, *Demographic Collapse*, p. 111.
3 Denevan, *The Native Population*, pp. xxi–xxiii.
4 For the term, Henige, "Native American population," passim.
5 Cook and Borah, *Essays*, vol. 1, p. 376.
6 Ibid., vol. 3, pp. 1, 100. The lower figure for 1548 is a suggested correction by Zambardino, "Mexico's Population," p. 14.
7 Cook, *Demographic Collapse*, p. 253.
8 Sánchez-Albornoz, "Population," p. 7; Wightman, *Indigenous Migration*, pp. 63–73.
9 E.g. Cook and Borah, "The historical demography of interior tribes of Colombia"; or Newson, "Demographic catastrophe in sixteenth-century Honduras".
10 Review of Alchon, *Native Society*, by Karen M. Powers, in *HAHR* 73, 4 (November 1993), p. 695.
11 An immense bibliography exists on this topic. Sources used here: Cook, *Demographic Collapse*; Gibson, *The Aztecs*; Whitmore, *Disease and Death*; Borah, "Epidemics"; Henige, "Native American population".
12 Alchon, *Native Society*, pp. 20–5.
13 Cook, *Demographic Collapse*, p. 253.
14 Whitmore, *Disease and Death*, p. 214.
15 Sánchez-Albornoz, "Population," pp. 17–18; the following discussion draws heavily on this essay.
16 Burkholder and Johnson, *Colonial Latin America*, p. 105.
17 Konetzke, "La emigración," pp. 13, 24.
18 Garcilaso de la Vega, *Royal Commentaries*, vol. 2, p. 734.

19 Martín, *Daughters*, p. 35.
20 Curtin, *The Atlantic Slave Trade*, p. 116; Palmer, *Slaves*, p. 27.
21 Bowser, *The African Slave*, pp. 286–7.
22 Quoted by Mörner, *Estratificación*, p. 13.
23 Morse, "Claims of political tradition," in *New World Soundings*, p. 104.
24 Domínguez Ortiz, *El antiguo régimen*, pp. 104–5. Discussion of Spanish society draws on chapter 6 of this work.
25 Ots Capdequí, *El estado español*, p. 25.
26 *Recopilación*, 6.1.27.
27 Borah, *Justice by Insurance*.
28 Discussion of changes in native society here draws on: Borah, *Justice by Insurance*, chapter 3; Gibson, *The Aztecs*, chapter 6; Lockhart, *The Nahua*, chapter 4; Ramírez, "El *Dueño de Indios*"; Stern, *Peru's Indian Peoples*, chapter 4.
29 See, for example, Murra, "Aymara lords".
30 Ramírez, "*El Dueño de Indios*," p. 609.
31 Lockhart, *The Men of Cajamarca*, p. 32.
32 Ibid., p. 38.
33 Lockhart, *Spanish Peru*, chapter 2.
34 Himmerich, "The encomenderos", p. 167.
35 Mörner, *Estratificación*, p. 15.
36 Padden, *The Hummingbird*, p. 230.
37 Figures rounded from those given in Cook and Borah, *Essays*, vol. 2, p. 197.
38 Ibid., p. 197.
39 Burkholder and Johnson, *Colonial Latin America*, p. 105.
40 Cook, *Demographic Collapse*, p. 151.
41 Palmer, *Slaves*, p. 46.
42 Cook and Borah, *Essays*, vol. 2, pp. 197–8.
43 Klein, *African Slavery*, p. 32; Cook, *Demographic Collapse*, p. 151; Bowser, *The African Slave*, p. 11.
44 Parry and Keith, *New Iberian World*, I, p. 418.
45 Saignes and Bouysse-Cassagne, "Dos confundidas identidades," pp. 14–15.
46 Israel, *Race*, p. 66.
47 Ibid., p. 64.
48 Lockhart, *Spanish Peru*, p. 182; and chapter 10 generally for Blacks in the sixteenth century.
49 *Recopilación*, 7.5.15.
50 Carroll, "Africans in mainland Spanish America," p. 113.
51 Hakluyt, *Voyages*, p. 162.
52 Phelan, *The Kingdom*, pp. 7 ff.
53 Israel, *Race*, pp. 69–71.
54 Mota y Escobar, *Descripción*, p. 66.
55 Palmer, *Slaves*, p. 178.
56 Pagden, *The Fall*, p. 18.
57 Morse, "The urban development," p. 74.
58 Fraser, *The Architecture*, p. 155; also pp. 36 ff.
59 Ibid., p. 41.
60 Morse, "The urban development," p. 82.
61 Ibid., p. 90.
62 Konetzke, "La emigración," pp. 2–4, 7.
63 Altman, *Emigrants*, pp. 127–9.

Chapter 10: Economy: Ships and Silver

1 *Recopilación*, 8.8.1.
2 For example, Parker, *Philip II*, p. 75.
3 Bakewell, *Silver and Entrepreneurship*, p. 188, n. 32.
4 Kamen, *Spain*, p. 166.
5 Lockhart, *The Men of Cajamarca*, p. 13.
6 Muro, "Bartolomé de Medina," p. 209.
7 Garner, "Long-term," p. 902. Other numerical estimates here are from the opening pages of this article.
8 TePaske, "The search," table 1. At Professor TePaske's suggestion, New Granadan production has been increased here by 30 percent over the amounts shown in that table, to allow for a greater non-registration of gold than he at first postulated.
9 Ibid.
10 Bakewell, "Notes," tables 2(a) and 2(b).
11 Salvucci, *Textiles*, p. 48.
12 Bennett and Hoffman, "Ranching," p. 99.
13 Cf. Borah, *Silk Raising*.
14 Viqueira and Urquiola, *Los obrajes*, p. 40.
15 Ibid., pp. 136–9; Bakewell, "Notes," tables 3(a)–(d).
16 Viqueira and Urquiola, *Los obrajes*, pp. 14, 26.
17 Romero, *Historia económica*, I, pp. 207–16.
18 Tyrer, *Historia*, p. 125; and chapters 2 and 3 generally.
19 Watts, *The West Indies*, pp. 104, 112–14.
20 Chevalier, *Land*, p. 78. Discussion of sugar in New Spain here also draws from Barrett, *The Sugar Hacienda*, chapters 1, 2, 6, 10.
21 Romero, *Historia económica*, p. 182. Discussion here also draws on Borah, *Early Colonial Trade*, pp. 85–6, and McAlister, *Spain*, p. 224.
22 Chevalier, *Land*, pp. 76, 78; for sugar refining, Barrett, *The Sugar Hacienda*, chapter 6, and Cushner, *Lords*, pp. 67–8.
23 Florescano, "The formation," p. 155.
24 Chevalier, *Land*, pp. 73–4.
25 Hamnett, *Politics*, pp. 9–10.
26 Borah, *Early Colonial Trade*, p. 5, and pp. 1–7 generally.
27 Lockhart, *Spanish Peru*, p. 97; and chapter 6 generally.
28 Ibid.
29 Ibid., p. 107.
30 Crosby, "Metamorphosis," p. 82.
31 Bakewell, *Silver Mining*, pp. 68–9.
32 Chevalier, *Land*, p. 94.
33 Crosby, "Metamorphosis," p. 83.
34 Florescano, "The formation," p. 154.
35 McNeill, "American food crops," p. 47.
36 McAlister, *Spain and Portugal*, p. 157.
37 Ots Capdequí, *El estado*, pp. 36–7.
38 Florescano, "The formation," pp. 159–64, and Mörner, "Rural economy," pp. 190–2. The following discussion draws heavily on these two essays.
39 Chevalier, *Land*, p. 60.
40 Florescano, "The formation," p. 157, citing Simpson, *Exploitation*.
41 Gibson, *The Aztecs*, pp. 225–6.

42 Ibid., p. 231.
43 MacLeod, "Aspects," p. 261.
44 Villamarín and Villamarín, *Indian Labor*, pp. 50ff. Generalizations here about labor on the periphery draw heavily on this work.
45 Bowser, "Africans," p. 366.
46 Sempat Assadourian, *El sistema*, p. 291.
47 Chaunu, *Sevilla*, p. 199. This, or its French original *Séville et l'Amérique, XVIe–XVIIe siècle*, is a convenient partial summation of the immense original by Pierre and Huguette Chaunu, *Séville et l'Atlantique (1504–1650)*, 8 vols, Paris, 1955–9.
48 Ibid., p. 203.
49 Ibid., p. 239; and generally, pp. 217–39.
50 Atwell, "International bullion flows," p. 82.
51 Lynch, *The Hispanic World*, pp. 340–2; Elliott, "Spain and America," p. 325.
52 Hoberman, *Mexico's Merchant Elite*, p. 220.
53 Semo, *Historia*, p. 172; quoting from Enrique Otte, "La Nueva España en 1529," *Historia y sociedad en el mundo de habla española*, El Colegio de México, Mexico City, 1970, pp. 103–6.
54 A random selection of items that notarized contracts show as arriving in Potosí in 1589.
55 For this, and other points raised here, McAlister, *Spain and Portugal*, pp. 212–13.
56 Ibid., p. 360.

Chapter 11: The Seventeenth Century: a Slacker Grip

1   Elliott, *Imperial Spain*, p. 283. For losses in the Armada, Martin and Parker, *The Spanish Armada*, pp. 258–60.
2   Lynch, *The Hispanic World*, p. 6.
3   Kamen, *Spain*, pp. 155–7.
4   Lynch, *The Hispanic World*, p. 7.
5   Goslinga, *The Dutch*, p. 54.
6   Ibid., p. 62.
7   Lynch, *The Hispanic World*, pp. 261–7; Pérez-Mallaína and Torres Ramírez, *La Armada*, pp. 222–9; and generally for foreign presence on the west coast of South America in the 1600s, Bradley, *The Lure of Peru*, passim.
8   Rich, "The European nations," pp. 702–4.
9   Boxer, *Salvador de Sá*, pp. 171–2.
10 *Licenciado* Juan Bautista Monzón to the king, Lima, December 17, 1567, in AGI Lima 92.
11 Cf. Israel, *Race*, chapter 3.
12 Baltasar Dorantes de Carranza, *Sumaria relación*, pp. 113–14, quoted by Brading, *The First America*, p. 296.
13 Aguirre Beltrán, *La población negra*, cited by MacLachlan and Rodríguez, *The Forging*, p. 197.
14 Peña, *Oligarquía*, p. 220, and chapters 5 and 6 generally; Israel, *Race*, pp. 80–3.
15 Burkholder, "Bureaucrats," p. 89.
16 Parry, *The Sale*, p. 12.
17 Ibid., p. 24.
18 Burkholder, "Bureaucrats," p. 82. The following paragraphs draw heavily on this article.

19 Ibid., p. 84.
20 Ibid., p. 93.
21 Andrien, *Crisis*, p. 117.
22 Burkholder, "Bureaucrats," p. 86; Andrien, *Crisis*, p. 119.
23 Ibid., pp. 87–91.
24 Hoberman, *Mexico's Merchant Elite*, p. 91.
25 Israel, *Race*, p. 158; and chapter 5 generally for this contest.
26 Cf. Andrien, *Crisis*, pp. 100–1.
27 Muro Romero, "La administración," p. 282, and passim.
28 Elliott, *The Count-Duke*, pp. 410, 418.
29 For trends and commentary, Garner, "Long-term silver mining trends," esp. pp. 900–5; also Bakewell, "Mining".
30 Data on Lima income given here are from Andrien, *Crisis*, pp. 52–61.
31 Totals, to the nearest thousand, calculated from TePaske et al., *La Real Hacienda*, annual summaries for the years shown.
32 Andrien, *Crisis*, p. 67.
33 Ruiz Rivera, "Remesas," pp. 24–30.
34 Bakewell, *Silver Mining*, p. 232.
35 TePaske and Klein, "The seventeenth-century crisis," p. 133; and passim.
36 Morineau, *Incroyables gazettes*, pp. 105ff., 262.
37 Lynch, *The Hispanic World*, p. 281. Discussion of trade here is largely based on chapter 7 of this work, esp. pp. 277–86.
38 Ibid., pp. 278–9; Chaunu, *Sevilla*, pp. 242–3.
39 Pérez-Mallaína and Torres Ramírez, *La Armada*, p. 44.
40 Tyrer, *Historia*, pp. 132, 136, 145.
41 Salvucci, *Textiles*, pp. 136–44, 150; Super, "The agricultural near north," p. 232; and his *La vida*, pp. 226–7.
42 Ramírez, *Provincial Patriarchs*, part 2.
43 Davies, *Landowners*, p. 91, and passim.
44 Information on commercial agriculture here is partly from Lynch, *The Hispanic World*, pp. 289, 302, 313–4.
45 Ferry, "Encomienda," pp. 611–13; Conniff, "Guayaquil," pp. 390–2.
46 Wortman, *Government*, p. 15.
47 Morilla Critz, "Crisis," p. 271.
48 Ibid., p. 264.
49 Vila Vilar, "Las ferias," p. 26.
50 *Recopilación*, 6.1.12 for the 1536 law; for later limitations, 6.3.18–19, and 6.7.7.
51 Jaramillo, "Migraciones," pp. 270–3, 284–5, 306–8.
52 Swann, "Migration," p. 145.
53 Gibson, *Aztecs*, p. 247.
54 Cook, "Migration," p. 56; for Cuzco, Wightman, *Indigenous Migration*, p. 6. The following remarks on *forasteros* are drawn mainly from Wightman.
55 Wightman, *Indigenous Migration*, pp. 112, 146–7.
56 Ibid., p. 124.
57 Lockhart, *The Nahuas*, pp. 304–18.
58 Ibid., p. 412; for *títulos* generally, ibid., pp. 410–18.
59 MacCormack, *Religion*, pp. 408–10, 417–19, and pp. 406–33 generally for seventeenth-century Andean native cult.
60 MacCormack, *Religion*, pp. 420–1.
61 Lockhart, *The Nahuas*, pp. 209, 245.
62 Ibid., pp. 236–7.

63 Cf. Mills, *An Evil*, pp. 74–5.
64 Lockhart, *The Nahuas*, p. 248; and, generally for Guadalupe, Taylor, "The Virgin".
65 Taylor, "The Virgin," p. 11; Lockhart, *The Nahuas*, pp. 245, 252.
66 McFarlane, *Colombia*, p. 24. This discussion of seventeenth-century New Granada draws heavily on chapter 1 of this work; and also on Villamarín and Villamarín, *Indian Labor*, pp. 80–92.
67 Ferry, "Encomienda," pp. 614, 618–22, 632–5.
68 Gutiérrez, *When Jesus Came*, p. 107; and chapter 3 generally for seventeenth-century New Mexico.
69 Farriss, *Maya Society*, p. 92; and chapters 1, 2, and 3 generally for seventeenth-century Yucatan.
70 Farriss, *Maya Society*, pp. 64, 427 n. 21.
71 Caraman, *The Lost Paradise*, p. 36; and passim for Jesuit missions.
72 Ibid., p. 235.
73 For Paraguay, Lockhart and Schwartz, *Early Latin America*, pp. 260–5; Villamarín and Villamarín, *Indian Labour*, pp. 104–10.
74 Zulawski, "Social differentiation," p. 104; and generally for urban work by native women.
75 Wightman, *Indigenous Migration*, p. 117.
76 Lockhart, *Spanish Peru*, chapter 9.
77 Lavrin, "Women," p. 331. The following draws widely on this chapter.
78 Ibid., pp. 327–8.
79 Ibid., p. 333; McCaa, "Marriageways," pp. 24–5.
80 Höller, "Elena", p. 14.
81 Lavrin, "Female religious," p. 188; the following draws widely on this chapter.
82 Martín, *Daughters*, pp. 172, 177; Lavrin, "Female religious," p. 175.
83 Lavrin, "Female religious," p. 182.
84 Paz, *Sor Juana*, pp. 64ff.
85 Brading, *The First America*, p. 372.
86 Translated by Pauline Cook, *The Pathless Grove*, and quoted by Leonard, *Baroque Times*, p. 176.
87 Paz, *Sor Juana*, p. 463. For her ideas, ibid., chapters 11–12, and Leonard, *Baroque Times*, pp. 186–92. For Rodríguez, Trabulse, "Un científico mexicano," p. 150.
88 Brading, *The First America*, p. 338 for this point and others here on Rosa; Martín, *Daughters*, pp. 282–94; Graziano, "Rosa de Lima".
89 Leonard's *Baroque Times* is an obvious example.
90 Bayón, "The Architecture," pp. 724, 744.
91 Stevenson, "The music," p. 785, and pp. 780–7 generally.
92 Bayón, "The Architecture," p. 742.
93 Kubler and Soria, *Art*, p. 96.
94 Brading, *The First America*, pp. 277, 280–1.
95 Ibid., pp. 362–71; and also for Kircher and Egypt, Paz, *Sor Juana*, pp. 175–8.
96 Gibson, "Indian societies," p. 416.

Chapter 12: Eighteenth-century Spanish America: Reformed or Deformed?

1 For Utrecht and the *asiento*, Walker, *Spanish Politics*, p. 67ff.; for the war, Lynch, *Bourbon Spain*, pp. 22–45.
2 Lynch, *Bourbon Spain*, pp. 8–10 and passim.

3   For New Granada, MacFarlane, *Colombia*, pp. 34, 37; for Chile, Carmagnani, "Colonial Latin American demography," passim; for Mexico, Garner, *Economic Growth*, p. 15; for the revisionist view of the central Andes, Tandeter, "Población," p. 12.

4   Lockhart and Schwartz, *Early Latin America*, p. 338.

5   Garner, "Long-term silver mining trends," pp. 900–5.

6   For the European valuation of bullion, Tandeter, *Coercion and Market*, pp. 5–10. The same work also analyses closely the benefits to Potosí of the continued *mita*. For Mexican labor costs, Garner, *Economic Growth*, pp. 128–31. For production at Almadén, Matilla Tascón, *Historia . . . de Almadén*, vol. 2, pp. 105, 354. For blasting, Bakewell, *Silver and Entrepreneurship*, pp. 76–7.

7   For comments on rising output before the reform era: TePaske, "General tendencies," p. 329, and Coatsworth, "The Mexican mining industry," p. 29.

8   McFarlane, *Colombia*, p. 78; for production and slavery in New Granada, ibid., chapter 3 generally. For gold in Mexico and Chile, Bakewell, "Mining," pp. 143, 149–50.

9   Salvucci, *Textiles*, pp. 139–43.

10   Malamud, "La economía colonial," p. 154.

11   Deans-Smith, *Bureaucrats*, pp. 24, 211.

12   Borah, *Early Colonial Trade*, pp. 124, 158 n. 35.

13   Malamud, "La economía colonial," p. 150.

14   Larraín, "Gross national product," pp. 116–21.

15   Cooney and Whigham, "Paraguayan commerce," pp. 216–20.

16   Rock, *Argentina*, pp. 42–7, 64.

17   Ferry, "The price of cacao," pp. 317–28.

18   Malamud, "La economía colonial," pp. 112–13.

19   Parry, Sherlock, and Maingot, *A Short History*, p. 146; for ranking of producers, Malamud, "La economía colonial," p. 113, citing Moreno Fraginals, *El ingenio*, pp. 40–2; also Watts, *The West Indies*, pp. 298–300.

20   Malamud, "La economía colonial," pp. 190–2.

21   Ibid., pp. 192–5.

22   For these reforms, ibid., pp. 168–73.

23   Walker, *Spanish Politics*, pp. 206–10.

24   Ibid., pp. 217–23; García-Baquero, *Cádiz*, vol. 1, pp. 540–3, vol. 2, gráfico 7.

25   Fisher, *Commercial Relations*, pp. 87–9.

26   Ibid., pp. 49–53, 88.

27   McFarlane, *Colombia*, pp. 187–97.

28   Rock, *Argentina*, pp. 61–2.

29   Lynch, *Bourbon Spain*, p. 350.

30   Gálvez to Areche, in Brading, *The First America*, p. 479.

31   Burkholder, "Bureaucrats," p. 90. For Gálvez, Brading, "Bourbon Spain," p. 404.

32   Van Bath, *Real Hacienda*, p. 24.

33   Brading, "Bourbon Spain," p. 408, for conservative estimates; growth rates from Garner, *Economic Growth*, pp. 217–18; for loans and inflation, TePaske, "General tendencies," pp. 323–5.

34   Malamud, "La economía colonial," p. 157.

35   For various estimates, see Brading, "Bourbon Spain," p. 409; Lynch, *Bourbon Spain*, pp. 349–50; Barbier, "Peninsular finance," p. 23. For New Granada, McFarlane, *Colombia*, p. 223.

36   Burkholder and Johnson, *Colonial Latin America*, p. 238.

37 Jorge de Escobedo, quoted in Barbier, "Peninsular finance," p. 33.

38 Cf. MacLachlan, *Spain's Empire*, pp. 123ff.

39 Payne, *Spanish Catholicism*, p. 64.

40 Céspedes del Castillo, *América*, p. 391. For a succinct account of the Mexican church under Charles III, see Farriss, *Crown and Clergy*, chapter 4.

41 Lynch, *Bourbon Spain*, pp. 261–8 (p. 266 for Charles III).

42 Royal *Instrucción* of 1768, quoted in Dussel, *Historia General*, p. 701.

43 Herr, "Disentailment," in Kern, *Historical Dictionary*, p. 170.

44 Anna, *The Fall of Royal Government*, p. 11. For New Spain, Hamnett, "The appropriation," passim.

45 Lynch, *Bourbon Spain*, p. 106.

46 Brading, *Miners*, pp. 234–5.

47 For Mexico, Archer, *The Army*, pp. 8–38; for Peru, Campbell, "The army," pp. 50–7.

48 Marchena Fernández, "The social world," p. 57; for Humboldt's comment, ibid., p. 59; for Venezuela, Brading, "Bourbon Spain," p. 401.

49 For Buenos Aires, Rock, *Argentina*, p. 44; for comparisons of cities, Sánchez-Albornoz, *La población*, p. 121; for summary population figures, Burkholder and Johnson, *Colonial Latin America*, pp. 263–4.

50 For peninsular migration, Sánchez-Albornoz, "The population of colonial Spanish America," pp. 31–2; for Spaniards in Mexico, Burkholder and Johnson, *Colonial Latin America*, p. 264.

51 See the issue of *Artes de México* for summer 1990 (nueva época, No. 8), "La pintura de castas."

52 Cf. Cope, *The Limits*, pp. 54–7.

53 Hoberman, "Conclusion," p. 316.

54 Cf. Seed, *To Love*, pp. 156–7.

55 Ladd, *The Mexican Nobility*, pp. 17, 28; Anna, *The Fall*, p. 22.

56 Cope, *The Limits*, chapter 7.

57 Florescano, *Precios del maíz*, pp. 159–72.

58 Taylor, *Drinking*, p. 122; and chapter 4 passim.

59 O'Phelan, *Rebellions*, p. 87. The discussion here of Andean revolts draws heavily on this book.

60 For messianism in, particularly, the far south of Mexico in the eighteenth century, see Florescano, *Memory*, pp. 146–83.

61 Stern, "The age," p. 43; and following pages generally for the revolt.

62 Spalding, *Huarochirí*, chapter 9.

63 For Peru, O'Phelan, *Rebellions*, Appendix 1; comparison with Mexico in Coatsworth, "Patterns," p. 32.

64 Juan and Ulloa, *Discourse*, p. 75.

65 O'Phelan, *Rebellions*, pp. 125–6.

66 Ibid., p. 164.

67 For this, and events recounted in this paragraph, Campbell, "Ideology," pp. 124–35.

68 For the term and the figure, Stern, "The age," pp. 34–5.

69 Fisher, *Government*, pp. 92ff.

70 Campbell, "Ideology," p. 126.

71 McFarlane, "The rebellion," p. 197 and passim.

72 McFarlane, *Colombia*, pp. 51–71, which offers a succinct analysis of the *comunero* affair.

73 Cf. Phelan, *The People*, p. 87–8.

74 Brading, *The First America*, pp. 428–32, and chapter 19 generally; and, for de Pauw, Gerbi, *The Dispute*, chapter 3.

75 Brading, *The First America*, p. 459, and chapter 20 generally.

76 For these stones see, for example, Carrasco and Matos Moctezuma, *Montezuma's Mexico*; for León y Gama, Brading, *The First America*, pp. 462–4.

77 Lynch, *The Spanish American Revolutions*, p. 34.

78 Discussion on music here draws from Stevenson, "The music," pp. 790–7. For Stampiglia, Grout, *A Short History of Opera*, p. 213.

79 Cf. Alain Pacquier's notes to Gabriel Garrido (Director), *De l'Altiplano a l'Amazone: Lima-La Plata, Missions Jésuites*, a recording of compositions by Zipoli, Torrejón y Velasco, and other composers in Spanish America in the seventeenth and eighteenth centuries (joint production by K617 and Association Française d'Action Artistique).

80 Palmer, *Sculpture*, chapters 8, 9; Vargas and Crespo Toral, *Arte de Ecuador*, pp. 62–72.

81 Kelemen, *Baroque*, p. 81. For Legarda, Palmer, *Sculpture*, chapter 8.

82 Fernández, *Mexican Art*, p. 40 and plate 36.

83 Kelemen, *Baroque*, p. 38.

84 Mesa and Gisbert, *Bolivia*, pp. 53–5.

85 Bayón, "The architecture," p. 717; Burke, "The academy," pp. 487–90.

Chapter 13: Colonial Brazil: Slaves, Sugar, and Gold

1 For a summary of Vespucci's activities and influence, Parry, *The Discovery*, pp. 215–19.

2 Johnson, "The Portuguese settlement," p. 259; the present account of early Brazil draws heavily from this chapter.

3 Hemming, *Red Gold*, p. 36; for Sousa, also Johnson, "The Portuguese settlement," p. 260; and Cortesão and Calmon, *Brasil*, pp. 345–55.

4 Parry and Keith, *New Iberian World*, vol. 5, pp. 42–4. For the origins of São Paulo, see Morse, *The Bandeirantes*, pp. 7, 10–11.

5 Johnson, "The Portuguese settlement," p. 261.

6 For a sample donation (that of the Pernambuco captaincy to Duarte Coelho in 1534), see Parry and Keith, *New Iberian World*, vol. 5, pp. 44–52. This is analyzed by Johnson in "The Portuguese settlement," pp. 261–2.

7 McAlister, *Spain and Portugal*, pp. 260–4.

8 Johnson, "The Portuguese settlement," p. 270; and pp. 269ff. in general for the following.

9 Cf. Schwartz, *Sugar Plantations*, pp. 33–7.

10 Hemming, *Red Gold*, pp. 98–9.

11 Ibid, pp. 102–3.

12 Johnson, "The Portuguese settlement," p. 272; for Sá and the Tupí, Hemming, *Red Gold*, pp. 83–5.

13 Hemming, *Red Gold*, pp. 85–6.

14 This discussion of disease draws on ibid., pp. 139–45.

15 Sánchez-Albornoz, *La población*, p. 83.

16 José de Anchieta, SJ, quoted by Hemming, *Red Gold*, p. 142.

17 Oliveira Marques, *A History*, vol. 1, p. 311.

18 For the slavery question from the 1566 junta on, Hemming, *Red Gold*, pp. 148–51.

19 Schwartz, *Sugar Plantations*, p. 13. The account given here of the rise of Brazilian sugar draws largely on this work, pp. 15–27.

20 Ibid., pp. 18–19.

21 Mintz, *Sweetness*, p. 96; production and export figures from Schwartz, *Sugar Plantations*, p. 165.

22 The account given here of sugar making is taken from Schwartz, *Sugar Plantations*, chapter 5, which refers primarily to Bahia.

23 For the *safra* and work, Schwartz, ibid., pp. 99–106.

24 Ibid., pp. 118, 216.

25 For Pernambuco, Schwartz, "Colonial Brazil," p. 437; for Bahia, Schwartz, *Sugar Plantations*, pp. 70–1.

26 Schwartz, *Sugar Plantations*, p. 54.

27 For 1535, Marcílio, "The population," p. 53; for 1538, Burns, *A History*, p. 38.

28 Schwartz, *Sugar Plantations*, pp. 65, 71, 339 (for the trade); for African sources, Mauro, *Le Portugal*, p. 171ff.

29 Figures from Johnson, "The Portuguese settlement," p. 279. See also discussion by Marcílio, "The population," p. 45.

30 Hemming, *Red Gold*, appendix, pp. 487–501; for Amazonia, Marcílio, "The population," p. 39, citing William M. Denevan, "The aboriginal population of Amazonia," in Denevan (ed.), *The Native Population*.

31 McAlister, *Spain and Portugal*, p. 282; Marcílio, "The population," pp. 38–41.

32 Schwartz, *Sovereignty*, p. 28. For the legal structure of Portugal and the empire in the sixteenth century, see chapters 2–4 of that work. They are the source for the discussion here.

33 Ibid., p. 38.

34 Ibid., p. 50.

35 Ibid., p. 64; and pp. 62–7 for the structure of the high court.

36 Schwartz, *Sugar Plantations*, pp. 17, 204.

37 Boxer, *The Dutch in Brazil*, p. 20.

38 Vogt, *Portuguese Rule*, p. 145; and, for this discussion, chapter 6 in general.

39 Boxer, *The Portuguese Seaborne Empire*, p. 110–11, for this and other Dutch attacks on Portuguese holdings; for the same, Oliveira Marques, *History of Portugal*, chapter 7.

40 For the Dutch attacks, Boxer, *The Dutch in Brazil*, chapters 1, 2.

41 Ibid., pp. 147–8; and chapter 4 generally for the following.

42 Ibid., p. 113; and chapter 4 of that work generally for Johan Maurits.

43 Ibid., p. 119.

44 Ibid., p. 151.

45 Cf. Rodrigues, *Brasil*, p. 76.

46 For this, and the following, Burns, *A History*, pp. 47–8; also Rodrigues, *Brasil*, p. 79, and Cortesão and Calmon, *Brasil*, pp. 459–60.

47 Boxer, *The Dutch in Brazil*, p. 243.

48 Schwartz, *Sugar Plantations*, pp. 125, 183.

49 Oliveira Marques, *History*, vol. 1, p. 305; and Hemming, *Red Gold*, p. 213.

50 Hemming, *Red Gold*, pp. 223–8, and chapter 11 generally for Portuguese exploration of the Amazon in the seventeenth century. For a brief summary, also Burns, *A History*, p. 51ff.

51 Simonsen, *Historia economica*, vol. 2, p. 138.

52 Cortesão and Calmon, *Brasil*, p. 483.

53 Morse, *The Bandeirantes*, pp. 22–3, citing Cortesão, *Rapôso Tavares*, pp. 70–7.

54 Hemming, *Red Gold*, p. 42.

55 Nazzari, *Disappearance*, p. 10.

56 This account of early São Paulo draws on Morse, *The Bandeirantes*, pp. 10–21.

57 Ellis, "The *bandeiras*," p. 49. The following discussion of the chronology of *bandeiras* is based on this account.

58 Morse, *The Bandeirantes*, p. 19. For the size of slaving *bandeiras*, Ellis, "The *bandeiras*," p. 53.

59 Russell-Wood, "Colonial Brazil," pp. 547–8, 560–1.

60 Buarque de Holanda, "The monsoons," p. 155, for this and other points on these expeditions.

61 Burns, *A History*, pp. 64–5. Discussion of cattle here draws generally on this work, pp. 64–8.

62 Hemming, *Red Gold*, p. 352; and chapter 16 generally for cattle in the seventeenth century.

63 Ibid., pp. 352, 371.

64 Ibid., chapter 16, passim.

65 Population figures here from: Marcílio, "The population," pp. 47, 54; McAlister, *Spain and Portugal*, p. 351; Schwartz, *Sugar Plantations*, pp. 86, 349–50; Schwartz, *Sovereignty*, pp. 105–6, 242.

66 Cf. Schwartz, *Sugar Plantations*, pp. 69, 249–50, 322; also his "Colonial Brazil," pp. 491–2.

67 Schwartz, *Sugar Plantations*, p. 391. For a summary of slave demography, ibid., p. 350; and chapters 13 and 14 passim for family, marriage, mortality and other life events among Bahian slaves. For a shorter and simpler account, see Conniff and Davis, *Africans*, chapter 5.

68 Conniff and Davis, *Africans*, pp. 97–8; Hemming, *Red Gold*, p. 393; generally on seventeenth-century slave resistance, Schwartz, *Sugar Plantations*, pp. 468–72. For suicide, etc., ibid. pp. 370–1. For fraternities, Schwartz, "Colonial Brazil," p. 493.

69 Schwartz, *Sugar Plantations*, pp. 330–2; Conniff and Davis, *Africans*, p. 97.

70 Hemming, *Red Gold*, pp. 317–18. This account of the Jesuits' efforts in the north of Brazil, and of Vieira's part in it, draws heavily from chapter 15 of that book.

71 Burns, *A Documentary History*, p. 83.

72 Hemming, *Red Gold*, p. 319.

73 Ibid., p. 337.

74 Schwartz, "Colonial Brazil," p. 498.

75 Schwartz, *Sovereignty*, pp. 346–7, 352, 382ff.

76 Ibid., p. 340; and chapter 13 (on which this discussion draws) generally for links between officials and colonials.

77 Ibid., p. 342.

78 Nazzari, *Disappearance*, p. 5.

79 Schwartz, *Sovereignty*, pp. 328–9; and generally for this discussion of marriage and illicit activities, ibid., pp. 162–3, 324–56.

80 Ibid., pp. 220–1.

81 Ibid., pp. 229–30, and chapter 10 generally for explanations of the suppression; for Brandônio's points and Fernandes Brandão, the latter's *Dialogues*, pp. 9, 42–4.

82 Ibid., p. 353; for the restoration of the court, ibid. pp. 234–42.

83 Schwartz, *Sugar Plantations*, p. 184; for Pernambuco and Bahia, ibid., p. 178. For exports and prices, Mauro, *Le Portugal*, pp. 278–80, 600–1.

84 Mauro, *Le Portugal*, p. 426.

85 Ibid., pp. 433–4; and pp. 426–32 for other products of the land.

86 Ibid., pp. 47–54 for this, and other information here about shipbuilding.

87 For seventeenth-century trade in the Río de la Plata, see Moutoukias, "Power," passim (here, p. 772). For the San Ildefonso treaty, and the defining of Brazil's limits generally, Mansuy-Diniz Silva, "Portugal," pp. 472–5.

88 Cf. Simonsen, *Historia econômica*, vol. 2, pp. 184–7; Boxer, *Portuguese Seaborne Empire*, pp. 223–5; Schwartz, *Sugar Plantations*, pp. 181–2.

89 McAlister, *Spain and Portugal*, p. 386.

90 Russell-Wood, "Colonial Brazil," p. 554. The following discussion draws heavily on this essay.

91 Ibid., p. 560.

92 Hemming, "The Indians and the frontier," pp. 536–8.

93 Luís Gomez Ferreira, quoted by Boxer, *The Golden Age*, p. 184. See pp. 38–9, 182–5, 216–17 of this for practices of gold and diamond extraction in eighteenth-century Brazil.

94 Russell-Wood, "Colonial Brazil," pp. 553, and 577–8 for local production.

95 Ibid., p. 594, for production, drawing on Virgílio Noya Pinto, *O ouro brasileiro e o comércio anglo-português*, São Paulo, 1979, p. 144; arrivals from Morineau, *Incroyables gazettes*, p. 139.

96 Cf. Prado, *The Colonial Background*, pp. 196–7; Russell-Wood, "Colonial Brazil," p. 582; Boxer, *The Golden Age*, p. 312.

97 For Portuguese trade and manufacture, Mauro, "Portugal and Brazil," pp. 460–8; Mansuy-Diniz Silva, "Portugal and Brazil," pp. 502–7.

98 Schwartz, *Sugar Plantations*, pp. 422–34; Alden, "Late colonial Brazil," pp. 627–31.

99 Alden, "Late colonial Brazil," p. 646; and for agricultural production and exports generally, ibid., pp. 626–53.

100 Ibid., p. 609. For the population figures cited here, and eighteenth-century demography in general, pp. 602–23; and for agriculture, trade, and economic change, pp 627–53.

101 Maxwell, *Pombal*, pp. 21–4.

102 The Chevalier des Courtils, quoted in Maxwell, *Pombal*, p. 48.

103 Mansuy-Diniz Silva, "Portugal," pp. 491–2; and ibid., pp. 479–94, generally for the following.

104 Maxwell, *Pombal*, pp. 76–7.

105 Mansuy-Diniz Silva, "Portugal and Brazil," p. 495.

106 Ibid., pp. 484–5.

107 Cf. Maxwell, *Pombal*, pp. 52–4.

108 Alden, "Late colonial Brazil," p. 616, and pp. 612–19 generally; Maxwell, *Pombal*, pp. 72–3, 84.

109 Ibid., pp. 96–108.

110 Cf. Barman, *Brazil*, chapter 1, passim.

111 Burns, "The intellectuals," p. 231; and pp. 217–19, 229–42, generally for this description of the academies.

112 Stevenson, "A note," p. 802, and pp. 799–803 generally. For a listing of works of colonial literature, Bethell, "A note," passim.

113 Kubler and Soria, *Art*, p. 190.

114 Keleman, *Baroque*, vol. 1, p. 253; and pp. 239–55 generally for Brazilian baroque and rococo.

115 Kubler and Soria, *Art*, p. 194; and pp. 118–19, 194–5 generally for Aleijadinho.

116 Ibid., p. 195.

Chapter 14: Independence

1 For a succinct account of Miranda, Robertson, *Rise*, chapter 2.
2 Ibid., p. 145, and chapter 5 generally for Moreno; also on free trade in Buenos Aires, Puiggrós, *Historia económica*, chapter 7, and Rock, *Argentina*, pp. 73–6.
3 For this and the following, Lynch, *Bourbon Spain*, pp. 388–95.
4 Whitaker, *The United States*, pp. 6ff.; and for trade with neutrals, Lynch, *Bourbon Spain*, pp. 367–8.
5 For France and Spain in these years, Lynch, *Bourbon Spain*, pp. 403–7, 419–21.
6 Payne, *A History*, vol. 2, p. 423.
7 Kern and Dodge, *Historical Dictionary*, p. 164. For Spanish resistance, juntas, and the cortes, see also Payne, *A History*, vol. 2, pp. 422–6, and Carr, *Spain*, pp. 81–105.
8 Lynch, *The Spanish American Revolutions*, pp. 304–6.
9 Arnade, *The Emergence*, p. 28.
10 Lynch, *The Spanish American Revolutions*, p. 237; for Buenos Aires, Socolow, *The Merchants*, p. 132.
11 Lombardi, *Venezuela*, p. 124.
12 Rock, *Argentina*, pp. 73–6.
13 For New Granada, Lynch, *The Spanish American Revolutions*, pp. 239–40; for Chile, Loveman, *Chile*, pp. 110–11.
14 For Hidalgo, Hamill, *The Hidalgo Revolt*, passim; succinct accounts in Anna, "The independence," pp. 61–5; Bazant, *A Concise History*, pp. 10–21; Villoro, "La revolución," pp. 325–31.
15 Dates are from relevant entries in Tenenbaum (ed.), *Encyclopedia*.
16 Cf. Lynch, *The Spanish American Revolutions*, pp. 105–18.
17 Johnson, *Simón Bolívar*, p. 37. This is a sound summary of Bolívar's life and beliefs, with selections of his writings. For a full narrative biography, Masur, *Simón Bolívar*; for a recent, succinct account of Bolívar's career and political ideas, see Brading, *The First America*, chapter 27.
18 Brading, *The First America*, p. 609.
19 Quoted in Trend, *Bolívar*, p. 41.
20 Chronology condensed from Bushnell, *The Liberator*, pp. xxii–xxxiv.
21 Quoted in Bushnell, *The Liberator*, p. 86.
22 Rojas, *El Santo*, p. 46.
23 For the liberation of Chile, Robertson, *Rise*, pp. 183–91; Lynch, *The Spanish American Revolutions*, pp. 139–41.
24 Quoted in Lynch, *The Spanish American Revolutions*, p. 177.
25 Domínguez, *Insurrection*, pp. 261–2.
26 Cf. Lynch, *The Spanish American Revolutions*, pp. 175–84.
27 Rojas, *El Santo*, p. 503.
28 For Morelos, Timmons, *Morelos*.
29 Archer, " 'La Causa Buena'," pp. 27–9.
30 The following draws heavily on Anna, "The independence," pp. 82–9.
31 Domínguez, *Insurrection*, p. 161.
32 For Cuban affairs and loyalty, Domínguez, *Insurrection*, pp. 101–6, 140, 161; also Thomas, "Cuba," pp. 281–6.
33 Barman, *Brazil*, p. 34; and pp. 18–41 generally for the late colonial years.
34 Ibid., p. 27.
35 Bethell, "The independence," p. 165.

36 Entry for "Inconfidência dos alfaiates" in Tenenbaum (ed.), *Encyclopedia*, vol. 3, p. 259; the quotation, in Barman, *Brazil*, p. 36.
37 Cf. Barman, *Brazil*, pp. 46–7, and chapter 2 generally for changes in Brazil in John's time.
38 Bethell, "The independence," p. 174.
39 Barman, *Brazil*, p. 49.
40 Ibid., pp. 56–61.
41 Ibid., pp. 55, 61–4.
42 Bethell, "The independence," p. 183; and pp. 179–87 for the final phase of Brazilian independence.
43 Ibid., p. 187.
44 Ibid., pp. 188–90.

Chapter 15: Adrift in Storms: *Caudillos* and Penury

1 *Bosquejo Estadístico de Bolivia*. For the quotation, p. 207.
2 Calderón de la Barca, *Life*, p. 462.
3 Numbers taken from entries, by country, for constitutions in Tenenbaum (ed.), *Encyclopedia*.
4 Cf. Lynch, *Caudillos*, p. 275, and chapter 7 generally.
5 Ibid., pp. 241–4, and chapter 6 generally for Rosas.
6 Ibid., p. 261.
7 Ibid., pp. 267–72, for this account of Rosas's fall.
8 For Santa Anna in the 1850s and later, Jones, *Santa Anna*, pp. 130ff.; also, generally, Lynch, *Caudillos*, chapter 8.
9 For folk *caudillos*, Burns, *Latin America*, pp. 118–24.
10 Lynch, *Caudillos*, p. 309.
11 Safford, "Politics," pp. 360–1; this discussion of post-independence politics draws primarily on Safford's treatment.
12 For Maximilian, Haslip, *The Crown*.
13 Safford, "Politics," p. 406.
14 The Visconde de Albuquerque, quoted by Burns in *Latin America*, p. 129.
15 Bazant, *A Concise History*, pp. 42–3.
16 Vázquez, "Los primeros tropiezos," pp. 26–7.
17 Callcott, *Church*, p. 102.
18 Bushnell and Macaulay, *The Emergence*, pp. 214–17.
19 Hamnett, *Juárez*, p. 96.
20 Bazant, *A Concise History*, pp. 74–5; for New Granada, Bushnell and Macaulay, *The Emergence*, p. 213; for Bolivia, Klein, *Haciendas*, pp. 117–18.
21 From Bulmer-Thomas, *The Economic History*, with adjustments from Lockhart and Schwartz, *Early Latin America*, p. 338. The following discussion of production is based on Bulmer-Thomas, chapter 2, and Halperín Donghi, "Economy and society."
22 Halperín Donghi, "Economy and society," p. 320.
23 For guano exports, Gootenberg, *Between Silver and Guano*, p. 162; and generally for effects in Peru.
24 Bazant, "Mexico," pp. 434ff; also, for the industry, Halperín Donghi, "Economy," pp. 327–8.
25 Tenenbaum (ed.), *Encyclopedia*, vol. 2, pp. 588–9.

26 Bethell, "The independence," pp. 173–4.
27 Halperín Donghi, "Economy," pp. 299–303.
28 Ibid., pp. 327–9.
29 Bulmer-Thomas, *The Economic History*, pp. 37–8, citing, for comparison of exports between 1829–31 and 1850, P. Bairoch and B. Etemard, *Commodity Structure of Third World Exports*, Librairie Droz, Geneva, 1985, table 1.5.
30 Tenenbaum, *The Politics*, p. 183.

Chapter 16: Calmer Waters and a New Course: Oligarchs and Exports

1   Halperín Donghi, *The Contemporary History*, pp. 131–6.
2   Stein, *Populism*, p. 23.
3   Pike, *The Modern History*, p. 93. See ibid., chapter 4 generally, for Castilla.
4   Bulmer-Thomas, *The Economic History*, pp. 63, 433. The following discussion of exports and other economic matters after the mid-nineteenth century draws mainly on this work, chapters 3, 4 and 5.
5   Cf. Fifer, *Bolivia*, p. 136ff.
6   Scobie, *Argentina*, p. 116.
7   For export percentages, Bulmer-Thomas, *The Economic History*, pp. 58–9.
8   These percentages from ibid., p. 74.
9   Ibid., pp. 76–7, for import shares.
10 Population figures from ibid., p. 432; rates of change calculated by author.
11 For these calculations, ibid., pp. 50–3, 61–8.
12 Ibid., p. 65; for other discussion of prices and terms of trade, pp. 66, 78–82.
13 For southern Mexican conditions, Tutino, *From Insurrection*, pp. 288–9, 295–6.
14 Cf. Tenenbaum (ed.), *Encyclopedia*, vol. 5, pp. 127–9.
15 Bulmer-Thomas, *The Economic History*, pp. 88–9.
16 Ibid., p. 90; for other migrant numbers, Glade, "Latin America," pp. 34–6.
17 Cf. Bulmer-Thomas, *The Economic History*, pp. 90–2.
18 Rock, *Argentina*, p. 144.
19 Bulmer-Thomas, *The Economic History*, p. 98; and pp. 96–108 generally for banking and investment.
20 These figures from ibid., p. 104.
21 Rock, *Argentina*, p. 169.
22 Cf. Glade, "Latin America," p. 43.
23 For this point, and the following, Glade, "Latin America," pp. 42–6.
24 Cf. Bulmer-Thomas, *The Economic History*, pp. 130–9.
25 Glade, "Latin America," pp. 43–6.
26 Balmori et al., *Notable Family Networks*, p. 46.
27 Francisco Cosmes, quoted in Zea, "Positivism," p. 72. Also see, generally, Zea, *Positivism in Mexico*.
28 Balmori et al., *Notable Family Networks*, p. 4; and Introduction and chapter I generally for the following.
29 Cf. Bauer, *Chilean Rural Society*, p. 16.
30 Loveman, *Chile*, p. 187, and chapter 6 generally.
31 Bauer, *Chilean Rural Society*, p. 206, quoting George McBride, *Chile. Land and Society* (American Geographical Society, New York, 1936), p. 207. This discussion of the Chilean oligarchy draws largely on Bauer, chapter 8.

32 For this and the class proportions, Knight, *The Mexican Revolution*, vol. 1, p. 44.
33 Bulmer-Thomas, *The Economic History*, p. 86.
34 Cf. Burns's rare and succinct discussion of the middle classes in *Latin America*, pp. 177–93.
35 Hall and Spalding, "The urban working class," p. 327; the following discussion draws heavily on this chapter.
36 Ibid., pp. 340–2.
37 For strikes and repression, ibid., pp. 330–1, 347–50; for the Mexican strikes, Anderson, *Outcasts*, chapters 3, 4.
38 Bauer, "Rural Spanish America," p. 165. Discussion of rural workers here draws largely on this admirable and succinct account.
39 Ibid., p. 171.
40 Ibid., p. 170; for Bulnes's observation, Katz, "Labor Conditions," p. 1, n. 1.
41 *The Autumn (El otoño del patriarca)*, p. 215.
42 Parkes, *A History*, p. 249.
43 Cumberland, *Mexico*, p. 191; for 1896–8, Sánchez-Albornoz, "The population ... 1850–1930," p. 141.
44 Ibid., pp. 204–5.
45 Cockcroft, *Intellectual Precursors*, p. 93.
46 Ibid., p. 133.
47 Knight, *The Mexican Revolution*, vol. 1, pp. 49–55.
48 Quirk, *The Mexican Revolution*, pp. 9–10.
49 Lieuwen, *Mexican Militarism*, p. 43.
50 Bazant, *A Concise History*, p. 149.
51 Tannenbaum, *Peace*, pp. 168–9.
52 Lieuwen, *Mexican Militarism*, p. 48.
53 Halperín, *The Contemporary History*, pp. 188–91.
54 Pike, *The Modern History*, pp. 198–201, 217–49.
55 Bulmer-Thomas, *The Economic History*, p. 155 ff.
56 Ibid., pp. 162, 183.
57 Ibid., p. 167 and ff.
58 Cf. export tables by value in Wilkie, *Statistics*, p. 259 ff.
59 Bulmer-Thomas, *The Economic History*, p. 38.
60 Burns, *A History*, p. 103.
61 Barman, *Brazil*, pp. 121–3, and chapter 8 generally.
62 Ibid., p. 239.
63 Ibid., p. 234.
64 Lombardi and Lombardi, *Latin American History . . . Atlas*, p. 59; also, for land and population losses, Tenenbaum (ed.), *Encyclopedia*, vol. 5, p. 445. For the war generally, a succinct account in Lynch, "The River Plate Republics," pp. 670–3.
65 Skidmore and Smith, *Modern Latin America*, p. 160.
66 Darío, *Selected Poems*, p. 45. Quoted by permission of the University of Texas Press.
67 Catlin, "Traveller-Reporter Artists," p. 48.
68 Martin, "The Literature," p. 807; Scobie, "The Growth," pp. 256–61.
69 Cf. Ades, *Art*, p. 28 ff.
70 Cf. Ramírez, "Apogeo del nacionalismo académico," *passim*.
71 Ades, *Art*, pp. 31–5.
72 Ibid., pp. 105–6.
73 See, e.g., Vargas and Crespo Toral (eds), *Arte de Ecuador*, pp. 226–34.

74 Ades, *Art*, pp. 137–42, for Figari, and chapter 5 for Posada; also for Posada, *Mexico. Splendors*, pp. 539–50.

75 Vasconcelos, *La raza cósmica*, pp. 52–3.

76 José Vasconcelos, *Hernán Cortés, creador de la nacionalidad* [1941], Editorial Jus, Mexico City, 1985.

77 Vasconcelos, *La raza cósmica*, p. 19.

78 Moreno Fraginals, "Plantation economies," p. 207.

79 Halperín, *The Contemporary History*, p. 175.

80 "To Roosevelt," in *Selected Poems*, pp. 69–70.

81 Blasier, *The Hovering Giant. U.S. Responses to Revolutionary Change in Latin America*.

Chapter 17: People, Politics, and Economies Since 1930

1 All population figures here are from Wilkie, *Statistical Abstract*, vol. 35, tables 501–20.

2 All immigrant numbers here are from Sánchez Albornoz, *La población . . .* (1994), pp. 135–8.

3 Wilkie, *Statistical Abstract*, vol. 35, table 702.

4 Merrick, "The Population," pp. 12–17.

5 Ibid., p. 19.

6 Wrigley, *Population and History*, p. 180 ff.

7 Merrick, "The Population," p. 20.

8 Ibid., pp. 20–2, 54; Thorp, *Progress, Poverty, and Exclusion*, p. 24; Wilkie, *Statistical Abstract*, vol. 35, table 903.

9 Wilkie, *Statistics and National Policy* (1974), p. 140.

10 Wilkie, *Statistical Abstract*, vol. 35, table 531.

11 Merrick, "The Population," pp. 3, 31.

12 Wilkie, *Statistical Abstract*, vol. 35, tables 1016–19; Thorp, *Progress, Poverty, and Exclusion*, pp. 14, 318; Bulmer-Thomas, "The Latin American Economies," p. 97; Ffrench-Davis, "The Latin American Economies," p. 189.

13 Ffrench-Davis, "The Latin American Economies," pp. 162, 166.

14 Bulmer-Thomas, *The Economic History*, p. 417; Wilkie, *Statistical Abstract*, vol. 35, table 1022.

15 Bulmer-Thomas, "The Latin American economies," pp. 89–91. Discussion of the 1930s here draws heavily on this chapter. See also Thorp, *Progress, Poverty, and Exclusion*, pp. 110–17.

16 Bulmer-Thomas, "The Latin American Economies," p. 105.

17 Thorp, "The Latin American Economies," p. 141.

18 This paragraph closely follows Thorp, *Progress, Poverty, and Exclusion*, pp. 117–20.

19 Thorp, "The Latin American Economies," p. 140.

20 For a fuller account of Prebisch's thought, see Love, "Economic Ideas," pp. 409–16.

21 Ffrench-Davis, "The Latin American economies," pp. 162, 198–9. The following discussion draws mainly on this chapter in *CHLA*, vol. VI, 1.

22 Wilkie, *Statistical Abstract*, vol. 35, tables 1700–1722 (for cars, 1712).

23 Sources for this paragraph: Thorp, *Progress* pp. 159, 169; Ffrench-Davis. "The Latin American economies," pp. 181, 190–1, 229.

24 For these regional markets, see Ffrench-Davis, "The Latin American economies," pp. 209–21.

25 Manzetti, "The Political Economy of Mercosur," passim; Wilkie, *Statistical Abstract*, vol. 35, table 2608.

26 For a critical view of inward-directed development, see, e.g., Bulmer-Thomas, *The Economic History*, pp. 283, 288.

27 Ffrench-Davis, "The Latin American economies," p. 235.

28 Thorp, *Progress, Poverty*, p. 206. Discussion here of borrowing and the subsequent crisis draws on Thorp, pp. 205–16; and on Ffrench-Davis, "The Latin American economies," pp. 181–6, 230–7.

29 Thorp, *Progress*, p. 215.

30 The numbers given in this paragraph are from Wilkie, *Statistical Abstract*, vol. 35, tables 3400, 3406; and Thorp, *Progress*, pp. 220–1.

31 Thorp, *Progress*, p. 225; also pp. 218–19, and Ffrench-Davis, "The Latin American economies," pp. 240–7, for Latin American policies in reaction to the debt crisis.

32 Wilkie, *Statistical Abstract*, vol. 35, tables 2902, 2907.

33 Thorp, *Progress*, p. 227; also pp. 226–35 generally for neo-liberal reforms.

34 For GDP, Wilkie, *Statistical Abstract*, vol. 35, table 3406; for exports, Bulmer-Thomas, *The Economic History*, pp. 385–7.

35 Wilkie, *Statistical Abstract*, vol. 17, table 500.

36 For income inequality, Wilkie, *Statistical Abstract*, vol. 35, table 1417; Thorp, *Progress*, p. 351–2; Bulmer-Thomas, *The Economic History*, pp. 423–5; Ward, *Latin America*, pp. 48–53; Mamalakis, "Income Distribution."

37 This paragraph draws on Ward, *Latin America*, pp. 63–77; Thorp, *Progress*, 353–61; Wilkie, *Statistical Abstract*, vol. 35, pp. 188–91; Ffrench-Davis, "The Latin American economies," pp. 243–4.

38 For Rio in 1995, Wilkie, *Statistical Abstract*, vol. 35, table 527; all other data here are from Ward, "Cities," pp. 166, 168.

39 Quoted in Marett, *Peru*, p. 154.

40 Alexander, *Aprismo*, p. 32.

41 Information on APRA and Haya de la Torre offered here is mainly from Klarén, *Modernization*, chapters. 2, 6, and 7, and his "Peruvian Aprista Party."

42 For this labor legislation, see Burns, *A History*, p. 302. Information on Vargas summarized here is taken from Burns, pp. 290–306; Poppino, "Vargas;" Levine and Crocitti, *The Brazil Reader*, part IV (esp. pp. 149–55).

43 Levine and Crocitti, *The Brazil Reader*, pp. 154–5.

44 Burns, *A History*, pp. 295–6.

45 Levine and Crocitti, *The Brazil Reader*, pp. 154–5.

46 The preceding draws on Bazant, *A Concise History*, pp. 170–2.

47 Knight, "Mexico," p. 11; the following paragraphs on Cárdenas are drawn mostly from this essay.

48 Bazant, *A Concise History*, p. 175; also, Knight, "Mexico," p. 9.

49 Knight, "Mexico," p. 19.

50 Ibid., pp. 20–6; also, generally for land policy, Hansen, *The Politics*.

51 Knight, "Mexico," pp. 35–8.

52 For the expropriation, Knight, "Mexico," pp. 41–6.

53 Krauze, *Mexico*, p. 480. Chapter 16 of this book, from which this quotation comes, is an attractive vignette of Cárdenas's career.

54 Rock, *Argentina*, pp. 232–3. For this period generally, see this work, chapter 6 (from which the present account is largely taken).

55 Ibid., pp. 232–4.
56 Winn, *Americas*, p. 130. This account of Perón's regime draws on chapter 4 of Winn's work; also on Torre and Riz, "Argentina."
57 Winn, *Americas*, pp. 138–9.
58 Torre and Riz, "Argentina," p. 79. For politics and economic affairs generally, ibid., pp. 78–82.
59 Ibid., pp. 81–2.
60 Ibid., p. 83.
61 Rock, *Argentina*, p. 264.
62 Well evoked, particularly in its more bizarre aspects, by Tomás Eloy Martínez's novel *Santa Evita* (tr. Helen Lane), Vintage Books, 1997.
63 Rock, *Argentina*, pp. 314–15.
64 For dates, Tenenbaum (ed.), *Encyclopedia*, vol. 5, p. 466.
65 Needler, *Politics and Society*, pp. 47–9.
66 Ackroyd, "Military Professionalism."
67 Wilkie, *Statistical Abstract*, vol. 35, table 3405.
68 Halperín, *The Contemporary History*, p. 286–7.
69 Pérez, "Cuba," pp. 449–52.
70 For an ambitious attempt to understand the mentality of the leaders of this Argentina regime, see Frank Graziano, *Divine Violence*. For summaries of the military regimes, Halperín Donghi, *The Contemporary History*, chapter 9. The discussion here draws heavily on that chapter.
71 Klein, *Bolivia*, p. 248.
72 Palmer, "Peru," in Wiarda and Kline, *Latin American Politics*, pp. 208–9
73 Ibid., p. 209.
74 For a summary of the *Sendero Luminoso*, Winn, *Americas*, pp. 536–49; for a full account, Stern, *Shining and Other Paths*; for a vivid fictional impression, Vargas Llosa, *Death in the Andes*.
75 Kline, "Colombia," p. 189.
76 See, e.g., Wilkie, *Statistical Abstract*, vol. 35, table 1313.
77 Thiessen, "Nicaragua," p. 187. For a general summary, Booth, "Nicaragua: Revolution and Retrenchment."
78 Winn, *Americas*, pp. 266, 527.
79 Ibid., pp. 268–9; Skidmore and Smith, *Modern Latin America*, (ed. of 2001), pp. 353–4, and chapter 10 generally.

Epilogue

1 *The Santa Fe New Mexican*, February 9, 10, 11, 1996.
2 *The New York Times*, February 18, 2002.
3 For the early 1960s, Esteva Fábregat, *El mestizaje*, pp. 378–9; for *c*.1990, *The Cambridge Encyclopedia*, p. 161.

BIBLIOGRAPHY

A Brief General Orientation

Almost all the topics touched on in this book, and many that are not, are discussed in one or more volumes of *The Cambridge History of Latin America*. (See the list below for bibliographical information.) Volume 11 of that work, published in 1995, consists of a set of bibliographical essays that are undoubtedly the most comprehensive guide now available to what has been written on Latin American history. An older, but still useful, work, is Charles C. Griffin (ed.), *Latin America. A Guide to the Historical Literature* (University of Texas Press, Austin, 1971). A continuing guide to new writing is the *Handbook of Latin American Studies* (annually from the Hispanic Division, Library of Congress, Washington DC).

For quicker reference, the five volumes of the *Encyclopedia of Latin American History and Culture* (see full reference below) are invaluable. Also most useful, and well illustrated, is the *Cambridge Encyclopedia of Latin America and the Caribbean*.

Several single-volume histories of Latin America, from Columbus to the present, exist. Most of them have been written for North American undergraduates. Perhaps the most interesting, for its unusual views, is *Latin America. A Concise Interpretive History*, by E. Bradford Burns.

More specific suggestions for further reading may be found in a note at the beginning of each section of this book.

Works referred to in Notes

The Cambridge History of Latin America is abbreviated here as *CHLA*, the *Encyclopedia of Latin American History and Culture* as Tenenbaum (ed.), *Encyclopedia*, and the *Hispanic American Historical Review* as *HAHR*.

Ackroyd, William S., "Military professionalism and nonintervention in Mexico," *Armed Forces and Society* 18: 1 (Fall, 1991); also reproduced in Rodríguez, Linda A. (ed.), *Rank and Privilege. The Military and Society in Latin America*, Scholarly Resources, Wilmington (Delaware) 1994, pp. 219–230.

Ades, Dawn, *Art in Latin America*, Yale University Press, New Haven, CT, 1989.

Aguirre Beltrán, Gonzalo, *La población negra de México*, Fondo de Cultura Económica, Mexico City, 1972.

Ahlfeld, Federico E., *Geografía física de Bolivia*, Los Amigos del Libro, La Paz-Cochabamba (Bolivia), 1969.

Aiton, Arthur S., *Antonio de Mendoza, First Viceroy of New Spain*, Duke University Press, Durham NC, 1927.

Alchon, Suzanne A., *Native Society and Disease in Colonial Ecuador*, Cambridge University Press, Cambridge, 1991.

Alden, Dauril, "Late Colonial Brazil, 1750–1808," in *CHLA, volume 2*, pp. 601–60.

Alexander, Robert J., *Aprismo. The Ideas and Doctrines of Víctor Raúl Haya de la Torre*, Kent State University Press, 1973.

Altman, Ida, *Emigrants and Society. Extremadura and America in the Sixteenth Century*, University of California Press, Berkeley and Los Angeles, 1989.

Altman, Ida, and Lockhart, James, *Provinces of Early Mexico. Variants of Spanish American Regional Evolution*, UCLA Latin American Center Publications, Los Angeles, 1976.

Anderson, Rodney D., *Outcasts in their Own Land. Mexican Industrial Workers, 1906–1911*, Northern Illinois University Press, DeKalb, 1976.

Andrien, Kenneth J., *Crisis and Decline. The Viceroyalty of Peru in the Seventeenth Century*, University of New Mexico Press, Albuquerque, 1985.

Andrien, Kenneth, and Johnson, Lyman L. (eds), *The Political Economy of Spanish America in the Age of Revolution, 1750–1850*, University of New Mexico Press, Albuquerque, 1994.

Anna, Timothy E., *The Fall of Royal Government in Peru*, University of Nebraska Press, Lincoln, 1979.

Anna, Timothy E., "The independence of Mexico and Central America," in *CHLA, volume 3*, pp. 51–94.

Archer, Christon I., *The Army in Bourbon Mexico, 1760–1810*, University of New Mexico Press, Albuquerque, 1977.

Archer, Christon I., " 'La Causa Buena': the Counterinsurgency Army of New Spain and the Ten Years' War," in Rodríguez (ed.), *Rank and Privilege*, pp. 11–35.

Arnade, Charles W., *The Emergence of the Republic of Bolivia*, University of Florida Press, Gainesville, 1957.

Arregui, Domingo Lázaro de, *Descripción de la Nueva Galicia*, Gobierno de Jalisco, Guadalajara (Mexico), 1980.

Artes de México, "La pintura de castas," in *Artes de México* (nueva época), Mexico City, no. 8 (summer 1990).

Atwell, William S., "International bullion flows and the Chinese economy *circa* 1530–1650," *Past & Present* 95 (May 1982), pp. 68–90.

Bakewell, Peter, *Silver Mining and Society in Colonial Mexico. Zacatecas, 1546–1700*, Cambridge University Press, Cambridge, 1971.

Bakewell, Peter, "Notes on the Mexican silver mining industry in the 1590s," *Humanitas* (Universidad de Nuevo León, Monterrey), no. 19 (1978), pp. 383–409.

Bakewell, Peter, *Miners of the Red Mountain. Indian Labor in Potosí, 1545–1650*, University of New Mexico Press, Albuquerque, 1984.

Bakewell, Peter, *Silver and Entrepreneurship in Seventeenth-Century Potosí. The Life and Times of Antonio López de Quiroga*, University of New Mexico Press, 1988 (repr. Southern Methodist University Press, Dallas, 1994).

Bakewell, Peter, "La maduración del gobierno del Perú en la década de 1560," *Historia Mexicana* 39:1 (July–Sept. 1989), pp. 41–70.

Bakewell, Peter, "Mining in Colonial Spanish America," in *CHLA, volume 2*, pp. 110–51.

Balmori, Diana, Voss, Stuart F., and Wortman, Miles, *Notable Family Networks in Latin America*, University of Chicago Press, Chicago, 1984.

Barbier, Jacques A., "Peninsular finance and colonial trade: the dilemma of Charles IV's Spain," *Journal of Latin American Studies*, 12:1 (May 1980), pp. 21–37.

Barman, Roderick J., *Brazil. The Forging of a Nation, 1798–1852*, Stanford University Press, Stanford, 1988.

Barnadas, Josep M., "The Catholic Church in colonial Spanish America," in *CHLA*, volume 1, pp. 511–40.

Barrett, Ward, *The Sugar Hacienda of the Marqueses del Valle*, University of Minnesota Press, Minneapolis, 1970.

Bataillon, Marcel, "Les colons du Pérou contre Charles Quint: Analyse du mouvement pizarriste (1544–1548)," *Annales ESC*, 22:3 (May–June 1967), pp. 479–94.

Baudot, Georges, *Utopía e historia en México. Los primeros cronistas de la civilización mexicana (1520–1569)*, Espasa-Calpe, Madrid 1983 (tr. of *Utopie et Histoire au Mexique*, Edouard Privat, Toulouse, 1977).

Bauer, Arnold, *Chilean Rural Society from the Spanish Conquest to 1930*, Cambridge University Press, Cambridge, 1975.

Bauer, Arnold, "Rural Spanish America, 1870–1930," in *CHLA*, volume 4, pp. 151–86.

Bayón, Damián, "The architecture and art of colonial Spanish America," in *CHLA*, volume 2, pp. 709–45.

Bazant, Jan, *A Concise History of Mexico, from Hidalgo to Cárdenas, 1805–1940*, Cambridge University Press, Cambridge, 1977.

Bazant, Jan, "Mexico from Independence to 1867," in *CHLA*, volume 3, pp. 423–70.

Bennassar, Bartolomé, "Por el Estado, contra el Estado," in his *Inquisición española*, pp. 321–36.

Bennassar, Bartolomé, (ed.), *Inquisición española: poder político y control social*, Editorial Crítica, Barcelona, 1981.

Bennett, Deb, and Hoffmann, Robert S., "Ranching in the New World," in Viola and Margolis, *Seeds of Change*, pp. 90–111.

Bennett, Wendell C., and Bird, Junius B., *Andean Culture History. The Archaeology of the Central Andes from Early Man to the Incas*, 2nd edn, American Museum of Natural History, The Natural History Press, Garden City, New York, 1964.

Bethell, Leslie, "A note on literature and intellectual life in colonial Brazil," in *CHLA*, volume 2, pp. 705–7.

Bethell, Leslie, "The independence of Brazil," in *CHLA*, volume 3, pp. 157–96.

Blakemore, Harold, and Smith, Clifford T. (eds), *Latin America. Geographical Perspectives*, 2nd edn, Methuen, London, 1983.

Blasier, Cole, *The Hovering Giant. U.S. Responses to Revolutionary Change in Latin America*, University of Pittsburgh Press, Pittsburgh, 1976.

Booth, John A., "Nicaragua: revolution and retrenchment," chapter 19 in Wiarda and Kline, *Latin American Politics*.

Borah, Woodrow W., *Silk Raising in Colonial Mexico*, Ibero-Americana 20, University of California Press, Berkeley and Los Angeles, 1943.

Borah, Woodrow W., *Early Colonial Trade and Navigation between Mexico and Peru*, Ibero-Americana 38, University of California Press, Berkeley and Los Angeles, 1954.

Borah, Woodrow W., *Justice by Insurance. The General Indian Court of Colonial Mexico and the Legal Aides of the Half-Real*, University of California Press, Berkeley and Los Angeles, 1983.

Borah, Woodrow W., "Representative institutions in the Spanish Empire in the sixteenth century," *The Americas*, 12:3 (Jan. 1956), pp. 246–57.

Borah, Woodrow W., "Epidemics in the Americas: major issues and future research," *Latin American Population History Bulletin*, 19 (Spring 1991), pp. 2–13.

Bowser, Frederick P., *The African Slave in Colonial Peru, 1524–1650*, Stanford University Press, Stanford, 1974.

Bowser, Frederick P., "Africans in Spanish American colonial society," in *CHLA*, volume 2, pp. 357–79.

Boxer, C. R., *Salvador de Sá and the Struggle for Brazil and Angola, 1602–1686*, Athlone Press, University of London, London, 1952.

Boxer, C. R., *The Dutch in Brazil, 1624–1654*, Clarendon Press, Oxford, 1957.

Boxer, C. R., *The Golden Age of Brazil, 1695–1750*, University of California Press, Berkeley and Los Angeles, 1969.

Boxer, C. R., *The Portuguese Seaborne Empire, 1415–1825*, Hutchinson & Co., London, 1969.

Brading, D. A., *Miners and Merchants in Bourbon Mexico, 1763–1810*, Cambridge University Press, Cambridge, 1971.

Brading, D. A., *The First America. The Spanish Monarchy, Creole Patriots, and the Liberal State, 1492–1867*, Cambridge University Press, Cambridge, 1991.

Brading, D. A., "Bourbon Spain and its American empire," in *CHLA*, volume 1, pp. 389–439.

Bradley, Peter T., *The Lure of Peru. Maritime Intrusion into the South Sea, 1598–1701*, Macmillan, Basingstoke and London, 1989.

Broda, Johanna, Carrasco, David, and Matos Moctezuma, Eduardo, *The Great Temple of Tenochtitlan. Center and Periphery in the Aztec World*, University of California Press, Berkeley and Los Angeles, 1987.

Brundage, Burr Cartwright, *A Rain of Darts. The Mexica Aztecs*, University of Texas Press, Austin, 1972.

Brundage, Burr Cartwright, *Two Earths, Two Heavens. An Essay Contrasting the Aztecs and the Incas*, University of New Mexico Press, Albuquerque, 1975.

Buarque de Holanda, Sérgio, "The Monsoons," in Morse (ed.), *The Bandeirantes*, pp. 152–66.

Bulmer-Thomas, Victor, *The Economic History of Latin America since Independence*, Cambridge University Press, Cambridge, 1994.

Bulmer-Thomas, Victor, "The Latin American economies, 1929–1939," in *CHLA*, volume 6, part 1, pp. 65–115.

Burke, Marcus, "The academy, neoclassicism, and independence," in John P. O'Neill (ed.), *Mexico. Splendors of Thirty Centuries*, pp. 487–96.

Burkholder, Mark A., "Bureaucrats," chapter 4 in Louisa Schell Hoberman and Susan M. Socolow (eds), *Cities and Society in Colonial Latin America*, University of New Mexico Press, Albuquerque, 1986.

Burkholder, Mark A., and Johnson, Lyman L., *Colonial Latin America*, Oxford University Press, New York, 1990.

Burns, E. Bradford (ed.), *A Documentary History of Brazil*, Alfred A. Knopf, New York, 1966.

Burns, E. Bradford, *A History of Brazil*, Columbia University Press, New York, 1970.

Burns, E. Bradford, "The intellectuals as agents of change and the independence of Brazil, 1724–1822," in Russell-Wood, *From Colony to Nation*, pp. 211–46.

Burns, E. Bradford, *Latin America. A Concise Interpretive History*, 6th edn, Prentice Hall/Simon and Schuster, Englewood Cliffs, NJ, 1994.

Bushnell, David (ed.), *The Liberator, Simón Bolívar. Man and Image*, Alfred A. Knopf, New York, 1970.

Bushnell, David, and Macaulay, Neill, *The Emergence of Latin America in the Nineteenth Century*, Oxford University Press, Oxford and New York, 1988.

Calderón de la Barca, Frances, *Life in Mexico*, University of California Press, Berkeley and Los Angeles, 1982.

Callcott, Wilfrid H., *Church and State in Mexico, 1822–1857*, Duke University Press, Durham, NC, 1926.

Calnek, Edward E., "Patterns of empire formation in the Valley of Mexico, late postclassic period, 1200–1521," in Collier *et al.* (eds), *The Inca and Aztec States*, pp. 43–62.

The Cambridge Encyclopedia of Latin America (Simon Collier, Thomas E. Skidmore, and Harold Blakemore, eds), 2nd edn, Cambridge University Press, Cambridge, 1992.

The Cambridge History of Latin America, volume *1–11*, Leslie Bethell (ed.), Cambridge University Press, Cambridge, 1984–95.

Campbell, Leon G., "The army of Peru and the Túpac Amaru revolt, 1780–1783," *HAHR*, 56:1 (Feb. 1976), pp. 31–57.

Campbell, Leon G., "Ideology and factionalism during the Great Rebellion, 1780–1782," in Stern (ed.), *Resistance, Rebellion, and Consciousness in the Andean Peasant World*, pp. 110–39.

Caraman, Philip, *The Lost Paradise. The Jesuit Republic in South America*, Seabury Press, New York, 1976.

Carmagnani, Marcello, "Colonial Latin American demography: growth of Chilean population, 1700–1830," *Journal of Social History*, 1:2 (Winter 1967), pp. 179–91.

Carr, Raymond, *Spain, 1808–1975*, 2nd edn, Clarendon Press, Oxford, 1982.

Carrasco, David, and Matos Moctezuma, Eduardo, *Moctezuma's Mexico. Visions of the Aztec World*, University Press of Colorado, Niwot, CO, 1992.

Carrasco, Pedro, "The political economy of the Aztec and Inca states," in Collier et al. (eds.) *The Inca and Aztec States*, pp. 23–40.

Carroll, Patrick, "Africans in mainland Spanish America," in Michael L. Conniff and Thomas J. Davis (eds), *Africans in the Americas. A History of the Black Diaspora*, St. Martin's Press, New York, 1994, pp. 107–21.

Catlin, Stanton L., "Traveller-reporter artists and the empirical tradition in post-independence Latin America," in Dawn Ades, *Art in Latin America*, pp. 41–61.

Céspedes del Castillo, Guillermo, *América Hispánica, 1492–1898*, volume VI of Manuel Tuñón de Lara (ed.), *Historia de España*, Editorial Labor, Madrid, 1983.

Chaunu, Pierre, *Conquête et exploitation des nouveaux mondes (XVIe siècle)*, Nouvelle Clio, Presses Universitaires de France, Paris, 1969.

Chaunu, Pierre, *Sevilla y América, siglos XVI y XVII*, University of Seville, Seville, 1983.

Chaunu, Pierre, *L'expansion européenne, du XIIIe au Xve siècle*, 2nd edn, Nouvelle Clio, Presses Universitaires de France, Paris, 1989.

Chevalier, François, *Land and Society in Colonial Mexico. The Great Hacienda*, University of California Press, Berkeley and Los Angeles, 1966.

Clancy, Flora S., and Harrison, Peter D. (eds), *Vision and Revision in Maya Studies*, University of New Mexico Press, Albuquerque, 1990.

Clapperton, Chalmers, "Tectonic history and structure," in *The Cambridge Encyclopedia of Latin America*, pp. 12–18.

Clendinnen, Inga, *Ambivalent Conquests. Maya and Spaniard in Yucatan, 1517–1570*, Cambridge University Press, Cambridge, 1987.

Clendinnen, Inga, *Aztecs. An Interpretation*, Cambridge University Press, Cambridge, 1991.

Clendinnen, Inga, "'Fierce and unnatural cruelty': Cortés and the Conquest of Mexico," *Representations* 33 (Winter 1991), pp. 65–100.

Coatsworth, John H., "The Mexican mining industry in the eighteenth century," in Jacobsen and Puhle, *The Economies of Mexico and Peru*, pp. 26–45.

Coatsworth, John H., "Patterns of rural rebellion in Latin America: Mexico in colonial perspective," in Katz (ed.), *Riot, Rebellion, and Revolution*, pp. 21–62.

Cockcroft, James D., *Intellectual Precursors of the Mexican Revolution, 1900–1913*, University of Texas Press, Austin, 1968.

Collier, George A., Rosaldo, Renato I., and Wirth, John D. (eds), *The Inca and Aztec States, 1400–1800. Anthropology and History*, Academic Press, New York, 1982.

Conniff, Michael L., "Guayaquil through independence: urban development in a colonial system," *The Americas*, 33:3 (Jan. 1977), pp. 385–410.

Conniff, Michael L., and Davis, Thomas J., *Africans in the Americas. A History of the Black Diaspora*, New York, St. Martin's Press, 1994.

Conrad, Geoffrey W., and Demarest, Arthur A., *Religion and Empire. The Dynamics of Aztec and Inca Expansionism*, Cambridge University Press, Cambridge, 1984.

Cook, Noble David, *Demographic Collapse: Indian Peru, 1520–1620*, Cambridge University Press, Cambridge, 1981.

Cook, Noble David, "Disease and the depopulation of Hispaniola, 1492–1518," *Colonial Latin American Review*, 2:1–2 (1993), pp. 211–45.

Cook, Noble David, "Migration in colonial Peru: an overview," chapter 3 in Robinson, *Migration in Colonial Spanish America*.

Cook, Pauline, *The Pathless Grove*, Decher Press, Prairie City, IL, 1951.

Cook, Sherburne F., and Borah, Woodrow, *Essays in Population History*, 3 volumes, University of California Press, Berkeley and Los Angeles, 1971–9.

Cook, Sherburne F., "The historical demography of the interior tribes of Colombia in the studies of Juan Friede and Germán Colmenares," in *Essays in Population History, volume 1*, pp. 411–29.

Cooney, Jerry W., and Whigham, Thomas L., "Paraguayan commerce with the outside world," chapter 10 in Andrien and Johnson, *The Political Economy of Spanish America*.

Cope, R. Douglas, *The Limits of Racial Domination. Plebeian Society in Colonial Mexico City*, University of Wisconsin Press, Madison, 1994.

Cortés, Hernán, *Letters from Mexico*, A. R. Pagden (tr. and ed.), Orion Press, New York, 1971.

Cortesão, Jaime, *Rapôso Tavares e a formação territorial do Brasil*, Rio de Janeiro, 1958.

Cortesão, Jaime, and Calmon, Pedro, *Brasil*, volume 26 of A. Ballesteros (ed.), *Historia de América*, Salvat Editores, Barcelona, 1956.

Crosby, Alfred W., "Metamorphosis of the Americas," in Viola and Margolis, *Seeds of Change*, pp. 70–89.

Cumberland, Charles C., *Mexico. The Struggle for Modernity*, Oxford University Press, New York, 1968.

Curtin, Philip D., *The Atlantic Slave Trade. A Census*, University of Wisconsin Press, Madison, 1969.

Cushner, Nicholas P., *Lords of the Land. Sugar, Wine, and Jesuit Estates of Coastal Peru, 1600–1767*, State University of New York Press, Albany, 1980.

Dalence, José M., *Bosquejo estadistico de Bolivia*, Universidad Mayor de San Andrés, La Paz, 1975.

Darío, Rubén, *Selected Poems*, (tr. Lysander Kemp), University of Texas Press, Austin, 1965.

Davies, Keith A., *Landowners in Colonial Peru*, University of Texas Press, Austin, 1984.

Davies, Nigel, *The Aztecs. A History*, University of Oklahoma Press, Norman, 1980.

Dealy, Glen C., *The Latin Americans. Spirit and Ethos*, Westview Press, Boulder, 1992.

Deans-Smith, Susan, *Bureaucrats, Planters, and Workers. The Making of the Tobacco Monopoly in Bourbon Mexico*, University of Texas Press, Austin, 1992.

Denevan, William M. (ed.), *The Native Population of the Americas in 1492*, 2nd edn, University of Wisconsin Press, Madison, 1992.

Díaz del Castillo, Bernal, *Historia verdadera de la conquista de la Nueva España*, 3 volumes, Espasa-Calpe Mexicana, S.A., Mexico City, 1950.

Díaz del Castillo, Bernal, *The Conquest of New Spain*, tr. J. M. Cohen, Penguin Books, Harmondsworth, 1963.

Diffie, Bailey W., and Winius, George D., *Foundations of the Portuguese Empire, 1415–1580*, University of Minnesota Press, Minneapolis, 1977.

Dobyns, Henry F., and Doughty, Paul L., *Peru. A Cultural History*, Oxford University Press, New York, 1976.

Domínguez, Jorge I., *Insurrection or Loyalty. The Breakdown of the Spanish American Empire*, Harvard University Press, Cambridge, MA, 1980.

Domínguez Ortiz, Antonio, *El Antiguo Régimen: Los Reyes Católicos y los Austrias*, Alianza Editorial, Madrid, 1973.

Dorantes de Carranza, *Sumaria relación de las cosas de la Nueva España*, ed. José María de Agreda y Sánchez, Mexico City, 1970.

Dussel, Enrique D., *Historia general de la Iglesia en América Latina. volume I/1. Introducción general a la historia de la Iglesia en América Latina*, Salamanca, Ediciones Sígueme, 1983.

Edmonson, Munro S., *Sixteenth-Century Mexico. The Work of Sahagún*, School of American Research and University of New Mexico Press, Albuquerque, 1974.

Elliott, J. H., *Imperial Spain, 1469–1716*, Edward Arnold, London, 1963.

Elliott, J. H., *The Count-Duke of Olivares. The Statesman in an Age of Decline*, Yale University Press, New Haven, 1986.

Elliott, J. H., "The Spanish conquest and settlement of America," in *CHLA, volume 1*, pp. 149–206.

Ellis, Myriam, "The Bandeiras in the geographical expansion of Brazil," in Morse (ed.), *The Bandeirantes*, pp. 48–63.

Encyclopedia of Latin American History and Culture, Barbara A. Tenenbaum (ed.), 5 volumes, Simon and Schuster Macmillan, New York, 1995.

Esteva Fábregat, Claudio, *El mestizaje en Iberoamérica*, Alhambra, Madrid, 1988.

Farriss, N[ancy] M., *Crown and Clergy in Colonial Mexico, 1759–1821*, Athlone Press, University of London, 1968.

Farriss, N[ancy] M., *Maya Society under Colonial Rule. The Collective Enterprise of Survival*, Princeton University Press, Princeton, 1984.

Fernandes Brandão Ambrósio (attrib'd), *Dialogues of the Great Things of Brazil*, (tr. Frederick A. H. Hall, William F. Harrison, Dorothy W. Welker), University of New Mexico Press, Albuquerque, 1987.

Fernández, Justino, *Mexican Art*, Spring Books, London, 1965.

Fernández-Armesto, Felipe, *Columbus*, Oxford University Press, Oxford, 1991.

Fernández-Armesto, Felipe, *Ferdinand and Isabella*, Dorset Press, New York, 1991.

Ferry, Robert J., "Encomienda, African slavery, and agriculture in seventeenth-century Caracas," *HAHR*, 61:4 (Nov. 1981), pp. 609–35.

Ferry, Robert J., "The price of Cacao, its export, and rebellion in eighteenth-century Caracas: boom, bust, and the Basque monopoly," chapter 10 in Johnson and Tandeter, *Essays on the Price History of Eighteenth-Century Latin America*.

Ffrench-Davis, Ricardo, "The Latin American economies, 1950–1990," in *CHLA, volume 6*, part i, pp. 159–249.

Fifer, J. Valerie, *Bolivia: Land, Location, and Politics since 1825*, Cambridge University Press, Cambridge, 1972.

Fisher, J. R., *Government and Society in Colonial Peru. The Intendant System, 1784–1814*, Athlone Press, University of London, 1970.

Fisher, J. R., *Commercial Relations between Spain and Spanish America in the Era of Free Trade, 1778–1796*, Centre for Latin American Studies, University of Liverpool, Liverpool, 1985.

Fisher, J. R., Kuethe, Alan J., and McFarlane, Anthony, (eds), *Reform and Insurrection in Bourbon New Granada and Peru*, Louisiana State University Press, Baton Rouge, 1990.

Floyd, Troy S., *The Columbus Dynasty in the Caribbean, 1492–1526*, University of New Mexico Press, Albuquerque, 1973.

Florescano, Enrique, *Precios del maíz y crisis agrícolas en México (1708–1810)*, El Colegio de México, Mexico City, 1969.

Florescano, Enrique, *Memory, Myth, and Time in Mexico, from the Aztecs to Independence*, University of Texas Press, Austin, 1994.

Florescano, Enrique, et al., *Atlas histórico de México*, 2nd edn, Siglo Veintiuno Editores, Mexico City, 1984.

Florescano, Enrique, "The formation and economic structure of the Hacienda in New Spain," in *CHLA, volume 2*, pp. 153–88.

Fraser, Valerie, *The Architecture of Conquest. Building in the Viceroyalty of Peru, 1535–1635*, Cambridge University Press, Cambridge, 1990.

Galloway, J. H., "Brazil," in Blakemore and Smith, *Latin America. Geographical Perspectives*, pp. 325–82.

García-Baquero González, Antonio, *Cádiz y el Atlántico, 1717–1778 (El comercio colonial español bajo el monopolio gaditano)*, 2 volume, Escuela de Estudios Americanos, Seville, 1976.

García Márquez, Gabriel, *The Autumn of the Patriach*, tr. Gregory Rabassa, Harper and Rowe, New York, 1991.

Garcilaso de la Vega, El Inca, *Royal Commentaries of the Incas and General History of Peru*, tr. Harold V. Livermore, 2 volumes, University of Texas Press, Austin, 1966.

Garner, Richard L., *Economic Growth and Change in Bourbon Mexico*, University Press of Florida, Gainesville, 1993.

Garner, Richard L., "Long-term silver mining trends in Spanish America: a comparative analysis of Peru and Mexico," *American Historical Review* 93:4 (1988), pp. 898–935.

Garrido, Gabriel (Director), *De l'Altiplano à l'Amazone. Lima–La Plata, Missions Jésuites*, Compact Disk, K617 and Association Française d'Action Artistique, no place, 1992.

Garrido Aranda, Antonio, *Moriscos e indios. Precedentes hispánicos de la evangelización de México*, Universidad Nacional Autónoma de México, Mexico City, 1980.

Gerbi, Antonello, *The Dispute of the New World. The History of a Polemic, 1750–1900*, University of Pittsburgh Press, Pittsburgh, 1973.

Gibson, Charles, *The Aztecs under Spanish Rule. A History of the Indians of the Valley of Mexico, 1519–1810*, Stanford University Press, Stanford, 1964.

Gibson, Charles, "Indian societies under Spanish rule," in *CHLA, volume 2*, pp. 381–419.

Glade, William, "Latin America and the international economy," in *CHLA., volume 4*, c.*1870–1930*, pp. 1–56.

Gómara – see López de Gómara.

Góngora, Mario, *Studies in the Colonial History of Spanish America*, Cambridge University Press, Cambridge, 1975.

Gootenberg, Paul, *Between Silver and Guano. Commercial Policy and the State in Post-independence Peru*, Princeton University Press, 1989.

Graziano, Frank, *Divine violence. Spectacle, Psychosexuality, and Radical Christianity in the Argentine "Dirty War,"* Westview Press, Boulder, CO and Oxford (UK), 1992.

Graziano, Frank, "Rosa de Lima and the tropes of sanctity," *Public* 8, Public Access, Toronto, 1993, pp. 49–55.

Grout, Donald J., *A Short History of Opera*, 3rd edn, Columbia University Press, New York, 1988.

Gutiérrez, Ramón A., *When Jesus Came, the Corn Mothers Went Away. Marriage, Sexuality, and Power in New Mexico, 1500–1846*, Stanford University Press, Stanford, 1991.

Hakluyt, Richard, *Voyages to the New World. A Selection* (David F. Hawke, ed.), Bobbs-Merrill, Indianapolis, 1972.

Hall, Michael M., and Spalding, Hobart A., Jr., "The urban working class and early Latin American labour movements, 1880–1930," in *CHLA, volume 4*, pp. 325–65.

Halperín Donghi, Tulio, *The Contemporary History of Latin America* (John C. Chasteen, ed. and tr.), Duke University Press, Durham, 1993.

Halperín Donghi, Tulio, "Economy and society in post-independence Spanish America," in *CHLA, volume 3*, pp. 299–345.

Hamill, Hugh M., Jr., *The Hidalgo Revolt: Prelude to Mexican Independence*, University of Florida Press, Gainesville, 1966.

Hammond Comparative World Atlas, Hammond Incorporated, Maplewood, NJ, 1989.

Hamnett, Brian R., *Politics and Trade in Southern Mexico, 1750–1821*, Cambridge University Press, Cambridge, 1971.

Hamnett, Brian R., *Juárez*, Longman, London and New York, 1994.

Hamnett, Brian R., "The appropriation of Mexican church wealth by the Spanish Bourbon government – the 'Consolidación de Vales Reales,' 1805–1809," *Journal of Latin American Studies*, 1:2 (Nov. 1969), pp. 85–113.

Hanke, Lewis, *The Spanish Struggle for Justice in the Conquest of America*, American Historical Association/Little, Brown and Co., Boston, 1965 (repr., Southern Methodist University Press, Dallas, 2002).

Hansen, Roger D., *The Politics of Mexican Development*, Johns Hopkins University Press, Baltimore, 1971.

Haring, Clarence H., *The Spanish Empire in America*, New York, Oxford University Press, 1947.

Haslip, Joan, *The Crown of Mexico. Maximilian and his Empress Carlota*, Holt, Rinehart and Winston, New York, 1971.

Hassig, Ross, *Aztec Warfare. Imperial Expansion and Political Control*, University of Oklahoma Press, Norman, 1988.

Helms, Mary W., "The Indians of the Caribbean and circum-Caribbean at the end of the fifteenth Century," in *CHLA, volume 1*, pp. 37–57.

Hemming, John, *The Conquest of the Incas*, Harcourt, Brace, Jovanovich, San Diego and New York, 1973.

Hemming, John, *Red Gold. The Conquest of the Brazilian Indians*, Harvard University Press, Cambridge, MA, 1978.

Hemming, John, "The Indians of Brazil in 1500," in *CHLA, volume 1*, pp. 119–43.

Hemming, John, "The Indians and the frontier in colonial Brazil," in *CHLA, volume 2*, pp. 501–45.

Henige, David, "Native American population at contact: standards of proof and styles of discourse in the debate," *Latin American Population History Bulletin*, 22 (Fall 1992), pp. 2–23.

Henshall, Janet D., and Momsen, R. P., *A Geography of Brazilian Development*, Bell, London, 1974.

Herr, Richard, "Disentailment," in Robert Kern (ed.), *Historical Dictionary of Modern Spain*, pp. 168–73.

Hidalgo, Jorge, "The Indians of southern South America in the middle of the sixteenth century," in *CHLA, volume 1*, pp. 37–57.

Himmerich, Robert T., *The Encomenderos of New Spain, 1521–1555*, PhD dissertation, University of California, Los Angeles, 1984.

Historia General de México, comp. Daniel Cosío Villegas, 4 volumes, El Colegio de México, Mexico City, 1977.

Hoberman, Louisa Schell, *Mexico's Merchant Elite, 1590–1660. Silver, State, and Society*, Duke University Press, Durham, NC, 1991.

Hoberman, Louisa Schell, "Conclusion," in Hoberman and Socolow (eds), *Cities and Society in Colonial Latin America*.

Hoberman, Louisa Schell, and Socolow, Susan M. (eds), *Cities and Society in Colonial Latin America*, University of New Mexico Press, Albuquerque, 1986.

Hóller, Jacqueline Z., *I, Elena de la Cruz: Heresy, Gender, and Crisis in Mexico City, 1568*, MA thesis, Simon Fraser University, Vancouver, 1992.

Hulme, Peter, *Colonial Encounters. Europe and the Native Caribbean, 1492–1797*, Methuen, London and New York, 1986.

Hyslop, John, *The Inka Road System*, Academic Press, New York, 1984.

Isbell, William H., "City and state in middle horizon Huari," in *Peruvian Prehistory. An Overview of Pre-Inca and Inca Society*, Richard W. Keatinge (ed.), Cambridge University Press, Cambridge, 1988, pp. 164–89.

Israel, J. I., *Race, Class and Politics in Colonial Mexico, 1610–1670*, Oxford University Press, Oxford, 1975.

Jacobsen, Nils, and Puhle, Hans-Jürgen, *The Economies of Mexico and Peru during the Late Colonial Period, 1760–1810*, Colloquium Verlag, Berlin, 1986.

James, Preston E., *Latin America*, 4th edn, Bobbs-Merrill, Indianapolis, 1975.

Jaramillo, Miguel, "Migraciones y formación de mercados laborales: La fuerza de trabajo indígena de Lima a comienzos del siglo XVII," *Economía* nos. 29–30 (Jun–Dec. 1992), pp. 265–320.

Johnson, H. B., "The Portuguese settlement of Brazil, 1500–1580," in *CHLA, volume 1*, pp. 249–86.

Johnson, John J., *Simón Bolívar and Spanish American Independence, 1783–1830*, D. Van Nostrand Co., Princeton, NJ, 1968.

Johnson, Lyman L., and Tandeter, Enrique, *Essays on the Price History of Eighteenth-Century Latin America*, University of New Mexico Press, Albuquerque, 1990.

Jones, Oakah L., *Santa Anna*, Twayne Publishers, New York, 1968.

Josephy, Alvin M., Jr., *America in 1492. The World of the Indian Peoples before the Arrival of Columbus*, Alfred A. Knopf, New York, 1992.

Juan y Santacilia, Jorge, and Ulloa, Antonio de, *Discourse and Political Reflections on the Kingdoms of Peru* (tr. John J. TePaske and Besse E. Clement), University of Oklahoma Press, Norman, 1978.

Kamen, Henry, *The Spanish Inquisition*, Meridian Books, New American Library, New York, 1965.

Kamen, Henry, *Spain, 1469–1714. A Society of Conflict*, Longman, London and New York, 1983.

Katz, Friedrich, (ed.), *Riot, Rebellion, and Revolution. Rural Social Conflict in Mexico*, Princeton University Press, Princeton, 1988.

Katz, Friedrich, "Labor conditions on haciendas in Porfirian Mexico: some trends and tendencies," *HAHR*, 54:1 (Feb. 1974), pp. 1–47.

Keatinge, Richard W. (ed.), *Peruvian Prehistory. An Overview of Pre-Inca and Inca Society*, Cambridge University Press, Cambridge, 1988.

Kelemen, Pál, *Baroque and Rococo in Latin America*, 2 volumes, Dover Publications, New York, 1967.

Kern, Robert W., and Dodge, Meredith D., *Historical Dictionary of Modern Spain, 1700–1988*, Greenwood Press, Westport, CT, 1990.

Kicza, John E. (ed.), *The Indian in Latin American History. Resistance, Resilience, and Acculturation*, Scholarly Resources Books, Wilmington, Delaware, 1993.

Klarén, Peter F., *Modernization, Dislocation, and Aprismo. Origins of the Peruvian Aprista Party, 1870–1932*, University of Texas Press, Austin, 1973.

Klarén, Peter F., "Peruvian Aprista Party," in *ELAH, volume 4*, pp. 379–80.

Klein, Herbert S., *African Slavery in Latin America and the Caribbean*, Oxford University Press, New York, 1986.

Klein, Herbert S., *Bolivia. The Evolution of a Multi-Ethnic Society*, 2nd edn, Oxford University Press, Oxford and New York, 1992.

Klein, Herbert S., *Haciendas and "Ayllus." Rural Society in the Bolivian Andes in the Eighteenth and Nineteenth Centuries*, Stanford University Press, Stanford, 1993.

Kline, Harvey F., "Colombia: the attempt to replace violence with democracy," chapter 9 in Wiarda and Kline (eds), *Latin American Politics and Development*.

Knight, Alan, *The Mexican Revolution*, 2 volumes, (Cambridge University Press, 1986), University of Nebraska Press, Lincoln, 1990.

Knight, Alan, "Mexico, c. 1930–46," in *CHLA, volume 7*, pp. 2–82.

Konetzke, Richard, "La emigración de mujeres españolas a América durante la época colonial," in *Revista Internacional de Sociología, volume 3* (Madrid, 1945), pp. 123–50; repr. in *Lateinamerika. Gesammelte Aufsätze von . . .*, Böhlau Verlag, Cologne and Vienna, 1983, pp. 1–28.

Kubler, George, *Mexican Architecture of the Sixteenth Century*, 2 volumes, Yale Historical Publications, Newhaven, 1948.

Kubler, George, "The behavior of Atahualpa, 1531–1533," *HAHR*, 25:4 (Nov. 1945), pp. 413–27.

Kubler, George, and Soria, Martín, *Art and Architecture in Spain and Portugal and their American Dominions, 1500–1800*, Penguin Books, Baltimore, 1969.

Ladd, Doris M., *The Mexican Nobility at Independence, 1780–1826*, Institute of Latin American Studies, University of Texas, Austin, 1976.

Lafaye, Jacques, "Literature and intellectual life in colonial Spanish America," in *CHLA, volume 2*, pp. 663–704.

Lamb, Ursula, *Frey Nicolás de Ovando, gobernador de las Indias (1501–1509)*, Consejo Superior de Investigaciones Científicas, Madrid, 1956.

Lanning, Edward P., *Peru before the Incas*, Prentice-Hall, Englewood Cliffs, 1967.

Larraín, José, "Gross national product and prices. The Chilean case in the seventeenth and eighteenth centuries," chapter 5 in Johnson and Tandeter, *Essays on the Price History of Eighteenth-Century Latin America*.

Larson, Brooke, *Colonialism and Agrarian Transformation in Bolivia. Cochabamba, 1550–1900*, Princeton University Press, Princeton, 1988.

Lavrin, Asunción, "Female religious," in Hoberman and Socolow, *Cities and Society in Colonial Latin America*, pp. 165–95.

Lavrin, Asunción, "Women in Spanish American colonial society," in *CHLA*, *volume 2*, pp. 321–55.

Le Flem, Jean-Paul, et al., *La frustración de un imperio (1476–1714)*, volume V of *Historia de España* (Manuel Tuñón de Lara, ed.), Editorial Labor, Barcelona, 1984.

León Portilla, Miguel (ed.), *The Broken Spears. The Aztec Account of the Conquest of Mexico*, Beacon Press, Boston, 1966.

Leonard, Irving A., *Baroque Times in Old Mexico. Seventeenth-Century Persons, Places, and Practices*, University of Michigan Press, Ann Arbor, 1959.

Levine, Robert M., and Crocitti, John J., (eds), *The Brazil Reader. History, Culture, Politics*, Duke University Press, Durham, 1999.

Leyes y ordenanzas nuevamente hechas por su Magestad para la gobernación de las Indias y buen tratamiento y conservación de los indios: que se han de guardar en el Consejo y Audiencias Reales que en ellas residen: y por todos los otros gobernadores, jueces y personas particulares de ellas, Antonio Muro Orejón (ed.), Escuela de Estudios Hispanoamericanos, Seville, 1961.

Lieuwen, Edwin, *Mexican Militarism*, University of New Mexico Press, Albuquerque, 1968.

Liss, Peggy K., *Mexico under Spain, 1521–1556*, University of Chicago Press, Chicago, 1975.

Lockhart, James, *Spanish Peru, 1532–1560. A Colonial Society*, University of Wisconsin Press, Madison, 1968.

Lockhart, James, *The Men of Cajamarca. A Social and Biographical Study of the First Conquerors of Peru*, Institute of Latin American Studies, University of Texas, Austin, 1972.

Lockhart, James, *The Nahuas after the Conquest. A Social and Cultural History of the Indians of Central Mexico, Sixteenth through Eighteenth Centuries*, Stanford University Press, Stanford, 1992.

Lockhart, James, and Schwartz, Stuart B., *Early Latin America. A History of Colonial Spanish America and Brazil*, Cambridge University Press, Cambridge, 1983.

Lohmann Villena, Guillermo, *El corregidor de indios en el Perú bajo los Austrias*, Ediciones Cultura Hispánica, Madrid, 1957.

Lohmann Villena, Guillermo, and Sarabia Viejo, María Justina, *Francisco de Toledo. Disposiciones gubernativas para el Virreinato del Perú*, 2 volumes, Escuela de Estudios Hispanoamericanos, Seville, 1986–9.

Lombardi, John V., *Venezuela. The Search for Order, the Dream of Progress*, Oxford University Press, New York, 1982.

Lombardi, John V., and Lombardi, Cathryn L., *Latin American History. A Teaching Atlas*, University of Wisconsin Press, Madison, 1983.

López de Gómara, Francisco, *Cortés. The Life of the Conqueror by his Secretary*, (Lesley B. Simpson, tr. and ed.), University of California Press, Berkeley and Los Angeles, 1966.

López Lara, Ramón, "Los Hospitales de la Concepción," in *Vasco de Quiroga: Educador de adultos*, El Colegio de Michoacán and CREFAL, Pátzcuaro, 1984, pp. 113–28.

Love, Joseph L., "Economic ideas and ideologies in Latin America since 1930," in *CHLA, volume 6, 1*, pp. 393–460.

Loveman, Brian, *Chile. The Legacy of Hispanic Capitalism*, 2nd edn, Oxford University Press, New York, 1988.

Lunenfeld, Marvin, *The Council of the Santa Hermandad. A Study of the Pacification Forces of Ferdinand and Isabella*, University of Miami Press, Coral Gables, 1970.

Lynch, John, *The Spanish American Revolutions, 1808–1826*, 2nd edn., W.W. Norton and Co., New York, 1986.

Lynch, John, *Bourbon Spain, 1700–1808*, Blackwell, Oxford, 1989.

Lynch, John, *Caudillos in Spanish America, 1800–1850*, Clarendon Press, Oxford, 1992.

Lynch, John, *The Hispanic World in Crisis and Change, 1598–1700*, Blackwell, Oxford, 1992.

MacCormack, Sabine, *Religion in the Andes. Vision and Imagination in Early Colonial Peru*, Princeton University Press, Princeton, 1991.

MacLachlan, Colin M., *Spain's Empire in the New World. The Role of Ideas in Institutional and Social Change*, University of California Press, Berkeley and Los Angeles, 1988.

MacLeod, Murdo J., "Aspects of the internal economy of colonial Spanish America: labour; taxation; distribution and exchange," in *CHLA, volume 2*, pp. 219–64.

Malamud Rikles, Carlos D., *La economía colonial americana en el siglo XVIII*, in *La época de la Ilustración, Las Indias en el siglo XVIII, volume 31*, part 2 of *Historia de España Menéndez Pidal* (José María Jover Zamora, ed.), Espasa-Calpe, Madrid, 1988.

Mamalakis, Markos J., "Income distribution," in *ELAH, volume 3*, pp. 251–9.

Mansuy-Diniz Silva, Andrée, "Portugal and Brazil. Imperial re-organization, 1750–1808," in *CHLA, volume 1*, pp. 469–508.

Manzetti, Luigi, "The political economy of Mercosur," *Journal of Inter-American Studies and World Affairs*, 35:4 (1993–4), pp. 101–41.

Marchena Fernández, Juan, "The social world of the military in Peru and New Granada. The colonial oligarchies in conflict, 1750–1810," in Fisher, Kuethe and McFarlane (eds), *Reform and Insurrection in Bourbon New Granada and Peru*, pp. 54–95.

Marcílio, Maria Luiza, "The population of colonial Brazil," in *CHLA, volume 2*, pp. 37–63.

Marett, Robert, *Peru*, Praeger, New York and Washington, 1969.

Martín, Luis, *Daughters of the Conquistadores. Women of the Viceroyalty of Peru*, Southern Methodist University Press, Dallas, 1983.

Martin, Gerald, "The literature, music and art of Latin America from independence to c.1870," in *CHLA, volume 3*, pp. 797–839.

Marzahl, Peter, *Town in the Empire. Government, Politics, and Society in Seventeenth-Century Popayán*, Institute of Latin American Studies, University of Texas, Austin, 1978.

Mason, J. Alden, *The Ancient Civilizations of Peru*, Penguin Books, Harmondsworth, 1957.

Masur, Gerhard, *Simón Bolívar*, University of New Mexico Press, Albuquerque, 1969.

Matilla Tascón, Antonio, *Historia de las minas de Almadén. Volume 2. Desde 1646 a 1799*, Minas de Almadén y Arrayanes, S.A., and Instituto de Estudios Fiscales, Madrid, 1987.

Mauro, Frédéric, *Le Portugal, le Brésil et l'Atlantique au XVIIe siècle (1570–1670), Etude Economique*, Fondation Calouste Gulbenkian, Centre Culturel Portugais, Paris, 1983.

Mauro, Frédéric, "Portugal and Brazil. Political and economic structures of empire, 1580–1750," in *CHLA, volume 1*, pp. 441–68.

Maxwell, Kenneth, *Pombal, Paradox of the Enlightenment*, Cambridge University Press, Cambridge, 1995.

McAlister, Lyle N., *Spain and Portugal in the New World, 1492–1700*, University of Minnesota Press, 1984.

McCaa, Robert, "Marriageways in Mexico and Spain, 1500–1900," *Continuity and Change* 9:1 (1994), pp. 11–43.

McFarlane, Anthony, *Colombia before Independence. Economy, Society, and Politics under Bourbon Rule*, Cambridge University Press, Cambridge, 1993.

McFarlane, Anthony, "The rebellion of the *Barrios*: urban insurrection in Bourbon Quito," in Fisher, Kuethe, and McFarlane (eds), *Reform and Insurrection in Bourbon New Granada and Peru*.

McLachlan, Colin M., and Rodríguez, Jaime O., *The Forging of the Cosmic Race. A Reinterpretation of Colonial Mexico*, University of California Press, Berkeley and Los Angeles, 1980.

McNeill, William H., "American food crops in the Old World," in Viola and Margolis, *Seeds of Change*, pp. 43–59.

Mendieta, Gerónimo de, *Historia eclesiástica indiana*, Porrúa, Mexico City, 1971.

Merrick, Thomas W., "The population of Latin America, 1930–1990," in *CHLA, volume 6, 1*. pp. 3–61.

Mesa, José de, and Gisbert, Teresa, *Bolivia. Monumentos históricos y arqueológicos*, Instituto Panamericano de Geografía e Historia, Mexico City, 1970.

Mexico. Splendors of Thirty Centuries. See O'Neill, John P.

Mills, Kenneth R., *Idolatry and its Enemies. Colonial Andean Religion and Extirpation*, Princeton University Press, Princeton, 1997.

Mills, Kenneth R., *An Evil Lost to View? An Investigation of Post-Evangelisation Andean Religion in Mid-colonial Peru*, Monograph Series no. 18, Institute of Latin American Studies, University of Liverpool, Liverpool, 1994.

Mintz, Sidney W. *Sweetness and Power. The Place of Sugar in Modern History*, Penguin Books, Harmondsworth, 1986.

Miranda, Francisco, "El Pátzcuaro de Don Vasco: un modelo de integración étnica y cultural," in *Vasco de Quiroga: Educador de adultos*, El Colegio de Michoacán and CREFAL, Pátzcuaro, 1984, pp. 78–96.

Mora Mérida, José Luis, *Historia social de Paraguay, 1600–1650*, Escuela de Estudios Hispanoamericanos, Seville, 1973.

Morales Padrón, Francisco, *Historia del Descubrimiento y Conquista de América*, Editora Nacional, Madrid, 1963.

Moreno Fraginals, Manuel, *El ingenio: complejo económico-social cubano del azúcar*, 3 volumes, Havana, 1978.

Moreno Fraginals, Manuel, "Plantation economies and societies in the Spanish Caribbean, 1860–1930," in *CHLA, volume 4*, pp. 187–231.

Morilla Critz, Jos, "Crisis y transformación de la economía de Nueva España en el siglo XVII. Un ensayo crítico," *Anuario de Estudios Americanos*, 45 (1988), pp. 241–72.

Morineau, Michel, *Incroyables gazettes et fabuleux métaux. Les retours des trésors américains d'après les gazettes hollandaises (XVIe–XVIIIe siècles)*, Maison des Sciences de l'Homme, Paris, and Cambridge University Press, Cambridge, 1985.

Morison, Samuel E., *Admiral of the Ocean Sea. A Life of Christopher Columbus*, Little, Brown and Co., Boston, 1942.

Mörner, Magnus, *Estratificación social hispanoamericana durante el periodo colonial*, Research Paper Series, no. 28, Institute of Latin American Studies, Stockholm, 1980.

Mörner, Magnus, "The rural economy and society of colonial Spanish South America," in *CHLA, volume 2*, pp. 189–217.

Morris, Craig, "Progress and prospect in the archaeology of the Inca," in *Peruvian Prehistory. An Overview of Pre-Inca and Inca Society*, Richard W. Keatinge (ed.), Cambridge University Press, Cambridge, 1988, pp. 233–56.

Morse, Richard M., *New World Soundings. Culture and Ideology in the Americas*, Johns Hopkins University Press, Baltimore, 1989.

Morse, Richard M. (ed.), *The Bandeirantes. The Historical Role of the Brazilian Pathfinders*, Alfred A. Knopf, New York, 1965.

Morse, Richard M., "The urban development of colonial Spanish America," in *CHLA*, volume 2, pp. 67–104.

Mota y Escobar, Alonso de la, *Descripción geográfica de los Reynos de Nueva Galicia, Nueva Vizcaya y Nuevo León* [1605], Instituto Jalisciense de Antropología e Historia, Guadalajara, 1966.

Moutoukias, Zacarías, "Power, corruption, and commerce: the making of the local administrative structure in seventeenth-century Buenos Aires," *HAHR*, 68:4 (Nov. 1988), pp. 771–801.

Muro, Luis, "Bartolomé de Medina, introductor del beneficio de patio en Nueva España," in Elías Trabulse (ed.), *Historia de la ciencia y la tecnología*, El Colegio de México, Mexico City, 1991, pp. 203–17.

Muro Romero, Fernando, "La administración de Indias. De la unidad imperial a la diversidad americana. El tránsito del siglo XVII," in *Unité et Diversité de l'Amérique Latine*, volume 1, Maison des Pays Ibériques, Université de Bordeaux III, 15–18 September 1982, pp. 275–99.

Murra, John V., "Aymara lords and their European agents at Potosí," *Nova Americana* I (Turin, 1978), pp. 231–43.

Nazzari, Muriel, *Disappearance of the Dowry. Women, Families, and Social Change in São Paulo, Brazil, 1600–1900*, Stanford University Press, Stanford, 1991.

Needler, Martin C., *Politics and Society in Mexico*, University of New Mexico Press, Albuquerque, 1971.

Newson, Linda A., "Demographic catastrophe in sixteenth-century Honduras," in *Studies in Spanish-American Population History*, David J. Robinson (ed.), Westview Press, Boulder, CO, 1981, pp. 217–41.

Newson, Linda A., "Indian population patterns in colonial Spanish America," *Latin American Research Review*, 20:3 (1985), pp. 41–74.

O'Callaghan, Joseph F., *A History of Medieval Spain*, Cornell University Press, Ithaca, 1975.

Oliveira Marques, A. H. de, *History of Portugal*, 2nd edn., Columbia University Press, New York, 1976.

O'Neill, John P. (ed.), *Mexico. Splendors of Thirty Centuries*, Metropolitan Museum of Art (New York), Little, Brown and Co., Boston, 1990.

O'Phelan Godoy, Scarlett, *Rebellions and Revolts in Eighteenth Century Peru and Upper Peru*, Böhlau Verlag, Cologne, 1985.

Ots Capdequí, J. M., *El estado español en las Indias*, Fondo de Cultura Económica, Mexico City, 1965.

Padden, R. C., *The Hummingbird and the Hawk. Conquest and Sovereignty in the Valley of Mexico, 1503–1541*, Harper and Rowe, New York, 1970.

Padden, R. C., "Cultural adaptation and militant autonomy among the Araucanians of Chile," in *The Indian in Latin American History. Resistance, Resilience and Acculturation*, John E. Kicza (ed.), Scholarly Resources Books, Wilmington, Delaware, 1993, pp. 69–88 (orig. pub. in *Southwestern Journal of Anthropology*, 13:1 (Spring 1957), pp. 103–21).

Pagden, Anthony, *The Fall of Natural Man. The American Indian and the Origins of Comparative Ethnology*, Cambridge University Press, Cambridge, 1986.

Palmer, Colin A., *Slaves of the White God. Blacks in Mexico, 1570–1650*, Harvard University Press, Cambridge, MA, 1976.

Palmer, David S., "Peru: the enduring authoritarian legacy," chapter 10 in Wiarda and Kline, *Latin American Politics*

Palmer, Gabrielle G., *Sculpture in the Kingdom of Quito*, University of New Mexico Press, Albuquerque, 1987.

Parker, Geoffrey, *Philip II*, Little, Brown and Co., Boston, 1978.

Parkes, Henry B., *A History of Mexico*, Eyre and Spottiswoode, London, 1962.

Parry, John H., *The Audiencia of New Galicia in the Sixteenth Century. A Study in Spanish Colonial Government*, Cambridge University Press, Cambridge, 1948.

Parry, John H., *The Sale of Public Office in the Spanish Indies under the Hapsburgs*, Ibero-Americana 37, University of California Press, Berkeley and Los Angeles, 1953.

Parry, John H., *The Age of Reconnaissance*, New American Library, New York, 1964.

Parry, John H., *The Discovery of the Sea*, University of California Press, Berkeley and Los Angeles, 1981.

Parry, John H., and Keith, Robert G. (eds), *New Iberian World. A Documentary History of the Discovery and Settlement of Latin America to the Early Seventeenth Century*, 5 volumes, Times Books and Hector & Rose, New York, 1984.

Parry, John H., Sherlock, Philip, and Maingot, Anthony, *A Short History of the West Indies*, 4th edn., St. Martin's Press, New York, 1987.

Patterson, Thomas C., *The Inca Empire. The Formation and Disintegration of a Pre-Capitalist State*, Berg, Oxford and New York, 1991.

Payne, Stanley G., *A History of Spain and Portugal*, 2 volumes., University of Wisconsin Press, Madison, 1973.

Payne, Stanley G., *Spanish Catholicism. An Historical Overview*, University of Wisconsin Press, Madison, 1984.

Paz, Octavio, *Sor Juana; Or, the Traps of the Faith*, Harvard University Press, Cambridge, MA, 1988.

Peña, José de la, *Oligarquía y propiedad en Nueva España, 1550–1624*, Fondo de Cultura Económica, Mexico City, 1983.

Pendergast, David M., "Up from the dust: the central lowlands postclassic as seen from Lamanai and Marco González, Belize," in Flora S. Clancy and Peter D. Harrison (eds), *Vision and Revision in Maya Studies*, University of New Mexico Press, Albuquerque, 1990, pp. 169–77.

Pérez, Louis. A., "Cuba, *c.*1930–59," in *CHLA, volume 7*, pp. 419–55.

Pérez-Mallaina, Pablo E., and Torres Ramírez, Bibiano, *La Armada del Mar del Sur*, Escuela de Estudios Hispanoamericanos, Seville, 1987.

Phelan, John L., *The Kingdom of Quito in the Seventeenth Century. Bureaucratic Politics in the Spanish Empire*, University of Wisconsin Press, Madison, 1967.

Phelan, John L., *The Millennial Kingdom of the Franciscans in the New World*, 2nd edn., University of California Press, Berkeley and Los Angeles, 1970.

Phelan, John L., *The People and the King. The Comunero Revolution in Colombia, 1781*, University of Wisconsin Press, Madison, 1978.

Phillips, William D., and Rahn, Carla, *The Worlds of Christopher Columbus*, Cambridge University Press, Cambridge, 1992.

Pike, Fredrick B., *The Modern History of Peru*, Frederick A. Praeger, New York, 1967.

Poppino, Rollie E., "Vargas, Getúlio Dornelles," in *ELAH, volume 5*, pp. 362–5.

Prado, Junior, Caio, *The Colonial Background of Modern Brazil* (tr. Suzette Macedo), University of California Press, Berkeley and Los Angeles, 1969.

Prescott, William H., *The Conquest of Mexico*, 2 volumes, Dent, London, 1962.

Puiggrós, Rodolfo, *Historia económica del Río de la Plata*, Ediciones Siglo Veinte, Buenos Aires, 1948.

Quirk, Robert E., *The Mexican Revolution, 1914–1915*, Citadel Press, New York, 1963.

Ramírez, Fausto, "Apogeo del nacionalismo académico: el arte entre 1877 y 1900," Museo Nacional del Arte, Instituto Nacional de Bellas Artes, Mexico City, n.d.

Ramírez, Susan, *Provincial Patriarchs. Land Tenure and the Economics of Power in Colonial Peru*, University of New Mexico Press, Albuquerque, 1986.

Ramirez, Susan, "El *Dueño de Indios*: thoughts on the consequences of the shifting bases of power of the *Curaca de los viejos antiguos* under the Spanish in sixteenth-century Peru," *HAHR* 67:4 (Nov. 1987), pp. 575–610.

Recopilación de Leyes de los Reinos de las Indias, mandadas imprimir, y publicar, por la Magestad Católica del Rey Don Carlos II, 4 volumes, Madrid, 1681 (facsimile ed., Ediciones Cultura Hispánica, Madrid, 1973).

Ricard, Robert, *The Spiritual Conquest of Mexico. An Essay on the Apostolate and the Evangelizing Methods of the Mendicant Orders in New Spain, 1523–1572*, (orig. edn, Paris, 1933) tr. Lesley B. Simpson, University of California Press, Berkeley and Los Angeles, 1966.

Rich, E. E., "The European nations and the Atlantic," in J. P. Cooper (ed.), *The New Cambridge Modern History, volume 4, The Decline of Spain and the Thirty Years War, 1609–48/59*, Cambridge University Press, Cambridge, 1970, pp. 672–706.

Riley, G. Micheal, *Fernando Cortés and the Marquesado in Morelos, 1522–1547. A Case Study in the Socioeconomic Development of Sixteenth-Century Mexico*, Albuquerque, University of New Mexico Press, 1973.

Robertson, William S., *Rise of the Spanish-American Republics as told in the Lives of their Liberators*, Collier Books, New York, 1961.

Robinson, David J. (ed.), *Migration in Colonial Spanish America*, Cambridge University Press, Cambridge, 1990.

Rock, David, *Argentina, 1516–1987. From Spanish Colonization to Alfonsín*, University of California Press, Berkeley and Los Angeles, 1987.

Rodrigues, José Honório, *Brasil. Período colonial*, Instituto Panamericano de Geografía e Historia, Comisión de Historia, Mexico City, 1953.

Rodríguez, Linda A. (ed.), *Rank and Privilege. The Military and Society in Latin America*, Scholarly Resources, Wilmington, DE, 1994.

Rojas, José Luis de, *México Tenochtitlan. Economía y sociedad en el siglo XVI*, El Colegio de Michoacán and Fondo de Cultura Económica, Zamora and Mexico City, 1986.

Rojas, Ricardo, *El santo de la espada. Vida de San Martín*, Editorial Losada, Buenos Aires, 1940.

Romero, Emilio, *Historia económica del Perú, volume 1*, 2nd edn, Editorial Universo, Lima, n.d.

Rostworowski de Diez Canseco, María, *Historia del Tahuantinsuyu*, Instituto de Estudios Peruanos, Lima, 1988.

Rostworowski de Diez Conseco, María, *History of the Inca Realm*, (tr. Harry B. Iceland), Cambridge University Press, Cambridge, 1999.

Rouse, Irving, *The Tainos. Rise and Decline of the People who greeted Columbus*, Yale University Press, New Haven and London, 1992.

Ruiz Medrano, Ethelia, *Gobierno y Sociedad en Nueva España. Segunda Audiencia y Antonio de Mendoza*, El Colegio de Michoacán, Zamora, 1991.

Ruiz Rivera, Julián, "Remesas de caudales del Nuevo Reino de Granada en el XVII," *Anuario de Estudios Americanos*, 34 (1977), pp. 241–71.

Russell-Wood, A. J. R., "Colonial Brazil: the gold cycle, *c.*1690–1750," in *CHLA*, volume 2, pp. 547–600.

Russell-Wood, A. J. R., (ed.), *From Colony to Nation. Essays on the Independence of Brazil*, The Johns Hopkins University Press, Baltimore, 1975.

Safford, Frank, "Politics, ideology and society in post-independence Spanish America," in *CHLA*, volume 3, pp. 347–421.

Sahagún, Bernardino de, *The Florentine Codex: General History of the Things of New Spain*, 12 books in 13 volumes, tr. Arthur J. O. Anderson and Charles Dibble, School of American Research, Santa Fe, NM, 1950–82.

Saignes, Thierry, and Bouysse-Cassagne, Thérèse, "Dos confundidas identidades: mestizos y criollos del siglo XVII," in Tomoeda and Millones (eds), *500 años de mestizaje en los Andes*, pp. 14–26.

Salvucci, Richard J., *Textiles and Capitalism in Mexico. An Economic History of the Obrajes, 1539–1840*, Princeton University Press, Princeton, 1987.

Sánchez-Albornoz, Nicolás, *La población de América Latina. Desde los tiempos precolombinos hasta el año 2000*, Alianza Editorial, Madrid, 1973 (2nd edn, Madrid, 1994).

Sánchez-Albornoz, Nicolás, "The population of colonial Spanish America," in *CHLA*, volume 2, pp. 3–35.

Sánchez-Albornoz, Nicolás, "The population of Latin America, 1850–1930," in *CHLA*, volume 4, pp. 121–52.

Sánchez Bella, Ismael, *La organización financiera de las Indias. Siglo XVI*, Escuela de Estudios Hispanoamericanos, Seville, 1968.

Sanderlin, George (tr. and ed.), *Bartolomé de las Casas. A Selection of his Writings*, Alfred A. Knopf, New York, 1971.

Sauer, Carl O. *The Early Spanish Main*, University of California Press, Berkeley and Los Angeles, 1966.

Sauer, Carl O., *Sixteenth Century North America. The Land and the People as seen by the Europeans*, University of California Press, Berkeley and Los Angeles, 1971.

Schäfer, Ernst, *El Consejo Real y Supremo de las Indias: Su historia, organización y labor administrativa hasta la terminación de la Casa de Austria*, 2 volumes, Escuela de Estudios Hispanoamericanos, Seville, 1935–47.

Schele, Linda, and Freidel, David, *A Forest of Kings. The Untold Story of the Ancient Maya*, William Morrow, New York, 1990.

Schwaller, John F., *The Church and Clergy in Sixteenth-Century Mexico*, University of New Mexico Press, Albuquerque, 1987.

Schwartz, Stuart B., *Sovereignty and Society in Colonial Brazil. The High Court of Bahia and its Judges, 1609–1751*, University of California Press, Berkeley and Los Angeles, 1973.

Schwartz, Stuart B., *Sugar Plantations in the Formation of Brazilian Society. Bahia, 1550–1835*, Cambridge University Press, Cambridge, 1985.

Schwartz, Stuart B., *Slaves, Peasants, and Rebels. Reconsidering Brazilian Slavery*, University of Illinois Press, Urbana and Chicago, 1992.

Schwartz, Stuart B., "Rethinking Palmares: slave resistance in colonial Brazil," in his *Slaves, Peasants, and Rebels*, chapter 4.

Schwartz, Stuart B., "Colonial Brazil, *c.*1580–*c.*1750: Plantations and Peripheries," in *CHLA*, volume 2, pp. 423–99.

Scobie, James R., *Argentina. A City and a Nation*, Oxford University Press, New York, 1964.

Scobie, James R, "The growth of Latin American cities," in *The Cambridge History of Latin America*, volume 4, *c.*1870–1930, pp. 233–65.

Seed, Patricia, *To Love, Honor and Obey in Colonial Mexico. Conflicts over Marriage Choice, 1574–1821*, Stanford University Press, Stanford, 1988.

Semo, Enrique, *Historia del capitalismo en México*, Lecturas Mexicanas, Secretaría de Educación Pública, Mexico City, 1987 (English tr. by Lidia Lozano, *The History of Capitalism in Mexico. Its Origins, 1521–1763*, University of Texas Press, Austin, 1993).

Sempat Assadourian, Carlos, *El sistema de la economía colonial. Mercado interno, regiones, y espacio económico*, Instituto de Estudios Peruanos, Lima, 1982.

Simmons, Marc, *Albuquerque. A Narrative History*, University of New Mexico Press, Albuquerque, 1984.

Simonsen, Roberto S., *Historia economica do Brasil, 1500–1820*, Companhia Editora Nacional, São Paulo, 1937.

Simpson, Lesley B., *Exploitation of Land in Central Mexico in the Sixteenth Century*, Ibero-Americana 13, University of California Press, Berkeley and Los Angeles, 1952.

Simpson, Lesley B., *The Encomienda in New Spain. The Beginning of Spanish Mexico*, University of California Press, Berkeley and Los Angeles, 1966.

Skidmore, Thomas E., and Smith, Peter H., *Modern Latin America*, 3rd edn, Oxford University Press, New York, 1992 (and later eds).

Skidmore, Thomas E., *Brazil. Five Centuries of Change*, Oxford University Press, New York and Oxford, 1999.

Socolow, Susan M., *The Merchants of Buenos Aires, 1778–1810. Family and Commerce*, Cambridge, Cambridge University Press, 1978.

Spalding, Karen, *Huarochirí. An Andean Society under Inca and Spanish Rule*, Stanford University Press, Stanford, 1984.

Spate, O. H. K., *The Spanish Lake* (volume 1 of *The Pacific since Magellan*), University of Minnesota Press, Minneapolis, 1979.

Stein, Steve, *Populism in Peru. The Emergence of the Masses and the Politics of Social Control*, University of Wisconsin Press, Madison, 1980.

Stern, Steve J., *Peru's Indian Peoples and the Challenge of Spanish Conquest. Huamanga to 1640*, University of Wisconsin Press, Madison, 1982.

Stern, Steve J., (ed.), *Resistance, Rebellion, and Consciousness in the Andean Peasant World, 18th to 20th Centuries*, University of Wisconsin Press, Madison, 1987.

Stern, Steve J., (ed.), *Shining and Other Paths. War and Society in Peru, 1980–1995*, Duke University Press, Durham, NC, 1998.

Stern, Steve J., "The age of Andean insurrection, 1742–1782: a reappraisal," in Stern (ed.), *Resistance, Rebellion, and Consciousness*, pp. 34–93.

Stevenson, Robert, "The music of colonial Spanish America," in *CHLA, volume 2*, pp. 771–98.

Stevenson, Robert, "A note on the music of colonial Brazil," in *CHLA, volume 2*, pp. 799–803.

Super, John C., *La vida en Querétaro durante la colonia, 1531–1810*, Fondo de Cultura Económica, Mexico City, 1983.

Super, John C., "The agricultural near north: Querétaro in the seventeenth century," chapter 9 in Altman and Lockhart (eds), *Provinces of Early Mexico*.

Swann, Michael M., "Migration, mobility, and the mining towns of colonial northern Mexico," chapter 8 in Robinson, *Migration in Colonial Spanish America*.

Tannenbaum, Frank, *Peace by Revolution. Mexico after 1910*, Columbia University Press, 1966 (1933).

Tandeter, Enrique, *Coercion and Market. Silver Mining in Colonial Potosí, 1692–1826*, University of New Mexico Press, Albuquerque, 1993.

Tandeter, Enrique, "Población y economía en los Andes (siglo XVIII)," *Revista Andina* (Cuzco) 13:1 (July 1995), pp. 7–42.

Taylor, William B., *Drinking, Homicide, and Rebellion in Colonial Mexican Villages*, Stanford University Press, Stanford, 1979.

Taylor, William B., "The Virgin of Guadalupe in New Spain: an inquiry into the social history of Marian devotion," *American Ethnologist*, 14 (Feb. 1987), pp. 9–33.

Tenenbaum, Barbara A., *The Politics of Penury. Debts and Taxes in Mexico, 1821–1856*, University of New Mexico Press, Albuquerque, 1986.

TePaske, John J., "General tendencies and secular trends in the economies of Mexico and Peru, 1750–1810: the view from the *Cajas* of Mexico and Lima," in Jacobsen and Puhle, *The Economies of Mexico and Peru*, pp. 316–39.

TePaske, John J., "The search for El Dorado: gold production in New Granada, New Spain, and Peru, 1521–1810," unpublished paper.

TePaske, John J., and Hernández Palomo, José and Mariluz, *La Real Hacienda de Nueva España: La Real Caja de México (1576–1816)*, Instituto Nacional de Antropología e Historia, Mexico City, 1976.

TePaske, John J., and Klein, Herbert S., "The seventeenth-century crisis in New Spain: myth or reality?," *Past and Present* 90 (Feb. 1981), pp. 116–35.

Thiessen, Heather K., "Nicaragua," in *ELAH*, *volume 4*, pp. 182–8.

Thomas, Hugh, "Cuba from the middle of the eighteenth century to *c*.1870," in *CHLA*, *volume 3*, pp. 277–96.

Thorp, Rosemary, *Progress, Poverty and Exclusion. An Economic History of Latin America in the Twentieth Century*, Inter-American Development Bank, New York, 1998.

Thorp, Rosemary, "The Latin American economies, 1939–*c*.1950," in *CHLA*, *volume* 6, part i, pp. 117–58.

Timmons, Wilbert H., *Morelos: Priest, Soldier, Statesman of Mexico*, Texas Western College Press, El Paso, 1963.

Todorov, Tzvetan, *The Conquest of America. The Question of the Other*, Harper and Row, New York, 1985.

Tomoeda, Hiroyasu, and Millones, Luis (eds), *500 años de mestizaje en los Andes*, Senri Ethnological Studies No. 33, National Museum of Ethnology, Osaka, 1992.

Torre, Juan Carlos, and Riz, Liliana de, "Argentina since 1946," in *CHLA*, *volume 8*, pp. 73–193.

Trabulse, Elías, "Un científico mexicano del siglo XVII: Fray Diego Rodríguez y su obra," in Trabulse (ed.), *Historia de la ciencia y la tecnología*, El Colegio de México, Mexico City, 1991, pp. 146–79.

Trend, J. B., *Bolívar and the Independence of Spanish America*, Bolivarian Society of Venezuela/Macmillan, New York, 1951.

Tutino, John, *From Insurrection to Revolution in Mexico. Social Bases of Agrarian Violence, 1750–1940*, Princeton University Press, Princeton, 1986.

Tyler, S. Lyman, *Two Worlds. The Indian Encounter with the European, 1492–1509*, University of Utah Press, Salt Lake City, 1988.

Tyrer, Robson B., *Historia demográfica y económica de la Audiencia de Quito: Población indígena e industria textil, 1600–1800*, Banco Central de Ecuador, Quito, 1988.

Vaillant, George C., *The Aztecs of Mexico*, Penguin Books, Harmondsworth, 1961.

van Bath, B. H. Slicher, *Real Hacienda y economía en Hispanoamérica, 1541–1820*, Centrum voor Studie en Documentatie van Latijns Amerika, Amsterdam, 1989.

Vargas, José María, *Historia del Ecuador. Siglo XVI*, Universidad Católica, Quito, 1977.

Vargas, José María, and Crespo Toral, Hernán, *Arte de Ecuador (siglos XVIII–XIX)*, Salvat Editores Ecuatoriana S.A., Quito, 1977.

Vargas Llosa, Mario, *Death in the Andes*, (tr. Edith Grossman), Penguin Books, New York, 1997.

Vasconcelos, José, *La raza cósmica*, Espasa-Calpe Mexicana S.A., Mexico City, 1948.

Vasconcelos, José, *Hernán Cortés, creador de la nacionalidad*, [1941] Editorial Jus, Mexico City, 1985.

Vázquez, Josefina Z., "Los primeros tropiezos," in *Historia General de México, volume 3*, pp. 1–84.

Vega Carpio, Félix Lope de, *Arauco domado*, Editorial Zig-Zag, Santiago de Chile, 1954.

Vigneras, Louis-André, *The Discovery of South America and the Andalusian Voyages*, Newberry Library/University of Chicago Press, Chicago, 1976.

Vila Vilar, Enriqueta, "Las ferias de Portobelo: Apariencia y realidad del comercio con Indias," *Anuario de Estudios Hispanoamericanos*, 39, pp. 275–340.

Villamarín, Juan A. and Judith E., *Indian Labor in Mainland Colonial Spanish America*, Latin American Studies Program, University of Delaware, Newark , 1975.

Villoro, Luis, "La revolución de independencia," in *Historia General de México, volume 2*, pp. 303–56.

Viola, Herman J., and Margolis, Carolyn (eds), *Seeds of Change. A Quincentennial Commemoration*, Smithsonian Institution Press, Washington DC, 1992.

Viqueira, Carmen, and Urquiola, José Ignacio *Los obrajes en la Nueva España: 1530–1630*, Consejo Nacional para la Cultura y las Artes, Mexico City, 1990.

Vogt, John, *Portuguese Rule on the Gold Coast, 1469–1682*, University of Georgia Press, Athens, GA, 1979.

Wagner, Henry Raup, *The Life and Writings of Bartolom de las Casas*, University of New Mexico Press, Albuquerque, 1967.

Walker, Geoffrey J., *Spanish Politics and Imperial Trade, 1700–1789*, Indiana University Press, Bloomington, 1979.

Ward, John, *Latin America. Development and Conflict since 1945*, Routledge, London and New York, 1997.

Ward, Peter M., "Cities and Urbanization," in *ELAH, volume 2*, pp. 164–9.

Watts, David, *The West Indies. Patterns of Development, Culture and Environmental Change since 1492*, Cambridge University Press, Cambridge, 1987.

West, Robert C., and Augelli, John P., *Middle America. Its Lands and Peoples*, Prentice-Hall, Englewood Cliffs, 1966.

Whitaker, Arthur P., *The United States and the Independence of Latin America, 1800–1830*, W.W. Norton & Co., New York, 1964.

Whitmore, Thomas M., *Disease and Death in Early Colonial Mexico: Simulating Amerindian Depopulation*, Westview Press, Boulder, 1992.

Wiarda, Howard J., and Kline, Harvey F. (eds), *Latin American Politics and Development*, 4th edn, Westview Press, Boulder, C., 1996.

Wightman, Ann M., *Indigenous Migration and Social Change. The Forasteros of Cuzco, 1520–1720*, Duke University Press, Durham, NC, 1990.

Wilkerson, Jeffrey K., "The ethnographic works of Andrés de Olmos, precursor and contemporary of Sahagún," chapter 3 in Edmonson, *Sixteenth-Century Mexico*.

Wilkie, James W., *Statistics and National Policy*, Latin American Center, University of California, Los Angeles, 1974.

Wilkie, James W., *Statistical Abstract of Latin America, volume 17*, Latin American Center, University of California, Los Angeles, 1976.

Wilkie, James W., *Statistical Abstract of Latin America, volume 35*, Latin American Center, University of California, Los Angeles, 1999.

Wilson, Samuel M., *Hispaniola. Caribbean Chiefdoms in the Age of Columbus*, University of Alabama Press, Tuscaloosa, 1990.

Wortman, Miles L., *Government and Society in Central America, 1680–1840*, Columbia University Press, New York, 1982.

Wrigley, E. A., *Population and History*, Weidenfeld and Nicholson, London, 1969.

Zambardino, Rudolph A., "Mexico's population in the sixteenth century: demographic anomaly or mathematical illusion?," *Journal of Interdisciplinary History*, 11:1 (Summer 1980), pp. 1–27.

Zavala, Silvio, *La encomienda indiana*, 2nd edn, Editorial Porrúa, Mexico City, 1973.

Zavala, Silvio, "Ideario de Vasco de Quiroga," in *Recuerdo de Vasco de Quiroga*, Editorial Porrúa, Mexico City, 1965, pp. 45–74.

Zavala, Silvio, "La 'Utopía' de Tomás Moro en la Nueva España," in *Recuerdo de Vasco de Quiroga*, Editorial Porrúa, Mexico City, 1965, pp. 11–40.

Zavala, Silvio, "Sir Thomas More in New Spain: a utopian adventure of the Renaissance," in *Recuerdo de Vasco de Quiroga*, Editorial Porrúa, Mexico City, 1965, pp. 101–16.

Zea, Leopoldo, *Positivism in Mexico*, (tr. Josephine H. Schulte), University of Texas Press, Austin, 1974.

Zea, Leopoldo, "Positivism in Mexico," in Ralph L. Woodward (ed.), *Positivism in Latin America, 1850–1900*, Boston, 1971, pp. 65–78.

Zepeda, Tomás, *La República Mexicana. Geografía y Atlas*, Editorial Progreso, Mexico City, 1962.

Zimmerman, Arthur F., *Francisco de Toledo, Fifth Viceroy of Peru, 1569–1581*, Caxton Printers, Caldwell, ID, 1938, and repr., Greenwood Press, New York, 1968.

Zulawski, Ann, "Social differentiation, gender, and ethnicity. Urban Indian women in colonial Bolivia, 1640–1725," *Latin American Research Review*, 25:2 (1990). pp. 93–113.

INDEX

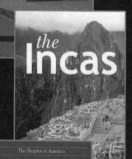
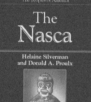